STRUCTURED BASIC

FUNDAMENTALS AND STYLE

for the IBM® PC
and Compatibles

Programming books from boyd & fraser

Structuring Programs in Microsoft BASIC
BASIC Fundamentals and Style
Applesoft BASIC Fundamentals and Style
Complete BASIC: For the Short Course
Fundamentals of Structured COBOL
Advanced Structured COBOL: Batch and Interactive
Comprehensive Structured COBOL
Pascal
WATFIV-S Fundamentals and Style
VAX Fortran
Fortran 77 Fundamentals and Style
Learning Computer Programming: Structured Logic, Algorithms, and Flowcharting
Structured BASIC Fundamentals and Style for the IBM® PC and Compatibles
C Programming
dBASE III PLUS Programming

Also available from boyd & fraser

Database Systems: Management and Design
Using Pascal: An Introduction to Computer Science I
Using Modula-2: An Introduction to Computer Science I
Data Abstraction and Structures: An Introduction to Computer Science II
Fundamentals of Systems Analysis with Application Design
Data Communications for Business
Data Communications Software Design
Microcomputer Applications: Using Small Systems Software
The Art of Using Computers
Using Microcomputers: A Hands-On Introduction
A Practical Approach to Operating Systems
Microcomputer Database Management Using dBASE III PLUS
Microcomputer Database Management Using R:BASE System V
Office Automation: An Information Systems Approach
Microcomputer Applications: Using Small Systems Software, 2/e
Mastering Lotus 1-2-3
Using Enable: An Introduction to Integrated Software
PC-DOS Simplified

Shelly, Cashman, and Forsythe books from boyd & fraser

Computer Fundamentals with Application Software
Workbook and Study Guide to accompany Computer Fundamentals with Application Software
Learning to Use SUPERCALC®3, dBASE III®, and WORDSTAR® 3.3: An Introduction
Learning to Use SUPERCALC®3: An Introduction
Learning to Use dBASE III®: An Introduction
Learning to Use WORDSTAR® 3.3: An Introduction
BASIC Programming for the IBM® Personal Computer
Workbook and Study Guide to accompany BASIC Programming for the IBM® Personal Computer
Structured COBOL — Flowchart Edition
Structured COBOL — Pseudocode Edition
Turbo Pascal Programming

STRUCTURED BASIC

FUNDAMENTALS AND STYLE

for the IBM® PC and Compatibles

James S. Quasney
John Maniotes

Purdue University Calumet

Dedication

To our wives: **Linda** and **Mary**
The Quasney tribe: **Lisa**, **Jeff**, **Marci**, **Jodi**, **Amanda**, and **Nikole**
The Maniotes clan: **Dionne**, **Sam**, and **Andrew**

Credits:

Publisher: Tom Walker
Editor: Donna Villanucci
Director of Production: Becky Herrington
Design/Cover: Becky Herrington
Cover Photo: ©David Hughes/Stock Boston
Manufacturing Director: Erek Smith

3 4 5 6 7 8 9 K 5 4 3 2 1 0 9

Library of Congress Cataloging-in-Publication Data

```
Quasney, James S.
    Structured BASIC fundamentals and style / James S. Quasney, John
Maniotes.
        p.   cm.
    Includes index.
    ISBN 0-87835-289-9
    1. BASIC (Computer program language)  2. Structured programming.
I. Maniotes, John.  II. Title.
QA76.73.B3Q376 1988
005.13'3--dc19                                              87-29968
                                                              CIP
```

PREFACE

OBJECTIVES OF THIS BOOK

This book was developed specifically for an introductory computer programming course that utilizes Microsoft BASIC on an IBM PC, IBM PS/2, or compatible system. The objectives of this book are as follows:

1. To acquaint the reader with the proper and correct way to design and write high-quality programs. The top-down approach and structured programming are emphasized early and are consistently used throughout the book. The GOTO statement is not used in any program examples.
2. To teach the fundamentals of the Microsoft BASIC programming language.
3. To familiarize the reader with the operational procedures of the IBM PC, IBM PS/2, and compatible systems.
4. To teach good problem-solving techniques that can be used in advanced computing and information processing courses.
5. To emphasize interactive applications and menu-driven programs, the most popular type of programming in today's world.
6. To develop an exercise-oriented approach that allows the reader to learn by example.
7. To use practical problems to illustrate the applications of computers.
8. To encourage independent study and help those who are working alone on their own personal computer systems.

LEVEL OF INSTRUCTION

This book is designed to be used in a one-semester course in BASIC programming or in independent study by those who are working alone. No previous experience with a computer is assumed, and no mathematics beyond the high school freshman level is required. The book is written specifically for the student with average ability, for whom continuity, simplicity, and practicality are characteristics we consider essential. Numerous insights, based on the authors' fifty cumulative years of experience in teaching and consulting in the field of data processing, are implicit throughout the book. For the past ten consecutive years, we have both taught introductory programming courses using BASIC.

FUNDAMENTAL TOPICS ARE PRESENTED IN DETAIL

Besides introducing students to the proper and correct way to design and write programs by means of structured and top-down techniques, this book presents fundamental topics concerning computers and programming which should be covered in any introductory programming class. These include the stored program concept; getting on the computer; editing programs; input/output operations; variables and constants; simple and complex computations; the use of functions and subroutines; decision making; the use of counters and running totals; rounding and truncation; looping and end-of-file tests; counter-controlled loops; the use of logical operators; string manipulation; and graphics. Other essential topics include data validation; control breaks; paging reports; table processing; sequence checking; selection; searching; matching; merging; sorting; file processing; and the differences between batch and interactive applications. Every one of these topics is covered in detail in this book.

DISTINGUISHING FEATURES

The distinguishing features of this book include the following:

A Proven Book

This book has evolved over the past decade and is based on the authors' four prior books on BASIC programming. Many instructors who have used our books have shared with us their comments and suggestions for improvement as new programming techniques have been developed. They have done much to shape the contents of this book, which reflects modern programming practices.

Early Presentation of the Top-Down (Modular) Approach and the Structured Programming Approach

Students are introduced to the top-down approach early, before they learn about looping and decision making. By the time they get to the larger and more complex programs, they are solving problems top-down by habit.

Particular attention is given to designing proper programs by means of the three logic structures of structured programming: Sequence, Selection (If-Then-Else and Case), and Repetition (Do-While and Do-Until). A disciplined method for implementing the structured design is adhered to throughout the book.

GOTOless Textbook

The GOTO and ON-GOTO statements are discussed briefly. However, they are not used in this book to write programs. All looping is implemented by means of either the WHILE and WEND statements or the FOR and NEXT statements. GOSUB statements are used when IF statements require more than three physical lines.

Early and Complete Coverage of File Processing

Complete coverage of sequential, random, and simulated-indexed files provides the reader with knowledge that is central to a real programming environment. Topics include creating all three types of files; file maintenance (matching and merging operations) and an information retrieval system that features simulated-indexed files. Sequential file processing is covered immediately following the presentation of the top-down approach and structured programming.

Student Interaction With Programs on the Student Diskette

The Student Diskette that accompanies this book contains all the executable programs and data files. Following the discussion of a program, the student is often asked to load the program from the Student Diskette and alter one or more statements to generate new results. We use the heading Try It Yourself to signal this activity. Instructors are encouraged to add to these short but meaningful exercises.

In our opinion, this interaction with the program has great educational value. Students quickly realize the significance of a statement by reviewing the results due to its modification. Interacting with a program also allows the student to experiment with changes without having to type the entire program. Furthermore, students may use a program from a particular chapter as a shell to solve a problem that is presented at the end of that chapter.

The use of a shell program will save keying time. Finally, the instructor will not be deluged with students requesting copies of data files when exercises requiring them are assigned, since each student will already have his or her own personal copy of all the referenced data files.

BASIC Programming Problems with Sample Input and Output

A total of 60 challenging field-tested BASIC Programming Problems are included at the end of the chapters. Each of the 60 problems includes a statement of purpose, a problem statement, sample input data, and the corresponding output results. Solutions to these problems are given in the *Instructor's Manual and Answer Book* and are also available from the publisher on an IBM PC-compatible diskette.

Interactive Applications (Menu-Driven Programs)

Although examples of batch processing are presented, the primary emphasis is on interactive processing. The reader is introduced to the INPUT, PRINT, and CLS (Clear Screen) statements early in Chapter 2. The LOCATE statement is presented in Chapter 4 and thereafter is used extensively to build screens. Several menu-driven programs are illustrated to familiarize the reader with the type of programming that is proliferating today.

Emphasis on the Program Development Cycle

The program development cycle is presented early in Chapter 1 and is used throughout the book. Good design habits are reinforced, and special attention is given to testing the design *before* attempting to implement the logic in a program.

Emphasis on Fundamentals and Style

Heavy emphasis is placed on the fundamentals of producing well-written and readable programs. A disciplined style is consistently used in all program examples. Thorough documentation and indentation standards illuminate the implementation of the Selection and Repetition logic structures.

Summary of the Microsoft BASIC Language on a Reference Card

A summary of the statements, commands, functions, special variables, special keys, operators, and reserved words can be found on a reference card at the back of this book. This summary is invaluable to the beginning student as a quick reference piece.

Presentation of Programming Case Studies

This book contains 26 completely solved and annotated case studies, illuminating the use of Microsoft BASIC and personal computers in the real world. Emphasis is placed on problem analysis, program design, and an in-depth discussion of the program solution. The program solutions to these Programming Case Studies, as well as all other programs found throughout the book, are on the accompanying Student Diskette.

Program Design Aids

Since the authors recognize top-down charts and flowcharts as excellent pedagogical aids and as the tools of an analyst or programmer, many of the Programming Case Studies include both top-down charts and program flowcharts to demonstrate programming style, design, and documentation. For the student's convenience, line numbers have been placed at the top-left corner of the symbols to better illustrate the relationship between the logic diagrams and the program.

Debugging Techniques and Programming Tips

A characteristic of a good programmer is that he or she has confidence that a program will work the first time it is executed. This confidence implies that careful attention has been given to the design and that the design has been fully tested. Still, errors do occur, and when they do, they must be corrected. Throughout this book, especially in Appendix C, efficient methods for locating and correcting errors are introduced. Tracing, as well as other debugging techniques, is discussed in detail. The section in Appendix C which deals with programming tips serves as an excellent reference, facilitating the writing of efficient, readable code.

Applications-Oriented Approach

Over 150 Microsoft BASIC programs, illustrating a wide range of practical applications, along with many partial programs, are used to introduce specific statements and the proper and correct way to write high-quality programs.

Emphasis on Data Validation

Most abnormal terminations in a production environment are due to user errors and not programmer errors. This is especially true for programs that interact with the user or are executed on personal computers. Good programmers will attempt to trap as many user errors as possible. This book pays particular attention to the illustration of various data validation methods for ensuring that incoming data is reasonable or within limits.

What You Should Know

Each chapter contains a succinct, list-formatted review entitled What You Should Know, reinforcing key concepts and data processing terminology.

Test Your BASIC Skills

A set of short-answer exercises identified as Test Your BASIC Skills, appears at the end of each chapter. Over 200 problems, many of which are complete programs, are included for practice. Through the use of these exercises, students can master the concepts presented and instructors are afforded a valuable diagnostic tool. Answers for even-numbered Test Your BASIC Skills exercises are included at the end of the book, before the index. Answers to the odd-numbered exercises can be found in the *Instructor's Manual and Answer Book*.

Graphics and Sound

Chapter 10 covers all the graphics statements and functions in Microsoft BASIC that are central to understanding what can be done with graphics on the PC. The topics provide the student with knowledge of how to create, change, display, and store graphic designs and animation sequences. Furthermore, the necessary sound and music statements are discussed and are applied to various applications.

Additional PC Information

Besides a general introduction to the IBM PC and IBM PS/2 in Chapter 1, Appendix D includes diskette formatting and operating instructions, and a list of popular magazines, newspapers, and manuals to help keep the student abreast of the many new developments in the personal computer field.

ANCILLARY MATERIALS

A comprehensive instructor's support package accompanies *Structured BASIC Fundamentals and Style for the IBM PC and Compatibles*. These ancillaries are available upon request from the publisher.

Instructor's Manual and Answer Book

The *Instructor's Manual and Answer Book* includes the following:

- Lecture outlines for each chapter
- Transparency masters from each chapter of the text
- Chapter-by-chapter objectives and vocabulary lists
- Answers to the odd-numbered Test Your BASIC Skills exercises
- Program solutions to the 60 programming assignments in the book
- Test bank, including true/false, short answer, fill-in, and multiple-choice questions for quizzes and tests

ProTest: An Easy-to-Use Computerized Test-Generating Package

Boyd & Fraser's state-of-the-art test-generating package, ProTest, has been designed specifically for this book. ProTest is an easy-to-use menu-driven package that is supplied on an IBM PC-compatible diskette. ProTest allows an instructor to create a customized test on the PC in a matter of minutes. The large test bank that accompanies ProTest includes field-tested true/false and multiple-choice questions. A user may also enter his or her own questions into the test bank.

ProTest will run on any IBM PC, IBM PS/2, or compatible system with two floppy-diskette drives or a hard disk.

Instructor Diskette

The Instructor Diskette includes the solutions to the 60 programming assignments found at the end of Chapters 2 through 10.

ACKNOWLEDGMENTS

We would like to thank and express our appreciation to the many fine and talented individuals who have contributed to the success of this book. We were fortunate to have a group of reviewers whose critical evaluations of our first four BASIC books, *Standard BASIC Programming, BASIC Fundamentals and Style, Complete BASIC for the Short Course,* and *Applesoft BASIC Fundamentals and Style,* were of great value during the preparation of these books. Special thanks again go to Professor James N. Haag, University of San Francisco; Professor R. Waldo Roth, Taylor University; Professor David Bradbard, Auburn University; Professor Donald L. Muench, St. John Fisher College; Professor Jerry Lameiro, Colorado State University; Professors John T. Gorgone, and I. Englander of Bentley College; Professor Chester Bogosta, Saint Leo College; Professor John J. Couture, San Diego City College; Professor Syed Shahabuddin, Central Michigan University; Sumit Sircar, University of Texas at Arlington; Marilyn Markowitz; and James Larson, director of computer services for the Homewood Flossmoor High School District in Homewood, Illinois. We are also very grateful to the following individuals, who reviewed the manuscript for *Structured BASIC Fundamentals and Style for the IBM PC and Compatibles:* Professor Al Schroeder, Richland College; Professor Dave Talsky, University of Wisconsin-Milwaukee; Professors George Fowler and Louise Darcey, Texas A&M University; Professor William Bailey, Casper College; Professor John Grillo, Bentley College; Professor Riki Kucheck, Orange Coast College; Professor Michael Walton, Miami-Dade Community College North;

Professor Dorelyn F. Anderson, Saint Cloud University; and Marjorie Leeson. The instructional staff of the Information Systems and Computer Programming Department of Purdue University Calumet provided many helpful comments and suggestions, and to them we extend our sincere thanks.

No book is possible without the motivation and support of an editorial staff. Therefore, our final acknowledgment and greatest appreciation are reserved for the following at Boyd & Fraser: Tom Walker, editor-in-chief, for the opportunity to write this book and for his constant encouragement; Donna Villanucci, who turned in an incredible developmental editing job; Becky Herrington, director of production, for her patience, diligence, and especially her creative talents; and finally, special praise for Toni Jean Rosenberg, for her invaluable editorial assistance.

Hammond, Indiana   James S. Quasney
January 1988   John Maniotes

NOTES TO THE STUDENT

1. The first occurrence of a computer or programming term is printed in **boldface**. Its definition can be found nearby, usually in the same paragraph.
2. Beginning in chapter 4, line numbers appear near symbols in top-down charts and program flowcharts, in order to show their relationship to the corresponding program.
3. Every chapter ends with an important and useful review section called What You Should Know.
4. The answers to all the even-numbered Test Your BASIC Skills questions are at the back of the book, before the index.
5. All the executable programs in the text are on the Student Diskette that accompanies this book. The programs on the Student Diskette which correspond to those in the text begin with the prefix PRG, followed by the chapter and program numbers. For example, PRG2-8 refers to the eighth executable program in chapter 2.

    Often, following the discussion of a program in the book, you will find a section labeled Try It Yourself. Follow the directions and load, modify, and execute the program. These short exercises will help you understand the significance of various Microsoft BASIC statements and how slight modifications to a program can affect the results.

    You will also find the programs on the Student Diskette helpful when you are solving assigned programming problems. These programs can be retrieved from the diskette, and statements can be added, modified, or deleted to arrive at a solution.
6. An easy-to-use reference card at the back of this book contains a summary of the Microsoft BASIC statements, commands, functions, special variables, special keys, operators, and reserved words.
7. Appendix A, "Program Flowcharting and Top-Down Design," and Appendix B, "Pseudocode and Other Logic Design Tools," provide you with additional valuable logic-design methods.
8. Appendix C, "Debugging Techniques, Programming Tips, and Chaining," suggests efficient methods for locating and correcting errors in a program. It also includes tips on how to write efficient, readable code and how to handle large programs.

LIST OF PROGRAMMING CASE STUDIES

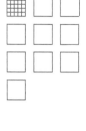

COMPUTERS AND PROBLEM SOLVING: AN INTRODUCTION

A **computer** is a machine that can accept data, process the data at high speeds, and give the results of these processes in an acceptable form. A more formal definition of a computer is given by the American National Standards Institute (ANSI), which defines it as a device that can perform substantial computation, including numerous arithmetic and logic operations, without intervention by a human operator.

The key phrases in the ANSI definition are "substantial computation," "logic operations," and "without intervention by a human operator." These phrases point out the differences between computers and desk calculators.

The act of instructing a computer is known as **programming**. It involves writing precise instructions in a language the computer understands.

*Advantages
of a Computer*

The major advantages of a computer are its speed and accuracy, as well as its ability to store and have ready for immediate recall vast amounts of data. Today's computers can also accept data from anywhere via telephone line or satellite communications. They can generate usable output, like reports, paychecks, and invoices, at a speed of several thousand lines per minute.

A recent statement made by James A. Allen of the public affairs division of Ford Motor Company illustrates the speed and accuracy of a computer. Mr. Allen's remarks concerned an engine control microcomputer system called Electronic Engine Control (EECIV), which the company says "can read seven engine parameters and change seven engine functions in less than one engine revolution — three-hundredths of a second. The computations performed during each minute of engine operation would take a human an estimated forty-five years or more using a manually operated calculator." This microcomputer system is made up of two chips, each less than a quarter of an inch square. In 1960, a computer with less capability than these two chips would have filled a room, and in 1970 it would have filled the trunk of a car.

Computers can handle tedious and time-consuming work and large amounts of data without ever tiring, which makes them indispensable for most businesses. In fact, computers have been among the most important forces in the modernization of business, industry, and society since World War II. Keep in mind, however, that with all their capabilities, computers are not built to think or reason. They extend our intellect, but they do not replace thinking.

⊞ **1.2**

COMPUTER
HARDWARE

Computer hardware is the physical equipment of a computer system. The equipment may consist of mechanical, magnetic, optical, electrical, or electronic devices. Although many computers have been built in different sizes, speeds, and costs, and with different internal operations, most of them have the same five basic subsystems, as shown in Figures 1.1 and 1.2.

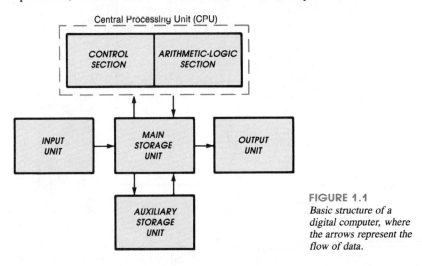

FIGURE 1.1
Basic structure of a digital computer, where the arrows represent the flow of data.

Input   An **input unit** is a device that allows **programs** (instructions to the computer) and **data** (like rate of pay, hours worked, and number of dependents) to enter the computer system. This device converts the incoming data into electrical impulses, which are then sent to the other units of the computer. A computer system usually has a **keyboard** for input. Other common input devices include a **joystick**, **mouse**, and **floppy diskette unit**. The keyboard and floppy diskette unit are shown in Figure 1.2.

Main Storage   After the instructions and data have entered the computer through an input unit, they are stored in the computer's **main storage** unit. Since computers can process vast amounts of data in a short time, and since some can perform millions of calculations in just one second, the storage unit must be able to retain large amounts of data and make any single item rapidly available for processing.

FIGURE 1.2
The IBM Personal Computer (PC) (Courtesy IBM Corp.).

Main storage in a computer is divided into locations called **bytes**, each having an **address**. Each byte can hold a single character, like the letter A, or a digit, like the number 5. A byte may also hold a code that has special meaning to the computer, like the type of instruction to execute.

When instructions and data are entered, they are stored in various locations of main storage. The computer leaves data in a storage location until it is instructed to replace it with new data. While a data item is in storage, the computer can "look it up" as often as it is needed. Thus, when data is retrieved from a storage location, the stored contents remain unaltered. When you instruct the computer to put new data in that location, it replaces old data.

Central Processing Unit (CPU)

The **CPU** controls and supervises the entire computer system and performs the actual arithmetic and logic operations on data, as specified by the written program. The CPU is divided into the **arithmetic-logic section** and the **control section**, as shown in Figure 1.1.

The arithmetic-logic section performs such operations as addition, subtraction, multiplication, division, transferring, storing, and setting the algebraic sign of the results. Depending on the cost and storage capacity of the computer, the speed of the arithmetic unit will range from several thousand to many millions of operations per second.

The arithmetic-logic section also carries out the decision-making operations required to change the sequence of instruction execution. These operations include testing various conditions, for example, deciding the algebraic sign of a number or comparing two characters for equality. The result of these tests causes the computer to take one of two or more alternate paths through the program.

The control section directs and coordinates the entire computer system according to the program developed by the programmer and placed in main storage. The control section's primary function is to analyze and initiate the execution of instructions. This means that it has control over all other subsystems in the computer system. It can control the input of data and output of information and routing of data and information between auxiliary storage and main storage or between main storage and the arithmetic-logic section.

Auxiliary Storage

The function of the **auxiliary storage unit** is to store data and programs that are to be used over and over again. Common auxiliary storage devices are the **magnetic tape**, the **hard disk** and the **floppy diskette**.

These auxiliary storage devices can be used to store programs and data for as long as desired. A new program entering the system erases the previous program and data in main storage, but the previous program and data may be permanently stored on an auxiliary storage device for recall by the computer.

In a business, files containing employee records, customer records, accounts receivable or payable data, and inventory data are stored on magnetic tape, hard disk, or floppy diskette. Programs written to print paychecks, invoices, and management reports are also stored on these auxiliary storage devices. Without auxiliary storage, all programs and data would have to be entered manually through an input device every time an application was processed.

Output

When instructed by a program, the computer can communicate the results of a program to output units. A computer usually has a **video display device** for output. Other common output devices include a **printer**, a **plotter**, and a **floppy diskette unit**.

The video display device, also called a **CRT** or **VDT** or **monitor** or **screen**, is similar to the tube in a television set and can be used to display the output results in the form of words, numbers, graphs, or drawings. The video display device is shown in Figure 1.2.

⊞ **1.3**

THE PC AND PS/2
FAMILY

In 1981, IBM introduced the IBM Personal Computer (PC), a fully assembled, easy-to-use computer that has become the *de facto* personal computer standard throughout the world (see Figure 1.2).

Since that time, the original PC has undergone many enhancements, and additional models have been produced. These models include the following:

- IBM PC XT (Figure 1.3)
- IBM PCjr
- IBM Portable PC
- IBM Convertible or Laptop
- IBM PC AT (Figure 1.4)
- IBM Personal System/2 (PS/2) (Figure 1.5)

Since 1981, several million IBM PCs and their clones have been manufactured. Currently, there are over two hundred vendors worldwide who provide PC-compatible systems and peripherals.

Figure 1.6 shows what the internals of an IBM PC look like when the cover of the system unit is removed. Note the arrangement of the various units, slots, chips, and built-in speaker for audio and music applications.

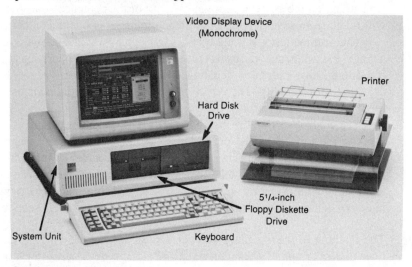

FIGURE 1.3
The IBM PC XT System (Courtesy IBM Corp.).

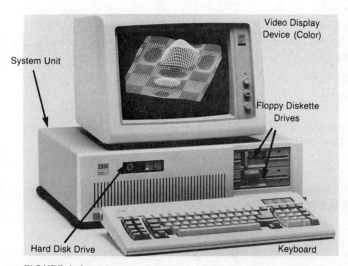

FIGURE 1.4
The IBM PC AT System (Courtesy IBM Corp.).

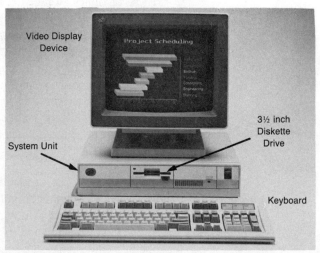

FIGURE 1.5
The IBM PS/2 System (Courtesy IBM Corp.).

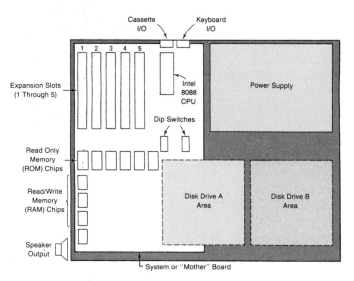

FIGURE 1.6
*A Top View of the
Internals of an IBM PC
System Unit.*

Figure 1.7 shows the front and rear views of the IBM PC. The figure illustrates the position of the On/Off power switch and the openings for some of the peripheral devices.

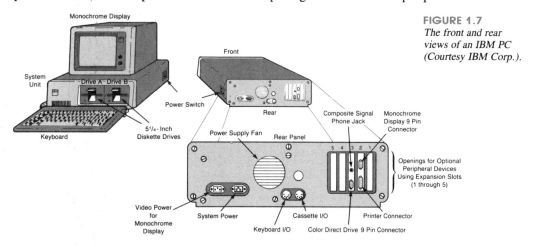

FIGURE 1.7
*The front and rear
views of an IBM PC
(Courtesy IBM Corp.).*

Many accessories and peripheral devices can be connected to the IBM PC family. This is possible because when IBM introduced the PC, it incorporated expansion slots so that users would be able to add enhancements at will. This "open architecture" has permitted many vendors to manufacture devices that enhance the performance of the PC.

The Keyboard   Figure 1.8 shows the IBM PC keyboard, which is similar to that of an ordinary typewriter and which is used to enter programs' and data into the main storage unit. Numeric, alphabetic, and special characters appear in the standard typewriter format on the keyboard, which contains eighty-three keys.

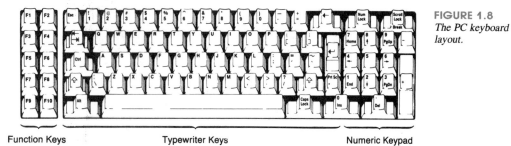

FIGURE 1.8
*The PC keyboard
layout.*

Function Keys   Typewriter Keys   Numeric Keypad

Note the layout of the function keys, the typewriter keys, and the numeric keypad. These keys will be explained in chapter 2. Exercise 1 in section 1.10 at the end of this chapter is designed to acquaint you with some of the important keys on your IBM PC keyboard.

Figure 1.9 shows how you can adjust the tilt position of your keyboard for typing comfort. There is one adjustable leg handle at each end of the keyboard.

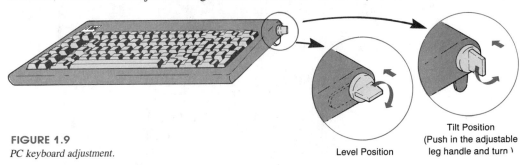

FIGURE 1.9
PC keyboard adjustment.

Level Position

Tilt Position
(Push in the adjustable
leg handle and turn)

Video Display Device

There are two types of video display devices — monochrome and color. Figure 1.10 shows the various control knobs on these display devices.

Monochrome displays come in black and white, green, or amber. Color displays come in sixteen colors. Either device can display 40 or 80 characters per horizontal line. There are 25 lines on the screen. The monochrome and color pin connectors on the system unit are shown in Figure 1.7 on the previous page.

FIGURE 1.10
Monochrome and color video display devices.

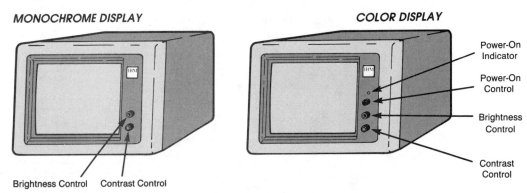

MONOCHROME DISPLAY

Brightness Control   Contrast Control

COLOR DISPLAY

Power-On Indicator

Power-On Control

Brightness Control

Contrast Control

When a PC contains a color/graphics board connected to a color display device, interesting graphics like plots, line drawings, and animation can be displayed. Chapter 10 presents a discussion on color and graphics for the PC.

CPU and Main Storage Unit

All IBM PCs and compatibles contain a 16-bit Intel 8088 CPU, called a microprocessor, which is miniaturized on a **silicon chip**, typically a fraction of an inch long. This microprocessor is shown in Figure 1.6 on the previous page. The IBM PC AT and compatibles contain an Intel 80286 CPU, and the advanced models of the IBM PS/2 and compatibles contain an Intel 80386 CPU.

The CPU and main storage unit are contained on the system board (see Figure 1.6). Main storage is sometimes called read/write memory, or **RAM**. The PC can contain a minimum of 16K (16,384) bytes of main storage, or RAM. The letter K represents 1,024. Most PCs contain at least 256K bytes of main storage. Additional main storage may be added, up to 640K bytes for the PC and 3 MB (3,145,728 bytes) for the PC AT.

Read Only Memory (**ROM**) is another form of storage. It is used to store the BASIC interpreter, disk loader, patterns for graphics characters, and so on (see Figure 1.6).

Auxiliary Storage

The IBM PC and compatibles use a 5¼-inch **flexible (floppy) diskette** for storing and retrieving information. Early PC's used one diskette unit containing a single-sided (SS), single-density (SD) diskette with approximately 160K bytes of storage.

Nowadays, most PCs use one or two diskette units, each containing a double-sided (DS), double-density (DD) diskette with approximately 360K bytes of storage. Hence, on a double-sided diskette, you can file away the contents of at least 125 8½-by-11 inch sheets of paper.

The IBM PS/2 uses 3½-inch diskettes containing 720K bytes. Examples of 5¼-inch and 3½-inch diskettes are shown in Figure 1.11.

FIGURE 1.11
A 5¼-inch and a 3½-inch diskette (Courtesy IBM Corp.).

A floppy diskette is a thin, circular media coated with a magnetic substance, and it comes in a permanent protective jacket. When not in use, the diskette is placed in a sleeve or diskette envelope. Figure 1.12 shows the various parts of a diskette.

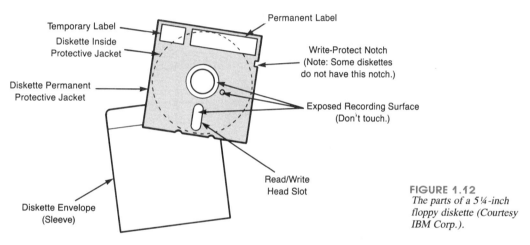

FIGURE 1.12
The parts of a 5¼-inch floppy diskette (Courtesy IBM Corp.).

The procedure for inserting a diskette to start up a PC is shown graphically in Figure 1.13 (follow the numbers 1 through 5) and is further described in Table 2.6 on page 32.

When a floppy diskette is inserted into a diskette unit, the floppy is made to spin inside its permanent protective jacket. A read/write head in the diskette unit comes into magnetic contact with the recording surface through the slot hole in the diskette's permanent protective jacket (see Figure 1.12).

FIGURE 1.13
Procedure for inserting a diskette to start up a PC.

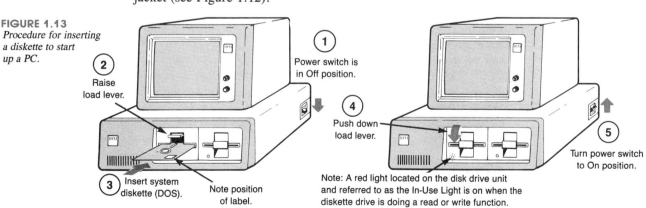

Many diskettes come with a **write-protect notch** (see Figure 1.12). If the notch is not covered with tape, the PC can read from as well as write on the diskette. If the notch *is* covered with tape, the PC can read only from the diskette. Important programs, such as the operating system, come in protective jackets with a no write-protect notch, thereby ensuring that the PC will not destroy any programs by writing on the diskette.

Floppy diskettes are delicate and should be handled and stored with care. Do not place diskettes near heat, cold, or magnetic field sources such as magnets. Do not bend or fold diskettes. Never touch the exposed recording surface; always hold the diskette by its protective jacket. If you need to write on the temporary label of a diskette, use only a felt-tip pen. A pencil or ballpoint pen, when pressed firmly, can damage the diskette and therefore should not be used for this purpose.

For additional auxiliary storage, a 5¼-inch **hard disk**, containing approximately 10 MB (10 million bytes) of storage can be used with a PC. This storage capacity is equivalent to 5,500 double-spaced typewritten pages. As the technology advances, 20MB, 30MB, and 50MB hard disks are becoming popular.

Network System   Some schools have opted to install a **network** that allows a printer, a disk drive, and other peripheral devices to be used by many interconnected personal computers. As shown in Figure 1.14, PCs in a network do not always require their own individual diskette drives or printers.

With a network, as many as seventy-two students operating PCs can be connected to an instructor-controlled PC. A network also allows students to access their programs from the instructor's disk drives and to use the printer. All processing of programs is done by the students on their assigned PC. When the students finish their work, they can store their programs on the instructor's diskette drives or hard disk drives.

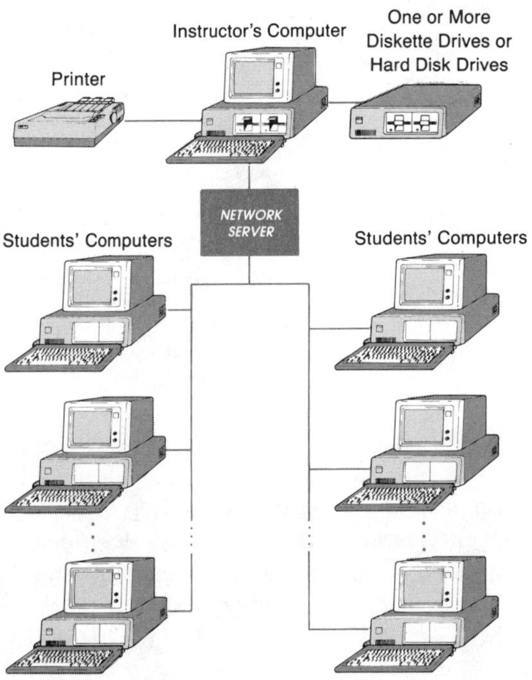

FIGURE 1.14
A network of personal computers.

PC Compatibles   Since IBM introduced the PC, more than two hundred companies worldwide have manufactured PC lookalikes, also called clones or compatibles. To compete against IBM, some of these companies add features to their models and increase their performance, while others undercut their competitors' prices. Some of the manufacturers have gone out of business as fast as they came in. A list of some of the popular PC compatibles is given in Table 1.1 (opposite).

As a potential user of a PC compatible, you should be aware that there are varying degrees of IBM PC compatibility. No one computer is 100 percent IBM PC compatible except, of course, an IBM PC. However, many are 99+ percent IBM PC compatible. The difference lies in the proprietary code that resides in the ROM chips and that controls the computer's operation (see Figure 1.6 on page 5).

_____TABLE 1.1 Some Popular IBM PC Compatibles_____

VENDOR	MODEL NUMBER	VENDOR	MODEL NUMBER
Apple Computer	*Macintosh II*	*Hewlett-Packard*	*HP PC*
	Macintosh SE	*ITT*	*Xtra Family*
AT&T	*PC 6300 Family*	*Leading Edge*	*Model D*
Compaq Computer	*PC Family*	*Radio Shack*	*Tandy 1000/2000/3000/*
Digital Equipment	*DEC VAXmate*		*4000 Family*
Epson	*Equity Family*	*Sperry*	*PC Family*
		Zenith Data Systems	*Z-100 PC Series*

All IBM PC compatibles should run the standard programs, like dBASE III™ and dBASE III PLUS™, Lotus 1-2-3™, MS Word™, and Sub Logic's Flight Simulator™ (see Table 1.2). If they don't, then they are not IBM PC compatible.

⊞ 1.4
THE STORED PROGRAM CONCEPT

Before a computer can take action and produce a desired result, it must be given a step-by-step description of the task to be accomplished. The step-by-step description is a series of precise instructions called a **program**. When these instructions are placed in the main storage unit of a computer, they are called the **stored program**. Main storage not only stores data but also stores the instructions that tell the computer what to do with the data. The stored program gives the computer a great deal of flexibility. Without it, the computer's ability to handle tasks would be reduced to that of a desk calculator.

Once the program is stored, the first instruction is located and sent to the control section, where it is interpreted and executed. Then the next instruction is located, sent to the control section, interpreted, and executed. This process continues automatically, instruction by instruction, until the program is completed or until the computer is instructed to halt.

In order for the computer to perform still another job, a new program must be stored in main storage. Hence, a computer can easily process a large number of different jobs.

⊞ 1.5
COMPUTER SOFTWARE

Computer software is a set of programming languages and programs concerned with the operation of a computer system. Some essential computer software comes with the purchase of a computer system. Additional software is either purchased or written by the user in a programming language that the computer understands. Table 1.2 lists some popular software packages and their functions. These packages do not require that you know how to program. They may be purchased at any computer store that sells personal computer systems.

_____TABLE 1.2 Some Popular Software Packages and Their Functions_____

SOFTWARE PACKAGE	FUNCTION
Harvard Presentation Graphics™	*A graphics program used to create line graphs, bar graphs, pie charts, and 3-D graphic images.*
Microsoft Word™	*A word processing program used to write, revise, and edit letters, reports, and manuscripts with efficiency and economy.*
Lotus 1-2-3™	*An electronic spreadsheet program used to organize data that can be defined in terms of rows and columns. Formulas can be applied to current rows or columns to create new rows and columns of information. Graphic images can be produced on the basis of the data in the spreadsheet. The 1-2-3 refers to the spreadsheet, database, and graphics features of this package.*
dBASE III PLUS™	*A data base system used to organize data on an auxiliary storage device. It also allows for the generation of reports and for easy access to the data.*

Programming languages are classified as **low-level languages** (like machine language and assembly language) and **high-level languages** (like BASIC, C, Pascal, COBOL, FORTRAN, and PL/I). Early-generation computers required programmers to program in machine language, and this language was different for each computer manufacturer's system.

Currently, most applications for the PC are programmed in one of the many popular high-level languages listed in Table 1.3. A high-level language is generally machine- or computer-independent; this means that programs written in a high-level language like BASIC can easily be transferred from one computer system to another, with little or no change in the programs.

TABLE 1.3 Some Popular High-Level Languages and Their Appropriate Area of Usefulness

LANGUAGE	AREA OF USEFULNESS
BASIC	*Beginner's All-purpose Symbolic Instruction Code is a very simple problem-solving language that is used with personal computers or with terminals in a time-sharing environment. BASIC is used for both business and scientific applications.*
C	*This is a procedure-oriented language that includes features like pointers, which allow access to many assembly-language capabilities. C is useful for writing applications packages and systems software, like operating systems.*
COBOL	*The COmmon Business Oriented Language is an English-like language that is suitable for business data-processing applications. It is especially useful for file and table handling and extensive input and output operations. COBOL is a very widely used programming language.*
FORTRAN	*FORmula TRANslation is a problem-solving language designed primarily for scientific data processing, engineering, and process-control applications.*
Pascal	*Pascal, named in honor of the French mathematician Blaise Pascal, is a programming language that allows for the formulations of algorithms and data in a form that clearly exhibits their natural structure. It is used primarily for scientific applications and systems programming and to some extent for business data processing.*
PL/I	*Programming Language/I is a problem-solving language designed for both business and scientific data processing. This language incorporates some of the best features of FORTRAN, COBOL, and other languages.*

Programming Case Study 1: *Computing an Average*

Program 1.1 illustrates a program written in BASIC. It instructs the PC to compute the average of three numbers, 17, 23, and 50.

PROGRAM 1.1

BASIC Program
```
100 ' Program 1.1
110 ' Computing an Average
120 ' *******************
130 AVG = (17 + 23 + 50) / 3
140 PRINT "The average is"; AVG
150 END
```

System Command
```
RUN
```

Displayed Result
```
The average is 30
```

The displayed answer, found below the word RUN, is 30. Even though we are deferring detailed explanations about this program until the next chapter, Program 1.1 gives you some indication of how to instruct a PC to calculate a desired result using BASIC. This program can be entered and processed on the IBM PC, PS/2, and all of the compatibles listed in Table 1.1 on the previous page.

The Operating System (MS DOS)

The operating system for the PC was designed by the Microsoft Corporation, one of the largest microcomputer software companies in the world. The operating system is called **PC DOS** for the IBM PC and **MS DOS** for the PC compatibles. MS DOS stands for Microsoft Disk Operating System.

This operating system, through a series of enhancements and new versions, has become the standard operating program for all IBM and IBM-compatible personal computer systems. MS DOS is permanently stored on the diskette that is supplied with every PC. This diskette is referred to either as **DOS** or as the **system diskette**.

MS DOS helps to act as an internal "traffic cop" by directing the flow of data into and out of the PC and the peripheral devices (see Figure 1.1 on page 2).

⊞ 1.6

PROBLEM SOLVING AND PROGRAM DEVELOPMENT

Every action the PC is expected to make toward solving a problem must be spelled out in detail in the program. The step-by-step procedures listed below will help you set up problems for the PC to solve. These procedures make up what is called the **program development cycle**.

1. **Problem Analysis** — Define the problem to be solved precisely, including the form of the input, the form of the output, and a description of the transformation of input to output.
2. **Program Design** — Devise an **algorithm**, or a method of solution, for the computer to use. This method must be a complete procedure for solving the specified problem in a finite number of steps. There must be no ambiguity (no chance that something can be interpreted in more than one way).

   Develop a detailed logic plan, using **flowcharts**, **pseudocode**, or some other logic tool to describe each step that the PC must perform to arrive at the solution. As far as possible, the flowcharts or pseudocode must describe *what* job is to be done and *how* the job is to be done.

   Develop good **test data**. As best you can, select data that will test for erroneous input.
3. **Test the Design** — Step by step, go through the flowchart or pseudocode, using the test data as if you were the PC. If the logic plan does not work, repeat steps 1 through 3.
4. **Code the Program** — Code the program in a computer language, like BASIC (see Table 1.3), according to the logic specified in the flowchart or pseudocode. Include program documentation, like comments and explanation, within the program.
5. **Review the Code** — Carefully review the code. Put yourself in the position of the PC and step through the entire program.
6. **Enter the Program** — Submit the program to the PC via a keyboard or other input device.
7. **Test the Program** — Test the program until it is error free and until it contains enough safeguards to ensure the desired result.
8. **Formalize the Solution** — Run the program, using the input data to generate the results. Review, and, if necessary, modify the documentation for the program.

Flowcharts

A **program flowchart** is a popular logic tool that is used for showing an algorithm in graphic form. By depicting a procedure for arriving at a solution, a program flowchart also shows how the application or job is to be accomplished.

A programmer prepares a flowchart *before* he or she begins coding the solution in BASIC. Eight basic symbols are used in program flowcharting. They are given in Table 1.4 on the following page with their respective names and meanings and with some of the BASIC statements that are represented by them.

___TABLE 1.4___ Flowchart Symbols and Their Meanings_____

SYMBOL	NAME	MEANING
▭	Process Symbol	Represents the process of executing a defined operation or group of operations which results in a change in value, form, or location of information. Examples: LFT, DIM, RESTORE, DEF, and other processing statements. Also functions as the default symbol when no other symbol is available.
▱	Input/Output (I/O) Symbol	Represents an I/O function, which makes data available for processing (input) or for displaying (output) of processed information. Examples: READ, INPUT, and PRINT.
Left to Right / Right to Left / Top to Bottom / Bottom to Top	Flowline Symbol	Represents the sequence of available information and executable operations. The lines connect other symbols, and the arrowheads are mandatory only for right-to-left and bottom-to-top flow
⌐▭	Annotation Symbol	Represents the addition of descriptive information, comments, or explanatory notes as clarification. The vertical line and the broken line may be placed on the left, as shown, or on the right. Example: REM or '.
◇	Decision Symbol	Represents a decision that determines which of a number of alternative paths is to be followed. Examples: IF and ON-GOSUB statements.
▭	Terminal Symbol	The beginning, the end, or a point of interruption or delay in a program. Examples: STOP, RETURN, and END statements.
○	Connector Symbol	Any entry from, or exit to, another part of the flowchart. Also serves as an off-page connector.
▯	Predefined Process Symbol	Represents a named process consisting of one or more operations or program steps that are specified elsewhere. Example: GOSUB.

One rule that is basic to all flowcharts concerns direction. In constructing a flowchart, start at the top (or left-hand corner) of a page. The flow should be top to bottom or left to right. If the flow takes any other course, arrowheads must be used. A plastic template can be obtained from most computer stores or bookstores. This template can be used to help you draw the flowchart symbols. Figure 1.15 on the opposite page shows a flowchart that illustrates the computations required to compute the average commission paid to a company's sales personnel. For an in-depth discussion on flowcharts, see Appendix A.

Pseudocode   Pseudocode is an alternative to program flowcharts which uses standard English and resembles BASIC code. It allows for the logic of a program to be formulated without diagrams or charts. Following are some examples of operations in pseudocode:

Clear screen

Discount = rate × sale price

If male
    Then Add 1 to male counter
    Else Add 1 to female counter
End-If

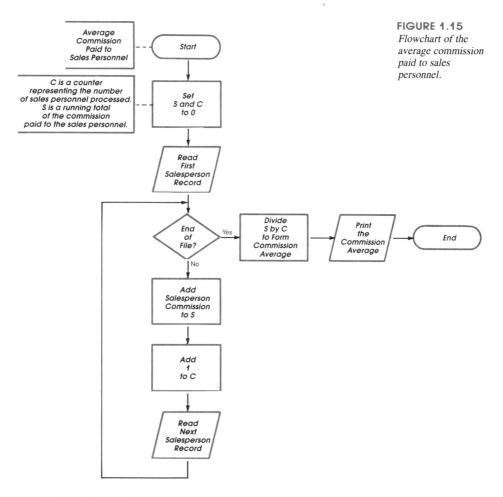

FIGURE 1.15
*Flowchart of the
average commission
paid to sales
personnel.*

Figure 1.16 shows a pseudocode version of the flowchart solution presented in Figure 1.15.

Program: Average Commission Paid to Sales Personnel
Set salesperson counter to 0
Set total commission to 0
Read first salesperson record
Do-While not end-of-file
    Add salesperson commission to total commission
    Add 1 to salesperson counter
    Read next salesperson record
End-Do
Commission average = total commission / salesperson counter
Display commission average
End: Average Commission Paid to Sales Personnel

FIGURE 1.16
*Pseudocode version of
the average commission
paid to sales personnel.*

Although pseudocode has few formal rules, we have listed some of the commonly accepted ones, along with several examples of their use, in section B.2 of Appendix B.

Appendix B also includes a discussion of some other powerful logic tools, like **Nassi-Schneiderman charts** and **Warnier-Orr diagrams**. Chapter 3 presents **top-down charts**. All of these logic tools have their strengths and weaknesses. As you solve problems in the later chapters of this book, we suggest you try all of the logic tools, and then choose the one that best suits you. Of course, your instructor may have something to say about the logic tool you use for the required assignments.

⊞ **1.7**

ADDITIONAL
INFORMATION ON
PERSONAL
COMPUTERS

You are encouraged to seek additional information on personal computers. To assist you in that search, Appendix D includes

- a list of magazines and newspapers oriented to the PC; both provide current information on what is taking place with personal computers.
- a list of PC manuals.

⊞ **1.8** WHAT YOU SHOULD KNOW

To help you study this chapter, a summary of the topics covered in it is listed below. These statements apply to all computers, including the PC. This is not a test that includes both true and false statements; all of the statements in this list are true.

1. A computer is a device that can perform substantial computation, including numerous arithmetic and logic operations, without intervention by a human operator.
2. The major advantages of a computer are its speed, accuracy, and ability to store and have ready for immediate recall vast amounts of data.
3. However fast, computers are not built to think or reason. They extend our intellect, but they do not replace thinking.
4. Computer hardware is the physical equipment of a computer system.
5. Most computers have five basic subsystems — input, output, main storage, auxiliary storage, and the central processing unit (CPU).
6. An input unit allows programs and data to enter the computer system.
7. Main storage is the computer's primary storage unit, where instructions and data are stored for processing purposes.
8. The central processing unit (CPU) controls and supervises the entire computer system and performs the actual arithmetic and logic operations on data, as specified by the written program. The CPU is made up of two sections — the arithmetic-logic section and the control section.
9. The arithmetic-logic section performs the arithmetic operations and carries out the decision-making operations required by a program.
10. The control section directs and coordinates the entire computer system.
11. The auxiliary storage unit stores data and programs that are to be used over and over again.
12. An output unit is used by the computer to communicate the results of a program.
13. A computer program is a series of instructions required to complete a procedure or task. When these instructions are placed in the main storage unit of a computer, they become a stored program.
14. Computer software is a program or a set of programs written for a computer.
15. Software packages that do not require a person to know how to program are available for word processing, electronic spreadsheets, data base management, and graphics.
16. Programming languages are classified as low-level languages (like machine language and assembly language) and high-level languages (like BASIC, C, Pascal, COBOL, FORTRAN, and PL/I).
17. The program development cycle is a set of step-by-step procedures for solving a problem.
18. In problem analysis, defining the problem is the first step in solving it.
19. Program design is made up of three steps — devising a method of solution, drawing logic diagrams, and selecting good test data.
20. A BASIC program should be coded only after the design is complete and has been carefully reviewed and tested.
21. A program flowchart is a popular logic tool used for showing an algorithm in graphic form.
22. Pseudocode is an alternative to program flowcharts which allows for the logic of a program to be formulated through the use of standard English, without diagrams or charts.

⊞ **1.9** TEST YOUR BASIC SKILLS (Even-numbered answers are at the back of the book, before the index.)

1. State three major advantages that computers have over the manual computation of problems.
2. What are the basic subsystems of a computer system? Briefly describe the function of each subsystem.
3. What makes up the central processing unit (CPU)?
4. Name two devices that serve both as input and output devices.
5. Name five IBM personal computer models.
6. What is meant by the term hardware? Software?
7. IBM PC monitors display either _____ or _____ characters per horizontal line on the screen.
8. What does the letter K represent when used to denote the amount of main storage?
9. A double-density floppy diskette for the IBM PC has a diameter of _____ inches and stores approximately _____ K bytes.
10. A system for sharing a disk drive and printer is also known as a _____ system.

11. Draw one flowchart that enables the Mechanical Man to accomplish efficiently the objectives set forth in phases 1 and 2 of Figure 1.17.

FIGURE 1.17
The two phases of the Mechanical Man.

OBJECTIVES:

Phase 1: The mechanical man is seated at an unknown integer number (0,1,2,...) of steps from the wall. He will stand up and walk forward until he touches the wall with his fingertips. When he is in a seated position with arms raised, his fingertips are aligned with the tips of his shoes.

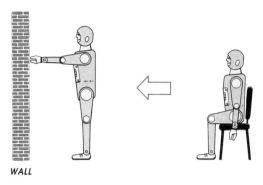

WALL

Phase 2: After touching the wall, the mechanical man will return to his chair. Since the chair is too low for him to sense by touch, he can get to it only by going back exactly as many steps as he came forward.

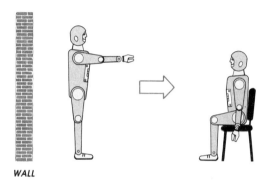

WALL

The Mechanical Man possesses the following properties:

• He is restricted to carrying out a limited repertoire of instructions.
• He does *nothing* unless given a specific instruction.
• He must carry out any instructions he is given *one at a time*.
• He understands the following instructions:

a. Physical Movement:
1. Stand up (into an erect position without moving feet).
2. Sit down (into a sitting position without moving feet).
3. Take one step (forward only; length of steps is always the same, and Mechanical Man can take a step only if he is standing up).
4. Raise arms (into one fixed position, straight ahead).
5. Lower arms (into one fixed position, straight down at his sides).
6. Turn right (in place without taking a step; can be done only if he is standing up; all right turns are 90-degree turns).

b. Arithmetic:
1. Add one (to a total that is being developed).
2. Subtract one (from a total that is being developed).
3. Record total (any number of totals can be remembered in this way).

c. Logic: The Mechanical Man can decide what instruction he will carry out next on the basis of answers to the following questions:
1. Arithmetic results
a. Is the result positive?
b. Is the result negative?
c. Is the result zero?
d. Is the result equal to a predetermined amount?

2. Physical status
a. Are the fingertips of the raised arms touching anything?

12. After reviewing the following three files with their specified records, answer the questions below:

	Record Number	Salesperson Number	Salesperson Commission
File 1	1	246	$ 400
	2	501	1100
	3	876	600
File 2	1	123	$ 300
File 3	This file is empty; that is, there are no records.		

     a. According to Figures 1.15 or 1.16 on page 13, what is the value of the commission average after File 1 is processed and the program terminates?

     b. Same as (a), but refer to File 2.

     c. Same as (a), but refer to File 3.

13. Same as problem 11, but use pseudocode to develop the logic that enables the Mechanical Man to accomplish efficiently the objectives shown in Figure 1.17 on the previous page.

14. Construct the flowchart to calculate a weekly payroll, using the following rules:

     a. Time and a half is paid for hours worked in excess of 40.

     b. $38.46 is allowed as nontaxable income for each dependent claimed.

     c. The withholding tax is 20 percent of the taxable income.

     d. Assume that end of file is defined as the condition in which the value for the number of hours worked is negative.

For each employee, input the following information:

     a. Name   b. Hourly rate of pay

     c. Number of hours worked   d. Number of dependents

For each employee, output the following information:

     a. Name   b. Gross pay

     c. Net pay   d. Income tax withheld

⊞ 1.10   PC HANDS-ON EXERCISES

The following exercises are designed to get you acquainted with your personal computer system. Consult with your instructor before running these exercises on your PC. Also consult Appendix D, which contains some of the operating instructions for the PC.

1. Identification of Keys on Keyboard

Find the following important keys on your keyboard. Make a check in the third column as you find each key.

TABLE 1.5 Special Keys on Keyboard

KEY	SYMBOL	CHECK	KEY	SYMBOL	CHECK	KEY	SYMBOL	CHECK
Enter	↵		Print Screen	PrtSc *		Home	7 Home	
Escape	Esc		Capital Lock	Caps Lock		End	1 End	
Tab	⇤ ⇥		Numeral Lock	Num Lock		Insert Key	0 Ins	
Control	Ctrl		Scroll Lock	Scroll Lock		Function Key 1	F1	
Shift	⇧		Alternate	Alt		Delete	• Del	
Backspace	←							

2. Sample Programs

With the assistance of your instructor, obtain and insert into Drive A the floppy diskette titled DOS or the system diskette (see Figure 1.13 on page 7). Insert into Drive B the diskette titled DOS Supplemental Programs.

See Table 2.6 on page 33, steps 1 to 8, for the initial PC start-up procedure. After the A> prompt appears, enter

```
B:
```

After the B> prompt appears, enter

```
A:BASICA
```

After the system displays the DOS version number and the following prompt:

```
ok
```

enter the command

```
RUN "SAMPLES"
```

Follow the self-explanatory instructions that appear on the screen. The DOS Supplemental Programs diskette will display various colors and animation on the screen, and will allow you to interact with the PC.

Try the following sample programs by entering the appropriate letter code:

Code	Sample Programs	Code	Sample Programs
A	Music	E	Donkey
B	Art	G	Ball
D	Circle	H	Colorbar

When you want to terminate a sample program, press the Escape (Esc) key.

3. Formatting a Diskette

When a diskette is purchased, it is blank, (that is, it has nothing recorded on its surface). In order for programs or data to be placed on a diskette, it must first be formatted. Obtain a blank diskette and format it by carefully following the instructions in section D.2 of Appendix D.

DO NOT FORMAT THE STUDENT DISKETTE THAT ACCOMPANIES THIS BOOK.

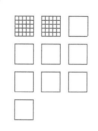

MICROSOFT BASIC: AN INTRODUCTION

The purpose of this chapter is to explain some of the rules that are common to all BASIC programs and to introduce some fundamental BASIC statements. We will concentrate on "simple" program illustrations, input/output operations, and system commands. Upon successful completion of this chapter, you should be able to develop some elementary programs written in Microsoft (MS) BASIC which will run on an IBM PC or compatible.

General Characteristics of a Microsoft BASIC Program

An MS BASIC program is composed of a sequence of lines. Each line contains a unique **line number** that serves as a label for the statement as shown in Figure 2.1. The line may contain up to 255 characters, although it usually contains considerably fewer.

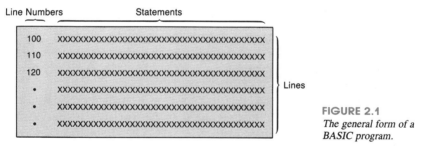

FIGURE 2.1
The general form of a BASIC program.

A line begins with a line number and ends when the Enter key is pressed, as indicated by the example below.

Programming Case Study 2, on the next page, illustrates the composition of an MS BASIC program.

Programming Case Study 2: Determining a Salesperson's Commission

Most salespeople work on a commission basis. Their earned commissions are often determined by multiplying their assigned commission rate by the amount of dollar sales. The dollar sales amount is computed by deducting any returned sales from the sum of their weekly sales. Given a biweekly pay period, the earned commission can be determined from the following formula:

Earned Commission = Rate × (Week 1 Sales + Week 2 Sales − Returns)

Let's assume that for the biweekly period, a salesperson's assigned commission rate is 15%, and sales are $1200 the first week, $1500 the second week. The returned sales are $75.

Program 2.1 instructs the PC to compute the earned amount and display it on the screen. The earned commission of 393.75 is just below the **system command** RUN.

PROGRAM 2.1

BASIC Program
```
100 LET COMMISSION = 0.15 * (1200 + 1500 - 75)
110 PRINT COMMISSION
120 END
```

System Command   RUN

Displayed Result   393.75

Keywords

There are three lines in this program. The first contains a LET statement. The LET statement consists of the **keyword** LET, a **variable name** COMMISSION, an **equal sign**, four **constants** (0.15, 1200, 1500, and 75), and three **arithmetic operators** (*, +, and −).

A keyword is a predefined word that has special meaning to MS BASIC. It describes the type of statement to be executed. In Program 2.1, there are three keywords: LET, PRINT, and END. Keywords are also called **reserved words**. See the reference card at the back of this book for a complete list of the MS BASIC keywords.

If a statement does not begin with a keyword and does contain an equal sign, then MS BASIC assumes it is a LET statement. For example, line 100 may be written in the following form:

```
100 COMMISSION = 0.15 * (1200 + 1500 - 75)
```

Even though line 100 does not contain the keyword LET, it is still called a LET statement. It may also be referred to as an **assignment statement**. Except for Program 2.1, in this book all LET statements will be written without the keyword LET.

Variable Names and Constants

In programming, a **variable** is a location in main storage whose value can change as the program is executed. In Program 2.1, the **variable name** COMMISSION references the storage location assigned to it by MS BASIC. Line 100 instructs the PC to complete the arithmetic operations and assign the resulting value of 393.75 to the storage location assigned to COMMISSION. A variable name begins with a letter and may be followed by up to 39 letters, digits, and decimal points. Keywords like LET, PRINT, and END that have special meaning to MS BASIC may not be used as variable names.

The equal sign in any LET statement means that the value of the variable to the left of the equal sign is to be replaced by the final value to the right of the equal sign.

Constants, like 0.15, 1200, 1500, and 75, represent ordinary numbers that do not change during the execution of a program. Both constants and variables are covered in detail in chapter 3.

Arithmetic Operators

The **plus sign** (+) in Program 2.1 signifies addition between the two constants that represent the weekly sales. The **minus sign** (–) indicates subtraction of the returned sales from the sum of the weekly sales. The **asterisk** (∗) indicates multiplication between the rate and the actual sales. The seven MS BASIC arithmetic operators are given in Table 2.1. As in mathematics, a set of parentheses is used to override the normal sequence of arithmetic operations.

_____TABLE 2.1 The Seven Arithmetic Operators_____

ARITHMETIC OPERATOR	MEANING	EXAMPLES OF USAGE	MEANING OF THE EXAMPLES
^	*Exponentiation*	2 ^ 3	*Raise 2 to the third power, which in this example is 8.*
∗	*Multiplication*	60.00 ∗ A1	*Multiply the value of A1 by 60.00.*
/	*Division*	H / 10	*Divide the value of H by 10.*
\	*Integer Division*	5 \ 3	*The integer quotient of 5 divided by 3, which in this example is 1. (Operands are rounded to whole numbers.)*
MOD	*Modulo*	16 MOD 5	*The integer remainder of 16 divided by 5, which in this example is 1.*
+	*Addition*	3.14 + 2.9	*Add 3.14 and 2.9.*
–	*Subtraction*	S - 35.4	*Subtract 35.4 from the value of S.*

The PRINT Statement

The second statement in Program 2.1 is called a PRINT statement. PRINT statements instruct the PC to bring a result out from main storage and display it on an output device. The statement causes the PC to display 393.75, the value of COMMISSION. The PRINT statement is covered in detail in chapter 4.

The END Statement

The last line of Program 2.1 contains the END statement. When executed, the END statement instructs the PC to stop executing the program. While the END statement is not required, it is recommended that you always include one.

Line Numbers

Every line in an MS BASIC program must begin with a unique line number. A line number must be a whole number between 0 and 65529. It must not contain a leading sign, embedded spaces, commas, decimal points, or any other punctuation. Line numbers are used in MS BASIC to

1. indicate the sequence of statement execution;
2. provide control points for branching, a topic discussed in chapter 3; and
3. add, change, and delete statements within a program.

Many experienced BASIC programmers begin with 100 or 1000 and then increase the line number of each new statement by 10. This leaves room to insert up to 9 possible extra statements between the numbers at a later time.

The system command RUN, found just below Program 2.1, instructs the PC to execute the program. It is not part of the program itself and, therefore, does not have a line number. For now, remember that BASIC statements have line numbers and system commands don't.

Line Rule 1: A line begins with a line number and ends when the Enter key is pressed. A line may contain up to 255 characters.

Line Rule 2: A line number must be be an integer between 0 and 65529. It must not contain a leading sign, embedded spaces, commas, decimal points, or any other punctuation.

Line Rule 3: BASIC statements have line numbers; system commands don't.

Some Relationships Between Statements

The PRINT statement in Program 2.1 would display a result of zero if, earlier in the program, we had failed to instruct the PC to assign a value to the variable COMMISSION. In other words, the PC cannot correctly display the value of COMMISSION before it determines this value. Therefore, if Program 2.1 were incorrectly written, as below, the PC would not display the correct results, unless by chance the earned commission were zero.

```
100 PRINT COMMISSION
110 COMMISSION = 0.15 * (1200 + 1500 - 75)   } Invalid
120 END
```

The following program is incorrect for the same reason:

```
100 PAY = 0.15 * (1200 + 1500 - 75)
110 PRINT COMMISSION                  } Invalid
120 END
```

The variable COMMISSION in line 110 has not been assigned a value earlier in the above program. The PC will calculate a value of 393.75 for the variable PAY but will display a result of zero. MS BASIC initially assigns all variables in a program a value of zero when the system command RUN is issued.

The correct program can be written as Program 2.1 or as Program 2.2 below.

PROGRAM 2.2

```
100 PAY = 0.15 * (1200 + 1500 - 75)
110 PRINT PAY
120 END

RUN

 393.75
```

Using the variable name PAY is no different from using the variable name COMMISSION, as long as the same name is used consistently. The relationship between output statements, like the PRINT statement, and other statements in a program can now be stated as follows:

Output Rule 1: Every variable appearing in an output statement should have been previously defined in the program.

Structured Style

Although the flexibility of the language permits certain statements to be placed anywhere in a program, logic, common sense, and **structured style** dictate where these statements are placed. Structured style is nothing more than disciplined, consistent programming. Discipline and consistency help programmers construct readable, maintainable, and reliable programs.

⊞ **2.2**

THE INPUT
STATEMENT

One of the major tasks of any computer program is to integrate the data that is to be processed into the program. In Program 2.1, the data was included directly in the LET statement as constants.

```
100 LET COMMISSION = 0.15 * (1200 + 1500 - 75)
110 PRINT COMMISSION
120 END
```
Data as Constants

This technique has its limitations. For example, line 100 must be modified each time a new salesperson is processed. An alternative method of integrating the data into the program is shown in Program 2.3 below.

PROGRAM 2.3

```
100 RATE = 0.15
110 WEEK1 = 1200
120 WEEK2 = 1500
130 RETURNS = 75
140 COMMISSION = RATE * (WEEK1 + WEEK2 - RETURNS)
150 PRINT COMMISSION
160 END

RUN

 393.75
```
Data as Constants

In this new program, data in the form of constants has been assigned to the variables RATE, WEEK1, WEEK2, and RETURNS. Line 140, used to calculate the earned commission, contains the variables that have been assigned the data in lines 100 through 130. When it executes Program 2.3, the PC must be informed of the numeric values for RATE, WEEK1, WEEK2, and RETURNS before it can calculate a value for COMMISSION. This can be generalized as the following rule:

> *Arithmetic Rule 1:* Every variable appearing to the right of the equal sign in a LET statement should have been previously defined in the program.

This second method of integrating the data into the program has the same limitations as Program 2.1. That is, lines 100 through 130 would have to be modified in order to process a new salesperson. The only advantage of Program 2.3 is that the LET statement itself in line 140 will work for any salesperson.

A third way to integrate data into the program is through the use of the INPUT statement. The INPUT statement provides for assignment of data to variables from a source outside the program during execution. The data is supplied to the program after the command RUN has been entered.

Through the use of the INPUT statement, the solution to Programming Case Study 2 can be made more general for calculating the earned commission for any salesperson, no matter what his or her commission rate, weekly sales, or returned sales. One version of the rewritten program is shown as Program 2.4 on the following page.

PROGRAM 2.4

```
100 INPUT RATE, WEEK1, WEEK2, RETURNS
110 COMMISSION = RATE * (WEEK1 + WEEK2 - RETURNS)
120 PRINT COMMISSION
130 END
RUN                                    Data Entered in Response to the
                                       Input Prompt
? 0.15, 1200, 1500, 75
 393.75
```

The function of the INPUT statement in line 100 is to display an **input prompt** and suspend execution of the program until data has been supplied. MS BASIC displays a **question mark** (?) for the input prompt. Then it is up to the user to supply the data. It is necessary that the Enter key be pressed following entry of the data.

Once the necessary data has been supplied, line 110 determines the earned commission, line 120 displays the earned commission, and, finally, line 130 terminates the program.

This third way of integrating data into a program, by means of the INPUT statement, is far more efficient than the other two ways, because we can process other sales personnel without modifying statements within the program. For example, to determine the earned commission for three salespeople, we can run the program three times, as shown below.

PROGRAM 2.4

```
100 INPUT RATE, WEEK1, WEEK2, RETURNS
110 COMMISSION = RATE * (WEEK1 + WEEK2 - RETURNS)
120 PRINT COMMISSION
130 END
RUN                        Execute Program for Salesperson 1

? 0.15, 1200, 1500, 75
 393.75

RUN                        Execute Program for Salesperson 2

? 0.10, 1000, 1300, 30
 227

RUN                        Execute Program for Salesperson 3

? 0.20, 2000, 4500, 0
 1300
```

It is important that the variables in the INPUT statement and the data supplied in response to the input prompt be separated by commas. A comma is used to establish a **list**, which is a set of distinct elements, each separated from the next by a comma. The comma must be used so that the PC can distinguish how many variables or data elements occur in each list. The order of the list of variables in the INPUT statement is also important. The INPUT statement in Program 2.4,

```
100 INPUT RATE, WEEK1, WEEK2, RETURNS
```

may have been written as

```
100 INPUT RETURNS, WEEK2, WEEK1, RATE
```

If so, however, the data supplied for Salesperson 1 must be entered as

```
? 75, 1500, 1200, 0.15
```

It is also important that the user respond with numeric data. For example, if the value 1AB were entered as the first item, rather than 75, then the PC would respond with the following message:

```
Redo from start
```

The same message will appear if too few or too many data items are entered in response to the INPUT statement.

Input Prompt Message

To ensure that the data is entered in its proper order, MS BASIC allows for an **input prompt message** to be placed in the INPUT statement. When the PC executes an INPUT statement containing an input prompt message, the message, rather than the question mark, is displayed on the screen. Execution is then suspended until the data is supplied. The following program requests one entry per INPUT statement:

PROGRAM 2.5

```
100 INPUT "Commission rate =====> ", RATE
110 INPUT "Week 1 sales ========> ", WEEK1
120 INPUT "Week 2 sales ========> ", WEEK2
130 INPUT "Return sales ========> ", RETURNS
140 COMMISSION = RATE * (WEEK1 + WEEK2 - RETURNS)
150 PRINT COMMISSION
160 END

RUN

Commission rate =====> 0.15
Week 1 sales ========> 1200
Week 2 sales ========> 1500
Return sales ========> 75
 393.75
```

When line 100 is executed in Program 2.5, the PC displays this input prompt message:

```
Commission rate =====>
```

After displaying the message requesting the commission rate, the PC suspends execution of the program until a response is entered.

If an acceptable response is then entered, the PC displays the next input prompt message and suspends execution again. This process continues until the last INPUT statement has been executed.

After the last data item is entered for line 130, line 140 determines the earned commission. Then line 150 displays the earned commission, and, finally, line 160 terminates the program.

The **quotation marks** surrounding the input prompt message and the comma separating the message from the variable in lines 100 through 130 are required punctuation. If a **semicolon** is used to separate the message from the variable, then a question mark will be displayed immediately after the input prompt message. For example, the following INPUT statement,

```
100 INPUT "What is the commission rate"; RATE
```

will display the message followed by the question mark, as shown here:

```
What is the commission rate?
```

Table 2.2, on the following page, gives the general form of the INPUT statement. The INPUT statement consists of the keyword INPUT, followed by an optional input prompt message, followed by a list of variables separated by mandatory commas. Here is the rule for determining the placement of the INPUT statement in a program:

> **Input Rule 1:** Every variable appearing in the program whose value is directly obtained through input must be listed in an INPUT statement before it is used elsewhere in the program.

You may enter the keyword INPUT by pressing simultaneously the Alt (lower left side of the keyboard) and the letter I keys. Using this combination of keys will speed program entry.

——————**TABLE 2.2** The INPUT Statement——————

General Form:	INPUT *variable, . . ., variable* *or* INPUT *"input prompt message", variable, . . ., variable*
Purpose:	*Provides for the assignment of values to variables from a source external to the program, like the keyboard.*
Keyword Entry:	*Simultaneously press the Alt and I keys on your keyboard. (See page 4 of the reference card at the back of this book for a list of all keyword entries using the Alt key.)*

Examples:		**Data from an External Source**
	INPUT Statements	
	`100 INPUT A`	`23.5`
	`115 INPUT X, Y, Z`	`2, 4, 6`
	`300 INPUT A$, B`	`Gross, -2.73`
	`400 INPUT "Please enter the sales tax: ", T`	`0.05`
	`500 INPUT "What is your name"; N$`	`John`
	`600 INPUT "Part number ====> ", P`	`1289`

Note:	*In the second General Form, a question mark is displayed immediately after the input prompt message if a semicolon, rather than a comma, follows the message within quotation marks.*

The INPUT statement allows the user complete interaction with the PC while the program is executed. The main use of the INPUT statement is found in applications that involve

1. small amounts of data to be entered into a program;
2. data input that is dependent on the output or conditions of previous parts of a program; or
3. the processing of data as it occurs in an interactive or on-line processing environment.

This section on the INPUT statement has introduced you to one method of assigning values to variables in a program. Later, we will discuss two other methods that are used to process data, the READ statement (chapter 4) and the use of data files (chapters 6 and 9).

⊞ 2.3
THE PRINT, CLS, AND WIDTH STATEMENTS

One of the functions of the PRINT statement is to display the values of variables that have been defined earlier in a program. You should understand by now that the following:

```
100 X = 99
110 PRINT X
```

displays 99, which is the value of X, not the letter X. The PRINT statement can also be used to display messages that identify a program result, as shown by line 150 in Program 2.6 on the opposite page.

PROGRAM 2.6

```
100 INPUT "Commission rate =====> ", RATE
110 INPUT "Week 1 sales ========> ", WEEK1
120 INPUT "Week 2 sales ========> ", WEEK2
130 INPUT "Return sales ========> ", RETURNS
140 COMMISSION = RATE * (WEEK1 + WEEK2 - RETURNS)
150 PRINT "Earned commission ===>"; COMMISSION
160 END

RUN

Commission rate =====> 0.15
Week 1 sales ========> 1200
Week 2 sales ========> 1500
Return sales ========> 75
Earned commission ===> 393.75
```

As with the INPUT statement, it is necessary in a PRINT statement to begin and end a message with quotation marks. The quotation marks in a PRINT statement inform MS BASIC that the item to be displayed is a message rather than a variable.

The semicolon following the message in line 150 instructs the PC to keep the **cursor** on the same line instead of positioning it on the next line. The cursor is a movable, blinking marker on the screen which indicates where the next point of character entry, change, or display will be. For example, the contents of line 150 can be written on two separate lines:

```
150 PRINT "Earned commission ===>"
155 PRINT COMMISSION
160 END
```

The PC displays the message found in line 150 and positions the cursor on the left margin of the next line. The value of COMMISSION is then displayed on the line below the message:

```
Earned commission ===>
 393.75
```

MS BASIC displays a numeric value that consists of a sign, the decimal representation, and a **trailing space**. Appearing immediately before the number, the sign is a **leading space** if the number is positive and a leading minus sign if the number is negative. The space following the message displayed by line 150 in Program 2.6 represents the sign of the variable COMMISSION, as shown below:

```
Earned commission ===> 393.75
```

A space here indicates that 393.75 is positive.

Clearing the Screen — The CLS Statement

One of the responsibilities of the programmer is to ensure that the prompt messages and results are meaningful and easy to read. A cluttered screen can make it difficult for you to locate necessary information. To clear the screen, MS BASIC includes the CLS statement, which erases the information on the screen and places the cursor in the upper left corner. The general form of the CLS statement is illustrated in Table 2.3 on the following page.

_____TABLE 2.3_ The CLS Statement_____

General Form:	CLS
Purpose:	*Erases the information on the first 24 lines of the screen and places the cursor in the upper left corner.*
Example:	100 CLS
Note:	*The 25th line of the screen may be erased with the* KEY *statement, which is discussed in section 2.7.*

The CLS statement is usually one of the first statements to be executed in a program, as it is in Program 2.7. The statement CLS may also be entered without a line number. This is called the **immediate mode**. Without a line number, the PC executes the statement as soon as it is entered; it is not made part of the current program. For example, the statement

    CLS

causes the PC to immediately clear the first 24 lines of the screen.

Consider now Program 2.7 below, which includes the CLS statement in line 100. When the RUN command is issued for this program, the PC clears the screen and then displays the input prompt message

    Commission rate =====>

on line 1. After obtaining a response through the keyboard, the PC displays the next input prompt message on line 2, and the rest of the program is executed.

PROGRAM 2.7

```
100 CLS
110 INPUT "Commission rate =====> ", RATE
120 INPUT "Week 1 sales ========> ", WEEK1
130 INPUT "Week 2 sales ========> ", WEEK2
140 INPUT "Return sales ========> ", RETURNS
150 COMMISSION = RATE * (WEEK1 + WEEK2 - RETURNS)
160 PRINT
170 PRINT "Earned commission ===>"; COMMISSION
180 END

RUN

Commission rate =====> 0.15
Week 1 sales ========> 1200
Week 2 sales ========> 1500
Return sales ========> 75

Earned commission ===> 393.75
```

The CLS statement clears the screen, including the image of the program, but it does not clear main storage. After you have entered the RUN command and the output results are displayed, you may again display the program by entering the LIST command. A detailed discussion of the LIST command can be found in section 2.7.

Line 160, which contains a PRINT statement without a list, shows how to instruct the PC to display a blank line in order to separate the input prompt messages from the results. A **null list** like this causes the PRINT statement to display a blank line.

A general flowchart that corresponds to Program 2.7 is shown in Figure 2.2 on the opposite page. A flowchart does not have to include a symbol for each statement in the program. For example, the four INPUT statements in Program 2.7 are represented by the single input/output (I/O) symbol "Input Salesperson Data," which follows the "Clear Screen" symbol in the flowchart in Figure 2.2.

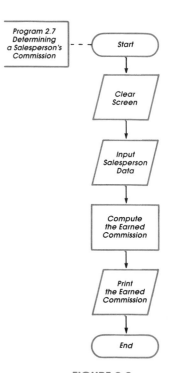

The WIDTH Statement

The PC automatically sets the width of each of the 25 lines on the screen to 80 characters. You can switch from the 80-column display mode to the 40-column display mode by entering the following statement:

        100 WIDTH 40

In the 40-column display mode, the characters are displayed in a larger form and, therefore, are easier to read. However, the PC can display only half as many characters in this mode.

You can switch back to the 80-column display mode by entering a statement similar to the following:

        200 WIDTH 80

The PC will remain in its current display mode until instructed to change to the other. Each time the WIDTH statement is executed, it clears the first 24 lines of the screen before switching display modes.

Like the CLS statement, the WIDTH statement is often entered prior to the execution of a program and without a line number. For example,

        WIDTH 40

instructs the PC to display 40 characters to a line. The following statement entered without a line number

        WIDTH 80

immediately switches the PC back to the 80-column display mode.

The general form of the WIDTH statement is given in Table 2.4 below.

FIGURE 2.2
A general flowchart for Program 2.7.

————TABLE 2.4 The WIDTH Statement————

General Form:	WIDTH *size* *where size has a value of 40 or 80.*
Purpose:	*Clears the first 24 lines of the screen and sets the display mode of the screen to 40 or 80 characters per line.*
Keyword Entry:	*Simultaneously press the Alt and W keys on your keyboard.*
Examples:	100 WIDTH 40 200 WIDTH 80
Note:	WIDTH 40 *is not valid for the IBM Monochrome Display.*

⊞ 2.4

CODING AND DOCUMENTING

In the preceding programs, only one BASIC statement is written on each line, and the first letter in each statement is always written under the first letter of the statement above it. A program written in such a form is usually easier to read and debug; as you will discover now, however, this is — in certain respects — an optional practice.

Coding Techniques

A BASIC program may be written on an ordinary sheet of paper. However, it is sometimes more convenient to write it on a specially printed sheet of paper called a **coding form**. Figure 2.3, on the following page, shows Program 2.8 written on a coding form.

The coding form is divided into columns that are identified by the numbers near the top of the form. When constructing a BASIC statement, you would place the first digit of the line number in column one. The first letter in each statement, like the P in PRINT, is customarily printed after spacing over one position from the line number.

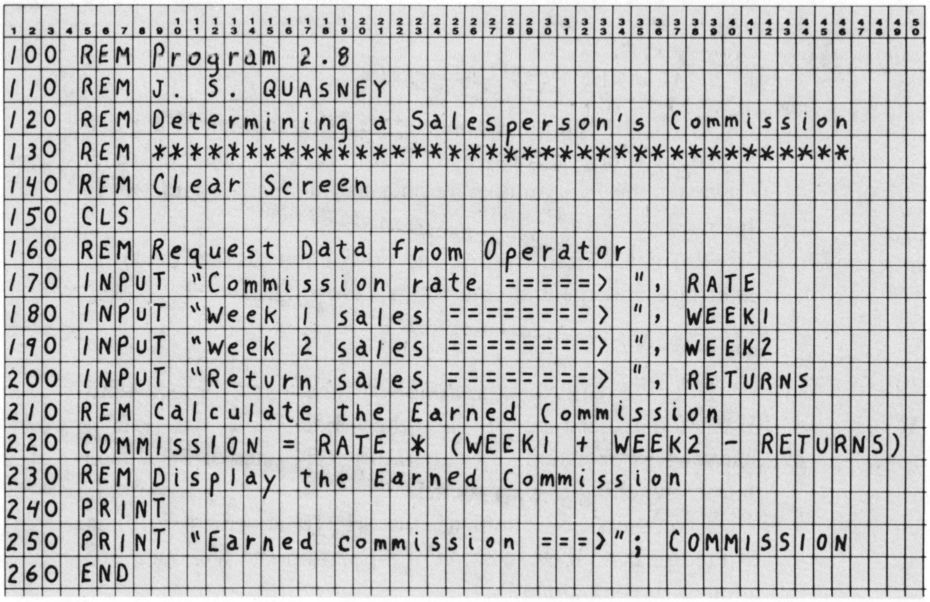

FIGURE 2.3
Program 2.8 on a coding form.

```
100 REM Program 2.8
110 REM J. S. QUASNEY
120 REM Determining a Salesperson's Commission
130 REM **********************************************
140 REM Clear Screen
150 CLS
160 REM Request Data from Operator
170 INPUT "Commission rate =====> ", RATE
180 INPUT "Week 1 sales =========> ", WEEK1
190 INPUT "Week 2 sales =========> ", WEEK2
200 INPUT "Return sales =========> ", RETURNS
210 REM Calculate the Earned Commission
220 COMMISSION = RATE * (WEEK1 + WEEK2 - RETURNS)
230 REM Display the Earned Commission
240 PRINT
250 PRINT "Earned Commission ===>"; COMMISSION
260 END
```

The **space**, or **blank**, is also a character. It is obtained on a keyboard by pressing the space bar once for each blank character desired. The blank character may be used freely to improve the appearance of the program. A useful rule of thumb for blank characters is this: Leave spaces in a BASIC statement in the same places where you would leave spaces in an English sentence. Spaces in line 100 of Program 2.1 yield the following:

```
100 LET COMMISSION = 0.15 * (1200 + 1500 - 75)
```

which is much more readable than

```
100LETCOMMISSION=0.15*(1200+1500-75)
```

Spaces should not appear within line numbers, within keywords, within numeric constants, or within variable names.

Documenting a Program — The REM Statement

Documentation is the readable description of what a program or procedure within a program is supposed to do. More often than not, programmers are asked to support the programs they write by means of **internal comments**. Documentation is used to identify programs and clarify parts of a program that would otherwise be difficult for others to understand.

The REM statements in Program 2.8, lines 100 through 140 and lines 160, 210, and 230, are called **remark lines**. The remark line consists of an internal comment, or explanation, intended solely for humans. The keyword REM, when present after a line number, designates the line as a remark line.

REM statements are nonexecutable, which means they have no effect on the results of a BASIC program. Program 2.8, which includes REM statements, and Program 2.7, which does not, both produce the same results. REM statements do take up space in main storage.

MS BASIC permits you to use an **apostrophe** (') as an abbreviation for the keyword REM. MS BASIC also permits the placement of a remark on the right-hand side of a BASIC statement by requiring the insertion of an apostrophe before the comment. The following two lines are valid:

```
140 ' Initialization Routine
150 CLS        ' Clear Screen
```

PROGRAM 2.8

```
100 REM Program 2.8
110 REM J. S. Quasney
120 REM Determining a Salesperson's Commission
130 REM **************************************
140 REM Clear Screen
150 CLS
160 REM Request Data from Operator
170 INPUT "Commission rate =====> ", RATE
180 INPUT "Week 1 sales ========> ", WEEK1
190 INPUT "Week 2 sales ========> ", WEEK2
200 INPUT "Return sales ========> ", RETURNS
210 REM Calculate the Earned Commission
220 COMMISSION = RATE * (WEEK1 + WEEK2 - RETURNS)
230 REM Display the Earned Commission
240 PRINT
250 PRINT "Earned commission ===>"; COMMISSION
260 END

RUN

Commission rate =====> 0.15
Week 1 sales ========> 1200
Week 2 sales ========> 1500
Return sales ========> 75

Earned commission ===> 393.75
```

The general form for the REM statement is found in Table 2.5 below.

TABLE 2.5 The REM Statement

General Form:	REM comment *or* ' comment
Purpose:	Provides for the insertion of comments in a program.
Examples:	110 REM J. S. Quasney 160 REM Determine the Balance Due 200 REM Program 2.8 250 ' 300 ' ************************** 310 ' Compute Gross Pay 320 PRINT ANSWER ' Display result

Shown below are a few basic suggestions for including explanatory remarks in a program.

1. Write and include your remarks as you code the program.
2. Write a prologue, including the program name, date, author, and any other desirable remarks, at the beginning of each program (see section 2.12 on page 48).
3. Remark lines should come before any major procedure in a program.
4. Variable names should be defined when it is not apparent what they represent.
5. Remark lines should be inserted into areas of a program only where the code is not self-explanatory. Do not insert remarks for their own sake. Insert them to make your program readable.
6. For the sake of appearance, highlight a group of remark lines by adding a series of asterisks or other special characters as the last remark line.

Multiple Statements Per Line

MS BASIC allows you to write multiple statements per line. That is, Program 2.2 can be rewritten as the following:

```
100 ' Program 2.2
110 PAY = 0.15 * (1200 + 1500 - 75) : PRINT PAY : END
```

The statements in line 110 are separated by **colons**. The purpose of the colon is to inform MS BASIC that one statement has ended and a new statement follows on the same line.

Do not precede any statement with a REM statement when using multiple statements per line. MS BASIC considers all characters following the keyword REM or apostrophe (') to be a comment, including the colon. The following entire version of Program 2.2 is a comment line.

```
100 ' Program 2.2 : PAY = 0.15 * (1200 + 1500 - 75) : PRINT PAY : END
```

⊞ 2.5

GETTING ON THE PC

To enter a BASIC program like Program 2.8 into the PC, you must first familiarize yourself with the procedures for getting on the PC. Table 2.6 presents a step-by-step procedure for getting to the point where you can begin entering a BASIC program. This procedure is sometimes called "booting the PC."

Terminating a Session with BASICA

To terminate your session with BASICA, enter the command SYSTEM. The SYSTEM command instructs the PC to return to MS DOS. When the A> or B> sign reappears, raise the load levers on disk drives A and B and carefully remove your diskettes from the disk drive units.

NEVER REMOVE A DISKETTE WHEN THE DISK DRIVE LIGHT IS ON.

Turn the video display device power switch to Off. If using a printer, turn the printer's power switch to Off. Finally, turn the PC's power switch to Off.

TRY IT YOURSELF

Boot the PC, using the **Cold Start** procedure described in step 5 of Table 2.6. Carefully follow the first eight steps outlined in the table. In step 2 of Table 2.6, insert the Student Diskette that accompanies this book into drive B. **Do not format the Student Diskette.**

After step 8, enter the command B:README.

Reboot the PC, using the the **Warm Start** procedure as described in step 5 of Table 2.6.

After step 9, enter the command SYSTEM; carefully remove the diskettes and place them in their respective envelopes; and turn all the PC units off.

⊞ 2.6

EDITING MICROSOFT BASIC PROGRAMS

Microsoft BASIC programs are entered one line at a time into the PC via a keyboard. Pressing the Enter key signals to MS BASIC that a line is complete. During the process of entering a program, you will quickly learn that it is easy to make **keyboard** and **grammatical errors** because of your inexperience with the BASIC language and your unfamiliarity with the keyboard. **Logical errors** can also occur in a program if you have not considered all the details associated with the problem.

_____TABLE 2.6 Initial PC Start-Up Procedures_____

1. *Obtain a floppy diskette titled* **DOS**, *also known as the* **system diskette**, *from your instructor. A system diskette contains the operating system (* **MS DOS** *or* **PC DOS** *) and* **BASICA**. BASICA *is the advanced version of Microsoft BASIC. Also obtain a formatted diskette for storing programs. If the second diskette is new, it must be formatted before proceeding. (See section D.2 in Appendix D for a discussion on how to format a diskette.)*

2. *Raise (open) the load lever of disk drive A (left drive) and insert the system diskette (see Figure 1.13 on page 7). Lower (close) the load lever of disk drive A. If your PC has a second drive, raise the load lever on disk drive B (right drive) and insert the properly formatted diskette. Lower the load lever of disk drive B.*

3. *Adjust the leg handles at each end of the keyboard, if desired (see Figure 1.9 on page 6).*

4. *Turn the video display device power switch to On. Adjust the Brightness Control and Contrast Control knobs accordingly (see Figure 1.10 on page 6).*

5. **Cold Start:** *Turn the PC's power switch to On (see Figure 1.13 on page 7). After a brief period, the light on disk drive A will come on. Drive A will spin for a few seconds and you will hear a "whirling" sound.*
    Or,
    Warm Start: *If your PC is initially On, press and hold the Control (Ctrl) and Alt keys, and then press the Del key. Finally, release these three keys. After a brief period of time, the light on disk drive A will come on. Drive A will spin for a few seconds and you will hear a "whirling" sound.*

6. *If using a printer, turn the printer's power switch to On.*

7. *When MS DOS is loaded from the system diskette, it displays the date in a manner similar to this:*
    Current date is Tue 1-01-1980
    Enter new date:
    If today's date is September 30, 1990, enter the date as follows:
    09-30-1990 *(Press the Enter key.)*

8. *After the date is entered, MS DOS displays the time in a manner similar to this:*
    Current time is 0:01:23.45
    Enter new time:
    The time display is in this form: Hours:Minutes:Seconds.Hundredths of a Second
    If the new time is 10:46 am, enter
    10:46 *(Press the Enter key.)*
    If the new time is 2:34 pm, enter
    14:34 *(Press the Enter key.)*
    Your PC may have a battery-run clock that maintains the date and time when it is not in use. In this case, the date and time are automatically loaded and, therefore, steps 7 and 8 are not required.

9. *For a one-diskette drive system or a network system: When MS DOS displays its prompt (A>), enter the command* BASICA *and press the Enter key. For example,*
    A> BASICA *(Press the Enter key.)*
    ok *(MS BASIC responds that it is ready.)*
    For a two-diskette drive system: When MS DOS displays its prompt (A>), enter the command B: *and press the Enter key. For example,*
    A> B: *(Press the Enter key.)*
    When MS DOS displays its prompt (B>), enter the command A:BASICA *and press the Enter key. For example,*
    B> A:BASICA *(Press the Enter key.)*
    ok *(MS BASIC responds that it is ready.)*

10. *You may begin entering your program.*

Some of these errors can be eliminated if you use coding forms and flowcharts or pseudocode and if you carefully review your design and program before you enter it into the PC. Any remaining errors are resolved by **editing** the BASIC program.

The right side of the keyboard, including the numeric keypad, shown in Figure 2.4 below, contains several keys that are specially designed to aid you in editing BASIC programs. The four arrow keys (←, ↑, →, ↓), also known as the **cursor control keys**, are used to move the cursor on the screen in the indicated direction.

Each time the delete key (Del) is pressed, the PC erases the character located within the cursor.

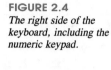

FIGURE 2.4
The right side of the keyboard, including the numeric keypad.

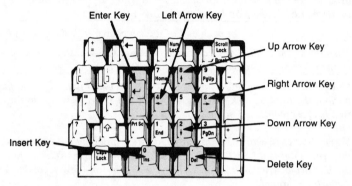

When pressed, the Insert key (Ins) places the PC in the **insert mode** and allows you to insert characters at the current cursor position. As characters are entered, existing ones are "pushed" to the right. To change back to the **overtype mode**, press any arrow key or the Ins key again.

Table 2.7 illustrates the features used most commonly in editing a BASIC program. You will find these features both powerful and easy to use.

TABLE 2.7 Commonly Used Features in Editing BASIC Programs

1. *Correct an error in the line being keyed before the Enter key is pressed.*	*Use the ← and → cursor control keys to move to the left and right within a line. You may also insert characters between any two adjacent characters by first pressing the Insert (Ins) key.* *Or,* *Press the Enter key and reenter the entire line.*
2. *Replace a line in an existing program.*	*Key in the new statement, using the line number of the line to be replaced.* *Or,* *Use the ↑ or ↓ key to position the cursor on the line to be replaced and follow the instructions in number 1 above. Be sure to press the Enter key when you are finished editing the line.*
3. *Insert a new line in an existing program.*	*Key in the statement, using a line number that will cause MS BASIC to place the statement in the desired sequence.*
4. *Delete a line in an existing program.*	*Key in the line number of the line to be deleted and press the Enter key.*
5. *Delete a sequence of lines.*	*Enter the system command* DELETE, *followed by the beginning line number and ending line number separated by a hyphen. For example,* DELETE 250-370
6. *Copy or move a line.*	*Use the arrow keys to move the cursor to the line number of the line to be copied or moved. Change the line number to one that will position the line at the desired location and press the Enter key. This will copy the line at the new location. If it is a move operation, use step 4 to delete the unwanted line.*
7. *Add, delete, or change characters in a line previously entered.*	*Move the cursor to the line to be edited and follow the instructions in number 1 above. Be sure to press the Enter key when you are finished editing the line.*

⊞ **2.7**

SYSTEM
COMMANDS AND
HARD-COPY OUTPUT

As indicated earlier, two types of instructions are used with MS BASIC. One type consists of BASIC statements, like LET, PRINT, and INPUT. The second type consists of the system commands, like RUN and SYSTEM. Before we discuss system commands, it is important that you understand the concept of a file specification.

File Specifications

Several system commands require the use of a **file specification**. A file specification, also called a **filespec**, is used to identify programs and data files that are placed in auxiliary storage. A filespec is made up of a **device name**, a **file name**, and an **extension**, all included with quotation marks, as shown below.

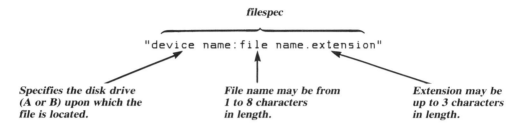

The device name refers to the disk drive, where A identifies the left-hand drive and B identifies the right-hand drive — or the top and bottom drives, respectively (see Figure 1.7 on page 5). BASIC programs are usually stored on disk drive B. If no device is specified, then the filespec refers to the default drive of the PC at the time of execution. If a device name is included in the file specification, it must be followed by a colon.

File names may be anywhere from 1 to 8 characters in length. Valid characters are upper- or lowercase A–Z, 0–9, and certain special characters ($ & # @ ! % " ( ) – { } _ / \). If an extension is used, then the file name must be followed by a period.

An extension that is up to 3 characters in length may be used to classify a file. Valid characters are the same as for a file name. With MS BASIC, the default extension is BAS. That is, when you use system commands that refer to files, MS BASIC will automatically append an extension of BAS if one is not included. However, it is possible to reference programs without ever using an extension.

Examples of valid filespecs include B:PAYROLL, B:LAB2-1.BAS, Accounts, and S123. The first two examples reference files on drive B. The latter two examples reference files on the default drive. See Table 2.11 on page 40 for additional examples of the use of file names.

The PC does not differentiate between the upper- and the lowercase characters. That is, B:LAB2-1.BAS and b:lab2-1.bas refer to the same file.

The RUN Command

Perhaps the most important system command for a beginner is RUN. If this command is not issued, the BASIC program will not be executed.

It is possible to initiate execution at a line number other than the lowest in a program. Whereas the system command

    RUN

instructs the PC to execute the current program in main storage at the lowest line number, the command

    RUN 200

instructs the PC to execute the program beginning at line 200. What do you think happens if RUN 200 is entered and there is no line 200 in the program?

A third form of the RUN command loads and executes a program that is stored in auxiliary storage. The following,

```
RUN "b:lab2-1"
```

causes the PC to load lab2-1 into main storage from drive B and executes lab2-1. At the time the command is issued, the current program in main storage is erased.

The LIST Command   Another useful system command is LIST. It instructs the PC to display all or part of the BASIC program. This command is especially useful in those circumstances where changes have been made to statements in the BASIC program and a new listing of the program is desired. Versions 1 and 2 of Program 2.9 illustrate the use of the RUN and LIST system commands.

PROGRAM 2.9   Version 1

```
LIST
100 ' Program 2.9
110 INPUT A, B
120 C = A - B
130 PRINT "The difference is:"; C
140 END

RUN

? 159, 62
The difference is: 97
```

If the following statement is entered,

```
120 C = B - A
```

line 120 is changed. The new line 120 replaces the original line 120. If a LIST command is followed by RUN, Program 2.9 appears and is executed:

PROGRAM 2.9   Version 2

```
LIST
100 ' Program 2.9
110 INPUT A, B
120 C = B - A
130 PRINT "The difference is:"; C
140 END

RUN

? 159, 62
The difference is:-97

LIST 130
130 PRINT "The difference is:"; C

LIST 110-130
110 INPUT A, B
120 C = B - A
130 PRINT "The difference is:"; C
```

The command LIST can be used to list a program at a point other than the first statement of the program. LIST 130 lists line 130 only. LIST 110-130 lists lines 110 through 130, inclusive. To list from the start of the program through line 120, use LIST-120. Use LIST 120- to list from line 120 to the end of the program.

Pressing the Control (Ctrl) and Num Lock keys simultaneously causes the PC to temporarily stop an activity like a program listing. Pressing any key thereafter (except Shift,

Break and Ins) causes the PC to continue an activity like the listing of a program.

Pressing the Control (Ctrl) and Break keys simultaneously causes the PC to permanently stop a program listing.

Listing Program Lines to the Printer

If you have a printer connected to your PC, you may list all or parts of your program to the printer by using the command LLIST. The command LLIST is similar to the LIST command. The only difference is that LIST displays the lines on the screen and LLIST displays the lines on the printer.

Listing Program Lines to a File

The LIST command may be used to copy lines from the current program in main storage to a file in auxiliary storage. For example,

    LIST 110-130, "b:lab2-3"

will copy lines 110 through 130 to the file lab2-3 on drive B. The command

    LIST, "b:lab2-3"

will store the entire program in main storage on drive B under the name lab2-3.

The NEW Command

Another command that is of considerable importance is NEW. It instructs the PC to erase or delete the last program that was keyed into main storage. Without this command, statements from the old program may mix with the statements of the new one.

Table 2.8 summarizes the system commands most often used.

_____**TABLE 2.8** Summary of the Most Often Used System Commands_____

SYSTEM COMMAND	KEYWORD ENTRY	FUNCTION
LIST	F1	*Causes all or part of the BASIC program currently in main storage to be displayed on the screen. The LIST command may also be used to copy lines to a file in auxiliary storage.*
LLIST	L and F1	*Causes all or part of the BASIC program currently in main storage to be displayed on the printer.*
NEW		*Causes the BASIC program currently in main storage to be erased and indicates the beginning of a new program to be created in main storage.*
RUN	F2 or Alt and R	*Causes the BASIC program currently in main storage to be executed. This command may also be used to begin execution at a specified line number of the program in main storage or to load and execute a program from auxiliary storage.*
SYSTEM		*Causes the PC to permanently exit BASICA and returns control to the operating system MS DOS.*

Use of the Function Keys and the KEY Statement

The PC has ten **function keys**, also called **PF** keys, which are located on the far left side of the keyboard. They are labeled F1 through F10, as shown in Figure 2.5 below.

Each function key is assigned a sequence of characters that is displayed on the 25th line of the screen when the PC is running under BASIC. This is shown in Figure 2.6 on the following page. When you press one of the function keys, its assigned sequence of characters is entered into the PC. For example, if you press F1, the system command LIST is displayed on the screen and is entered into the PC. Pressing F2 is the same as keying in the command RUN and pressing the Enter key.

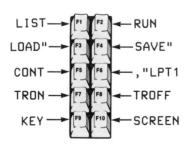

FIGURE 2.5
The function keys on the left side of the keyboard.

Besides the function keys, the PC allows you to enter keywords through the use of the Alt key and one of the letter keys. You will recall from Table 2.2, on page 26, that when you hold down the Alt key and press the I key, the keyword `INPUT` is entered into the PC.

The 25th line on the screen, containing the description of the function keys, can be erased through the use of the `KEY` statement. For example,

100 KEY OFF

instructs the PC to erase the 25th line. To redisplay the line, use the following statement:

200 KEY ON

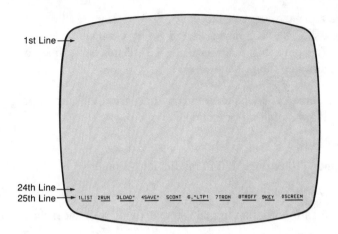

FIGURE 2.6

The display of the 10 PF keys on the 25th line of the screen.

This statement is most frequently used in tandem with the `CLS` statement to completely clear the screen. For example,

300 CLS : KEY OFF   ' Clear Screen

The first statement in line 300 clears the first 24 lines. The second statement clears the 25th line. The apostrophe indicates that a comment follows. You can press the F9 key or press the Alt and K keys simultaneously to enter the keyword `KEY`.

The general form of the `KEY` statement is found in Table 2.9 below.

_____TABLE 2.9 The KEY Statement_____

General Form:	KEY *switch* *where switch is equal to* ON *or* OFF.
Purpose:	KEY ON *causes the display of the ten PF keys on the 25th line of the screen.* KEY OFF *clears the 25th line of the screen.*
Keyword Entry:	*Press the F9 key or press simultaneously the Alt and K keys on your keyboard.*
Example:	100 KEY OFF 500 KEY ON 700 CLS : KEY OFF ' Clear Screen
Note:	*The* KEY *statement may also be used to redefine the function of the ten PF keys. For more information, check the MS BASIC user's manual.*

This statement is often used in the immediate mode. For example,

KEY ON

displays the function of the ten PF keys on the 25th line of the screen. Likewise,

KEY OFF

erases the 25th line.

Additional System Commands

The system commands summarized in Table 2.8 are the ones most commonly used by BASIC programmers. Additional system commands that you will have to become familiar with are listed in Table 2.10 on the following page.

The LOAD and SAVE
Commands

Programs are not always completed during a single session with the PC. As Figure 2.7 illustrates, through the use of the SAVE and LOAD commands, it is possible with MS BASIC to store an incomplete program in auxiliary storage and at a later time retrieve the program.

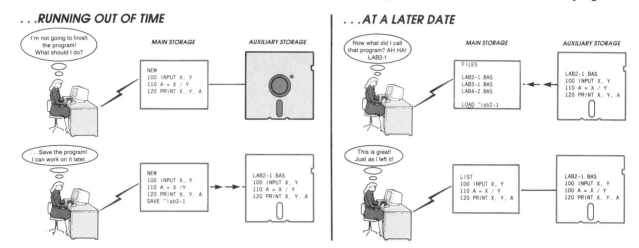

FIGURE 2.7
Storing a program in auxiliary storage and later loading the program LAB2-1 into main storage. Assume B drive is the default drive.

As described in the table below, the SAVE command allows you to save BASIC programs into auxiliary storage for later use. The LOAD command allows you to load BASIC programs from auxiliary storage into main storage. Also see Table 2.11, on the following page, for examples of the use of these two commands.

TABLE 2.10 Summary of Additional System Commands

SYSTEM COMMAND	KEYWORD ENTRY	FUNCTION
AUTO *number, increment*	*ALT and A*	*Automatically starts a BASIC line with a line number. Each new line is assigned a systematically incremented line number. Pressing the Control and Break keys terminates the* AUTO *activity.*
CLEAR		*Assigns all numeric variables the value zero and all string variables the null value.*
CONT	*F5*	*Resumes a system activity, like the execution of a program, following interruption due to pressing the Control and Break keys simultaneously or execution of the* STOP *or* END *statement.*
DELETE *lineno₁–lineno₂*	*ALT and D*	*Deletes line numbers lineno$_1$ through lineno$_2$ in the current program.*
EDIT *line number*		*Displays a line for editing purposes.*
FILES *"device name:*		*Lists the names of all programs and data files in auxiliary storage.*
KILL *"filespec*		*Deletes a previously stored program or data file from auxiliary storage.*
LOAD *"filespec*	*F3*	*Loads a previously stored program from auxiliary storage into main storage.*
MERGE *"filespec*		*Merges the lines from a program in auxiliary storage with the program in main storage. The program in auxiliary storage must have been saved in character format (ASCII) with the A parameter.*
NAME *"old filespec" AS "new filespec"*		*Changes the name of a program or data file in auxiliary storage to a new name.*
RENUM *start,,increment*		*Renumbers the entire program uniformly.*

(continued)

_____TABLE 2.10_ Summary of Additional System Commands _(continued)_._____

SYSTEM COMMAND	KEYWORD ENTRY	FUNCTION
SAVE "filespec	F4	_Saves the current program into auxiliary storage for later use. The command_ SAVE "filespec", A _saves the file in character format (ASCII) instead of binary format._
SHELL		_Places the current_ BASICA _session in a temporary wait state and returns control to the operating system. When the operating system prompt appears, you may enter DOS commands. To return to the_ BASICA _session, type_ EXIT.
TRON	F7	_Turns on the program trace feature (see Appendix C)._
TROFF	F8	_Turns off the program trace feature (see Appendix C)._

The FILES Command

The FILES command is used to display the names of the files (both programs and data files) that are stored on the diskette in drive A or B. The following command, entered in upper- or lowercase, displays the names of all the files stored on the diskette in drive A, which is assumed to be the default drive:

    FILES   or   FILES "a:

The following command displays the names of the files on the diskette in drive B:

    FILES "b:

The quotation mark preceding the device name B and the colon following it are required punctuation. See Table 2.11 below for additional examples of the FILES command.

The AUTO Command

Another important command in Table 2.10 is the AUTO command. It is used primarily when you first enter a program. It will automatically display the next line number and, therefore, can save keying time. For example, if you enter

    AUTO 100, 10

the PC will automatically display line 100. Once you complete the line and press the Enter key, the PC will display 110 on the following line. It will continue to display line numbers, incrementing each by 10, until you simultaneously press the Control (Ctrl) and Break keys.

_____TABLE 2.11_ Examples of System Commands with File Specifications_____

SYSTEM COMMAND WITH FILESPEC	COMMENT
FILES "b:lab*.bas	_Lists all files whose name begins with LAB and has an extension of BAS stored on the diskette in drive B. The_ **asterisk (*)** _is called a_ **wild character** _in programming._
FILES "b:*.bas	_Lists the names of all files with an extension of BAS stored on the diskette in drive B._
LOAD "b:payroll	_Loads a program named PAYROLL.BAS, stored on the diskette in drive B, into main storage._
LOAD "lab4-1	_Loads a program named LAB4-1.BAS, stored on the diskette in the default drive, into main storage._
SAVE "b:lab3-2	_Saves the current program in main storage on the diskette in drive B in binary format under the name LAB3-2.BAS._
SAVE "b:lab5-3", a	_Saves the current program in main storage on the diskette in drive B in character format (ASCII) under the name LAB5-3.BAS._
Note:	_It is not required to end the filespec with a quotation mark unless the system command requires additional information following the filespec._

TRY IT YOURSELF

Boot the PC, following the instructions in Table 2.6 on page 33. Place the Student Diskette in the B drive. Using the function keys described in Figure 2.5 on page 37, do the following:

1. Load Program 2.8 (PRG2-8) from the Student Diskette.
2. Use the LIST command to display various parts of the program. Try LIST, LIST 100, LIST 210-230, and LIST 160-
3. Execute the program and see what happens. Enter the same data that was used with Program 2.8 on page 31.
4. Delete lines 100 to 160 and repeat step 3.
5. Enter 165 WIDTH 40
6. Replace the comma that appears in each INPUT statement (lines 170 to 200) with a semicolon and repeat step 3.
7. Enter CLS : FILES
8. Enter WIDTH 80
9. Beginning with line 1000 and incrementing each line by 10, renumber the program. Enter the command LIST. Use the command SYSTEM to return to MS DOS.
10. Finally, remove the diskettes and turn the PC off.

PC Hard-Copy Output

Most BASIC programmers use a keyboard for input and a video display device for output. In many instances, it is desirable to list the program and the results on a printer. A listing of this type is **hard-copy output**. To obtain a listing on the printer of the program itself, use the system command LLIST.

To obtain a listing of both the program and output results, simultaneously press the Control (Ctrl) key and Print Screen (PrtSC) key, and enter the system commands LIST and RUN, as shown below.

> Press simultaneously the Ctrl and PrtSc keys.
> LIST
> RUN
> Press simultaneously the Ctrl and PrtSc keys again.

When pressed simultaneously, the Control and Print Screen keys serve as a toggle switch. Pressing the two keys once instructs the PC to direct output to the printer as well as to the screen. Pressing the two keys following the completion of an operation instructs the PC to terminate transmission to the printer.

Sometimes it is desirable to obtain a hard-copy output of exactly what is on the screen. To do this, simply press simultaneously the Shift and Prt Sc keys. The PC will print the contents of the screen, starting with line 1. This activity can easily be observed by following the movement of the cursor.

When you enter BASICA, the PC also sets the mode of the printer to 80 characters per line. Although the WIDTH statement changes the number of characters that are displayed on the screen, it *does not* change the number of characters printed per line. If you plan to print the larger characters seen on the screen in the 40-column display mode, you must check your printer manual for the instructions for setting the printer to the 40-column print mode. For example, using the Epson FX-80 printer, if you enter the following statement in the immediate mode,

```
LPRINT CHR$(27); "W1"
```

the printer will be set to the 40-column print mode. Everything sent to the printer will be printed in the expanded 40-column print mode. You may reset the Epson FX 80 printer to the 80-column print mode by entering the following statement in the immediate mode:

```
LPRINT CHR$(27); "WO"
```

⊞ 2.8
SPECIAL KEYS

In this chapter, you have been introduced to a variety of special keys. Included on page 4 of the reference card at the back of this book is a table of the special keys and their functions. You will find this table useful as you begin entering and executing BASIC programs.

⊞ 2.9
PROGRAMMING TIPS

Having read the first eight sections of this chapter, you are ready to write your first program to use a PC for solving a problem. At the end of chapter 2 are several BASIC Programming Problems. Each problem includes a short statement of the problem, suggested input data, and the corresponding output results. Collectively, these items are the **program specifications**. Following the sample BASIC Programming Problem below, we have suggested a step-by-step procedure for solving the problem. You will find this helpful when you begin solving problems on your own. You will also find it helpful to review section 1.6 on page 11.

Sample BASIC Programming Problem: Computation of State Tax

Problem: Construct a program that will compute the state tax owed by a taxpayer. The state determines the amount of tax owed by taking a person's yearly income, subtracting $500.00 for each dependent, and then multiplying the result by 2%. Use the following formula:

$$\text{Tax} = 0.02 * (\text{Income} - 500 * \text{Dependents})$$

Code the program so that it will request that the taxpayer's income and the number of dependents be entered through the keyboard.

Input Data: Use the following sample input data.

> Taxpayer's income: $73,000.00
> Number of dependents: 8

Output Results: The following results are displayed.

```
Taxpayer's income ========> 73000
Number of dependents ======> 8

State Tax Due ============> 1380
```

The following systematic approach to solving this exercise as well as the other BASIC Programming Problems in this textbook is recommended. In essence, this list is the same as the program development cycle in section 1.6.

Step 1: Problem analysis.

Review the program specifications until you thoroughly understand the problem to be solved. Ascertain the form of input, the form of output, and the type of processing that must be performed. For this problem, you should have determined the following.

> *Input*: The program must allow for the user to supply the data through the use of INPUT statements. There are two data items: taxpayer's income and number of dependents.
> *Processing*: The formula $\text{Tax} = 0.02 * (\text{Income} - 500 * \text{Dependents})$ will determine the state tax.
> *Output*: The required results include the input prompt messages and the state tax due.

Step 2: Program design.

Develop a method of solution the PC will use. One way to do this is to list the program tasks sequentially. For this exercise, the **program tasks** are as follows:

1. Clear the screen.
2. Prompt the user for the necessary data.
3. Calculate the state tax.
4. Display the state tax.

Once the program tasks have been determined, select the variable names you plan to use in the program solution. Three variable names are required. We will use the following:

INCOME for taxpayer's income
DEPENDENTS for number of dependents
TAX for state tax

Next, draw a program flowchart or write pseudo-code that shows how the program will accomplish the program tasks. The flowchart for the sample programming problem is shown in Figure 2.8.

Step 3: Test the design.

Carefully review the design by stepping through the program flowchart or pseudocode to ensure that it is logically correct.

Step 4: Code the program.

Code the program, as shown in Figure 2.9 below, according to the program design.

Step 5: Review the code.

Carefully review the coding. Put yourself in the position of the PC and step through the program. This is sometimes referred to as **desk checking** your code. Be sure the syntax of each instruction is correct. Check to be sure that the sequence of the instructions is logically correct. **You want to be confident that the program will work the first time it is executed.**

Step 6: Enter the program.

Enter the program into the PC, as shown in Figure 2.10 on the following page. Before starting this step, you should be familiar with the system commands and the method for getting on the PC (see Table 2.6 on page 33).

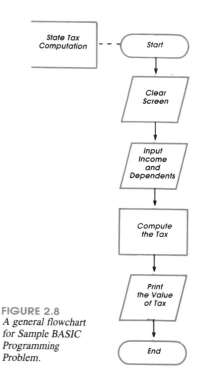

FIGURE 2.8
A general flowchart for Sample BASIC Programming Problem.

```
100  '  CLS :60, DIV. 01, BASIC Programming
110  '  J. S. Quasney
120  '  September 30, 1990
130  '  Sample Basic Programming Problem
140  '  Computation of State Tax
150  '  *******************************************
160  CLS : KEY OFF    ' Clear Screen
170  INPUT "Taxpayer's income =========>", INCOME
180  INPUT "Number of dependents ======>", DEPENDENTS
190  ' Calculate Tax
200  TAX = 0.02 * (INCOME - 500 * DEPENDENTS)
210  PRINT
220  PRINT "State tax due ===========>"; TAX
230  END
```

FIGURE 2.9
Program solution for Sample BASIC Programming Problem on coding form.

Step 7: Test the program.

Test the program by executing it, as shown in Figure 2.11. If the input data does not produce the expected results, the program must be reviewed and corrected. (See Appendix C for debugging techniques.)

Step 8: Formalize the solution.

Obtain a **hard copy** (a listing) of the source program and the output results. If the program logic was modified in steps 4 through 6, revise the documentation and redraw the program flowchart or rewrite the pseudocode to include the changes.

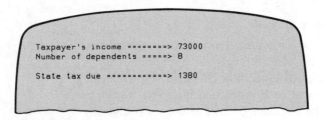

```
100 ' CIS 160, Div. 01, BASIC Programming
110 ' J. S. Quasney
120 ' September 30, 1990
130 ' Sample BASIC Programming Problem
140 ' Computation of State Tax
150 ' **********************************
160 CLS : KEY OFF  ' CLEAR SCREEN
170 INPUT "Taxpayer's income ========> ", INCOME
180 INPUT "Number of dependents ======> ", DEPENDENTS
190 ' Calculate Tax
200 TAX = 0.02 * (INCOME - 500 * DEPENDENTS)
210 PRINT
220 PRINT "State tax due ============>"; TAX
230 END

RUN
```

FIGURE 2.10

Program solution to Sample BASIC Programming Problem entered in the PC.

FIGURE 2.11

The display from executing the program solution to the Sample BASIC Programming Problem.

```
Taxpayer's income ========> 73000
Number of dependents ======> 8

State tax due ============> 1380
```

⊞ 2.10 WHAT YOU SHOULD KNOW

The following list summarizes this chapter.

1. A BASIC program is composed of a sequence of lines, each of which contains a unique line number.
2. A keyword informs BASIC of the type of statement to be executed. LET, PRINT, and END are keywords. The keyword LET is optional in a LET statement.
3. In programming, a variable is a location in main storage whose value can change as the program is executed.
4. A variable name begins with a letter and may be followed by up to 39 letters, digits, and decimal points. It is invalid to use a keyword as a variable name.
5. The LET statement is used to assign a value to a variable on the left-hand side of the equal sign.
6. The equal sign in any LET statement means that the value of the variable to the left of the equal sign is to be replaced by the final value to the right of the equal sign.
7. Constants represent ordinary numbers that do not change during the execution of a program.
8. The PRINT statement instructs the PC to bring a result out from its main storage area and display it on an output device.
9. The line containing the END statement terminates the program's execution.
10. Each program should contain an END statement.

11. Every line in a BASIC program must begin with a unique line number. A line number must be an unsigned whole number between 0 and 65529.
12. Each succeeding line must begin with a line number greater than the line number of the preceding statement.
13. Every variable appearing in an output statement should appear at least once earlier in the program in such a way that its value can be determined.
14. Although most BASIC statements can be placed anywhere in a given program, logic, common sense, and structured style dictate where these statements are placed.
15. Every variable appearing to the right of the equal sign in a LET statement should appear at least once earlier in the same program in such a way that its value can be determined.
16. The INPUT statement provides for assignment of data to variables from a source outside the program during execution.
17. The function of the INPUT statement is to display an input prompt and to suspend execution of the program until data has been supplied. The input prompt must be followed by a comma or a semicolon separator. If a semicolon follows the input prompt, then a question mark is displayed following the input prompt when the INPUT statement is executed.
18. In response to an INPUT statement, it is important that the Enter key be pressed following entry of the data.
19. A comma is used to establish a list, which is a set of distinct elements. In a PRINT or INPUT statement, each element is separated from the next one by a comma.
20. Every variable appearing in the program whose value is directly obtained through input must be listed in an INPUT statement before it is used elsewhere in the program.
21. In a PRINT statement, like 110 PRINT X, the PC displays the value of X, not the letter X.
22. The PRINT statement can be used to display messages as well as the values of variables.
23. The CLS statement causes all the information on the first 24 lines of the screen to be erased and places the cursor in the upper left corner of the screen. The KEY statement may be used to erase or display the 25th line, which contains a description of the ten PF keys.
24. In a PRINT statement, the semicolon separator instructs the PC to maintain the current position of the cursor.
25. After displaying the list of items, a PRINT statement causes the cursor to return to the leftmost position on the next line, unless the list ends with a punctuation mark. If the PRINT statement ends with a punctuation mark, like the semicolon, the PC keeps the cursor on the same line.
26. A null list in a PRINT statement causes the PC to display a blank line.
27. A line in a program can contain more than one statement if colons are used to separate them.
28. Spaces should appear in a BASIC statement in the same places that spaces appear in an English sentence. Spaces should not be placed within line numbers, within keywords, within numeric constants, or within variable names.
29. The REM statement, used to document a program, has no effect on the execution of the program. The apostrophe (') is an abbreviation for REM. It may also be used to insert a comment on the right-hand side of a BASIC statement.
30. Before you can enter a program into the PC, you must familiarize yourself with how to get on the PC.
31. Keyboard and grammatical errors can be corrected by editing the BASIC program. For example, you can correct errors while keying in a line. Lines can also be replaced, inserted, or deleted.
32. BASIC statements have line numbers; system commands do not. When a statement is entered without a line number, the PC treats the statement like a system command and executes it immediately. This is called the immediate mode.
33. A file specification, also called a filespec, is used to identify programs and data files that are placed in auxiliary storage. A filespec is made up of a device name, a file name, and an extension.
34. The RUN command is used to execute a BASIC program.
35. The LIST command is used to display all or part of a BASIC program on the screen. The LLIST command displays all or part of a BASIC program on the printer.
36. The NEW command deletes the current BASIC program and indicates the beginning of a new program to be created in main storage.
37. The system commands described in Table 2.8, on page 37, and Table 2.10, on page 39, facilitate program development; SAVE stores a program into auxiliary storage and LOAD loads a stored program into main storage.
38. The PC has ten function keys, which are located on the far left side of the keyboard. These keys have been assigned a sequence of characters. When a key is pressed, the sequence of characters displays on the screen and they are entered into the system.
39. The program and output results can be displayed on the printer, one after the other, through the use of the Control (Ctrl) and Print Screen (PrtSc) keys.

⊞ 2.11 TEST YOUR BASIC SKILLS (Even-numbered answers are at the back of the book, before the index.)

1. Which of the following are invalid line numbers for MS BASIC programs?

   a. 3-1/2   b. 10   c. 9999.   d. 0   e. 1,321
   f. 100033   g. 1,000   h. 10.   i. + 10   j. −10

2. Put yourself in the place of the PC and record for each line number the current values of W, X, and Y. (Hint: The value of a variable does not change until the program instructs the PC to change it.)

```
100 W = 4
110 X = 2
120 Y = 6
130 PRINT Y
140 W = W + 1
150 X = W * Y
160 PRINT X
170 X = 9
180 Y = Y - 2
190 PRINT Y
200 X = X - 9
210 PRINT X
220 END
```

Line	W	X	Y	Displayed
100				
110				
120				
130				
140				
150				
160				
170				
180				
190				
200				
210				
220				

3. For each program below, construct a table similar to the one in exercise 2. Record for each line number the current values of the variables and the results displayed by the PRINT statements.

a.
```
100 A = 1
110 B = 3
120 PRINT A
130 A = A + 1
140 B = B - 1
150 PRINT B
160 A = A + 1
170 B = B - 1
180 PRINT A
190 END
```

b. A is assigned the value 4 and B is assigned the value 2.
```
100 C = 4
110 PRINT C
120 INPUT A, B
130 C = A \ B + C + 8 MOD 4
140 A = A - 3
150 B = C ^ A
160 PRINT B
170 END
```

c. A is assigned the value 7 and B is assigned the value 2.
```
100 INPUT A, B
110 C = A * A
120 PRINT C
130 D = A - B
140 PRINT D
150 E = 1
160 PRINT E
170 D = D - 3
180 X = E / D
190 PRINT X
200 END
```

d. PRINCIPAL is assigned the value 500 and RATE is assigned the value 10.
```
100 INPUT PRINCIPAL, RATE
110 RATE = RATE / 100
120 DISCOUNT = PRINCIPAL * RATE
130 RATE = RATE * 100
140 ' Display Results
150 PRINT "Discount rate"; RATE; "%"
160 PRINT "Price"; PRINCIPAL; "Dollars"
170 PRINT "Discount"; DISCOUNT; "Dollars"
180 END
```

4. Write LET statements for each of the following:

   a. Assign T the value of 3.
   b. Assign X the value of T less 2.
   c. Assign P the product of T and X.
   d. Triple the value of T.
   e. Assign A the quotient of P divided by X.
   f. Increment X by 1.
   g. Cube the value of R.

5. Fill in the missing word in each of the following:

   a. An output statement must contain the word _____ .
   b. Every BASIC program should contain the _____ statement.
   c. Every LET statement must contain an _____ sign.

6. Correct the errors in the following programs.

```
a. 100 PRINT Y          b. 100 S = 3 / 5000      c. 100 X = 3003 x 4004
   110 END                 110 PRINT                110 PRINT X
   120 Y = 21              120 END
```

```
d. 100 S = 23 - 901      e. 100 A1 = 999 / 888    f. 100 Z = 1
    95 PRINT S              110 PRINT S              110 PRINT Z1
   110 END                 120 DEND                 120 END
```

7. Identify the BASIC arithmetic operators for the following:

   a. Addition   b. Subtraction   c. Multiplication   d. Division
   e. Exponentiation f. Integer Division g. Modulo

8. Describe three techniques presented in chapter 2 for integrating data into a program.
9. Explain in one sentence the purpose of pressing the Control (Ctrl) and Break keys simultaneously.
10. Explain in one sentence each the purpose of the following system commands: AUTO, FILES, LIST, NEW, RUN, RENUM.
11. What does the following program display when the value 10 is entered in response to the first INPUT statement and 8 is entered in response to the second INPUT statement?

```
100 ' Exercise 2.11
110 INPUT "What is the length"; LONG
120 INPUT "What is the width"; WIDE
130 AREA = LONG * WIDE
140 PRINT "A rectangle with dimensions"; LONG; "and"; WIDE
150 PRINT "has an area of"; AREA; "."
160 END
```

12. Is it possible to issue a RUN command more than once for the same program?
13. In an MS BASIC program, how do you instruct the PC to display two consecutive blank lines?
14. A program requests the user to input the hours worked (40) and the rate of pay ($6.75). The program determines the gross pay by multiplying the two values together and displays the gross pay. Is the following program solution logically correct for the problem stated?

```
100 ' Exercise 2.14
110 INPUT "Hours worked ===> ", HOURS
120 INPUT "Rate of pay ====> ", RATE
130 PAY = RATE * HOURS   ' Compute the Gross Pay
140 PRINT "The gross pay is 270"
150 END
```

15. What is wrong with the following program?

```
100 ' Exercise 2.15
110 INPUT X
120 X = A / B
130 PRINT "The answer is"; X
140 END
```

16. How would you delete line 150 from an MS BASIC program?
17. In the following program, indicate which lines are not required and, if deleted, would not alter the results.

```
100 ' Exercise 2.17
110 ' Calculate the Sales Tax
120 INPUT SALES
130 TAX = 0.04 * SALES
140 PRINT "The sales tax is"; TAX
150 END
```

18. If the following program is entered as shown, will it be accepted or rejected by MS BASIC?

```
130 END
120 PRINT X
110 X = 4 * 5 * 6 \ 3
100 ' Exercise 2.18
```

19. Use the Student Diskette to complete the Try It Yourself exercises on pages 32 and 41.

⊞ 2.12   BASIC PROGRAMMING PROBLEMS

So that your computer programs are documented properly, you can use the following identification format at the beginning of each BASIC source program:

```
100 ' Department, Course Number, Division, Course Name
110 ' Your Name
120 ' Date
130 ' Problem Number
140 ' A Short Description of the Problem
150 ' ************************************************
```

In line 130, for example, use the comment "Problem 2-1" to represent the first problem in chapter 2. In line 140, use the title of the problem as the comment.

Upon completion of each problem, turn in to your instructor the following items:

1. a logic diagram in flowchart form or in pseudocode, as required
2. a listing of the source program
3. the output results

See section 2.7, page 41, on how to obtain a hard copy of your source program and output results. Use meaningful variable names in all the programs. Each major section of the program should be documented with appropriate remark lines.

When you enter a program for the first time, use the AUTO command, which automatically starts a BASIC line with a line number. If additional lines are inserted later, use the RENUM command to begin the program with line 100 or 1000 and increment each line number by 10. Be sure to use the SAVE command to store all program solutions in auxiliary storage in the form of SAVE "LABc-n", where c represents the chapter number and n represents the problem number.

> *Note:* All programming problems in this book include partial or complete sample output results and, when applicable, sample input data. Learn to select good test data to evaluate the logic of your program. Check your design and program against the sample output, and select your own data for additional testing purposes.

1. Computation of a Sum

Purpose: To gain confidence in keying and executing your first BASIC program.

Problem: Key in and execute the following program, which determines the sum of three numbers. Replace the verbiage in lines 100 to 120 with your course identification and name and today's date, as described earlier.

```
100 ' Course Identification
110 ' Your Name
120 ' Today's Date
130 ' Problem 2-1
140 ' Computation of a Sum
150 ' *******************
160 SUM = 25.65 + 13.75 + 15.25
170 PRINT "The sum is"; SUM
180 END
```

Input Data: None.

Output Results: The following results are displayed.

```
The sum is 54.65
```

2. Determining the Selling Price

Purpose: To become familiar with elementary uses of the INPUT, PRINT, and LET statements.

Problem: Merchants are in the retail business to buy goods from producers, manufacturers, and wholesalers and to sell the merchandise to their customers. To make a profit, they must sell their merchandise for more than the cost plus the overhead (taxes, store rent, upkeep, salaries, and so forth). The margin is the sum of the overhead and profit. The selling price is the sum of the margin and cost. Write a program, following the steps outlined in section 2.9 on page 42, that will determine the selling price of an item that costs $48.27 and has a margin of 25%. Develop your solution by loading and modifying program PRG2-10 on the Student Diskette. Use the following formula:

$$\text{Selling Price} = \left(\frac{1}{1-\text{Margin}}\right)\text{Cost}$$

Input Data: Use the following data in response to INPUT statements.

> Cost: $48.27
> Margin: 25%

Output Results: The following results are displayed.

```
What is the cost? 48.27
What is the margin in percent? 25

The selling price is 64.36
```

3. The Optimal Investment

Purpose: To familiarize the student with the use of the CLS, INPUT, KEY, PRINT, and LET statements and to perform multiple runs on the same program.

Problem: Three local banks have undertaken an advertising campaign to attract savings-account customers. The specifics of their advertisements are shown in Table 2.12 below.

Construct a single program, following the steps outlined in section 2.9 on page 42, whose execution will employ the RUN command three times, once for each bank. The program is to compute and display the amount of a $500 investment for a period of one year. A comparison of the results will show the optimal investment. Clear the entire screen before displaying any output. Develop your solution by loading and modifying program PRG2-10 on the Student Diskette. Use the following formula:

$$\text{Amount} = \text{Principal} * (1 + \text{Rate} / T)\;\hat{}\;T$$

where T = number of times the investment is compounded per year (i.e., the conversions).

TABLE 2.12 Interest Rates Charged by Three Local Banks

BANK 1	BANK 2	BANK 3
Interest 6⅞%	Interest 6¾%	Interest 6⅝%
Compounded annually	Compounded semiannually	Compounded quarterly

Input Data: Enter the data found in Table 2.12 in response to INPUT statements. For example, for Bank 1, enter the following.

> Bank: 1
> Principal: $500.00
> Rate: 0.06875
> Conversions: 1

Output Results: The following results are displayed for Bank 1.

```
Please enter:

        Bank number ============> 1
        Principal ===============> 500
        Rate in decimal =========> 0.06875
        Number of conversions ===> 1
Amount of investment after one year for bank 1 =====> 534.375
```

4. Payroll Problem I: Gross Pay Computations

Purpose: To become familiar with some of the grammatical and logical rules of MS BASIC and to demonstrate the basic concepts of executing an MS BASIC program.

Problem: Construct a program, following the steps outlined in section 2.9 on page 42, that will clear the screen, then compute and display the gross pay for an employee working 80 hours during a biweekly pay period at an hourly rate of $12.50.

Version A: Insert the data, 80 and 12.50, directly into a LET statement that determines the gross pay.

Version B: Assign the data, 80 and 12.50, to variables in LET statements and then compute the gross pay in a separate LET statement.

Version C: Enter the data, 80 and 12.50, in response to INPUT statements.

Output Results: The following results are displayed for Version B.

```
Hours worked ===> 80
Rate of pay ====> 12.5
Gross pay ======> 1000
```

CALCULATIONS, STRINGS, AND AN INTRODUCTION TO THE TOP-DOWN APPROACH

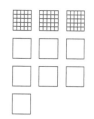

3.1

INTRODUCTION

In chapter 2, you were introduced to a few simple computer programs that demonstrated some of the grammatical rules of the Microsoft BASIC language. Also presented were examples of programs that interact with the user through the INPUT and PRINT statements. This chapter continues to develop straight-line programs, with more complex computations and manipulation of data.

The focus in this chapter is on constants, variables, expressions, functions, and statements that assign values. This chapter also expands on the type of data that can be assigned to variables by introducing **string values**, examples of which include a word, a phrase, or a sentence.

Finally, chapter 3 presents the top-down (modular) approach to solving problems. The top-down approach is a useful methodology for solving larger and more complex problems than those presented in chapter 2. Included in the presentation are the GOSUB and RETURN statements.

Upon successful completion of this chapter, you will be able to write programs that manipulate string expressions and numeric expressions. You will also be able to solve problems by first breaking them into smaller and more manageable subproblems.

Programming Case Study 3: *Tailor's Calculations*

Program 3.1, on the following page, determines the average neck, hat, and shoe size of a male customer. The program uses the following formulas:

$$\text{Neck Size} = 3\left(\frac{\text{Weight}}{\text{Waistline}}\right) \qquad \text{Hat Size} = \frac{\text{Neck Size}}{2.125} \qquad \text{Shoe Size} = 50\left(\frac{\text{Waistline}}{\text{Weight}}\right)$$

Program 3.1 computes the average neck size (15), hat size (7.058824), and shoe size (10) for Mike, who has a 35-inch waistline and weighs 175 pounds. Even though it is not used in the computations, the customer name is requested in the program, because it helps identify the measurements when more than one set of computations is involved.

PROGRAM 3.1

```
100 ' Program 3.1
110 ' Tailor's Computations
120 ' Determine Neck Size, Hat Size and Shoe Size
130 ' *******************************************
140 CLS : KEY OFF   ' Clear Screen
150 INPUT "Customer's first name"; FIRST.NAME$
160 INPUT "Waistline"; WAIST
170 INPUT "Weight"; WEIGHT
180 NECKSIZE = 3 * WEIGHT / WAIST
190 HATSIZE  = NECKSIZE / 2.125
200 SHOESIZE = 50 * WAIST / WEIGHT
210 PRINT
220 PRINT FIRST.NAME$; "'s neck size is"; NECKSIZE
230 PRINT FIRST.NAME$; "'s hat size is"; HATSIZE
240 PRINT FIRST.NAME$; "'s shoe size is"; SHOESIZE
250 END

RUN

Customer's first name? Mike
Waistline? 35
Weight? 175

Mike's neck size is 15
Mike's hat size is 7.058824
Mike's shoe size is 10
```

Program 3.1 contains a sequence of LET statements (lines 180 through 200) with expressions that are more complex than those encountered in chapter 2. Furthermore, line 150 contains a variable, FIRST.NAME$, that is assigned a string of letters, Mike, rather than a numeric value. The value of FIRST.NAME$ is displayed along with the results because of lines 220 through 240. The following pages introduce some additional formal definitions and special rules for constructing constants, variables, and LET statements, and for manipulating strings.

TRY IT YOURSELF

Load Program 3.1 (PRG3-1) from the Student Diskette. Display and execute the program. Enter your name and measurements in place of Mike's. How close did the PC and Program 3.1 come in estimating your neck, hat, and shoe size?

Now rerun the program, using the figures 36 and 190 for Mike's waistline and weight.

⊞ 3.2

CONSTANTS

You will recall from chapter 2 that constants are values that do not change during the execution of a program. Two different kinds of constants are valid for use in BASIC programs: **numeric constants** and **string constants**. Numeric constants represent ordinary numbers. A string constant is a sequence of letters, digits, and special characters enclosed in quotation marks. They are used for such nonnumeric purposes as representing an employee name, a social security number, an address, or a telephone number.

Numeric Constants

A numeric constant can have one of the three following forms in MS BASIC:

1. **Integer:** a positive or negative whole number with no decimal point, like –174 or 5903 or 0 or –32768.

2. **Fixed Point:** a positive or negative real number with a decimal point, like 713.1417 or 0.0034 or 0.0 or –35.1 or 1923547463.34.
3. **Floating Point** or **Exponential Form:** A number written as an integer or fixed point constant, followed by the letter D or E and an integer. D or E stands for "times ten to the power." (An explanation of the difference between using a D or an E follows shortly.) Examples are 793E19, 62E–23, 1E0, –2.3D–3, and + 12.34789564D + 7.

Examples of numeric constants in Program 3.1 are 3, 2.125, and 50, found in lines 180, 190, and 200. A line number like 210 is not considered to be a constant in MS BASIC.

```
180 NECKSIZE = 3 * WEIGHT / WAIST

190 HATSIZE  = NECKSIZE / 2.125          Numeric Constants

200 SHOESIZE = 50 * WAIST / WEIGHT
```

To write the constant three and a half in a BASIC program, you may not use 3–1/2 or 3&1/2 or 3 and 1/2 or three & 1/2. You may validly write 3.5 or 3.50 or 3.50000 or 3.5E0 or 0.35E1 or 35E–1 or 3.5D0.

Table 3.1 lists some ordinary numbers and shows how they may be expressed as valid numeric constants in MS BASIC. Examples 1, 3, and 9 of Table 3.1 show that special characters like $, ¢, @, and commas are not allowed in numeric constants.

Examples 3 and 6 show that you may write an integer in any of the three forms. If a number is negative, as in example 5, the minus sign must precede the number. If a number is positive, as in example 8, the plus sign is optional.

TABLE 3.1 Examples of Numeric Constants

EXAMPLE	ORDINARY NUMBERS	NUMERIC CONSTANTS IN MS BASIC
1.	$3.14	3.14 or 3.140
2.	512.71	512.71 or 512.710 or 0512.71
3.	4¢	4 or 4. or 4.00 or 04 or 4E0
4.	1.7321	1.7321 or 1.73210
5.	–29.7822	–29.7822 or –2.97822E1
6.	0	0 or 0. or 000 or 0E0 or 0D0
7.	–39.5	–39.5 or –39.50 or –0039.50 or –.395E2
8.	+ 12,768.5	+ 12768.5 or 12768.5
9.	1000,000@	100000 or 100000. or 1.E5 or 1E5 or 1D5
10.	6.02257×10^{23}	6.02257E23 or + 6.02257D + 23

Examples 8 and 9 indicate that *commas must not be inserted into numeric constants.* Example 7 illustrates that high-order zeros (to the left of the first significant digit) have no effect on the number. Finally, spaces should not occur in numeric constants.

Programming Case Study 4: Banker's Simple Interest

Program 3.2, on the next page, uses the following formula

$$\text{Banker's Interest} = P \times R \left(\frac{\text{Exact No. of Days}}{360} \right)$$

to determine the ordinary simple interest for a loan of $4,850 at 15.6% for 90 days.

PROGRAM 3.2

```
100 ' Program 3.2
110 ' Banker's Simple Interest
120 ' ***********************
130 CLS : KEY OFF  ' Clear Screen
140 RATE = 0.156
150 INPUT "Principal ========> ", PRINCIPAL
160 INPUT "Time in days =====> ", TIME
170 INTEREST = PRINCIPAL * RATE * TIME / 360
180 PRINT
190 PRINT "Interest =========> $"; INTEREST
200 END

RUN

Principal ========> 4850
Time in days =====> 90

Interest =========> $ 189.15
```

The answer that results from the execution of this program is 189.15 (dollars). Lines 140 and 170 each include a numeric constant. In line 140, the variable RATE (the rate of interest) is set equal to the value of 0.156. In line 170, the numeric constant 360 is used to determine the time factor. The numeric data items, 4850 and 90 days, entered in response to the INPUT statements in lines 150 and 160, must take the form of numeric constants. This leads to the following rule:

> **Input Rule 2:** Numeric data that is assigned to numeric variables through the use of the INPUT statement must take the form of numeric constants.

Program 3.2 could have been made more general if RATE had been assigned the interest rate through the use of the INPUT statement. A LET statement was used to assign RATE the value 0.156 in order to illustrate the makeup of a numeric constant.

TRY IT YOURSELF

Load Program 3.2 (PRG3-2) from the Student Diskette. Display the program and change line 140 to accept a value for the rate (RATE) through an INPUT statement similar to the one in line 150. Execute the program. Enter the same data used with Program 3.2.

Computer Precision

Numeric constants are stored in main storage in one of three forms: integer, single precision, or double precision.

The PC requires 2 bytes of main storage to store an integer constant, 4 bytes to store a single-precision constant, and 8 bytes to store a double-precision constant.

We tell the PC how to store a value, like a numeric constant, by the way we write it. For example, a numeric constant is stored in integer form if it is between –32768 and +32767 and does not contain a decimal point or does include a trailing percent sign (%).

The PC stores a constant in single precision if one of the following is true:

1. it is outside the range for an integer and contains seven or fewer digits;
2. it contains a decimal point and has seven or fewer digits;
3. it is written in exponential form, using E; or
4. it includes a trailing exclamation point (!).

With single precision, the PC maintains seven significant digits.

The PC uses double precision to store a constant if one of the following is true:

1. it has eight or more digits;
2. it is written in exponential form, using D; or
3. it includes a trailing number sign (#).

With double precision, the PC will store up to seventeen digits. With single or double precision, you can represent any number (positive or negative) from 2.9×10^{-39} to 1.7×10^{38}. Table 3.2 shows several examples of constants as well as the form used by the PC to store them.

TABLE 3.2 Numeric Constants and the Form Used to Store Them

NUMERIC CONSTANT	STORED AS
−128	Integer
1	Integer
4.923458%	Integer; stored as the constant 5.
5125	Integer
3E−4	Single Precision
1.	Single Precision
4.67	Single Precision
67.45637681902!	Single Precision; stored as 67.45638.
345612	Single Precision
3D−4	Double Precision
87.3#	Double Precision
899045637.87957	Double Precision

The precision with which numeric values are stored can also play an important role in determining the type of arithmetic the PC will use to compute the value of an expression. Generally speaking, integer arithmetic is faster than single-precision arithmetic, which in turn is faster than double-precision arithmetic.

For the most part, you can let the PC handle the precision with which it stores values, as was done in chapter 2 and in Programs 3.1 and 3.2. *That is, write numeric constants in a BASIC program the same way you would in algebra.* However, you should be aware that it is possible for the BASIC programmer to control both the way a numeric constant is stored and the type of arithmetic the PC will use.

Numeric Constants in Exponential Form

Numeric constants may be written in **exponential form**. This form is similar to **scientific notation**. It is a shorthand way of representing very large and very small numbers in a program. If a result exceeds the precision under which it is stored, the PC displays it in exponential form. For these two reasons, it is important to have some idea of how to read and write numbers in this form.

With exponential notation, a number, regardless of its magnitude, is expressed as a value between 1 and 10 that is multiplied by a power of 10. For example, 1,500,000 can be expressed as 1.5×10^6 in scientific notation or can be written as an exponential-type constant in the form of 1.5E6. The positive power of 10 in the exponential notation of 1.5×10^6 shows that the decimal point was previously moved 6 places to the left. That is,

$$1.\underset{\curvearrowleft}{500000}.$$

6 places to left

In order to write 1.5×10^6 as an exponential-type constant in a BASIC program, either the letter D (double precision) or E (single precision), which both stand for "times ten to the power," is substituted for the "$\times$ 10." Hence, the exponential-type constant may be written as 1.5E6 in single precision or 1.5D6 in double precision.

In the same way, a small number like 0.000000001234 can be expressed as 1.234×10^{-9} or 1.234E–9 or 1.234D–9. The negative power of 10 in 1.234×10^{-9} signifies that the decimal point was moved 9 places to the right, as follows:

0.000000001.234

9 places to right

Program 3.3 represents the use of exponential notation in computing the banker's interest for a 90-day loan of $1,500,000. This program is nearly the same as Program 3.2, except that the numeric constant (0.156) assigned to the variable RATE in line 140 is written in exponential form, and the principal is entered in exponential form in response to line 150.

PROGRAM 3.3

```
100 ' Program 3.3
110 ' Banker's Simple Interest
120 ' ***********************
130 CLS : KEY OFF   ' Clear Screen
140 RATE = 1.56E-1
150 INPUT "Principal ========> ", PRINCIPAL
160 INPUT "Time in days =====> ", TIME
170 INTEREST = PRINCIPAL * RATE * TIME / 360
180 PRINT
190 PRINT "Interest =========> $"; INTEREST
200 END

RUN

Principal ========> 1.5E6        Principal of $1,500,000
Time in days =====> 90           Entered in Exponential Form

Interest =========> $ 58500
```

Table 3.3 lists some ordinary numbers and shows how they may be expressed in scientific notation and as exponential-type constants in MS BASIC.

TABLE 3.3 Examples of Scientific Notation and Exponential-Type Constants

ORDINARY NUMBERS	SCIENTIFIC NOTATION	POSSIBLE EXPONENTIAL-TYPE CONSTANTS
10,000,000	1×10^7	*1E7 or 1.E+7 or 0.01E9*
0.0000152	1.52×10^{-5}	*1.52E–5 or +152D–7*
0.001	1×10^{-3}	*1E–3 or 0.001E0*
–6000000000000	-6×10^{12}	*–6E+12 or –6D12 or –0.6E13*
–0.005892	-5.892×10^{-3}	*–5.892E–3 or 5892E–6*
186,000	1.86×10^5	*1.86E+5 or 0.186D6*

TRY IT YOURSELF

Load Program 3.3 (PRG3-3) from the Student Diskette. Execute the program with a time factor of 90 days for each of the following principals: 15E5, 0.0015E9, 1500000, 150000E1, and 15000000000E-4. Does each execution of the program result in an interest of $58,500?

String Constants   A string constant has as its value the string of all characters between surrounding quotation marks. The length of a string constant may be between 0 and 255 characters. A string with a length of zero is a **null string** or an **empty string**. The quotation marks indicate the beginning and end of the string constant and are not considered to be part of the value.

The messages that have been incorporated in INPUT statements to prompt for the required data and in PRINT statements to identify results are examples of string constants. For example, string constants appear in lines 150, 160, and 190 of Program 3.3.

```
150 INPUT "Principal ========> ", PRINCIPAL

160 INPUT "Time in days =====> ", TIME        String Constants

190 PRINT "Interest ========> $"; INTEREST
```

String constants can be assigned to variables in a LET statement, as is shown in the following program.

PROGRAM 3.4

```
100 ' Program 3.4
110 ' Examples of String Constants
120 ' **************************
130 MODEL$ = "Q1937A"
140 PART$ = "12AB34"
150 DESCRIPTION$ = "Nylon, Disc"
160 PRINT "Model number: "; MODEL$
170 PRINT "Part number: "; PART$
180 PRINT "Description: "; DESCRIPTION$
190 END

RUN

Model number: Q1937A
Part number: 12AB34
Description: Nylon, Disc
```

In line 130 of Program 3.4, the variable MODEL$ is assigned the value Q1937A. In line 140, PART$ is assigned the value 12AB34, and in line 150, DESCRIPTION$ is assigned the value Nylon, Disc.

String constants are used in a program to represent values that name or identify a person, place, or thing. They are also used to represent report and column headings and output messages. The ability to manipulate data of this type is important in the field of business data processing. As you will see later in this chapter as well as in chapter 8, MS BASIC also includes **string functions** for manipulating strings.

Table 3.4 lists sequences of letters, digits, and special characters and shows how they may be expressed as valid string constants.

TABLE 3.4 Examples of String Constants

STRING OF CHARACTERS	CORRESPONDING STRING CONSTANT IN MS BASIC
844-0520 (Telephone Number)	"844-0520"
Nikole Zigmund	"Nikole Zigmund"
Blank (Space)	" "
EMPLOYEE FILE LIST	"EMPLOYEE FILE LIST"
310386024 (Social Security No.)	"310386024"
A Null or Empty String	""

Be careful not to include a quotation mark within a string. For example,

```
100 MESSAGE$ = "She Said, "No""    ' Invalid Statement
```

is invalid because the second quotation mark ends the string. An apostrophe is recommended for cases where a quotation mark is needed in a string. For example,

```
100 MESSAGE$ = "She Said, 'No'"
```

is valid. The message

```
She Said, 'No'
```

can later be displayed by a statement such as

```
500 PRINT MESSAGE$
```

⊞ 3.3

VARIABLES

In chapter 2, you learned that in programming, a **variable** is a location in main storage whose value can change as the program is executed. In a program, the variable is referenced by a variable name. Variables are declared in a BASIC program by incorporating variable names in statements. For example, the LET statements,

```
100 RANK = 4
110 SCHOOL$ = "Purdue"
```

instruct MS BASIC to set up independent storage areas for RANK and SCHOOL$ as well as the constants 4 and Purdue.

Although it may appear to you that RANK is being assigned the value 4 when you enter the statement through your keyboard, this does not occur until the program is executed. You'll recall from chapter 1 that a BASIC program must be translated into equivalent machine language instructions before it can be executed. During this translation, the variables and numeric constants of a program are assigned particular storage areas in main storage. Figure 3.1 illustrates the storage areas for RANK and SCHOOL$ before and after execution of lines 100 and 110 in the partial program above.

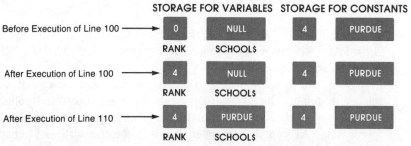

STORAGE FOR VARIABLES   STORAGE FOR CONSTANTS

Before Execution of Line 100 ⟶ | 0 RANK | NULL SCHOOL$ | 4 | PURDUE |

After Execution of Line 100 ⟶ | 4 RANK | NULL SCHOOL$ | 4 | PURDUE |

After Execution of Line 110 ⟶ | 4 RANK | PURDUE SCHOOL$ | 4 | PURDUE |

FIGURE 3.1
The assignment of values to variables in main storage.

Unlike a constant, a variable may be redefined (that is, its value may be changed) during the execution of a program. However, its value may remain unchanged in a BASIC program if you so desire. For example, if in the previous partial program another line is added after line 110, as shown here:

```
100 RANK = 4
110 SCHOOL$ = "Purdue"
120 RANK = 2
```

then the value of RANK changes from 4 to 2 when line 120 is executed. MS BASIC recognizes that the two variable names are the same and during translation does not attempt to create an independent storage location for the second one. In other words, there can be only one variable with the name RANK in a program; however, it can be referenced and the value changed as often as needed.

Two categories of variables are valid for use in a BASIC program. These are **simple variables** and **subscripted variables**. Simple variables are used to store single values, while subscripted variables are used to store groups of values, like one- or two-dimensional arrays.

Our discussion here concerns simple variables; subscripted variables will be discussed in chapter 7.

As with constants, there are two types of simple variables: **numeric** and **string**. A numeric variable may be assigned only a numeric value, and a string variable may be assigned only a string of characters.

When the system command RUN is issued for a program, all numeric variables are assigned an initial value of zero and all string variables are assigned a null value. The LET statement may be used to assign a variable a constant value or the result of a calculation. Variables may also be assigned values through INPUT statements.

Selection of Variable Names A variable name begins with a letter and may be followed by up to 39 letters, digits, and periods.

If a variable name ends with a dollar sign ($), then MS BASIC establishes a location in main storage to receive a string value. If a variable name does not end with a dollar sign, then MS BASIC establishes a location in main storage to receive a numeric value.

Keywords like, LET, PRINT, and END or any other **reserved word** that has special meaning to MS BASIC may not be used as a variable name. See the reference card at the back of this book for a list of the reserved words. Some examples of numeric and string variable names, invalid if written as given, are listed in Tables 3.5 and 3.6.

_____TABLE 3.5 Invalid Numeric Variables and the Corresponding Valid Forms_____

INVALID NUMERIC VARIABLES	TYPE OF ERROR	VALID NUMERIC VARIABLES
1P	*First character must be a letter.*	PAY1 *or* PAY
LET	LET *is a keyword.*	LETS
QUANTITY*	*Special characters other than the period are invalid.*	QUANTITY
FNNUM	*A variable name may not begin with the characters* FN. *(To be discussed in chapter 8.)*	NUM
RATE$	*A numeric variable must not end with a $.*	RATE

_____TABLE 3.6 Invalid String Variables and the Corresponding Valid Forms_____

INVALID STRING VARIABLES	TYPE OF ERROR	VALID STRING VARIABLES
EMP.NAME	*Appended dollar sign necessary.*	EMP.NAME$
WIDTH$	WIDTH *is a keyword.*	WIDE$
CUSTOMER $	*Blank character not permitted.*	CUSTOMER$

When you compose variable names, make them as meaningful as possible. It is far easier for a person to read the various statements in a program if meaningful names are used. For example, let's assume that the formula for gross pay is given by

Gross Pay = Rate × Hours

The following statement may represent the formula in a BASIC program:

    150 A = B * C

However, it is more meaningful to write

    150 G = R * H

It is even more meaningful to say

```
150 GROSS = RATE * HOURS
```

Some BASIC programmers apply the period to group variable names, as shown below:

Group name.Specific name

For example, if several variable names are needed to describe data in an employee record, then EMP may be used as the group name. The part of the variable name that follows the period differentiates between the variable names that begin with the group name, as shown here:

```
EMP.NUMBER$
EMP.NAME$
EMP.ADDRESS$
EMP.SALARY
EMP.CODE$
```

Develop a structured style for choosing meaningful variable names for a program. During the program design stage, establish guidelines for how variable names will be selected, and rigorously follow these guidelines when coding the program. Of course, you must abide by the rules that may restrict or enhance the ways you make up variable names.

Undefined Variables

Nearly every serious BASIC program, when first written, contains errors. Microsoft BASIC will detect many of the more common types of BASIC statement errors, and it will display appropriate diagnostic messages.

One of the most common errors beginners make is not to define variables for computation. An **undefined variable** has no value assigned to it by the programmer during the execution of the program. Undefined variables are not detected during the process of translating a BASIC program into its equivalent machine-language instructions. All numeric variables are assigned a value of zero and all string variables are assigned the null string when the system command RUN is issued for the program.

It is recommended that you assign all variables valid values through the use of the LET or INPUT statement, instead of relying on MS BASIC to **initialize** them for you. Assigning variables a valid value before they are used for computation purposes will decrease your debugging effort and increase your confidence in the program. Furthermore, defining variables is an excellent habit, because few other programming languages automatically initialize variables to a valid value.

Program 3.5 represents a program with an undefined variable, X, in lines 160 and 170.

PROGRAM 3.5

```
100 ' Program 3.5
110 ' Example of a Program
120 ' With an Undefined Variable
130 ' **************************
140 SIDE1 = 4
150 SIDE2 = 6
160 SUM = SIDE1 + SIDE2 + X
170 PRINT "The value of X is"; X
180 PRINT "The value of SUM is"; SUM
190 END

RUN

The value of X is 0
The value of SUM is 10
```

To avoid the problems that are brought on by undefined variables in a program, make sure all variables are assigned initial values.

Declaring Variable Types

The name of a variable determines whether it is string or numeric, and, if numeric, what its precision is.

As the last character in a variable name, the dollar sign ($) declares that the variable will represent a string. If the dollar sign is absent at the end of the variable name, then the variable is declared to be numeric. As with numeric constants, numeric variables may be declared type integer, single precision, or double precision.

If there is no trailing special character in a variable name, then MS BASIC defines it as single precision. Variable names like SUM, EMP.SALARY, and PRODUCT are single-precision numeric variables. All of the numeric variables used thus far in this book have been of this type.

You may also declare a variable to be single precision explicitly by appending an exclamation point (!) to the variable name. Variable names like NUMBER!, MEAN!, and ASSESSMENT! are examples of explicitly declared single-precision variables. Also see the third and fourth examples in Table 3.7.

Single-precision variables can store up to 7 significant digits. If a value being assigned to a single-precision variable contains 8 or more digits, the system will round it to 7. For this reason, the 7th digit may not always be exact. The numeric values that may be assigned to a single-precision variable are restricted to the range (positive or negative) 2.9×10^{-39} to 1.7×10^{38}.

An integer variable is declared by ending the variable name with a percent sign (%). The first two examples in Table 3.7 illustrate integer-type variables. Integer variables take up less space in main storage and for that reason are often used in programs to count the number of times something has occurred. Integer variables can hold only an integer value that is between –32,768 and +32,767. If you assign an integer variable a noninteger value, MS BASIC will round the noninteger value to an integer. For example,

```
100 GPA% = 3.7
```

results in GPA% being assigned the value 4. Likewise, the following partial program

```
100 SIDE1 = 5.4345
110 SUM% = SIDE1
```

is valid and results in SUM% being assigned a value of 5. The PC rounds the value 5.4345, assigned to SIDE1 in line 100, to 5 in line 110, because SUM% can hold only an integer value.

If you attempt to assign an integer variable a value outside the range –32,768 to +32,767, the PC will display the diagnostic message

```
Overflow in line number
```

where line number is the number of the line in which the overflow occurred.

A double-precision variable is declared by appending a number sign (#) to the variable name. Examples of variables declared double precision include DISTANCE#, QUOTIENT#, and TEMP#. A variable declared double precision may hold up to 17 significant digits and may be assigned numeric values in the same range as single-precision variables.

Table 3.7 shows several examples of numeric variables and the type declared.

The following program illustrates the difference, in terms of the results displayed, between assigning the double-precision constant

TABLE 3.7 Declaring the Type of Numeric Variable

NUMERIC VARIABLE	DECLARED TYPE
CODE%	*Integer*
POINT%	*Integer*
DEVIATION	*Single Precision*
ERROR!	*Single Precision*
SPECS#	*Double Precision*
WEIGHT#	*Double Precision*

123,456,789,012,345,678 to a single-precision variable SINGLE and a double-precision variable DOUBLE#.

```
100 SINGLE  = 123456789012345678
110 DOUBLE# = 123456789012345678
120 PRINT "The value in single precision is"; SINGLE
130 PRINT "The value in double precision is"; DOUBLE#
140 END

RUN

The value in single precision is 1.234568E17
The value in double precision is 1.234567890123457D17
```

With single precision, the PC displays 7 digits in the integer portion of the result. As with double-precision constants, double-precision variables can maintain up to 17 significant digits. However, as illustrated in the previous example, the PC displays up to 16 digits rounded when more than 16 digits are assigned to the double-precision variable.

Although single-precision variables are adequate for most applications, some situations, especially in the areas of science and finance, require double-precision variables for accuracy.

TRY IT YOURSELF

Load Program 3.3 (PRG3-3) from the Student Diskette. Append the character % at the end of each variable name and execute the program with the same data that was used with Program 3.3. Are the results the same for the modified version of Program 3.3 as they were for the original? Next, substitute the character # in place of the character % at the end of each variable name, and repeat the above steps.

Regions of Overflow and Zero

As previously stated, when you attempt to assign an integer variable a value that is outside the range –32,768 to +32,767, the PC will display a diagnostic message.

The same applies in the case where you attempt to assign a fixed-point or floating-point variable a value outside the range -1.7×10^{38} to $+1.7 \times 10^{38}$. This **overflow condition** exists when a numeric expression gives a value greater than the largest permissible value allowed in MS BASIC for either integer, fixed-point, or floating-point values.

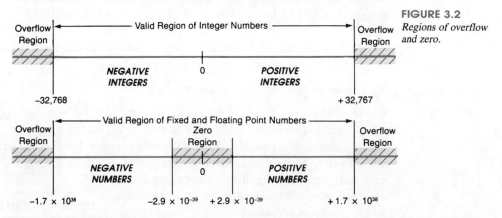

FIGURE 3.2
Regions of overflow and zero.

Figure 3.2 represents various regions of overflow and zero conditions for integer, fixed-point, and floating-point values in MS BASIC. A zero condition exists in MS BASIC when the value of a numeric expression is within the range –2.9E–39 to +2.9E–39. When that condition occurs, the PC assigns the numeric expression a value of zero. For example,

```
100 DIST = 2.9E-40
```

results in DIST being assigned a value of zero.

Assigning Numeric Variables Values Through the INPUT Statement

A number that is entered in response to the INPUT statement and assigned to a single-precision or double-precision variable may have as many digits as required, up to a maximum of 38. However, the PC will keep only the number of digits that is specified by the type of variable receiving the value. That is, if the following number, containing 38 digits,

12345678901234567890123456789012345678

is entered in response to each of the following INPUT statements,

```
220 INPUT AMT
230 INPUT AMT#
```

the PC stores the number as

12345680000000000000000000000000000000   or   1.234568E+37

for AMT, and

12345678901234567000000000000000000000   or   1.2345678901234567D+37

for AMT#. The value of AMT (single precision) is rounded to 7 significant digits, and the value of AMT# (double precision) is truncated to 17 significant digits. In both instances, the PC maintains the magnitude of the number.

Assigning Values to String Variables Through the INPUT Statement

The following program requests that string data be entered in response to the INPUT statements.

PROGRAM 3.6

```
100 ' Program 3.6
110 ' Entering String Data in
120 ' Response to the INPUT Statement
130 ' *****************************
140 INPUT "Model number: ", MODEL$
150 INPUT "Part number: ", PART$
160 INPUT "Description: ", DESCRIPTION$
170 PRINT
180 PRINT "The model number is "; MODEL$
190 PRINT "The part number is "; PART$
200 PRINT "The description is "; DESCRIPTION$
210 END

RUN

Model number: "Q1937A"          ⎫   Quoted String Data
Part number: "345123"           ⎬   Entered in Response to the
Description: "Nylon, Disc"      ⎭   Program's INPUT Statements

The model number is Q1937A
The part number is 345123
The description is Nylon, Disc
```

In Program 3.6, the string variables MODEL$, PART$, and DESCRIPTION$ are assigned quoted strings, following the rules for string constants. In general, surrounding a string with quotation marks is optional when an INPUT statement is used to assign the string to a string variable, but there are certain exceptions. Examine the output from Program 3.6 when unquoted strings are entered along with one quoted string, in contrast to the original output, in which all three strings were quoted:

```
RUN

Model number: Q1937A          ⎫ ──────  Unquoted Strings
Part number: 345123           ⎬
Description: "Nylon, Disc" ◄──── Quoted String

The model number is Q1937A
The part number is 345123
The description is Nylon, Disc
```

The first two string data items, Q1937A and 345123, are entered as unquoted strings. The third data item Nylon, Disc is entered within quotes because it contains an embedded comma. Quotation marks are necessary only if one of the following two characteristics is true of the string data item:

1. either the string contains leading or trailing spaces, or
2. the string contains a comma or colon.

The following rule summarizes the assignment of string data items through the use of the INPUT statement.

> **Input Rule 3:** String data that is assigned to string variables through the use of the INPUT statement may be entered with or without surrounding quotation marks, provided the string contains no leading or trailing spaces or embedded commas or colons. If the string contains leading or trailing spaces or embedded commas or colons, it must be surrounded with quotation marks.

Displaying String Variables

MS BASIC does not add leading or trailing spaces when it displays a string value. Therefore, when a semicolon is used as the separator between string items in a PRINT statement, a space should be included to separate the displayed values. Line 180 of the following partial program includes a space that follows the word is in the string constant. This causes the PC to display the value of MODEL$ one space after the word is.

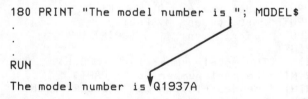

```
180 PRINT "The model number is "; MODEL$
        .
        .
        .
RUN

The model number is Q1937A
```

If the space after the last character in the string is omitted, the PC displays the value of MODEL$ right next to it, as shown here:

```
180 PRINT "The model number is"; MODEL$
        .
        .
        .
RUN

The model number isQ1937A
```

⊞ **3.4**

THE LET STATEMENT

The LET statement in MS BASIC is used to assign a value to a variable. The general form of the LET statement is given in Table 3.8. Each LET statement consists of the optional keyword LET, followed by a variable, followed by an equal sign, and then by an expression.

_____TABLE 3.8 The LET Statement_____

General Form:	LET *numeric variable* = *numeric expression* *or* LET *string variable* = *string expression*
Purpose:	*Causes the evaluation of the expression, followed by the assignment of the resulting value to the variable to the left of the equal sign.*

Examples:	```100 LET PERIMETER = 2 * SIDE1 + 2 * SIDE2```
	```150 LET Q = (B + A) / 2 - Q + R```
	```200 COUNT = COUNT + 1```
	```250 OPPOSITE = -OPPOSITE```
	```300 ARRAY.1(Y, 4) = 0```
	```350 DESCRIPTION$ = "PLIER"```
	```400 HYPOTENUSE = (BASE ^ 2 + HEIGHT ^ 2) ^ (1/2)```
	```450 P(I) = C(K) + P(J)```
	```500 E = M * C^2```
	```550 NUMBER$ = PREFIX$ + "0520"```

Note:	*The keyword* LET *is optional.*

The execution of the LET statement is not a one-step process for the PC. The execution of a LET statement requires two steps: evaluation of the expression and assignment of the result to the variable to the left of the equal sign.

Although the equal sign is employed in MS BASIC, it does not carry all the properties of the equal sign in mathematics. For example, the equal sign in MS BASIC does not allow for the symmetric relationship. That is,

```
100 LET A = B
```

cannot be written as

```
100 B = LET A
```

The equal sign in MS BASIC can best be described as meaning "is replaced by." Therefore,

```
160 INTEREST = PRINCIPAL * RATE * TIME / 360
```

means that the old value of INTEREST is replaced by the value determined from the expression to the right of the equal sign.

Programming Case Study 5A: *Finding the Single Discount Rate*

Program 3.7, on the following page, determines the single discount rate that is equal to the series of discount rates of 40%, 20%, and 10%, using the following formula:

$$\text{Rate} = 1 - (1 - \text{rate}_1)(1 - \text{rate}_2)(1 - \text{rate}_3) \ldots (1 - \text{rate}_n)$$

where Rate is the single discount rate, and rate_1, rate_2 ...rate_n is the series of discount rates. The number of factors of $(1 - \text{rate}_n)$ that are used to determine the single discount rate is dependent on the number of discounts. Program 3.7 is written to find the single discount rate for a series of three discount rates.

After the three discount rates are assigned their decimal values in Program 3.7, line 180 determines the value of the single discount from the expression found to the right of the equal sign. Specifically, the expression is evaluated and the final value 0.568 is assigned to the variable RATE. Line 200 displays the value for RATE before the program ends.

PROGRAM 3.7

```
100 ' Program 3.7
110 ' Finding the Single Discount Rate
120 ' ******************************
130 CLS : KEY OFF  ' Clear Screen
140 PRINT "Enter in Decimal Form:"
150 INPUT "          First Discount ======> ", RATE1
160 INPUT "          Second Discount =====> ", RATE2
170 INPUT "          Third Discount ======> ", RATE3
180 RATE = 1 - (1 - RATE1) * (1 - RATE2) * (1 - RATE3)
190 PRINT
200 PRINT "Single Discount ================>"; RATE
210 END

RUN

Enter in Decimal Form:
          First Discount ======> 0.40
          Second Discount =====> 0.20
          Third Discount ======> 0.10

Single Discount ================> .568
```

When dealing with rates that usually occur in percent form, it is often preferable to have the program accept the data and display the results in percent form. Program 3.8 shows how you can write a solution to Programming Case Study 5A that accomplishes this task.

PROGRAM 3.8

```
100 ' Program 3.8
110 ' Finding the Single Discount Rate
120 ' ******************************
130 CLS : KEY OFF  ' Clear Screen
140 PRINT "Enter in Percent Form:"
150 INPUT "          First Discount ======> ", RATE1
160 INPUT "          Second Discount =====> ", RATE2
170 INPUT "          Third Discount ======> ", RATE3
180 RATE1 = RATE1 / 100
190 RATE2 = RATE2 / 100
200 RATE3 = RATE3 / 100
210 RATE = 1 - (1 - RATE1) * (1 - RATE2) * (1 - RATE3)
220 RATE = 100 * RATE
230 PRINT
240 PRINT "Single Discount ================>"; RATE; "%"
250 END

RUN

Enter in Percent Form:
          First Discount ======> 40
          Second Discount =====> 20
          Third Discount ======> 10

Single Discount ================> 56.8 %
```

In Program 3.8, the INPUT statements (lines 150 through 170) prompt the user to enter the discount rates in percent form. In lines 180 through 200, the rates are changed from percent form to decimal form by dividing RATE1, RATE2, and RATE3 by 100. The single discount is then determined by line 210. Line 220 replaces the assigned value of RATE (0.568) with 100 times RATE. In other words, line 220 changes the value of RATE from decimal form to percent form. Line 240 then displays the value of RATE. The string constant % that is found at the end of line 240 helps identify the result as a percent value.

Program 3.8 includes two concepts that many beginners have difficulty understanding. The first is that the same variable — RATE1, for example, in line 180 — can be found on both sides of an equal sign. The second concerns the reuse of a variable that had been assigned a value through computations in an earlier LET statement. In Program 3.8, RATE1, RATE2, and RATE3 are reused in line 210 after having been assigned values in earlier LET statements. At the end of this chapter, you will find several exercises that will help you to better understand these important concepts.

TRY IT YOURSELF

Load Program 3.8 (PRG3-8) from the Student Diskette. In lines 180 through 200, instead of dividing the discounts by 100, multiply them by 0.01. Execute the program. Enter the same data that was used with Program 3.8. Are the results for the modified version of Program 3.8 the same as they were for the original?

⊞ 3.5

EXPRESSIONS

Expressions may be either numeric or string. **Numeric expressions** consist of one or more numeric constants, numeric variables, and numeric function references, all of which are separated from each other by parentheses and arithmetic operators.

The seven valid arithmetic operators and examples of their use are shown in Table 2.1 on page 21. They include exponentiation (^), multiplication (∗), division (/), integer division (\), modulo (MOD), addition (+), and subtraction (−).

You'll recall that exponentiation is the raising of a number to a power. For example, 4 ^ 2 is equal to 16, and 3 ^ 4 is equal to 81. In programming, the asterisk (∗) means "times" and the slash means "divided by." Therefore, 8 ∗ 4 is equal to 32, and 8 / 4 is equal to 2. For addition and subtraction, the traditional signs are used.

Two arithmetic operators that may be unfamiliar to you are the backslash (\) and MOD. The backslash instructs the PC first to round the dividend and the divisor to integers and then to truncate any decimal portion of the quotient. For example, 5 \ 3 is equal to 1, and 6.8 \ 3.2 is equal to 2.

The modulo operator returns the integer remainder of integer division. For example, 34 MOD 6 is equal to 4, and 23 MOD 12 is equal to 11.

String expressions consist of one or more string constants, string variables, and string function references separated by the **concatenation operator** (+), which combines two strings into one. No other operators are allowed in string expressions.

A programmer must be concerned with both the formation and the evaluation of an expression. It is necessary to consider what an expression is, as well as what constitutes validity in an expression, before it is possible to write valid BASIC statements with confidence.

Formation of Numeric Expressions

The definition of a numeric expression dictates the manner in which it is to be validly formed. For example, it may be perfectly clear to you that the following invalid statement has been formed to assign A twice the value of B.

```
100 A = 2B   ' Invalid Statement
```

However, the PC will reject the statement, because a constant and a variable within the same expression must be separated by an arithmetic operator. The statement can validly be written as follows:

```
100 A = 2 * B
```

An example of another invalidly formed numeric expression is shown in the following statement:

```
100 A = B + -2 * A   ' Invalid Statement
```

This statement is invalid because no two successive characters may be arithmetic operators in a numeric expression. That is, the " + -" makes the above expression invalid, which makes the entire statement invalid. In order to be validly formed, the numeric expression must be rewritten either as B - 2 * A or as -2 * A + B. To state this in another way, we can say that in a numeric expression, the arithmetic operators must always be separated from each other by constants, variables, function references, or parentheses.

Finally, it is invalid to use a string variable or string constant in a numeric expression. The following are invalid numeric expressions:

```
6 + "DEBIT" / C
A$ / B + C$ - 19
```
Invalid Numeric Expressions

Pay close attention to the formation of valid numeric expressions. Remember that your PC is dealing with the program in its translation and execution stages and is not some sort of electronic human being. You may assert your individuality by selecting one variable name over another, but not by using

```
2 - -A
```

instead of

```
2 + A
```

in a numeric expression.

Evaluation of Numeric Expressions

Formation of complex expressions involving several arithmetic operations can sometimes create problems. For example, consider the following statement:

```
100 A = 8 / 4 / 2
```

Does this assign a value of 1 or 4 to A? The answer depends on how the system evaluates the expression. If it completes the operation 8 / 4 first and only then completes 2 / 2, the expression yields the value 1. If the system completes the second operation, 4 / 2, first and only then completes 8 / 2, it yields 4.

In MS BASIC the evaluation of an expression — the assigning of a value to that expression — follows the normal algebraic rules. Therefore, the expression 8 / 4 / 2 yields a value of 1.

The order in which the operations in an expression are evaluated is given by the following rule:

> **Precedence Rule 1:** Unless parentheses dictate otherwise, reading from left to right in a numeric expression, all exponentiations are performed first, then all multiplications and/or divisions, then all integer divisions, then all modulo arithmetic, and finally all additions and/or subtractions.

This order of operations is sometimes called the **rules of precedence**, or the **hierarchy of operations**. The meaning of these rules can be made clear with some examples. For instance, the expression 18 / 3 ^ 2 + 4 * 2 is evaluated as follows:

```
18 / 3 ^ 2 + 4 * 2 = 18 / 9 + 4 * 2
                   = 2       + 4 * 2
                   = 2       + 8
                   = 10
```

If you had trouble following the logic behind this evaluation, use this technique: Whenever a numeric expression is to be evaluated, "look" or "scan" from *left to right* five different times, applying Precedence Rule 1. On the first scan, every time you encounter an ^ operator, you perform exponentiation. In this example, 3 is raised to the power of 2, yielding 9.

On the second scan, moving from left to right again, every time you encounter the operators ∗ and /, perform multiplication and division. Hence, 18 is divided by 9, yielding 2, and 4 and 2 are multiplied, yielding 8.

On the third scan, from left to right, perform all integer division. On the fourth scan, from left to right, perform all modulo arithmetic. (In this example, there is no integer division or modulo arithmetic.)

On the fifth scan, moving again from left to right, every time you detect the operators + and −, perform addition and subtraction. In this example, 2 and 8 are added to form 10.

The following expression includes all seven arithmetic operators and yields a value of 2.

```
3 * 9 MOD 2 ^ 2 + 5 \ 5 / 2 - 3 = 3 * 9 MOD 4 + 5 \ 4.8 / 2 - 3    (at end
                                                                    of first scan)
                                = 27 MOD 4 + 5 \ 2.4 - 3            (at end
                                                                    of second scan)
                                = 27 MOD 4 + 2 - 3                  (at end
                                                                    of third scan)
                                = 3 + 2 - 3                         (at  end
                                                                    of fourth scan)
                                = 2                                 (at end
                                                                    of fifth scan)
```

The expression below yields the value of −2.73, as follows:

```
2 - 3 * 4/5 ^ 2 + 5/4 * 3 - 2 ^ 3 = 2 - 3 * 4/25 + 5/4 * 3 - 8    (at end
                                                                   of first scan)
                                  = 2 - 0.48 + 3.75 - 8            (at end of
                                                                   second scan)
                                  = -2.73                          (at end of fifth scan)
```

The Effect of Parentheses in the Evaluation of Numeric Expressions Parentheses may be used to change the order of operations. In MS BASIC, parentheses are normally used to avoid ambiguity and to group terms in a numeric expression; they do not imply multiplication. The order in which the operations in an expression containing parentheses are evaluated is given in the following rule:

> **Precedence Rule 2:** When parentheses are inserted into an expression, the part of the expression within the parentheses is evaluated first, and then the remainder of the expression is evaluated according to Precedence Rule 1.

If the first example contained parentheses, as does $(18 / 3) \char94 2 + 4 * 2$, then it would be evaluated in the following manner:

```
(18 / 3) ^ 2 + 4 * 2 = 6 ^ 2 + 4 * 2
                     = 36 + 4 * 2
                     = 36 + 8
                     = 44
```

The rule is: *Make five scans from left to right within each pair of parentheses, and only after this make the standard five passes over the entire numeric expression.*

The expression below yields the value of 1.41, as follows:

```
(2 - 3 * 4/5)^2 + 5/(4 * 3 - 2^3) = (2 - 3 * 4 / 5)^2 + 5 / (4 * 3 - 8)
                                   = (2 - 2.4)^2 + 5 / (12 - 8)
                                   = (-0.4)^2 + 5 / 4
                                   = 0.16 + 5 / 4
                                   = 0.16 + 1.25
                                   = 1.41
```

Use parentheses freely when in doubt as to the formation and evaluation of a numeric expression. For example, if you wish to have the PC divide 8 ∗ D by 3 ^ P, the expression may correctly be written as 8 / D / 3 ^ P, but you may also write it as (8 ∗ D) / (3 ^ P) and feel more certain of the result.

For more complex expressions, MS BASIC allows parentheses to be contained within other parentheses. When this occurs, the parentheses are said to be **nested**. In this case, MS BASIC evaluates the innermost parenthetical expression first and then goes on to the outermost parenthetical expression. Thus, 18 / 3 ^ 2 + (3 ∗ (2 + 5)) would be broken down in the following manner:

```
18 / 3 ^.2 + (3 * (2 + 5)) = 18 / 3 ^ 2 + (3 * 7)
                           = 18 / 3 ^ 2 + 21
                           = 18 / 9 + 21
                           = 2 + 21
                           = 23
```

Table 3.9 gives examples of the MS BASIC equivalent of some algebraic statements. Study each example carefully. Two of the most common errors beginners make are surrounding the wrong part of an expression with parentheses and not balancing the

TABLE 3.9 MS BASIC Equivalent Statements

ALGEBRAIC STATEMENTS	EQUIVALENT LET STATEMENTS
$H = \sqrt{X^2 + Y^2}$	`130 H = (X ^ 2 + Y ^ 2) ^ 0.5`
$S = AL^P K^{1-P}$	`170 S = A * L ^ P * K ^ (1 - P)`
$Q = \dfrac{-b + \sqrt{b^2 - 4ac}}{2a}$	`220 Q = (-B + (B ^ 2 - 4 * A * C) ^ 0.5) / (2 * A)`
$A = F\left[\dfrac{r}{(1 + r)^n - 1}\right]$	`350 A = F * (R / (((1 + R) ^ N) - 1))`
$P = \sqrt[3]{(x - p)^2 + y^2}$	`600 P = ((X - P) ^ 2 + Y ^ 2) ^ (1 / 3)`
$Z = \dfrac{ab}{x + \sqrt{x^2 - a^2}}$	`810 Z = A * B / (X + (X ^ 2 - A ^ 2) ^ 0.5)`

parentheses. Be sure that an expression has as many closed parentheses as open parentheses. When operations of the same precedence are encountered, Precedence Rule 1 applies. For example,

```
A - B - C        is interpreted as (A - B) - C
A / B / C        is interpreted as (A / B) / C
A ^ B ^ C        is interpreted as (A ^ B) ^ C
A \ B \ C        is interpreted as (A \ B) \ C
A MOD B MOD C    is interpreted as (A MOD B) MOD C
```

To illustrate the order of operations and the use of parentheses, here is a third solution to Programming Case Study 5A.

PROGRAM 3.9

```
100 ' Program 3.9
110 ' Finding the Single Discount Rate
120 ' *********************************
130 CLS : KEY OFF  ' Clear Screen
140 PRINT "Enter in Percent Form:"
150 INPUT "        First Discount ======> ", RATE1
160 INPUT "        Second Discount =====> ", RATE2
170 INPUT "        Third Discount ======> ", RATE3
180 RATE = 1 - (1 - RATE1 / 100) * (1 - RATE2 / 100) * (1 - RATE3 / 100)
190 RATE = 100 * RATE
200 PRINT
210 PRINT "Single Discount ================>"; RATE; "%"
220 END

RUN

Enter in Percent Form:
        First Discount ======> 40
        Second Discount =====> 20
        Third Discount ======> 10

Single Discount ================> 56.8 %
```

Program 3.9 is similar to Program 3.8 on page 66 in that both the data entered and the result displayed are in percent form. The major difference is that in this new solution all the computations have been incorporated into a single LET statement. Lines 180 through 210 in Program 3.8 have been replaced by a new line 180 in Program. 3.9.

The programmer's ability to control the sequence of operations with the use of parentheses is obvious in Program 3.9. If you have a mathematical background, you will surely find the method employed in Program 3.9 to your liking. If you have less confidence in your mathematical ability, you may prefer the technique of using multiple LET statements, as shown in Program 3.8.

The arithmetic rules discussed in this section are summarized below.

> ***Arithmetic Rule 2:*** A numeric expression is a sequence of one or more numeric constants, numeric variables, and function references separated from each other by parentheses and arithmetic operators.

> ***Arithmetic Rule 3:*** A numeric expression may not contain two consecutive arithmetic operators.

> ***Arithmetic Rule 4:*** The formation and evaluation of numeric expressions follow the normal algebraic rules.

Construction of Error-Free Numeric Expressions   Once you have written a numeric expression that observes the precedence rules, the PC is capable of translating it; no error messages will be generated. However, this is no guarantee that the PC will be able to execute the instructions. In other words, although a numeric expression may be validly formed, your PC may not be able to evaluate it because of the numbers involved. When error conditions arise, the PC will do one of two things, depending on the type of error. The **fatal error** causes the PC to terminate execution of the program.

The **nonfatal error** causes the PC to supply a value to the expression; the value depends on the type of error. Applying the following rules to your program will help you to avoid such hazards.

1. Do not attempt to divide by zero.
2. Do not attempt to determine the square root of a negative value.
3. Do not attempt to raise a negative value to a nonintegral value.
4. Do not attempt to compute a value that is greater than the largest permissible value or less than the smallest nonzero permissible value (see Figure 3.2 on page 62).

By way of a dramatic summary, Figure 3.3 illustrates some of the combinations that should be avoided in numeric expressions written in a BASIC program.

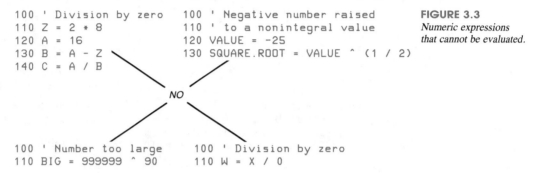

```
100 ' Division by zero        100 ' Negative number raised
110 Z = 2 * 8                 110 ' to a nonintegral value
120 A = 16                    120 VALUE = -25
130 B = A - Z                 130 SQUARE.ROOT = VALUE ^ (1 / 2)
140 C = A / B

                        NO

100 ' Number too large        100 ' Division by zero
110 BIG = 999999 ^ 90         110 W = X / 0
```

FIGURE 3.3
Numeric expressions that cannot be evaluated.

TRY IT YOURSELF

Load Program 3.2 (PRG3-2) from the Student Diskette. In line 170, replace the constant 360 with zero. Execute the program, using the same data that was used with Program 3.2. Note the diagnostic message displayed on the third line and the unusual value displayed for the interest.

You should also understand that the evaluation of a numeric expression by the PC gives as a value an approximation of the mathematical value represented by each operation in a numeric expression. In most cases, the approximation is the same as the expected result. However, in some instances this can cause problems — especially with respect to values smaller than 0.01. For example, you would expect the following partial program to display the value 0.09.

```
100 X = 9 / 100
110 PRINT X
    .
    .
    .
RUN

9.000001E-2
```

The quotient 9.000001E-2, assigned to X in line 100, is equivalent to 0.0900001. This is an approximation of the actual quotient, 0.09. Although the approximation is close, the result is difficult to interpret, especially for non-technical personnel.

You should also understand that owing to precision limitations, some of the mathematical laws with which you are familiar may not apply, especially when small decimal fraction numbers are involved. Consider the following partial program, which deals with the associative law of mathematics:

```
200 X = (.021 * .005) * .065
210 Y = .021 * (.005 * .065)
220 PRINT X, Y
       .
       .
       .
RUN

 6.825E-06      6.824999E-06
```

These problems have remedies. One technique is to use the PRINT USING statement, which will be discussed in chapter 4.

String Expressions   The ability to process strings of characters is an essential part of any programming language that is to be used for business applications. Letters, words, names, and a combination of letters and numbers can play an important role in generating readable reports and easing communication between non-technical personnel and the computer.

In MS BASIC, string expressions include string constants, string variables, string function references, and a combination of the three, separated by the concatenation operator (+). Consider the following program:

PROGRAM 3.10

```
100 ' Program 3.10
110 ' Examples of String Expressions
120 ' ******************************
130 CLS : KEY OFF  ' Clear screen
140 INPUT "Area code ===============> ", AREA.CODE$
150 INPUT "Local number ============> ", LOCAL$
160 TEMP$ = AREA.CODE$
170 COMMENT$ = "Telephone number "
180 NUMBER$ = AREA.CODE$ + "-" + LOCAL$
190 PRINT
200 PRINT COMMENT$; "========> "; NUMBER$
210 PRINT "Area code ===============> "; TEMP$
220 END

RUN

Area code ===============> 219
Local number ============> 844-0520

Telephone number ========> 219-844-0520
Area code ===============> 219
```

Examples of string expressions in Program 3.10 include the following:

1. the string variable AREA.CODE$ in line 160, which is assigned to TEMP$;
2. the string constant Telephone number in line 170, which is assigned to COMMENT$; and
3. the string expression AREA.CODE$ + "-" + LOCAL$ in line 180, which is assigned to NUMBER$.

In line 180, the plus sign is the concatenation operator. When strings are concatenated, they are joined in the order in which they are found. The result is a single string. The value of NUMBER$, which is displayed by line 200, is illustrated in the output results of Program 3.10.

Use of LEFT$, LEN,
MID$, and RIGHT$
String Functions

Although concatenation is the only valid string operation, MS BASIC includes functions that allow for additional string manipulation. The most often used string functions are presented in Table 3.10; other string functions are presented in chapter 8.

_____TABLE 3.10 Some Common String Functions_____

FUNCTION	FUNCTION VALUE
LEFT$(X$, N)	*Returns the leftmost N characters of the string argument X$.*
LEN(X$)	*Returns the number of characters in the value associated with the string argument X$.*
MID$(X$, P, N)	*Returns N characters of the string argument X$ beginning at P.*
RIGHT$(X$, N)	*Returns the rightmost N characters of the string argument X$.*
Where X$ is a string expression, and N and P are numeric expressions.	

The following program illustrates the use of the functions found in Table 3.10.

PROGRAM 3.11

```
100 ' Program 3.11
110 ' Example of Referencing String Functions
120 ' ****************************************
130 CLS : KEY OFF  ' Clear screen
140 ' ****** Request Telephone Number *******
150 INPUT "Complete telephone number =====> ", NUMBER$
160 AREA.CODE$ = LEFT$(NUMBER$, 3)
170 PREFIX$ = MID$(NUMBER$, 5, 3)
180 LOCAL$ = RIGHT$(NUMBER$, 4)
190 COUNT = LEN(NUMBER$)
200 PRINT
210 PRINT "Area code ============> "; AREA.CODE$
220 PRINT "Prefix ===============> "; PREFIX$
230 PRINT "Last four digits =====> "; LOCAL$
240 PRINT "Character count in "; NUMBER$; " =====>"; COUNT
250 END

RUN

Complete telephone number =====> 219-844-0520

Area code ============> 219
Prefix ===============> 844
Last four digits =====> 0520
Character count in 219-844-0520 =====> 12
```

In Program 3.11, the function LEFT$ in line 160 assigns the three leftmost characters of NUMBER$ to AREA.CODE$. AREA.CODE$ is assigned the string 219. In line 170, the MID$ function assigns 3 characters beginning with the fifth character 8 in NUMBER$ to PREFIX$. PREFIX$ is assigned the string 844. In line 180, the function RIGHT$ assigns the last four characters of NUMBER$ to LOCAL$. LOCAL$ is assigned the string 0520. Finally, in line 190, the numeric variable COUNT is assigned a value equal to the number of characters in NUMBER$. COUNT is assigned the numeric value 12.

For a more detailed discussion on the operation of concatenation and the LEFT$, LEN, MID$, and RIGHT$ functions, see chapter 8, section 8.2.

TRY IT YOURSELF

Load Program 3.11 (PRG3-11) from the Student Diskette. Use the EDIT command to change line 170 so that the telephone number prefix displayed by line 220 includes the surrounding dashes. Execute the program using the same data used with Program 3.11.

⊞ **3.6**

THE TOP-DOWN (MODULAR) APPROACH AND THE GOSUB AND RETURN STATEMENTS

Before we move on to larger and more complex problems, it is appropriate that we introduce you to a popular programming methodology called **top-down** or **modular programming**. The objective of top-down programming is to break down a problem into smaller and more manageable subproblems. In other words, to solve a problem top-down, you divide and conquer.

Top-down programming is a methodology that is recommended by nearly all computer scientists. The claim is that a program written top-down is reliable; has simplicity of design; and is easy to read and maintain, or modify.

At first, top-down programming may appear to be cumbersome, especially for the simple problems discussed thus far. However, for large, complex problems, it is the only logical way to program. We are introducing this methodology early because most programmers find it difficult to change their plan of attack, that is, unlearn less sophisticated programming habits. By the time we get to the more sophisticated problems, we want to be sure that you are solving problems top-down by habit.

The idea of solving a problem by dividing it into subproblems is not new. In his *Discourse on Method*, written some three hundred years before the first computer was built, René Descartes made this very same point. In essence, he said that the resolution of a problem can be achieved if a person (1) divides each of the difficulties into as many parts as possible, and (2) thinks in an orderly fashion, beginning with those matters which are simplest and easiest to understand and gradually working toward those which are more complex.

The Top-Down Chart

A graphic representation of the top-down approach is called a **top-down chart**, which is also known as a **hierarchy chart** or a **VTOC — Visual Table of Contents**. Figure 3.4 represents a top-down chart in which the problem or task presented in Programming Case Study 5A on page 65 is broken down into subtasks. The overall task and each of the subtasks are represented by a process symbol with a short description written inside it. The top-down chart is read from top to bottom, and in general from left to right.

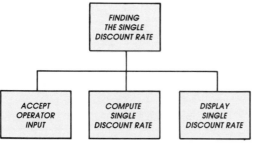

FIGURE 3.4
A top-down chart for the problem presented in Programming Case Study 5A.

A top-down chart differs from a program flowchart, or pseudocode, in that it does not show decision-making logic or flow of control. A program flowchart, or pseudocode, shows *procedure*, but a top-down chart shows *organization*. A top-down chart allows you to concentrate on defining *what* needs to be done in the program before deciding *how* and *when* it is to be done, which is represented in a program flowchart or by pseudocode.

A top-down chart is very similar to a company's organization chart; each subtask carries out a function for its superior. Think of the higher-level subtasks as vice presidents of the organization, who perform the controlling functions of that organization. The top-down chart in Figure 3.4 resembles a small company in that there is only one level below the president. As a company grows and becomes more complex, additional levels are appended to the organizational chart to carry out the tasks for that organization. Likewise, as problems become larger and more complex, additional levels are appended to the top-down chart. For further information on top-down charts, see Appendix A, section A.7.

Implementing a Top-Down Design – Internal Subroutines (Modules)

Once the larger, more complex problem has been decomposed into smaller pieces, a solution to each subtask can be designed, coded, and tested independently. The group of statements that is associated with a single programming task within a BASIC program is called an **internal subroutine** or a **module**.

An internal subroutine is executed only if referenced (*called*) by an explicit instruction from some other part of the program, as illustrated in Figure 3.5. Following execution of the internal subroutine, control passes back to the statement that immediately follows the instruction that activated the subroutine.

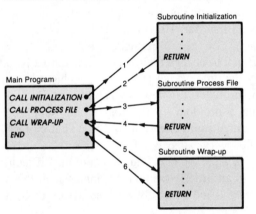

FIGURE 3.5
A conceptual view of control transferring to an internal subroutine and eventually returning to the statement that immediately follows the instruction that activated the subroutine.

The GOSUB and RETURN Statements

A subroutine is called by a GOSUB statement. The keyword GOSUB is immediately followed by a line number to which control is transferred. The last statement executed in a subroutine must be the RETURN statement. The RETURN statement returns control to the next executable statement following the corresponding GOSUB statement. A subroutine, therefore, can exit only through a RETURN statement. When a GOSUB statement is executed,

1. the main program calls or transfers control to the subroutine;
2. the called subroutine executes and performs a particular or recurring task for the main program; and
3. the RETURN statement of the subroutine transfers control back to the first executable statement following the GOSUB that referenced it.

The general forms for the GOSUB and RETURN statements are shown in Tables 3.11 and 3.12.

_____TABLE 3.11 The GOSUB Statement_____

General Form:	GOSUB *line number* *where the line number represents the first line of a subroutine.*
Purpose:	*Causes control to transfer to the subroutine that is represented by the specified line number. Causes the location of the next executable statement following the GOSUB to be retained.*
Examples:	1250 GOSUB 1600 1900 GOSUB 2000

_____TABLE 3.12 The RETURN Statement_____

General Form:	RETURN
Purpose:	*Causes control to transfer from the subroutine back to the first executable statement immediately following the* GOSUB *statement that referenced it.*
Examples:	1700 RETURN 2100 RETURN
Note:	*The* RETURN *statement may be followed by a line number. (This option is not used in this book.)*

Consider the following top-down approach to Programming Case Study 5A, Finding the Single Discount Rate, on page 65. The solution corresponds to the top-down chart in Figure 3.4 on page 75.

PROGRAM 3.12

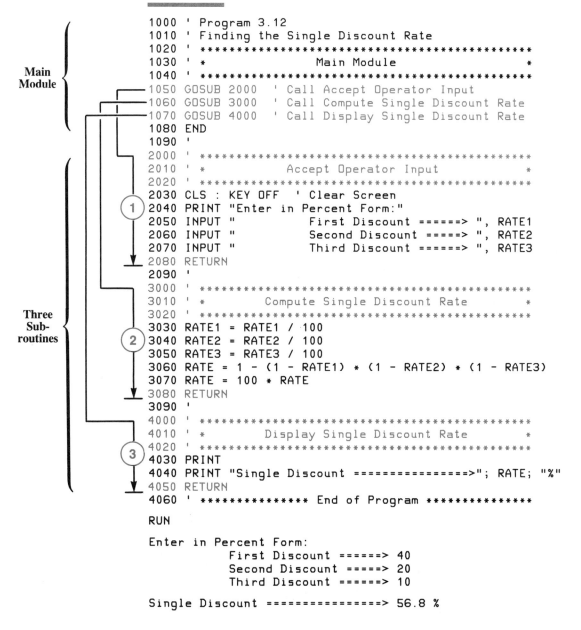

```
1000 ' Program 3.12
1010 ' Finding the Single Discount Rate
1020 ' *********************************************
1030 ' *              Main Module                  *
1040 ' *********************************************
1050 GOSUB 2000   ' Call Accept Operator Input
1060 GOSUB 3000   ' Call Compute Single Discount Rate
1070 GOSUB 4000   ' Call Display Single Discount Rate
1080 END
1090 '
2000 ' *********************************************
2010 ' *           Accept Operator Input           *
2020 ' *********************************************
2030 CLS : KEY OFF  ' Clear Screen
2040 PRINT "Enter in Percent Form:"
2050 INPUT "        First Discount ======> ", RATE1
2060 INPUT "        Second Discount =====> ", RATE2
2070 INPUT "        Third Discount ======> ", RATE3
2080 RETURN
2090 '
3000 ' *********************************************
3010 ' *       Compute Single Discount Rate        *
3020 ' *********************************************
3030 RATE1 = RATE1 / 100
3040 RATE2 = RATE2 / 100
3050 RATE3 = RATE3 / 100
3060 RATE = 1 - (1 - RATE1) * (1 - RATE2) * (1 - RATE3)
3070 RATE = 100 * RATE
3080 RETURN
3090 '
4000 ' *********************************************
4010 ' *       Display Single Discount Rate        *
4020 ' *********************************************
4030 PRINT
4040 PRINT "Single Discount =================>"; RATE; "%"
4050 RETURN
4060 ' ************** End of Program **************
RUN

Enter in Percent Form:
        First Discount ======> 40
        Second Discount =====> 20
        Third Discount ======> 10

Single Discount =================> 56.8 %
```

Main Module

Three Sub-routines

When the RUN command is issued for Program 3.12, the GOSUB statement in line 1050 transfers control to the Accept Operator Input Module, which begins at line 2000. This module clears the screen and accepts the three discounts. The RETURN statement in line 2080 returns control to line 1060. Line 1060 represents the next executable statement following the GOSUB in the Main Module, which referenced the Accept Operator Input Module.

The GOSUB in line 1060 calls the Compute Single Discount Rate Module, which begins at line 3000. Once the single discount RATE has been determined, the RETURN statement in line 3080 returns control to line 1070 in the Main Module. Line 1070, in turn, transfers control to the Display Single Discount Rate Module. Following the display of the single discount RATE, the RETURN statement in line 4050 returns control to line 1080 of the Main Module. The END statement in line 1080 halts the execution of the program.

Note also that by placing the END statement in line 1080, we prevent the Accept Operator Input Module from being executed again.

Prior to Program 3.12, all programs used the END statement as the *physical* end of the program. In Program 3.12, the END statement, line 1080, is used to indicate the *logical* end of the program and line 4060, a remark line, is used to indicate the physical end of the program. It should now be apparent that MS BASIC does not require a physical END statement.

Recommended Style and Tips When Using The Top-Down Approach

Consider the following tips when using the top-down approach.

1. A subroutine does not have a unique *initial* statement to differentiate it from other subroutines or from the Main Module. In order to highlight the beginning of first-level subroutines, use a boxed-in remark before the first executable statement, as illustrated by lines 2000 to 2020 in Program 3.12.

2. Begin the Main Module with line 1000 and each subsequent first-level subroutine with 2000, 3000, 4000, and so on. Begin lower-level subroutines called by the first-level subroutine beginning at 2000, with 2200, 2400, 2600, and so on. Don't concern yourself with consistent line numbering until your program is working properly. When you are ready to renumber your program, use the RENUM command. For example,

   ```
   RENUM 1000
   ```

   will renumber the entire program, beginning with line 1000 and using increments of 10. After renumbering the program, list the first 20 lines (LIST 1000-1200). Renumber the program again; only this time, renumber beginning with the subroutine that follows the Main Module. If the subroutine begins with line 1150, then the following command will renumber beginning at line 1150, with a starting line number of 2000 and with increments of 10:

   ```
   RENUM 2000, 1150
   ```

   List the next 20 lines, beginning with line 2000, and continue the process until the entire program has been renumbered as suggested.

3. For purposes of readability, insert a comment line, using the apostrophe after each module, as shown in Program 3.12, lines 1090, 2090, and 3090.

4. With the GOSUB statement, you have the choice of referencing the first remark line or the first executable statement of the subroutine. In this book, we will reference the first remark line of the subroutine, as illustrated in line 1050 of Program 3.12. The GOSUB references line 2000, which is a remark line. When control transfers to a remark line, the PC automatically passes control to the first executable statement following the remark line.

5. So that lower-level modules can be located easily for debugging purposes, they should be placed below the module that calls them and in the order in which they are called.

*More About
Subroutines*

The last statement of a subroutine should always be the RETURN statement. Any attempt to execute a RETURN statement without executing an earlier corresponding GOSUB statement results in the display of the **diagnostic message**

        RETURN without GOSUB in line number

and the termination of the program. This can be summarized by the following rule:

> **RETURN Rule 1:** A GOSUB statement must be executed before its corresponding
> RETURN statement can be executed.

*Flowchart
Representation of
GOSUB, RETURN,
and Referenced
Subroutine*

The program flowchart representation of Program 3.12, including the GOSUB statement and the referenced subroutine, is shown in Figure 3.6. Remember that a top-down chart, as shown in Figure 3.4, is not a program flowchart. A top-down chart shows *what* must be done to solve a problem, and a program flowchart shows *how* to solve the problem.

The GOSUB statement, which calls the subroutine, is represented by the **predefined process symbol**, which was defined in Table 1.4 on page 12. The predefined process symbol consists of a set of vertical lines within the rectangle and indicates that the program steps of the subroutine are specified elsewhere. In Figure 3.6, the first subroutine is represented by the flowchart to the right of the Main Module, and the RETURN statement is represented by the terminal symbol.

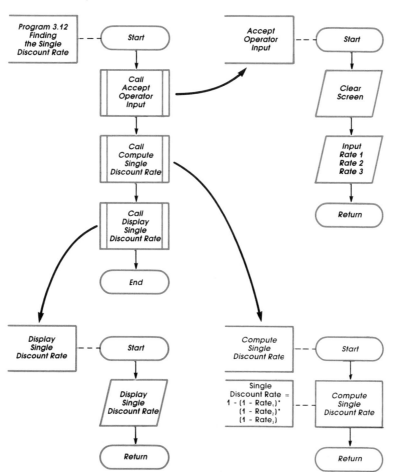

FIGURE 3.6
*General flowcharts for
the Main Module and
subroutines for
Program 3.12.*

Nested Subroutines   One subroutine may call another subroutine, which may in turn call another, and so on. However, each subroutine must terminate with a RETURN statement. Program 3.13 illustrates the flow of control from the Main Module to the nested subroutines. The lines and numbers represent the flow of control.

PROGRAM 3.13

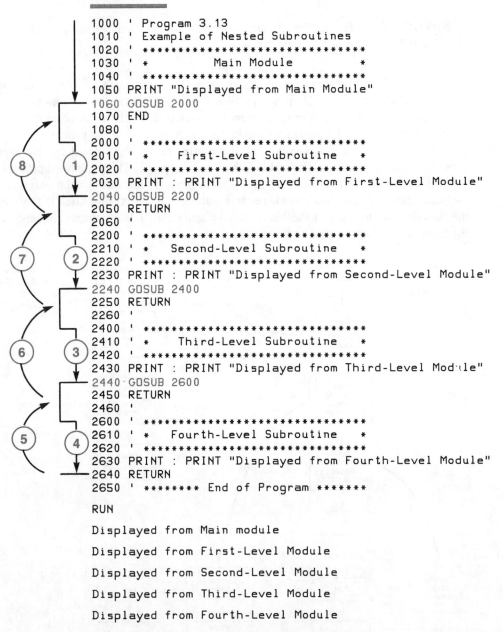

```
1000 ' Program 3.13
1010 ' Example of Nested Subroutines
1020 ' *****************************
1030 ' *          Main Module          *
1040 ' *****************************
1050 PRINT "Displayed from Main Module"
1060 GOSUB 2000
1070 END
1080 '
2000 ' *****************************
2010 ' *      First-Level Subroutine      *
2020 ' *****************************
2030 PRINT : PRINT "Displayed from First-Level Module"
2040 GOSUB 2200
2050 RETURN
2060 '
2200 ' *****************************
2210 ' *    Second-Level Subroutine    *
2220 ' *****************************
2230 PRINT : PRINT "Displayed from Second-Level Module"
2240 GOSUB 2400
2250 RETURN
2260 '
2400 ' *****************************
2410 ' *      Third-Level Subroutine      *
2420 ' *****************************
2430 PRINT : PRINT "Displayed from Third-Level Module"
2440 GOSUB 2600
2450 RETURN
2460 '
2600 ' *****************************
2610 ' *      Fourth-Level Subroutine      *
2620 ' *****************************
2630 PRINT : PRINT "Displayed from Fourth-Level Module"
2640 RETURN
2650 ' ******* End of Program *******
```

```
RUN

Displayed from Main module

Displayed from First-Level Module

Displayed from Second-Level Module

Displayed from Third-Level Module

Displayed from Fourth-Level Module
```

It might help you to understand nested subroutines if you thought of a **control stack**. MS BASIC maintains a control stack to keep track of the location of the next executable statement following the GOSUB to which control is returned. Each time a GOSUB statement is executed, the address location of the first executable statement following the GOSUB is placed on top of the stack. When a RETURN statement is executed, the address location at the top of the stack is removed and control is directed to the statement at that address location in the program.

The nesting of subroutines, as illustrated in Program 3.13, is limited only by the amount of available main storage. The PC displays the following message when available main storage is exhausted:

```
Out of Memory
```

TRY IT YOURSELF

Load Program 3.13 (PRG3-13) from the Student Diskette and complete the following:

1. Add the line 1055 GOSUB 2400. Execute the program and see what happens. Do you agree that it is possible to reference a subroutine from several points in a program?

2. Reload Program 3.13. Delete line 1070. Execute the program and see what happens. Do you understand the importance of the END statement in line 1070?

3. Reload Program 3.13 again. Execute the program. Keeping in mind that the last statement executed was the END statement in line 1070, enter the system command CONT. Do you now understand the importance of RETURN Rule 1?

3.7 WHAT YOU SHOULD KNOW

1. Constants are values that do not change during the execution of a program.
2. There are two types of constants: numeric constants and string constants.
3. Numeric constants represent ordinary numbers. A numeric constant may be written in one of three forms: integer, fixed point, or floating point.
4. An integer constant is a positive or negative whole number with no decimal point.
5. A fixed-point constant is a constant with a decimal point.
6. A floating-point constant, also called exponential form, is a constant that is written as an integer or as a fixed-point constant, followed by the letter D or E and an integer. D or E stands for "times ten to the power."
7. Depending on how it is written in a program, a numeric constant is stored as type integer, single precision (7 digits), or double precision (17 digits).
8. With double precision, the PC will store up to 17 digits. With single or double precision, you can represent any number (positive or negative) from 2.9×10^{-39} to 1.7×10^{38}.
9. The only special characters allowed in a numeric constant are a leading sign (+ or – or blank), the decimal point, and the letter D or E.
10. String constants represent strings of characters enclosed in quotation marks. A string constant can have between 0 and 255 characters.
11. In programming, a variable is a location in main storage that can be referenced by a variable name and whose value can change as the program is executed.
12. There are two types of variables in BASIC: simple variables and subscripted variables. Simple variables are used to store single values. Subscripted variables are used to store groups of values. Either of the two can be defined as numeric or string.
13. A variable name begins with a letter and may be followed by up to 39 letters, digits, and periods. It is invalid to use a keyword as a variable name.
14. You should develop a structured style for choosing meaningful variable names in a program.
15. All variables that are used in a program should be assigned an initial value.
16. The name of a variable determines whether it is string or numeric. As the last character in a variable name, the dollar sign ($) declares that the variable will represent a string. If the last character is not a dollar sign, then the variable is numeric.
17. If a variable name ends with an exclamation point (!) or with no special character, then it is declared single precision. If a variable name ends with a percent sign (%), then the variable is declared integer. If the variable name ends with a number sign (#), then it is declared double precision.

18. While integer variables take up 2 bytes of main storage, single-precision variables take up 4 bytes and double-precision variables take up 8 bytes of main storage.
19. Numeric data that is assigned to numeric variables through the use of the INPUT statement must take the form of numeric constants.
20. String data that is assigned to string variables through the use of the INPUT statement must be surrounded with quotation marks if the string contains leading or trailing blanks or embedded commas or colons.
21. The LET statement causes evaluation of the expression to the right of the equal sign, followed by assignment of the resulting value to the variable to the left of the equal sign.
22. The equal sign in BASIC can best be described as meaning "is replaced by."
23. It is invalid to assign a string expression to a numeric variable or a numeric expression to a string variable.
24. A numeric expression is a sequence of one or more numeric constants, numeric variables, and numeric function references that are separated from each other by parentheses and arithmetic operators.
25. A string expression is a sequence of one or more string constants, string variables, or string function references that are separated by the concatenation operator.
26. The formation and evaluation of numeric expressions follow the normal algebraic rules.
27. Unless parentheses dictate otherwise, reading from left to right in a numeric expression, all exponentiations are performed first, then all multiplications and/or divisions, then all integer divisions, then all modulo arithmetic, and finally all additions and/or subtractions. This order is called the hierarchy of operations or the rules of precedence.
28. When parentheses are inserted into an expression, the part of the expression within the parentheses is evaluated first, and then the remaining expression is evaluated according to the rules of precedence.
29. No numeric expression can be evaluated if it requires a value that is not mathematically defined. For example, do not divide a number by 0 in your program.
30. Concatenation generates a single string value that is the result of combining the values of each of the terms in the order in which they are found in the expression.
31. The string functions LEFT$, LEN, MID$, and RIGHT$ are used to access and manipulate groups of characters (substrings) within a string.
32. The top-down approach is a popular method for solving large, complex problems.
33. A top-down chart is a graphic representation of a task that has been broken down into subtasks.
34. An internal subroutine is a group of statements that is associated with a single programming task within a BASIC program.
35. Subroutines, or modules, as they can also be called, are useful for solving large, complex problems, because they allow a problem to be subdivided into smaller and more manageable subproblems, which can then be solved by means of the appropriate subroutines.
36. A subroutine is referenced by a GOSUB statement.
37. The RETURN statement is always the last statement to be executed in a subroutine. Its function is to cause control to transfer from the subroutine back to the first executable statement following the corresponding GOSUB statement.
38. A subroutine may call another subroutine, which may in turn call another, and so on.

⊞ 3.8 TEST YOUR BASIC SKILLS (Even-numbered answers are at the back of the book, before the index.)

1. Which of the following are invalid constants if each appeared exactly as written in a valid location in a BASIC statement?

   a. 6.4   b. 7$ c. +.319#
   d. 0   e. 1,976!   f. 179F4
   g. 9.613%   h. $1.75   i. 1E1
   j. 987.6D-25   k. 0E0   l. 4.56-

2. Write the number 568,962,482,176 to the greatest possible accuracy using a precision of seven significant digits. What is the error in this value?

3. Which arithmetic operation is performed first in the following numeric expressions?

   a. 9 / 5 * 6   b. X - Y + A
   c. 3 * (A + 8)   d. (X * (2 + Y)) ^ 2 + Z ^ (2 ^ 2) - 6 MOD 3
   e. X / Y \ Z   f. (B ^ 2 - 4 * A * C) / (2 * A)

4. Evaluate each of the following:

   ```
   a. 4 * 5 * 3 / 6 - 7 ^ 2 / 3
   b. (2 - 4) + 5 ^ 2
   c. 12 \ 6 / 2 + 7 MOD 3 + 3
   ```

5. Calculate the numeric value for each of the following valid numeric expressions if A = 3, B = 4, C = 5, W = 3, T = 4, X = 1, and Y = 2.

   ```
   a. (A + B / 2) + 6.2
   b. 3 * (A ^ B) / C
   c. (A / (C + 1) * 4 - 5) / 2 + ( 4 MOD 3 \ 3)
   d. X + 2 * Y * W / 3 - 7 / (T - X / Y) - W ^ T
   ```

6. Which of the following are invalid variables in Microsoft BASIC? Why?

a. A	b. SALE!	c. INT	d. P.1#	e. 39
f. PRINT	g. 7F	h. FOR$	i. Q$	j. Q9%

7. Consider the valid programs below. What is displayed if each program is executed?

   ```
   a. 100 ' Exercise 3.7a          b. 100 ' Exercise 3.7b
      110 A = 2.5                     110 COUNT = 0
      120 B = 4 * A / 2 * A + 5       120 GOSUB 300
      130 PRINT B                     130 PRINT COUNT
      140 B = 4 * A / (2 * A + 5)     140 GOSUB 300
      150 PRINT B                     150 PRINT COUNT
      160 A = -A                      160 GOSUB 300
      170 PRINT A                     170 PRINT COUNT
      180 A = -A                      180 COUNT = COUNT - 3
      190 PRINT A                     190 PRINT COUNT
      200 END                         200 END
                                      300 ' ** Increment Count **
                                      310 COUNT = COUNT + 1
                                      320 RETURN
                                      330 ' *** End of Program **
   ```

   ```
   c. 100 ' Exercise 3.7c          d. Assume SEED is assigned the value 1.
      110 X% = 4.4
      120 Y% = 2 / 3                  100 ' Exercise 3.7d
      130 A% = X% + Y%                110 INPUT "Enter seed number ===> ", SEED
      140 PRINT A%                    120 SEED = SEED * (SEED + 1)
      150 B% = Y% - X%                130 PRINT SEED
      160 PRINT B%                    140 SEED = SEED * (SEED + 1)
      170 C% = A% + B% - X%           150 PRINT SEED
      180 PRINT C%                    160 SEED = SEED * (SEED + 1)
      190 D% = 2 * (A% + B% + C%) / 4 170 PRINT SEED
      200 PRINT D%                    180 SEED = SEED * (SEED + 1)
      210 END                         190 PRINT SEED
                                      200 END
   ```

8. What is the distinction between the formulation of a numeric expression and the evaluation of a numeric expression?
9. Can a validly formed numeric expression always be executed by a computer?
10. Calculate the numeric value for each of the following numeric expressions if X = 2, Y = 3, and Z = 6.

    ```
    a. X + Y ^ 2       b. Z / Y / X           c. 12 / (3 + Z) - X
    d. X ^ Y ^ Z       e. X * Y + 2.5 * X + Z f. (X ^ (2 + Y)) ^ 2 + Z ^ (2 ^ 2)
    ```

11. Repeat exercise 10 for the case of X = 4, Y = 6, and Z = 2.

12. Write a valid LET statement for each of the following algebraic statements.

   a. $q = (d + e)^{1/3}$

   b. $d = (A^2)^{3.2}$

   c. $b = \dfrac{20}{6 - S}$

   d. $Y = a_1 x + a_2 x^2 + a_3 x^3 + a_4 x^4$

   e. $h = X + \dfrac{X}{X - Y}$

   f. $S = 19.2X^3$

   g. $V = 100 - (2/3)^{100 - B}$

   h. $t = \sqrt{76{,}234/(2.37 + D)}$

   i. $V = 0.12340005M - \left[\dfrac{(0.123458)^3}{M - N} \right]$

   j. $Q = \dfrac{(F - M1000)^{2B}}{4M} - \dfrac{1}{E}$

13. If necessary, insert parentheses so that each numeric expression results in the value indicated.

   a. `8 / 2 + 2 + 12 --> 14`

   b. `8 ^ 2 - 1 --> 8`

   c. `3 / 2 + 0.5 + 3 ^ 1 --> 5`

   d. `12 MOD 5 \ 2 + 1 ^ 2 + 1 * 2 * 3 / 4 - 3 / 2 --> 0`

   e. `12 - 2 - 3 - 1 - 4 --> 10`

   f. `7 * 3 + 4 ^ 2 - 3 / 13 --> 22`

   g. `3 * 2 - 3 * 4 * 2 + 3 --> -60`

   h. `3 * 6 - 3 + 2 + 6 * 4 - 4 / 2 ^ 1 --> 33`

14. Which of the following are invalid LET statements?

   a. `100 X = 9 / B(A + C)`

   b. `200 X + 5 = Y`

   c. `-40 X = 17`

   d. `750 P = 4 * 3 -+6`

   e. `260 FOR = 4`

   f. `290 X = -X * (((1 + R) ^ 2 - N) ^ 2 + (2 + X)`

   g. `300 GET Q = R ^ S ^ Q ^ T`

   h. `400 P = +4`

   i. `500 G = 4(-2 + A)`

   j. `600 X = X + 1`

15. Calculate the numerical value for each of the following validly formed LET statements if A = 2 and B = 3.

   a.
   ```
   100 D = (A ^ 6 / A * B) - (8 * B / 4)
   110 D = D + 1
   ```

   b.
   ```
   100 E1 = A * B
   110 E1 = A ^ (6 / E1)
   120 E2 = B * 8
   130 E3 = 4 + 1
   140 E2 = E2 / E3
   150 A = E1 - E2
   ```

16. Repeat exercise 15 for the case where the value of A is 1 and the value of B is 2.

17. Correct the logic and syntax errors in the following programs.

   a.
   ```
   100 ' Exercise 3.17a
   110 PRINT "Values for A and B":
   120 INPUT B, A
   130 GET TAB# = AB
   140 PRINT "The product" is": TAB
   150 DONE
   ```

   b.
   ```
   100 ' Exercise 3.17b
   110 3 = X
   120 B = X & Y
   130 C = 4 * (X + B / 3) / 3 + Y
   140 C PRINT
   150 END
   ```

18. Correct the logic errors in the following programs.

   a.
   ```
   100 ' Exercise 3.18a
   110 A = 3
   120 B = 6
   130 A = A - 3
   140 C = B / A
   150 PRINT C
   160 END
   ```

   b.
   ```
   100 ' Exercise 3.18b
   110 X = - 2
   120 Y = 0.5
   130 Z = X ^ Y
   140 PRINT Z
   150 END
   ```

19. If the string John R. Blakely is entered in response to the INPUT statement, what is displayed by the following program?

```
100 ' Exercise 3.19
110 INPUT "Name ===> ", S$
120 A$ = LEFT$(S$, 4)
130 B$ = RIGHT$(S$, 7)
140 C$ = MID$(S$, 6, 2)
150 D$ = LEFT$(S$, 1) +  MID$(S$, 7, 1)
160 D$ = D$ + " " +  MID$(S$, 6, 3) +  RIGHT$(S$, 7)
170 E = LEN(S$)
180 PRINT S$
190 PRINT A$
200 PRINT B$
210 PRINT C$
220 PRINT D$
230 PRINT E
240 END
```

20. Consider the valid program listed below. What is displayed when it is executed? Assume that PRINCIPAL is assigned the value 100 and RATE is assigned 15.

```
1000 ' Exercise 3.20
1010 ' *************************
1020 ' *        Main Module       *
1030 ' *************************
1040 GOSUB 2000   ' Accept Operator Input
1050 GOSUB 3000   ' Compute Amount
1060 GOSUB 4000   ' Display Amount
1070 END
1080 '
2000 ' *************************
2010 ' * Accept Operator Input *
2020 ' *************************
2030 INPUT "Principal ===> ", PRINCIPAL
2040 INPUT "Rate in % ===> ", RATE
2050 RETURN
2060 '
3000 ' *************************
3010 ' *     Compute Amount     *
3020 ' *************************
3030 RATE = RATE / 100
3040 AMOUNT = PRINCIPAL + RATE * PRINCIPAL
3050 RETURN
3060 '
4000 ' *************************
4010 ' *     Display Amount     *
4020 ' *************************
4030 PRINT "Amount ======>"; AMOUNT
4040 RETURN
4050 ' ***** End of Program ****
```

21. Is the following partial program valid or invalid? If it is invalid, indicate why.

```
1000 ' Exercise 3.21
1010 ' ** Main Module **
      .
      .
      .
1100 GOSUB 2000
1110 '
2000 ' ** Compute Square **
2010 X = X ^ 2
2020 RETURN
2030 END
```

22. Use the Student Diskette to complete the Try It Yourself exercises on pages 52, 54, 56, 62, 67, 72, 75, and 81.

⊞ 3.9 BASIC PROGRAMMING PROBLEMS

1. Service Charge Computations

Purpose: To become familiar with the use of constants and variables and with the INPUT, PRINT, and LET statements.

Problem: Write a program to determine the new service charge. Use the following formula:

New Service Charge = Old Service Charge + 2% × Old Service Charge

Input Data: Use the old service charge, 114.26, as the sample data in response to the appropriate INPUT statement.

Output Results: The following results are displayed.

```
Old service charge ====> 114.26
New service charge ====> 116.5452
```

2. Computing the Six-Month Dow-Jones Average

Purpose: To become familiar with entering data items in response to an INPUT statement; declaring integer, single-precision, and double-precision variables; and calculating an average.

Problem: Construct a program to input the end-of-month Dow-Jones closings for the last six months; compute the average in various precision modes from these six numbers; and print the average.

Version A: Perform all inputs, computations, and outputs in single-precision mode.
Version B: Perform all inputs, computations, and outputs in double-precision mode.
Version C: Perform all inputs, computations, and outputs in integer mode.

Input Data: Use the following sample data: 2259.45, 2133.45, 2209.53, 2199.98, 2211.91, 2231.41

Output Results: The following results are displayed.

For Version A (Single Precision):

```
Last six-month closings: 2259.45, 2133.45, 2209.53, 2199.98, 2211.91, 2231.41
The six-month Dow-Jones average is 2207.622
```

For Version B (Double Precision):

```
Last six-month closings: 2259.45, 2133.45, 2209.53, 2199.98, 2211.91, 2231.41
The six-month Dow-Jones average is 2207.621666666667
```

For Version C (Integer Precision):

```
Last six-month closings: 2259.45, 2133.45, 2209.53, 2199.98, 2211.91, 2231.41
The six-month Dow-Jones average is 2208
```

3. Maturity Value of an Investment Converted Quarterly

Purpose: To become familiar with the concepts associated with arithmetic operations; with parentheses in expressions; and with the use of INPUT, LET, and PRINT statements.

Problem: Write a program to determine the maturity value of an investment of P dollars for N years at I percent converted quarterly. Use the following formula:

$$S = P \left(1 + \frac{I}{M}\right)^{NM}$$

where S = maturity value
P = investment
I = nominal rate of interest
N = time of years
M = number of conversions per year

Input Data: Use the following sample data in response to the appropriate INPUT statements.

Investment:	$10,500
Interest:	11.5%
Time:	4 years 6 months
Conversions:	4

(Hint: The program must include a statement to change the rate from percent form to decimal form.)

Output Results: The following results are displayed.

```
Please enter the:
        Investment ===========> 10500
        Nominal rate in % ====> 11.5
        Time in years ========> 4.5
        No. of Conversions ===> 4

Maturity value ==============> $17489.05
```

4. Determining the Monthly Payment on a Loan

Purpose: To become familiar with the hierarchy of operations in a LET statement; the use of the INPUT and PRINT statements; and the top-down approach.

Problem: Using the top-down chart in Figure 3.7, write a program to determine the monthly payment for a loan where the annual interest rate (expressed in percent), the amount of the loan, and the number of years are entered via INPUT statements. The monthly payment for the loan is computed from the following relationship:

$$P = \left(\frac{r(1 + r)^n}{(1 + r)^n - 1}\right) \times L$$

where P = payment
L = amount of the loan
r = monthly interest rate
n = number of payments

Determine the total interest paid by using the following formula:

Total Interest Paid = nP – L

Input Data: Use the following sample data.

Loan:	$8000.00
Interest rate:	12.8%
Time:	4 years

(**Hint:** The annual interest must be divided by 1200, and the time must be multiplied by 12. Also see Program 3.12 on page 77.)

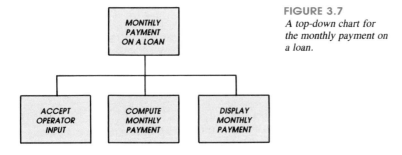

FIGURE 3.7
A top-down chart for the monthly payment on a loan.

Output Results: The following results are displayed.

```
Amount of loan =================> 8000
Interest rate (in percent) ====> 12.8
Time in years =================> 4

Monthly payment ===============> $ 213.8282
Total interest paid ==========> $ 2263.753
```

5. Extracting Substrings

Purpose: To become familiar with the string functions.

Problem: Construct a program to prompt you to enter the alphabet and assign it to a string variable. Using the MID$ string function and concatenation operator, have the program string the selected letters from the alphabet together to form and display your first name and determine the number of characters in your first name.

Input Data: Prepare and use the following data.

ABCDEFGHIJKLMNOPQRSTUVWXYZ

Output Results: The following results are displayed for a person with the first name John.

```
Enter the alphabet: ABCDEFGHIJKLMNOPQRSTUVWXYZ

My first name is: JOHN
The number of letters in my first name is: 4
```

(**Note:** Answers will vary.)

6. Payroll Problem II: Federal Withholding Tax Computations

Purpose: To become familiar with the top-down approach; with nested subroutines; and with executing a program for several sets of data.

Problem: Modify Payroll Problem I in chapter 2 on page 49 (BASIC Programming Problem 4) to accept by means of INPUT statements an employee number, number of dependents, hourly rate of pay, and hours worked during a biweekly pay period. Use the following formulas to compute the gross pay, federal withholding tax, and net pay:

1. Gross pay = hours worked × hourly rate of pay
2. Federal withholding tax = 0.2 × (gross pay – dependents × 38.46)
3. Net pay = gross pay – federal withholding tax

Execute the program for each employee described under the Input Data for this problem. Have the program clear the screen before accepting any data. Use the top-down chart in Figure 3.8.

(**Hint:** See Program 3.12 on page 77.)

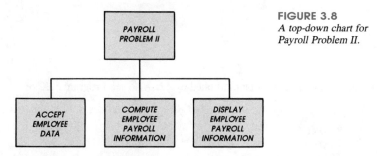

FIGURE 3.8
A top-down chart for Payroll Problem II.

Input Data: Use the following sample data.

Employee Number	Number of Dependents	Hourly Rate of Pay	Hours Worked
123	2	$12.50	80
124	1	8.00	100
125	1	13.00	80
126	2	4.50	20

Output Results: The following results are displayed for employee number 123.

```
Employee number ============> 123
Number of dependents =======> 2
Hourly rate of pay =========> 12.50
Hours worked ===============> 80

Gross pay ==================> 1000
Federal withholding tax ===> 184.616
Net pay ====================> 815.3841
```

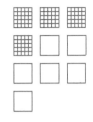

LOOPING AND INPUT/OUTPUT PROCESSING

The programs discussed in the previous chapters are classified as **straight-line programs**. Up to this point, therefore, we have not utilized the complete power of the PC; essentially, we have used it as a high-speed calculator. However, the power of a PC is derived both from its speed and its ability to do repetitive tasks. In regard to the second of these two capacities, one of the purposes of this chapter is to introduce you to the WHILE and WEND statements. These two statements allow you to instruct the PC to loop and repeat a task in a program.

The programs developed in chapters 2 and 3 also processed only small amounts of data. In this chapter we will present a technique for integrating data into a program through the use of the READ and DATA statements. The READ and DATA statements are usually preferred over the INPUT statement when a program has to process large amounts of data that are part of the program itself.

The third topic to be discussed in this chapter is the generation of tabular reports. To write programs that can produce meaningful information in a form that is easy to read and understand, you need to know more about the PRINT statement. You will also learn about the PRINT USING and LOCATE statements, which give you even more control over the output than the PRINT statement does.

Upon successful completion of this chapter, you will be able to write programs that can process data that is part of the program itself, and you will be able to generate readable reports. Furthermore, you will be able to write programs that can repeat the same task over and over.

Programming Case Study 6: *Determining the Sale Price*

Program 4.1, on page 91, computes the discount amount and sale price for each of a series of products. The discount amount is determined from the following formula:

$$\text{Discount Amount} = \frac{\text{Discount Rate}}{100} \times \text{Original Price}$$

The sale price is determined from the formula:

$$\text{Sale Price} = \text{Original Price} - \text{Discount Amount}$$

The product data includes the product identification number, the original price, and the discount rate, as shown below:

	Product Number	Original Price	Discount Rate in Percent
	112841A	$115.00	14
	213981B	100.00	17
	332121A	98.00	13
	586192X	88.00	12
	714121Y	43.00	8
Trailer Record →	EOF	0	0

The top-down chart and flowchart that correspond to Program 4.1 are given in Figure 4.1. For your convenience in following the logic, line numbers have been placed on the top left-hand corner of the symbols in order to illustrate the relationship between the top-down chart, the program flowcharts and Program 4.1.

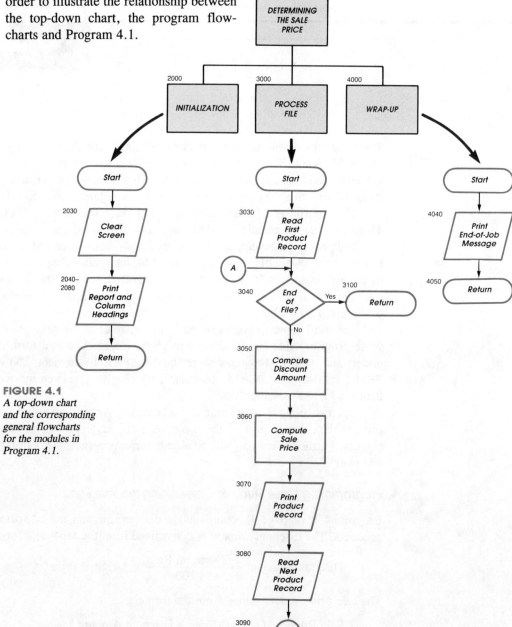

FIGURE 4.1
A top-down chart and the corresponding general flowcharts for the modules in Program 4.1.

PROGRAM 4.1

```
1000 ' Program 4.1
1010 ' Determining the Sale Price
1020 ' **********************************************
1030 ' *                Main Module                 *
1040 ' **********************************************
1050 GOSUB 2000   ' Call Initialization
1060 GOSUB 3000   ' Call Process File
1070 GOSUB 4000   ' Call Wrap-up
1080 END
1090 '
2000 ' **********************************************
2010 ' *              Initialization                *
2020 ' **********************************************
2030 CLS: KEY OFF   ' Clear Screen
2040 PRINT TAB(21); "Determine the Sale Price"
2050 PRINT
2060 PRINT "Product", "Original", "Discount", "Discount", "Sale"
2070 PRINT "Number", "Price", "Rate in %", "Amount", "Price"
2080 PRINT
2090 RETURN
2100 '
3000 ' **********************************************
3010 ' *              Process File                  *
3020 ' **********************************************
3030 READ PRODUCT$, ORIGINAL.PRICE, RATE
3040 WHILE PRODUCT$ <> "EOF"
3050    DISCOUNT = RATE / 100 * ORIGINAL.PRICE
3060    SALE.PRICE = ORIGINAL.PRICE - DISCOUNT
3070    PRINT PRODUCT$, ORIGINAL.PRICE, RATE, DISCOUNT, SALE.PRICE
3080    READ PRODUCT$, ORIGINAL.PRICE, RATE
3090 WEND
3100 RETURN
3110 '
4000 ' **********************************************
4010 ' *               Wrap-up                      *
4020 ' **********************************************
4030 PRINT
4040 PRINT "End of Report"
4050 RETURN
4060 '
4070 ' *************** Data Follows ***************
4080 DATA 112841A, 115, 14
4090 DATA 213981B, 100, 17
4100 DATA 332121A,  98, 13
4110 DATA 586192X,  88, 12
4120 DATA 714121Y,  43,  8
4130 DATA EOF,       0,  0  : ' This Is the Trailer Record
4140 ' ************** End of Program **************
RUN
```

Determine the Sale Price

Product Number	Original Price	Discount Rate in %	Discount Amount	Sale Price
112841A	115	14	16.1	98.9
213981B	100	17	17	83
332121A	98	13	12.74	85.26
586192X	88	12	10.56	77.44
714121Y	43	8	3.44	39.56

End of Report

In Program 4.1, the Main Module includes three GOSUB statements. Each GOSUB calls a module that carries out a particular subtask. The GOSUB in line 1050 calls the Initialization Module that begins at line 2000. The Initialization Module clears the screen and displays the report and column headings before the RETURN statement in line 2090 returns control to the Main Module.

The PRINT statement in line 2040 of the Initialization Module includes the TAB function, which specifies that the report heading is to begin exactly in column 21. The two PRINT statements in lines 2060 and 2070 and the one in line 3070 contain a **comma separator** after each string constant or variable, instead of the semicolon separator used in previous programs. The use of the comma separator in PRINT statements causes the PC to produce output that is automatically positioned in a tabular format. These concepts are described in detail in section 4.4.

The second GOSUB statement in the Main Module, line 1060, calls the Process File Module, which begins at line 3000. Lines 3030 and 3080 contain READ statements that instruct the PC to assign values to PRODUCT$, ORIGINAL.PRICE, and RATE from the sequence of data created from DATA statements that begin at line 4080. Note that this data is part of Program 4.1 itself. The rules regarding the READ and DATA statements are presented in section 4.3.

Following the first READ statement in line 3030, lines 3040 through 3090 establish a **While loop**. In looping, a control statement, like the WEND statement in line 3090, automatically returns control to the corresponding WHILE statement in line 3040. The WHILE statement is the first of a series of statements that are executed repeatedly as long as PRODUCT$ does not equal the value EOF. When PRODUCT$ does equal the value EOF, the WHILE statement in line 3040 transfers control to line 3100, and control is finally returned to the Main Module. One execution of the While loop is called a **pass**. Note that the statements within the loop, lines 3050 through 3080, are indented by three spaces for the purpose of readability.

The Process File Module contains two READ statements, located in lines 3030 and 3080. The first READ statement, in line 3030, is executed only once. The other READ statement, in line 3080, is executed in each pass through the While loop. Although many programming styles exist, the programming style of using two READ statements and a While loop will be employed often in this book.

By now, the potential of the WHILE and WEND statements should be apparent. In Program 4.1, after the first three values in line 4080 are read by the READ statement in line 3030, the WHILE statement in line 3040 tests to see whether PRODUCT$ does not equal the value EOF. Since PRODUCT$ is equal to 112841A, execution continues with line 3050 and the data describing the first product is processed. At the bottom of the While loop, line 3080 reads the next three data values. These newly read values for PRODUCT$, ORIGINAL.PRICE, and RATE replace the three original values in the main storage unit. The PC then executes the WEND statement in line 3090. The WEND statement automatically returns control to its corresponding WHILE statement in line 3040.

As a result, the PC again tests to see whether it has read the trailer record represented by line 4130. Since the READ statement only assigned the second set of data items the previous time it was executed, another pass on the While loop is made. The PC continues this looping operation until all the values in the DATA statements have been read by the READ statement in line 3080 and all the computations and output have been completed.

The general forms for the WHILE and WEND statements are shown in Tables 4.1 and 4.2 on the opposite page.

As illustrated in the flowchart for the Process File Module in Figure 4.1, on page 90, the WHILE statement is represented in a flowchart by the diamond-shaped symbol. When

_____TABLE 4.1 The WHILE Statement_____

General Form:	WHILE condition
Purpose:	*Causes the statements between* WHILE *and* WEND *to be executed repeatedly while the condition is true. When the condition is false, control transfers to the line that follows the corresponding* WEND *statement.*
Keyword Entry:	*Press simultaneously the Alt and W keys on your keyboard.*
| **Examples:** | ```
100 WHILE COUNT = 0
200 WHILE EMP.NAME$ <> "EOF"
300 WHILE SIDE1 + SIDE2 < 5
400 WHILE EMP.NUMBER$ > "000000"
500 WHILE DISCOUNT >= 500
600 WHILE AMOUNT <= 125.25
``` |

you flowchart the branch called for by the WEND statement, you may wish to use a connector symbol, like the circled A in Figure 4.1, rather than long flowlines, an example of which can be seen in Figure A.3 of Appendix A.

With regard to the placement of the WHILE and WEND statements in a program, the WHILE statement *must* have a lower line number than the corresponding WEND statement.

_____TABLE 4.2 The WEND Statement_____

General Form:	WEND
Purpose:	*Identifies the end of a While loop. Automatically transfers control to the corresponding* WHILE *statement.*
| **Examples:** | ```
500 WEND
700 WEND
``` |

Testing for the End of File

Lines 4080 through 4120 contain data for only five products. The sixth product in line 4130 is the **trailer record**. It represents the end of file and is used to determine the point at which all the valid data has been processed. To incorporate an end-of-file test, a variable must be selected and a trailer record added to the data. In Program 4.1, the authors selected the product number as the test for end of file and the data value EOF. Since it guards against reading past end of file, the trailer record is also called the **sentinel record**. The value EOF is called the **sentinel value** and is clearly distinguishable from all the rest of the data assigned to PRODUCT$. This sentinel value is the same as the string constant that is found in line 3040.

After the READ statement in line 3080 assigns PRODUCT$ the value EOF, the WEND statement returns control to the WHILE statement. Since PRODUCT$ is equal to the value EOF, the WHILE statement causes the PC to branch forward to line 3100, which follows the corresponding WEND statement.

The RETURN statement in line 3100 returns control to the Main Module. Line 1070 then calls the Wrap-up Module. The Wrap-up Module displays the message End of Report and control is returned to the Main Module. Line 1080 causes the PC to terminate execution of the program. Lines 4000 through 4060 are also referred to as an **end-of-file routine**.

Three other points about establishing a test for end of file in a While loop are worthy of note:

1. It is important that the trailer record contain enough values for all the variables in the READ statement. In Program 4.1, if we added only the sentinel value EOF to line 4130, there would not be enough data to fulfill the requirements of the three variables in the READ statement. We arbitrarily assigned zero values to each.
2. The While loop requires the use of two READ statements. The first READ statement (line 3030) reads the first product record before the PC enters the While loop.

The second READ statement, found at the bottom of the While loop (line 3080), causes the PC to read the next data record. This READ statement reads the remaining data records, one at a time, until there are no more data records left. Note that if the first record contains the product EOF, the WHILE statement will immediately transfer control to the statement below the corresponding WEND statement.

3. Program 4.1 can process any number of products simply by placing each one in a DATA statement prior to the trailer record.

Conditions   In line 3040 of Program 4.1, the WHILE statement contains the **condition**

```
PRODUCT$ <> "EOF"
```

The condition is made up of two expressions and a **relational operator**. The condition specifies a relationship between expressions that is either true or false. If the condition is true, execution continues with the line that follows the WHILE statement. If the condition is false, control is transferred to the line that follows the corresponding WEND statement.

The PC makes a comparison between the two operators on the basis of the relational operator. Table 4.3 lists the six valid relational operators in MS BASIC.

TABLE 4.3 Relational Operators Used in Conditions

RELATIONS	MATH SYMBOL	BASIC SYMBOL	EXAMPLES
Equal To	=	=	200 WHILE CODE$ = "1"
Less Than	<	<	300 WHILE GROSS < 1000
Greater Than	>	>	400 WHILE RATE > 0.05
Less Than Or Equal To	≤	<= *or* =<	500 WHILE TAX <= 250
Greater Than Or Equal To	≥	>= *or* =>	600 WHILE COUNT >= 10
Not Equal To	=	<> *or* ><	700 WHILE NAME$ <> "End"

There are several important points to watch for in the application of conditions. For example, it is invalid to compare a numeric expression to a string expression. The following is invalid:

```
500 WHILE DOLLARS$ > 100    ' Invalid
```

Furthermore, the condition should ensure termination of the loop. If a logical error like

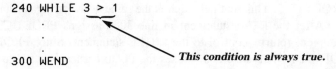

```
240 WHILE 3 > 1
    .
    .
    .
300 WEND
```

This condition is always true.

is not detected, a never-ending loop develops. The endless program execution cannot be stopped except by manual intervention, such as simultaneously pressing the Control and Break keys on your PC keyboard.

TRY IT YOURSELF

1. Load Program 4.1 (PRG4-1) from the Student Diskette. Execute Program 4.1 and note the results that are displayed. Move line 4130 to 4075. Remember, you may move a line by first changing the current line number (4130) to one (4075) that places it in the new location and then deleting the current line number (4130). After editing the program, execute it and see what happens.

(continued)

Try It Yourself (continued)

2. Reload PRG4-1. In line 3040, change the relational operator from < > to = ; execute the program; and see what happens. Note the importance of placing the correct relational operator in a WHILE statement.

3. Reload PRG4-1. Delete line 4130, the trailer record; execute the program; and see what happens. Note the importance of the trailer record in Program 4.1.

⊞ 4.3

THE READ, DATA, AND RESTORE STATEMENTS

In section 4.1, the READ and DATA statements were briefly introduced. This section will illustrate the rules of the READ, DATA, and RESTORE statements and will give further examples of their use, as well as explain their limitations.

The DATA Statement

The DATA statement provides for the creation of a sequence of data items for use by the READ statement. The general form of the DATA statement and some examples are given in Table 4.4.

___TABLE 4.4 The DATA Statement___

General Form:	DATA *data item, . . ., data item* *where each **data item** is either a numeric constant or a string constant.*
Purpose:	*Provides for the creation of a sequence of data items for use by the READ statement.*

Examples *(with READ statements):*	``110 DATA 2, -3.14, 0.025, -95``
	 ``120 READ A, B, C, D2``
	 -- 	
	 ``130 DATA 0.24E33, 0, -2.5D-12, 1.23, 2.46, 5``
	 ``140 READ E, F, G(J), X#, Y, Z%``
	 -- 	
	 ``150 DATA 15, , ",", YES, "2 + 7 = ", NO, 2.2, ""``
	 ``160 READ H, A$, B$(3), C$, D$, E$, I, F$``

Note:	*In line 160 of the last example, A$ and F$ are both assigned the null character.*

The DATA statement consists of the keyword DATA, followed by a list of data items that are separated by mandatory commas. The data items may be numeric or string and are formulated according to the following rules:

> ***DATA Rule 1:*** Numeric data items that are placed in a DATA statement must be formulated as numeric constants.

> ***DATA Rule 2:*** String data items that are placed in a DATA statement may be formulated with or without surrounding quotation marks, provided the string contains no trailing or leading blanks or embedded commas or colons. A string that contains a trailing or leading blank or an embedded comma or colon must be surrounded with quotation marks.

> ***DATA Rule 3:*** The apostrophe (') may not be used in a DATA statement to signify a comment. A comment may be placed at the end of a DATA statement by preceding the keyword REM or apostrophe (') with a colon (:).

Data items from all DATA statements in a program are collected in main storage into a single **data-sequence holding area**. The order in which the data items appear in the DATA statements determines their order in the single data sequence (see Figure 4.2). In other words, the ordering of the data items is based on two considerations: the ascending line numbers of the DATA statements, and the order from left to right of the data items within each DATA statement.

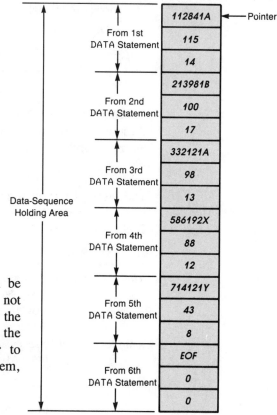

FIGURE 4.2
The order of data items as represented in main storage from the sequence of DATA statements in Program 4.1, lines 4080 to 4130.

The number of data items that can be represented in a DATA statement depends not only on the type of problem but also on the programming style that is adopted by the programmer. Some programmers prefer to write one DATA statement for each data item, like this:

```
110 DATA 310386024
120 DATA JOE NIKOLE
130 DATA -3.85
140 DATA -1E-15
150 READ SOC.SEC$, EMP.NAME$, AMOUNT, STANDARD
```

Others prefer to write as many data items in a DATA statement as there are variables in the READ statement that refers to that DATA statement. For example, the previous DATA and READ statements can be rewritten in this way:

```
140 DATA 310386024, JOE NIKOLE, -3.85, -1E-15
150 READ SOC.SEC$, EMP.NAME$, AMOUNT, STANDARD
```

The DATA statement, like the REM statement, is a nonexecutable statement; that is, if the execution of a program reaches a line that contains a DATA statement, it proceeds to the next line with no other effect. In this book, all DATA statements are placed at the end of programs as shown in Program 4.2 on the opposite page.

The READ Statement

The READ statement provides for the assignment of values to variables from a sequence of data items created from DATA statements. The general form of the READ statement is given in Table 4.5 on the opposite page. The READ statement consists of the keyword READ, followed by a list of variables that are separated by mandatory commas. The variables may be numeric or string variables.

———**TABLE 4.5** The READ Statement———

General Form:	READ *variable, . . ., variable* *where each* **variable** *is either a numeric variable or a string variable.*
Purpose:	*Provides for the assignment of values to variables from a sequence of data items created from* DATA *statements.*

Examples *(with* DATA *statements):   See Table 4.4.*

The READ statement causes the variables in its list to be assigned specific values, in order, from the data sequence that is formed by all of the DATA statements. In order to visualize the relationship between the READ statement and its associated DATA statement, think of a **pointer** that is associated with the data-sequence holding area, as shown in Figure 4.2. When a program is first executed, this pointer points to the first data item in the data sequence. Each time a READ statement is executed, the variables in the list are assigned specific values from the data sequence, beginning with the data item indicated by the pointer, and the pointer is advanced one value per variable, in a downward fashion, to point beyond the data used.

Program 4.2 illustrates the data-sequence holding area and pointer for a program that contains multiple READ and DATA statements. The pointer *initially* points to the location of 565.33 in the holding area. When line 150 is executed, the value of 565.33 is assigned to the variable MON.SAL; the pointer is advanced to the location of the next value, 356.45, which is assigned to the variable TUES.SAL; and the pointer is advanced to the location of the next value, 478.56. When line 160 is executed, the variable WED.SAL is assigned the value of 478.56, THUR.SAL the value of 756.23, and FRI.SAL the value of 342.23.

As this assignment occurs, the pointer advances one value per variable to point to a location beyond the data used, which is recognized by the PC as the end of the data-sequence holding area.

PROGRAM 4.2

```
100 ' Program 4.2
110 ' Determining the Average Daily Sales
120 ' with Multiple READ and
130 ' Multiple DATA Statements
140 ' ********************************
150 READ MON.SAL, TUES.SAL
160 READ WED.SAL, THUR.SAL, FRI.SAL
170 AVERAGE = (MON.SAL + TUES.SAL + WED.SAL + THUR.SAL + FRI.SAL) / 5
180 PRINT MON.SAL, TUES.SAL
190 PRINT WED.SAL, THUR.SAL, FRI.SAL
200 PRINT "The average is"; AVERAGE
210 ' ********** Data Follows **********
220 DATA 565.33, 356.45, 478.56
230 DATA 756.23, 342.23
240 END

RUN

  565.33        356.45
  478.56        756.23        342.23
The average is 499.76
```

Data-Sequence Holding Area

565.33	*356.45*	*478.56*	*756.23*	*342.23*	*Undefined*

Pointer *Before* the Execution of Line 150   Pointer *After* the Execution of Line 150   Pointer *After* the Execution of Line 160

In Program 4.2, the PC is unable to calculate AVERAGE correctly until it has the value of MON.SAL, TUES.SAL, WED.SAL, THUR.SAL, and FRI.SAL. The READ statement should occur somewhere *before* the LET statement in the program. This example can be generalized to give the following:

> **READ Rule 1:** Every variable that appears in the program whose value is directly obtained by a READ should be listed in a READ statement before it is used elsewhere in the program.

While the placement of the DATA statements in a program is immaterial, the placement of the READ statement is important. Furthermore, more than one DATA statement may be used to satisfy one READ statement, and more than one READ statement may be satisfied from one DATA statement.

> **READ Rule 2:** A program that contains a READ statement must also have at least one DATA statement.

If the number of data items to be assigned to the variables of a READ statement is insufficient, a diagnostic message appears, as shown in Program 4.3. However, excessive data items are ignored, as shown in Program 4.4.

PROGRAM 4.3	PROGRAM 4.4

```
100 ' Program 4.3           100 ' Program 4.4
110 ' Insufficient Data Items  110 ' Excessive Data Items
120 ' in a DATA Statement    120 ' in a DATA Statement
130 ' *********************   130 ' ******************
140 READ A, B, C, D          140 READ A, B, C
150 PRINT A, B, C, D         150 PRINT A, B, C
160 ' **** Data Follows *****  160 ' *** Data Follows ***
170 DATA 1, 2, 3             170 DATA 1, 2, 3, 4, 5
180 END                      180 END

RUN                          RUN

Out of DATA in 140            1          2          3
```

Finally, the type of data item in the data sequence must correspond to the type of variable to which it is to be assigned. If they do not agree, then the error message Syntax error displays.

> **READ Rule 3:** Numeric variables in READ statements require numeric constants as data items in DATA statements, and string variables require quoted strings or unquoted strings as data.

TRY IT YOURSELF

1. Load Program 4.2 (PRG4-2) from the Student Diskette. Display the program and then execute it. Change line 150 to include the three variables in line 160. Delete line 160. Execute the program and compare the display with the original one. Do you agree that adjacent READ statements may be combined, provided the variables maintain the same order?

(continued)

*T*RY *I*T *Y*OURSELF *(continued)*

2. Reload PRG4-2. Delete line 230 and execute the program. Now do you understand what happens when an insufficient number of data items is assigned to the variables of a READ statement?

3. Reload PRG4-2. Insert quotation marks around each of the data items in line 230, and execute the program. Now do you understand READ Rule 3?

The RESTORE Statement

Usually data items from a DATA statement are processed by a READ statement only once. If you want the PC to read all or some of the same data items later in the program, you must use the RESTORE statement to restore the data.

The RESTORE statement allows the data in a given program to be reread as often as is necessary by other READ statements. The general form of the RESTORE statement, with examples, is given in Table 4.6. The RESTORE statement consists of the keyword RESTORE, optionally followed by a line number. If no line number follows the keyword RESTORE, then the next READ statement accesses the first data item in the first DATA statement. If a line number follows RESTORE, the next READ statement accesses the first data item in the DATA statement that is referenced by the specified line number.

_____TABLE 4.6 The RESTORE Statement_____

General Form:	RESTORE line number where **line number** is optional.
Purpose:	Allows the data items in DATA statements to be reread. *If no line number follows the keyword RESTORE, then the next READ statement accesses the first data item in the first DATA statement.* *If a line number follows RESTORE, the next READ statement accesses the first data item in the DATA statement referenced by the specified line number.*
Examples:	500 RESTORE 600 RESTORE 450

The RESTORE statement causes the pointer to be moved back to a specified area in the data-sequence holding area. This is done so that the next READ statement executed will read the data from that point in the sequence once again.

The RESTORE statement is generally used when it is necessary to perform several types of computations on the same data items. Program 4.5, on the following page, illustrates the use of the RESTORE statement.

When the first READ statement, in line 130, is executed in Program 4.5, A is assigned the value of 1, B the value of 3, and C the value of 9. After a value for U is computed in line 140, the RESTORE statement in line 150 is executed. This resets the pointer to the beginning of the data-sequence holding area so that it points at the value of 1. When the second READ statement, in line 160, is executed, the values of 1, 3, and 9 are assigned to D, E, and F.

After a value of V is calculated, the third READ statement, in line 180, is executed, and 2, 4, and 12 are assigned to G, H, and I. After a value of W is calculated in line 190, the RESTORE 270 statement in line 200 is executed, and the pointer is reset to the first data item in line 270 (not line 260).

When the fourth READ statement, in line 210, is executed, 2, 4, and 12 are assigned J, K, and L. Finally, the value of X is calculated in line 220, and the values of all the variables used in the program are displayed. See BASIC Programming Problem 2 at the end of chapter 5 concerning the use of the RESTORE statement.

PROGRAM 4.5

```
100 ' Program 4.5
110 ' Use of the RESTORE Statement
120 ' ****************************
130 READ A, B, C
140 U = A ^ B ^ C
150 RESTORE
160 READ D, E, F
170 V = F / E / D
180 READ G, H, I
190 W = G * H * I
200 RESTORE 270
210 READ J, K, L
220 X = L \ K \ J
230 PRINT A, B, C, D, E
240 PRINT F, U, V, W, X
250 ' ******* Data Follows *******
260 DATA 1, 3, 9
270 DATA 2, 4, 12
280 END

RUN

1           3           9           1           3
9           1           3           96          1
```

⊞ 4.4

THE PRINT STATEMENT

The execution of the PRINT statement generates a string of characters for transmission to an external source like a video display device. The PRINT statement is commonly used to display the results from computations, to display headings and labeled information, and to plot points on a graph. In addition, the PRINT statement allows you to control the spacing and the format of the desired output.

The general form of the PRINT statement is given with examples in Table 4.7 on the opposite page. The PRINT statement consists of the keyword PRINT. It may also have an optional list of **print items**, separated by mandatory commas or semicolons or spaces. The print items may be numeric or string constants, variables, expressions, or null items. In addition, the print items may include useful function references, like the MID$ function described in chapter 3.

Print Zones and Print Positions

The most common use of the PRINT statement is to output values that have been defined earlier in a program. Every sample program presented thus far has included a PRINT statement. Listing items separated by commas within a PRINT statement, like the following

```
3070    PRINT PRODUCT$, ORIGINAL.PRICE, RATE, DISCOUNT, SALE.PRICE
```

causes the values of PRODUCT$, ORIGINAL.PRICE, RATE, DISCOUNT, and SALE.PRICE to be displayed on a *single* line. MS BASIC displays the five values in **print zones**.

In the 80-column display mode, there are five print zones per line. Each print zone has 14 positions, for a total of 70 positions per line. In the 40-column display mode, there are only two print zones per line, for a total of 28 positions. The **print positions** are numbered consecutively from the left, starting with position 1, as shown in Figure 4.3 on the opposite page.

_____TABLE 4.7 The PRINT Statement_____

General Form:	PRINT *item pm item pm . . . pm item* *where each **item** is a constant, variable, expression, function reference, or null and* *each **pm** is a comma, semicolon, or space.*
Purpose:	*Provides for the generation of labeled and unlabeled output or of output in a* *consistent tabular format from the program to the screen.*
Keyword Entry:	*Press the question mark (?) key or simultaneously the Alt and P keys on your* *keyboard.*
Examples:	100 PRINT 150 PRINT EMP.NAME$ 200 ? AMOUNT, CODE$ 250 PRINT COUNT; DISCOUNT, EMPLOYEE$; NUMBER 300 PRINT SEX.CODE$; " "; TIME; " "; MARITAL.STATUS$ 350 PRINT HEIGHT, WEIGHT; RACE$; JOB(8); 400 PRINT "X = "; X, "Y = "; Y 450 PRINT "The answer is $"; H, 500 PRINT TAB(10); (X + Y) / 4, INT(A) 550 ? ,, AREA, 10, 20 600 PRINT "The interest rate is"; I; "%" 650 PRINT X; " "; 2 * X; " "; 3 * X; " "; 4 * X 700 PRINT A B C
Note:	*One or more spaces between print items has the same effect as the semicolon.*

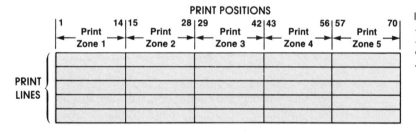

PRINT POSITIONS

FIGURE 4.3
*In the 80-column display
mode, the print line is
divided into five print
zones.*

Representation of Numeric Output

Numeric constants, variables, expressions, and function references are evaluated to produce a string of characters consisting of a sign, the decimal representation of the number, and a trailing space. The sign is a leading space if the number is positive and is a leading minus sign if the number is negative.

Representation of String Output

String constants, variables, expressions, and functions are displayed without any leading or trailing spaces. For example, when the following line,

    200 PRINT "BAS"; "IC"

is executed, the PC displays BASIC in print positions 1 through 5. Unlike the way it treats numeric output, the PC does not insert a trailing space following the string constants in the output.

Use of the Comma Separator

Punctuation marks like the comma, semicolon, and space are placed between print items. In this section, the role of the comma, or **comma separator**, is examined. As illustrated in Figure 4.4, on the following page, the comma separator allows you to produce output that is automatically positioned in tabular format. Each PRINT statement executed displays one line of information, *unless* one of the following two conditions is true:

1. the number of print zones required by the PRINT statement exceeds five (see Figure 4.4, line 270), or

2. the PRINT statement ends with a punctuation mark, like a comma or semicolon (see Figure 4.4, lines 190, 200, and 280).

All the numbers displayed in Figure 4.4 are negative and, therefore, a leading minus sign is automatically displayed as the first character in the various print zones. When a number is positive, a leading space is displayed in the first position of the print zone. Two or more consecutive commas may be included in a PRINT statement (see Figure 4.4, lines 240 and 250) as a means of tabulating over print zones.

FIGURE 4.4

The effect of commas with numeric and string expressions in PRINT statements.

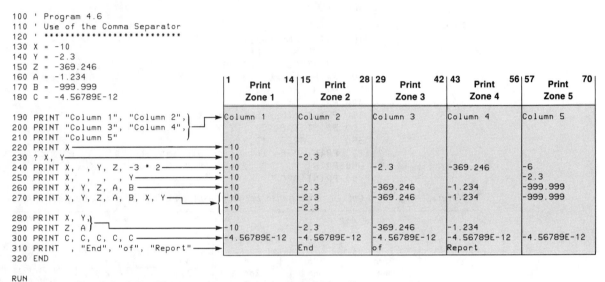

```
100 ' Program 4.6
110 ' Use of the Comma Separator
120 ' **************************
130 X = -10
140 Y = -2.3
150 Z = -369.246
160 A = -1.234
170 B = -999.999
180 C = -4.56789E-12

190 PRINT "Column 1", "Column 2",
200 PRINT "Column 3", "Column 4",
210 PRINT "Column 5"
220 PRINT X
230 ? X, Y
240 PRINT X, , Y, Z, -3 * 2
250 PRINT X, , , , Y
260 PRINT X, Y, Z, A, B
270 PRINT X, Y, Z, A, B, X, Y

280 PRINT X, Y,
290 PRINT Z, A
300 PRINT C, C, C, C, C
310 PRINT , "End", "of", "Report"
320 END

RUN
```

1 Print Zone 1 14	15 Print Zone 2 28	29 Print Zone 3 42	43 Print Zone 4 56	57 Print Zone 5 70
Column 1	Column 2	Column 3	Column 4	Column 5
-10				
-10	-2.3			
-10		-2.3	-369.246	-6
-10				-2.3
-10	-2.3	-369.246	-1.234	-999.999
-10	-2.3	-369.246	-1.234	-999.999
-10	-2.3			
-10	-2.3	-369.246	-1.234	
-4.56789E-12	-4.56789E-12	-4.56789E-12	-4.56789E-12	-4.56789E-12
	End	of	Report	

Use of the Semicolon and Space Separators

In this section, we will examine the identical role of the **semicolon** and **space separators** in the PRINT statement. Whereas the comma separator allows you to tab to the next print zone, the semicolon or space does not. Instead, the semicolon or space in a PRINT statement causes the display of the value immediately to the right of the preceding one. The semicolon or space enables you to display more than five items per line. Use of the semicolon or space is referred to as displaying values in a **packed** or **compressed format**. (Compare the compressed format in Figure 4.5, on the opposite page, with the tabular format in Figure 4.4.)

Program 4.7, as illustrated in Figure 4.5, shows the use of the semicolon and space separators. Whereas each numeric value displayed is preceded by a leading sign and a trailing space, string values are displayed with no spaces separating them (see line 180).

In line 190, all five print items are separated by the semicolon, and the values are all displayed within the first 20 print positions. Line 200 shows the use of the space separator in place of the semicolon separator. In line 210, the keyword PRINT is followed by a comma separator, which causes the value of A, the first print item, to be displayed beginning in print zone 2.

If a PRINT statement ends with a semicolon, as in line 240, the first item in the next PRINT statement (line 250) displays on the same line in compressed form.

Creating Blank Lines

If a PRINT statement contains a null list, then a blank line results. For example,

```
200 PRINT
```

contains no print items and results in the display of a blank line. Line 240 in Program 4.7 displays two blank lines before the values of A, B, and C are displayed.

PROGRAM 4.7

```
100 ' Program 4.7
110 ' Use of the Semicolon Separator
120 ' ****************************
130 A = -10
140 B = -20
150 C = -30
160 D = -40
170 E = -50
180 PRINT "The"; "value"; "of"; "A"; "is"; A
190 PRINT A; B; C; D; E
200 PRINT "The " "value " "of " "A " "is " A
210 PRINT , A; " "; B; " "; C; " "; D; " "; E
220 PRINT "The value of A is "; A
240 PRINT : PRINT : PRINT A, B; C;
250 PRINT D, E
260 END
```

RUN

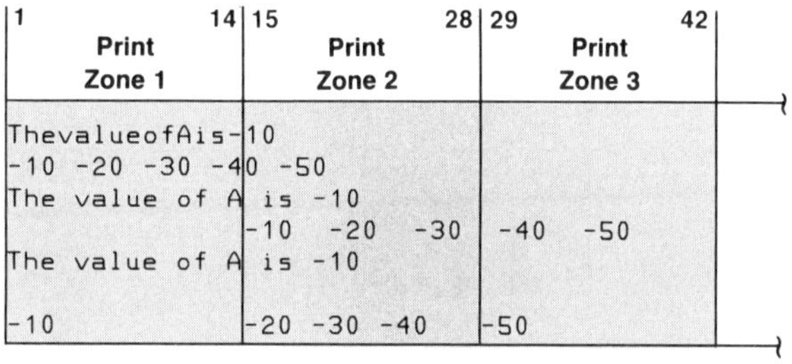

1 14	15 28	29 42
Print Zone 1	**Print Zone 2**	**Print Zone 3**
ThevalueofAis-10		
-10 -20 -30 -40 -50		
The value of A is -10		
	-10 -20 -30	-40 -50
The value of A is -10		
-10	-20 -30 -40	-50

FIGURE 4.5
The effect of semicolons and spaces with numeric and string expressions in PRINT statements.

Use of the TAB Function

Thus far, PRINT statements have contained the comma, semicolon, and space as separators among numeric and string expressions in order to display the values of these expressions in a readable format with correct spacing. Compact and exact spacing of output results can also be achieved by the use of the TAB and SPC functions.

The TAB function is used in the PRINT statement to specify the exact print positions for the various output results on a given line. Use of the TAB function as follows,

```
2040 PRINT TAB(21); "Determine the Sale Price"
```

causes the string to be displayed beginning in exactly print position 21. The form of the TAB function is

TAB(numeric expression)

where the numeric expression, the argument, may be a numeric constant, a variable, an expression, or a function reference. The value of the argument determines the position on the line of the next character to be displayed. The TAB function may be used in a PRINT, LPRINT, and PRINT #n statement. The LPRINT statement is discussed shortly, and the PRINT #n statement is discussed in chapter 6. Consider line 160 of Program 4.8 on the following page:

```
160 PRINT TAB(10); "PUC Company"
```

The function TAB(10) causes the PC to tab to print position 10 and display the string PUC Company in positions 10 through 20. Study closely the remaining examples of the TAB function in lines 190 through 260. Note that noninteger arguments are rounded.

PROGRAM 4.8

```
100 ' Program 4.8
110 ' Use of the TAB function
120 ' ***********************
130 A = 27
140 B = 4
150 C = 13
160 PRINT TAB(10); "PUC Company"
170 PRINT
180 PRINT
190 PRINT TAB(5); "Emp No"; TAB(22); "Rate"
200 PRINT TAB(5) 12345 TAB(22) 3.25
210 PRINT
220 PRINT
230 PRINT TAB(A / B + C); "Rate ="; 3.25
240 PRINT TAB(15); A; TAB(12); B
250 PRINT TAB(5); C
260 PRINT TAB(10), "End of Job"
270 END

RUN
```

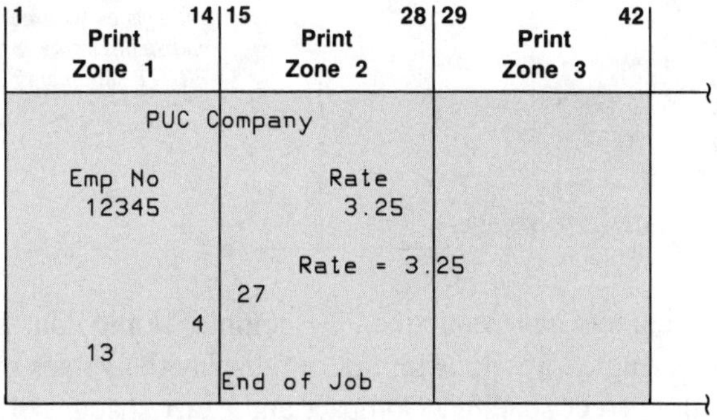

FIGURE 4.6
The use of the TAB function in PRINT statements.

The following rules summarize the use of the TAB function:

TAB Rule 1: The argument must evaluate to an integer between 1 and 255.

TAB Rule 2: A decimal argument is rounded to the nearest integer.

TAB Rule 3: Backspacing is not permitted with the TAB function.

Displaying Spaces — The SPC Function

The SPC function is similar to the space bar on a typewriter. It may be used in a PRINT statement to insert spaces between print items. The form of the SPC function is

SPC(numeric expression)

Consider the following:

```
240 PRINT "Column 1"; SPC(3); "Column 2"; SPC(5); "Column 3"
```

The SPC(3) causes the insertion of three spaces between Column 1 and Column 2. The SPC(5) inserts five spaces between Column 2 and Column 3. The spaces inserted between displayed results are often called **filler**. The SPC function may be used any number of times in the same statement. However, it may be used only in a PRINT, LPRINT, or PRINT #n statement.

Calculations Within the PRINT Statement

MS BASIC permits calculations to be made within the PRINT statement. For instance, the sum, difference, product, quotient, modulo, and exponentiation of two numbers, like 4 and 2, may be made in the conventional way by using LET statements or by using the PRINT statement, as in Program 4.9.

PROGRAM 4.9

```
100 ' Program 4.9
110 ' Calculations Within a PRINT Statement
120 ' *************************************
130 PRINT 4 + 2; SPC(4); 4 - 2; SPC(4); 4 * 2
140 PRINT 4 / 2; SPC(4); 4 \ 2; SPC(4); 4 MOD 2; SPC(4); 4 ^ 2
150 END

RUN

    6       2       8
    2       2       0       16
```

Using the Immediate Mode in MS BASIC

As described earlier in chapter 2, MS BASIC has an immediate mode of operation, which permits your PC to act as a powerful desk calculator. When you are in the immediate mode, BASIC statements like the PRINT statement can be executed individually, without being incorporated into a program. You merely enter the keyword PRINT, followed by any numeric expression. As soon as you press the Enter key, the PC immediately computes and displays the value of the expression. Line numbers are not used in the immediate mode.

The following example of calculating a complex expression uses the immediate mode of MS BASIC:

```
PRINT (2 - 3 * 4 / 5) ^ 2 + 5 / (4 * 3 - 2 ^ 3)
    1.41
```

The value displayed is 1.41. This expression was previously computed in section 3.5, on page 70, to illustrate the effect of parentheses and the rules of precedence with respect to the evaluation of numeric expressions.

MS BASIC also allows you to use the immediate mode to **debug** programs. For example, if a fatal error occurs, the PRINT statement can be used to display the values of variables used in the program that terminates. It is important that no other commands be issued between the time the program stops and the time the PRINT statement is entered. See Appendix C for a discussion of debugging a program that has errors.

The LPRINT Statement

While the PRINT statement displays results on the screen, the LPRINT statement prints the results on the printer. Everything that has been presented with respect to the PRINT statement in this chapter applies to the LPRINT statement as well. Obviously, to use this statement you must have a printer attached to your PC.

TRY IT YOURSELF

Load Program 4.6 (PRG4-6) from the Student Diskette. Display and execute the program. Replace all the PRINT statements with LPRINT statements. Turn on the printer and execute the program a second time. After the modified Program 4.6 terminates, enter the following two statements in the immediate mode:

```
PRINT TAB(10); X; SPC(5); Y
LPRINT TAB(10); X; SPC(5); Y
```

Study the displayed results and compare them to the values printed earlier for X and Y. Displaying the values of variables following the termination of execution of a program through the immediate mode is an important debugging tool.

4.5

THE PRINT USING
STATEMENT FOR
FORMATTED OUTPUT

The PRINT USING statement is far more useful than the PRINT statement in exactly controlling the format of a program's output. In section 4.4, you were introduced to the comma, the semicolon, the space and the TAB and SPC functions for print-control purposes. For most applications, these print-control methods will suffice. However, when you are confronted with generating readable reports for non-technical personnel, more control over the format of the output is essential. The PRINT USING statement gives you the desired capabilities to display information according to a predefined format instead of the free format provided by the PRINT statement. Through the use of the PRINT USING statement, you can do the following:

1. Specify the exact image of a line of output.
2. Force decimal-point alignment when displaying numeric tables in columnar format.
3. Control the number of digits that are displayed for a numeric result.
4. Specify that commas be inserted into a number. (Starting from the units position of a number and progressing toward the left, digits are separated into groups of three by a comma.)
5. Specify that the sign status of the number be displayed along with the number (+ or blank if positive, – if negative).
6. Assign a fixed or floating dollar sign ($) to the number displayed.
7. Force a numeric result to be displayed in exponential notation.
8. **Left-** or **right-justify** string values in a formatted field (i.e., align the left- or rightmost characters, respectively).
9. Specify that only the first character of a string be displayed.
10. Round a value automatically to a specified number of decimal digits.

The general form of the PRINT USING statement is given with examples in Table 4.8.

_____TABLE 4.8 The PRINT USING Statement_____

General Form:	PRINT USING *string expression; list*
	where **string expression** (sometimes called the **descriptor field** or **format field**)
	    is either a string constant or a string variable, and
	    list is a list of items to be displayed in the format specified by the descriptor field.

Purpose:	*Provides for controlling exactly the format of a program's output to the screen by specifying an image to which that output must conform.*
Keyword Entry:	*Simultaneously press the Alt and P keys for the keyword* PRINT. *Simultaneously press the Alt and U keys for the keyword* USING.
Examples:	150 PRINT USING "The answer is #,###.##"; COST 200 PRINT USING "## divided by # is #.#"; NUM, DEN, QUOT 300 FORMAT.1$ = "Total cost =======> $$,###.##-" 310 PRINT USING FORMAT.1$; TOTAL 350 FORMAT.2$ = "**,###.##" 360 PRINT USING FORMAT.2$; CHECK; 900 PRINT USING "\ \"; CUST.NAME$ 950 PRINT USING "!, !, \ \"; FIRST$, MIDDLE$, LAST$ 975 PRINT USING "Example _##"; NUMBER 999 PRINT USING "#.##^^^^"; DIS.1, DIS.2, DIS.3, DIS.4

Declaring the Format of the Output

To control the format of the displayed values, the PRINT USING statement is employed in conjunction with a string expression that specifies exactly the image to which the output must conform. The string expression is placed immediately after the words PRINT USING in the form of a string constant or string variable. If the format is described by a string variable, then the string variable must be assigned the format by a LET statement before the PRINT USING statement is executed in the program. Consider the following two methods:

Method 1:

```
100 ' Format Specified as a String in the PRINT USING Statement
110 PRINT USING "Employee ### has earned $$,###.##"; CLOCK, SALARY
```

Method 2:

```
100 ' Format Specified Earlier and Assigned to a String Variable
110 FORMAT$ = "Employee ### has earned $$,###.##"
        .
        .
        .
170 PRINT USING FORMAT$; CLOCK, SALARY
```

In Method 1, the string following the keywords PRINT USING in line 110 instructs the PC to display the values of CLOCK and SALARY, using the format found in that statement. In Method 2, the string constant has been replaced by the string variable FORMAT$, which was assigned the desired format in line 110. If CLOCK is equal to 000105 and SALARY is equal to 4563.20, then the results displayed from the execution of line 110 in Method 1 or line 170 in Method 2 are as follows:

```
Employee 105 has earned $4,563.20
```

Format Symbols

Table 4.9 includes the format symbols that are available with MS BASIC. One or more consecutive format symbols appearing in a string expression is a **descriptor field**, or **format field**.

TABLE 4.9 Format Symbols

SYMBOL	FUNCTION	EXAMPLES
#	*Grouped number signs define a numeric descriptor field and cause the display of a numeric value in integer form.*	# ### ####
.	*The period is used for decimal-point placement. A decimal point in a numeric descriptor field causes the display of a numeric value in fixed point form.*	###. ###.## .###
,	*The comma is used for automatic-comma placement. A comma in front of a decimal point in a numeric descriptor field causes the display of a numeric value with commas displayed to the left of the decimal point every three significant digits.*	#,###,### ###,###.## #######,.##
^ ^ ^ ^	*Four consecutive circumflexes to the right of a numeric descriptor field causes the display of a value in exponential notation (D or E format).*	##^^^^ #.###^^^^ -##.###^^^^
+	*A single plus sign to the left or right of a numeric descriptor field causes the display of a numeric value with a sign (plus or minus) immediately before or after the number.*	+##,###.## ###+ #,###.##+
−	*A single minus sign to the right of a numeric descriptor field causes the display of negative numbers with a trailing minus sign and positive numbers with a trailing space.*	##.##− ###− ###,###.##−

(continued)

_____TABLE 4.9 Format Symbols *(continued)*_____

SYMBOL	FUNCTION	EXAMPLES
$	A single leading dollar sign in a numeric descriptor field causes the display of a fixed dollar sign in that position, followed by a numeric value. (Note: The dollar sign may be substituted for any valid BASIC character listed in Table D.2 in Appendix D. Format symbols must be preceded by the underscore character.)	$### $##.## $#,###.##+
$$	Two leading dollar signs in a numeric descriptor field cause the display of a single dollar sign immediately to the left of the first significant digit of a numeric value.	$$##.## $$###.##− $$,###.##
**	Two leading asterisks in a numeric descriptor field cause the display of a numeric value with leading spaces, filled with asterisks, to the left of the numeric value.	**###.### **,###.## **.##
**$	Two leading asterisks followed by a single dollar sign in a numeric descriptor field combine the effects of the previous two symbols. These symbols (**$) cause the display of a numeric value with leading spaces filled with asterisks, followed by a floating dollar sign immediately to the left of the numeric value.	**$######## **$#,###.##+
&	The ampersand causes the display of a complete string value left-justified.	&
!	The exclamation point causes the display of the first character of a string value.	!
_	The underscore causes the display of the next character in the descriptor field as if the character were a string constant. Any of the format symbols in this table can be displayed as a string constant.	_& _! _# #_# _$$##.##_#
\n spaces\	Two backslashes separated by n spaces cause the display of a string of characters left-justified and equal in length to 2 plus the number of spaces (n).	\\ \ \ \ \ \ \

The Number Sign Symbol

The number sign (#) is the format symbol that is used to define a numeric descriptor field. Grouped number signs indicate exactly how many positions are desired in a numeric result during output. A number sign reserves space for a digit or sign. For example, in a numeric result,

- # indicates one position;
- ## indicates two positions;
- #### indicates four positions; and
- ####.## indicates six positions, two of which are decimal fractional positions.

It is your responsibility to ensure that enough number signs are in the descriptor field to fit the output results into the prescribed format.

Consider the following example, where A = 10, B = –11, C = 12.75, and D = 4565:

```
100 ' Format Specified Earlier and Assigned to a String Variable
110 FORMAT$ = " ####      ####      ##       ###"
        .
        .
        .
190 PRINT USING FORMAT$; A, B, C, D
```

The results that are displayed from the above sequence, where ƀ represents a blank character, are as follows:

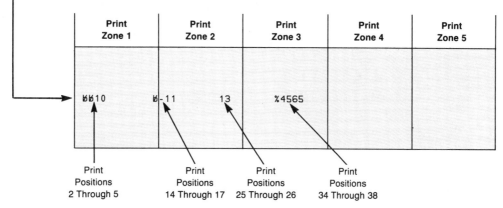

Table 4.10 summarizes the use of the number sign in the previous sample program. Program 4.10, on the following page, gives examples of the use of the number sign.

_____TABLE 4.10 Use of the Number Sign (#) in a Descriptor Field _____

DESCRIPTOR FIELD	DATA	OUTPUT	REMARKS
####	10	ƀƀ10	*Right-justify the digits in the field with leading spaces. Note the floating minus sign.*
####	-11	ƀ-11	
##	12.75	13	*The data is rounded to an integer, since only integers are specified by the descriptor field.*
###	4565	%4565	*Since the data is too large for the specified descriptor field, the value is displayed but is preceded by a percent sign (%) to indicate that an insufficient number of positions were reserved for this descriptor field.*

If the string expression referenced in a PRINT USING statement contains fewer descriptor fields than print items in the list, MS BASIC reuses the string expression. For example, when the following line is entered in the immediate mode,

```
PRINT USING "##   "; -5, -7, -9
```

the PC displays

```
-5   -7   -9
```

If the string expression contains more descriptor fields than print items in the list, MS BASIC ignores the excess. For example,

```
PRINT USING "##    ##    ##    ##"; -5
```

results in –5 being displayed in print positions 1 and 2.

The Decimal Point (Period) Symbol

The period (.) in a numeric descriptor field places a decimal point in the output record at that character position in which it appears, and the format of the numeric result is aligned with the position of the decimal point. When number signs (#) precede the decimal point in a descriptor field, any leading zeros appearing in the data are replaced by spaces, except for a single leading zero immediately preceding the decimal point.

When number signs follow the decimal point, unspecified decimal fractional positions are filled with trailing zeros. When the data contains more decimal fractional digits than the descriptor field allows, the decimal fraction is rounded to the limits of the field.

Table 4.11 and Program 4.10 illustrate the use of the decimal point in various descriptor fields.

TABLE 4.11 Use of the Decimal Point (.) in a Descriptor Field

DESCRIPTOR FIELD	DATA	OUTPUT	REMARKS
####.##	217.5	Ƅ217.50	*Unspecified decimal fraction positions are filled with trailing zeros.*
#####.##	-40	ƄƄ-40.00	
#####.##	23.458	ƄƄƄ23.46	*Decimal fractional digits are rounded.*
####.##	0.027	ƄƄƄ0.03	*The last leading zero before the decimal point is not suppressed.*

The Comma Symbol

A comma (,) to the left of the decimal point in a numeric descriptor field places a comma to the left of every third digit that is to the left of the decimal point. A comma specifies a digit position within the descriptor field. If there are fewer than four significant digits to the left of the decimal point, the PC displays a space in place of the comma symbol. Table 4.12 and Program 4.10 illustrate the use of the comma in various descriptor fields.

If the descriptor field that contains a comma has too few number signs, the comma is replaced by a digit.

TABLE 4.12 Use of the Comma (,) in a Descriptor Field

DESCRIPTOR FIELD	DATA	OUTPUT	REMARKS
#,###	4000	4,000	*Comma displayed.*
#,###,###	999999	ƄƄ999,999	*Comma displayed.*
#,###.##	-30.5	ƄƄ-30.50	*Space displayed for comma when leading digits are blank.*
########,.##	9876543.21	9,876,543.21	*Comma in front of a decimal point in descriptor field.*

PROGRAM 4.10

```
100 ' Program 4.10
110 ' Examples of the Use of the Number Sign,
120 ' Decimal Point and Comma in a Descriptor Field
130 ' ********************************************
140 FORMAT$ = "####   #,###   #,###.##   ########,.##"
150 READ VALUE, CONSTANT#
160 PRINT USING FORMAT$; VALUE, VALUE, VALUE, CONSTANT#
170 PRINT USING "####"; VALUE
180 PRINT USING "#,###"; VALUE
190 PRINT USING "#,###.##"; VALUE
200 ' ************* Data Follows ***************
210 DATA 1234.56, -1234567.89
220 END

RUN

1235    1,235   1,234.56   -1,234,567.89
1235
1,235
1,234.56
```

The Plus and Minus Sign Symbols

A plus sign (+) as either the first or last character in a numeric descriptor field causes a + to be displayed if the data item is positive or a – if the data item is negative. If the plus sign is the leftmost character, a **floating plus sign** is displayed immediately to the left of the first significant digit of the output item.

A plus sign to the right of the last character in a numeric descriptor field causes the sign to be displayed in that position. A minus sign (–) at the end of a numeric descriptor field causes negative numbers to be displayed with a trailing minus sign and positive numbers to be displayed with a trailing space. Table 4.13 gives examples of the use of the plus and minus signs in various numeric descriptor fields.

TABLE 4.13 Use of the Plus (+) or Minus (–) Sign in a Descriptor Field

DESCRIPTOR FIELD	DATA	OUTPUT	REMARKS
FIXED SIGNS			
###.##–	000.01	ƀƀ0.01ƀ	*The last leading zero before the decimal point is not suppressed.*
###.##+	20.5	ƀ20.50+	
###.##+	-8.236	ƀƀ8.24–	*Automatic rounding when length of data exceeds descriptor-field specification.*
###.##–	-456.0	456.00–	
FLOATING SIGNS			
+##.##	40.5	+40.50	
+##.##	7.07	ƀ+7.07	
+###.##	-0.236	ƀƀ-0.24	
+##.##	-456.0	%-456	

The Dollar Sign Symbol

A single leading dollar sign appearing to the left of a numeric descriptor field causes a $ to be displayed in that position of the line.

Two leading dollar signs at the left of a numeric descriptor field cause a single dollar sign to float. The single dollar sign will appear at the left of the first significant digit.

The leading dollar signs specify two positions in the numeric descriptor field. One position is filled by the dollar sign; the second dollar sign reserves a digit position. Table 4.14 gives examples of the use of the dollar sign in various numeric descriptor fields.

TABLE 4.14 Use of the Dollar Sign ($) in a Descriptor Field

DESCRIPTOR FIELD	DATA	OUTPUT	REMARKS
FIXED DOLLAR SIGN			
$###.##	123.45	$123.45	
$###.##	98.76	$ƀ98.76	
$###.##–	40.613	$ƀ40.61ƀ	
$#,###.##–	-40.613	$ƀƀƀ40.61–	
$#,###.##+	40.613	$ƀƀƀ40.61+	
FLOATING DOLLAR SIGN			
$$###.##	1.23	ƀƀƀ$1.23	
$$,###.##	1234.68	$1,234.68	*Second $ sign replaced by digit.*
$$##.##–	-1.0	ƀƀ$1.00–	

The Asterisk Symbol

Two asterisks (**) starting at the left side of a numeric descriptor field cause the value to be displayed in asterisk-filled format. The left side of the numeric field is filled with leading asterisks rather than leading spaces.

Leading asterisks are often used in place of number signs when checks are being printed or when the result must be protected. Hence, leading asterisks are sometimes called **check protection asterisks**, and their use prevents someone from physically adding digits to the left side of a number. Table 4.15 gives examples of the use of the asterisk in various numeric descriptor fields.

TABLE 4.15 Use of the Asterisk Sign (*) in a Descriptor Field

DESCRIPTOR FIELD	DATA	OUTPUT	REMARKS
**,###.##	10.15	****10.15	*Asterisk displayed for comma when leading digits are zero.*
**##-	-6.95	***7-	*Data is rounded to an integer.*
**###.##	4.58	****4.58	
**$#,###.##	50.258	*****$50.26	*Dollar sign floats and leading zeros are displayed as asterisks.*

Formatted Character String Output

Descriptor fields for string values are defined in terms of the ampersand (**&**), two backslashes (\\), the exclamation point (!), or the underscore (-), rather than the number sign (#). Table 4.9, on page 108, summarizes these four symbols.

As a descriptor field, the ampersand represents a variable-length string field. The number of positions used to display the string is dependent on the internal size of the string. The ampersand indicates the beginning position in which the string is displayed, and expansion is to the right in the line. Table 4.16 summarizes the use of the ampersand. Program 4.11, on the opposite page, gives examples of the use of the ampersand. Note that the underscore (-) is used in line 200 to precede the exclamation point (!). This informs the PC that the exclamation point is a string constant to be displayed, not a descriptor field.

TABLE 4.16 Use of the Ampersand (&) as a Descriptor Field

DESCRIPTOR FIELD	DATA	OUTPUT	REMARKS
&	ABC	ABC	*The character A is placed exactly in the line at the location specified by the ampersand. The B and C are placed in & + 1 and & + 2 positions of the line, respectively.*
&	ABCDE	ABCDE	
&	A	A	

The exact number of positions to use for displaying a string value can be specified by using two backslashes separated by zero or more spaces. The number of positions in the descriptor field, including the two backslashes, indicate how many positions are to be used to display the string value. The string value is aligned in the descriptor field left-justified. If the internal value of the string contains fewer characters than the descriptor field, the string value is filled with spaces on the right in the print line. If the internal value of the string contains more characters than the descriptor field, the string value is truncated on the right. Table 4.17, on the following page, summarizes the use of the backslash, and Program 4.12 gives examples of its use.

PROGRAM 4.11

```
100 ' Program 4.11
110 ' Use of the Ampersand and the
120 ' Underscore as Descriptor Fields
130 ' *****************************
140 CLS : KEY OFF  ' Clear Screen
150 SHORT$  = "REM"
160 MIDDLE$ = "Remark"
170 LONG$   = "Remarkable"
180 PRINT USING "The keyword &"; SHORT$
190 PRINT USING "represents  &."; MIDDLE$
200 PRINT USING "Isn't that  &_!"; LONG$
210 PRINT USING "So &"; SHORT$;
220 PRINT USING "&"; "arkable"
230 END

RUN

The keyword REM
represents  Remark.
Isn't that  Remarkable!
So REMarkable
```

___TABLE 4.17 Use of the Backslash (\) in a Descriptor Field___

DESCRIPTOR FIELD	NUMBER OF SPACES BETWEEN BACKSLASHES	DATA	OUTPUT	REMARKS
\ \	3	ABCDE	ABCDE	*Size of descriptor field and string value the same.*
\ \	1	ABCDE	ABC	*The last two characters are truncated.*
\\	0	ABCDE	AB	*The last three characters are truncated.*
\ \	6	ABCDE	ABCDEƀƀ	*Three spaces are appended to the right of the string value in the print line.*

PROGRAM 4.12

```
100 ' Program 4.12
110 ' Use of Two Backslashes in a Descriptor Field
120 ' *******************************************
130 CLS : KEY OFF  ' Clear Screen
140 PRINT      "Name     Address     City-State    Zip Code"
150 PRINT      "----     -------     ----------    --------"
160 FORMAT$ = "\     \ \      \ \      \ \      \"
170 READ CUST.NAME$, CUST.STREET$, CUST.CITY$, CUST.ZIP$
180 PRINT USING FORMAT$; CUST.NAME$, CUST.STREET$, CUST.CITY$, CUST.ZIP$
190 ' ************** Data Follows **************
200 DATA Jones J., 451 W 45th, "Munster, IN", 46321-0452
210 END

RUN

Name      Address     City-State     Zip Code
----      -------     ----------     --------
Jones J.  415 W 45th  Munster, IN    46321-0452
```

Study closely the method used in lines 140 through 160 in Program 4.12 to align the fields. The string constants in lines 140 and 150 are purposely started six positions to the right of the keyword PRINT so that the column headings align with the string constant in line 160. This technique will be used throughout this book.

The exclamation point is used as a descriptor field to specify a one-position field in the print line. If the internal value of the string to be displayed is longer than one character, only the leftmost character is displayed. Table 4.18 summarizes the use of the exclamation point, and Program 4.13 illustrates its use.

TABLE 4.18 Use of the Exclamation Point (!) as a Descriptor Field

DESCRIPTOR FIELD	DATA	OUTPUT	REMARKS
!	JOE	J	*First initial of name displayed.*
!	XYZ	X	

PROGRAM 4.13

```
100 ' Program 4.13
110 ' Use of the Exclamation Point as a Descriptor Field
120 ' ******************************************************
130 READ FIRST.NAME$, MIDDLE.NAME$, LAST.NAME$
140 PRINT USING "!. !. \          \"; FIRST.NAME$, MIDDLE.NAME$,LAST.NAME$
150 ' **************** Data Follows ******************
160 DATA George, Alfred, Smith
170 END

RUN

G. A. Smith
```

TRY IT YOURSELF

Load Program 4.12 (PRG4-12) from the Student Diskette. In line 160, replace each of the four sets of backslashes (\) with an exclamation point (!). Place the exclamation point at the beginning of each column heading. Execute the program and compare the results to those displayed by the original Program 4.12.

The LPRINT USING Statement

Like the LPRINT statement, the LPRINT USING statement prints the results on the printer. Everything that has been presented with respect to the PRINT USING statement also applies to the LPRINT USING statement. This statement gives you the capacity to print results according to a predefined format on the printer.

Programming Case Study 7: *Determining the Accounts Receivable Balance*

This problem and its program solution incorporate much of the information discussed so far in this chapter, including the following useful techniques for formatting a report:

1. Align the detail lines with the column headings.
2. Force decimal-point alignment.
3. Control the number of digits displayed in a result.
4. Specify that commas and decimal points are to be appropriately displayed in numeric results.

Problem: Ron's Family Discount House would like its PC to generate a management report for the accounts receivable balance for a monthly billing period. The following formula is used to determine the balance:

End of Month Balance = Beginning of Month Balance –
Payments + Purchases – Credits +
Service Charge on Ending Unpaid Balance

The following formula is used to compute the service charge:

Service Charge = 19.5% Annually on the Unpaid Balance
or
= 0.01625 ∗ (Beginning of Month Balance –
Payments – Credits) per Month

The input data for each customer includes customer number, beginning-of-month balance, payments, purchases, and credits. The following accounts receivable data is to be processed:

Customer Number	Beginning Balance	Payment	Purchases	Credit
14376172	$1,112.32	$35.00	$56.00	$ 0.00
16210987	30.00	30.00	15.00	0.00
18928384	125.50	25.00	0.00	12.50
19019293	120.00	12.00	12.00	23.00
19192929	10.00	7.00	2.50	1.50
EOF	0	0	0	0

The program should generate a report that includes report and column headings and a line of information for each customer. Each line is to include the five values read for each customer, the service charge, and end-of-month balance as described on the **printer spacing chart** shown in Figure 4.7. Lines 1 through 4 of the printer spacing chart define the report and column headings. Line 6 defines the **detail line** that is displayed for each record processed: the row of Xs on line 6 describes an area for a string value, and the groups of 9s, with commas and decimal points, describe areas for numeric values. Finally, line 8 describes the end-of-job message.

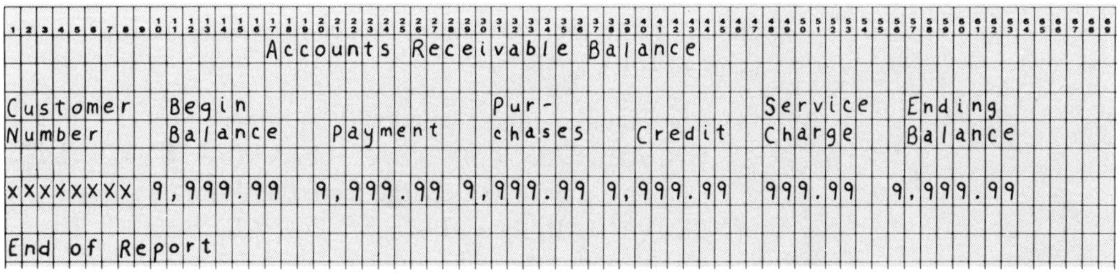

FIGURE 4.7
Output for Program 4.14, designed on a printer spacing chart.

Following are a top-down chart (Figure 4.8 on the following page); a list of the program tasks that correspond to the top-down chart; a program solution; and a discussion of the program solution.

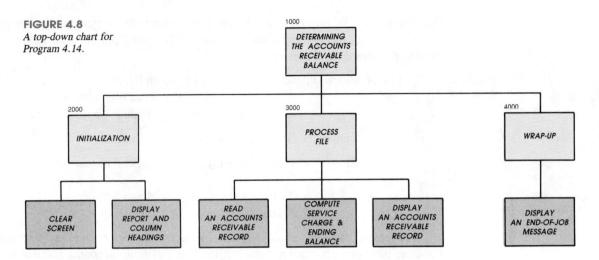

FIGURE 4.8
A top-down chart for Program 4.14.

Program Tasks The following program tasks correspond to the top-down chart in Figure 4.8.

1. Initialization

    a. Clear the screen.

    b. Display report and column headings described on the printer spacing chart in Figure 4.7.

    c. In a string expression, define the detail line described on the printer spacing chart in Figure 4.7.

2. Process File

    a. Read an accounts receivable record; use the following variable names:

        CUSTOMER$: Customer Number
        BEG.BAL: Beginning Balance
        PAYMENTS: Payments
        PURCHASES: Purchases
        CREDITS: Credits

    b. Use a `WHILE` statement to establish a loop. The condition within the `WHILE` statement should allow the loop to be executed as long as CUSTOMER$ does not equal the sentinel value EOF.

      (1) Compute the unpaid balance from this formula:
         UNPAID.BAL = BEG.BAL – PAYMENTS – CREDITS
      (2) Compute the service charge from this formula:
         SERV.CHARGE = 0.01625 * UNPAID.BAL
      (3) Compute the end-of-month balance from this formula:
         END.BAL = UNPAID.BAL + PURCHASES + SERV.CHARGE
      (4) Employ the `PRINT USING` statement to display the seven values pertaining to the customer.
      (5) Read the next accounts receivable record

3. Wrap-up — display the message `End of Report`.

Program Solution   The following program corresponds to the top-down chart in Figure 4.8 and the preceding tasks. The blue-colored symbols in Figure 4.8 are implemented in Program 4.14 as modules. The grey-colored symbols represent subtasks that have been moved into their superior modules in Program 4.14.

PROGRAM 4.14

```
1000 ' Program 4.14
1010 ' Determining the Accounts Receivable Balance
1020 ' *********************************************
1030 ' *                Main Module                *
1040 ' *********************************************
1050 GOSUB 2000   ' Call Initialization
1060 GOSUB 3000   ' Call Process File
1070 GOSUB 4000   ' Call Wrap-up
1080 END
1090 '
2000 ' *********************************************
2010 ' *              Initialization               *
2020 ' *********************************************
2030 CLS : KEY OFF  ' Clear Screen
2040 PRINT        "              Accounts Receivable Balance"
2050 PRINT
2060 PRINT        "Customer  Begin                 Pur-              Service   Ending"
2070 PRINT        "Number    Balance   Payment    chases   Credit  Charge    Balance"
2080 FORMAT$ = "\       \ #,###.##   #,###.## #,###.## #,###.##   ###.## #,###.##"
2090 PRINT
2100 RETURN
2110 '
3000 ' *********************************************
3010 ' *              Process File                 *
3020 ' *********************************************
3030 READ CUSTOMER$, BEG.BAL, PAYMENTS, PURCHASES, CREDITS
3040 WHILE CUSTOMER$ <> "EOF"
3050    UNPAID.BAL  = BEG.BAL - PAYMENTS - CREDITS
3060    SERV.CHARGE = .01625 * UNPAID.BAL
3070    END.BAL     = UNPAID.BAL + PURCHASES + SERV.CHARGE
3080    PRINT USING FORMAT$; CUSTOMER$, BEG.BAL, PAYMENTS, PURCHASES,
                            CREDITS, SERV.CHARGE, END.BAL
3090    READ CUSTOMER$, BEG.BAL, PAYMENTS, PURCHASES, CREDITS
3100 WEND
3110 RETURN
3120 '
4000 ' *********************************************
4010 ' *                Wrap-up                    *
4020 ' *********************************************
4030 PRINT
4040 PRINT "End of Report"
4050 RETURN
4060 '
4070 ' ************** Data Follows ****************
4080 DATA 14376172, 1112.32, 35,   56,    0
4090 DATA 16210987,      30, 30,   15,    0
4100 DATA 18928384,   125.5, 25,    0, 12.5
4110 DATA 19019293,     120, 12,   12,   23
4120 DATA 19192929,      10,  7,  2.5,  1.5
4130 DATA EOF,           0,  0,    0,    0
4140 ' ************** End of Program **************
RUN
```

The output results for Program 4.14 are shown on the following page.

Accounts Receivable Balance

Customer Number	Begin Balance	Payment	Pur-chases	Credit	Service Charge	Ending Balance
14376172	1,112.32	35.00	56.00	0.00	17.51	1,150.83
16210987	30.00	30.00	15.00	0.00	0.00	15.00
18928384	125.50	25.00	0.00	12.50	1.43	89.43
19019293	120.00	12.00	12.00	23.00	1.38	98.38
19192929	10.00	7.00	2.50	1.50	0.02	4.02

End of Report

Discussion of the Program Solution

When the RUN command is issued for Program 4.14, control transfers to the Initialization Module. The PC clears the screen and then executes the PRINT statements (lines 2040 and 2070) that display the report and column headings. Line 2080 assigns FORMAT$ the descriptor field for the detail line described on the printer chart in Figure 4.7. FORMAT$ is referenced later by the PRINT USING statement in line 3080. Note that line 3080 extends beyond 80 columns. When keying in a line that exceeds 80 characters, simultaneously press the Control (Ctrl) and Enter keys to advance the cursor to the next physical line.

After the Initialization Module is complete, the GOSUB statement in line 1060 calls the Process File Module. In line 3030, the READ statement causes the PC to read the first record found in line 4080. Since the first record is not the end of file, the WHILE statement in line 3040 passes control to line 3050 and customer 14376172 is processed.

After the second record is read, the WEND statement in line 3080 instructs the PC to loop back to line 3040 to test for end of file. The second record is processed and displayed before the PC reads the next record. This process continues until all of the accounts receivable records have been processed. When the trailer record is read, control returns to the Main Module, which then calls the Wrap-up Module. After the message End of Report is displayed, control returns to the Main Module and Program 4.14 is terminated by line 1080.

The report shows that through the use of the PRINT USING statement in line 3080, Program 4.14 displays all monetary values rounded to the nearest cent, with decimal points aligned and right-justified below the column headings. The customer number, which is defined as a string item, is displayed left-justified. The significance of taking the time to lay out the report on a printer spacing chart should be apparent in Programming Case Study 7. Once the printer spacing chart is complete, the format of the report can be copied directly into the program, as shown in lines 2040 through 2080 of the Initialization Module in Program 4.14.

With the output techniques discussed thus far in this chapter, you can now begin to dress up the output. Programmers often forget that most people who use the results of computer-generated reports are unfamiliar with computers and are confused by poorly formatted output. You now have the capacity in MS BASIC to produce high-quality reports that are meaningful and easy to read.

TRY IT YOURSELF

Load Program 4.14 (PRG4-14) from the Student Diskette. Display and execute the program. Modify line 2080 by removing the commas and displaying the numeric values to the nearest dollar. Execute the program and see what happens.

⊞ 4.6

THE LOCATE STATEMENT

The LOCATE statement may be used to position the cursor on the screen. It may also be used to make the cursor a block or an underscore. In the 80-column display mode, MS BASIC defines the screen as having 25 rows and 80 columns (see Figure 2.6 on page 38). The LOCATE statement can position the cursor precisely on any one of the two thousand print positions on the screen.

The general form of the LOCATE statement is shown in Table 4.19. The values that follow the keyword LOCATE are called **parameters**.

————**TABLE 4.19** The LOCATE Statement————

General Form:	LOCATE row, column, cursor where **row** represents the row and is a numeric expression between 1 and 25; **column** represents the column and is a numeric expression between 1 and 80 for the 80-column display mode and between 1 and 40 for the 40-column display mode; and **cursor** is a numeric expression equivalent to 0 or 1. Zero makes the cursor a block and 1 makes the cursor an underscore.
Purpose:	Positions the cursor precisely on the screen and makes the cursor a block or an underscore.
Keyword Entry:	Simultaneously press the Alt and L keys.
Examples:	100 LOCATE 5, 10 200 LOCATE 1, 1 300 KEY OFF : LOCATE 25, 4 400 LOCATE 7 500 LOCATE , 50 600 LOCATE 4, 6, 0 700 LOCATE , , 1
Note:	The LOCATE statement may also be used to control the size of the cursor. For further information on controlling the size of the cursor, see the MS BASIC user's manual.

In Table 4.19, line 100 moves the cursor to column 10 on line 5. It makes no difference whether the cursor is above or below line 5 or to the right or left of column 10; when line 100 is executed, the cursor is moved to the specified location.

Line 200 moves the cursor to the home position: leftmost column on line 1. The cursor is located at column 4 on line 25 following the execution of line 300 in Table 4.19. It is important that the KEY OFF statement be executed to clear line 25 before the LOCATE statement is executed. If the display of the description of the function keys is not turned off, then the execution of line 300 will result in the following error message:

```
Illegal function call
```

One of the interesting characteristics of line 25 is that unlike the other 24 lines, it does not scroll. For this reason, line 25 is often used to display messages that are of a more permanent nature. Line 400 in Table 4.19 moves the cursor directly up or down to the same column on line 7. In line 500, the row is left blank, and in this case, the PC moves the cursor to column 50 of the current line. When the parameters row, column, or cursor in the LOCATE statement are left blank, the PC uses the current value.

Line 600 of Table 4.19 causes the PC to position the cursor in column 6 of line 4. Furthermore, the third parameter, zero, instructs the PC to make the cursor a block. With line 700, the cursor remains at the current position and is made an underscore.

The following revised version of Programming Case Study 5A illustrates the use of the PRINT USING and LOCATE statements. In addition, a new procedure for displaying messages on the screen is presented.

Programming Case Study 5B: *Finding the Single Discount Rate with a Fixed-Screen Format and an End-of-File Test*

Let's consider a refined program solution to Programming Case Study 5A, Finding the Single Discount. Add the following to the original program specifications presented in chapter 3 on page 65.

1. Redesign the output results so that they agree with the format shown on the **screen layout form** in Figure 4.9. A screen layout form is similar to a printer spacing chart in that it allows you to construct a skeleton of the output results for a video display device.
2. Format the single discount in the manner shown in Figure 4.9.
3. Allow the operator to decide whether he or she wants to enter another series of discounts or terminate execution of the program.

FIGURE 4.9
Output for Program 4.15, designed on a screen layout form.

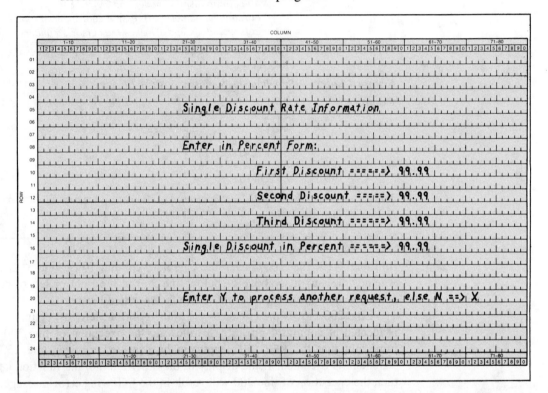

Following are a top-down chart (see Figure 4.10 on the opposite page); a list of the additional program tasks; a program solution; and a discussion of the program solution.

Additional Program Tasks

1. Use the LOCATE statement to position the cursor for each line displayed. Display all instructions and messages once in the Initialization Module. Leave the instructions and messages on the screen for the duration of execution of the program. Use the LOCATE statement and SPC function to blank out the results to the right of the instructions before processing another series of discounts.
2. Use the PRINT USING statement to format the single discount.
3. Establish a While loop within the Process Request Module. Just prior to the WHILE statement, assign the variable (CONTROL$) used in the condition in the WHILE statement a value (Y) that will ensure at least one pass through the While loop.
4. Following the display of the single discount, call upon a module that uses the INPUT statement to accept a response from the operator as to whether he or she wants to determine another single discount. After accepting the response, clear the screen of the previous inputs and results.

FIGURE 4.10
*A top-down chart for
Program 4.15.*

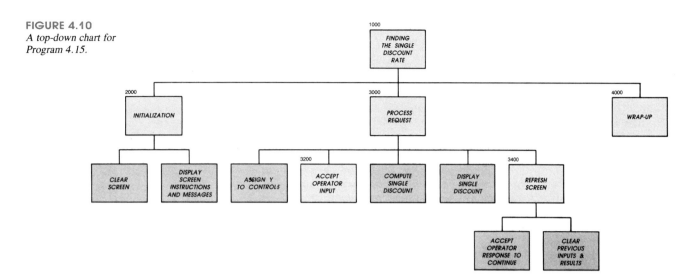

Program Solution   The following program corresponds to the top-down chart in Figure 4.10 and the preceding tasks.

PROGRAM 4.15

```
1000 ' Program 4.15
1010 ' Finding the Single Discount Rate
1020 ' **********************************************
1030 ' *                Main Module                 *
1040 ' **********************************************
1050 GOSUB 2000    ' Call Initialization
1060 GOSUB 3000    ' Call Process Request
1070 GOSUB 4000    ' Call Wrap-up
1080 END
1090 '
2000 ' **********************************************
2010 ' *               Initialization               *
2020 ' **********************************************
2030 CLS : KEY OFF   ' Clear Screen
2040 LOCATE   5, 25 : PRINT "Single Discount Rate Information"
2050 LOCATE   8, 25 : PRINT "Enter in Percent Form:"
2060 LOCATE  10, 37 : PRINT "First Discount ======> "
2070 LOCATE  12, 37 : PRINT "Second Discount =====> "
2080 LOCATE  14, 37 : PRINT "Third Discount ======> "
2090 LOCATE  16, 25 : PRINT "Single Discount in Percent ======>"
2100 LOCATE  20, 25 : PRINT "Enter Y to process another request, else N ==>"
2110 RETURN
2120 '
3000 ' **********************************************
3010 ' *               Process Request              *
3020 ' **********************************************
3030 CONTROL$ = "Y"   '  Initialize CONTROL$ to Ensure One Pass on Loop
3040 WHILE CONTROL$ = "Y"
3050    GOSUB 3200   ' Call Accept Operator Input
3060    RATE = 1 - (1 - RATE1 / 100) * (1 - RATE2 / 100) * (1 - RATE3 / 100)
3070    RATE = 100 * RATE
3080    LOCATE 16, 59 : PRINT USING " ##.##"; RATE
3090    GOSUB 3400   '  Call Refresh Screen
3100 WEND
3110 RETURN
3120 '
```

(continued)

```
3200 ' *********************************************
3210 ' *             Accept Operator Input          *
3220 ' *********************************************
3230 LOCATE 10, 60 : INPUT "", RATE1
3240 LOCATE 12, 60 : INPUT "", RATE2
3250 LOCATE 14, 60 : INPUT "", RATE3
3260 RETURN
3270 '
3400 ' *********************************************
3410 ' *                Refresh Screen              *
3420 ' *********************************************
3430 LOCATE 20, 72 : INPUT "", CONTROL$
3440 LOCATE 10, 60 : PRINT SPC(7)
3450 LOCATE 12, 60 : PRINT SPC(7)
3460 LOCATE 14, 60 : PRINT SPC(7)
3470 LOCATE 16, 60 : PRINT SPC(7)
3480 LOCATE 20, 72 : PRINT SPC(7)
3490 RETURN
3500 '
4000 ' *********************************************
4010 ' *                   Wrap-up                  *
4020 ' *********************************************
4030 CLS ' Clear Screen
4040 LOCATE 12, 25 : PRINT "End of Program — Have a Nice Day"
4050 RETURN
4060 ' ************* End of Program ***************
RUN
```

Discussion of the Program Solution

When the RUN command is issued for Program 4.15, the GOSUB 2000 in line 1050 transfers control to the Initialization Module. In the top-down chart in Figure 4.10, the Initialization Module has two subtasks. Line 2030 clears the screen and lines 2040 through 2100 display *all* of the instructions and messages specified on the screen layout form described in Figure 4.9. The display from these lines is shown in Figure 4.11. Line 3030 of the process Request Module assigns CONTROL$ the value Y. This ensures that the WHILE statement in line 3040 of the Process Request Module will allow the PC to execute the statements within the While loop at least once.

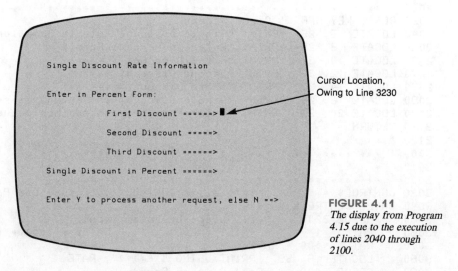

FIGURE 4.11
The display from Program 4.15 due to the execution of lines 2040 through 2100.

It is not necessary to place all of the subtasks of the Initialization Module and Process Request Module shown in Figure 4.10 in separate subroutines. Remember that a top-down chart, like the one in Figure 4.10, shows what must be done to solve the problem. At coding time, potential modules that contain only a few lines of code may be placed directly in the superior module. The decision as to whether a subtask in a top-down chart should be a separate module in a program becomes easier to make with experience.

In the Accept Operator Input Module, lines 3230 through 3250 employ the LOCATE and INPUT statements to accept the three discounts from the operator. You'll recall that the LOCATE statement is capable of moving the cursor back to the end of the corresponding instruction, which is already displayed. Each INPUT statement has the null string as the prompt message. The null string is employed so that we can use the comma to eliminate the question mark that is displayed when no prompt message is used.

Once the single discount has been determined by lines 3060 and 3070, line 3080 displays the formatted result. The INPUT statement in line 3430 of the Refresh Screen Module causes the PC to halt execution until a response to continue is entered by the operator. This gives the operator time to read the results. When the operator finishes reading the results, he or she enters a response. If the operator enters a Y, as shown in Figure 4.12, then the PC will make another pass through the While loop. On the other hand, if the operator enters an N (or presses any key other than a Y), control returns to the Main Module, and the Wrap-up Module displays a message before the END statement in line 1080 terminates execution of the program. Note that in line 4040 of the Wrap-up module, a pleasant message to the operator is displayed as part of the end-of-job routine.

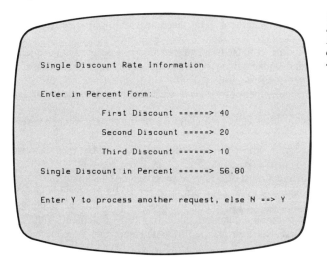

FIGURE 4.12
Screen display from Program 4.15 when entering discounts of 40%, 20%, and 10%.

The last important point regarding Program 4.15 concerns lines 3430 through 3480 in the Refresh Screen Module. These lines are used to refresh the screen in preparation for the next set of data to be entered by the operator. In each of these lines, the LOCATE statement is used to move the cursor to the exact position where previous data entered by the operator is displayed on the screen. Following each LOCATE statement, the SPC function is used in a PRINT statement to blank out the previous data. SPC(7) blanks out seven positions to the right, beginning with the location of the cursor. If you plan to use this procedure to build screens, it is important to remember that the LOCATE statement does not clear the screen. Any old data will remain on the screen unless it is cleared. Clearing the data from the screen is the purpose of lines 3430 through 3480.

TRY IT YOURSELF

Load Program 4.15 (PRG4-15) from the Student Diskette. Display and execute the program. Enter the following sets of data:

Set 1: 10%, 15%, 25%   Set 3: 22.25%, 34.55%, 46.99%
Set 2: 2%, 4%, 6%   Set 4: 99.99%, 99.99%, 99.99%

Step through the program and try to determine which statement the PC is attempting to execute when it suspends execution to accept the data.

⊞ 4.7 WHAT YOU SHOULD KNOW

1. A loop in a program instructs the PC to repeat a series of instructions. A loop that is defined by the WHILE and WEND statements is called a While loop. The WHILE statement indicates the beginning of the loop; the WEND statement indicates the end of the loop.
2. One execution of a loop is a pass.
3. A condition is a relationship that is either true or false. A condition is made up of two expressions that are separated by a relational operator. There are six valid relational operators: greater than (>); less than (<); equal to (=); greater than or equal to (>=); less than or equal to (<=); and not equal to (<>).
4. The DATA statement provides for the creation of a sequence of data items for use by the READ statement.
5. The DATA statement consists of the keyword DATA followed by a list of data items, which can be either numeric or string. If string data contains a leading or trailing blank or an embedded comma or colon, the data must be enclosed in quotation marks.
6. The DATA statement is a nonexecutable statement. The placement of DATA statements has no bearing on the execution of the program.
7. Data items from all DATA statements are collected and placed into one single data-sequence holding area. The order in which the data items appear among all DATA statements determines the order of the data items in the single data-sequence holding area.
8. The READ statement provides for the assignment of values to variables from a sequence of data items created from DATA statements.
9. The READ statement consists of the keyword READ followed by a list of variables that are separated by mandatory commas.
10. Every variable appearing in the program whose value is directly obtained by a READ must be listed in a READ statement before it is used in the program.
11. A program that contains a READ statement must also have at least one DATA statement.
12. The RESTORE statement allows the data in a given program to be reread by READ statements as often as necessary.
13. The RESTORE statement consists of the keyword RESTORE followed by an optional line number. If the line number is not present, the pointer is restored to the first data item in the first DATA statement. If the line number is present, then the pointer is restored to the first data item in the DATA statement that is referenced by the specified line number.
14. The PRINT statement consists of the keyword PRINT. It may also have an optional list of print items that are separated by mandatory commas, semicolons, or spaces. The print items may be numeric or string constants, variables, expressions, or null items. In addition, the print items may include useful functions like TAB and SPC.
15. The comma separator in a PRINT statement allows you to display output automatically positioned in a tabular format that is determined by five print zones in the 80-column display mode and two print zones in the 40-column display mode. Each print zone has 14 positions.
16. If a PRINT statement contains no list of print items, then a blank line results.
17. The semicolon separator can be used to generate output in a compressed or packed format. Any number of spaces between two print items is the same as the semicolon separator.
18. The TAB function is used in the PRINT statement to specify the exact print positions for the various output results on a given print line.
19. The SPC function is used to insert spaces (filler) between print items.
20. MS BASIC allows calculations to be made within the PRINT statement.
21. In immediate mode, MS BASIC permits the PC to be used as a powerful desk calculator.
22. The PRINT USING statement is useful in controlling the output format.
23. One or more consecutive format symbols appearing in a string expression comprise a descriptor field or field format.

24. Depending on the type of editing desired, numeric descriptor fields can include a number sign, decimal point, comma, dollar sign, plus or minus sign, asterisk, and four consecutive circumflexes.
25. Descriptor fields for string values use the exclamation point, ampersand, underscore, and two backslashes separated by n spaces (which reserve n + 2 positions in the line) to display a string.
26. While the PRINT and PRINT USING statements display results on the screen, the LPRINT and LPRINT USING statements print the results on a printer.
27. In the 80-column display mode, the display screen has 25 lines. Each line has 80 columns. In the 40-column display mode, the display screen has 40 columns in each of 25 rows. The LOCATE statement is used to position the cursor on the screen.

⊞ 4.8 TEST YOUR BASIC SKILLS (Even-numbered answers are at the back of the book, before the index.)

1. Consider the valid programs listed below. What is displayed if each program is executed?

a.
```
100 ' Exercise 4.1a
110 ' MPG Comparison
120 READ CAR.MODEL$, MILES, GALLONS
130 WHILE CAR.MODEL$ <> "EOF"
140    MPG = MILES / GALLONS
150    PRINT "Car model ===> "; CAR.MODEL$
160    PRINT "Miles =======>"; MILES
170    PRINT "Gallons =====>"; GALLONS
180    PRINT "Mpg =========>"; MPG
190    PRINT
200    READ CAR.MODEL$, MILES, GALLONS
210 WEND
220 PRINT "Job Finished"
230 ' *** Data Follows ***
240 DATA A,   1275, 41.7
250 DATA B,    685, 23.2
260 DATA C,   1650, 62.5
270 DATA EOF, 0,    0
280 END
```

b.
```
100 ' Exercise 4.1b
110 READ X, Y
120 WHILE X <> -1
130    PRINT "Old value of X ="; X
140    PRINT "Old value of Y ="; Y
150    T = X
160    X = Y
170    Y = T
180    PRINT "New value of X ="; X
190    PRINT "New value of Y ="; Y
200    PRINT
210    READ X, Y
220 WEND
230 LOCATE 13, 7 : PRINT "Job Finished"
240 ' *** Data Follows ***
250 DATA  4, 6
260 DATA  3, 7
270 DATA -1, 0
280 END
```

c.
```
1000 ' Exercise 4.1c
1010 ' ******* Main Module ********
1020 GOSUB 2000   ' Call Initialization
1030 GOSUB 3000   ' Call Process File
1040 GOSUB 4000   ' Call Wrap-up
1050 END
1060 '
2000 ' ******* Initialization ******
2010 CLS : KEY OFF  ' Clear Screen
2020 A = 0
2030 B = 0
2040 COUNT = 0
2050 RETURN
2060 '
3000 ' ******** Process File *******
3010 READ X, Y
3020 WHILE Y >= 0
3030    A = A + X
3040    B = B + Y
3050    COUNT = COUNT + 1
3060    PRINT COUNT; A; B
3070    READ X, Y
3080 WEND
3090 RETURN
3100 '
4000 ' ********* Wrap-up ***********
4010 LOCATE 1, 14, 0
4020 PRINT USING "Count ====> ###"; COUNT
4030 LOCATE 3, 14, 1 : PRINT "FINIS"
4040 RETURN
4050 '
4060 ' ******* Data Follows *******
4070 DATA 4, 9, 6, 10, 8, 12, 0, -1
4080 ' ****** END OF PROGRAM ******
```

d.
```
100 ' Exercise 4.1d
110 ' Displaying Hi!
120 CLS : KEY OFF  ' Clear Screen
130 ROW = 12
140 COLUMN = 31
150 CURSOR = 0
160 WHILE ROW < 20
170    COLUMN = COLUMN + 4
180    LOCATE ROW , COLUMN, CURSOR : PRINT "Hi!"
190    ROW = ROW + 1
200 WEND
210 END
```

e.
```
100 ' Exercise 4.1e
110 ' Nested While Loops
110 CLS : KEY OFF  ' Clear Screen
120 ROW = 0
130 WHILE ROW < 10
140    ROW = ROW + 1
150    COLUMN = 0
160    WHILE COLUMN < 40
170       COLUMN = COLUMN + 1
180       LOCATE ROW, COLUMN : PRINT "*"
190    WEND
200 WEND
210 END
```

2. Which of the following are true?

   a. Backspacing on the same line is permissible with the TAB function.
   b. It is invalid to have a DATA statement without a READ statement in a program.
   c. Every program must have a PRINT statement.
   d. It is invalid to have a WHILE statement with a higher line number than its corresponding WEND statement in a program.
   e. It is invalid to have more data items in a DATA statement than are required by a READ statement.
   f. The LOCATE statement is used to position the cursor vertically and horizontally on the screen.
   g. The RESTORE statement instructs the system to execute the program beginning at the lowest line number.
   h. It is valid to have two adjacent commas in a DATA statement.
   i. The LOCATE statement is used to clear a specific position on the screen.

3. How many values will be read from a DATA statement by the following READ statement?

   a. 110 READ A, B   b. 120 READ J, K, K, J

4. Write a sequence of LOCATE and PRINT statements that will display the value of A in column 7 of the first line and the value of B in column 45 of the fourth line.

5. Write a single PRINT statement to compute and display:

   a. $\sqrt{Y}$ b. $\sqrt[3]{Y}$ c. $\sqrt[4]{Y}$

6. Write a PRINT USING statement that includes the string constant for the purpose of displaying the message The amount is followed by the value of AMOUNT. Include a numeric descriptor field with the following characteristics:

   a. five digit positions, two to the right of the decimal point;
   b. a floating dollar sign;
   c. a sign status to the right of the number; and
   d. three or more check protection asterisks.

7. Determine whether the conditions below are true or false, given the following: CREDIT.UNION = 25, INS.DED = 20, and SALARY = 900

   a. CREDIT.UNION >= 25   b. SALARY / INS.DED < CREDIT.UNION
   c. INS.DED = CREDIT.UNION - 5   d. SALARY <> 800
   e. 875 + CREDIT.UNION <= SALARY f. INS.DED > 20

8. Write a sequence of statements that will clear the screen and display the value 6 in print position 6 of line 6.

9. Write a LOCATE and PRINT statement that will cause the the following to be displayed starting in column 20 of line 7:

   ```
   Customer name =====>
   ```

10. Indicate the location of the cursor immediately after line 110 is executed in the partial program below.

    ```
    100 LOCATE 5, 12, 1 : PRINT "PC"
    110 LOCATE 14
    ```

11. Consider the valid programs listed below. What is displayed if each program is executed?

    ```
    a. 100 ' Exercise 4.11a
       110 PRINT "Net"; "    "; "Pay"
       120 PRINT TAB(11); "Net Pay"
       130 PRINT
       140 PRINT "N"; SPC(3); "e"; SPC(3); "t"; SPC(3); "P";
       150 PRINT SPC(3); "a"; SPC(3); "y"
       160 END
    ```

```
b. 100 ' Exercise 4.11b
   110 PRINT "Hours", "Gross", "FICA", "FIT"
   120 PRINT "Hours"; "Gross"; "FICA"; "FIT"
   130 PRINT
   140 PRINT 10, 20, 30, 30 - 10
   150 PRINT 10; 20; 30; 30 - 10
   160 PRINT
   170 PRINT TAB(10); "Hours"
   180 PRINT "Hours"; TAB(40); "Gross"
   190 END
```

12. What kind of graphic output displays from this program?

```
   100 ' Exercise 4.12
   110 CLS : KEY OFF   ' Clear Screen
   120 LOCATE 10, 3 : PRINT "VVVVV"
   130 LOCATE 11, 2 : PRINT "X"; TAB(8); "X"
   140 LOCATE 12, 1 : PRINT "X"; TAB(4); "O"; TAB(6); "O"; TAB(9); "X"
   150 LOCATE 13, 1 : PRINT "X"; TAB(9); "X"
   160 LOCATE 14, 1 : PRINT "X"; TAB(5); "U"; TAB(9); "X"
   170 LOCATE 15, 1 : PRINT "X"; TAB(3); "("; TAB(7); ")"; TAB(9); "X"
   180 LOCATE 16, 1 : PRINT "X"; TAB(5); "-"; TAB(9); "X"
   190 LOCATE 17, 2 : PRINT "X"; TAB(8); "X"
   200 LOCATE 18, 3 : PRINT "XXXXX"
   210 END
```

13. Write a program that will generate the following graphic output. Use the LOCATE statement to position the upper-leftmost asterisk in column 33 of line 8.

```
* * * * * * * * * * * *
*  B  A  S  I  C  *
B  L           N  B
A     E     R     A
S        A        S
I     E     R     I
C  L           N  C
*  B  A  S  I  C  *
* * * * * * * * * * * *
```

14. Write a PRINT USING statement that displays the value of LAST.NAME$ beginning in position 1, as follows:

   a. only the first character of LAST.NAME$ is displayed;
   b. all of LAST.NAME$ is displayed;
   c. the first six characters of LAST.NAME$ are displayed; and
   d. the first two characters of LAST.NAME$ are displayed.

15. Write a sequence of LOCATE and PRINT statements to display the following triangle, with the vertex at print position 20 on line 9. Clear the screen before displaying the triangle.

16. For each of the following descriptor fields and corresponding data, indicate what the computer displays. Use the letter b̶ to indicate the space character.

	Descriptor Field	Data	Result		Descriptor Field	Data	Result
a.	###	25		b.	#,###.##	38.4	
c.	$$,###.##-	-22.6		d.	$#,###.##-	425.89	
e.	**#,###.##	88.756		f.	#,###.#	637214	
g.	##.##-	3.975		h.	###.##	-123.8	
i.	##,###.###	12.6143		j.	##.##^^^^	265.75	
k.	!	ABCD		l.	&	ABCD	
m.	\\ (zero spaces)	ABCD		n.	\ \ (2 spaces)	ABCD	

17. Use the Student Diskette to complete the Try It Yourself exercises on pages 94, 98, 105, 114, 118, and 124.

⊞ 4.9 BASIC PROGRAMMING PROBLEMS

1. Determining the Price/Earnings Ratio

Purpose: To become familiar with the top-down approach, READ, DATA, and PRINT statements, and While loops.

Problem: Construct a top-down program to compute and display the Price/Earnings (P/E) ratio for companies whose current stock prices and earnings per share are known. Process the companies listed in the table below until the stock name is equal to the value EOF. Use the top-down chart illustrated in Figure 4.1 on page 90 as a guide to solving this problem.

The P/E ratio is a useful tool that is employed by stock-market analysts in evaluating the investment potential of various companies. The P/E ratio is determined by dividing the price of a share of stock by the company's latest earnings per share.

Input Data: Prepare and use the following sample data.

	Stock Name	Price per Share	Latest Earnings
	Cray	125-⅛	4.00
	Digital	162-½	6.50
	DataGn	32-⅛	0.30
	IBM	154	7.70
Trailer	Prime	21-⅞	0.95
Record ⟶	EOF	0	0

Output Results: The following results are displayed.

```
              P/E Ratio Report

Stock         Price per    Latest      P/E
Name          Share        Earnings    Ratio
-----         ---------    --------    -----

Cray          125.125      4           31.28125
Digital       162.5        6.5         25
DataGn        32.125       .3          107.0833
IBM           154          7.7         20
Prime         21.875       .95         23.02632

End of Stock Report
```

Alternative Formatted Output Results: Employ the PRINT USING statement to display all numeric fields to the nearest hundredth place. Align all numeric fields on the decimal point. Under the column headings, left-justify string values and right-justify numeric values. The following formatted results are displayed.

```
              P/E Ratio Report

Stock         Price per    Latest      P/E
Name          Share        Earnings    Ratio
-----         ---------    --------    -----

Cray          125.13       4.00        31.28
Digital       162.50       6.50        25.00
DataGn         32.13       0.30        107.08
IBM           154.00       7.70        20.00
Prime          21.88       0.95        23.03

End of Stock Report
```

2. Inflation Gauge

Purpose: To become familiar with gauging inflation and the use of the WHILE, WEND, READ, DATA, and PRINT statements.

Problem: Write a top-down program to input today's current price, the previous price, and the number of weeks between price quotes. Compute the sample annual inflation rate and the expected price of the item one year from today's current price. For each item processed, display the item, current price, computed annual inflation rate, and expected price in one year. Use the top-down chart illustrated in Figure 4.8 on page 116 as a guide to solving this problem.

Input Data: Prepare and use the following sample data.

Item	Current Price	Previous Price	Number of Weeks
1 doz. eggs	$0.93	$0.92	13
1 lb. butter	2.59	2.50	15
1 gal. milk	1.92	1.85	18
1 loaf bread	1.10	1.07	6

Output Results: The following results are displayed.

```
                 Inflation Gauge Report

                 Current      Inflation     Expected
  Item           Price        Rate in %     Price in 1 Yr
  ----           -------      ---------     -------------

  1 doz. eggs    .93          4.301071      .97
  1 lb. butter   2.59         12.04632      2.902
  1 gal. milk    1.92         10.5324       2.122222
  1 loaf bread   1.1          23.63634      1.36

  Job Finished
```

Alternative Formatted Output Results: Employ the PRINT USING statement to align the decimal points and display all numeric results to the nearest hundredth place, right-justified under their column headings.

3. Determining the Point of Intersection

Purpose: To become familiar with While loops, testing for end of file, and the READ, DATA, and PRINT statements.

Problem: Maximum profit or minimum cost can often be determined from equations based on known facts concerning a product. The point of intersection of the equations is significant. Write a top-down program to find the point of intersection for two first-degree equations in two variables (that is, two equations and two unknowns). The general form for two equations is as follows:

$$a_1x + b_1y = c_1 \qquad a_2x + b_2y = c_2$$

Its solutions are expressed by the following equations:

$$x = \frac{c_1b_2 - c_2b_1}{a_1b_2 - a_2b_1} \qquad\qquad y = \frac{c_2a_1 - c_1a_2}{a_1b_2 - a_2b_1}$$

The program should read the coefficients (a_1, b_1, c_1, a_2, b_2, and c_2, in this order) from a DATA statement; solve for x and y; and display the values of a_1, b_1, and c_1 on one line and a_2, b_2, c_2, x, and y on the next line. The program should loop back and process the set of data for the next system of equations. Terminate the While loop within the Process File Module when a_1 is equal to –999.999. Use the top-down chart illustrated in Figure 4.8 on page 116 as a guide to solving this problem. Also, make your program efficient by computing the denominator of x and y only once.

Input Data: Prepare and use the following sample data.

System	Equation 1 Coefficients			Equation 2 Coefficients		
	a	b	c	a	b	c
1	1	1	5	1	–1	1
2	2	–7	8	3	1	–8
3	0.6	–0.75	–8	0.6	–0.125	2

Output Results: The following results are displayed.

```
    <-----------Equations------------>    <----Intersection--->

    Coeff A      Coeff B      Coeff C     X Value      Y Value
    -------      -------      -------     -------      -------

      1            1            5
      1           -1            1          3            2

      2           -7            8
      3            1           -8         -2.086957    -1.73913

      .6          -.75         -8
      .6          -.125         2          6.666667     16

    End of Report
```

Alternative Formatted Output Results: Employ the PRINT USING statement to display the results of x and y to the nearest thousandth place, right-justified under the column headings and with decimal points aligned.

4. Determining the Eventual Cash Value of an Annuity

Purpose: To become familiar with the LOCATE statement; looping; the hierarchy of operations in a complex LET statement; and building a screen for data entry.

Problem: An annuity, or installment plan, is a series of payments made at equal intervals of time. Examples of annuities are pensions and premiums on life insurance. More often than not, the interest conversion period is unequal to the payment interval. The following formula determines the eventual cash value of an annuity of R dollars paid per year in P installments for N years at an interest rate of J percent converted M times a year.

$$S = R \left[\frac{\left(1 + \frac{J}{M}\right)^{MN} - 1}{P\left[\left(1 + \frac{J}{M}\right)^{M/P} - 1\right]} \right]$$

where
S = eventual cash value
R = payment per year
P = number of installments per year
N = duration of the annuity in years
J = nominal interest rate
M = conversions per year

Write a top-down program to determine the eventual cash value of an annuity. After processing the first annuity, loop back to process the next annuity.

Prior to processing the first annuity, clear the screen and use the LOCATE statement to center the instructions and messages. Display the instruction and message portions only *once*. After the results for the first set of data are displayed, request that the operator enter Y to process another set of data and N to terminate the program. If Y is entered, use the SPC function to clear the numeric values, and then request the operator to enter the next set of data. (**Hint:** See the top-down chart in Figure 4.10 and Program 4.15 on page 121.)

Input Data: Prepare and use the following sample data.

Data

Description	Set 1	Set 2	Set 3
Payment per year	$2000	$3000	$4000
Installments per year	12	12	12
Time in years	20	20	20
Interest rate in %	13	14	15
Conversions per year	2	4	6

Output Results: The results shown below are displayed for set 1. Begin the screen title on line 5, column 25. After that, skip a line between each line displayed. Skip three lines prior to the last line. When the operator requests that the program terminate, clear the screen and display an appropriate message. The Eventual Cash Value for sets 2 and 3 are $318,119.80 and $492,591.70.

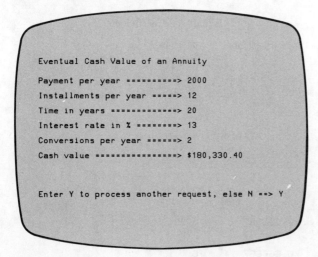

```
Eventual Cash Value of an Annuity

Payment per year ==========> 2000

Installments per year ======> 12

Time in years ==============> 20

Interest rate in % =========> 13

Conversions per year ======> 2

Cash value ================> $180,330.40



Enter Y to process another request, else N ==> Y
```

5. Payroll Problem III: Biweekly Payroll Report

Purpose: To become familiar with looping and the use of the PRINT USING, READ, and DATA statements.

Problem: Modify Payroll Problem II in chapter 3 on page 88 (BASIC programming problem 6) to generate a report with column headings and a line of information for each employee. Each line is to include employee number, gross pay, federal withholding tax, and net pay.

Input Data: Use the sample data found in Payroll Problem II. Add a trailer record. Select your own sentinel value.

Output Results: The following results are displayed.

```
                  Biweekly Payroll Report
      Employee
      Number      Gross Pay      Fed. Tax      Net Pay
      --------    ---------      --------      -------

        123       1,000.00        184.62        815.38
        124         800.00        152.31        647.69
        125       1,040.00        200.31        839.69
        126          90.00          2.62         87.38

      End of Payroll Report
```

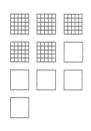

STRUCTURED PROGRAMMING AND MENU-DRIVEN PROGRAMS

It is appropriate at this time to introduce some important concepts related to **structured programming**.

Structured programming is a methodology according to which all program logic can be constructed from a combination of the following three basic logic structures:

1. **Sequence.** The most fundamental of the logic structures, it provides for two or more actions to be executed in the order in which they appear.
2. **If-Then-Else** or **Selection.** Provides a choice between two alternative actions.
3. **Do-While** or **Repetition.** Provides for the repeated execution of a loop.

The following are two common extensions to these logic structures:

4. **Do-Until** or **Repeat-Until.** An extension of the Do-While logic structure.
5. **Case.** An extension of the If-Then-Else logic structure, in which the choice includes more than two alternatives.

So far in this book, the Sequence and Do-While logic structures have been used, even though they have not been identified by their formal names.

The use of structured programming offers definite advantages. Computer scientists have found that when it is applied correctly in the construction of programs, structured programming confers the following benefits:

1. Programs are clearer and more readable.
2. Less time is spent debugging, testing, and modifying the program.
3. The programmer's productivity is increased.
4. The quality, reliability, and efficiency of the program are improved.

Clearly, there are important payoffs in the use of structured programming.

Logic Structures

In the previous chapter, the programs performed precisely the same computation for every set of data items that was processed. In some applications, it is not always desirable to process each set of data items in exactly the same way. For example, in a program that computes gross pay, some employees may be eligible for overtime (the number of hours they worked in a given week is greater than 40), while others may not. Therefore, in a payroll computation, a decision must be made concerning which of two gross pay formulas to use.

The sequential flow of control within modules used in previous programs and shown in Figure 5.1 is not sufficient to solve problems that involve **decision making.** To develop an algorithm that requires deviation from sequential control, we need another logic structure. This new structure, called If-Then-Else, is shown in Figure 5.2. It is also described in detail in Appendix A, section A.4.

FIGURE 5.1
Sequence structure.

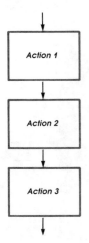

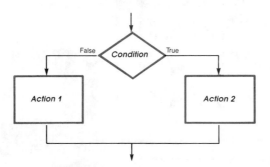

FIGURE 5.2
If-Then-Else structure.

The flowchart representation of a decision is the diamond-shaped symbol. One flowline will always be shown entering the symbol, and two lines will always be shown leaving the symbol. A condition that must be either true or false is written within the decision symbol. Such a condition asks, for example, whether two variables are equal or whether an expression is within a certain range. If the condition is true, one path is taken; if not, the other path is taken.

To instruct the PC to select actions on the basis of the values of variables, as illustrated in Figure 5.2, MS BASIC includes the IF statement. This chapter presents a number of examples to illustrate how IF statements are used to implement If-Then-Else structures.

The ON-GOSUB statement may be used to implement an extension of the If-Then-Else structure, in which selection of one of many alternatives is based on an integer test. This extended version of the If-Then-Else structure is called the Case structure; it is illustrated in Figure 5.3 and described in Appendix A, section A.4. As we shall see later in this chapter, the Case structure is commonly used to implement **menu-driven programs**. A menu-driven program is one in which a **menu** or series of menus is used to guide an operator through a multifunction interactive program. The menu itself lists the functions that a program or a section of a program can perform.

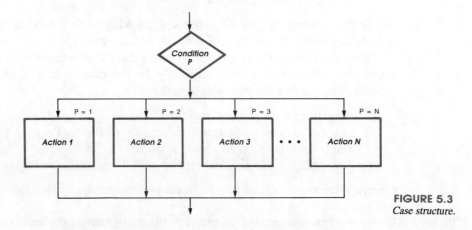

FIGURE 5.3
Case structure.

As we saw in chapter 4 with looping, it is necessary to include within the repeatedly executed process a decision to terminate the loop after a sufficient number of repetitions has occurred. Most computer scientists agree that the decision to terminate a loop should be located at the very top or very bottom of the loop. A loop that has the termination decision at the top is called a Do-While structure (see Figure 5.4). All of the loops presented in chapter 4 were of this variety.

A loop that has the termination decision at the bottom is called a Do-Until structure (see Figure 5.5). The major difference between the two structures lies in the minimum number of times the loop may be executed. With the Do-While structure, where the decision is at the top of the loop, it is possible that the body of the loop may be executed zero times. With the Do-Until structure, the body of the loop is always executed at least once. See Appendix A, section A.4 for additional information on the Do-While and Do-Until logic structures.

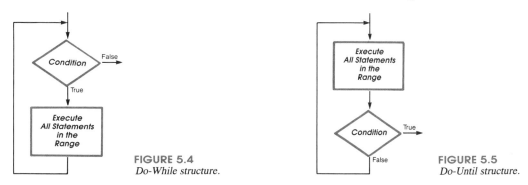

FIGURE 5.4
Do-While structure.

FIGURE 5.5
Do-Until structure.

Combining Conditions

Logical operators, like AND, OR, and NOT, may be used to combine conditions in order to reduce the number of statements required to implement certain If-Then-Else structures. In this chapter, we shall discuss these three logical operators and three others — XOR, EQV, and IMP.

Logical operators are often used in programs to verify that the data entered by the operator is within a range that will generate valid results when the program is run. This is called **data validation**.

Top-Down Versus Structured

In chapter 3, you studied concepts associated with the top-down or modular approach. In this chapter, you will study structured programming. Do not confuse structured programming with top-down programming; they are *not* the same.

When the expression *top-down* is used with any data-processing task associated with analysis, design, programming, testing, debugging, maintenance, or documentation, it describes a strategy for solving large, complex problems. To solve a problem top-down, you divide and conquer. For example, **top-down design** is a design strategy that breaks large, complex problems into smaller, less complex problems and then breaks down each one of these — decomposes them — into even smaller problems. In **top-down (modular) programming**, high-level modules are coded as soon as they are designed, generally before the low-level modules have been designed.

For now, you should know that whenever the word *structured* is appended to any of these data-processing tasks, it is used to describe a task that is well organized, rigorous, and formal. Structured programming is used within modules to generate disciplined code. We improve the clarity and reduce the complexity of our code when we use only these five constructs: Sequence, If-Then-Else, Do-While, Do-Until, and Case.

In designing a solution top-down, we use a top-down chart to determine *what must be done*, as described in chapter 3. In designing a structured programming solution for a subtask, we use the program flowchart or some other logic tool to resolve the question of *how to implement* the subtask. Emphasis is placed on decision making and looping. Besides program flowcharts, the common logic tools used by programmers are pseudocode, Nassi-Schneiderman charts, and Warnier-Orr diagrams. For a discussion of these alternative logic tools, see Appendix B.

Upon successful completion of this chapter, you will be able to apply concepts related to structured programming and top-down design. You will also be able to develop algorithms and write programs that include decisions, controlled loops, accumulators, logical operators, data-validation techniques, and menus.

⊞ 5.2

THE IF STATEMENT

The IF statement is commonly regarded as the most powerful statement in MS BASIC. The major function of this statement is to perform selection. In selection, the IF statement is used to let a program choose between two alternative paths, as illustrated earlier in Figure 5.2. The general form of the IF statement is given in Table 5.1.

——TABLE 5.1 The IF Statement——

General Form:	IF *condition* THEN *clause* ELSE *clause* *or* IF *condition* THEN *clause* where **condition** *is a relationship that is either true or false, and* **clause** *is a statement or series of statements (separated by colons).*
Purpose:	*If the condition is true, the PC executes the statement or series of statements following the keyword* THEN. *If the condition is false, the PC executes the statement or series of statements following the keyword* ELSE. *After either clause is executed, control passes to the next numbered line following the* IF *statement.*
Keyword Entry:	*For the keyword* THEN, *simultaneously press the Alt and T keys on your keyboard. For the keyword* ELSE, *simultaneously press the Alt and E keys on your keyboard.*
| ***Examples:*** | ```
100 IF TAX >= 0
        THEN SWITCH = 0
200 IF LABEL.1$ <> LABEL.2$
        THEN PRINT LABEL.1$ : RESTORE
300 IF 2 * A * B <= 0
        THEN PRINT Q : READ W
        ELSE GOSUB 3000
400 IF A$ = "YES"
        THEN GOSUB 2000
500 IF LABEL$ <> "275"
        THEN PRINT LABEL.1$ : PRINT : GOSUB 6000
        ELSE PRINT LABEL.2$ : PRINT : GOSUB 7000
600 IF SEX.CODE$ = "M"
        THEN MALE = MALE + 1
        ELSE FEMALE = FEMALE + 1
700 IF J > 5
        THEN IF J < 10 THEN PRINT E
                            ELSE PRINT G
``` |
| ***Note:*** | 1. *All of the* IF *statements in this table include more than one physical line with indention used for the purpose of readability. To end a physical line with fewer than 80 characters displayed, simultaneously press the Ctrl and Enter keys. Press the Enter key to end the last physical line.*
2. *In the general form, either clause may be a line number to which the PC transfers control. This option will not be used in this book.* |

As indicated in Table 5.1, the IF statement is used to specify a decision. The condition appears between the keywords IF and THEN. As with the WHILE statement in chapter 4, the condition specifies a relationship between expressions which is either true or false. The relationship is a comparison between one numeric expression and another or between one string expression and another. In determining whether or not a condition is true, the PC first determines the single value of each expression in the condition and then evaluates them both with respect to the relational operator. Table 4.3 in chapter 4, on page 94, lists the six relational operators that are used to indicate the type of comparison.
```

If the condition in an IF statement is true, the PC acts upon the THEN clause. If the condition is false, the PC acts upon the ELSE clause. In either case, or if no ELSE clause exists and the condition is false, control passes to the next numbered line following the IF statement.

The following partial flowchart illustrates the use of the If-Then-Else structure to resolve a gross pay computation in which employees are paid a fixed rate per hour for hours worked less than or equal to 40 and time and a half for hours worked greater than 40.

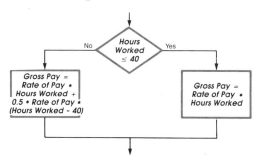

The gross pay computation illustrated in the partial flowchart may be written as a module in MS BASIC as follows:

```
3400 ' ********** Compute Gross Pay - Style 1 **********
3410 IF HOURS <= 40
        THEN GROSS = HOURS * RATE
        ELSE GROSS = HOURS * RATE + 0.5 * RATE * (HOURS - 40)
3420 RETURN
3430 '
```

Line 3410 selects a LET statement to compute the gross pay (GROSS). If hours worked (HOURS) is less than or equal to 40, the gross pay is computed by means of the LET statement following THEN. If the condition, HOURS <= 40, is false, then the gross pay is computed by means of the LET statement following ELSE. In either case, control passes to the RETURN statement in line 3420.

Note the programming style that was used to write the Gross Pay Computation Module. The THEN and ELSE clauses are on separate lines without line numbers. Furthermore, for the sake of readability, the keywords THEN and ELSE are indented three spaces in relation to the keyword IF. This programming style will be used to write most of the IF statements in this book.

The Gross Pay Computation Module could also have been written with the following programming style:

```
3400 ' ********** Compute Gross Pay - Style 2 **********
3410 IF HOURS<=40 THEN GROSS=HOURS*RATE ELSE GROSS=HOURS*RATE+0.5*RATE*(HOURS-40)
3420 RETURN
3430 '
```

This style of cramming the characters is valid but somewhat awkward to read.

Logical Versus Physical Lines

MS BASIC differentiates between a **logical line** and a **physical line**. A logical line is composed of a line number that is followed by one or more physical lines that have no line numbers. Each logical line may contain up to 255 characters (254 plus the Enter key). Each physical line, except for the last, contains 80 characters. The last physical line contains the exact number of characters displayed and the Enter key. Therefore, a logical line may have a maximum of four physical lines. The last physical line may have up to 15 characters.

To terminate a physical line with fewer than 80 characters displayed, press simultaneously the Ctrl and Enter keys. This combination of keys causes the PC to fill the remainder of the physical line with blank characters and to move the cursor to column 1 of the next physical line. You end the last physical line by pressing the Enter key. Consider again the first version of line 3410, presented on the previous page:

Press simultaneously the Ctrl and Enter keys.

```
One      { 3410 IF HOURS <= 40
Logical  {         THEN GROSS = HOURS * RATE
Line     {         ELSE GROSS = HOURS * RATE + 0.5 * RATE * (HOURS - 40)
```

Press the Enter key.

As illustrated here, line 3410 is a logical line that is comprised of three physical lines.

We may state the following rules in regard to logical versus physical lines.

> ***Line Rule 1:*** A logical line is composed of a line number followed by one or more physical lines that have no line numbers. Each logical line may contain up to 255 characters (254 plus the Enter key).

> ***Line Rule 2:*** Each physical line, except for the last, contains 80 characters. The last physical line contains the exact number of characters displayed and the Enter key.

> ***Line Rule 3:*** To end a physical line with fewer than 80 characters displayed, press simultaneously the Ctrl and Enter keys. To end the last physical line, press the Enter key.

Comparing Numeric Expressions

If the condition in an IF statement includes two numeric expressions, the comparison is based on the algebraic values of the two expressions. That is, the PC evaluates not only the magnitude of each resultant expression but also its sign. Lines 100 through 400 in Table 5.2, on the next page, illustrate several examples of IF statements that include conditions made up of numeric expressions.

Comparing String Expressions

If the condition in an IF statement includes two string expressions, the PC evaluates the two strings from left to right, one character at a time. Two string expressions are considered equal if they are of the same length and contain an identical sequence of characters. As soon as one character in an expression is different from the corresponding character in the other expression, the comparison stops and the PC decides which expression has a lower value, generally on the basis of numerical and alphabetical order. In other words, the PC evaluates two string expressions the same way you would. For example,

> DOE is less than JOE
> JEFF is greater than JAFF
> NO is not equal to No
> YES is equal to YES
> TAPE is greater than TAP

The PC determines which characters are "less" than others on the basis of the code that is used to store data in main storage. This code is called the **ASCII code (American Standard Code for Information Interchange)**. A total of 256 different characters can be entered into main storage. The ASCII code and the **collating sequence** of the 256 characters are shown in Appendix D, Table D.2. The collating sequence is the position of a character in relation to other characters. As Table D.2 shows, numbers are less than uppercase letters in value, which are in turn less than lowercase letters in value. The null character is considered to have the least value in the collating sequence.

Lines 500 through 800 in Table 5.2 illustrate examples of IF statements that include conditions made up of string expressions.

_____TABLE 5.2_ Examples of IF Statements_____

THE STATEMENT	VALUE OF VARIABLES	RESULT

100 IF X < Y
        THEN PRINT A : TAX = TAX + 10
        ELSE PRINT B : TAX = TAX + 5
	X = 7
	Y = 9
		The value of A is displayed, TAX is incremented by 10, and control passes to the line number following 100.

200 IF D <> A - B - 6 THEN PRINT S	D = 23 A = 14 B = -15	*Control passes to the line number following 200.*

300 IF 12.7 <= S
        THEN
        ELSE PRINT Y : PRINT Z
	S = 12.7	*The* THEN *clause is null. Control passes to the line number following 300.*

400 IF A + B >= 2
        THEN EMP.CNT1 = EMP.CNT1 + 1
        ELSE
	A = 3
	B = 2
		EMP.CNT1 is incremented by 1 and control passes to the line number following 400. Note that the ELSE *clause is null.*

500 IF A$ = "NO" THEN PRINT A$	A$ = "No"	*The line following 500 is executed, since "No" and "NO" are not the same string.*
600 IF B$ <= H$ + J$ THEN S = S - 1	B$ = "abx" H$ = "a" J$ = "by"	*S is decremented by 1 and control passes to the line following 600.*

700 IF "Sh2" > V$
        THEN B = 10
        ELSE READ A
	V$ = "Sh1"	*B is assigned a value of 10 and control passes to the line number following 700.*

800 IF A$ + B$ < C$ + MID$(A$,1,2)
        THEN READ A$, B$
        ELSE READ B$, A$
	A$ = "12"
	B$ = "12"
	C$ = "12"
		Values are assigned to B$ and A$, in that order. Control passes to the line number following 800.

⊞ 5.3

ACCUMULATORS

Most programs require **accumulators**, which are used to develop totals. Accumulators are initialized to a value of zero in the Initialization Module, then incremented within the loop in the Process File Module, and then manipulated or displayed in the Wrap-up Module. Although the PC automatically initializes numeric variables to zero, good programming practice demands that this be done in the program. There are two types of accumulators: counters and running totals. Both types are discussed in the sections that follow.

Counters

A **counter** is an accumulator that is used to count the number of times some action or event is performed. For example, appropriately placed within a loop, the statement

```
3050 EMP.COUNT = EMP.COUNT + 1
```

causes the counter EMP.COUNT to increment by 1 each time a record is read. Associated with a counter is a statement placed in the Initialization Module which initializes the counter to some value. In most cases the counter is initialized to zero.

Running Totals

A **running total** is an accumulator that is used to sum the different values that a variable is assigned during the execution of a program. For example, appropriately placed within a loop, the statement

```
3070 CMPY.SALARY = CMPY.SALARY + EMP.SALARY
```

causes CMPY.SALARY (company monthly salary) to increase by the value of

EMP.SALARY. CMPY.SALARY is called a running total. If a program is processing an employee file and the variable EMP.SALARY is assigned the employee's monthly salary each time a record is read, then variable CMPY.SALARY in line 3070 below represents the running total of the monthly salaries paid to all the employees in the file. As with a counter, a running total must be initialized to some predetermined value in the Initialization Module.

Consider the following partial program, which includes both counters and a running total. Assume that each time a record is read, EMP.SEX$ is assigned a value of M or F and EMP.SALARY is assigned the employee's monthly salary.

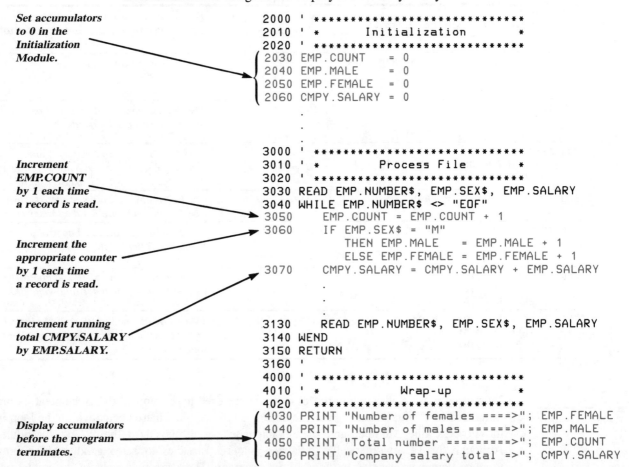

Set accumulators to 0 in the Initialization Module.

```
2000 ' ****************************
2010 ' *        Initialization        *
2020 ' ****************************
2030 EMP.COUNT    = 0
2040 EMP.MALE     = 0
2050 EMP.FEMALE   = 0
2060 CMPY.SALARY = 0
     .
     .
     .
3000 ' ****************************
3010 ' *          Process File          *
3020 ' ****************************
3030 READ EMP.NUMBER$, EMP.SEX$, EMP.SALARY
3040 WHILE EMP.NUMBER$ <> "EOF"
3050     EMP.COUNT = EMP.COUNT + 1
3060     IF EMP.SEX$ = "M"
             THEN EMP.MALE    = EMP.MALE + 1
             ELSE EMP.FEMALE = EMP.FEMALE + 1
3070     CMPY.SALARY = CMPY.SALARY + EMP.SALARY
     .
     .
     .
3130     READ EMP.NUMBER$, EMP.SEX$, EMP.SALARY
3140 WEND
3150 RETURN
3160 '
4000 ' ****************************
4010 ' *              Wrap-up              *
4020 ' ****************************
4030 PRINT "Number of females ====>"; EMP.FEMALE
4040 PRINT "Number of males ======>"; EMP.MALE
4050 PRINT "Total number =========>"; EMP.COUNT
4060 PRINT "Company salary total =>"; CMPY.SALARY
```

Increment EMP.COUNT by 1 each time a record is read.

Increment the appropriate counter by 1 each time a record is read.

Increment running total CMPY.SALARY by EMP.SALARY.

Display accumulators before the program terminates.

Lines 2030 through 2060 in the Initialization Module initialize the accumulators to zero. Each time a record is read, line 3050 increments EMP.COUNT by 1. The PC then compares EMP.SEX$ to the string value M and the THEN or ELSE clause is executed. Line 3070 increments the company monthly salary running total (CMPY.SALARY) by the employee's monthly salary (EMP.SALARY). Finally, in the Wrap-up Module, lines 4030 through 4060 display the values of EMP.FEMALE, EMP.MALE, EMP.COUNT, and CMPY.SALARY.

Programming Case Study 8A: *Weekly Payroll and Summary Report*

The following example incorporates both a counter and a running total, as well as some of the concepts discussed earlier in this section. Furthermore, instead of the report and column headings being displayed in the Initialization Module, an alternative method is presented, in which the report format and the display of the report and column headings are executed in separate modules, called from the Initialization Module.

Problem: A payroll application requires that the employee number, the hours worked, the rate of pay, and the gross pay be displayed for each of the following employees.

Employee Number	Hours Worked	Rate of Pay
124	40	$5.60
126	56	5.90
128	38	4.60
129	48.5	6.10

Also, the total gross pay, the total number of employees, and the average gross pay for this payroll are to be displayed. The required report is described on the printer spacing chart shown in Figure 5.6.

FIGURE 5.6
Output for Program 5.1 designed on a printer spacing chart.

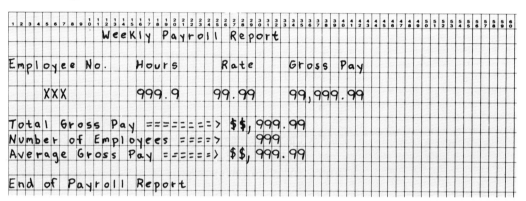

The gross pay is determined by multiplying the hours worked by the hourly rate of pay. Overtime (hours in excess of 40) is paid at 1.5 times the hourly rate.

Following are the program tasks in outline form; a top-down chart with two program flowcharts of subtasks; a program solution; and a discussion of the program solution.

Program Tasks   The following program tasks correspond to the top-down chart in Figure 5.7 on the following page.

1. Initialization

    a. Initialize a counter (EMP.COUNT) and running total (TOTAL.GROSS) to zero. Use the counter to determine the total number of employees processed. Use the running total to determine the total gross pay.
    b. Clear the screen.
    c. Initialize the report format — assign the heading lines, the detail line, and the total lines, described in Figure 5.6, to string variables.
    d. Display the report and column headings.

2. Process File

    a. Read an employee record. Use the following variable names for the employee record:

        EMP.NUMBER$: employee number
        EMP.HOURS: employee hours
        EMP.RATE: employee hourly rate

b. Use a `WHILE` statement to establish a loop for processing the employee records until EMP.NUMBER\$ equals the value EOF. If end of file, return control to the Main Module. If not end of file, do the following:

    (1) Determine the gross pay and increment accumulators.

        (a) Increment the counter EMP.COUNT by 1.

        (b) Compute the employee overtime (EMP.OVERTIME).

        (c) Determine the gross pay (EMP.GROSS). If EMP.OVERTIME is less than or equal to zero, use this formula:

$$\text{EMP.GROSS} = \text{EMP.HOURS} * \text{EMP.RATE}$$

If EMP.OVERTIME is greater than zero, use this formula:

$$\text{EMP.GROSS} = \text{EMP.HOURS} * \text{EMP.RATE} + 0.5 * \text{EMP.RATE} * \text{EMP.OVERTIME}$$

        (d) Increment the running total (TOTAL.GROSS) by the employee gross pay (EMP.GROSS).

    (2) Display an employee record.

    (3) Read the next employee record.

3. Wrap-up

    a. Compute the average employee gross pay (AVERAGE.GROSS).

    b. Display the accumulators (TOTAL.GROSS and EMP.COUNT) and average employee gross pay (AVERAGE.GROSS).

    c. Display an end-of-job message.

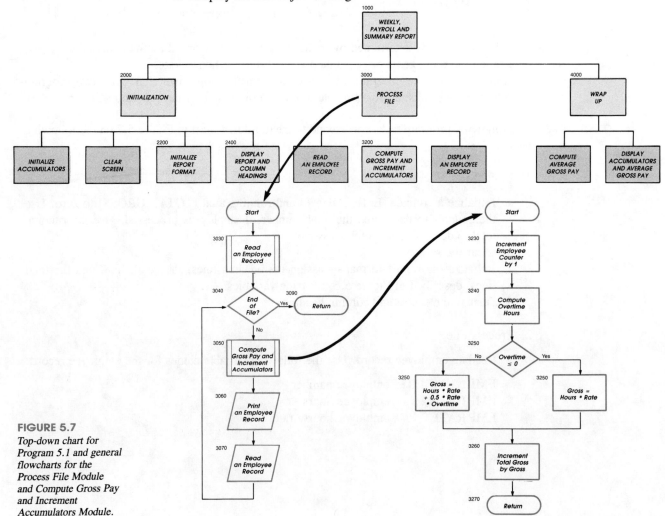

FIGURE 5.7

Top-down chart for Program 5.1 and general flowcharts for the Process File Module and Compute Gross Pay and Increment Accumulators Module.

Program Solution   The following program corresponds to the preceding tasks and to the top-down chart in Figure 5.7.

PROGRAM 5.1

```
1000 ' Program 5.1
1010 ' Weekly Payroll and Summary Report
1020 ' ****************************************************
1030 ' *                 Main Module                      *
1040 ' ****************************************************
1050 GOSUB 2000   ' Call Initialization
1060 GOSUB 3000   ' Call Process File
1070 GOSUB 4000   ' Call Wrap-up
1080 END
1090 '
2000 ' ****************************************************
2010 ' *                Initialization                    *
2020 ' ****************************************************
2030 EMP.COUNT   = 0
2040 TOTAL.GROSS = 0
2050 CLS : KEY OFF   ' Clear Screen
2060 GOSUB 2200   ' Call Initialize Report Format
2070 GOSUB 2400   ' Call Display Report and Column Headings
2080 RETURN
2090 '
2200 ' ****************************************************
2210 ' *            Initialize Report Format              *
2220 ' ****************************************************
2230 HEAD.LN1$ = "        Weekly Payroll Report"
2240 HEAD.LN2$ = "Employee No.   Hours     Rate     Gross Pay"
2250 DETL.LN$  = "    \     \        ###.#    ##.##     ##,###.##"
2260 TOT.LN1$  = "Total Gross Pay ========> $$,###.##"
2270 TOT.LN2$  = "Number of Employees ====>     ###"
2280 TOT.LN3$  = "Average Gross Pay ======> $$,###.##"
2290 TOT.LN4$  = "End of Payroll Report"
2300 RETURN
2310 '
2400 ' ****************************************************
2410 ' *       Display Report and Column Headings         *
2420 ' ****************************************************
2430 PRINT HEAD.LN1$
2440 PRINT
2450 PRINT HEAD.LN2$
2460 PRINT
2470 RETURN
2480 '
3000 ' ****************************************************
3010 ' *                Process File                      *
3020 ' ****************************************************
3030 READ EMP.NUMBER$, EMP.HOURS, EMP.RATE
3040 WHILE EMP.NUMBER$ <> "EOF"
3050    GOSUB 3200   ' Call Compute Gross Pay & Increment Accums.
3060    PRINT USING DETL.LN$; EMP.NUMBER$, EMP.HOURS,
                              EMP.RATE, EMP.GROSS
3070    READ EMP.NUMBER$, EMP.HOURS, EMP.RATE
3080 WEND
3090 RETURN
3100 '
3200 ' ****************************************************
3210 ' *  Compute Gross Pay & Increment Accumulators      *
3220 ' ****************************************************
3230 EMP.COUNT = EMP.COUNT + 1
3240 EMP.OVERTIME = EMP.HOURS - 40
```

(continued)

```
3250 IF EMP.OVERTIME <= 0
         THEN EMP.GROSS = EMP.HOURS * EMP.RATE
         ELSE EMP.GROSS = EMP.HOURS * EMP.RATE + .5 * EMP.RATE * EMP.OVERTIME
3260 TOTAL.GROSS = TOTAL.GROSS + EMP.GROSS
3270 RETURN
3280 '
4000 ' **************************************************
4010 ' *                    Wrap-up                     *
4020 ' **************************************************
4030 AVERAGE.GROSS = TOTAL.GROSS / EMP.COUNT
4040 PRINT
4050 PRINT USING TOT.LN1$; TOTAL.GROSS
4060 PRINT USING TOT.LN2$; EMP.COUNT
4070 PRINT USING TOT.LN3$; AVERAGE.GROSS
4080 PRINT
4090 PRINT TOT.LN4$
4100 RETURN
4110 '
4120 ' ************** Data Follows *****************
4130 DATA 124, 40,   5.60
4140 DATA 126, 56,   5.90
4150 DATA 128, 38,   4.60
4160 DATA 129, 48.5, 6.10
4170 DATA EOF, 0,    0    : ' This is the trailer record
4180 ' ************** End of Program ***************

RUN

              Weekly Payroll Report

   Employee No.   Hours    Rate    Gross Pay

       124        40.0     5.60       224.00
       126        56.0     5.90       377.60
       128        38.0     4.60       174.80
       129        48.5     6.10       321.77

   Total Gross Pay ========> $1,098.17
   Number of Employees ====>       4
   Average Gross Pay ======>    $274.54

   End of Payroll Report
```

Discussion of the
Program Solution
The solution to the Weekly Payroll and Summary Report, as represented by the top-down chart in Figure 5.7 and the corresponding Program 5.1, includes a few significant points that did not appear in previous programs. They are as follows:

1. The use of a counter (EMP.COUNT) and a running total (TOTAL.GROSS). Both are both initialized to zero (lines 2030 and 2040) and are incremented each time an employee record is read. The counter is used to keep track of the total number of employees and is incremented in line 3230. The running total is used to sum the gross pay and is incremented by the individual employee gross pay in line 3260.

2. The Initialization Module calls two modules. The first one, Initialize Report Format (lines 2200 through 2310), assigns each output line, described on the printer spacing chart in Figure 5.6, to a string variable. Later, these string variables are used in PRINT and PRINT USING statements to display the required output. The second module (lines 2400 through 2480) displays the report and column headings according to the format established in the Initialize Report Format Module.

3. A decision is made in line 3250 to determine which one of the two formulas is to be used to compute the gross pay. If EMP.OVERTIME is less than or equal to zero, the PC uses the THEN clause. If EMP.OVERTIME is greater than zero, the PC uses the ELSE clause.

4. The Wrap-up Module (lines 4000 to 4110) involves calculating an average that is based on the total gross pay (TOTAL.GROSS) and the number of employees (EMP.COUNT) and displaying these totals and the average.

5. By calculating the overtime in line 3240 and assigning it to the variable EMP.OVERTIME, we are able to eliminate the recomputation of this value. Whenever a value is required several times in a program, it is better to compute it once and assign it a variable that can be referenced later, as in line 3250, than to recompute it every time it is needed.

Try It Yourself

1. Load Program 5.1 (PRG5-1) from the Student Diskette. Display the program and execute it. After the results are displayed, modify the program by changing line 2070 and line 3060 to comments so that PRG5-1 displays only the summary totals.

2. Reload PRG5-1. Modify it by changing lines 4130 through 4160 to comments. Execute the modified version of Program 5.1. Now do you understand why it is important to have at least one line of data (excluding the trailer record) for this program?

Programming Styles

You should be aware that there are several ways to modularize and code Program 5.1. For example, some programmers prefer to place the single statement that reads a record (line 3030 or line 3070 in Program 5.1) and the statement that prints the detail line (line 3060 in Program 5.1) in separate subroutines. The authors did not follow this programming style since it tends to increase the complexity of a program and creates confusion by containing too many unnecessary levels of subroutines.

The authors believe a program should be easy to read and understand while still maintaining its structure. We do not believe in using unnecessary subroutines merely for the sake of subroutine usage.

⊞ 5.4

IMPLEMENTING THE DO-WHILE AND DO-UNTIL LOGIC STRUCTURES

In designing and implementing a loop, think carefully about where to place the decision to terminate the loop. As mentioned earlier, most computer scientists recommend that the decision to terminate should be at the very top or very bottom of the loop.

If, in the design of a solution, the decision to terminate is at the top of the loop (Do-While), then use the WHILE and WEND statements to implement the loop. The program flowchart in Figure 5.7 on page 142 has the decision to terminate at the very top of the loop. It is the same logic structure that we used in chapter 4. In each case, we used the WHILE and WEND statements to implement the loop.

Keep in mind that with the Do-While loop, the body of the loop may be executed a minimum of zero times. This would be the case, for example, if the first DATA statement in a program contained the trailer record, as shown in part 2 of the above Try It Yourself.

If, in the design of a solution, the decision to terminate is at the bottom of the loop (Do-Until), then you can only simulate the Do-Until structure in MS BASIC; there is no UNTIL statement. Simulating a Do-Until structure may be accomplished through the use of the WHILE and WEND statements and a LET statement. The LET statement, located just before the WHILE statement, assigns the variable in the condition of the WHILE statement a value that ensures that the body of the loop is executed at least once.

Consider the Do-Until structure in the flowchart in Figure 5.8, as well as the corresponding partial BASIC program. By assigning CONTROL$ a value of Y in line 2150, we ensure that the body of the loop is executed at least once. The minimum number of times the body of the loop may be executed is the key difference between a Do-While and a Do-Until structure. For another example of the implementation of a Do-Until structure with the technique described in Figure 5.8, see Program 4.15 in chapter 4, on page 121.

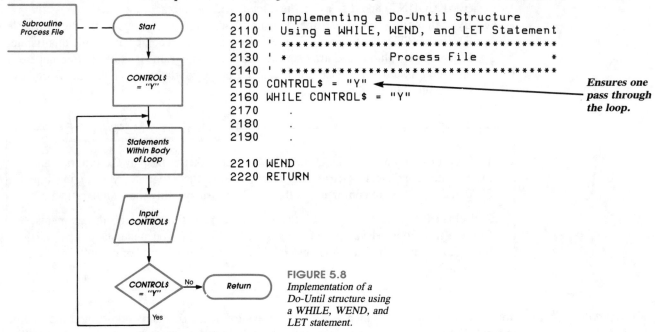

```
2100 ' Implementing a Do-Until Structure
2110 ' Using a WHILE, WEND, and LET Statement
2120 ' ****************************************
2130 ' *            Process File             *
2140 ' ****************************************
2150 CONTROL$ = "Y"        ← Ensures one pass through the loop.
2160 WHILE CONTROL$ = "Y"
2170    .
2180    .
2190    .

2210 WEND
2220 RETURN
```

FIGURE 5.8
Implementation of a Do-Until structure using a WHILE, WEND, and LET statement.

5.5

IMPLEMENTING THE IF-THEN-ELSE STRUCTURE

This section describes the various forms of the If-Then-Else structure and the use of IF statements to implement them in MS BASIC.

Simple Forms of the If-Then-Else Structure

Consider the If-Then-Else structure in Figure 5.9 and the corresponding methods of implementing the logic in MS BASIC. Assume that REG$ represents a person's voter-registration status. If REG$ is equal to the value Y, the person is registered to vote. If REG$ does not equal Y, the person is not registered to vote. REG.CNT and NREG.CNT are counters that are incremented as specified in the flowchart.

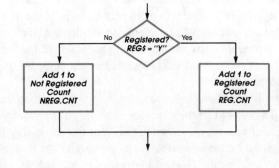

FIGURE 5.9
Implementation of the If-Then-Else structure, with alternative processing for the true and false cases.

Method 1: Using a single IF statement.

```
200 IF REG$ = "Y"
        THEN REG.CNT  = REG.CNT  + 1
        ELSE NREG.CNT = NREG.CNT + 1
210
```

Method 2: Using two IF statements.

```
200 IF REG$ = "Y"
        THEN REG.CNT  = REG.CNT  + 1
210 IF REG$ <> "Y"
        THEN NREG.CNT = NREG.CNT + 1
```

In the first method of solution shown in Figure 5.9, an IF statement resolves the logic indicated in the partial flowchart. Line 200 compares REG$ to the value Y. If REG$ is equal to Y, then REG.CNT is incremented by 1 in the THEN clause. If REG$ does not equal Y, NREG.CNT is incremented by 1 in the ELSE clause. Regardless of the counter incremented, control passes to line 210, the next numbered line following line 200. Line 210 is said to be the **structure terminator**, since both the true and false tasks pass control to this line.

In method 2, REG$ is compared to the value Y twice. In line 200, if REG$ is equal to Y, then the counter REG.CNT is incremented by 1. In line 210, the counter NREG.CNT is incremented by 1 if REG$ does not equal Y.

Although both methods are valid, and both satisfy the If-Then-Else structure, the first method is more efficient, as it involves fewer lines of code and less execution time. Therefore, the first method is recommended over the second.

As shown in Figures 5.10, 5.11, and 5.12, the If-Then-Else structure can take on a variety of appearances. In Figure 5.10, there is a task only if the condition is true.

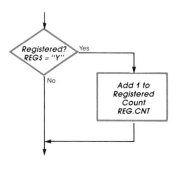

Method 1: Using an IF statement with no ELSE clause.

```
200  IF REG$ = "Y"
         THEN REG.CNT = REG.CNT + 1
210
```

Method 2: Using an IF statement with a null ELSE clause.

```
200  IF REG$ = "Y"
         THEN REG.CNT = REG.CNT + 1
         ELSE
210
```

In Figure 5.10, the first method is preferred over the second, since it is more straightforward and involves fewer lines of code. Note that the second method involves a null ELSE clause.

The If-Then-Else structure in Figure 5.11 illustrates the incrementation of the counter NREG.CNT when the condition is false.

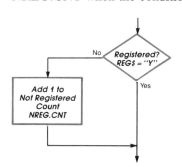

Method 1: Negating the condition in the decision symbol and using an IF statement.

```
200  IF REG$ <> "Y"
         THEN NREG.CNT = NREG.CNT + 1
210
```

Method 2: Using an IF statement with a null THEN clause.

```
200  IF REG$ = "Y"
         THEN
         ELSE NREG.CNT = NREG.CNT + 1
210
```

In method 1, the relation in the condition that is found in the partial flowchart has been negated. The condition REG$ = "Y" has been modified to read REG$ <> "Y" in the BASIC code. Negating the relation is usually preferred when additional tasks must be done as a result of the condition being false. In method 2, the relation is the same as in the decision symbol. When the condition REG$ = Y is true, the null THEN clause simply passes control to line 210. Either method is acceptable. Some programmers prefer always to include both a THEN and an ELSE clause, even when one of them is null. On the other hand, some prefer to negate the condition rather than include a null clause.

The If-Then-Else structure in Figure 5.12 includes alternative tasks for both the true and false cases. Each task is made up of several statements.

Method 1: Using the IF statement and colons.

```
200 IF REG$ = "Y"
        THEN REG.CNT  = REG.CNT  + 1 : PRINT "Registered"
        ELSE NREG.CNT = NREG.CNT + 1 : PRINT "Not Registered"
```

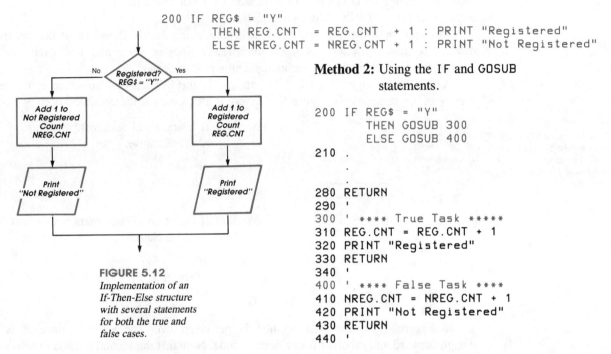

Method 2: Using the IF and GOSUB statements.

```
200 IF REG$ = "Y"
        THEN GOSUB 300
        ELSE GOSUB 400
210 .
    .
    .
280 RETURN
290 '
300 ' **** True Task *****
310 REG.CNT = REG.CNT + 1
320 PRINT "Registered"
330 RETURN
340 '
400 ' **** False Task ****
410 NREG.CNT = NREG.CNT + 1
420 PRINT "Not Registered"
430 RETURN
440 '
```

FIGURE 5.12
Implementation of an If-Then-Else structure with several statements for both the true and false cases.

In method 1 of Figure 5.12, if the condition REG$ = "Y" is true, the two statements in the THEN clause are executed. If the condition is false, the two statements in the ELSE clause are executed.

In method 2, the IF and GOSUB statements are used to implement the If-Then-Else structure. If the condition is true, control passes to line 300 and the true task is executed. If the condition in line 200 is false, control passes to line 400 and the false task is executed. In either case, control returns to line 210, the structure terminator.

Although both methods satisfy the If-Then-Else structure, the first method is more straightforward and involves fewer lines of code. Therefore, for this example, the first method is recommended over the second method. However, since MS BASIC allows for only 255 characters in a line, method 2 should be used when many physical lines are involved in the THEN or ELSE clause.

Nested Forms of the If-Then-Else Structure

A nested If-Then-Else structure is one in which the action to be taken for the true or false case includes yet another If-Then-Else structure. The second If-Then-Else structure is considered to be nested or layered within the first.

Study the partial program that corresponds to the nested If-Then-Else structure in Figure 5.13 on the next page.

```
200 IF AGE >= 18
        THEN GOSUB 300
        ELSE NELIG.CNT = NELIG.CNT + 1 : PRINT "Not Eligible to Register"
210 RETURN
220 '
300 ' ********* True Task *********
310 IF REG$ = "Y"
320     THEN REG.CNT  = REG.CNT  + 1 : PRINT "Registered"
330     ELSE ELIG.CNT = ELIG.CNT + 1 : PRINT "Eligible and Not Registered"
340 RETURN
350 '
```

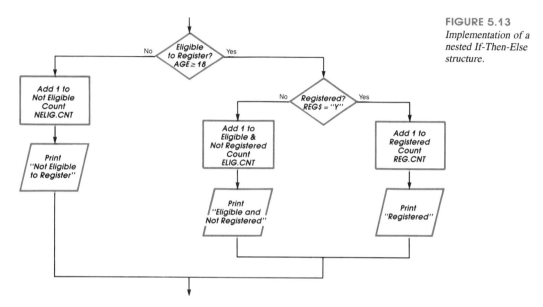

FIGURE 5.13
Implementation of a nested If-Then-Else structure.

In this figure, if the condition AGE >= 18 is true, the true task is executed and control passes to line 300. If the condition is false, the ELSE clause in line 200 is executed. The true task is implemented as a subroutine and it contains a second IF statement, which corresponds to the inner If-Then-Else structure in the flowchart. Note in Figure 5.13 that only one of the three alternative tasks is executed for each record processed. Regardless of the path taken, control eventually returns to the structure terminator in line 210.

If-Then-Else structures can be nested to any depth, but readability decreases as nesting increases. Consider the nested structure in Figure 5.14 on the following page and the corresponding implementation in MS BASIC. Figure 5.14 contains three nests of If-Then-Else structures and six counters. The counters can be described in the following manner:

NE.MALE: totals the number of males not eligible to register
NE.FEM: totals the number of females not eligible to register
NR.MALE: totals the number of males who are old enough to vote but have not registered
NR.FEM: totals the number of females who are old enough to vote but have not registered
NVOTE: totals the number of individuals who are eligible to vote but did not vote
VOTE: totals the number of individuals who voted

In the partial BASIC program in Figure 5.14, line 3430 corresponds to the decision at the very top of the flowchart. The subroutine beginning at line 3600 handles the true case to the right in the flowchart. The subroutine beginning at line 3800 fulfills the false case to the left in the flowchart. Incorporating the logic and concepts found in Figure 5.14 into a complete program is left as an exercise for you at the end of this chapter (see BASIC Programming Problem 3 on page 181).

```
3400 ' ****************************************
3410 ' *          Increment Running Total        *
3420 ' ****************************************
3430 IF AGE >= 18
         THEN GOSUB 3600
         ELSE GOSUB 3800
3440 RETURN
3450 '
3600 ' ************** True Task *************
3610 IF REG$ = "Y"
         THEN IF VOTE$ = "Y" THEN VOTE = VOTE + 1     ELSE NVOTE   = NVOTE + 1
         ELSE IF SEX$ = "F" THEN NR.FEM = NR.FEM + 1 ELSE NR.MALE = NR.MALE + 1
3620 RETURN
3630 '
3800 ' ************** False Task *************
3810 IF SEX$ = "F"
         THEN NE.FEM  = NE.FEM + 1
         ELSE NE.MALE = NE.MALE + 1
3820 RETURN
3830 '
```

FIGURE 5.14

Implementation of a nested If-Then-Else structure with several layers.

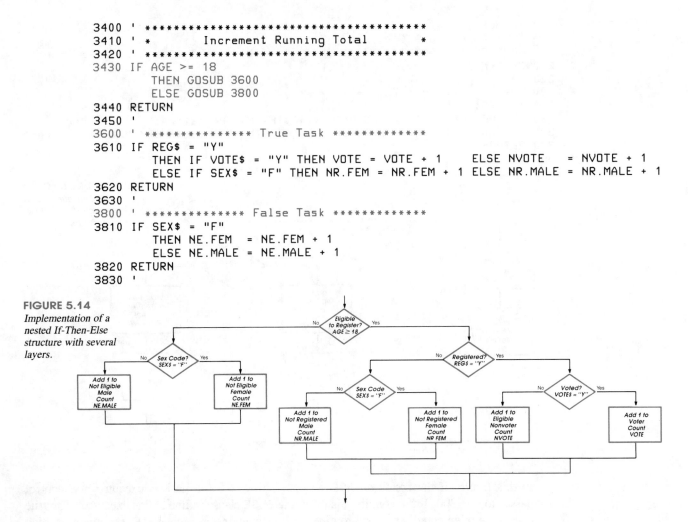

GOTO — A Dangerous Four-Letter Word

As with most programming languages, MS BASIC includes the infamous GOTO statement. The general form of the GOTO statement is

GOTO line number

The GOTO statement may be used to transfer control backward or forward to any line in the same program. In other words, you can instruct the PC to jump around from one routine to another without any return. It is a statement that should be avoided unless all other means fail. We introduce it at this juncture in the book because sooner or later someone will suggest it as a quick fix for your program. Don't listen!

The GOTO statement may appear quite innocent the first time you use it. It is not. All too often, beginning programmers get caught up in a solution and start branching from one routine to another. Before you know it, the program resembles a bowl of spaghetti. Even the original author of the program no longer understands the logic. The result is a program solution that is inefficient, unreliable, difficult to follow, and difficult to maintain. Experience has shown that error-free, reliable, and efficient programs can be constructed by avoiding the use of the GOTO statement. For this reason, we strongly recommend that you not use the GOTO statement and that you follow the examples given in Figures 5.9 through 5.14 when implementing If-Then-Else structures. On the positive side, the GOTO statement may be used in the immediate mode to reenter the current program at any line. This can be useful in debugging. Furthermore, the GOTO statement may be used to transfer control to an error-handling routine that then terminates the program.

5.6
PAIRING OF NESTED IF STATEMENTS

Line 3610 of Figure 5.14 is called a **nested** IF statement. A nested IF statement is one in which another IF statement immediately follows the keyword THEN or ELSE. In the following statement, two ELSEs follow two IFs:

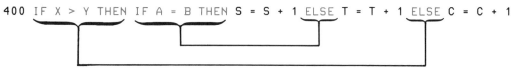

```
400  IF X > Y THEN IF A = B THEN S = S + 1 ELSE T = T + 1 ELSE C = C + 1
```

The relationship between a specific IF-THEN and the ELSE to which it is paired can be determined by the following rule:

> **Nested IF Rule 1:** Each ELSE is matched with the closest previous unmatched IF-THEN.

In line 400, reading from left to right, the first ELSE belongs to IF A = B THEN. The second ELSE is paired with IF X > Y THEN.

If X is greater than Y, the condition A = B is evaluated. If A equals B, S is incremented by 1. If X is greater than Y and A does not equal B, T is incremented by 1. If X is not greater than Y, C is incremented by 1.

It is not necessary that a nested IF statement have as many ELSE clauses as THEN clauses. For example, the statement

```
550  IF X = Y
        THEN IF A = B
             THEN IF C = D THEN T = T + 1 ELSE S = S + 1
```

contains three THEN clauses and one ELSE clause. The ELSE belongs to IF C = D THEN. Therefore, if all three conditions are true, the counter T is incremented by 1. If the first two conditions are true and the third condition is false, S is incremented by 1 and control passes to the next numbered line following 550. If either of the first two conditions is false, control passes to the next numbered line following 550.

On the other hand, it is invalid to have more ELSE clauses than THEN clauses in a single nested IF statement. Thus, the following nested IF statement is invalid:

```
750  IF S > T
        THEN GOSUB 800
        ELSE GOSUB 850 ELSE GOSUB 900
```
Invalid Owing to Unbalanced ELSE

Nested IF statements tend to increase the complexity of a program significantly. This is especially true if more than two IF statements are located within the same IF statement. If the number exceeds two, we suggest that you use logical operators or consider breaking the number up by using a subroutine, as illustrated in Figures 5.12, 5.13, and 5.14.

5.7
LOGICAL OPERATORS

In many instances, a decision to execute one alternative or another is based upon two or more conditions. In previous examples that involved two or more conditions, we tested each condition in a separate decision statement. In this section, we will discuss combining conditions within one decision statement by means of the logical operators AND, OR, XOR, EQV, and IMP. When two or more conditions are combined by these logical operators, the expression is called a **compound condition**. The logical operator NOT allows you to write a condition in which the truth value is **complemented**, or reversed.

The AND Logical Operator

The AND operator requires that both conditions be true for the compound condition to be true. Consider the following IF statements:

Method 1: Using the AND logical operator.

```
200 IF SEX$ = "M" AND AGE > 20
        THEN PRINT EMP.NAME$
210
```

Method 2: Using nested IF statements.

```
200 IF SEX$ = "M"
        THEN IF AGE > 20
                THEN PRINT EMP.NAME$
210
```

If SEX$ is equal to the value M and AGE is greater than 20, then EMP.NAME$ is displayed before control passes to line 210. If either one of the conditions is false, then the compound condition is false and control passes to line 210 without EMP.NAME$ being displayed. Although both methods are equivalent, method 1 is more efficient, more compact, and more straightforward than method 2.

Like a single condition, a compound condition can be only true or false. To determine the truth value of the compound condition, the PC must evaluate and assign a truth value to each individual condition. Then the truth value is determined for the compound condition.

For example, if X equals 4 and Y$ equals "1", the PC evaluates the following compound condition in the manner shown:

```
300 IF X = 3 AND Y$ = "1" THEN GOSUB 3400
```
1. false   2. true

3. false

The PC first determined the truth value for each condition, then concluded that the compound condition was false because of the AND operation.

A compound condition can be made up of several conditions separated by AND operators. The flowchart in Figure 5.15 indicates that all three variables (T1, T2, and T3) must equal zero to increment COUNT by 1. Line 3400 in Figure 5.15 illustrates the use of a compound condition to implement the logic. The AND operator requires that all three conditions be true for COUNT to be incremented by 1. If any one of the three conditions is false, control is transferred to line 3410 and COUNT is not incremented by 1.

FIGURE 5.15
Use of two AND operators.

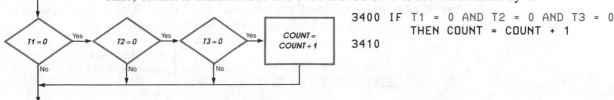

```
3400 IF T1 = 0 AND T2 = 0 AND T3 = 0
        THEN COUNT = COUNT + 1
3410
```

The following rule summarizes the use of the logical operator AND:

> **Logical Operator Rule 1:** The logical operator AND requires that all conditions be true for the compound condition to be true.

The OR Logical Operator

The OR operator requires that only one of the two conditions be true for the compound condition to be true. If both conditions are true, the compound condition is also true. The use of the OR operator is illustrated below.

Method 1: Using the OR logical operator.

```
500 IF DIV = 0 OR EXPO > 1E30
        THEN PRINT "WARNING" : END
510
```

Method 2: Using two IF statements.

```
500 IF DIV = 0
        THEN PRINT "WARNING" : END
505 IF EXPO > 1E30
        THEN PRINT "WARNING" : END
510
```

In line 500 of method 1, if either DIV equals 0 or EXPO is greater than 1E30, the THEN clause is executed. If both conditions are true, the THEN clause is also executed. If both conditions are false, the THEN clause is bypassed and control passes to the next numbered line. Method 2 employs two IF statements to resolve the same problem. Again, both methods are equivalent. However, method 1 is more straightforward than method 2. Can you write a single nested IF statement without a logical operator which results in the same logic described in methods 1 and 2?

Figure 5.16 illustrates a partial flowchart and the use of two OR operators to implement it.

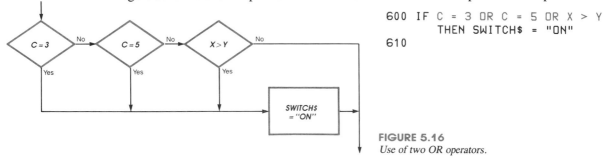

```
600 IF C = 3 OR C = 5 OR X > Y
       THEN SWITCH$ = "ON"
610
```

FIGURE 5.16
Use of two OR operators.

As with the logical operator AND, the truth values of the individual conditions in line 600 of Figure 5.16 are first determined, then the truth values for the conditions containing the logical operator OR are evaluated. For example, if C equals 4, X equals 4.9, and Y equals 4.8, the following condition is true:

```
600 IF   C = 3   OR   C = 5   OR   X > Y   THEN SWITCH$ = "ON"
         1. false      2. false      3. true

                 4. false

                      5. true
```

In line 600, the PC first evaluates the individual conditions (steps 1, 2, and 3). The first and second conditions are false and the third condition is true. Next, the PC evaluates the leftmost OR (step 4). Since the truth values of the first two conditions are false, the truth value of C = 3 OR C = 5 is also false.

Finally, the PC evaluates the truth value of the condition resulting from step 4 and the condition resulting from step 3 for the rightmost logical operator OR. Since the condition resulting from step 3 has a truth value of true, the entire condition is determined to be true.

The following rule summarizes the use of the logical operator OR:

> ***Logical Operator Rule 2:*** The logical operator OR requires that *only one* of the conditions be true for the compound condition to be true. If both conditions are true, the compound condition is also true.

The Logical Operators XOR, ' EQV, and IMP

Three logical operators that are not used very often but are a part of MS BASIC are XOR (exclusive OR), EQV (equivalence), and IMP (implication).

The XOR operator requires that one of the two conditions be true for the compound condition to be true. If both conditions are true, the compound condition is false. For example, if C = 3 and D = 4, then the following compound condition is false.

```
C = 3 XOR D > 3
1. true      2. true

      3. false
```

The EQV operator requires that both conditions be true or both conditions be false for the compound condition to be true. For example, if C = 4 and D = 3, then the following compound condition is true.

```
C = 3 EQV D > 3
  1. false    2. false
       3. true
```

The IMP operator requires that both conditions be true or both conditions be false or the first condition be false and the second condition be true for the compound condition to be true. For example, if C = 4 and D = 5, then the following compound condition is true.

```
C = 3 IMP D > 3
  1. false   2. true
      3. true
```

The NOT Logical Operator

A condition made up of two expressions and a relational operator is sometimes called a **relational expression**. A relational expression that is preceded by the logical operator NOT forms a condition that is false when the relational expression is true. If the relational expression is false, then the condition is true. Consider the following IF statements:

Method 1: Using the NOT logical operator.

Method 2: Using other relations to complement.

Method 3: Using a null THEN.

```
700 IF NOT A > B
       THEN READ A
```

```
700 IF A <= B
       THEN READ A
```

```
700 IF A > B
       THEN
       ELSE READ A
```

If A is greater than B (the relational expression is true), then the condition NOT A > B is false. If A is less than or equal to B (the relational expression is false), then the condition is true. All three methods are equivalent; however, methods 1 and 2 are preferred.

Because the logical operator NOT can increase the complexity of the decision statement significantly, use it sparingly. As illustrated in Table 5.3, with MS BASIC you may write the complement, or reverse, of a condition by using other relations.

TABLE 5.3 Use of Other Relations to Complement a Condition

CONDITION	COMPLEMENT OF CONDITION	
	METHOD 1	METHOD 2
A = B	A <> B	NOT A = B
A < B	A >= B	NOT A < B
A > B	A <= B	NOT A > B
A <= B	A > B	NOT A <= B
A >= B	A < B	NOT A >= B
A <> B	A = B	NOT A <> B

The following rule summarizes the use of the logical operator NOT.

> *Logical Operator Rule 3:* The logical operator NOT requires that the relational expression be false for the condition to be true. If the relational expression is true, then the condition is false.

Truth Tables   Truth tables for the six logical operators discussed in this section are summarized in Table 5.4. A summary of the order of precedence of all MS BASIC operators, including arithmetic, relational, and logical, can be found on page 4 of the reference card in the back of this book.

——TABLE 5.4 Truth Tables for Logical Operators Where A and B Represent Conditions, T Represents True, and F Represents False——

LOGICAL OPERATOR NOT			LOGICAL OPERATOR XOR		
VALUE OF A	VALUE OF NOT A		VALUE OF A	VALUE OF B	VALUE OF A XOR B
T	F		T	T	F
F	T		T	F	T
			F	T	T
			F	F	F

LOGICAL OPERATOR AND			LOGICAL OPERATOR IMP		
VALUE OF A	VALUE OF B	VALUE OF A AND B	VALUE OF A	VALUE OF B	VALUE OF A IMP B
T	T	T	T	T	T
T	F	F	T	F	F
F	T	F	F	T	T
F	F	F	F	F	T

LOGICAL OPERATOR OR			LOGICAL OPERATOR EQV		
VALUE OF A	VALUE OF B	VALUE OF A OR B	VALUE OF A	VALUE OF B	VALUE OF A EQV B
T	T	T	T	T	T
T	F	T	T	F	F
F	T	T	F	T	F
F	F	F	F	F	T

Combining Logical Operators   Logical operators can be combined in a decision statement to form a compound condition. The formation of compound statements that involve more than one type of logical operator can create problems unless you fully understand the order in which the PC evaluates the entire condition. Consider the following decision statement:

```
800 IF X > Y OR T = D AND H < 3 OR NOT Y = R
       THEN COUNT = COUNT + 1
```

Does the PC evaluate operators from left to right or right to left or one type of operator before another?

The order of evaluation is a part of what is called the **rules of precedence**. Just as we have rules of precedence for arithmetic operations (chapter 3, pages 68 and 69), we also have rules of precedence for logical operators.

> ***Precedence Rule 3:*** Unless parentheses dictate otherwise, reading from left to right, conditions containing arithmetic operators are evaluated first; then those containing relational operators; then those containing NOT operators; then those containing AND operators; then those containing OR or XOR operators; then those containing EQV operators; and finally those containing IMP operators.

The compound condition found earlier in line 800, then, is evaluated as follows. Assume that D = 3, H = 3, R = 2, T = 5, X = 3, and Y = 2:

```
X > Y   OR   T = D   AND   H < 3   OR   NOT Y = R
1. true       2. false      3. false       4. true
                     6. false              5. false
             7. true
                          8. true
```

If you have trouble following the logic behind this evaluation, use this technique: Applying the rules of precedence, look or scan from *left to right* four different times. On the first scan, determine the truth value of each condition that contains a relational operator. On the second scan, moving from left to right again, evaluate all conditions that contain NOT operators. Y = R is true and NOT Y = R is false. On the third scan, moving again from left to right, evaluate all conditions that contain AND operators. T = D is false, as is H < 3; therefore, T = D and H < 3 is false. On the fourth scan, moving from left to right, evaluate all conditions that contain OR operators. The first OR yields a truth value of true. The second OR yields, for the entire condition, a final truth value of true.

The Effect of Parentheses in the Evaluation of Compound Conditions

Parentheses may be used to change the order of precedence. In MS BASIC, parentheses are normally used to avoid ambiguity and to group conditions with a desired logical operator. When there are parentheses in a compound condition, the PC evaluates that part of the compound condition within the parentheses first and then continues to evaluate the remaining compound condition according to the rules of precedence. For example, suppose variable C (below) has a value of 6 and D has a value of 3. Consider the compound condition:

```
C = 7   AND   D < 4   OR   D <> 0
1. false       2. true       3. true
           4. false
                  5. true
```

Following the order of precedence for logical operators, the compound condition yields a truth value of true. If parentheses surround the latter two conditions in the compound condition, then the OR operator is evaluated before the AND condition, and the compound condition yields a truth value of false, as shown below:

```
C = 7   AND   (D < 4   OR   D <> 0)
4. false        1. true       2. true
                     3. true
           5. false
```

Parentheses may be used freely when the evaluation of a compound condition is in doubt. For example, if you wish to evaluate the compound condition

```
C > D AND S = 4 OR X < Y AND T = 5
```

you may incorporate it into a decision statement as it stands. You may also write it as

```
(C > D AND S = 4) OR (X < Y AND T = 5)
```

and feel more certain of the outcome of the decision statement.

Programming Case Study 9: *Employee Analysis and Summary Report*

This problem illustration requires the use of an If-Then-Else structure with the logical operators AND and OR.

Problem: The records of an employee file are to be displayed if they meet one of the following two criteria:

1. sex code is female and service is greater than 10 years, or
2. sex code is male and age is greater than or equal to 35 years and service is less than 10 years.

A summary of the total number of employees who meet the criteria and the average salary paid to these selected employees are to be displayed in the Wrap-up Module. The employee file is as follows:

Name	Sex	Service	Age	Annual Salary
Babjack, Bill	M	3	41	$19,500
Knopf, Louis	M	19	53	29,200
Taylor, Jane	F	12	38	26,000
Droopey, Joe	M	4	36	28,000
Lane, Lyn	F	9	44	19,800
Lis, Frank	M	1	44	21,000
Bye, Ed	M	1	42	15,000
Braion, Jim	M	19	35	26,500

Following are a list of the program tasks; a top-down chart, including flowcharts of the Process File Module and Process Selected Employee Record Module (see Figure 5.17 on the following page); a program solution; and a discussion of the program solution.

Program Tasks The following program tasks correspond to the top-down chart in Figure 5.17.

1. Initialization

   a. Initialize a counter (EMP.COUNT) to zero. This counter will keep track of the number of employees who meet the criteria. Initialize a running total (TOTAL.SALARY) to zero. This running total will be used to sum the selected salaries.
   b. Clear the screen.
   c. Initialize the report format.
   d. Display the report and column headings.

2. Process File

   a. Read the first employee record. The name (EMP.NAME$), sex code (EMP.SEX$), service (EMP.SERVICE), age (EMP.AGE), and annual salary (EMP.SALARY) are values read from DATA statements.
   b. Establish a While loop that repeats while EMP.NAME$ does not equal the value EOF. Within the While loop, if the record represents an employee who is female (EMP.SEX$ = "F") and whose service is greater than 10 years (EMP.SERVICE > 10) or an employee who is male (EMP.SEX$ = "M"), who is at least 35 years old (EMP.AGE >= 35), and who has fewer than 10 years of service (EMP.SERVICE < 10), then the following is done:
      (1) EMP.COUNT is incremented by 1.
      (2) TOTAL.SALARY is incremented by the salary (EMP.SALARY).
      (3) The record is displayed.
   c. Read the next employee record.

3. Wrap-up

   a. Calculate the average salary by dividing TOTAL.SALARY by EMP.COUNT.
   b. Display the employee count (EMP.COUNT).
   c. Display the average salary (TOTAL.SALARY).
   d. Display an end-of-job message.

FIGURE 5.17
A top-down chart for Program 5.2 and general flowcharts of the Process File Module and Process Selected Employee Record Module.

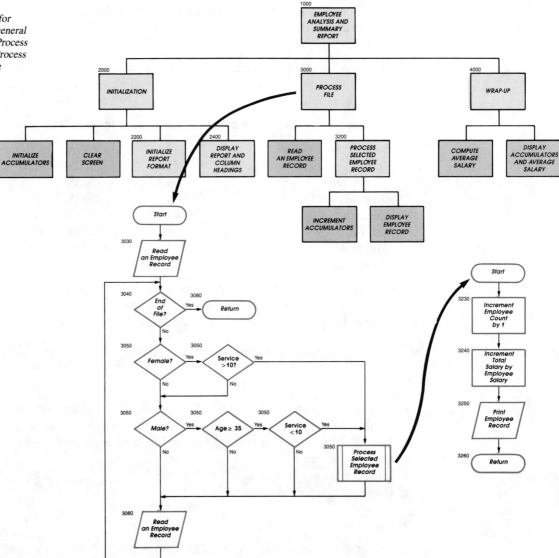

Program Solution The following program corresponds to the preceding tasks and to the top-down chart in Figure 5.17.

PROGRAM 5.2

```
1000 ' Program 5.2
1010 ' Employee Analysis and Summary Report
1020 ' *****************************************************************
1030 ' *                         Main Module                          *
1040 ' *****************************************************************
1050 GOSUB 2000   ' Call Initialization
1060 GOSUB 3000   ' Call Process File
1070 GOSUB 4000   ' Call Wrap-up
1080 END
1090 '
2000 ' *****************************************************************
2010 ' *                       Initialization                         *
2020 ' *****************************************************************
2030 EMP.COUNT = 0
2040 TOTAL.SALARY = 0
2050 CLS : KEY OFF   ' Clear Screen
2060 GOSUB 2200   ' Call Initialize Report Format
2070 GOSUB 2400   ' Call Display Report and Column Headings
2080 RETURN
2090 '
2200 ' *****************************************************************
2210 ' *                   Initialize Report Format                   *
2220 ' *****************************************************************
2230 HEAD.LN1$ = "         Employee Analysis and Summary Report"
2240 HEAD.LN2$ = "            Sex = Female, Service > 10"
2250 HEAD.LN3$ = "                         Or"
2260 HEAD.LN4$ = "        Sex = Male, Age >= 35, Service < 10"
2270 HEAD.LN5$ = "Employee Name    Sex    Service    Age    Annual Salary"
2280 DETL.LN$  = "\          \    !       ##        ##      ###,###.##"
2290 TOT.LN1$  = "Number of employees meeting criteria ===> ##"
2300 TOT.LN2$  = "Average salary of employees meeting criteria ===> $$#,###.##"
2310 TOT.LN3$  = "End of Employee Analysis Report"
2320 RETURN
2330 '
2400 ' *****************************************************************
2410 ' *              Display Report and Column Headings              *
2420 ' *****************************************************************
2430 PRINT HEAD.LN1$
2440 PRINT HEAD.LN2$
2450 PRINT HEAD.LN3$
2460 PRINT HEAD.LN4$
2470 PRINT
2480 PRINT HEAD.LN5$
2490 PRINT
2500 RETURN
2510 '
3000 ' *****************************************************************
3010 ' *                       Process File                           *
3020 ' *****************************************************************
3030 READ EMP.NAME$, EMP.SEX$, EMP.SERVICE, EMP.AGE, EMP.SALARY
3040 WHILE EMP.NAME$ <> "EOF"
3050    IF (EMP.SEX$ = "F" AND EMP.SERVICE > 10) OR
           (EMP.SEX$ = "M" AND EMP.AGE >= 35 AND EMP.SERVICE < 10)
           THEN GOSUB 3200   ' Call Process Selected Employee Record
3060    READ EMP.NAME$, EMP.SEX$, EMP.SERVICE, EMP.AGE, EMP.SALARY
3070 WEND
3080 RETURN
3090 '
```

(continued)

```
3200 ' ****************************************************************
3210 ' *              Process Selected Employee Record              *
3220 ' ****************************************************************
3230 EMP.COUNT = EMP.COUNT + 1
3240 TOTAL.SALARY = TOTAL.SALARY + EMP.SALARY
3250 PRINT USING DETL.LN$; EMP.NAME$, EMP.SEX$, EMP.SERVICE,
                          FMP.AGE, EMP.SALARY
3260 RETURN
3270 '
4000 ' ****************************************************************
4010 ' *                         Wrap-up                            *
4020 ' ****************************************************************
4030 AVERAGE = TOTAL.SALARY / EMP.COUNT
4040 PRINT
4050 PRINT USING TOT.LN1$; EMP.COUNT
4060 PRINT USING TOT.LN2$; AVERAGE
4070 PRINT
4080 PRINT TOT.LN3$
4090 RETURN
4100 '
4110 ' ******************** Data Follows ***********************
4120 DATA Babjack Bill, M,  3, 41, 19500
4130 DATA Knopf Louis,  M, 19, 53, 29200
4140 DATA Taylor Jane,  F, 12, 38, 26000
4150 DATA Droopey Joe,  M,  4, 36, 28000
4160 DATA Lane Lyn,     F,  9, 44, 19800
4170 DATA Lis Frank,    M,  1, 44, 21000
4180 DATA Bye Ed,       M,  1, 42, 15000
4190 DATA Braion Jim,   M, 19, 35, 26500
4200 DATA EOF,           ,   ,   ,
4210 ' ******************** End of Program ***********************


        RUN


              Employee Analysis and Summary Report
                  Sex = Female, Service > 10
                              Or
              Sex = Male, Age >= 35, Service < 10

    Employee Name    Sex    Service    Age    Annual Salary

    Babjack Bill      M        3        41       19,500.00
    Taylor Jane       F       12        38       26,000.00
    Droopey Joe       M        4        36       28,000.00
    Lis Frank         M        1        44       21,000.00
    Bye Ed            M        1        42       15,000.00

    Number of employees meeting criteria ===>  5
    Average salary of employees meeting criteria ===> $21,900.00

    End of Employee Analysis Report
```

Discussion of the Program Solution

The top-down chart and flowchart of the Process File Module in Figure 5.17 and the corresponding Program 5.2 represent a solution to the Employee Analysis and Summary Report. The If-Then-Else structure in the flowchart is implemented in line 3050 of the Process File Module with logical AND and OR operators. If an employee record passes the criteria, then the subroutine beginning at line 3200 is executed. Within the subroutine, both accumulators are incremented and the record is displayed. If a record fails to pass the test, it is not processed any further; rather, the next record is read.

Finally, since the AND operator is evaluated before the OR operator, the parentheses in line 3050 of Program 5.2 are not required. We inserted parentheses strictly for the purpose of readability.

TRY IT YOURSELF

1. Load Program 5.2 (PRG5-2) from the Student Diskette. Display the program and execute it. Replace line 3050 with the following series of IF statements:

```
3050    IF EMP.SEX$ = "F"
            THEN IF EMP.SERVICE > 10
                    THEN GOSUB 3200
3055    IF EMP.SEX$ = "M"
            THEN IF EMP.AGE >= 35
                    THEN IF EMP.SERVICE < 10 THEN GOSUB 3200
```

Execute the program and see what happens. Although the results are the same, in the authors' estimation the use of logical operators, as illustrated in the original Program 5.2, significantly decreases the complexity of the solution.

2. Reload PRG5-2 and display it. Will the same output result if line 3050 is replaced by the following IF statement:

```
3050 IF NOT(EMP.SEX$ = "M" OR EMP.SERVICE <= 10) OR
        NOT(EMP.SEX$ = "F" OR EMP.AGE < 35 OR EMP.SERVICE >= 10)
        THEN GOSUB 3200
```

(**Hint:** See Test Your BASIC Skills exercise 11, regarding DeMorgan's laws, at the end of this chapter.)

5.8

DATA VALIDATION TECHNIQUES

Data validation is a technique used to ensure that valid data is assigned to a program. It should be apparent that the information produced by a computer is only as accurate as the data it processes. In data processing, GIGO (Garbage In—Garbage Out, pronounced GI-GOH) is used to describe the generation of inaccurate information from the input of invalid data. A good program always validates the data at initial input, especially when the INPUT statement is used.

In this section, some definitions and techniques for data validation will be formalized so that you will write programs that are characterized by GDGI (Garbage Doesn't Get In) rather than GIGO. The following four data-validation techniques are used:

1. the reasonableness check
2. the range check
3. the code check
4. the digit check

Before describing these data-validation techniques, we will examine the BEEP statement and its use in validation routines.

The BEEP Statement

When executed, the BEEP statement causes the PC's speaker (see Figure 1.9 on page 5) to beep for a quarter of a second; several successive BEEP statements produce a constant beeping sound. For example, the following statement causes the PC to beep for one second.

```
220 BEEP : BEEP : BEEP : BEEP
```

The BEEP statement is often used in validation routines to alert the operator that something is wrong. The general form of the BEEP statement is given in Table 5.5.

———**TABLE 5.5** The BEEP Statement———————————————————————

General Form:	BEEP
Purpose:	*Causes the PC's speaker to beep for a quarter ot a second.*
Examples:	100 BEEP
	200 BEEP : BEEP : BEEP : BEEP : BEEP : BEEP

Additional examples of the BEEP statement are presented in the remainder of this section.

The Reasonableness Check

The **reasonableness check** ensures the legitimacy of data items that are entered from an external source. For example, a program may check a string variable to ensure that a specific number of characters is assigned to it. Or a program may check a numeric variable representing a person's age to ensure that it is positive. If the data is not reasonable, the program can request that the data be reentered or it can note the error in a report.

The following partial program requests that the user enter a 5-character part number. If the string data item does not contain 5 characters, the user is requested to reenter the part number.

```
200 INPUT "Five character Part Number =====> "; PART$
210 WHILE LEN(P$) <> 5
220    BEEP : BEEP : BEEP : BEEP
230    PRINT "Part Number "; PART$; " in error, please reenter"
240    INPUT "Five character Part Number =====> "; PART$
250 WEND
```

An Invalid Part Number

```
RUN

Five character Part Number =====> 436A
Part Number 436A in error, please reenter
Five character Part Number =====> 436A2
```

Line 200 requests that the user enter a part number. Line 210 uses the LEN function to test the length of the entry. If the length of PART$ is 5, control transfers to the line following line 250. If the length of PART$ is not 5, the PC enters the body of the While loop. Within the loop, the speaker is beeped for one second; a diagnostic message is displayed; and the operator is requested to reenter the part number. The PC remains in the loop until a valid part number is entered or until the program is manually terminated.

If the LOCATE statement is used to specify exactly where the prompt message in the first INPUT statement is displayed on the screen, then the following routine may be used in place of the previous one.

```
200 LOCATE 14, 10 : INPUT "Five character Part Number =====> "; PART$
210 WHILE LEN(P$) <> 5
220    BEEP : BEEP : BEEP : BEEP
230    LOCATE 15, 10 : PRINT "Part Number "; PART$;
                              " in error, please reenter"
240    LOCATE 14, 44 : PRINT SPC(10)
250    LOCATE 14, 44 : INPUT "", PART$
260    LOCATE 15, 10 : PRINT SPC(40)
270 WEND
```

In this example, if an invalid entry is made, line 230 displays the diagnostic message; line 240 erases the previous operator entry; and line 250 positions the cursor to the right of the prompt message displayed earlier by line 200. Following the next operator entry, line 260 erases the diagnostic message displayed earlier by line 230.

The Range Check The **range check** ensures that data items entered from an external device fall within a range of valid values. A company may have a rule that all purchase order amounts must be less than $500.00. If so, then the program that processes the purchase order should check the amount on the order to verify that it is greater than zero and less than $500.00. This range check is shown in the following partial program.

```
200 INPUT "Purchase Order Amount ($0.00 < Amount < $500.00) =====> "; AMT
210 WHILE AMT <= 0 OR AMT >= 500
220    BEEP : BEEP : BEEP : BEEP
230    PRINT "Amount"; AMT; "is in error, please reenter"
240    INPUT "Purchase Order Amount ($0.00 < Amount < $500.00) =====> "; AMT
250 WEND
```

An Out-of-Range Purchase Order Amount

```
RUN

Purchase Order Amount ($0.00 < Amount < $500.00) =====> 525.45
Amount 525.45 is in error, please reenter
Purchase Order Amount ($0.00 < Amount < $500.00) =====> 425.45
```

The range check, defined by the condition in the WHILE statement in line 210, verifies that the value of the purchase order amount is positive and less than $500.00. If the purchase amount is within range, the While loop is bypassed and control transfers to the line following the WEND statement in line 250. If the purchase amount is out of range, the PC enters the body of the While loop. Line 220 beeps the speaker for one second. Line 230 displays a diagnostic message, and line 240 requests that the operator enter a valid amount. Note that the PC remains in the While loop until a valid amount is entered or until the program is manually terminated.

The Code Check The **code check** ensures that codes entered from an external source are valid. In a school registration system, for example, the value for class standing may be F for freshman, S for sophomore, J for junior, and G for senior, with all other codes considered invalid.

The following partial program requests that the user enter the class standing.

```
200 INPUT "Class Standing (F, S, J, OR G) =====> "; CLASS$
210 WHILE CLASS$ <> "F" AND CLASS$ <> "S" AND
         CLASS$ <> "J" AND CLASS$ <> "G"
220    BEEP : BEEP : BEEP : BEEP
230    PRINT "Class Standing "; CLASS$; " is invalid, please reenter"
240    INPUT "Class Standing (F, S, J, OR G) =====> "; CLASS$
250 WEND
```

An Invalid Class-standing Code

```
RUN

Class Standing (F, S, J, OR G) =====> B
Class Standing B is invalid, please reenter
Class Standing (F, S, J, OR G) =====> J
```

As illustrated in the compound condition in line 210, since the codes are seldom contiguous (they seldom follow one another in the alphabet or, for that matter, in sequence), the logical operator AND and the relational operator <> are normally used to form the compound condition. If CLASS$ equals F, S, J, or G, control does not enter the While loop; rather, it transfers to the line following line 250.

Any other value assigned to CLASS$ causes the PC to enter the While loop. Line 220 beeps the speaker; line 230 displays the diagnostic message; and line 240 requests the operator to enter a valid class standing.

The Digit Check   The **digit check** verifies the assignment of a special digit to a number. A company may use a procedure whereby all part numbers of items sold begin with the digit 2. The partial program below illustrates how the string function LEFT$ can be used to accept only part numbers that begin with a 2.

```
200 INPUT "Part Number =====> "; PART$
210 WHILE LEFT$(PART$, 1) <> "2"
220    BEEP : BEEP : BEEP : BEEP
230    PRINT "Part Number must begin with a 2, please reenter"
240    INPUT "Part Number =====> "; PART$
250 WEND
```

                                                        An Invalid
                                                        Part Number

```
RUN

Part Number =====> 12389
Part Number must begin with a 2, please reenter
Part Number =====> 22389
```

In line 210, the expression LEFT$(PART$, 1) is equal to the first character of PART$. If the first character in PART$ is a 2, control bypasses the While loop. If the first character is not a 2, control enters the While loop. The PC beeps the speaker and displays a diagnostic message, and the operator is requested to reenter the part number.

⊞ 5.9
THE ON-GOSUB STATEMENT AND MENU-DRIVEN PROGRAMS

The GOSUB statement is defined as an unconditional subroutine call, because each time such a statement is executed, control is always transferred to the specified subroutine. In contrast, the ON-GOSUB statement allows for selected subroutine calls. Depending on the current value of the numeric expression that is associated with this statement, control will be transferred to one of two or more subroutines.

The ON-GOSUB statement can be used to implement an extension of the If-Then-Else structure, in which selection of one of many alternatives is based on an integer test. This extended version of the If-Then-Else structure is called the Case structure; it is illustrated in Figure 5.3 on page 134 and described in Appendix A, section A.4.

The condition in the ON-GOSUB statement may be a numeric variable or a numeric expression (never a string variable or string expression). The condition is placed between the keywords ON and GOSUB. Depending on the value of the condition, control transfers to one of several subroutines that are defined by line numbers appearing in a list that follows the keyword GOSUB. The general form of the ON-GOSUB statement is given in Table 5.6.

———TABLE 5.6 The ON-GOSUB Statement———

General Form:	ON *numeric expression* GOSUB *lineno$_1$, lineno$_2$, . . ., lineno$_n$*
Purpose:	*Causes control to transfer to the subroutine represented by the selected line number, where n is the current value of the numeric expression. Also causes the location of the next statement following the ON-GOSUB to be retained.*
Examples:	1300 ON CODE GOSUB 2000, 3000, 4000, 5000 1500 ON AGE / 10 + 1 GOSUB 2500, 3500, 2500, 2500, 3500 1750 ON A MOD B GOSUB 1850, 1950, 2050, 2050, 2050
Note:	*If the value of the numeric expression is 0 or greater than the number of line numbers (but less than or equal to 255), execution continues with the next statement following the ON-GOSUB.*
	If the value of the numeric expression is less than 0 or greater than 255, the program is terminated following the display of the message Illegal function call.

When the ON-GOSUB statement is executed, control transfers to one of the subroutines that are represented by the line numbers in the list following the keyword GOSUB. Commas are mandatory punctuation in the list of line numbers in the ON-GOSUB statement. The PC reads the line numbers in the ON-GOSUB statement from left to right, beginning with the first one in the list. If the value of the condition is 1, then control is transferred to the first line number in the list; if 2, then control is transferred to the second line number; and so on. Consider the following example.

```
1200 ON CODE GOSUB 2300, 2300, 2300, 2400, 2400, 2500, 2300, 2600
```

      Condition   List of line numbers representing subroutines
                                   to which control is transferred depending on
                                   the value of the condition.

If the value of CODE is 1 at the instant of the execution of line 1200, control will be transferred to line number 2300. The same thing will take place whenever CODE has the integer value of 2, 3, or 7. When CODE is equal to 4 or 5, control will pass to the subroutine that is represented by line 2400. When CODE is equal to 6, control will pass to the subroutine that begins at line number 2500. Finally, when CODE is equal to 8, control will be transferred to the subroutine at line number 2600.

The numeric expression in an ON-GOSUB statement is evaluated and rounded to obtain an integer whose value is then used to select a line number from the list following the keyword GOSUB. Consider the following example:

```
3000 ON A * B - C / D + E GOSUB 3200, 3400, 3600
```

If the value of the expression $A * B - C/D + E$ is 2.64, it will be rounded to an integer value of 3 and control will be transferred to line number 3600, which is the subroutine represented by the third line number in the list following the GOSUB.

In a BASIC program, you should never permit the value of an expression in an ON-GOSUB statement to be negative or zero. Furthermore, the value of the expression should not exceed the total number of line numbers in the list of the ON-GOSUB statement. A value that is negative, zero, or too large cannot be used to select a line number from the list. An IF or a WHILE statement may be used to prevent an error condition like this by validating the value of the expression just before the ON-GOSUB statement is executed. Thus, the following portion of a program can be used to test for all of the nonpermissible values of CODE:

```
2230 LOCATE 22, 19 : INPUT "Enter a Code 1 through 7 =======> ", CODE
2240 WHILE CODE < 1 OR CODE > 7
2250    BEEP : BEEP : BEEP : BEEP
2260    LOCATE 23, 19 : PRINT "Code Out of Range, Please reenter"
2270    LOCATE 22, 52 : PRINT SPC(10)
2280    LOCATE 22, 52 : INPUT "", CODE
2290    LOCATE 23, 19 : PRINT SPC(34)    ' Erase diagnostic message
2300 WEND
```

In this program, a nonpermissible value assigned to CODE will cause the PC to execute the body of the While loop. Within the loop, line 2250 beeps the speaker; line 2260 displays a diagnostic message; line 2270 clears the invalid entry from the screen; and line 2280 requests that a value be reentered for CODE. Following the next operator entry, line 2290 erases the diagnostic message displayed earlier by line 2260.

The suggested restrictions on the value of the expression in an ON-GOSUB may be summarized as the following rule:

> **ON-GOSUB Rule 1:** At the instant of execution of the ON-GOSUB statement, the integer obtained as the value of the expression must never be negative or greater than 255. Furthermore, the value of the expression should not be equal to zero or exceed the total number of line numbers in the list of the ON-GOSUB statement.

In addition, the ON-GOSUB statement must refer to an existing line number in the program; otherwise, the diagnostic message Undefined line number will be displayed, followed by termination of the program.

It is easy to see why programmers use the ON-GOSUB statement. An ON-GOSUB statement is used when the design of a program includes a Case structure (see Figure 5.3 on page 134) and the condition in the decision symbol can be equated to an integer test. The following Programming Case Study illustrates a major use of the ON-GOSUB statement.

Programming Case Study 10: *A Menu-Driven Program*

It is not at all uncommon for programs to have multiple functions. A **menu**, which is a list of the functions that a program can perform, is often used to guide an operator through a multifunction program. We call a program that displays a menu of functions a **menu-driven program**. Such a program displays a menu like the one illustrated on the screen layout form in Figure 5.18. The operator can then choose the desired function from the list by entering a corresponding code. Once the request is satisfied, the program again displays the menu. As illustrated in Figure 5.18, one of the codes (in this case 7) terminates execution of the program.

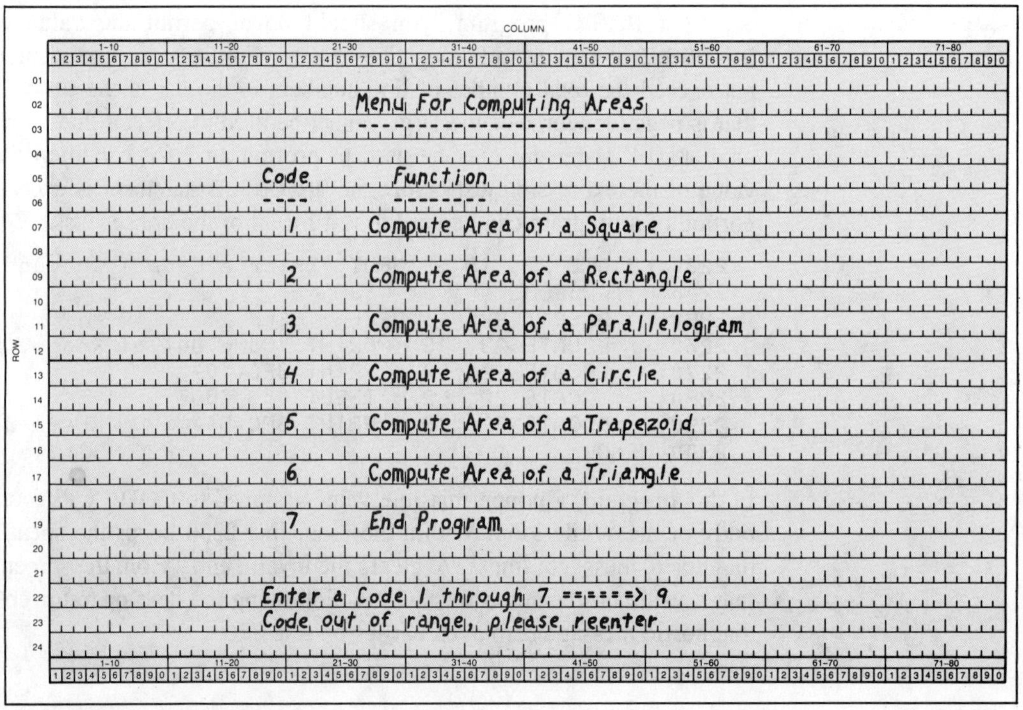

FIGURE 5.18

A menu of program functions designed on a screen layout form.

The following problem uses the menu illustrated in Figure 5.18.

Problem: A menu-driven program is to compute the area of a square, rectangle, parallelogram, circle, trapezoid, and triangle. The program should display the menu shown in Figure 5.18. Once a code is entered, the program must do a range check to ensure that the code corresponds to one of the menu functions. After the selection of the proper function, the program should prompt the operator for the necessary data, compute the area, and display it accordingly. The displayed results are to remain on the screen until the Enter key on the keyboard is pressed. After that, the program should display the menu again.

Use the following formulas for the areas:

1. Area of a square: $A = S * S$, where S is the length of a side of the square.
2. Area of a rectangle: $A = L * W$, where L is the length and W is the width of the rectangle.
3. Area of a parallelogram: $A = B * H$, where B is the length of the base and H is the height of the parallelogram.
4. Area of a circle: $A = 3.141593 * R * R$, where R is the radius of the circle.
5. Area of a trapezoid: $A = \dfrac{H(B1 + B2)}{2}$, where H is the height, B1 is the length of the primary base, and B2 is the length of the secondary base of the trapezoid.
6. Area of a triangle: $A = \dfrac{B * H}{2}$, where B is the base and H is the height of the triangle.

Following is a list of the program tasks that correspond to the top-down chart; the top-down chart itself (Figure 5.19); a program solution; and a discussion of the program solution.

Program Tasks   The following program tasks correspond to the top-down chart in Figure 5.19, on the next page.

1. Process Request

   a. Call the Display Menu Module. Within this module, do the following:
     (1) Clear the screen.
     (2) Use the `LOCATE` and `PRINT` statements to display the menu shown in Figure 5.18.
   b. Call the Accept a Code Module. Within this module, do the following:
     (1) Request the operator to enter a code (CODE).
     (2) Use a While loop to validate the code. If the code is invalid, beep the speaker, display an appropriate diagnostic message, and again ask the operator to select a function.
     (3) When a valid code is entered, clear the screen and return to the Process Request Module.
   c. Establish a While loop that is executed until CODE equals 7. Within the loop, do the following:
     (1) Use an `ON-GOSUB` statement to transfer control to the subroutine that carries out the requested function. In this case, implement each of the six different area computations in separate subroutines. Within each subroutine, do the following:
       (a) Use one or more `INPUT` statements to request the data.
       (b) Compute the area.
       (c) Display the results.
       (d) Prior to returning to the Process Request Module, call a subroutine (Return to Menu) to beep the speaker in order to alert the operator to press the Enter key. Use the following prompt message to redisplay the menu:

```
Press Enter key to return to the menu...
```

     (2) Call the Display Menu Module described in step 1a.
     (3) Call the Accept a Code Module described in step 1b.

2. Wrap-up

   a. Clear the screen.

   b. Display a pleasant message prior to terminating the program.

     The general flowchart of the Process Request Module in Figure 5.19 illustrates the six independent functions of Program 5.3. Each subroutine reference includes its own input, processing, and output statements.

FIGURE 5.19
A top-down chart and general flowchart for the Process Request Module for Program 5.3.

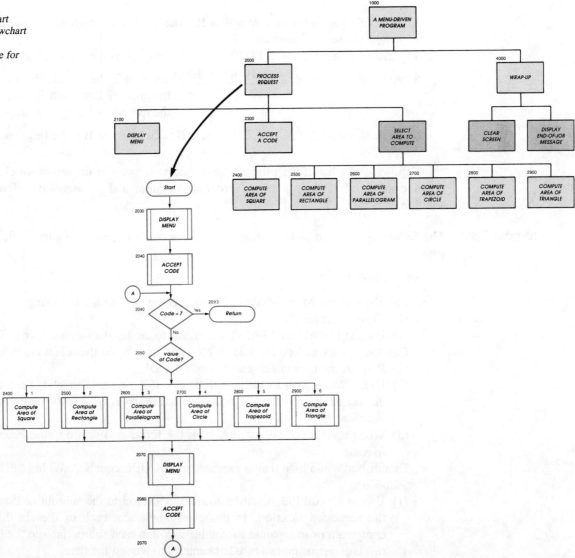

Discussion of the Program Solution When Program 5.3, on the following page, is first executed, line 1050 calls the Process Request Module. In this module, line 2030 calls the Display Menu Module.

     In the Display Menu Module, line 2130 clears the screen, and lines 2140 through 2240 display the menu illustrated in Figure 5.20 on page 171. The last line of Figure 5.20 is displayed by line 2330 of the Accept a Code Module. Assume that function 3 is selected, as shown in the lower right corner of Figure 5.20.

Program Solution The following program corresponds to the preceding tasks and to the top-down chart in Figure 5.19.

PROGRAM 5.3

```
1000 ' Program 5.3
1010 ' A Menu-Driven Program
1020 ' ************************************************************
1030 ' *                    Main Module                          *
1040 ' ************************************************************
1050 GOSUB 2000  ' Call Process Request
1060 GOSUB 4000  ' Call Wrap-up
1070 END
2000 ' ************************************************************
2010 ' *                  Process Request                        *
2020 ' ************************************************************
2030 GOSUB 2100  ' Call Display Menu
2040 GOSUB 2300  ' Call Accept a Code
2050 WHILE CODE <> 7
2060    ON CODE GOSUB 2400, 2500, 2600, 2700, 2800, 2900  ' Call Compute Area
2070    GOSUB 2100  ' Call Display Menu
2080    GOSUB 2300  ' Call Accept a Code
2090 WEND
2093 RETURN
2095 '
2100 ' ************************************************************
2110 ' *                  Display Menu                           *
2120 ' ************************************************************
2130 CLS : KEY OFF  ' Clear Screen
2140 LOCATE  2, 27 : PRINT "Menu for Computing Areas"
2150 LOCATE  3, 27 : PRINT "------------------------"
2160 LOCATE  5, 19 : PRINT "Code     Function"
2170 LOCATE  6, 19 : PRINT "----     --------"
2180 LOCATE  7, 19 : PRINT "  1      Compute Area of a Square"
2190 LOCATE  9, 19 : PRINT "  2      Compute Area of a Rectangle"
2200 LOCATE 11, 19 : PRINT "  3      Compute Area of a Parallelogram"
2210 LOCATE 13, 19 : PRINT "  4      Compute Area of a Circle"
2220 LOCATE 15, 19 : PRINT "  5      Compute Area of a Trapezoid"
2230 LOCATE 17, 19 : PRINT "  6      Compute Area of a Triangle"
2240 LOCATE 19, 19 : PRINT "  7      End Program"
2250 RETURN
2260 '
2300 ' ************************************************************
2310 ' *                  Accept a Code                          *
2320 ' ************************************************************
2330 LOCATE 22, 19 : INPUT "Enter a Code 1 through 7 ======> ", CODE
2340 WHILE CODE < 1 OR CODE > 7
2350    BEEP : BEEP : BEEP : BEEP
2360    LOCATE 23, 19 : PRINT "Code out of range, please reenter"
2370    LOCATE 22, 52 : PRINT SPC(10)
2380    LOCATE 22, 52 : INPUT "", CODE
2390    LOCATE 23, 19 : PRINT SPC(40)
2392 WEND
2394 CLS
2396 RETURN
2398 '
2400 ' ************************************************************
2410 ' *              Compute Area of a Square                   *
2420 ' ************************************************************
2430 LOCATE 5, 24 : PRINT "Compute Area of a Square"
2440 LOCATE 8, 24 : INPUT "Length of Side of Square ====> ", SIDE
2450 AREA = SIDE * SIDE
```

(continued)

```
2460 LOCATE 10, 24 : PRINT "Area of Square ===============>" ; AREA; "Square Units"
2470 GOSUB 3000  ' Call Return to Menu
2480 RETURN
2490 '
2500 ' ****************************************************************
2510 ' *              Compute Area of a Rectangle                    *
2520 ' ****************************************************************
2530 LOCATE  5, 24 : PRINT "Compute Area of a Rectangle"
2540 LOCATE  8, 24 : INPUT "Length of Rectangle =====> ", LONG
2550 LOCATE 10, 24 : INPUT "Width of Rectangle ======> ", WIDE
2560 AREA = LONG * WIDE
2570 LOCATE 12, 24 : PRINT "Area of Rectangle =======>"; AREA; "Square Units"
2580 GOSUB 3000  ' Call Return to Menu
2590 RETURN
2595 '
2600 ' ****************************************************************
2610 ' *            Compute Area of a Parallelogram                  *
2620 ' ****************************************************************
2630 LOCATE  5, 24 : PRINT "Compute Area of a Parallelogram"
2640 LOCATE  8, 24 : INPUT "Base of Parallelogram =====> ", BASE
2650 LOCATE 10, 24 : INPUT "Height of Parallelogram ===> ", HEIGHT
2660 AREA = BASE * HEIGHT
2670 LOCATE 12, 24 : PRINT "Area of Parallelogram =====>"; AREA; "Square Units"
2680 GOSUB 3000  ' Call Return to Menu
2690 RETURN
2695 '
2700 ' ****************************************************************
2710 ' *              Compute Area of a Circle                       *
2720 ' ****************************************************************
2730 LOCATE  5, 24 : PRINT "Compute Area of a Circle"
2740 LOCATE  8, 24 : INPUT "Radius of Circle =====> ", RADIUS
2750 AREA = 3.141593 * RADIUS * RADIUS
2760 LOCATE 10, 24 : PRINT "Area of Circle =======>"; AREA; "Square Units"
2770 GOSUB 3000  ' Call Return to Menu
2780 RETURN
2790 '
2800 ' ****************************************************************
2810 ' *              Compute Area of a Trapezoid                    *
2820 ' ****************************************************************
2830 LOCATE  5, 24 : PRINT "Compute Area of a Trapezoid"
2840 LOCATE  8, 24 : INPUT "Primary Base of Trapezoid =====> ", BASE1
2850 LOCATE 10, 24 : INPUT "Secondary Base of Trapezoid ===> ", BASE2
2860 LOCATE 12, 24 : INPUT "Height of Trapezoid ============> ", HEIGHT
2870 AREA = HEIGHT * (BASE1 + BASE2) / 2
2880 LOCATE 14, 24 : PRINT "Area of Trapezoid ==============>";AREA; "Square Units"
2890 GOSUB 3000  ' Call Return to Menu
2893 RETURN
2895 '
2900 ' ****************************************************************
2910 ' *              Compute Area of a Triangle                     *
2920 ' ****************************************************************
2930 LOCATE  5, 24 : PRINT "Compute Area of a Triangle"
2940 LOCATE  8, 24 : INPUT "Base of Triangle =====> ", BASE
2950 LOCATE 10, 24 : INPUT "Height of Triangle ===> ", HEIGHT
2960 AREA = BASE * HEIGHT / 2
2970 LOCATE 12, 24 : PRINT "Area of Triangle =====>"; AREA; "Square Units"
2980 GOSUB 3000  ' Call Return to Menu
2990 RETURN
2995 '
```

(continued)

```
3000 '  ***************************************************************
3010 ' *                     Return to Menu                          *
3020 '  ***************************************************************
3030 BEEP : BEEP : BEEP : BEEP
3040 LOCATE 20, 24 : INPUT "Press Enter key to return to menu...", A$
3050 RETURN
3060 '
4000 '  ***************************************************************
4010 ' *                       Wrap-up                               *
4020 '  ***************************************************************
4030 CLS
4040 LOCATE 12, 24 : PRINT "End of Program - Have a Nice Day!"
4050 RETURN
4060 ' ****************** End of Program *********************

RUN
```

FIGURE 5.20
The menu displayed by the Display Menu and Accept Code Modules in Program 5.3.

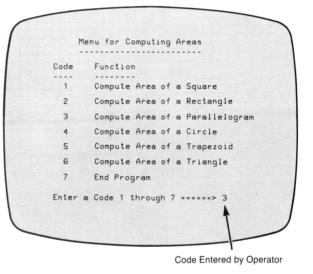

Code Entered by Operator

When the Enter key is pressed, lines 2340 through 2392 validate the code. Once a valid code is entered, line 2394 again clears the screen before control is returned to the Process Request Module.

Since CODE is not equal to 7, the WHILE statement in line 2050 allows control to pass to the ON-GOSUB statement in line 2060. With CODE equal to 3, control passes to the Compute Area of a Parallelogram Module (lines 2600 through 2695). Figure 5.21, for example, shows a base of 10 units and a height of 4 units to have been entered, which results in an area of 40 square units for the parallelogram. The subroutine (Return to Menu) called by line 2680 allows the operator to view the results on the screen for as long as he or she wishes. Note that the speaker is beeped four times (this produces one constant beep that lasts for a second). Once the Enter key is pressed in response to line 3040, the PC returns control to line 2070 and again displays the menu shown in Figure 5.20.

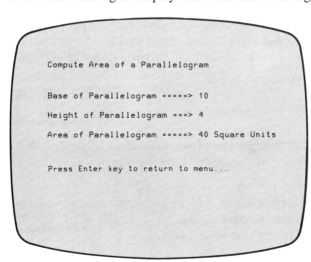

FIGURE 5.21
The display from the selection of code 3 (Compute Area of a Parallelogram).

Figure 5.22 shows an out-of-range code, which causes the PC to beep before displaying a diagnostic message. The beeping and the display of the diagnostic message are due to lines 2350 and 2360. Line 2370 is used to refresh that part of the screen where the incorrect code is displayed so that another code may be entered. After a valid code is entered in response to line 2380, the screen is again cleared by line 2394 and control is returned to the Process Request Module.

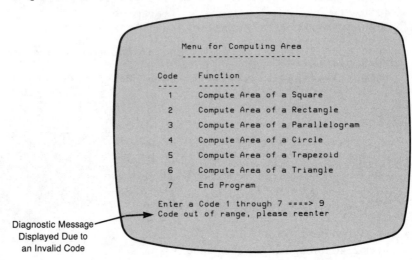

FIGURE 5.22
Diagnostic message displayed by line 2360, owing to the invalid code 9.

```
           Menu for Computing Area
           -----------------------

   Code      Function
   ----      --------
    1        Compute Area of a Square

    2        Compute Area of a Rectangle

    3        Compute Area of a Parallelogram

    4        Compute Area of a Circle

    5        Compute Area of a Trapezoid

    6        Compute Area of a Triangle

    7        End Program

Enter a Code 1 through 7 ====> 9
Code out of range, please reenter
```

Diagnostic Message Displayed Due to an Invalid Code

If the operator enters a code of 5 to compute the area of a trapezoid with a primary base of 18, a secondary base of 9, and a height of 5, the display shown in Figure 5.23 occurs.

FIGURE 5.23
The display from the selection of code 5 (Compute Area of a Trapezoid).

```
Compute Area of a Trapezoid

Primary Base of Trapezoid =====> 18

Secondary Base of Trapezoid ===> 9

Height of Trapezoid ===========> 5

Area of Trapezoid =============> 67.5 Square Units

Press Enter key to return to the menu...
```

To terminate execution of Program 5.3, a code of 7 is entered. Line 1060 in the Main Module calls upon the Wrap-up Module, which displays an appropriate message before line 1070 terminates execution of the program.

The preceding problem could have been solved by replacing the ON-GOSUB statement with a series of consecutive IF statements. Usually, however, when a series of three or more integer tests are to be performed in succession, the ON-GOSUB statement is the better alternative.

Try It Yourself

Load Program 5.3 (PRG5-3) from the Student Diskette. List the program and then execute it. When requested, enter the following:

Data Set 1: Code = 4, Radius = 5
Data Set 2: Code = 0 (A diagnostic message should display.)
Data Set 3: Code = 6, Base = 4, Height = 6
Data Set 4: Code = 7 (End program.)

The ON-GOTO Statement — Another Statement to Avoid

The `ON-GOTO` statement may also be used to implement the Case structure. The general form of the `ON-GOTO` statement is

> `ON` numeric expression `GOTO` lineno$_1$, lineno$_2$, ..., lineno$_n$

The `ON-GOTO` statement is similar to the `ON-GOSUB` statement; when it is executed, control transfers to the selected line number, where n is the current value of the numeric expression. The major difference between the two statements is that the `ON-GOSUB` causes the PC to retain the location of the next statement following it, whereas the `ON-GOTO` does not. Therefore, `GOTO` statements are required to return control to the statement following the `ON-GOTO`. For this reason, it is strongly recommended that the `ON-GOSUB` statement be used to implement the Case structure, as illustrated in the previous Programming Case Study.

⊞ 5.10
A STANDARD FORM OF PROGRAM ORGANIZATION FOR A MENU-DRIVEN PROGRAM

Programs are often classified as being batch or interactive in mode. A **batch program** is one that generates information on the basis of data that has been collected over a period of time. The data is placed in `DATA` statements or into a file and is made available to the program via `READ` statements. Most of the programs presented in chapter 4 and the first two programs presented in chapter 5 were batch programs.

An **interactive program** is one that generates information on the basis of data as it occurs; the data is usually entered into the program by the operator via `INPUT` statements. Most of the programs presented in chapters 2 and 3 were of the interactive type. A special instance of the interactive program is the menu-driven program, as illustrated by Program 5.3.

The top-down chart and general flowchart of the Process Request Module in Figure 5.19 illustrate the logic used in Program 5.3. Many menu-driven programs call for similar logic. The following steps will handle most problems requiring a menu-driven program:

1. Main Module

    a. Call Process Request.
    b. Call Wrap-up.

2. Process Request

    a. Display menu.
       (1) Clear the screen.
       (2) Display the acceptable codes and their functions.
    b. Accept operator request.
       (1) In a friendly manner, prompt the operator to enter a response.
       (2) Validate the response.
       (3) If the response is valid, clear the screen and transfer control to the appropriate function or to another menu.
       (4) If the response is invalid, in a clear and courteous manner notify the operator of the incorrect response and request him or her to enter a new response.
    c. Perform the chosen function.
       (1) If the function is another menu, repeat steps 2a and 2b.
       (2) If the function is interactive, input the data and execute the function accordingly.
       (3) Include a statement, like `INPUT`, to halt the PC so that the operator can view the screen. When the function is completed, prompt the operator to enter a response to the main menu or another menu.
       (4) If the function is batch, follow the general logic pattern for batch programs.
    d. Repeat steps 2a through 2c as necessary.
    e. Enter a response to terminate the program.

3. Wrap-up — display an appropriate end-of-job message.

⊞ 5.11   WHAT YOU SHOULD KNOW

1. Structured programming is a methodology according to which all program logic can be constructed from a combination of the following three basic logic structures: Sequence, Selection (If-Then-Else or Case), Repetition (Do-While or Do-Until).
2. The If-Then-Else structure is used in program design to specify a selection between two alternative paths.
3. The Case structure is an extension of the If-Then-Else structure, in which the choice includes more than two alternatives.
4. Most computer scientists agree that the decision statement to terminate a loop should be located at the top or bottom of the loop.
5. A loop that has the termination decision statement at the top is called a Do-While structure.
6. A loop that has the termination decision statement at the bottom is called a Do-Until structure.
7. Top-down programming and structured programming are not the same. Top-down programming describes a strategy for solving large, complex problems. To solve a problem top-down, you divide and conquer. Structured programming is used within modules to generate disciplined code. We improve the clarity and reduce the complexity by using only the five constructs Sequence, If-Then-Else, Case, Do-While, and Do-Until.
8. The IF statement is used to implement If-Then-Else structures.
9. In an IF statement, if the condition is true, the PC executes the statement or series of statements following the keyword THEN and control passes to the next numbered line following the IF statement. If the condition is false, the PC executes the statement or series of statements following the keyword ELSE and control passes to the next numbered line following the IF statement. If the condition is false and no ELSE clause in included in the IF statement, then the PC passes control to the next numbered line following the IF statement.
10. If a condition contains two numeric expressions, then the comparison is based on the algebraic values of the two expressions.
11. If a condition contains two string expressions, the PC evaluates the two strings from left to right, one character at a time. As soon as one character in one expression is different from the corresponding character in the other expression, the PC decides which expression has a lower value.
12. The PC uses the ASCII code to represent characters in main storage. It is the collating sequence of the ASCII code which determines the position of a character in relation to other characters.
13. A null THEN or null ELSE clause is valid.
14. A counter is an accumulator that is used to count the number of times some action or event is performed.
15. A running total is an accumulator that is used to sum the different values that a variable is assigned during the execution of a program.
16. All accumulators should be initialized to some value before they are used in a statement that tests the accumulator or adds to its value.
17. Depending on the problem to be solved, an If-Then-Else structure can have alternative processing for both the true case and the false case, alternative processing only for the true case, or alternative processing only for the false case.
18. Negating the relation in the condition of an If-Then-Else structure can sometimes simplify and clarify the IF statement.
19. A nested If-Then-Else structure is one in which the action to be taken for the true or false case includes yet another If-Then-Else structure.
20. In an IF statement, each ELSE is matched with the closest previous IF-THEN.
21. When two or more conditions are combined by the logical operators AND, OR, XOR, EQV, and IMP, the expression is a compound condition.
22. The truth value of a condition is complemented by the logical operator NOT.
23. The logical operator NOT requires that the relational expression be false for the condition to be true. If the relational expression is true, then the condition is false.
24. The logical operator AND requires that both conditions be true for the compound condition to be true.
25. The logical operator OR requires that only one of the two conditions be true for the compound condition to be true. If both conditions are true, the compound condition is also true.
26. The XOR (exclusive OR) operator requires that one of the two conditions be true for the compound condition to be true. If both are true, the condition is false.
27. The IMP (implication) operator requires that both conditions be true or both conditions be false or the first condition be false and the second true for the compound condition to be true.

28. The EQV (equivalence) operator requires that both conditions be true or both conditions be false for the compound condition to be true.

29. Unless parentheses dictate otherwise, reading from left to right, conditions containing arithmetic operators are evaluated first; then those containing relational operators; then those containing NOT operators; then those containing AND operators; then those conditions containing OR and XOR operators; then those containing IMP operators; and finally those containing EQV operators.

30. Data validation is a technique used to ensure that valid data is assigned to a program. Data can be validated, or checked, for reasonableness, range, code, and digit.

31. A reasonableness check is a technique used to ensure that data items are legitimate.

32. A range check is a technique used to ensure that data items fall within a range of valid values.

33. A code check is a technique used to ensure that codes entered from an external source are valid.

34. A digit check is a technique used to verify the assignment of a special digit to a number.

35. The BEEP statement causes the PC's speaker to beep for a quarter of a second.

36. The ON-GOSUB can be used to implement a Case structure, provided the decision is based on an integer test.

37. The condition in the ON-GOSUB statement may be a numeric variable or a numeric expression. Depending on the value of the condition, control transfers to one of several line numbers following the keyword GOSUB.

38. In a BASIC program, you must never permit the value of an expression in an ON-GOSUB statement to be negative or greater than 255. Furthermore, the value of the expression should not equal zero or exceed the total number of line numbers in the list of the ON-GOSUB statement.

39. A batch program is one that generates information on the basis of data that has been collected over a period of time.

40. An interactive program is one that generates information on the basis of data as it occurs; the data is usually entered into the program by the operator via INPUT statements in response to questions.

41. A menu is a list of the functions that a program can perform. When a menu-driven program is first executed, it displays a menu of functions. Each time a requested function is satisfied, the program redisplays the menu.

⊞ 5.12 TEST YOUR BASIC SKILLS (Even-numbered answers are at the back of the book, before the index.)

1. Consider the valid programs below. What is displayed if each program is executed?

```
a. 1000 ' Exercise 5.1a
   1010 ' ****** Main Module ******
   1020 GOSUB 2000   ' Call Initialization
   1030 GOSUB 3000   ' Call Process File
   1040 GOSUB 4000   ' Call Wrap-up
   1050 END
   1060 '
   2000 ' ***** Initialization *****
   2010 COUNT1 = 0
   2020 COUNT2 = 0
   2030 RETURN
   2040 '
   3000 ' ****** Process File ******
   3010 READ AGE, WEIGHT
   3020 WHILE  AGE >= 0
   3030    COUNT1 = COUNT1 + 1
   3040    IF AGE >= 21 AND WEIGHT >= 120
              THEN COUNT2 = COUNT2 + 1
   3050    READ AGE, WEIGHT
   3060 WEND
   3070 RETURN
   3080 '
   4000 ' ******** Wrap-up ********
   4010 PRINT "Number of People Evaluated:"; COUNT1
   4020 PRINT "Number of Adults Weighing "
   4030 PRINT "120 Pounds or more:"; COUNT2
   4040 RETURN
   4050 '
   4060 ' ****** Data Follows ******
   4070 DATA 10, 125, 24, 130, 21, 150, 30, 120
   4080 DATA 51, 225, 47, 175, 18, 130, -1, 0
   4090 ' ***** End of Program *****
```

```
b. 1000 ' Exercise 5.1b
   1010 A = 1
   1020 PRINT A
   1030 WHILE A > 0
   1040    IF A - 2 < 0
              THEN A = 2
              ELSE GOSUB 1200
   1050    PRINT A
   1060 WEND
   1070 END
   1200 ' *** Subroutine 1 ***
   1210 IF A - 2 = 0
          THEN A = 3
          ELSE GOSUB 1400
   1220 RETURN
   1400 ' *** Subroutine 2 ***
   1410 IF A - 4 < 0
          THEN A = 4
          ELSE GOSUB 1600
   1420 RETURN
   1600 ' *** Subroutine 3 ***
   1610 IF A - 4 = 0
          THEN A = 5
          ELSE A = 1
   1620 RETURN
   1630 ' ** End of Program **
```

```
c. 100 ' Exercise 5.1c          d. 100 ' Exercise 5.1d
   110 I = 1                        110 READ X, Y
   120 WHILE I <= 2                 120 WHILE X > 0
   130    J = 1                     130    IF X = Y AND Y >= 10
   140    WHILE J <= 2                        THEN PRINT "Both Conditions Are True"
   150       K = 1                  140    IF X = Y XOR Y >= 10
   160       WHILE K <= 2                     THEN PRINT "Only One of the Two Conditions Is True"
   170          PRINT I, J, K       150    IF NOT X = Y AND NOT Y >= 10
   180          K = K + 1                     THEN PRINT "Neither Condition Is True"
   190       WEND                   160    READ X, Y
   200       J = J + 1              170 WEND
   210    WEND                      180 PRINT "End of Job"
   220    I = I + 1                 190 ' ********* Data Follows **********
   230 WEND                         200 DATA 3, 5, 8, 10, 15, 15, 4, 4, -1, 0
   240 END                          210 END
```

2. Write a BASIC statement that will initialize X to 0 and another that will initialize T to 10. Also, write additional BASIC statements that will consecutively increment these variables by the following amounts:

   a. 1   b. 7   c. 2   d. double each value   e. minus 1

3. Determine the truth value of the compound conditions below, given the following:

   Employee number (E) = 500   Tax (T) = $60
   Salary (S) = $700   Insurance deduction (I) = $40
   Job code (J) = 1

   ```
   a. E < 400 OR J = 1               b. S = 700 AND T = 50
   c. S - T = 640 AND J = 1          d. T + I = S - 500 OR J = 0
   e. NOT J < 0                      f. NOT S > 500 AND NOT T > 80
   g. NOT (J = 1 OR T = 60)          h. J = 1 XOR E >= 500
   i. I <> 40 EQV S > 500            j. S = 700 IMP T = 60
   k. S < 300 AND I < 50 OR J = 1    l. S < 300 AND (I < 50 OR J = 1)
   m. NOT (NOT J = 1)
   ```

4. Determine the value of Q that will cause the condition in the IF statements below to be true.

   ```
   a. 100 IF Q > 8 OR Q = 3          b. 110 IF Q + 10 >= 7 AND NOT Q < 0
              THEN LET Z = Z / 10               THEN PRINT "THE ANSWER IS "; A

   c. 120 IF Q / 3 < 9               d. 130 IF Q <> 3 XOR Q = 3
              THEN COUNT = COUNT + 1            THEN SUM = SUM + AMT
   ```

5. Write a series of statements to perform the logic indicated below:

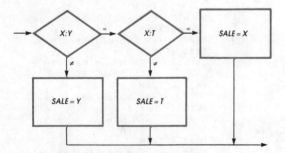

6. Construct partial programs for each of the following logic structures:

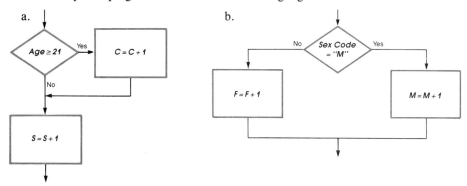

7. Construct partial programs for each of the logic structures found below and on the following page:

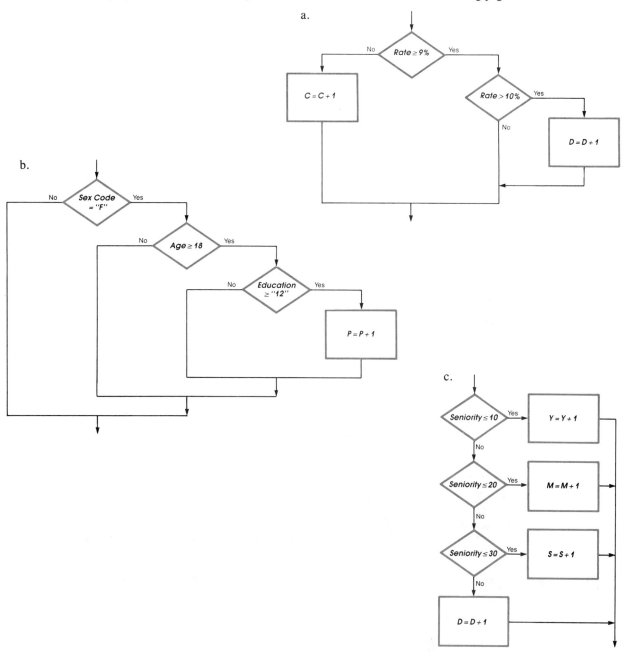

d.

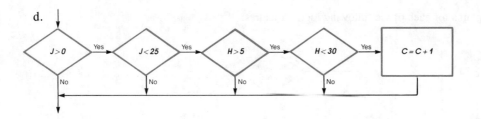

e.   f.

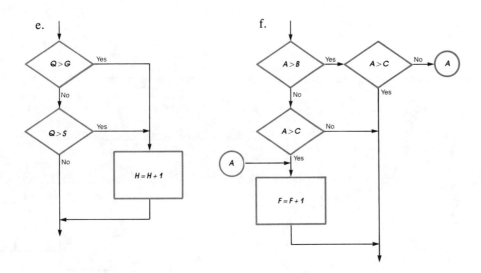

8. Construct a partial flowchart for each of the following:

  a. NOT(S = Q) AND (X > 1 OR C < 3)   b. (K = 9 AND Q = 2) OR NOT Z = 3 OR T = 0

9. Given S = 0, Y = 4, B = 7, T = 8, and X = 3, determine the action taken for each of the following.

<table>
<tr><td>

```
a. 100 IF S > 0
       THEN GOSUB 5000
```
</td><td>

```
b. 200 IF B = 4 OR T > 7
       THEN IF X > 1
           THEN GOSUB 5000
```
</td></tr>
<tr><td>

```
c. 300 IF X = 3 OR T > 2
       THEN IF Y > 7
           THEN GOSUB 5000
```
</td><td>

```
d. 400 IF X + 2 < 5
       THEN IF B < Y + X
           THEN GOSUB 5000
```
</td></tr>
<tr><td>

```
e. 500 IF B <> 7 AND NOT(T = 6)
       THEN GOSUB 5000
```
</td><td>

```
f. 600 IF T > X OR B <> S
       THEN GOSUB 5000
```
</td></tr>
</table>

10. The following situations all request the user to enter a value; write a partial program for each situation. After the value is entered, validate the value with a While loop. If the value is invalid, display an appropriate diagnostic message and request that the entry be reentered.

  a. Request a percent (PERCENT). If the percent is negative or greater than 25, request the user to reenter the value.

  b. Request a balance (BALANCE). Check if the balance is between \$550.99 and \$765.50 inclusive. If the balance is outside the range, request the user to reenter the value.

  c. Request a customer code (CODE\$). Check to ensure that the code is an A, D, E, or F. If the code is invalid, request the user to reenter the code.

  d. Request a customer number (CUSTOMER\$) and check to ensure that the third leftmost digit is a 4. If the third digit is not a 4, request the user to reenter the number.

11. Assume that P and Q are simple conditions. The following logical equivalences are known as DeMorgan's laws:

        NOT (P OR Q) is equivalent to NOT P AND NOT Q
        NOT (P AND Q) is equivalent to NOT P OR NOT Q

Use DeMorgan's laws to find a logical equivalent for each of the following:

a. NOT(P OR (NOT Q))
b. NOT((NOT P) OR Q)
c. NOT(NOT P AND Q)
d. NOT((NOT P) AND (NOT Q))

12. Write a program that determines the number of negative values N, number of zero values Z, and number of positive values P in the following data set: 4, 2, 3, –9, 0, 0, –4, –6, –8, 3, 2, 0, 0, 8, –3, 4. Use the sentinel value –1E37 to test for the end of file.
13. Given the four variables W, X, Y, and Z, with previously defined values, write a sequence of IF statements to increment the variable COUNT by 1 if all four variables have the exact value of 100. If one or more variables have a different value, execute line 300 instead.
14. The sequence of Fibonacci numbers begins with 1, 1 and continues endlessly, each number being the sum of the preceding two:

    1, 1, 2, 3, 5, 8, 13, 21, 34, ...

Construct a program to compute the first X numbers of the sequence where the value of X is entered in response to an INPUT statement.

15. Given two positive valued variables, A and B, write a sequence of statements to assign the variable with the larger value to GREATER and the variable with the smaller value to SMALLER. If A and B are equal, assign either one to EQUAL.
16. The values of three variables U, V, and W are positive and not equal to each other. Using IF statements, determine which has the smallest value and assign this value to SMALL.
17. The symbol N! represents the product of the first N positive integers: $N! = N * (N - 1) * (N - 2) * ... * 1$. When a result is defined in terms of itself, we call it a **recursive definition**. Construct a program that will accept from the keyboard a positive integer and compute its factorial. The recursive definition is as follows: If $N = 1$, then $N! = 1$; otherwise $N! = N(N - 1)!$.
18. Consider the following program and then answer the questions on the top of the next page.

```
1000 ' Exercise 5.18
1010 ' ****** Main Module ******
1020 GOSUB 2000   ' Initialization
1030 GOSUB 3000   ' Process File
1040 GOSUB 4000   ' Wrap-up
1050 END
1060 '
2000 ' ***** Initialization ******
2010 COUNT = 0
2020 SUM = 0
2030 RETURN
2040 '
3000 ' ****** Process File ******
3010 READ X, Y, Z
3020 WHILE X > 0
3030     IF X < Y + 2
             THEN COUNT = COUNT - 1
             ELSE GOSUB 3200
3040     READ X, Y, Z
3050 WEND
3060 RETURN
3070 '
3200 ' ****** False Task 1 ******
3210     IF X >= Z + 1
             THEN SUM = SUM + X * Z : COUNT = COUNT + 1 : PRINT SUM
             ELSE COUNT = COUNT - 2
3220 RETURN
3230 '
4000 ' ******** Wrap-up **********
4010 PRINT COUNT, SUM
4020 PRINT "End of Report"
4030 RETURN
4040 '
4050 ' ****** Data Follows ******
4060 DATA 4, 1, 15, 12, 7, 1, 8, 4, 7
4070 DATA 6, 8, 3, 1, 7, 2, -1, 0, 0
4080 ' ****** End of Program *****
```

a. Which variable is used to test for end of file?
b. What are the values of COUNT and SUM just before line 3040 is executed for the third time?
c. How many lines are displayed by this program?
d. What is the maximum value of SUM displayed?
e. What is the maximum value of COUNT displayed?

19. Given the following "unstructured" program, rewrite it by making it more "structured." Eliminate the two GOTO statements and use the WHILE and WEND statements for looping.

```
100 ' Exercise 5.19
110 TOTAL = 0
120 READ WEIGHT
130 IF WEIGHT < 0 THEN 180
140 IF WEIGHT > 1000 THEN 160
150 GOTO 120
160 TOTAL = TOTAL + WEIGHT
170 GOTO 120
180 PRINT TOTAL
190 ' *** Data Follows ***
200 DATA 1000, 120000, 80000, 22, -12345
210 END
```

20. Write a partial program to set A = -1 if C and D are both zero; set A = -2 if neither C nor D is zero; and set A = -3 if either, but not both, C or D is zero.

21. The WESAVU National Bank computes its monthly service charge on checking accounts by adding $0.25 to a value computed from the following:

a. $0.09 per check for the first ten checks   b. $0.08 per check for the next ten checks
c. $0.07 per check for the next ten checks   d. $0.06 per check for all the rest of the checks

Write a sequence of statements that includes an ON-GOSUB statement and a PRINT statement to display the account number (ACCOUNT), the number of checks cashed (CHECKS), and the computed monthly charge (CHARGE). Assume that the account number and the number of checks cashed are entered via INPUT statements prior to the execution of the ON-GOSUB statement.

22. In each of the following compound conditions, indicate the order of evaluation by the PC. (See the examples on page 156. Beginning with 1, use numbers to show the order of evaluation.)

a. S > 0 OR A > 0 OR T > 0   b. S > 0 AND A > 0 AND NOT T > 0
c. S > 0 IMP A > 0 EQV T > 0 AND P > 0   d. NOT S > 0 AND T > 0 XOR P > 0

23. Use the Student Diskette to complete the Try It Yourself exercises on pages 145, 161, and 172.

5.13 BASIC PROGRAMMING PROBLEMS

1. Employee Average Yearly Salary

Purpose: To illustrate the concepts of counter and running total initialization; counter and running total incrementation; looping; and testing for the last value in a set of data.

Problem: Construct a top-down program to read, count records, accumulate salaries, and display a sequence of data consisting of employee numbers and salaries for various employees in a payroll file. After the sentinel value (EOF) is processed, display the total number of employees and the average yearly salary of all the employees processed.

Input Data: Prepare and use the following sample data in DATA statements.

Employee Number	Employee Salary
123	$16,000
148	8,126
184	14,800
196	17,400
201	18,950
EOF	0

(**Hint:** See Program 5.1 on page 143.)

Output Results: The following results are displayed.

```
Employee      Employee
Number        Salary
--------      --------
   123        16,000.00
   148         8,126.00
   184        14,800.00
   196        17,400.00
   201        18,950.00

Number of Employees ===>    5
Average Salary ========> $15,055.20
```

2. Selecting the Best and Worst Salesperson

Purpose: To become familiar with exchanging the values of string variables and with using the RESTORE statement.

Problem: Construct a top-down program that will determine and display the best and worst salesperson on the basis of total sales from a salesperson file.

Input Data: Prepare and use the following sample data in DATA statements.

Salesperson Name	Total Sales
Franklin, Ed	$96,185
Smith, Susan	18,421
Stankie, Jim	97,856
Runaw, Jeff	32,146
Ray, Kathy	13,467
Doolittle, Frank	11,316
Zachery, Louis	48,615

Output Results: The following results are displayed.

```
Best Salesperson ======> Stankie, Jim
Total Sales ===========>  $97,856.00

Worst Salesperson =====> Doolittle, Frank
Total Sales ===========>  $11,316.00
```

3. Voter Analysis

Purpose: To become familiar with nested If-Then-Else structures.

Problem: Construct a top-down program that will clear the screen, analyze a citizen file, and generate the following totals.

1. number of males not eligible to register
2. number of females not eligible to register
3. number of males who are old enough to vote but have not registered
4. number of females who are old enough to vote but have not registered
5. number of individuals who are eligible to vote but did not vote
6. number of individuals who did vote
7. number of records processed

(Hint: See Figure 5.14 on page 150.)

Input Data: Prepare and use the following sample data in DATA statements.

Number	Age in Years	Sex Code	Registered	Voted
1614	18	F	N	N
1321	21	M	N	N
1961	33	M	Y	Y
1432	46	F	Y	Y
1721	25	M	Y	Y
1211	16	M	N	N
1100	38	F	Y	Y
4164	34	M	Y	N
2139	19	M	Y	N
8647	25	F	Y	Y
9216	13	M	N	N
7814	15	F	N	N

Output Results: The following results are displayed.

```
Voter Analysis

Males Not Eligible to Register ===================> 2
Females Not Eligible to Register ================> 1

Males Old Enough to Vote but Not Registered =====> 1
Females Old Enough to Vote but Not Registered ===> 1

Individuals Eligible to Vote but Did Not Vote ===> 2
Individuals that Voted ==========================> 5

Total Number of Records Processed ===============> 12

End of Report
```

4. Stockbroker's Commission

Purpose: To become familiar with the If-Then-Else structure and with methods used to determine a stockbroker's commission.

Problem: Write a top-down program that will read a stock transaction and determine the stockbroker's commission. Each transaction includes the following data: the stock name, price per share, number of shares involved, and the stockbroker's name.

The stockbroker's commission is computed in the following manner: if price per share P is less than or equal to $40.00, the commission rate is $0.15 per share; if P is greater than $40.00, the commission rate is $0.25 per share; and if the number of shares sold is less than 125, the commission is 1.5 times the rate per share.

Each line of output is to include the stock transaction data set and the commission paid the stockbroker. Test the stock name for the EOF. Display the total commission earned.

Input Data: Prepare and use the following sample data in DATA statements.

Stock Name	Price per Share	Number of Shares	Stockbroker Name
Crane	$32.50	200	Baker, G.
FstPa	17.50	100	Smith, J.
GenDyn	56.25	300	Smith, A.
Harris	40.00	125	Lucas, M.
BellCd	48.00	160	Soley, K.
BellHow	22.00	300	Jones, D.

Output Results: The following results are displayed.

```
                  Stockbroker's Commission

   Stock       Price       Number      Stockbroker
   Name        Per Share   Of Shares   Name           Commission
   -----       ---------   ---------   -----------    ----------
   Crane         32.50         200     Baker, G.          30.00
   FstPa         17.50         100     Smith, J.          22.50
   GenDyn        56.25         300     Smith, A.          75.00
   Harris        40.00         125     Lucas, M.          18.75
   BellCd        48.00         160     Soley, K.          40.00
   BellHow       22.00         300     Jones, D.          45.00

   Total Commission Earned ========>      $231.25

   End of Report
```

5. Aging Accounts

Purpose: To become familiar with the concepts of aging accounts receivable using Julian calendar dates (i.e., using a number between 1 and 365 to signify a date).

Problem: Write a top-down program to compute the total amount due and percentage of the total amount of receivables that are

1. less than 30 days past due (accounts due < 30 days);
2. past due between 30 and 60 days (30 ≤ accounts due ≤ 60);
3. past due over 60 days (accounts due > 60).

Include in the output the number of accounts in each category. The first input value will be today's Julian date. However, the account number, amount due, and the date due for each customer should be stored in one or more DATA statements.

Input Data: Prepare and use the following sample data in DATA statements. Assume today's Julian date is 155 (i.e., 155th day of the year).

Account Number	Amount Due	Date Due
1168	1495.67	145
2196	3211.16	15
3485	1468.12	130
3612	1896.45	98
7184	5.48	126
8621	965.10	75
9142	613.50	105

Output Results: The following results are displayed.

```
Please enter the Julian Date ======> 155

                Aging Accounts For Day 155

Accounts            Number of       Total           Percent of
Past Due            Accounts        Amount Due      Total Amount
--------            ---------       ----------      ------------
Less Than 30 Days       3           2,969.27            30.75
30 To 60 Days           2           2,509.95            26.00
Over 60 Days            2           4,176.26            43.25

Job Complete
```

6. A Menu-Driven Program with Multi-Functions

Purpose: To become familiar with a multifunction program and with the use of a menu.

Problem: Use top-down programming techniques to write a menu-driven program to compute the volume of a box, a cylinder, a cone, and a sphere. The program should display the menu that is shown under Output Results. Once a code is entered, it must be validated. After the selection of the proper function, the program should prompt the operator for the necessary data, then compute the volume and display it accordingly. The displayed results are to remain on the screen until the Enter key on the keyboard is pressed. After that, the program should redisplay the menu.

Use the following formulas for the volumes V:

1. Volume of a box: $V = L * W * H$, where L is the length, W is the width, and H is the height of the box.
2. Volume of a cylinder: $V = \pi * R * R * H$, where π equals 3.141593, R is the radius, and H is the height of the cylinder.
3. Volume of a cone: $V = (\pi * R * R * H)/3$, where π equals 3.141593, R is the radius of the base, and H is the height of the cone.
4. Volume of a sphere: $V = 4 * \pi * R * R * R$, where π equals 3.141593, and R is the radius of the sphere.

(Hint: See Program 5.3 on page 169.)

Input Data: Use the following sample data.

    Code: 3, Radius = 7, Height = 9
    Code: 4, Radius = 10
    Code: 1, Length = 4.5, Width = 6.7, Height = 12
    Code: 2, Radius = 8, Height = 15
    Code: 7 (This code should return a diagnostic message.)
    Code: 5 (This code ends the program.)

Output Results: The following menu is displayed.

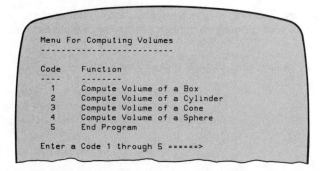

```
Menu For Computing Volumes
--------------------------


Code     Function
----     --------
   1     Compute Volume of a Box
   2     Compute Volume of a Cylinder
   3     Compute Volume of a Cone
   4     Compute Volume of a Sphere
   5     End Program

Enter a Code 1 through 5 ======>
```

7. Payroll Problem IV: Weekly Payroll Computations with Time and a Half for Overtime

Purpose: To become familiar with decision making and with some payroll concepts.

Problem: Modify in a top-down fashion Payroll Problem III in chapter 4, on page 131 (BASIC Programming Problem 3), to include the following conditions.

1. Overtime (hours worked > 80) is paid at 1.5 times the hourly rate.
2. Federal withholding tax is determined in the same manner as indicated in Payroll Problem III. However, assign a value of $0.00 if the gross pay is less than the product of the number of dependents and $38.46.
3. After processing the employee records, display the total gross pay, federal withholding tax, and net pay.

Input Data: Use the sample data found in Payroll Problem II in chapter 3, on page 88 (BASIC Programming Problem 2). Modify the data representing employee 126 so that the number of dependents equals 9.

(Hint: See Program 5.1 on page 143.)

Output Results: The following results are displayed.

```
                  Biweekly Payroll Report

     Employee
     Number       Gross Pay      Fed. Tax     Net Pay
     --------      ---------      --------     -------
        123        1,000.00        184.62      815.38
        124          880.00        168.31      711.69
        125        1,040.00        200.31      839.69
        126           90.00          0.00       90.00

     Total Gross Pay ========>   3,010.00
     Total Withholding Tax ==>     553.23
     Total Net Pay ==========>   2,456.77

     End of Payroll Report
```

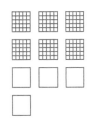

SEQUENTIAL FILES, PAGING REPORTS, AND CONTROL-BREAK PROCESSING

In the first five chapters of this book, we emphasized the importance of integrating data into the program. You learned that data may be entered into a program through the use of the LET statement, the INPUT statement, or the READ and DATA statements. This chapter presents a fourth method for entering data — the use of data files. With data files, the data is stored in auxiliary storage rather than in the program itself. This technique is used primarily for dealing with large amounts of data.

Processing large amounts of data often involves generating reports that are many pages in length. When the length of a report exceeds one page, the report and column headings, as well as a page number, should be printed at the top of each page. This chapter introduces you to writing programs that generate reports of more than one page.

The third topic presented in this chapter is **control breaks**. A control break is a technique that is used to generate subtotals within a report. Most businesses today are divided into units for the purpose of better management. To evaluate the performance of the units within each level, managerial reports are generated which show summaries or minor totals for each subunit. This chapter illustrates programming techniques for generating these types of reports.

At the conclusion of this chapter, you should be able to design programs that write reports to auxiliary storage; build data files; process data files; and generate reports with paging and control breaks.

⊞ **6.2**

DATA FILES

In previous chapters, program development was emphasized. Of equal concern are the organization and processing of data in the form of files. This is especially true in a business environment, for the following three reasons:

1. Business applications, such as payroll, billing, order entry, and inventory, involve the processing of extensive amounts of data.
2. Data must be continually updated if management reports are to be useful.
3. The same data is often required for several applications, such as payroll, personnel, pension plans, and insurance reporting.

Computer manufacturers have applied a great deal of effort toward the development both of hardware, like auxiliary storage devices, and software, like **file-handling statements**, in order to deal directly with the organization and processing of large amounts of data.

In programs in previous chapters, the LET statement, the INPUT statement, or the READ and DATA statements were used to enter data into the PC. A more efficient and convenient method of organizing data is to store it on an auxiliary storage device, like a floppy diskette, and keep it separate from the programs that will process the data. Data stored in this fashion is a **file**, a group of related records. The number of records making up a file may range from just a few to thousands or millions. Each record within the file contains related data items.

Figure 6.1 illustrates a partial list of data items that can be found within the records of a payroll file. Common data items occupy the same position in each record. This sequence within a record is important both for processing and updating a file.

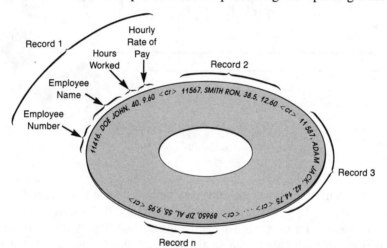

FIGURE 6.1

A conceptual view of a file stored on a diskette, with each data item separated by a comma and each record separated by a carriage return character <cr>.

Creating a data file that is separate from the program yet accessible to it means the following:

1. Data can be used by different programs without having to be reentered each time.
2. Records can be easily updated.
3. Many data files can be processed by a single program.
4. Programs can process a particular file for one run and another file for the next, provided the data items in the records of the files have some common order.

MS BASIC includes a set of file-handling statements that allow a user to do the following:

1. create data files;
2. define the data files to be used by a program;
3. open a file;
4. read data from a file;
5. write data to a file;
6. test for the end of file; and
7. close a file.

File Organization **File organization** is a method of arranging records on an auxiliary storage device. MS BASIC provides for two types of file organization: sequential and random.

A file that is organized sequentially is called a **sequential file** and is limited to sequential processing. This means that the records can be processed only in the order in which they are placed in the file. Conceptually, a sequential file is identical to the use of DATA statements within a BASIC program. For example, the fourteenth record in a sequential file cannot be processed until after the previous thirteen records have been processed. Similarly, the fourteenth data item in a DATA statement of a BASIC program cannot be processed until the previous thirteen data items have been processed.

Sequential organization can also be used to write reports to auxiliary storage instead of to an external device, such as a screen or a printer. Once the report is in auxiliary storage, it can be displayed at any time and as often as needed. Writing reports to auxiliary storage is a common practice, especially with programs that generate multiple reports. In such programs, each report is written to a separate file.

The second type of file organization, random files, will be discussed in chapter 9.

⊞ 6.3
SEQUENTIAL FILE PROCESSING

This section presents the file-handling statements required to create and process sequential files. Also, sample programs are presented to illustrate the following:

1. how reports can be written to auxiliary storage instead of to the screen or to the printer;
2. how to build sequential files that other programs can process; and
3. how reports can be generated from data that is located in sequential files.

Later, in chapter 9, we will show you how to update sequential files.

Opening Sequential Files

Before any file can be read from or written to, it must be opened by the OPEN statement. When executed, the OPEN statement carries out the following five basic functions:

1. It requests the PC to allocate a **buffer**. A buffer is a part of main storage through which data is passed between the program and auxiliary storage.
2. It identifies by name the file to be processed.
3. It indicates whether the file is to be read from or written to.
4. It assigns the file a filenumber.
5. It sets the pointer to the beginning of the file or to the end of the file.

The general form of the OPEN statement is shown in Table 6.1.

TABLE 6.1 The OPEN Statement for Sequential Files

General Form:	OPEN filespec FOR mode AS #filenumber
	where **filespec** *is the name of the file;*
	mode *is one of the following:*
	APPEND *specifies sequential output mode, where the pointer is positioned to the end of the file;*
	INPUT *specifies sequential input mode, where the pointer is positioned at the beginning of the file;*
	OUTPUT *specifies sequential output mode, where the pointer is positioned at the beginning of the file; and*
	filenumber *is a numeric expression whose value is between 1 and the maximum number of files allowed (3 by default). The filenumber is associated with the file (**filespec**) for as long as it is open. The filenumber may be used by other file-handling statements to refer to the specific file.*
Keyword Entry:	*Simultaneously press the Alt and O keys on your keyboard.*
Purpose:	*Allows a program to read records from or write records to a sequential file.*
Examples:	500 OPEN "B:EMPLOYEE.DAT" FOR INPUT AS #1
	600 OPEN "PAYROLL.LIS" FOR OUPUT AS #2
	700 OPEN "ACCOUNTS.DAT" FOR APPEND AS #3
	800 OPEN FILESPEC$ FOR INPUT AS #3
Note:	*MS BASIC provides for a second general form for the OPEN statement:*
	OPEN mode, #filenumber, filespec
	(This second general form is less contemporary than the general form specified at the top of this table, and will therefore not be used in this book.)

As described in Table 6.1 on the previous page, a sequential file may be opened for input, output, or append. Line 500 in the examples section of Table 6.1 opens the file EMPLOYEE.DAT for input as filenumber 1. The file is located on the B drive. Since EMPLOYEE.DAT is opened for input, the program can only read records from it. An attempt to write a record to EMPLOYEE.DAT will result in the following diagnostic message:

```
Bad file number
```

If an attempt is made to open a nonexistent file for input, the following diagnostic message displays:

```
File not found
```

Line 600 in Table 6.1 opens PAYROLL.LIS on the default drive for output. Since PAYROLL.LIS is opened for output, the program can only write records to the sequential file.

Opening a sequential file for output always creates a new file. If, for example, PAYROLL.LIS already exists, then it is deleted before it is opened. Since there are never any records in a newly opened file, the data pointer is positioned at the beginning of the file.

In the third example in Table 6.1, line 700 opens ACCOUNTS.DAT on the default drive for appending records to the end of the file. If ACCOUNTS.DAT exists, the data pointer is positioned after the last record. If ACCOUNTS.DAT does not exist, the PC creates ACCOUNTS.DAT and positions the data pointer at the beginning of the file.

The append mode (APPEND) should be used in the OPEN statement whenever records are added to a sequential file. For example, with an order-entry application, it may be desirable to maintain a weekly customer-order file. Orders entered on a daily basis are appended to those which have been previously entered. At the end of the week, the customer-order file will contain the orders for the week in the sequence entered.

The last example in Table 6.1, line 800, illustrates that the filespec may be defined in an OPEN statement as a string variable. This allows you to write an OPEN statement in a program without knowing the name of the sequential file. Of course, when the program is executed, the user must supply the filespec. This is usually done through the use of an INPUT statement. Consider the following partial program:

```
790 INPUT "File Specification of the File to Process ====> ", FILESPEC$
800 OPEN FILESPEC$ FOR INPUT AS #3
```

The OPEN statement in line 800 opens for input the file that corresponds to the string value assigned to FILESPEC$ in line 790. Note that the operator is responsible for the entire file specification — device name, file name, and file extension. Through the use of the concatenation operator, we can simplify the operator entry. For example:

```
890 INPUT "Name of the File to Process ====> ", FILENAME$
900 OPEN "B:" + FILENAME$ + ".DAT" FOR INPUT AS #3
```

In this case, the operator enters only the file name. The concatenation operators in line 900 append the device name to the front of the file name and the file extension to the back of the file name.

The filenumber in an OPEN statement must be an integer expression whose value is between 1 and the number of maximum files allowed. The default maximum number of files is three. If a program requires more than three different file numbers at any one time, you can increase the maximum number of files to fifteen by appending the /F parameter to the BASICA command. For more information on the use of this parameter, see the BASIC user's manual. Note that a program may reuse filenumbers that have been deallocated by the CLOSE statement.

The following rules summarize the use of the OPEN statement.

> ***OPEN Rule 1:*** A sequential file must be opened before it can be read from or written to.

> ***OPEN Rule 2:*** A program can only read records from a sequential file that has been opened for input.

> ***OPEN Rule 3:*** A sequential file must already exist if it is opened for input.

> ***OPEN Rule 4:*** A program can only write records to a sequential file that has been opened for output or append.

> ***OPEN Rule 5:*** A filenumber can be assigned to only one sequential file at a time.

Closing Sequential Files

When a program is finished reading or writing to a file, it must close the file with the CLOSE statement. The CLOSE statement terminates the association between the file and the filenumber assigned in the OPEN statement and deallocates the part of main storage that is assigned to the buffer. If a file is being written to, the CLOSE statement ensures that the last record is transferred from the buffer in main storage to auxiliary storage.

The general form of the CLOSE statement is shown in Table 6.2.

———TABLE 6.2 The CLOSE Statement———

General Form:	CLOSE *or* CLOSE #*filenumber₁*, ..., #*filenumberₙ*
Purpose:	*Terminates the association between a filenumber and a file that was established in a previously executed OPEN statement.* *If the file is opened for output, the CLOSE statement ensures that the last record is transferred from main storage to auxiliary storage.* *If no filenumbers follow the keyword CLOSE, then all opened files are closed.*
Examples:	600 CLOSE #1, #2, #3 700 CLOSE #1 800 CLOSE #2, #1 900 CLOSE

The CLOSE statement terminates access to a file. For example,

    4600 CLOSE #2, #3

causes the files assigned to filenumbers 2 and 3 to be closed. Any other files previously opened by the program remain open.

Following the close of a specified file, the filenumber may be assigned again to the same file or to a different file by an OPEN statement. For example, the partial program at the top of the following page is valid.

```
150 OPEN "INVEN.DAT" FOR INPUT AS #1
        .
        .
        .
500 CLOSE #1
510 OPEN "INVEN.DAT" FOR INPUT AS #1
        .
        .
        .
700 CLOSE #1
710 END
```

Line 150 opens INVEN.DAT for input as filenumber 1. After some processing, line 500 closes INVEN.DAT. Line 510 reopens INVEN.DAT for input as filenumber 1. When the file is opened for the second time, the data pointer is positioned to the first record in the file.

Opening and closing a file more than once in a program is quite common. For example, many applications involve reading and processing the records in a sequential data file to compute an average. The file is then processed a second time to evaluate each record against the average. In earlier chapters, the RESTORE statement was used with data located in DATA statements to process the data set a second time. The term **rewind** is sometimes used to describe the technique of closing and then opening the file to begin processing again with the first record. Note that when executed, the END statement closes all opened files before terminating execution of the program. In our opinion, it is good programming practice to close all opened files with the CLOSE statement, instead of relying on the execution of the END statement.

The following rule summarizes the CLOSE statement.

CLOSE Rule 1: A file must be opened before it can be closed.

Writing Reports to a Sequential File

The PRINT #n and PRINT #n, USING statements are used to write reports to sequential files. Once it has been written to a file, the report can be displayed or printed as often as desired without the program being reexecuted. The general forms of the PRINT #n and PRINT #n, USING statements are shown in Tables 6.3 and 6.4, respectively.

_____TABLE 6.3 The PRINT #n Statement_____

General Form:	PRINT #n, item pm item pm ... pm item
	
	where **n** is a filenumber assigned to a file defined in an OPEN statement;
	    item is a constant, variable, expression, function reference, or null; and
	    pm is a comma, semicolon, or space.

Purpose:	Provides for the generation of labeled and unlabeled output or of output in a consistent tabular format from the program to a sequential file in auxiliary storage.
Keyword Entry:	Press the question mark (?) key or simultaneously the Alt and P keys on your keyboard.
Examples:	100 PRINT #1, 200 PRINT #2, EMP.NAME$, AGE, WEIGHT 300 PRINT #1, TAB(10); "Total Sales ======>"; TOTAL 400 PRINT #2, X + Y/4, C * B 500 PRINT #3, Q1TAX, Q2TAX, Q3TAX, Q4TAX 600 PRINT #2, SUM;
Note:	One or more spaces between the print items have the same effect as the semicolon. The print items may be numeric or string.

_____TABLE 6.4 The PRINT #n, USING Statement_____

General Form:	`PRINT #n, USING` *string expression; list*

	*where **n** is a filenumber assigned to a file defined in an* `OPEN` *statement;*
	      string expression *(sometimes called the descriptor field or format field)*
	      is either a string constant or a string variable; and
	      list *is a list of items to be displayed in the format specified by the*
	      descriptor field.

Purpose:	*Provides for controlling exactly the format of a program's output to a sequential file by specifying an image to which that output must conform.*
Keyword Entry:	*Simultaneously press the Alt and P keys for the keyword* `PRINT`. *Simultaneously press the Alt and U keys for the keyword* `USING`.

Examples:	`550 PRINT #3, USING "The answer is #,###.##"; COST`
	`600 PRINT #2, USING "## divided by # is #.#"; NUM, DEN, QUOT`
	
	`650 FORMAT.1$ = "Total cost =======> $$,###.##-"`
	`700 PRINT #7, USING FORMAT.1$; TOTAL`
	
	`750 FORMAT.2$ = "**,###.##"`
	`760 PRINT #1, USING FORMAT.2$; CHECK;`
	
	`800 PRINT #2, USING "\   \"; CUST.NAME$`
	`850 PRINT #3, USING "!, !, \        \"; FIRST$, MIDDLE$, LAST$`
	`905 PRINT #4, USING "Example _##"; NUMBER`
	`950 PRINT #9, USING "#.##^^^^"; DIS.1, DIS.2, DIS.3, DIS.4`

Note:	*For more information on the descriptor field, see Table 4.9 on page 107.*

The `PRINT #n` and `PRINT #n, USING` statements work in exactly the same way as the `PRINT` and `PRINT USING` statements except that information is written to a sequential file in auxiliary storage rather than to the screen. For example, the statement

```
500 PRINT A, B, C
```

displays the values of A, B, and C on the screen in print zones 1, 2, and 3. Similarly, the statement

```
500 PRINT #1, A, B, C
```

creates and transmits a record image to the sequential file, assigned to filenumber 1, with the values of A, B, and C beginning in zones 1, 2, and 3 of the record.

Programming Case Study 8B: *Writing the Weekly Payroll and Summary Report to Auxiliary Storage*

In chapter 5, the Weekly Payroll and Summary Report (Programming Case Study 8A) was introduced. In the solution (Program 5.1 on pages 143-144), the `PRINT` and `PRINT USING` statements displayed the report on the screen. In the following modified solution, the report is written to a sequential file in auxiliary storage. Program 6.1 is identical to Program 5.1 except for some minor comments and the inclusion of the following:

1. line 2053, which displays a message on the screen indicating that the report is being written to auxiliary storage;
2. line 2056, which opens for output the sequential file REPORT.LIS on the B drive;
3. inclusion of filenumber 1 in each `PRINT` and `PRINT USING` statement writing the report;
4. line 4093, which closes REPORT.LIS; and
5. lines 4096 and 4099, which display end-of-job information on the screen.

Program Solution   The following program writes the weekly payroll and summary report to auxiliary storage.

PROGRAM 6.1

```
1000 ' Program 6.1
1010 ' Writing the Weekly Payroll and Summary Report
1013 ' to Auxiliary Storage
1016 ' Report File Name = REPORT.LIS
1020 ' ********************************************
1030 ' *                Main Module               *
1040 ' ********************************************
1050 GOSUB 2000   ' Call Initialization
1060 GOSUB 3000   ' Call Process File
1070 GOSUB 4000   ' Call Wrap-up
1080 END
1090 '
2000 ' ********************************************
2010 ' *              Initialization              *
2020 ' ********************************************
2030 EMP.COUNT = 0
2040 TOTAL.GROSS = 0
2050 CLS : KEY OFF   ' Clear Screen
2053 LOCATE 10, 20 : PRINT "Writing Payroll Report to Auxiliary Storage..."
2056 OPEN "REPORT.LIS" FOR OUTPUT AS #1
2060 GOSUB 2200   ' Call Initialize Report Format
2070 GOSUB 2400   ' Call Write Report and Column Headings
2080 RETURN
2090 '
2200 ' ********************************************
2210 ' *          Initialize Report Format        *
2220 ' ********************************************
2230 HEAD.LN1$ = "          Weekly Payroll Report"
2240 HEAD.LN2$ = "Employee No.   Hours     Rate     Gross Pay"
2250 DETL.LN$  = "     \  \           ###.#     ##.##      ##,###.##"
2260 TOT.LN1$  = "Total Gross Pay ========> $$,###.##"
2270 TOT.LN2$  = "Number of Employees ====>      ###"
2280 TOT.LN3$  = "Average Gross Pay ======> $$,###.##"
2290 TOT.LN4$  = "End of Payroll Report"
2300 RETURN
2310 '
2400 ' ********************************************
2410 ' *        Write Report and Column Headings   *
2420 ' ********************************************
2430 PRINT #1, HEAD.LN1$
2440 PRINT #1,
2450 PRINT #1, HEAD.LN2$
2460 PRINT #1,
2470 RETURN
2480 '
3000 ' ********************************************
3010 ' *                Process File              *
3020 ' ********************************************
3030 READ EMP.NUMBER$, EMP.HOURS, EMP.RATE
3040 WHILE EMP.NUMBER$ <> "EOF"
3050    GOSUB 3200   ' Call Compute Gross Pay and Increment Accums.
3060    PRINT #1, USING DETL.LN$; EMP.NUMBER$, EMP.HOURS,
                             EMP.RATE, EMP.GROSS
3070    READ EMP.NUMBER$, EMP.HOURS, EMP.RATE
3080 WEND
3090 RETURN
3100 '
```

(continued)

```
3200 ' ****************************************************
3210 ' * Compute Gross Pay and Increment Accumulators *
3220 ' ****************************************************
3230 EMP.COUNT = EMP.COUNT + 1
3240 EMP.OVERTIME = EMP.HOURS - 40
3250 IF EMP.OVERTIME <= 0
        THEN EMP.GROSS = EMP.HOURS * EMP.RATE
        ELSE EMP.GROSS = EMP.HOURS * EMP.RATE + .5 * EMP.RATE * EMP.OVERTIME
3260 TOTAL.GROSS = TOTAL.GROSS + EMP.GROSS
3270 RETURN
3280 '
4000 ' ****************************************************
4010 ' *                   Wrap-up                      *
4020 ' ****************************************************
4030 AVERAGE.GROSS = TOTAL.GROSS / EMP.COUNT
4040 PRINT #1,
4050 PRINT #1, USING TOT.LN1$; TOTAL.GROSS
4060 PRINT #1, USING TOT.LN2$; EMP.COUNT
4070 PRINT #1, USING TOT.LN3$; AVERAGE.GROSS
4080 PRINT #1,
4090 PRINT #1, TOT.LN4$
4093 CLOSE #1
4096 LOCATE 12, 20 : PRINT "Report Stored Under File Name REPORT.LIS"
4099 LOCATE 14, 20 : PRINT "End of Job"
4100 RETURN
4110 '
4120 ' *************** Data Follows *****************
4130 DATA 124, 40,   5.60
4140 DATA 126, 56,   5.90
4150 DATA 128, 38,   4.60
4160 DATA 129, 48.5, 6.10
4170 DATA EOF, 0,    0    : ' This is the trailer record
4180 ' ************** End of Program ****************

RUN
```

Discussion of the
Program Solution

When the RUN command is issued for Program 6.1, the information shown in Figure 6.2 is displayed on the screen to inform the operator that the report is being written to a sequential file in auxiliary storage under the name REPORT.LIS on the default drive.

FIGURE 6.2
The display from
the execution
of Program 6.1.

```
Writing Payroll Report to Auxiliary Storage...
Report Stored Under File Name REPORT.LIS
End of Job
```

The report written to auxiliary storage by Program 6.1 is illustrated in Figure 6.3

FIGURE 6.3
Results of Program 6.1
written to auxiliary
storage under the file
name REPORT.LIS and
displayed with the MS
DOS command TYPE.

```
            Weekly Payroll Report

Employee No.    Hours    Rate    Gross Pay

    124         40.0     5.60      224.00
    126         56.0     5.90      377.60
    128         38.0     4.60      174.80
    129         48.5     6.10      321.77

Total Gross Pay ========> $1,098.17
Number of Employees ====>        4
Average Gross Pay ======>   $274.54

End of Payroll Report
```

TRY IT YOURSELF

A copy of the sequential file REPORT.LIS is on the Student Diskette. Place the Student Diskette in the B drive and use the MS DOS command TYPE to list the contents of REPORT.LIS on the screen. For example, enter

```
B> TYPE REPORT.LIS
```

Use the MS DOS command PRINT to print the report on the printer. For example, enter

```
B> PRINT REPORT.LIS
```

Do you understand that once a report has been written to auxiliary storage, the TYPE and PRINT commands can be used to display and print the report as often as needed?

Flowchart of the OPEN and CLOSE Statements

The I/O symbol is used to represent the OPEN and CLOSE statements. Therefore, the flowchart symbol below on the left represents the OPEN statement in line 2056 of Program 6.1, and the flowchart symbol on the right represents the CLOSE statement in line 4093 of Program 6.1.

Writing Data to a Sequential File

In Program 6.1, the PRINT #n and PRINT #n, USING statements were employed to write a report to a sequential file in auxiliary storage. To write data to a sequential file, we use the WRITE #n statement. The WRITE #n statement writes data in a format required by the INPUT #n statement. The format requirement is similar to that of the READ and DATA statements — all data items are separated by commas. The WRITE #n statement even goes one step better by surrounding all string data items with quotation marks.

The following WRITE #n statement writes a record in the format required by the INPUT #n statement.

```
500 WRITE #2, EMP.NAME$, AGE, CODE$, SENIORITY
```

The WRITE #n statement in line 500 causes a comma to be placed between the data items. Quotation marks are placed around the values of EMP.NAME$ and CODE$ and a carriage return character <cr> is appended to the last data item written to form the record. For example, if EMP.NAME$ = John Smith, AGE = 46, CODE$ = 3, and SENIORITY = 12, then line 500 transmits the following record to the sequential file assigned to file number 2:

```
"John Smith",46,"3",12<cr>
```
Record Transmitted to Filenumber 2 by Line 500

Note that the string values are delimited with the quotation marks and that the usual leading and trailing spaces surrounding positive numbers are compressed out.

The general form of the WRITE #n statement is given in Table 6.5 on the opposite page.

_____TABLE 6.5 The WRITE #n Statement_____

General Form:	WRITE #n, *list of variables*
	where **n** *is a filenumber assigned to a sequential file opened for output.*
Purpose:	*Writes data items separated by commas to a sequential file in auxiliary storage.*
Examples:	1000 WRITE #1, COST, MARGIN, PRICE
	2000 WRITE #2, AMOUNT, DESCRIPTION$
	3000 WRITE #3, DEPENDENTS, TAX,

Programming Case Study 11: Creating a Sequential File

Problem: The PUC Company has requested that a sequential file (INVNTORY.DAT) be created from the inventory data below. The data must be written in a format that is consistent with the INPUT #n statement. Use a series of LOCATE and INPUT statements to display the screen shown in Figure 6.4.

In the following inventory data, each line represents an inventory record.

Stock Number	Warehouse Location	Description	Unit Cost	Selling Price	Quantity on Hand
C101	1	Roadhandler	97.56	125.11	25
C204	3	Whitewalls	37.14	99.95	140
C502	2	Tripod	32.50	38.99	10
S209	1	Maxidrill	88.76	109.99	6
S416	2	Normalsaw	152.55	179.40	1
S812	2	Router	48.47	61.15	8
S942	4	Radialsaw	376.04	419.89	3
T615	4	Oxford-Style	26.43	31.50	28
T713	2	Moc-Boot	24.99	29.99	30
T814	2	Work-Boot	22.99	27.99	56

FIGURE 6.4
The screen design for requesting operator entry of inventory records for Program 6.2.

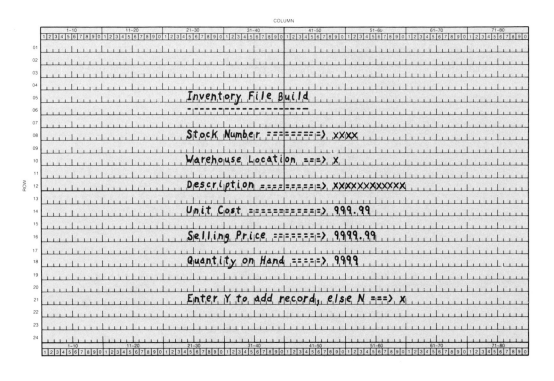

Following are a list of the program tasks in outline form; a program solution; and a discussion of the program solution.

Program Tasks

1. Initialization

   a. Set record count (RECORD.COUNT) to zero.
   b. Clear the 25th line of the screen.
   c. Open the file INVNTORY.DAT for output as filenumber 1.

2. Build File

   a. Call the Accept an Inventory Record Module. In this module, do the following:
      (1) Clear the screen and display a screen title.
      (2) Accept the stock number (STOCK$).
      (3) If STOCK$ does not equal the value EOF, then call the Accept Remaining Inventory Record Data Items Module. In this module, request the operator to enter the remaining data items (LOCATION$, DESC$, COST, PRICE, and QUANTITY) for the inventory record. Also request the operator to enter Y to add the record, else N. Assign the latter response to CONTROL$. (In the interest of brevity, we are omitting the validation of the codes Y, y, N, and n.)
   b. Establish a While loop that executes until STOCK$ is equal to the value EOF. Do the following within this loop:
      (1) If CONTROL$ is equal to the value Y or y, then call the Write an Inventory Record Module. In the Write an Inventory Record Module, do the following:
         (a) Use the WRITE #n statement to write the record to INVNTORY.DAT.
         (b) Increment the record count (RECORD.COUNT) by 1.
      (2) Call the Accept an Inventory Record Module described in step 2a.

3. Wrap-up

   a. Close the file.
   b. Clear the screen and display a message indicating that the file creation is complete.
   c. Display the number of records (RECORD.COUNT) written to INVNTORY.DAT.

Program Solution

The following program corresponds to the preceding tasks.

PROGRAM 6.2

```
1000 ' Program 6.2
1010 ' Creating a Sequential File
1020 ' Output File Name = INVNTORY.DAT
1030 ' ******************************************************************
1040 ' *                          Main Module                           *
1050 ' ******************************************************************
1060 GOSUB 2000   ' Call Initialization
1070 GOSUB 3000   ' Call Build File
1080 GOSUB 4000   ' Call Wrap-up
1090 END
1100 '
2000 ' ******************************************************************
2010 ' *                         Initialization                         *
2020 ' ******************************************************************
2030 RECORD.COUNT = 0
2040 KEY OFF   ' Clear 25th line
2050 OPEN "INVNTORY.DAT" FOR OUTPUT AS #1
2060 RETURN
2070 '
```

(continued)

```
3000 ' ********************************************************************
3010 ' *                            Build File                          *
3020 ' ********************************************************************
3030 GOSUB 3200      ' Call Accept an Inventory Record
3040 WHILE STOCK$ <> "EOF"
3050    IF CONTROL$ = "Y" OR CONTROL$ = "y"
            THEN GOSUB 3600  ' Call Write an Inventory Record
3060    GOSUB 3200  ' Call Accept an Inventory Record
3070 WEND
3080 RETURN
3090 '
3200 ' ********************************************************************
3210 ' *                  Accept an Inventory Record                    *
3220 ' ********************************************************************
3230 CLS  ' Clear Screen
3240 LOCATE  5, 25 : PRINT "Inventory File Build"
3250 LOCATE  6, 25 : PRINT "--------------------"
3260 LOCATE  8, 25 : INPUT "Stock Number =========> ", STOCK$
3270 IF STOCK$ <> "EOF"
        THEN GOSUB 3400  ' Accept Remaining Inventory Record Data Items
3280 RETURN
3290 '
3400 ' ********************************************************************
3410 ' *          Accept Remaining Inventory Record Data Items          *
3420 ' ********************************************************************
3430 LOCATE 10, 25 : INPUT "Warehouse Location ===> ", LOCATION$
3440 LOCATE 12, 25 : INPUT "Description ===========> ", DESC$
3450 LOCATE 14, 25 : INPUT "Unit Cost =============> ", COST
3460 LOCATE 16, 25 : INPUT "Selling Price ========> ", PRICE
3470 LOCATE 18, 25 : INPUT "Quantity on Hand =====> ", QUANTITY
3480 LOCATE 21, 25 : INPUT "Enter Y to add record, else N ===> ", CONTROL$
3490 RETURN
3500 '
3600 ' ********************************************************************
3610 ' *                  Write an Inventory Record                     *
3620 ' ********************************************************************
3630 WRITE #1, STOCK$, LOCATION$, DESC$, COST, PRICE, QUANTITY
3640 RECORD.COUNT = RECORD.COUNT + 1
3650 RETURN
3660 '
4000 ' ********************************************************************
4010 ' *                            Wrap-up                             *
4020 ' ********************************************************************
4030 CLOSE #1
4040 CLS  ' Clear Screen
4050 LOCATE 10, 15 : PRINT "Creation of Sequential File Is Complete"
4060 LOCATE 14, 15
4070 PRINT "Total Number of Records in INVNTORY.DAT ===>"; RECORD.COUNT
4080 RETURN
4090 ' ******************** End of Program **********************

RUN
```

Discussion of the Program Solution

When Program 6.2 is executed, line 2050 of the Initialization Module opens INVNTORY.DAT for output as filenumber 1.

In the Build File Module, line 3030 calls the Accept an Inventory Record Module. Figure 6.5 on the following page, shows the display due to the execution of this module for the first record entered by the operator. Owing to line 3270, the last five data items are requested only if STOCK$ does not equal the value EOF. If STOCK$ equals the value EOF, control returns to the Build File Module and the While loop is terminated.

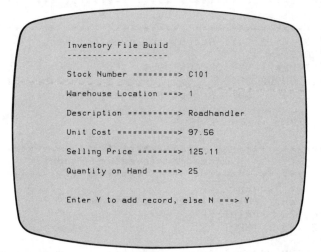

FIGURE 6.5
*The display from the
execution of the Accept
an Inventory Record
Module in Program 6.2.*

As shown in the last line of Figure 6.5, line 3480 requests that the operator enter Y to add the record displayed on the screen to INVNTORY.DAT. This request allows the operator to reject the record if an error is detected after the entries on the screen have been checked. Note that in line 3050 of the Build File Module, the Write an Inventory Record Module is called only if CONTROL$ equals the value Y or y.

In the Write an Inventory Record Module, line 3630 includes the WRITE #n statement. This statement writes the record to the sequential file INVNTORY.DAT in a format that is consistent with the INPUT #n statement. Figure 6.6 shows the format of the data written to INVNTORY.DAT by Program 6.2.

```
"C101","1","Roadhandler",97.56,125.11,25
"C204","3","Whitewalls",37.14,99.95,140
"C502","2","Tripod",32.5,38.99,10
"S209","1","Maxidrill",88.76,109.99,6
"S416","2","Normalsaw",152.55,179.4,1
"S812","2","Router",48.47,61.15,8
"S942","4","Radialsaw",376.04,419.89,3
"T615","4","Oxford-Style",26.43,31.5,28
"T713","2","Moc-Boot",24.99,29.99,30
"T814","2","Work-Boot",22.99,27.99,56
```

FIGURE 6.6
*A listing of
INVNTORY.DAT
created by Program 6.2.*

In the Wrap-up Module, line 4030 closes INVNTORY.DAT. This ensures that the last record entered by the operator is moved from the buffer to the file in auxiliary storage. Figure 6.7 shows the display due to lines 4040 through 4070 of the Wrap-up Module.

FIGURE 6.7
*The display due to the
execution of the
Wrap-up Module in
Program 6.2.*

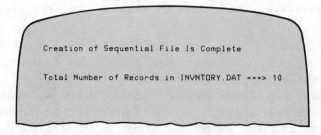

Data validation was purposely left out of the Case Study to present a clear-cut example of how to create a sequential file. In a production environment, reasonableness checks are always considered for the stock number (STOCK$); warehouse location (LOCATION$);

unit cost (COST); selling price (PRICE); quantity on hand (QUANTITY); and operator response (CONTROL$). Data should always be validated before it is placed in a file.

The INPUT #n Statement

The INPUT #n statement is used to read data from a sequential file that has been created by using the WRITE #n statement. The statement is the same as the READ statement except that it reads data from a file instead of from DATA statements. Line 2050 in the following partial program,

```
2050 OPEN "INVNTORY.DAT" FOR INPUT AS #1
          .
          .
          .
3210 INPUT #1, STOCK$, LOCATION$, DESC$, COST, PRICE, QUANTITY
```

reads six data items from the sequential file INVNTORY.DAT.

For data to be read from a sequential file, the following must be true:

1. The file must already exist.
2. The file must be opened for input.
3. The data items in the file must be separated by a comma or by a carriage return character (<cr>).

The general form of the INPUT #n statement is shown in Table 6.6.

_____TABLE 6.6 The INPUT #n Statement_____

General Form:	INPUT #n, *list of variables*
	*where **n** is a filenumber assigned to a sequential file opened for input.*
Purpose:	*Reads data items from a sequential file in auxiliary storage and assigns them to variables.*
Keyword Entry:	*Simultaneously press the Alt and I keys on your keyboard.*
Examples:	300 INPUT #1, SUM, FIX, DESC$, PRICE
	400 INPUT #2, AMOUNT
	500 INPUT #3, CODE$, SALARY, TAX, DEPENDENTS

The INPUT #n statement causes the variables in its list to be assigned specific values, in order, from the data sequence found in the sequential file assigned to filenumber n. In order to visualize the relationship between the INPUT #n statement and the associated file, think of a pointer associated with the data items, as discussed in chapter 4 on page 96. When the OPEN statement is executed, this pointer references the first data item in the data-sequence holding area. Each time an INPUT #n statement is executed, the variables in the list are assigned values from the data-sequence holding area, beginning with the data item that is indicated by the pointer, and the pointer is advanced one value per variable. Hence, the pointer points to the next data item to be assigned when the INPUT #n statement is executed.

The PC will display the diagnostic message

```
Type mismatch
```

if the data type of the data item to be assigned does not agree with the variable in the INPUT #n statement. For example, it is invalid to assign a string value to a numeric variable.

In determining the actual value of a data item, the PC scans in the following manner:

1. For a numeric value: Leading spaces and carriage return characters (<cr>) are ignored. The first character that is not a space or a carriage return character is assumed to be the start of the numeric data item. A comma, carriage return, or space terminates the numeric value.

2. For a string value: Leading spaces and carriage return characters are ignored. The first character that is not a space or a carriage return character is assumed to be the start of the string data item. Spaces within a string are valid characters. If the first character is a quotation mark, the string data item will consist of all characters between the first quotation mark and the second. Also, if the first character is a quotation mark, the string cannot not include a quotation mark. If the string is unquoted, the value terminates with a comma or a carriage return character.

The following rules summarize the material discussed in this section.

> **Input Rule 4:** Before the INPUT #n statement is executed, the filenumber n must be assigned to a sequential file that is opened for input.

> **Input Rule 5:** Numeric variables in INPUT #n statements require numeric constants as data items, and string variables require quoted strings or unquoted strings as data.

The EOF Function   When a sequential file that was opened for output is closed, the PC automatically adds an end-of-file mark after the last record written to the file. Later, when the same sequential file is opened for input, you can use the EOF(n) function to test for the end-of-file mark. The n indicates the file number assigned to the file in the OPEN statement.

If the EOF function senses the end-of-file mark, it returns a value of –1 (true). Otherwise, it returns a value of 0 (false). The EOF function can be used to control a While loop. For example, consider the following partial program.

```
2070 OPEN "INVNTORY.DAT" FOR INPUT AS #1
      .
      .
      .
3030 WHILE NOT EOF(1)
3040    INPUT #1, STOCK$, LOCATION$, DESC$, COST, PRICE, QUANTITY
3050    GOSUB 3200  ' Call Compute and Increment Accumulators
3060    GOSUB 3400  ' Call Print an Inventory Record
3070 WEND
```

In line 3030, the EOF(1) function is used to control the While loop (lines 3030 through 3070). Each time line 3030 is executed, the PC checks to see whether the data pointer is pointing to the end-of-file mark in INVNTORY.DAT.

When using the EOF function, it is important to organize your program so that the test for the end of file precedes the execution of the INPUT #n statement. Therefore, note in the previous partial program that only one INPUT #n statement is employed, and that this statement is placed inside at the top of the While loop as line 3040. This is different from our previous programs, which employed two READ statements — one prior to the While loop and one at the bottom of the While loop.

The logic exhibited by the While loop also works when the file is empty (i.e., when the file contains no records). If the INVNTORY.DAT file is empty, line 2070 in the partial program above will still open the file for input. However, when line 3030 is executed, the EOF function immediately detects the end-of-file mark on the empty file, thereby causing the While loop to pass control to the statement following line 3070.

Two additional points of concern regarding the EOF function:

1. It is invalid to precede the filenumber with a number sign (#). For example, the following is invalid:

```
3340 WHILE NOT EOF(#1)  ' Invalid due to #
```

2. Filenumber n must be opened for input. It is invalid to test for the end-of-file mark on a file that is opened for output.

The following rule summarizes the placement of the EOF function in a program.

> **EOF Function Rule 1:** The EOF function should test for the end-of-file mark prior to the execution of an INPUT #n statement.

See Programs 6.3, 6.4, and 6.5, later in this chapter, for examples on the use of the EOF function.

6.4
PAGING A REPORT

Processing large amounts of data often results in reports that are many pages long. In multiple-page reports, the report title, the column headings, and a page number should be displayed at the top of every page. This is called **paging** the report.

Additional programming logic is required for paging a report. For example, immediately after a detail or total line is printed, a **line counter** should be incremented to keep track of what line the printer is on. Prior to printing a detail or a series of total lines, an IF statement should be used to determine whether the paper in the printer should be advanced to the top of the next page. The condition in the IF statement compares the line counter to the maximum number of lines per page. The maximum number of lines per page is usually assigned to a variable in the Initialization Module.

Here is the logic for *single-spacing* detail lines in a report:

1. If the line counter is equal to the maximum lines per page, call the Print Report and Column Headings Module.
2. Print the detail line.
3. Increment the line counter by 1. (Increment the line counter by 2 for double-spacing and by 3 for triple-spacing.)

Here is the logic for the Print Report and Column Headings Module:

1. Increment the page counter by 1.
2. Advance the paper to the top of the page.
3. Print the report title, column headings, and page counter.
4. Set the line counter equal to the number of lines printed in this module plus 1.

It is also important that you are aware of some of the characteristics associated with most printers attached to PCs.

1. The paper in a printer is normally 8.5 inches wide and 11 inches long on continuous forms.
2. Printers print 6 or 8 lines per inch. The default value is 6 lines per inch.
3. When the printer is turned on, it establishes as the top of the page the line on the paper that the print head-mechanism (or the ribbon) is at. To ensure that the paper is aligned properly for a program, it is good practice to request, in the Initialization Module, that the operator align the paper to the top of the page.

    To align the paper, use the platen knob to advance it so the perforation between sheets is approximately 1 inch above the print-head mechanism. Next, press the reset button. If the printer has no reset button, turn the printer off and then back on. Remember, if the paper is not aligned properly, the page breaks will not align with the top of the page.
4. In the Print Report and Column Headings Module, we instruct the printer to advance to the top of the page by printing a Form Feed character. The ASCII code for the Form Feed character is 12. There is no single key on the keyboard for this code; however, we can transmit the **Form Feed character** by using the CHR$ function. This

function is discussed in detail in chapter 8 on page 288. The following LPRINT statement advances the paper to the top of the page:

```
4240 LPRINT CHR$(12);  ' Advance the paper to top of page
```

Once the paper has ejected, the semicolon instructs the printer to stay on the current line (line 1) rather than space down a line.

The following problem requires data to be read and processed from the sequential file created by Program 6.2. The program solution illustrates printing a report on the printer; paging a report; the INPUT #n statement; and the use of the EOF function.

Programming Case Study 12: *Processing a Sequential File and Paging a Report*

Problem: INVNTORY.DAT was created by Program 6.2; the contents of the sequential file are shown in Figure 6.6 on page 198.

For each record in INVNTORY.DAT, the following is to be printed on the printer by means of the LPRINT and LPRINT USING statements:

1. stock number
2. description
3. unit cost
4. selling price
5. quantity on hand
6. total item cost of a stock item (unit cost times quantity on hand)
7. total selling price of a stock item (selling price times quantity on hand)

Print the total inventory cost and the total inventory selling price after all records have been processed.

Print the report title, column headings, and a page number at the top of each page. Print the inventory records on every other line (in other words, double-space the report). Print a maximum of 20 lines per page.

The printer spacing chart in Figure 6.8 illustrates the design of the report to be printed.

FIGURE 6.8
The output for Program 6.3, designed on a printer spacing chart.

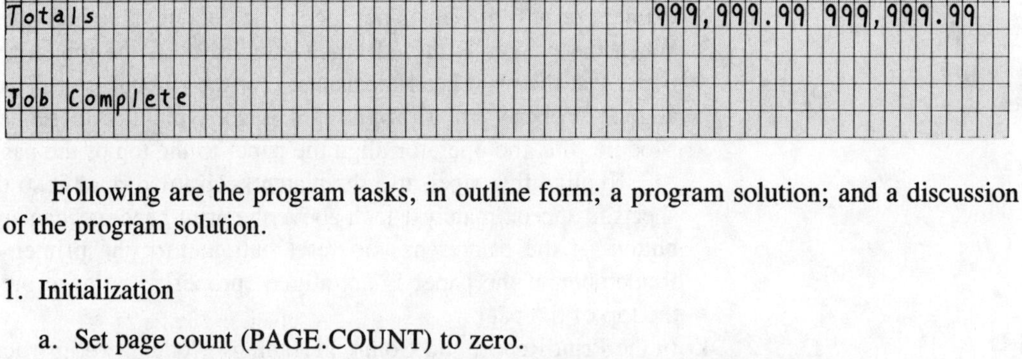

Following are the program tasks, in outline form; a program solution; and a discussion of the program solution.

Program Tasks

1. Initialization
   a. Set page count (PAGE.COUNT) to zero.
   b. Set the maximum lines per page (MAX.LINES.PER.PAGE) to 20.
   c. Set grand total cost (GRAND.TOTAL.COST) and grand total price (GRAND.TOTAL.PRICE) to zero.

d. Clear the screen.

e. Display a message on the screen which instructs the operator to set the paper in the printer to the top of the page.

f. Open the file INVNTORY.DAT for input as filenumber 1.

g. Call the Initialize Report Format Module.

h. Call the Print Report and Column Headings Module. Since this module is also called from any other module that prints lines on the printer, place the Print Report and Column Headings Module below the Wrap-up Module. In the Print Report and Column Headings Module, do the following:

(1) Increment PAGE.COUNT by 1.

(2) Advance the paper to the top of the page.

(3) Print the report title and PAGE.COUNT (see line 1 in Figure 6.8).

(4) Print the column headings (see lines 2 through 6 in Figure 6.8).

(5) Set LINE.COUNT to 7, the number of report title and heading lines printed plus 1. (Note that LINE.COUNT is set equal to the line that the print-head mechanism will be on after the report title and column headings are printed.)

2. Process File

a. Establish a While loop that executes until the EOF function detects the end-of-file mark in INVNTORY.DAT. Do the following within the loop:

(1) Use the INPUT #n statement to read an inventory record. Use the same variable names found in the WRITE #n statement in line 3630 of Program 6.2. (Consistent use of variable names between programs referencing the same file is not necessary, but it is good programming practice.)

(2) Call the Compute and Increment Accumulators Module. Compute the total cost (TOTAL.COST) and total price (TOTAL.PRICE). The total cost is determined by multiplying the unit cost by the quantity on hand. The total price is determined by multiplying the selling price by the quantity on hand. Increment the grand total cost (GRAND.TOTAL.COST) by the total cost and increment the grand total price (GRAND.TOTAL.PRICE) by the total price.

(3) Call the Print an Inventory Record Module. In this module, do the following:

(a) Compare the value of LINE.COUNT to MAX.LINES.PER.PAGE + 1. If the condition is true, call the Print Report and Column Headings Module. (Note that if LINE.COUNT is equal to 19 or less, the double-spaced detail line to be printed in this module will not exceed the value of MAX.LINES.PER.PAGE.)

(b) Use the LPRINT USING statement to print the inventory record. Also use a null LPRINT statement to double-space.

(c) Increment LINE.COUNT by 2.

3. Wrap-up

a. Close INVNTORY.DAT.

b. If LINE.COUNT is equal to MAX.LINES.PER.PAGE − 2, then call the Print Report and Headings Module. (LINE.COUNT is compared to MAX.LINES.PER.PAGE − 2 because there are two double-spaced lines printed in this module.)

c. Print the grand total cost (GRAND.TOTAL.COST) and grand total price (GRAND.TOTAL.PRICE).

d. Print an end-of-job message to conclude the report.

e. Display an end-of-job message on the screen.

Program Solution   The following program corresponds to the printer spacing chart in Figure 6.8 and to the preceding program tasks.

PROGRAM 6.3

```
1000 ' Program 6.3
1010 ' Processing a Sequential Data File and Paging a Report
1020 ' Input File Name = INVNTORY.DAT
1030 ' ************************************************
1040 ' *                 Main Module                 *
1050 ' ************************************************
1060 GOSUB 2000   ' Call Initialization
1070 GOSUB 3000   ' Call Process File
1080 GOSUB 4000   ' Call Wrap-up
1090 END
1100 '
2000 ' ************************************************
2010 ' *              Initialization                 *
2020 ' ************************************************
2030 PAGE.COUNT = 0
2040 MAX.LINES.PER.PAGE = 20
2050 GRAND.TOTAL.COST    = 0
2060 GRAND.TOTAL.PRICE   = 0
2070 CLS : KEY OFF   ' Clear Screen
2080 LOCATE 10, 20
2090 PRINT "Set the paper in the printer to the top of page."
2100 LOCATE 12, 20
2110 INPUT "Press the Enter key when the printer is ready...", CONTROL$
2120 OPEN "INVNTORY.DAT" FOR INPUT AS #1
2130 GOSUB 2200   ' Call Initialize Report Format
2140 GOSUB 4200   ' Call Print Report and Column Headings
2150 RETURN
2160 '
2200 ' ************************************************
2210 ' *           Initialize Report Format          *
2220 ' ************************************************
2230 HEAD.L1$="                         Inventory Analysis          Page: ##"
2240 HEAD.L2$="                                                        Total"
2250 HEAD.L3$="Stock                 Unit Selling Quantity Total     Selling"
2260 HEAD.L4$="No.   Description      Cost Price   On Hand  Item Cost Price"
2270 HEAD.L5$="---   -----------      ---- -------  -------- --------- -------"
2280 DETL.LN$="\ \ \              \ ###.## ####.##     #### ##,###.## ##,###.##"
2290 TOT.L1$ ="Totals                                    ###,###.## ###,###.##"
2300 TOT.L2$ ="Job Complete"
2310 RETURN
2320 '
3000 ' ************************************************
3010 ' *              Process File                   *
3020 ' ************************************************
3030 WHILE NOT EOF(1)
3040    INPUT #1, STOCK$, LOCATION$, DESC$, COST, PRICE, QUANTITY
3050    GOSUB 3200   ' Call Compute and Increment Accumulators
3060    GOSUB 3400   ' Call Print an Inventory Record
3070 WEND
3080 RETURN
3090 '
3200 ' ************************************************
3210 ' *      Compute and Increment Accumulators     *
3220 ' ************************************************
3230 TOTAL.COST  = COST  * QUANTITY
3240 TOTAL.PRICE = PRICE * QUANTITY
3250 GRAND.TOTAL.COST  = GRAND.TOTAL.COST  + TOTAL.COST
3260 GRAND.TOTAL.PRICE = GRAND.TOTAL.PRICE + TOTAL.PRICE
3270 RETURN
3280 '
```

(continued)

```
3400 ' *************************************************
3410 ' *          Print an Inventory Record          *
3420 ' *************************************************
3430 IF LINE.COUNT = MAX.LINES.PER.PAGE + 1
         THEN GOSUB 4200   ' Call Print Report and Column Headings
3440 LPRINT USING DETL.LN$; STOCK$, DESC$, COST, PRICE,
                              QUANTITY, TOTAL.COST, TOTAL.PRICE
3450 LPRINT
3460 LINE.COUNT = LINE.COUNT + 2
3470 RETURN
3480 '
4000 ' *************************************************
4010 ' *                   Wrap-up                   *
4020 ' *************************************************
4030 CLOSE #1
4040 IF LINE.COUNT = MAX.LINES.PER.PAGE - 2
         THEN GOSUB 4200   ' Call Print Report and Column Headings
4050 LPRINT
4060 LPRINT USING TOT.L1$; GRAND.TOTAL.COST, GRAND.TOTAL.PRICE
4070 LPRINT
4080 LPRINT TOT.L2$
4090 LOCATE 14, 20 : PRINT "Job Complete"
4100 RETURN
4200 ' *************************************************
4210 ' *        Print Report and Column Headings     *
4220 ' *************************************************
4230 PAGE.COUNT = PAGE.COUNT + 1
4240 LPRINT CHR$(12); ' Advance the paper to top of page
4250 LPRINT USING HEAD.L1$; PAGE.COUNT
4260 LPRINT
4270 LPRINT HEAD.L2$
4280 LPRINT HEAD.L3$
4290 LPRINT HEAD.L4$
4300 LPRINT HEAD.L5$
4310 LINE.COUNT = 7
4320 RETURN
4330 ' ************** End of Program ***************
RUN
```

Discussion of the Program Solution

When the RUN command is issued for Program 6.3, the report illustrated in Figure 6.9 on the following page is printed on the printer. The following points should be noted concerning the program solution represented by Program 6.3.

1. In line 2030, PAGE.COUNT is initialized to zero; later, in line 4230, it is incremented by 1 just prior to printing the report title. In line 2040, MAX.LINES.PER.PAGE is set equal to 20, the number of lines to be printed per page.

2. In line 2120, the OPEN statement opens INVNTORY.DAT for input as filenumber 1. The remaining file-handling statements, lines 3040 and 4030, reference INVNTORY.DAT by specifying the filenumber 1.

3. The While loop, lines 3030 through 3070 in the Process File Module, processes records until the end-of-file mark is detected by the EOF function.

4. The activity of printing an inventory record is in a separate module (lines 3400 through 3480), because it involves several lines of code. This module is called from line 3060 in the While loop. Study the Print an Inventory Record Module closely. Whenever a program pages a report, the line counter must be tested (line 3430) before the detail line is printed. After printing the detail line and double-spacing, the line counter is incremented by 2 (line 3460).

Note that the line counter (LINE.COUNT) is compared against a value that ensures that the required lines to be printed in the module will fit on the page. The problem specifications indicated that only 20 physical lines were to be printed per page. Since double-spacing is called for, LINE.COUNT is compared to MAX.LINES.PER.PAGE + 1.

5. The Print Report and Column Headings Module is called from lines 2140, 3430, and 4040. Top-down programming requires that a module called from two or more different places in a program be placed below the last call. Calls should always be made in a downward direction to a higher line number.

    The Print Report and Column Headings Module, beginning at line 4200, increments the page number (line 4230); prints the report and column headings (lines 4240 through 4300); and finally sets the line counter to 7 (line 4310). LINE.COUNT is set equal to the number of the line the print-head mechanism is on (the next line to be printed).

6. Even though the warehouse location is not manipulated or displayed by Program 6.3, it is necessary to include a variable (LOCATION$) that represents the warehouse location in the list of the INPUT #n statement (line 3040), since the data item is part of the record. You cannot be selective and input from a sequential file only those data items which you plan to manipulate or display. All data items within the record must be assigned to variables in the INPUT #n statement, as shown in line 3040.

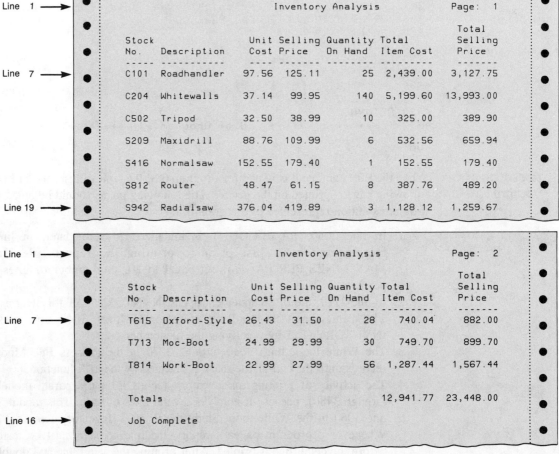

FIGURE 6.9
The report generated by Program 6.3.

TRY IT YOURSELF

1. Load Program 6.3 (PRG6-3) from the Student Diskette. Delete line 3460. Execute the program. Compare the results to those in Figure 6.9. Now do you understand why it is important to increment the line counter in line 3460?

2. Load Program 6.3 again. In line 2030, initialize PAGE.COUNT to 12. Execute the program and compare the page numbers on the report to those in Figure 6.9.

3. Same as (2) except initialize PAGE.COUNT to 99. Execute the program and examine the page numbers on the report. How would you adjust line 2230 to ensure that page numbers up to 999 will print correctly?

4. Load Program 6.3 again. In line 2040, set MAX.LINES.PER.PAGE to 15. Execute the program and compare the report to Figure 6.9. Do you agree that by modifying the value of this variable you can change the number of lines printed per page?

6.5
CONTROL-BREAK PROCESSING

Most businesses today are divided into smaller units for the purpose of better management. A retail company that is doing business on a national scale may have several levels of management, with the levels headed by such people as a district manager, a store manager, and a department manager. To evaluate the performance of the units within each level, managerial reports are generated, showing summaries or minor totals for each subunit. For example, a sales analysis report that is generated for the manager of a company often shows a summary sales total for each district within the company as well as a grand sales total for the company.

Programs that are written to generate levels of subtotals use a technique involving **control fields** and **control breaks**. A control field contains data that is to be compared from record to record. A control break occurs when the data in the control field changes.

A control break may be used to display a summary line each time a selected data item, common to all records in the file, changes value. The variable that is assigned to the selected data item is called the **control variable**. For this technique to work successfully, it is essential that the records be processed in sequence, according to the data item that determines the break. For example, to generate the Sales Analysis Report shown in Figure 6.10 on the following page, all the records that belong to district 1 must precede all the district 2 records.

With the sales records in sequence, the program solution can check each sales record to see whether it is the first record of a new district. If the sales record represents an item from the *old* district (i.e., if the current item and the previous one belong to the same district), then selected contents of that record are displayed, and the PC adds the sales amount for that item to a district sales accumulator.

When a sales record that belongs to a *new* district is read, a control break occurs and the current value of the district sales accumulator is displayed. In addition, asterisks are usually displayed to the right of the totals to indicate a summary. One asterisk indicates the lowest level, two asterisks the next level, and so on. Before processing the sales record that caused the control break, the PC must add the district sales to the company sales total, which is displayed after all records in the file have been processed.

Furthermore, the control variable must be assigned the value of the next district number before the processing of the record is resumed. Finally, the variable that is used to sum the district sales must be reset to zero after each control break so that it can be used to sum the sales for the next district.

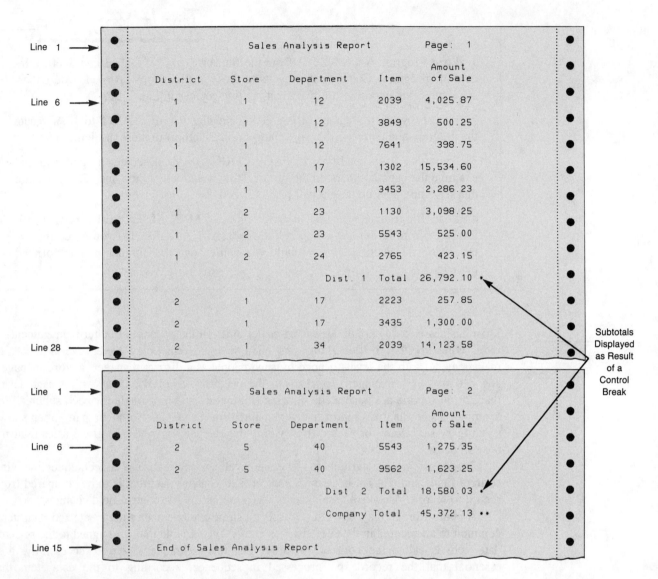

Line 1 →

Line 6 →

Line 28 →

Line 1 →

Line 6 →

Line 15 →

Subtotals Displayed as Result of a Control Break

```
              Sales Analysis Report        Page:  1

                                          Amount
   District    Store    Department    Item    of Sale
      1          1          12        2039   4,025.87
      1          1          12        3849     500.25
      1          1          12        7641     398.75
      1          1          17        1302  15,534.60
      1          1          17        3453   2,286.23
      1          2          23        1130   3,098.25
      1          2          23        5543     525.00
      1          2          24        2765     423.15
                             Dist.  1  Total  26,792.10 *
      2          1          17        2223     257.85
      2          1          17        3435   1,300.00
      2          1          34        2039  14,123.58
```

```
              Sales Analysis Report        Page:  2

                                          Amount
   District    Store    Department    Item    of Sale
      2          5          40        5543   1,275.35
      2          5          40        9562   1,623.25
                             Dist  2  Total  18,580.03 *

                           Company Total    45,372.13 **

End of Sales Analysis Report
```

FIGURE 6.10
Sales Analysis Report (report with a single-level control break).

The following Programming Case Study pertains to generating the report found in Figure 6.10.

Programming Case Study 13A: *Sales Analysis Report — Single-Level Control Break*

Problem: The Sales Analysis Department of the PUC Company has requested that a program be written to generate the Sales Analysis Report shown in Figure 6.10. Each record in the file includes a district, a store, a department, an item, and the sales amount, as shown on the following page.

District	Store	Dept.	Item	Amt. of Sales
1	1	12	2039	$ 4,025.87
1	1	12	3849	500.25
1	1	12	7641	398.75
1	1	17	1302	15,534.60
1	1	17	3453	2,286.23
1	2	23	1130	3,098.25
1	2	23	5543	525.00
1	2	24	2765	423.15
2	1	17	2223	257.85
2	1	17	3435	1,300.00
2	1	34	2039	14,123.58
2	5	40	5543	1,275.35
2	5	40	9562	1,623.25

The sales records are located in the data file SALES.DAT in ascending sequence by district, as illustrated in Figure 6.11. A data file like SALES.DAT may be created by a program that is similar to Program 6.2. Note that although the first four data items in each record of SALES.DAT are numeric, we have stored them as string values because we do not plan to do arithmetic on them.

FIGURE 6.11
A listing of SALES.DAT created by a program similar to Program 6.2.

```
"1","1","12","2039",4025.87
"1","1","12","3849",500.25
"1","1","12","7641",398.75
"1","1","17","1302",15534.6
"1","1","17","3453",2286.23
"1","2","23","1130",3098.25
"1","2","23","5543",525
"1","2","24","2765",423.15
"2","1","17","2223",257.85
"2","1","17","3435",1300
"2","1","34","2039",14123.58
"2","5","40","5543",1275.35
"2","5","40","9562",1623.25
```

The data items within each sales record are to be printed on the printer. Also to be printed are the sales total for each district before a new district is processed and the final sales total for the company after all sales records have been processed. Print 30 lines to a page. At the top of each new page, print the report title, page number, and column headings as illustrated in Figure 6.10.

Following are a top-down chart and a general flowchart of the Process File Module (Figure 6.12 on the following page); a list of the program tasks in outline form; a program solution; and a discussion of the program solution.

In the top-down chart in Figure 6.12, the process symbols with the upper-right-hand corner darkened identify recurring subtasks. Recurring subtasks are coded once and called as often as needed.

Program Tasks The following program tasks correspond to the top-down chart in Figure 6.12.

1. Initialization

    a. Set PAGE.COUNT to zero.
    b. Set MAX.LINES.PER.PAGE to 30.
    c. Two running totals are necessary. Set DIST.TOTAL (district sales accumulator) and CMPY.TOTAL (company sales accumulator) to zero.
    d. Clear the screen.
    e. Display a message instructing the operator to set the paper to the top of the page in the printer.
    f. Open the sequential data file SALES.DAT for input.
    g. Call the Initialize Report Format Module.
    h. Call the Print Report and Column Headings Module. In this module, increment PAGE.COUNT by 1, print the report and column headings, and set LINE.COUNT to 6.

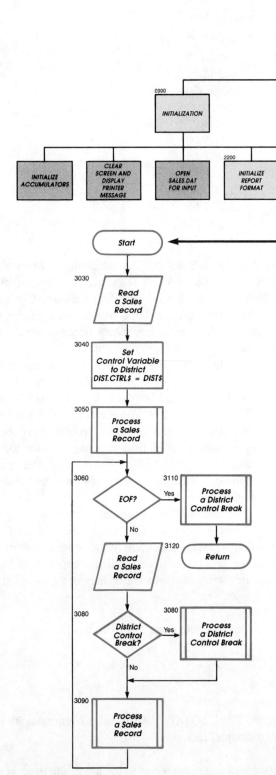

FIGURE 6.12
A top-down chart and a general flowchart of the Process File Module for Program 6.4.

2. Process File, if not end of file

   a. Use the INPUT #n statement to read the first sales record in SALES.DAT. Use the following variable names:

DIST$:	district
STORE$:	store
DEPT$:	department
ITEM$:	item number
AMOUNT:	amount of sales

   b. Assign the control variable, DIST.CTRL$, the value of DIST$. (This assignment is often called "priming the pump," since it sets DIST.CTRL$ equal to the first district.)

   c. Call the Process a Sales Record Module. Within this module, do the following:

   (1) Increment the district sales accumulator (DIST. TOTAL) by the amount of the sales (AMOUNT).

   (2) If LINE.COUNT is equal to MAX.LINES. PER.PAGE, then call the Print Report and Headings Module.

   (3) Print the five data values described in step 2a. Double-space the detail lines.

   (4) Increment LINE.COUNT by 2.

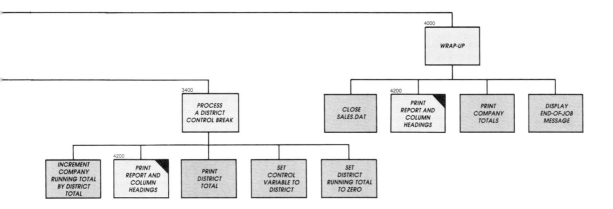

d. Establish a While loop that executes repeatedly until the end-of-file mark is reached. Use the EOF function to control the While loop. Within the While loop, do the following:

(1) Read the next sales record in SALES.DAT.

(2) Test for a control break. If DIST$ (district of sales record just read) does not equal DIST$.CTRL$ (district being processed), then call the Process a District Control Break Module. This module must do the following:

(a) Increment the company sales accumulator (CMPY.TOTAL) by the district sales accumulator (DIST.TOTAL).

(b) If LINE.COUNT is equal to MAX.LINES.PER.PAGE, then call the Print Report and Headings Module.

(c) Print the district sales accumulator (DIST.TOTAL).

(d) Set the control variable (DIST.CTRL$) equal to the new district (DIST$).

(e) Initialize the district sales accumulator (DIST.TOTAL) to zero.

(3) Call the Process a Sales Record Module described in step 2c.

e. Following the While loop, call the Process a District Control Break Module described in step 2d(2). This call ensures that the last district total is processed.

3. Wrap-up

a. Close SALES.DAT.

b. If LINE.COUNT is equal to MAX.LINES.PER.PAGE – 2, then call the Print Report and Headings Module.

c. Print the company sales accumulator (CMPY.TOTAL) and an end-of-job message.

d. Display an end-of-job message on the screen.

Program Solution   The program on the following page corresponds to the preceding program tasks and to the top-down chart in Figure 6.12.

PROGRAM 6.4

```
1000 ' Program 6.4
1010 ' Sales Analysis Report -- Single-Level Control Break
1020 ' Input File Name = SALES.DAT
1030 ' ****************************************************
1040 ' *                    Main Module                  *
1050 ' ****************************************************
1060 GOSUB 2000   ' Call Initialization
1070 IF NOT EOF(1)
        THEN GOSUB 3000   ' Call Process File
1080 GOSUB 4000   ' Call Wrap-up
1090 END
1100 '
2000 ' ****************************************************
2010 ' *                 Initialization                  *
2020 ' ****************************************************
2030 PAGE.COUNT = 0
2040 MAX.LINES.PER.PAGE = 30
2050 DIST.TOTAL = 0
2060 CMPY.TOTAL = 0
2070 CLS : KEY OFF   ' Clear Screen
2080 LOCATE 10, 20
2090 PRINT "Set the paper in the printer to the top of page."
2100 LOCATE 12, 20
2110 INPUT "Press the Enter key when the printer is ready...", CONTROL$
2120 OPEN "SALES.DAT" FOR INPUT AS #1
2130 GOSUB 2200     ' Call Initialize Report Format
2140 GOSUB 4200     ' Call Print Report and Column Headings
2150 RETURN
2160 '
2200 ' ****************************************************
2210 ' *             Initialize Report Format            *
2220 ' ****************************************************
2230 HEAD.L1$ = "              Sales Analysis Report          Page: ##"
2240 HEAD.L2$ = "                                              Amount"
2250 HEAD.L3$ = "District     Store     Department     Item     of Sale"
2260 DETL.LN$ = "   \\          \\            \\        \ \   ##,###.##"
2270 TOT.L1$  = "                              Dist. \\ Total ###,###.## *"
2280 TOT.L2$  = "                              Company Total ####,###.## _**"
2290 TOT.L3$  = "End of Sales Analysis Report"
2300 RETURN
2310 '
3000 ' ****************************************************
3010 ' *                 Process File                    *
3020 ' ****************************************************
3030 INPUT #1, DIST$, STORE$, DEPT$, ITEM$, AMOUNT
3040 DIST.CTRL$ = DIST$
3050 GOSUB 3200              ' Call Process a Sales Record
3060 WHILE NOT EOF(1)
3070    INPUT #1, DIST$, STORE$, DEPT$, ITEM$, AMOUNT
3080    IF DIST$ <> DIST.CTRL$
          THEN GOSUB 3400    ' Call Process a District Control Break
3090    GOSUB 3200           ' Call Process a Sales Record
3100 WEND
3110 GOSUB 3400              ' Call Process a District Control Break
3120 RETURN
3130 '
```

(continued)

```
3200 ' ********************************************************
3210 ' *              Process a Sales Record                *
3220 ' ********************************************************
3230 DIST.TOTAL = DIST.TOTAL + AMOUNT
3240 IF LINE.COUNT = MAX.LINES.PER.PAGE
         THEN GOSUB 4200  ' Print Report and Column Headings
3250 LPRINT USING DETL.LN$; DIST$, STORE$, DEPT$, ITEM$, AMOUNT
3260 LPRINT
3270 LINE.COUNT = LINE.COUNT + 2
3280 RETURN
3290 '
3400 ' ********************************************************
3410 ' *           Process a District Control Break         *
3420 ' ********************************************************
3430 CMPY.TOTAL = CMPY.TOTAL + DIST.TOTAL
3440 IF LINE.COUNT = MAX.LINES.PER.PAGE
         THEN GOSUB 4200  ' Call Print Report and Column Headings
3450 LPRINT USING TOT.L1$; DIST.CTRL$, DIST.TOTAL
3460 LPRINT
3470 LINE.COUNT = LINE.COUNT + 2
3480 DIST.CTRL$ = DIST$
3490 DIST.TOTAL = 0
3500 RETURN
3510 '
4000 ' ********************************************************
4010 ' *                    Wrap-up                         *
4020 ' ********************************************************
4030 CLOSE #1
4040 IF LINE.COUNT = MAX.LINES.PER.PAGE - 2
         THEN GOSUB 4200  ' Call Print Report and Column Headings
4050 LPRINT USING TOT.L2$; CMPY.TOTAL
4060 LPRINT : LPRINT : LPRINT TOT.L3$
4070 LOCATE 14, 20 : PRINT "Job Complete"
4080 RETURN
4090 '
4200 ' ********************************************************
4210 ' *          Print Report and Column Headings          *
4220 ' ********************************************************
4230 PAGE.COUNT = PAGE.COUNT + 1
4240 LPRINT CHR$(12); ' Advance the paper to top of page
4250 LPRINT USING HEAD.L1$; PAGE.COUNT
4260 LPRINT
4270 LPRINT HEAD.L2$
4280 LPRINT HEAD.L3$
4290 LPRINT
4300 LINE.COUNT = 6
4310 RETURN
4320 ' *************** End of Program ******************
RUN
```

Discussion of the Solution

When the RUN command is issued for Program 6.4, the PC prints the report shown in Figure 6.10 on page 208. Note the following important points regarding the control break process in Program 6.4.

1. In the Initialization Module, lines 2050 and 2060 initialize the district and company accumulators.

2. The Process File Module is called by line 1070 only if SALES.DAT is not empty. The IF statement is required in line 1070 because the first statement in the Process File Module (line 3030) is the INPUT #n statement.

3. In the Process File Module, line 3030 reads the first record. Line 3040 sets the control variable (DIST.CTRL$) equal to the first district (DIST$). Line 3050 causes the first sales record to be processed.

   The WHILE statement in line 3060 tests to determine whether there are any records left in SALES.DAT. Within the While loop, line 3070 reads the next record. Line 3080 compares the district of the most recently read sales record to the control variable. If they are different, a control break has occurred and the Process a District Control Break Module is called. Whether or not a control break occurs, line 3090 processes the sales record last read by line 3070.

   Following the processing of a record, line 3100 returns control to the WHILE statement in line 3060. When the end-of-file mark is finally detected, the WHILE statement transfers control to line 3110, and the totals for the last district in the file are processed.

4. In the Process a District Control Break Module, the four requirements for processing a control break are fulfilled in the following way:
   a. Line 3430 increments the company sales accumulator (CMPY.TOTAL) by the district sales accumulator (DIST.TOTAL).
   b. Line 3440 tests for a page break. Lines 3450 through 3470 print the value of the district sales accumulator and increment LINE.COUNT. Note that line 3450 uses the control variable (DIST.CTRL$) rather than the variable DIST$ to print the district number. Can you explain why we don't print DIST$?
   c. Line 3480 assigns the control variable (DIST.CTRL$) the value of the new district.
   d. Line 3490 sets the district sales accumulator (DIST.TOTAL) to zero.

5. In the Wrap-up Module, the company sales total (CMPY.TOTAL) is printed.

TRY IT YOURSELF

Load Program 6.4 (PRG6-4) from the Student Diskette. Display and execute Program 6.4. Delete line 3110 and execute the program a second time. Study the output results and explain the function of line 3110.

Programming Case Study 13B: Sales Analysis Report — Two Levels of Control Breaks

There are four classifications of control breaks: minor, intermediate, major, and multiple. A report may include one break (minor), as was the case in the previous example; two breaks (intermediate); three breaks (major); or multiple (more than three breaks).

   The next program solution illustrates the generation of a sales analysis report that is the same as the one shown in Figure 6.10 on page 208, except that it includes two levels of control breaks. The control breaks are store within district within company. Each control break causes a number of summaries to be displayed, depending on the level of the break. A store change (minor) causes one summary to be displayed. A district change (major) causes both the last store total and the district total to be displayed. When the end-of-file mark is sensed, all summaries that relate to the last store and district are displayed, along with the grand total sales for the company.

   The logic employed in a program involving multilevel control breaks is similar to that shown in Program 6.4. It makes little difference whether there are two, three, or more levels to consider. The program need only include additional decision statements and accumulators for each control-break summary. The comparison should be structured so that the major level is considered first, then the intermediate levels, and so forth down to the minor level. Finally, it is important that the sales records be in ascending sequence by store within district. That is, within each district, the stores must be in ascending sequence. Study carefully the sequence of the sales records in SALES.DAT shown in Figure 6.11 on page 209. For this report, print 36 lines to a page.

A list of the additional program tasks required to modify Program 6.4 so that it will generate the new report are listed below. The program solution, the Sales Analysis Report, and a discussion of the program solution follow.

Program Tasks
in Addition to
Those Listed for
Programming Case
Study 13A

1. Initialization

   a. Initialize an additional running total (STORE.TOTAL) to zero.
   b. In the Initialize Report Format Module, add an extra total line to print the value of STORE.TOTAL when a minor control break occurs.

2. Process File

   a. Immediately after the district number of the first record is assigned to the control variable (DIST.CTRL$), set a second control variable (STORE.CTRL$) equal to the store number (STORE$) in the first record.
   b. Within the While loop, add a test for a minor control break immediately after the test for the major control break.
   c. As the first statement in the Process a District Control Break Module, add a call to the Process a Store Control Break Module. (Whenever there is a district control break, there is a store control break.)
   d. Add the Process a Store Control Break Module. This module is nearly identical to the Process a District Control Break Module; the only difference is that the reference to all variables is at the store level rather than at the district level.

Program Solution Program 6.5, on the following page, contains the modifications to Program 6.4 described by the preceding additional tasks.

Discussion of the When the RUN command is issued for Program 6.5, the report shown in Figure 6.13, on page
Program Solution 218, is generated.

The main difference between the report in Figure 6.13 and the one in Figure 6.10 is that in Figure 6.13 there are two levels of control breaks. Following the processing of all store 1, district 1 records, a total for store 1 is displayed. Following a district control break, both the totals for the store and district are displayed. Printing the store and district totals each time they change continues until the entire file has been processed.

The following specific points should be noted concerning Program 6.5:

1. In the Process File Module, line 3090 tests for a district control break. If a district control break occurs, control transfers to the subroutine beginning at line 3400. The first instruction in this module, line 3430, transfers control to the Process a Store Control Break Module. Once the store control break has been processed, control returns to the Process a District Control Break Module and the district control break is processed. Line 3430 ensures that a store control break is processed whenever a district control break occurs.

2. After testing for a district control break in line 3090, line 3100 tests to determine whether there is a store control break. If there is a minor control break, control transfers to the Process a Store Control Break Module.

   When a sales record causes a district control break, the condition in line 3100 that tests for a store control break can never be true because STORE.CTRL$ is equal to STORE$, owing to the major control break.

PROGRAM 6.5

```
1000 ' Program 6.5
1010 ' Sales Analysis Report -- Two Levels of Control Breaks
1020 ' Input File Name = SALES.DAT
1030 ' *****************************************************
1040 ' *                  Main Module                     *
1050 ' *****************************************************
1060 GOSUB 2000   ' Call Initialization
1070 IF NOT EOF(1)
         THEN GOSUB 3000   ' Call Process File
1080 GOSUB 4000   ' Call Wrap-up
1090 END
1100 '
2000 ' *****************************************************
2010 ' *                Initialization                    *
2020 ' *****************************************************
2030 PAGE.COUNT     = 0
2040 MAX.LINES.PER.PAGE = 36
2050 STORE.TOTAL    = 0
2060 DIST.TOTAL     = 0
2070 CMPY.TOTAL     = 0
2080 CLS : KEY OFF  ' Clear Screen
2090 LOCATE 10, 20
2100 PRINT "Set the paper in the printer to the top of page."
2110 LOCATE 12, 20
2120 INPUT "Press the Enter key when the printer is ready...", CONTROL$
2130 OPEN "SALES.DAT" FOR INPUT AS #1
2140 GOSUB 2200      ' Call Initialize Report Format
2150 GOSUB 4200      ' Call Print Report and Column Headings
2160 RETURN
2170 '
2200 ' *****************************************************
2210 ' *           Initialize Report Format               *
2220 ' *****************************************************
2230 HEAD.L1$ = "            Sales Analysis Report        Page: ##"
2240 HEAD.L2$ = "                                          Amount"
2250 HEAD.L3$ = "District      Store      Department     Item     of Sale"
2260 DETL.LN$ = "   \\          \\            \\          \ \    ##,###.##"
2270 TOT.L1$  = "                              Store \\ Total ###,###.## *"
2280 TOT.L2$  = "                              Dist. \\ Total ###,###.## *_*"
2290 TOT.L3$  = "                              Company Total ####,###.## *_**"
2300 TOT.L4$  = "End of Sales Analysis Report"
2310 RETURN
2320 '
3000 ' *****************************************************
3010 ' *                Process File                      *
3020 ' *****************************************************
3030 INPUT #1, DIST$, STORE$, DEPT$, ITEM$, AMOUNT
3040 DIST.CTRL$  = DIST$
3050 STORE.CTRL$ = STORE$
3060 GOSUB 3200               ' Call Process a Sales Record
3070 WHILE NOT EOF(1)
3080    INPUT #1, DIST$, STORE$, DEPT$, ITEM$, AMOUNT
3090    IF DIST$ <> DIST.CTRL$
           THEN GOSUB 3400   ' Call Process a District Control Break
3100    IF STORE$ <> STORE.CTRL$
           THEN GOSUB 3600   ' Call Process a Store Control Break
3110    GOSUB 3200           ' Call Process a Sales Record
3120 WEND
3130 GOSUB 3400              ' Call Process a District Control Break
3140 RETURN
3150 '
```

(continued)

```
3200 ' ******************************************************
3210 ' *              Process a Sales Record               *
3220 ' ******************************************************
3230 STORE.TOTAL = STORE.TOTAL + AMOUNT
3240 IF LINE.COUNT = MAX.LINES.PER.PAGE
        THEN GOSUB 4200  ' Call Print Report and Column Headings
3250 LPRINT USING DETL.LN$; DIST$, STORE$, DEPT$, ITEM$, AMOUNT
3260 LPRINT
3270 LINE.COUNT = LINE.COUNT + 2
3280 RETURN
3290 '
3400 ' ******************************************************
3410 ' *          Process a District Control Break         *
3420 ' ******************************************************
3430 GOSUB 3600  ' Call Process a Store Control Break
3440 CMPY.TOTAL = CMPY.TOTAL + DIST.TOTAL
3450 IF LINE.COUNT = MAX.LINES.PER.PAGE
        THEN GOSUB 4200  ' Call Print Report and Column Headings
3460 LPRINT USING TOT.L2$; DIST.CTRL$, DIST.TOTAL
3470 LPRINT
3480 LINE.COUNT = LINE.COUNT + 2
3490 DIST.CTRL$ = DIST$
3500 DIST.TOTAL = 0
3510 RETURN
3520 '
3600 ' ******************************************************
3610 ' *           Process a Store Control Break           *
3620 ' ******************************************************
3630 DIST.TOTAL = DIST.TOTAL + STORE.TOTAL
3640 IF LINE.COUNT = MAX.LINES.PER.PAGE
        THEN GOSUB 4200  ' Call Print Report and Column Headings
3650 LPRINT USING TOT.L1$; STORE.CTRL$, STORE.TOTAL
3660 LPRINT
3670 LINE.COUNT  = LINE.COUNT + 2
3680 STORE.CTRL$ = STORE$
3690 STORE.TOTAL = 0
3700 RETURN
3710 '
4000 ' ******************************************************
4010 ' *                     Wrap-up                        *
4020 ' ******************************************************
4030 CLOSE #1
4040 IF LINE.COUNT = MAX.LINES.PER.PAGE - 2
        THEN GOSUB 4200  ' Call Print Report and Column Headings
4050 LPRINT USING TOT.L3$; CMPY.TOTAL
4060 LPRINT : LPRINT : LPRINT TOT.L4$
4070 LOCATE 14, 20 : PRINT "Job Complete"
4080 RETURN
4090 '
4200 ' ******************************************************
4210 ' *          Print Report and Column Headings         *
4220 ' ******************************************************
4230 PAGE.COUNT = PAGE.COUNT + 1
4240 LPRINT CHR$(12); ' Advance paper to top of page
4250 LPRINT USING HEAD.L1$; PAGE.COUNT
4260 LPRINT
4270 LPRINT HEAD.L2$
4280 LPRINT HEAD.L3$
4290 LPRINT
4300 LINE.COUNT = 6
4310 RETURN
4320 ' *************** End of Program ******************
RUN
```

As an addition to this program solution, in BASIC Programming Problem 6 you are asked to generate a triple-control-break report with the same file (SALES.DAT) that was used in Programming Case Studies 13A and 13B. The report requires three control breaks that include department within store within district. A close look at SALES.DAT in Figure 6.10 reveals that the file is in ascending sequence by department within store within district.

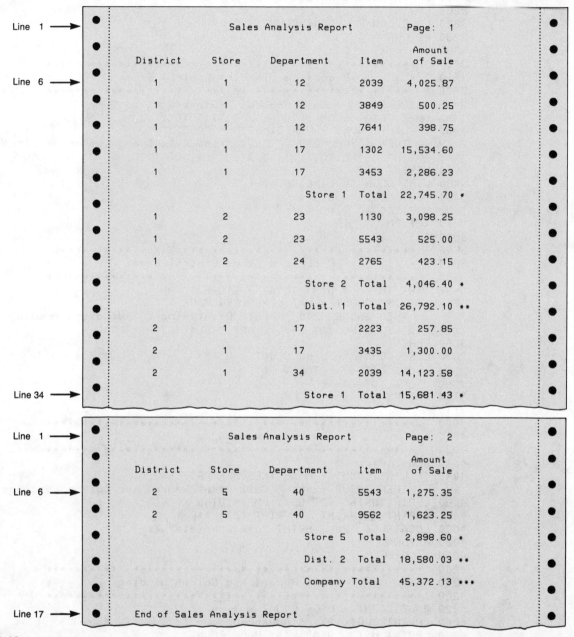

FIGURE 6.13
*Sales Analysis Report
(report with two levels
of control breaks).*

── TRY IT YOURSELF ──

Load Program 6.5 (PRG6-5) from the Student Diskette. Display and execute Program 6.5. Delete line 3430 and execute the program a second time. Study the output results. Do you understand that when there is a major control break, all lower-level control breaks must also be processed?

⊞ 6.6 Wʜᴀᴛ Yᴏᴜ Sʜᴏᴜʟᴅ Kɴᴏᴡ

1. In MS BASIC, there are four techniques that can be used to integrate data into a program, as follows:
   a. the INPUT statement and keyboard or any other external input device;
   b. the READ and DATA statements;
   c. the INPUT #n statement and data files; and
   d. the LET statement.
2. A file is a group of related records. Each record within the file contains related data items.
3. MS BASIC provides for two types of file organization: sequential and random. A file that is organized sequentially is limited to sequential processing. Random files will be discussed in chapter 9.
4. A filespec identifies a file in auxiliary storage.
5. Before a file can be read from or written to, it must be opened by the OPEN statement.
6. When a program is finished reading from or writing to a file, it should close the file with the CLOSE statement.
7. A sequential file can be opened for input, output, or append. If a file is opened for input, the pointer is placed at the beginning of the file and the program can only read records from it. If a file is opened for output, the pointer is placed at the beginning of the file and the program can only write records to the file. If a file is opened for append, the pointer is placed after the last record in the file and the program can only write records to the file.
8. If a file is opened for input, the file must already exist. If a file is opened for output and it already exists, the PC deletes the file before it opens it. The file may or may not exist prior to the execution of the OPEN statement for appending records. If the file exists, the pointer is placed after the last record in the file. If the file does not exist, then APPEND is the same as OUTPUT.
9. The PRINT #n and PRINT #n, USING statements are used to write information to a sequential file in the form of a report.
10. The WRITE #n statement is used to write data to a file in the format required by the INPUT statement. The format requirement is similar to that of the READ and DATA statements: all data items must be separated by commas.
11. The INPUT #n statement reads data from a sequential file.
12. When a file opened for output is closed by the CLOSE or END statement, an end-of-file mark is added after the last record. Later, when a program reads records from the file, the EOF(n) function may be used to test for the end-of-file mark on the file that is associated with filenumber n. It is important that the test be made prior to the attempt to read a record.
13. Paging a report involves printing the report and column headings along with a page number at the top of the first page and then each time after a predetermined number of lines has been printed.
14. Paging a report requires two accumulators: a line counter and a page counter.
15. Programs that are written to generate levels of subtotals use control fields and control breaks. A control field contains data that is to be compared from record to record. A control break occurs when the data in the same control field changes.
16. In order to display subtotals when control breaks occur, the records within a file must be in sorted sequence (ascending or descending), according to the control field.
17. There are four classifications of control breaks: one break (minor); two breaks (intermediate); three breaks (major); and multiple breaks (more than three).

⊞ 6.7 Tᴇsᴛ Yᴏᴜʀ Bᴀsɪᴄ Sᴋɪʟʟs (Even-numbered answers are at the back of the book, before the index.)

1. Consider the valid program listed below and to the right, then explain its function. Assume that the values in the table below and to the left are entered in response to the INPUT statements in the program.

Stock Item	Selling Price	Discount Code
138	$ 78.56	2
421	123.58	3
617	475.65	2
812	23.58	1
917	754.56	4
eof		

```
100 ' Exercise 6.1
110 CLS : KEY OFF   ' Clear Screen
120 OPEN "EX61A.DAT" FOR OUTPUT AS #1
130 INPUT "Stock Item ======> ", ITEM$
140 WHILE ITEM$ <> "eof"
150    INPUT "Selling Price ===> ", PRICE
160    INPUT "Discount Code ===> ", CODE$
170    WRITE #1, ITEM$, PRICE, CODE$
180    INPUT "Stock Item ======> ", ITEM$
190 WEND
200 CLOSE #1
210 PRINT : PRINT "Job Complete"
220 END
```

2. Fill in the blanks in the following sentences:

   a. The _____ statement with a mode of_____ or _____ must be executed before a `PRINT #n`, `PRINT #n`, `USING`, or `WRITE #n` statement is executed.

   b. The _____ statement with a mode of _____ must be executed before an `INPUT #n` statement is executed.

   c. A file can be opened as often as required, provided it is _____ before each subsequent open.

   d. The _____ function is used to test for the end-of-file mark with a sequential file.

   e. When records are to be added to the end of a sequential file, the _____ mode is used in the `OPEN` statement.

3. Explain the purpose of the `EOF` function. Also indicate where it should be located in a program in relation to the `INPUT #n` statement.

4. A program is to read records from one of three sequential files, SALES1.DAT, SALES2.DAT, and SALES3.DAT. The three files are stored on the diskette in the B drive. Write three `OPEN` statements that would allow the program to read records from any of the three sequential files.

5. Construct a `WRITE #n` statement that would write the values of A, B, X$, and D to a sequential file in the format required by the `INPUT #n` statement.

6. Which of the following are invalid file-handling statements? Why?

   a. `100 OPEN FOR OUTPUT "B:SAL.DAT" AS #1`   b. `200 OPEN FILE$ FOR APPEND AS #3`
   c. `300 PRINT #1,`   d. `400 PRINT #1, A,`
   e. `500 PRINT #1 USING "####.##"; COST`   f. `600 CLOSE`
   g. `700 WHILE NOT EOF(#2)`   h. `800 INPUT #2, AMOUNT,`

7. Assume that line 3440 below is located in the Print a Detail Line Module and prints the detail line for a report. Write the line that would immediately follow line 3440 if double-spacing were required; if triple-spacing were required.

   `3440 LPRINT EMP.NUMBER$, EMP.NAME$, EMP.SOC.SEC$, EMP.SALARY`

8. Write a statement that would properly increment the line counter (LINECOUNT) for each of the requirements below (this statement would follow line 3440 in exercise 7 in the Print a Detail Line Module):

   a. single-space the detail line
   b. double-space the detail line
   c. triple-space the detail line

9. Write the `IF` statement that would test to determine whether the report title and column headings should be printed for each of the requirements below (this `IF` statement would precede line 3440 in exercise 7 in the Print a Detail Line Module):

   a. `MAX.LINES.PER.PAGE = 10` and triple-spacing
   b. `MAX.LINES.PER.PAGE = 45` and double-spacing
   c. `MAX.LINES.PER.PAGE = 54` and single-spacing

10. Use the Student Diskette to complete the Try It Yourself exercises on pages 194, 207, 214, and 218.

⊞ 6.8   BASIC PROGRAMMING PROBLEMS

1. Creating a Master File

Purpose: To become familiar with creating a sequential file that is consistent with the format required by the `INPUT` statement. Use of the `OPEN`, `CLOSE`, and `WRITE #n` statements is required.

Problem: Construct a top-down program to create a sequential file named EX61PAY.DAT that represents the payroll master file for the PUC Company. A **master file** is one that is for the most part permanent or includes data that is required each time an application such as payroll is processed. Each record in the file describes an employee, including the year-to-date (YTD) payroll information, as shown under the Input Data.

Write the data to the file in the format required by the `INPUT #n` statement. An employee number of EOF indicates there are no more payroll records to enter. As part of the end-of-job routine, display a message indicating that the file was created as well as the total number of records written to the file.

(Hint: See Program 6.2 on page 196.)

Input Data: Prepare and use the following sample data.

Employee		Depen-dents	Marital Status	Rate of Pay	Year-to-Date		
No.	Name				Gross Pay	Federal With. Tax	Social Security
123	Col, Joan	2	M	12.50	25,345.23	10,256.45	1,812.18
124	Fiel, Don	1	S	18.00	41,725.00	8,546.45	2,983.34
125	Dit, Lisa	1	S	13.00	42,115.23	11,035.78	3,003.00
126	Snow, Joe	9	M	4.50	11,510.05	854.34	822.97
134	Hi, Frank	0	M	8.75	9,298.65	2,678.25	664.85
167	Bri, Edie	3	S	10.40	8,190.45	17.50	585.62
210	Liss, Ted	6	M	8.80	7,098.04	2,120.55	507.51
234	Son, Fred	2	M	6.75	0.00	0.00	0.00

Output Results: The sequential file EX61PAY.DAT is created in auxiliary storage on the default drive. The following results are shown for the first payroll record.

```
Payroll File Build
------------------

Employee Number ======> 123

Employee Name ========> Col Joan

No. of Dependents =====> 2

Marital Status =======> M

Rate of Pay ==========> 12.50

YTD Gross Pay ========> 25345.23

YTD Withholding Tax ==> 10256.45

YTD Social Security ==> 1812.18

Enter Y to add record, else N ===> Y
```

The following is displayed prior to termination of execution of the program.

```
Creation of Sequential Data File Is Complete

Total Number of Records in EX61PAY.DAT ===> 8

Job Complete
```

2. Master File List

Purpose: To become familiar with reading records in a sequential file; printing the records on the printer; and paging a report. Use of the OPEN, CLOSE, INPUT #n, LPRINT, and LPRINT USING statements and the EOF function is required.

Problem: Write a top-down program that prints the data items found in each employee record of the sequential file EX61PAY.DAT created in BASIC Programming Problem 1. Page the report. Print a maximum of 17 lines to a page. Double-space the detail lines and single-space the total lines. As part of the end-of-job routine, display the following totals: employee-record count, YTD gross pay, YTD federal withholding tax, and YTD social security tax.

(Hint: See Program 6.3 on page 204.)

Input Data: Use the sequential file EX61PAY.DAT created in BASIC Programming Problem 1. (If you did not complete BASIC Programming Problem 1, then use EX61PAY.DAT found on the Student Diskette.)

Output Results: The following results are displayed.

```
                        Payroll File List           Page:  1

    Employee        Marital Rate of  <-------Year-to-Date-------->
    No. Name    Dep. Status  Pay     Gross Pay With. Tax Soc. Sec.
    --- -------- ---- ------- -------  ---------- ---------  ---------
    123 Col Joan  2    M      12.50   25,345.23 10,256.45  1,812.18

    124 Fiel Don  1    S      18.00   41,725.00  8,546.45  2,983.34

    125 Dit Lisa  1    S      13.00   42,115.23 11,035.78  3,003.00

    126 Snow Joe  9    M       4.50   11,510.05    854.34    822.97

    134 Hi Frank  0    M       8.75    9,298.65  2,678.25    664.85

    167 Bri Edie  3    S      10.40    8,190.45     17.50    585.62
```

```
                        Payroll File List           Page:  2

    Employee        Marital Rate of  <-------Year-to-Date-------->
    No. Name    Dep. Status  Pay     Gross Pay With. Tax Soc. Sec.
    --- -------- ---- ------- -------  ---------- ---------  ---------
    210 Liss Ted  6    M       8.80    7,098.04  2,120.55    507.51

    234 Son Fred  2    M       6.75        0.00      0.00      0.00

    Total Number of Records ========>        8
    Total YTD Gross Pay =============> 145,282.65
    Total YTD Wihtholding Tax ======>  35,509.32
    Total YTD Social Security ======>  10,379.47
    Job Complete
```

3. Writing a Report to Auxiliary Storage

Purpose: To become familiar with writing a report to a sequential file. Use of the OPEN, CLOSE, INPUT #n, PRINT #n, and PRINT #n, USING statements and the EOF function is required.

Problem: Same as BASIC Programming Problem 2, except write the report to the sequential file EX63RPT.LIS. Later, use the MS DOS command TYPE to display the report on the screen and the PRINT command to print the report on the printer.

Input Data: Use the sequential file EX61PAY.DAT that was created in BASIC Programming Problem 1. (If you did not complete BASIC Programming Problem 1, then use EX61PAY.DAT found on the Student Diskette.)

Output Results: The sequential file EX63RPT.LIS is created in auxiliary storage. The following is displayed at end-of-job time.

```
    Report Complete and Stored Under the File Name EX63RPT.LIS.
    Job Complete
```

4. Appending Records to the End of a File

Purpose: To become familiar with appending records to the end of a sequential file. Use of the OPEN, CLOSE, and WRITE #n statements is required.

Problem: The sequential file EX64PAY.DAT found on the Student Diskette is a duplicate of EX61PAY.DAT, created by BASIC Programming Problem 1. Append to EX64PAY.DAT the new employee records described under Input Data.

Input Data: Prepare and use the following sample data.

Employee Number	Employee Name	Dependents	Marital Status	Rate of Pay
345	Lie Jeff	2	M	6.60
612	Abe Mike	1	S	8.75

Since these are new employees, assign all year-to-date items a value of zero.

Output Results: The screen display should be the same as shown in the Output Results for BASIC Programming Problem 1. The following is displayed at end-of-job time.

```
Total Number of Records Added to EX64PAY.DAT ===> 2
Job Complete
```

5. Computing the Average Age of Employees with a Minor Control Break

Purpose: To become familiar with a method of testing for a control break in a file. Use of the OPEN, CLOSE, and INPUT #n statements and the EOF function is required.

Problem: Construct a top-down program that will find the average age of those employees less than 40 years old and the average age of those greater than or equal to 40 years old. The program should do the following:

1. Read a department number and a person's age from the sequential file EX65EMP.DAT found on the Student Diskette. The employee records found in EX65EMP.DAT are shown under Input Data.
2. Test to see whether the department number is the same as the previous one.
3. If it is the same department number, determine whether the age is greater than or equal to 40 or less than 40. Use an IF statement to transfer control so that the age is added to an appropriate total and a variable representing a counter has its value incremented by 1.
4. If the department number changes (control break occurs), transfer control to determine the average ages of those employees below 40 and of those 40 and above; display a summary line; then reset counters and the control variable and continue processing the next department.

(**Hint:** See Program 6.4 on page 212. No paging is required for this report.)

Input Data: The sequential file EX65EMP.DAT is stored on the Student Diskette. The file contains the following sample data:

Dept. No.	Age	Dept. No.	Age	Dept. No.	Age	Dept. No.	Age
1	26	1	64	2	65	2	25
1	38	1	19	2	18	3	21
1	22	1	38	2	37	3	23
1	40	2	46	2	41	3	34
1	51	2	48	2	43	3	56

Output Results: The following results are displayed.

```
                     Employee Average Age

              Below    Average Age    40 and    Average Age
Dept. No.     40       Below 40       Above     40 and Above
--------      -----    -----------    ------    ------------

    1           5          28.6         3           51.7
    2           3          26.7         5           48.6
    3           3          26.0         1           56.0

Employee Age Analysis Report Complete
```

6. Sales Analysis Report with Three Levels of Control Breaks

Purpose: To become familiar with paging a report; the LPRINT and LPRINT USING statements; and the concepts of multilevel control breaks and sequential file processing.

Problem: Write a top-down program that prints a report with three levels of control breaks. The program is to process the sequential data file SALES.DAT used earlier in the chapter by Program 6.4 and stored on the Student Diskette. Print totals for department, store, district, and company. A listing of SALES.DAT is shown in Figure 6.11 on page 209. Note that the records are in sequence by department within store within district. Page the report. Print a maximum of 36 lines per page.

(**Hint:** See Program 6.5 on page 216.)

Input Data: Use the sequential file SALES.DAT that is on the Student Diskette.

Output Results: The output results should be similar to the report shown in Figure 6.13 on page 218.

7. Checking the Sequence of Customer Numbers

Purpose: To devise an efficient method of checking the sequence in ascending order of records in a sequential file.

Problem: A sequential file (EX67CUS.DAT) on the Student Diskette contains customer records. Each record contains a customer number and the balance due. The records must be checked to ensure that all are in ascending sequence on the basis of the customer number. The program *must not* compare the first customer number against the customer number of 0 or 1 or any predetermined fixed number. Beginning with the second record, each customer number should be compared to the previous customer number in sequence.

If a customer record is out of order, the following is to be displayed:

```
Out of Order =====> XXXXX
```

where the Xs represent the customer number of the record that is out of order. If a duplicate customer number is detected, the following is to be displayed:

```
Duplicate ========> XXXXX
```

If the customer record is in ascending order, processing continues. Duplicate customer numbers are not out of order. When the last customer number is processed, display the total customer records that have been sequence-checked in ascending order.

Input Data: Use the sequential data file EX67CUS.DAT on the Student Diskette. Listed below are the first five records. You can use the TYPE command to display the entire file.

Customer Number	Balance Due
03000	$ 43.25
03012	132.00
03013	5.65
03015	354.98
03014	99.80

Output Results: The following partial results are shown.

```
Out of Order =====> 3014
Duplicate ========> 3018
Out of Order =====> 3037
          .
          .
          .
Out of Order =====> 3078
Out of Order =====> 3095

Customer Numbers in Sequence =====> 31

Job Finished
```

8. Payroll Problem V: Social Security Computations and Multiple-File Processing

Purpose: To become familiar with multiple-file processing and paging a report.

Problem: Modify Payroll Problem IV in chapter 5 on page 184 (BASIC Programming Problem 7), to determine the social security deduction. The social security deduction is equal to 7.15% of the gross pay, to a maximum of $3,003.00 (7.15% of $42,000) for the year. Modify the solution to Payroll Problem IV by adding this additional computation as a subroutine. Print the social security tax to the nearest cent. Also do the following:

1. Use the master payroll file (EX61PAY.DAT) created in BASIC Programming Problem 1 of this chapter to obtain year-to-date information and the rate of pay for each employee. (If you did not complete BASIC Programming Problem 1, then use EX61PAY.DAT found on the Student Diskette.)
2. Use the **transaction file** EX68TRA.DAT on the Student Diskette. A transaction file is one that contains temporary data. In this case, the temporary data is the employee number and hours worked for the pay period, as shown under Input Data.
3. Write a new master file (EX68PAY.DAT) that includes the updated year-to-date values for each employee.
4. Page the report. Print a maximum of 17 lines to a page.

You may assume that the records in EX61PAY.DAT and EX68TRA.DAT are in ascending sequence and that there is exactly one record in each file per employee (i.e., each record in EX61PAY.DAT has a match in EX68TRA.DAT).

Input Data: Use the sequential data files described below. Both files are stored on the Student Diskette.

1. EX61PAY.DAT as the master payroll file (see the Input Data for BASIC Programming Problem 1 on page 220).
2. EX68TRA.DAT as the transaction file. EX68TRA.DAT contains the following data:

Employee Number	Hours Worked	Employee Number	Hours Worked
123	88	134	80
124	96	167	70.5
125	72	210	80
126	80	234	32

Output Results: A new master payroll file is created as EX68PAY.DAT. The report below is printed on the printer.

```
                    Biweekly Payroll Report          Page:  1

   Employee
   Number        Gross Pay       Fed. Tax       Soc. Sec.      Net Pay
   --------      ---------       --------       ----------     -------
      123        1,150.00         214.62           82.23       853.16

      124        1,872.00         366.71           19.66     1,485.63

      125          936.00         179.51            0.00       756.49

      126          360.00           2.77           25.74       331.49

      134          700.00         140.00           50.05       509.95

      167          733.20         123.56           52.42       557.21
```

```
                    Biweekly Payroll Report          Page:  2

   Employee
   Number        Gross Pay       Fed. Tax       Soc. Sec.      Net Pay
   --------      ---------       --------       ----------     -------
      210          704.00          94.65           50.34       559.02

      234          216.00          27.82           15.44       172.74

   Total Gross Pay ========>      6,671.20
   Total Withholding Tax ==>      1,149.63
   Total Social Security ==>        295.88
   Total Net Pay ==========>      5,225.69

   End of Payroll Report
```

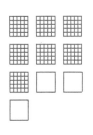

FOR LOOPS, ARRAYS, SORTING, AND TABLE PROCESSING

In earlier chapters, loops were implemented (coded) with the WHILE and WEND statements. This chapter presents a second method for implementing certain types of loops by means of the FOR and NEXT statements.

Also, in the previous chapters, the programs used simple variables like AMT, PRICE, and CODE$ to store and access data. Each variable was assigned a single value in an INPUT, LET, or READ statement. Another technique that can make a program shorter, easier to code, and more general is the use of arrays. In this chapter, we will discuss the advantages gained by grouping similar data into an array. An **array** is an ordered set of string or numeric data that is defined in terms of one or more dimensions. In mathematics, an array is sometimes called a matrix or a table, and each member of an array is called an **array element**.

In MS BASIC, an array is a variable that is allocated a specified number of storage locations, each of which can be assigned a unique value. In other words, an array allows a programmer to store more than one value under the same variable name. Conceptually, an array in MS BASIC is the same as an array in mathematics. Arrays are commonly used in programming for sorting and table processing, in which related data items are organized into rows and columns.

A report is usually easier to work with and more meaningful if the information is generated in some sequence, such as first to last, largest to smallest, or oldest to newest. Arranging data according to order or sequence is called **sorting**.

In data processing terminology, a **table** is a collection of data in which each item is uniquely identified by a label, by its position relative to other items, or by some other means. Income-tax tables, insurance tables, airline schedules, and telephone directories are examples of tables that present data that is concise yet easy to read and understand. Storing table elements in arrays allows a programmer to organize the entries and to write efficient code for retrieving each individual element.

Upon successful completion of this chapter, you will be able to code certain types of loops more efficiently. Furthermore, you will be able to develop programs that demand that large amounts of data, stored in an orderly fashion, be available to the PC during the entire execution of the program.

⊞ 7.2

THE FOR AND NEXT STATEMENTS

The FOR and NEXT statements make it possible to execute a section of a program repeatedly, with automatic changes in the value of a variable between repetitions.

In chapters 4, 5, and 6, the WHILE and WEND statements were used to implement a loop structure that executed a section of a program repeatedly. Whenever you have to develop a **counter-controlled loop** (a loop that is to be executed a specified number of times), the coding requires statements for initializing, incrementing, and testing of a counter. Any loop that involves this type of coding may be written with the FOR and NEXT statements. When these two statements are used to establish a counter-controlled loop, we call it a **For loop**.

The While Loop Versus the For Loop

Programs 7.1 and 7.2 illustrate the similarity between the use of the WHILE and WEND statements and the FOR and NEXT statements. Both programs compute the sum of the integers from 1 to 10.

PROGRAM 7.1

```
100 ' Program 7.1
110 ' Looping Using WHILE
120 ' and WEND Statements
130 ' *******************
140 SUM = 0
150 COUNT = 1
160 WHILE COUNT <= 10
170     SUM = SUM + COUNT
180     COUNT = COUNT + 1
190 WEND
200 PRINT "The sum is"; SUM
210 END

RUN

The sum is 55
```

While Loop brackets lines 160–190.

PROGRAM 7.2

```
100 ' Program 7.2
110 ' Looping Using FOR
120 ' and NEXT Statements
130 ' ******************
140 SUM = 0
150 FOR COUNT = 1 TO 10 STEP 1
160     SUM = SUM + COUNT
170 NEXT COUNT
180 PRINT "The sum is"; SUM
190 END

RUN

The sum is 55
```

For Loop brackets lines 150–170.

Program 7.1 uses the WHILE and WEND statements. Lines 140 and 150 initialize the running total (SUM) to 0 and the counter (COUNT) to 1. Line 160 tests to determine whether the value of COUNT is less than or equal to 10. If the condition is true, SUM is incremented by COUNT, and the counter COUNT is incremented by 1 before control transfers back to line 160. When the condition in the WHILE statement is false, the program terminates the loop, and line 200 displays the value of SUM.

Program 7.2 incorporates the FOR and NEXT statements to define the For loop (lines 150 through 170). Read through Program 7.2 carefully and note how compact it is and how superior it is to Program 7.1. Using a single FOR statement, as in line 150 of Program 7.2, we can consolidate the functions of lines 150, 160 and 180 of Program 7.1.

Besides using less main storage and being easier to read than Program 7.1, Program 7.2 is also more efficient; it executes faster than Program 7.1. In chapter 8, we will illustrate the performance difference between a While loop and a For loop.

The Execution of a For Loop

The execution of the For loop in Program 7.2 involves the following:

1. When the FOR statement is executed for the first time, the For loop becomes *active* and COUNT is set equal to 1.
2. The statements in the For loop, in this case line 160, are executed.
3. Control returns to the FOR statement, where the value of COUNT is incremented by a value of 1, which follows the keyword STEP.
4. If the value of COUNT is less than or equal to 10, execution of the For loop continues.
5. When the value of COUNT is greater than 10, control transfers to the statement (line 180) following the NEXT COUNT statement.

The general forms of the FOR and NEXT statements are given in Tables 7.1 and 7.2.

_____TABLE 7.1 The FOR Statement_____

General Form:	FOR k = *initial value* TO *limit value* STEP *increment value* *or* FOR k = *initial value* TO *limit value* *where **k** is a simple numeric variable called the **loop variable**, and the **initial value**, **limit value**, and **increment value** are numeric expressions.*
Purpose:	*Causes the statements between the FOR and NEXT statements to be executed repeatedly until the value of k exceeds the limit value. When k exceeds the limit value, control transfers to the line just after the corresponding NEXT statement.* *If the increment value is negative, the test is reversed. The value of k is decremented each time through the loop, and the loop is executed until k is less than the limit value.*
Keyword Entry:	*Simultaneously press the Alt and F keys on your keyboard.*
Examples:	250 FOR ITEM = 1 TO 20 350 FOR AMOUNT = -5 TO 15 STEP 2 400 FOR COUNT = 10 TO -5 STEP -3 450 FOR TAX = 0 TO 10 STEP 0.1 500 FOR TOTAL = START TO FINISH STEP INCREMENT 550 FOR S = A + 5 TO C/D STEP F * B 600 FOR I = 20 TO 20 650 FOR J = 20 TO 1
Note:	*If the keyword STEP is not used, then the increment value is 1.*

_____TABLE 7.2 The NEXT Statement_____

General Form:	NEXT k *where **k** is the same variable as the loop variable in the corresponding FOR statement.*
Purpose:	*Identifies the end of a For loop.*
Keyword Entry:	*Simultaneously press the Alt and N keys on your keyboard.*
Examples:	300 NEXT AMOUNT 380 NEXT ITEM

The terminology used to describe the FOR statement is shown below:

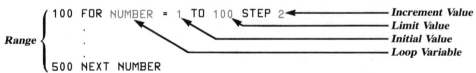

The **range** of a For loop is the set of repeatedly executed statements beginning with the FOR statement and continuing up to and including the NEXT statement that has the same loop variable.

TRY IT YOURSELF

Load Program 7.2 (PRG7-2) from the Student Diskette. Modify the initial, limit, and increment values according to the sets listed below. Execute Program 7.2 for each set. If the PC goes into an infinite loop, press the Control and Break keys simultaneously to terminate processing.

Set	Initial	Limit	Increment	Set	Initial	Limit	Increment
1	1	1000	2	6	1	10	0.1
2	25	75	5	7	1	–10	–1
3	5	5	1	8	1	10	0
4	5	1	1	9	–5	–20	Remove the
5	5	1	–1				keyword STEP

Flowchart Representation of a For Loop

The flowchart representation for a For loop corresponds to a Do-While structure (see Figure 7.1). In the first process symbol, the loop variable is assigned the initial value. Next a test is made. If the condition is true, the loop is terminated and control transfers to the statement that follows the Do-While structure.

If the condition is false, control passes into the body of the For loop. After the statements in the For loop are executed, the loop variable is incremented by the increment value and control transfers back up to the decision symbol again to test whether the loop variable exceeds the limit value.

If the increment value is negative, the test is reversed. The value of the loop variable is decremented each time through the loop, and the loop is executed until the loop variable is less than the limit value.

Figure 7.2 illustrates a flowchart that corresponds to Program 7.2.

FIGURE 7.1

General flowchart representation of a For loop.

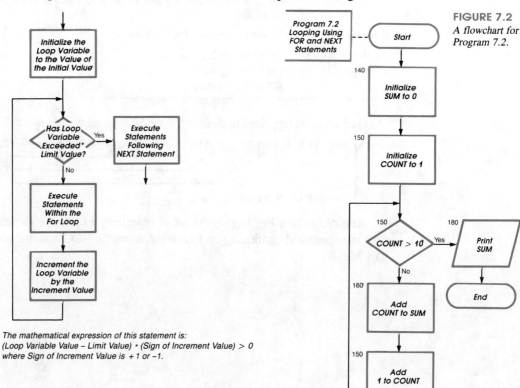

FIGURE 7.2

A flowchart for Program 7.2.

The mathematical expression of this statement is:
(Loop Variable Value – Limit Value) * (Sign of Increment Value) > 0
where Sign of Increment Value is +1 or –1.

Valid Values in the
FOR Statement

The examples presented in Table 7.1 indicate that the initial, limit, and increment values of a FOR statement can take on a variety of representations. This section is divided into subsections that illustrate these representations.

Stepping by 1. Many applications call for incrementing or **stepping** the control variable by 1 each time the For loop is executed. You may write such a FOR statement like this:

```
170 FOR RATE = 1 TO 12 STEP 1
```

or

```
170 FOR RATE = 1 TO 12
```

Program 7.3 computes the amount of an investment (AMOUNT), compounded annually, for the interest rate (RATE) between 1 and 12%, inclusive.

PROGRAM 7.3

```
100 ' Program 7.3
110 ' Stepping by 1 in a FOR Statement
120 ' *******************************
130 INPUT "Investment =====> ", PRINCIPAL
140 PRINT
150 PRINT     "Rate        Amount"
160 FORMAT$ = "##.#      ##,###.##"
170 FOR RATE = 1 TO 12
180    AMOUNT = PRINCIPAL * (1 + RATE / 100)
190    PRINT USING FORMAT$; RATE, AMOUNT
200 NEXT RATE
210 PRINT "Job Complete"
220 END

RUN

Investment =====> 500

Rate        Amount
 1.0        505.00
 2.0        510.00
 3.0        515.00
 4.0        520.00
 5.0        525.00
 6.0        530.00
 7.0        535.00
 8.0        540.00
 9.0        545.00
10.0        550.00
11.0        555.00
12.0        560.00
Job Complete
```

Line 130 in Program 7.3 requests that the operator enter the principal. Line 170 activates the For loop and assigns RATE a value of 1 (1%). Line 180 computes the amount of the investment, and line 190 displays the interest rate and amount. The control variable RATE is incremented by 1, and the loop is executed repeatedly until RATE exceeds 12. When this occurs, control transfers to line 210.

As with While loops, the statements in the For loop, except for the first and last statement, should be indented by three spaces for the purpose of readability (see lines 180 and 190). This style allows you to scan a For loop quickly, and it simplifies the debugging effort.

Stepping by a Value Other Than 1.   Some applications call for the loop variable to be incremented by a value other than 1. If line 170 of Program 7.3 is modified to

```
170 FOR RATE = 1 TO 12 STEP 3
```

the program computes the amount of an investment, compounded annually, for interest rates of 1%, 4%, 7%, and 10%. The loop terminates when the loop variable RATE becomes 13, since this is greater than the value of the limit. Table 7.3 (opposite) presents the output from Program 7.3 when line 170 is modified accordingly.

Initializing the Loop Variable to a Value Other Than 1.   It is not necessary to initialize the loop variable to 1. If line 170 of Program 7.3 is modified to

```
170 FOR RATE = 8 TO 16 STEP 2
```

the program generates a report that computes the even valued interest rates between 8 and 16% inclusive. Table 7.3 presents the output from Program 7.3 when line 170 is modified accordingly.

Some applications may call for the initialization of the loop variable to zero or some negative value. For example, the statements

```
500 FOR X = 0 TO 10
```

and

```
700 FOR Y = -6 TO 12
```

are both valid. Line 500 will cause the corresponding For loop to execute eleven times. Line 700 will cause the For loop to execute nineteen times.

Decimal Fraction Values in a FOR Statement.   The values in a FOR statement can be decimal fraction numbers. If line 170 of Program 7.3 is modified to

```
170 FOR RATE = 11.5 TO 12.5 STEP .1
```

the program computes the amount of an investment compounded annually for interest rates between 11.5 and 12.4%, inclusive, in increments of one-tenth of a percent. Table 7.3 presents the output from Program 7.3 when line 170 is modified accordingly.

Be careful with decimal fraction parameters, since the PC may not always store the exact binary representation of a decimal number. Stepping by a decimal number can, in some instances, result in one less or one more time through the loop than you expect. Note that in Table 7.3, the last Rate displayed is 12.4 and this is one-tenth less than the limit value of 12.5.

Negative Values in a FOR Statement.   The values in a FOR statement may be negative. If line 170 of Program 7.3 is modified to

```
170 FOR RATE = 8 TO 0 STEP -1
```

the program generates a report in which the interest rates are decremented from 8 to 0%. The negative value step in the FOR statement causes the test to be reversed, and the loop variable is decremented until it is less than the limit value. Table 7.3 presents the output from Program 7.3 when line 170 is modified accordingly.

Try It Yourself

Load Program 7.3 (PRG7-3) from the Student Diskette. Modify the initial, limit, and increment values in line 170 according to the values listed in Table 7.3. Execute Program 7.3 each time line 170 is modified, and compare your output to the output presented in Table 7.3. Don't forget to also enter the correct investment value.

TABLE 7.3 Modifications to and Outputs from Program 7.3

REPLACEMENT OF LINE 170 IN PROGRAM 7.3 BY:	INVESTMENT	OUTPUT OF MODIFIED PROGRAM 7.3	
170 FOR RATE = 1 TO 12 STEP 3	1000	Rate	Amount
		1.0	1,010.00
		4.0	1,040.00
		7.0	1,070.00
		10.0	1,100.00
170 FOR RATE = 8 TO 16 STEP 2	2000	Rate	Amount
		8.0	2,160.00
		10.0	2,200.00
		12.0	2,240.00
		14.0	2,280.00
		16.0	2,320.00
170 FOR RATE = 11.5 TO 12.5 STEP 0.1	1500	Rate	Amount
		11.5	1,672.50
		11.6	1,674.00
		11.7	1,675.50
		11.8	1,677.00
		11.9	1,678.50
		12.0	1,680.00
		12.1	1,681.50
		12.2	1,683.00
		12.3	1,684.50
		12.4	1,686.00
170 FOR RATE = 8 TO 0 STEP −1	2500	Rate	Amount
		8.0	2,700.00
		7.0	2,675.00
		6.0	2,650.00
		5.0	2,625.00
		4.0	2,600.00
		3.0	2,575.00
		2.0	2,550.00
		1.0	2,525.00
		0.0	2,500.00

Variable Values in a FOR Statement.   Program 7.4, on the following page, shows that the values in a FOR statement can be variables as well as numeric constants. Lines 130 through 150 request that the user enter the initial, terminal, and increment values.

Be careful that the increment value is assigned a value other than zero. An increment value of zero creates an infinite loop (endless loop) and forces you to press the Control and Break keys simultaneously to terminate further processing on the PC.

Expressions as Values in a FOR Statement.   The values in a FOR statement may be complex numeric expressions. For example, the following FOR statements are valid:

```
500 FOR X = A * B TO S ^ T STEP C * 2

600 FOR Y = (A + B) / C TO P * (F - G) ^ C STEP 5 * V
```

If C is zero, what do you think happens in line 500 and line 600 above?

PROGRAM 7.4

```
100 ' Program 7.4
110 ' Variable Values in a FOR Statement
120 ' *************************************
130 INPUT "Initial Rate (in %) =======> ", RATE1
140 INPUT "Limit Rate (in %) =========> ", RATE2
150 INPUT "Increment Rate (in %) =====> ", INCREMENT
160 INPUT "Investment ================> ", PRINCIPAL
170 PRINT
180 PRINT      "Rate          Amount"
190 FORMAT$ = "##.#      ##,###.##"
200 FOR RATE = RATE1 TO RATE2 STEP INCREMENT
210    AMOUNT = PRINCIPAL * (1 + RATE / 100)
220    PRINT USING FORMAT$; RATE, AMOUNT
230 NEXT RATE
240 PRINT "Job Complete"
250 END

RUN

Initial Rate (in %) =======> 10
Limit Rate (in %) =========> 12.5
Increment Rate (in %) =====> .5
Investment ================> 3000

Rate        Amount
10.0        3,300.00
10.5        3,315.00
11.0        3,330.00
11.5        3,345.00
12.0        3,360.00
12.5        3,375.00
Job Complete
```

TRY IT YOURSELF

Load Program 7.4 (PRG7-4) from the Student Diskette. Display and execute the program. Enter an initial value that is equal to the rate your bank pays. Enter a limit value 3 points higher than the initial value. Enter an increment value of 0.5. Finally, enter the amount in your savings account. See what effect the interest rate has on the amount after one year.

Your bank may compound the interest more than once a year. For a hint as to how to modify Program 7.4 so that it will take multiple conversions into consideration, see BASIC Programming Problem 3 at the end of chapter 2 on page 49.

Initial Entry into a For Loop

Control must not transfer into the range of a For loop from any statement outside its range. You cannot use a GOSUB or an ON-GOSUB to transfer into the range of a For loop without executing the FOR statement itself.

The following partial program (opposite) is invalid, since control is transferred into the range of a For loop, which means that the FOR statement is not executed to define the loop variable correctly.

```
 ┌─200 GOSUB 410        ╲
 │     .                 ╲
 │     .                  ╲  Invalid
 │     .                  ╱
 │ 400 FOR I = 1 TO 50   ╱
 └►410    PRINT I       ╱
   420 NEXT I          ╱
```

Loop Variable and Values Redefined

Once the FOR statement is executed, the initial, limit, and increment values are set and cannot be altered while the For loop is active. MS BASIC simply disregards any attempt to redefine them. For example, the following For loop executes ten times, even though the variables in the FOR statement are changed by lines 200 through 220.

```
100 A = 1
110 B = 10
120 C = 1
130 FOR I = A TO B STEP C
        .
        .
        .
200    A = 5
210    B = 1
220    C = 4
230 NEXT I
```

If A, B, and C are displayed after the second pass, they will be equal to 5, 1, and 4, respectively. However, the initial, limit, and increment values in the FOR statement are still equal to 1, 10, and 1, respectively.

On the other hand, the loop variable may be reassigned a value within the For loop for the purpose of terminating the loop. The following partial program, which modifies the value of the loop variable within the For loop, is valid.

```
300 FOR PERIOD = 1 TO 100 STEP 2
        .
        .
        .
390    IF AMOUNT = INTEREST
           THEN PERIOD = 100
400 NEXT PERIOD
410
```

When the For loop terminates, the loop variable is always equal to the sum of its value from the last time the NEXT statement was executed plus the increment value. In the previous example, PERIOD is equal to 102 when control is transferred to line 410.

Listed below are rules that summarize the FOR statement.

FOR Rule 1: If the increment value following the keyword STEP is positive, or if the keyword STEP is not used, then the PC executes the For loop until the loop variable exceeds the limit value. If the increment value is negative, the test is reversed. The value of the loop variable is decremented each time through the loop, and the loop is executed until the loop variable is less than the limit value.

FOR Rule 2: The value of the increment value must not be zero.

FOR Rule 3: A valid initial entry into a For loop can be accomplished only by transferring control to the FOR statement.

> ***FOR Rule 4:*** A normal exit from a For loop leaves the current value of the loop variable equal to the sum of its value the last time the `NEXT` statement was executed plus the increment value.

> ***FOR Rule 5:*** No statement that is located in the range of a For loop can change the initial, limit, and increment values.

Iterations in a For Loop

The number of **iterations** or repetitions specified by a `FOR` statement may be computed with the following formula:

$$\text{No. of Iterations} = \frac{\text{Limit value} - \text{Initial value}}{\text{Increment value}} + 1$$

where the ratio is performed in integer arithmetic so that the quotient is truncated to the next lowest integer.

How many iterations are performed by the following For loop?

```
400 FOR TEMP = -73 TO 987 STEP 7
         .
         .
         .
800 NEXT TEMP
```

Using the formula, the number of iterations is

$$\frac{987 - (-73)}{7} + 1 = 151 + 1 = 152$$

Note that the initial quotient was 151.42 but the decimal fraction 0.42 was truncated.

Another Look at the For Loop

The For loop in MS BASIC corresponds to a Do-While structure (see Figure 7.1 on page 230). Note that the test for whether the value of the loop variable exceeds the limit value is carried out at the beginning of the loop. This means that the body of the For loop will not be executed if the initial value is greater than the limit value.

For example, in the following partial program, control immediately transfers to line 240 when the `FOR` statement is encountered. The For loop is executed zero times, and the loop variable is equal to the initial value.

```
200 COUNT = 0
210 FOR I = 10 TO 1 STEP 2
220    COUNT = COUNT + 1
230 NEXT I
240 PRINT "The loop variable is equal to"; I
250 PRINT "The For loop is executed"; COUNT; "times"

RUN

The loop variable is equal to 10
The For loop is executed 0 times
```

On the other hand, if the increment value is –2 and line 210 is modified to

```
210 FOR I = 10 TO 1 STEP -2
```

the output becomes:

```
The loop variable is equal to 0
The For loop is executed 5 times
```

Reexamine Figure 7.1 and note that the mathematical expression used to terminate the looping in a For loop is

(Loop Variable Value – Limit Value) $*$ (Sign of Increment Value) > 0

where the sign of the increment value is either $+1$ or -1.

Nested For Loops Just as there are nested expressions and nested subroutines in MS BASIC, there are nested For loops. When the statements of one For loop lie within the range of another For loop, the loops are said to be **nested** or **embedded**. Furthermore, the outer For loop may be nested in the range of still another For loop, and so on.

Program 7.5 utilizes two nested For loops. The inner For loop, formed by lines 150 through 170, is written so that all the statements in its range also lie within the range of the outer For loop, lines 130 through 190.

When line 130 is executed, the outer For loop becomes active. The loop variable X is set to 1, and line 140 displays that value. When line 150 is executed, the inner For loop becomes active. The loop variable Y is set to 1, and line 160 displays the values of both X and Y. With X equal to 1, control remains within the inner loop, which is executed three times, until Y exceeds 3. At this point, the inner loop is satisfied and control passes to the outer For loop, which executes line 180.

Control then passes to line 130, where the loop variable X is incremented by 1 to become 2. After line 140 displays the new value of X, line 150 is executed and the inner For loop becomes active again. The loop variable Y is initialized to 1, and the process repeats itself.

PROGRAM 7.5

```
100 ' Program 7.5
110 ' Nested For Loops
120 ' ****************
130 FOR X = 1 TO 4
140     PRINT "Outer Loop - X ="; X
150     FOR Y = 1 TO 3
160         PRINT "    Inner Loop - X ="; X; "and Y ="; Y
170     NEXT Y
180     PRINT
190 NEXT X
200 END

RUN

Outer Loop - X = 1
    Inner Loop - X = 1   and Y = 1
    Inner Loop - X = 1   and Y = 2
    Inner Loop - X = 1   and Y = 3

Outer Loop - X = 2
    Inner Loop - X = 2   and Y = 1
    Inner Loop - X = 2   and Y = 2
    Inner Loop - X = 2   and Y = 3

Outer Loop - X = 3
    Inner Loop - X = 3   and Y = 1
    Inner Loop - X = 3   and Y = 2
    Inner Loop - X = 3   and Y = 3
Outer Loop - X = 4
    Inner Loop - X = 4   and Y = 1
    Inner Loop - X = 4   and Y = 2
    Inner Loop - X = 4   and Y = 3
```

Outer For Loop *Inner For Loop*

When the outer loop is satisfied, control passes to line 200. In Program 7.5, the outer For loop executes a total of 4 times, and the inner For loop executes a total of 3 * 4, or 12, times.

As another example of a program with nested For loops, consider Program 7.6 which generates the multiplication table. Each time the loop variable in the outer For loop (lines 160 through 220) is assigned a new value, the inner For loop (lines 180 through 200) computes and displays one row of the table. Note that the two loop variables, ROW and COLUMN, are multiplied together in line 190 to form the various products in the multiplication table.

The PRINT statements in lines 170 and 190 end with the semicolon separator. You'll recall from chapter 4 that when a PRINT statement ends with a semicolon, the cursor remains on the same line. Each time the inner loop is satisfied, the PRINT statement in line 210 prints blanks and moves the cursor to the beginning of the next line.

PROGRAM 7.6

```
100 ' Program 7.6
110 ' Generating the Multiplication Table
120 ' **********************************
130 CLS : KEY OFF  ' Clear Screen
140 PRINT " ×  !   0   1   2   3   4   5   6   7   8   9  10  11  12"
150 PRINT "----+-------------------------------------------------------"
160 FOR ROW = 0 TO 12
170    PRINT USING "###  _!"; ROW;
180    FOR COLUMN = 0 TO 12
190       PRINT USING "####"; ROW * COLUMN;
200    NEXT COLUMN
210    PRINT
220 NEXT ROW
230 PRINT
240 PRINT "End of Multiplication Table"
250 END
RUN
```

```
 ×  !   0   1   2   3   4   5   6   7   8   9  10  11  12
----+-------------------------------------------------------
 0  !   0   0   0   0   0   0   0   0   0   0   0   0   0
 1  !   0   1   2   3   4   5   6   7   8   9  10  11  12
 2  !   0   2   4   6   8  10  12  14  16  18  20  22  24
 3  !   0   3   6   9  12  15  18  21  24  27  30  33  36
 4  !   0   4   8  12  16  20  24  28  32  36  40  44  48
 5  !   0   5  10  15  20  25  30  35  40  45  50  55  60
 6  !   0   6  12  18  24  30  36  42  48  54  60  66  72
 7  !   0   7  14  21  28  35  42  49  56  63  70  77  84
 8  !   0   8  16  24  32  40  48  56  64  72  80  88  96
 9  !   0   9  18  27  36  45  54  63  72  81  90  99 108
10  !   0  10  20  30  40  50  60  70  80  90 100 110 120
11  !   0  11  22  33  44  55  66  77  88  99 110 121 132
12  !   0  12  24  36  48  60  72  84  96 108 120 132 144
End of Multiplication Table
```

TRY IT YOURSELF

Load Program 7.6 (PRG7-6) from the Student Diskette. Display and execute the program. Change the limit value to 15 in the FOR statements in lines 160 and 180. Execute the program and see what happens.

Valid Nesting of For Loops

When nesting occurs, all statements in the range of the inner For loop must also be in the range of the outer For loop. MS BASIC does not allow the range of an inner For loop to extend past the end of the range of an outer For loop. An example of this kind of invalid nest of For loops is shown below in Program 7.7.

PROGRAM 7.7

```
100 ' Program 7.7
110 ' Invalid Nest of For Loops
120 ' ************************
130 FOR X = 1 TO 3
140     PRINT "X ="; X
150     FOR Y = 11 TO 12
160         PRINT "    Y ="; Y
170     NEXT X
180 NEXT Y
190 END
```

Invalid Nesting of For Loops

```
RUN

NEXT without FOR in 180
```

The inner loop, which begins at line 150, extends past the NEXT statement that corresponds to the outer loop. The invalid nest of For loops may be rewritten, validly, as shown below in Program 7.8:

PROGRAM 7.8

```
100 ' Program 7.8
110 ' Valid Nest of For Loops
120 ' *********************
130 FOR X = 1 TO 3
140     PRINT "X ="; X
150     FOR Y = 11 TO 12
160         PRINT "    Y ="; Y
170     NEXT Y
180 NEXT X
190 END
```

```
RUN

X = 1
        Y = 11
        Y = 12
X = 2
        Y = 11
        Y = 12
X = 3
        Y = 11
        Y = 12
```

When one For loop is nested within another, the name of the loop variable for each For loop must be different. Figure 7.3 illustrates valid and invalid nesting of For loops.

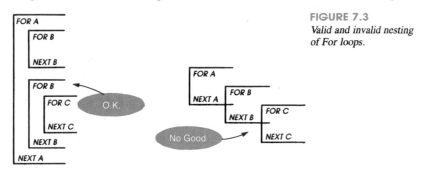

FIGURE 7.3
Valid and invalid nesting of For loops.

The number of levels of nested For loops allowed in MS BASIC is dependent on the available bytes of main storage when the program is executed. If the number of levels of nested For loops causes the PC to terminate execution, it will display the following diagnostic message:

```
Out of memory
```

If this error occurs, issue the CLEAR command and execute the program again. As demonstrated in Table 2.10 on page 39, the CLEAR command resets numeric variables to zero and string variables to null without erasing your program from main storage.

The usefulness of the FOR and NEXT statements for looping purposes should be apparent from the examples and illustrations presented thus far. However, you will see an even greater use for them in applications involving the manipulation of arrays, which are discussed in the following sections of this chapter. The material in this section can be summarized in the following rules:

> **FOR Rule 6:** If the range of a For loop includes another For loop, all statements in the range of the inner For loop must also be within the range of the outer For loop.

> **FOR Rule 7:** When one For loop is within another, the name of the loop variable for each For loop must be different.

⊞ 7.3
ARRAYS VERSUS SIMPLE VARIABLES

Arrays permit a programmer to represent many values with one variable name. The variable name assigned to represent an array is called the **array name**. The elements in the array are distinguished from one another by subscripts. In MS BASIC, the subscript is written inside a set of parentheses and is placed immediately to the right of the array name. You'll recall from chapter 3, page 58 that MS BASIC allows for two different types of variables: simple and subscripted. While simple variables are used to store and reference values that are independent of one another, subscripted variables are used to store and reference values that have been grouped into an array.

Consider the problem of writing a program that is to manipulate the 12 monthly sales for a company and generate a year-end report. Figure 7.4 illustrates the difference between using an array to store the 12 monthly sales and using simple variables.

FIGURE 7.4
Utilizing an array (1) versus simple variables (2).

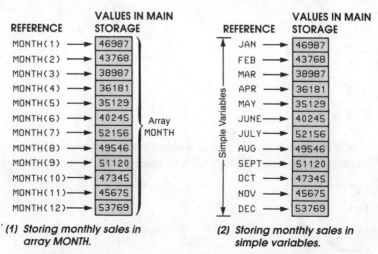

(1) *Storing monthly sales in array MONTH.*

(2) *Storing monthly sales in simple variables.*

The monthly sales stored in an array require the same storage allocation that the sales represented as independent variables do. The difference lies in the programming techniques that can access the different values. For example, the programmer may assign the values of simple variables in a READ statement in this manner:

```
150 READ JAN, FEB, MAR, APR, MAY, JUNE, JULY, AUG, SEPT, OCT, NOV, DEC
```

Each simple variable must explicitly appear in a LET or PRINT statement if the monthly sales are to be summed or displayed. Not only is the programming time consuming, but the variables *must* be properly placed in the program.

The same function can be accomplished by entering all 12 values into array MONTH:

```
140 FOR NUM = 1 TO 12
150    READ MONTH(NUM)
160 NEXT NUM
```

In line 140, the value of NUM is initialized to 1. In line 150, the first value in the data-holding area is assigned to MONTH(1) (read "MONTH sub 1"). Then NUM is incremented to 2, and the next value is assigned to MONTH(2). This continues until MONTH(12) is assigned the 12th value in the data-holding area.

MONTH2 and MONTH(2) are different from each other. MONTH2 is a simple variable, no different from SALE, INC, DIG, or COST. On the other hand, MONTH(2) is the second element in array MONTH, and the manner in which it is called upon in a program differs from the fashion in which a simple variable is called.

⊞ 7.4
DECLARING ARRAYS

Before arrays can be used, the amount of main storage to be reserved must be declared in the program. This is the purpose of the DIM statement. The keyword DIM is an abbreviation of **dimension**. The DIM statement also declares explicitly the **upper-bound value** and implicitly the **lower-bound value** of the subscript. The upper- and lower-bound values define the range of permissible values that a subscript may be assigned.

The DIM Statement

The main function of the DIM statement is to declare to the PC the necessary information regarding the allocation of storage locations for arrays used in a program. Good programming practice dictates that every program that utilizes array elements should have a DIM statement that properly defines the arrays.

The general form of the DIM statement is given in Table 7.4. Note that commas are required punctuation between the declared array elements.

TABLE 7.4 The DIM Statement

General Form:	DIM *array name(size), . . . , array name(size)* *where **array name** represents a numeric or string variable name, and **size** represents the upper bound value of each array. The size may be an integer or numeric variable for one-dimensional arrays. The size may be a series of integers or a series of numeric variables separated by commas for multidimensional arrays.*
Purpose:	*To reserve storage locations for arrays.*
Examples:	100 DIM BAL(4) 200 DIM PICK(6), JOB$(200), LOAN(N), TIME(20, 20) 300 DIM COST(10, 45), K$(X, Y, Z), AMT(2, 25, 7)
Note:	*In MS BASIC, the maximum number of dimensions an array may have is 255.*

To ensure the proper placement of DIM statements, most programmers put them at the beginning of the program.

> ***DIM Rule 1:*** The DIM statement may be located anywhere before the first use of an array element in a program.

In Table 7.4, line 100 reserves storage for a one-dimensional array BAL, which consists of 5 elements or storage locations. These elements — BAL(0), BAL(1), BAL(2), BAL(3) and BAL(4) — can be used in a program in much the same way that a simple variable can be used. For this DIM statement, elements BAL(5) or BAL(6) or BAL(–4) are considered not valid.

Line 200 declares three one-dimensional arrays, PICK, JOB$, and LOAN, and one two-dimensional array, TIME. Line 200 reserves storage locations for 7 elements for array PICK; 201 elements for array JOB$; N + 1 elements for array LOAN; and 441 elements for array TIME.

Line 300 in Table 7.4 declares three arrays. The first array, COST, is a two-dimensional array. The last two, K$ and AMT, are three-dimensional arrays. Multi-dimensional arrays like COST, K$, and AMT are discussed in section 7.6.

A single DIM statement will be sufficient for most programs in this chapter. If five different arrays are to be declared, all five arrays can be listed in the same DIM statement as follows:

```
200 DIM BALANCE(20), CODE(15, 28), TEMPERATURE(ROW, COLUMN, PLANE),
        DESC$(25), STATUS(12, 24, 48)
```

Five separate DIM statements can also be used in the program to declare the arrays individually:

```
200 DIM BALANCE(20)
210 DIM CODE(15, 28)
220 DIM TEMPERATURE(ROW, COLUMN, PLANE)
230 DIM DESC$(25)
240 DIM STATUS(12, 24, 48)
```

The OPTION BASE Statement

Unless otherwise specified, MS BASIC allocates the zero element for each one-dimensional array. For two-dimensional arrays, an extra row — the zero row — and an extra column — the zero column — are reserved. Thus,

```
130 DIM MONTH(12), TIME(20, 20)
```

actually reserves 13 elements for the array MONTH and 21 rows and 21 columns for the array TIME. The extra array element is MONTH(0) for array MONTH and the extra row and column is the 0th (read "zeroth") row and the 0th column for the array TIME. Although an additional element, row, or column will not present a problem to your program, the OPTION BASE statement allows you to control the lower-bound of arrays that are declared. The OPTION BASE statement can be used to set the lower bound value to 1 instead of the default 0, and this will avoid wasting main storage on unused array elements.

The general form of the OPTION BASE statement is found in Table 7.5.

———— **TABLE 7.5** The OPTION BASE Statement ————

General Form:	OPTION BASE *n* *where **n** is either 0 or 1.*
Purpose:	*To assign a lower bound of 0 or 1 to all arrays in a program.*
Examples:	100 OPTION BASE 0 120 OPTION BASE 1
Note:	*If the OPTION BASE statement is not used, the lower-bound value for all arrays is set to zero, the default value.*

The OPTION BASE statement can be used only once in a program. The effect of the OPTION BASE statement on arrays and its proper placement in a program are summarized in OPTION BASE Rules 1 and 2.

> **OPTION BASE Rule 1:** The OPTION BASE statement affects all arrays declared in a program.

> **OPTION BASE Rule 2:** The OPTION BASE statement must precede any DIM statement in a program.

The ERASE Statement

If you attempt to dimension an array more than once, the PC displays the following diagnostic message:

```
Duplicate definition
```

You can get around this diagnostic message through the use of the ERASE statement. When executed, the ERASE statement eliminates specified arrays from a program, thereby freeing main storage space.

The ERASE statement may be used, for example, if you are running short of main storage space or if you want to redimension an array.

Unlike the CLEAR command, which frees main storage space by setting *all* numeric variables to zero and string variables to null, the ERASE statement eliminates selected arrays. The general form of the ERASE statement is given in Table 7.6.

____TABLE 7.6 The ERASE Statement____

General Form:	ERASE array name$_1$, . . ., array name$_n$
Purpose:	To eliminate previously defined arrays from a program.
Examples:	2040 ERASE AMT
	3040 ERASE COST, PRICE

In Table 7.6, line 2040 eliminates array AMT. Following the execution of line 2040, the program may not reference elements of array AMT unless it is redimensioned. Line 3040 in Table 7.6 eliminates arrays COST and PRICE.

Dynamic Allocation of Arrays

Some applications call for arrays to have their upper bounds assigned **dynamically**. For example, a program may manipulate 60 elements of a one-dimensional array during one run, 100 elements the next time, and so on. Rather than modify the value of the size of a DIM statement each time the number of elements changes, MS BASIC permits the size of an array in a DIM statement to be written as a simple variable, as in

```
140 DIM CODE(SUB)
```

This DIM statement reserves a variable number of elements for the one-dimensional array CODE.

Usually an INPUT or a READ statement is used before the DIM statement to assign a value to the variable SUB. Once SUB is assigned a value, the DIM statement allocates the actual number of elements to array CODE. Any FOR statements involved in the manipulation of the array must contain as their limit value the same simple variable SUB.

⊞ **7.5**

MANIPULATING ARRAYS

In this section, several sample programs that manipulate the elements of arrays will be discussed. Before the programs are presented, however, it is important that you understand the syntax and limitations of subscripts.

Subscripts

As indicated in section 7.3, the elements of an array are referenced by assigning a subscript to the array name. The subscript is written within parentheses and is placed immediately to the right of the array name. The subscript may be any valid nonnegative number, variable, or numeric expression within the **range** of the array. The lower and upper bounds of an array should never be exceeded. For example, if an array TAX is declared as follows:

```
100 DIM TAX(50)
```

it is invalid to reference TAX(–3), TAX(51), or any others that are outside the lower and upper bounds of the array.

Noninteger subscripts are rounded to the nearest integer to determine the element to be manipulated. Table 7.7 illustrates some additional valid and invalid subscripts.

———**TABLE 7.7** Valid and Invalid Subscripts———

TAX(1)	*Valid.*
TAX(-3)	*Invalid. Negative subscripts are not permitted.*
TAX(X + Y)	*Valid, provided X + Y is within the range of the array.*
TAX(-X)	*Valid, provided –X is within the range of the array.*
TAX(12.7)	*Valid, provided the array has been declared to 13 or more elements.*
TAX(0)	*Valid, provided the zero element exists.*
TAX(COST(2))	*Valid, provided COST(2) is within the range of the array.*
TAX(X + Y/3 + 5^X)	*Valid, provided X + Y/3 + 5^X is within the range of the array.*

You must decide which variables will be subscripted in any program and then use them consistently throughout the program. For example, if the array element is MONTH(NUM), the subscript NUM should not be dropped to form the name MONTH, and the subscript NUM should not be replaced by multiple subscripts to form MONTHS(NUM1, NUM2) in the same program. On the PC, either of these two actions would cause the program to halt and display the diagnostic message

```
Subscript out of range
```

Program 7.9 reads data into an array and then displays the value of each element in the array.

PROGRAM 7.9

```
100 ' Program 7.9
110 ' Monthly Sales Analysis I
120 ' ************************
130 OPTION BASE 1
140 DIM MONTH(12)
150 CLS : KEY OFF  ' Clear Screen
160 FOR NUM =  1 TO 12
170    READ MONTH(NUM)
180 NEXT NUM
190 FOR NUM = 1 TO 12
200    PRINT MONTH(NUM),
210 NEXT NUM
220 ' ************ Data Follows **************
230 DATA 46987, 43768, 38987, 36181, 35129, 40245
240 DATA 52156, 49546, 51120, 47345, 45675, 53769
250 END

RUN

    46987        43768        38987        36181        35129
    40245        52156        49546        51120        47345
    45675        53769
```

In Program 7.9, line 130 sets the lower bound for all arrays dimensioned in the program to 1. Line 140 reserves 12 elements or storage locations for array MONTH. Valid subscripts for MONTH range from 1 to 12. Line 160 activates the first For loop and assigns NUM a value of 1. Line 170 reads the first data item, 46987, from the data-holding area and assigns it to MONTH(1). NUM is incremented to 2 and line 180 returns control to the FOR statement in line 160. The READ statement in line 170 then assigns the second data item to MONTH(2). This loop continues until MONTH(12) is assigned the 12th data item, 53769.

Line 190 activates the second For loop and resets NUM to 1. This For loop then proceeds to display the values assigned to array MONTH, as shown.

TRY IT YOURSELF

Load Program 7.9 (PRG7-9) from the Student Diskette. Delete line 140. Execute the program and see what happens.

Insert line 140 back into the program. Delete line 130. In line 190, insert the following statement:

```
190 FOR NUM = 12 TO 1 STEP -1
```

Execute the program. Compare the sequence of the monthly sales to the original results displayed by Program 7.9.

Summing the Elements of an Array

Many applications call for summing the elements of an array. In Program 7.10, the monthly sales are summed, an average is computed, and the sales are displayed, four to a line.

PROGRAM 7.10

```
100 ' Program 7.10
110 ' Monthly Sales Analysis II
120 ' ************************
130 OPTION BASE 1
140 DIM MONTH(12)
150 CLS : KEY OFF  ' Clear Screen
160 TOTAL.SALES = 0
170 FOR NUM = 1 TO 12
180    READ MONTH(NUM)
190    TOTAL.SALES = TOTAL.SALES + MONTH(NUM)
200 NEXT NUM
210 AVG.SALES = TOTAL.SALES / 12
220 PRINT USING "The average monthly sales is $$##,###.##"; AVG.SALES
230 PRINT
240 FOR NUM = 1 TO 12 STEP 4
250    PRINT MONTH(NUM), MONTH(NUM + 1), MONTH(NUM + 2), MONTH(NUM + 3)
260 NEXT NUM
270 PRINT
280 PRINT "Job Complete"
290 ' ************* Data Follows **************
300 DATA 46987, 43768, 38987, 36181, 35129, 40245
310 DATA 52156, 49546, 51120, 47345, 45675, 53769
320 END

RUN

The average monthly sales is  $45,075.67

  46987        43768        38987        36181
  35129        40245        52156        49546
  51120        47345        45675        53769

Job Complete
```

In Program 7.10, line 190 is used to sum the values of the array elements. For example, when line 170 activates the For loop, NUM is assigned the value of 1. Line 180 reads the first data item, 46987, and assigns it to MONTH(1). Line 190 increments TOTAL.SALES by MONTH(1). NUM is incremented to 2, and line 200 returns control to the FOR statement in line 170.

After the READ statement, TOTAL.SALES is assigned the sum of TOTAL.SALES and MONTH(2). This process continues until the 12th element is added to the sum of the first 11 elements of the array S. Line 210 computes the average, and line 220 displays it.

The For loop found in lines 240 through 260 displays the monthly sales, four to a line. The first time through the loop, NUM is equal to 1, and MONTH(1), MONTH(2), MONTH(3), and MONTH(4) display on one line. The next time through the loop, NUM is equal to 5, and MONTH(5), MONTH(6), MONTH(7), and MONTH(8) display on the next line. Finally, NUM is set equal to 9 and MONTH(9), MONTH(10), MONTH(11), and MONTH(12) display on the third line. The subscripts in line 250 are in the form of numeric expressions.

Programming Case Study 14: *Analysis of Monthly Sales*

The following programming case study illustrates the use of **parallel arrays** and the selection of elements that meet a certain criterion. Parallel arrays are two or more arrays that have corresponding elements. This case study also shows how arrays may be used to store data that is used many times during the execution of a program.

Problem   Ray's Roofing Company has stored the past year's monthly sales on a diskette in a sequential file called MONTHSAL.DAT. The contents of the file are illustrated below.

"January",46987	"July",52156
"February",43768	"August",49546
"March",38987	"September",51120
"April",36181	"October",47345
"May",35129	"November",45675
"June",40245	"December",53769

The company would like to have a program that generates an annual sales report. The following is to be included in the report:

1. the average monthly sales for the previous year;
2. a list of the months in which the sales exceeded the average monthly sales (include the sales figures for these months and their deviation from the average sales); and
3. the month name with the greatest sales and the month name with the least sales (assume that no two months have equal monthly sales).

A partial top-down chart (showing the first level of decomposition) and a flowchart for each subtask are illustrated in Figure 7.5. The program tasks that correspond to the top-down chart; a program solution; and a discussion of the program solution follow.

Program Tasks   The following program tasks correspond to the top-down chart in Figure 7.5 on page 248.

1. Initialization

   a. Use the OPTION BASE statement to set to 1 the lower bound of arrays defined in the program.
   b. Dimension two parallel arrays, MONTH$ and MONTH, to 12 elements. Use the array MONTH$ to store the 12 month names and the array MONTH to store the 12 monthly sales.

   c. Initialize a running total (TOTAL.SALES) to zero. Use TOTAL.SALES to sum the 12 monthly sales.
   d. Open the sequential data file MONTHSAL.DAT for input as file number 1.
   e. Clear the screen.

2. Fill Sales Array and Determine Average

   a. Use a For loop with an initial value of 1 and a limit value of 12 to read the 12 month names and corresponding sales into the parallel arrays MONTH$ and MONTH. Within the loop, increment TOTAL.SALES by each monthly sales.
   b. Close MONTHSAL.DAT file.
   c. Determine the average monthly sales (AVG.SALES) by dividing TOTAL.SALES by 12.
   d. Display the average monthly sales.

3. Display Months with Sales Above Average

   a. Display report title and column headings.
   b. With an initial value of 1 and limit value of 12, use a For loop to test each month's sales against the average monthly sales. If the month's sales are greater than the average monthly sales, display the month name, month's sales, and deviation of the month's sales from the average monthly sales.

4. Determine Month of Highest and Lowest Sales

   a. Assume that the first month has the highest and lowest sales.
      (1) Set the variable HIGH to the first month's sales. Initialize the variable SUBH to the value 1. SUBH is used later as a subscript to access the month name with the greatest sales.
      (2) Set the variable LOW to the first month's sales. Initialize the variable SUBL to the value 1. SUBL is used later as a subscript to access the month name with the least sales.
   b. Use a For loop with an initial value 2 and limit value 12 to test the sales of the second through twelfth month against the value of the variable HIGH. If a month's sales are greater than the value of HIGH, assign the month's sales to HIGH and the value of the loop variable (NUM) to SUBH. Also include within the For loop a test in which the month's sales are compared against the value of LOW. If the month's sales are less than the value of LOW, assign the month's sales to LOW and the value of the loop variable (NUM) to SUBL.
   c. Display the month with the greatest sales — MONTH$(SUBH).
   d. Display the month with the least sales — MONTH$(SUBL).

Program Solution   Program 7.11, on the following page, corresponds to the previously defined tasks and to the top-down chart in Figure 7.5.

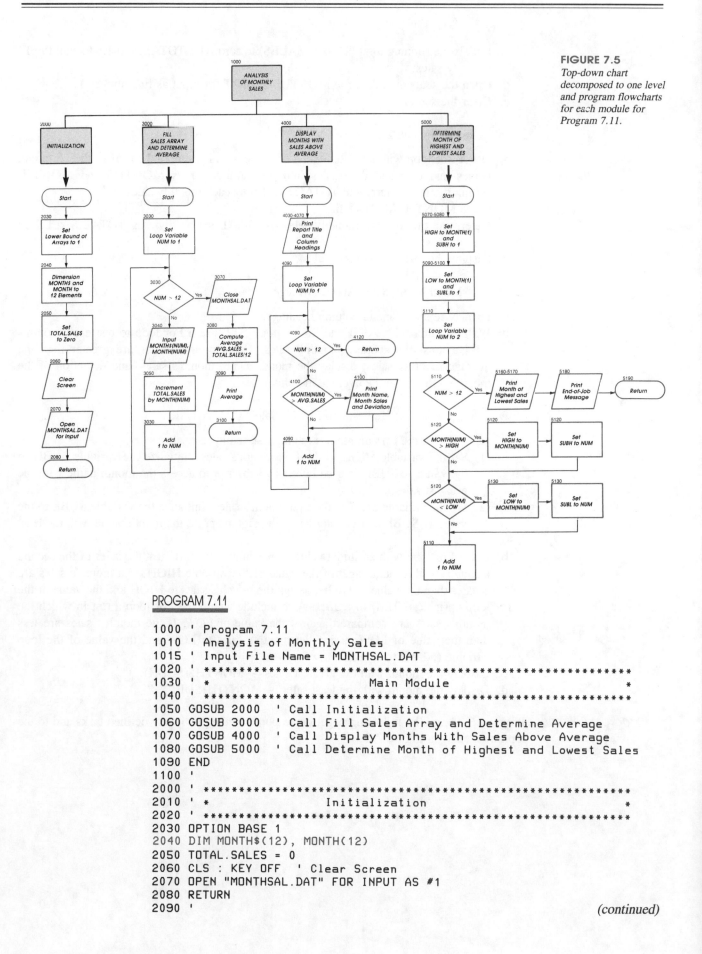

FIGURE 7.5
*Top-down chart
decomposed to one level
and program flowcharts
for each module for
Program 7.11.*

PROGRAM 7.11

```
1000 ' Program 7.11
1010 ' Analysis of Monthly Sales
1015 ' Input File Name = MONTHSAL.DAT
1020 ' *****************************************************************
1030 ' *                        Main Module                           *
1040 ' *****************************************************************
1050 GOSUB 2000    ' Call Initialization
1060 GOSUB 3000    ' Call Fill Sales Array and Determine Average
1070 GOSUB 4000    ' Call Display Months With Sales Above Average
1080 GOSUB 5000    ' Call Determine Month of Highest and Lowest Sales
1090 END
1100 '
2000 ' *****************************************************************
2010 ' *                      Initialization                          *
2020 ' *****************************************************************
2030 OPTION BASE 1
2040 DIM MONTH$(12), MONTH(12)
2050 TOTAL.SALES = 0
2060 CLS : KEY OFF   ' Clear Screen
2070 OPEN "MONTHSAL.DAT" FOR INPUT AS #1
2080 RETURN
2090 '
```

(continued)

```
3000 ' ********************************************************
3010 ' *            Fill Sales Array and Determine Average            *
3020 ' ********************************************************
3030 FOR NUM = 1 TO 12
3040    INPUT #1, MONTH$(NUM), MONTH(NUM)
3050    TOTAL.SALES = TOTAL.SALES + MONTH(NUM)
3060 NEXT NUM
3070 CLOSE #1
3080 AVG.SALES = TOTAL.SALES / 12
3090 PRINT USING "The average monthly sales is $$##,###.##"; AVG.SALES
3100 RETURN
3110 '
4000 ' ********************************************************
4010 ' *            Display Months with Sales Above Average            *
4020 ' ********************************************************
4030 PRINT : PRINT
4040 PRINT "Months in Which Sales Are Above Average"
4050 PRINT
4060 PRINT        "Month            Sales            Deviation"
4070 PRINT
4080 FORMAT$ = "\            \        ##,###.##            ##,###.##"
4090 FOR NUM = 1 TO 12
4100    IF MONTH(NUM) > AVG.SALES
            THEN PRINT USING FORMAT$; MONTH$(NUM), MONTH(NUM),
                                MONTH(NUM) - AVG.SALES
4110 NEXT NUM
4120 RETURN
4130 '
5000 ' ********************************************************
5010 ' *            Determine Month of Highest and Lowest Sales            *
5020 ' *                                                                  *
5030 ' * Assume First Month has the Highest and Lowest Sales            *
5040 ' * SUBH = Subscript of Highest Sales, HIGH = Highest Sales *
5050 ' * SUBL = Subscript of Lowest Sales,  LOW  = Lowest Sales  *
5060 ' ********************************************************
5070 HIGH = MONTH(1)
5080 SUBH = 1
5090 LOW  = MONTH(1)
5100 SUBL = 1
5110 FOR NUM = 2 TO 12
5120    IF MONTH(NUM) > HIGH
            THEN HIGH = MONTH(NUM) : SUBH = NUM
5130    IF MONTH(NUM) < LOW
            THEN LOW  = MONTH(NUM) : SUBL = NUM
5140 NEXT NUM
5150 PRINT
5160 PRINT "Month of Highest Sales - "; MONTH$(SUBH)
5170 PRINT "Month of Lowest Sales  - "; MONTH$(SUBL)
5180 PRINT : PRINT "Job Complete"
5190 RETURN
5200 ' ****************** End of Program *********************

RUN

The average monthly sales is  $45,075.67

Months in Which Sales Are Above Average

Month            Sales            Deviation

January        46,987.00            1,911.33
July           52,156.00            7,080.33
August         49,546.00            4,470.33
September      51,120.00            6,044.33
October        47,345.00            2,269.33
November       45,675.00              599.33
December       53,769.00            8,693.33

Month of Highest Sales - December
Month of Lowest Sales  - May

Job Complete
```

Discussion of the Program Solution

In Program 7.11, the Fill Sales Array and Determine Average Module is similar to Program 7.10. The For loop (lines 3030 through 3060) loads the two arrays with values and sums the monthly sales. Line 3070 closes MONTHSAL.DAT. At this point, the entire file is loaded into the parallel arrays MONTH$ and MONTH. Line 3080 computes the average, and line 3090 displays the average monthly sales.

The For loop, lines 4090 through 4110, tests each of the monthly sales found in array MONTH against the average monthly sales, AVG.SALES. If the value of an element in the array is greater than the average, then the PC is instructed to display the corresponding month name, the monthly sales, and the monthly sales deviation from the average (MONTH(NUM) - AVG.SALES).

In the last module of Program 7.11, lines 5070 through 5170 illustrate a technique that determines the month in which the sales are the highest and the month in which the sales are the lowest. In lines 5070 through 5100, the first month's sales are assumed to be the highest as well as the lowest. The For loop, lines 5110 through 5140, tests the remaining months against the highest sales (line 5120) and the lowest sales (line 5130).

If a month's sales (MONTH(NUM)) are greater than the current highest sales (HIGH), the month's sales are assigned as the current highest sales and the variable SUBH is assigned the value of the subscript NUM. When the For loop is satisfied, SUBH is the subscript that represents the element in array MONTH that has the highest sales. SUBL is the subscript that represents the element in array MONTH that has the lowest sales. Since MONTH$ and MONTH are parallel arrays, the corresponding month with the highest and lowest sales can be obtained by referencing MONTH$(SUBH) and MONTH$(SUBL).

7.6 MULTI-DIMENSIONAL ARRAYS

The dimension of an array is the number of subscripts required to reference an element in an array. Up to now, all the arrays were one dimensional, and an element was referenced by an integer, a variable, or a single expression in the parentheses following the array name. MS BASIC allows arrays to have up to 255 dimensions. One- and two-dimensional arrays are the most commonly used arrays. Three-dimensional arrays are used less frequently in business applications, and arrays with more than three dimensions are rarely used.

Manipulating Two-Dimensional Arrays

As illustrated in Table 7.4 on page 241, the number of dimensions is declared in the `DIM` statement. For example,

```
140 DIM COST(2, 5)
```

declares an array to be two-dimensional. A two-dimensional array usually takes the form of a table. The first subscript tells how many rows there are, and the second subscript tells how many columns. Figure 7.6 shows a 2 × 5 array (read "2 by 5 array"). COST(1, 1) — read "COST sub one one" — references the element found in the first row and first column. COST(2, 3) — read "COST sub two three" — references the element found in the second row and third column. Although Figure 7.6 does not show the zero row and zero column, they always exist unless the `OPTION BASE` statement is used to set the lower bound to 1.

ROWS \ COLUMNS	1	2	3	4	5
1	*COST(1, 1)*	*COST(1, 2)*	*COST(1, 3)*	*COST(1, 4)*	*COST(1, 5)*
2	*COST(2, 1)*	*COST(2, 2)*	*COST(2, 3)*	*COST(2, 4)*	*COST(2, 5)*

FIGURE 7.6 *Conceptual view of the storage locations reserved for a 2 × 5 two-dimensional array called COST, with the name of each element specified.*

ROWS \ COLUMNS	1	2	3	4	5
1	6	12	-52	3.14	0.56
2	8	2	5	6	2

FIGURE 7.7 *A 2 × 5 array with each element assigned a value.*

Assuming that the elements of array COST are assigned the values shown in Figure 7.7, the following statements are true:

COST(1, 2) is equal to 12
COST(2, 4) is equal to 6
COST(2, 2) is equal to 2
COST(1, 1) is equal to COST(2, 4)
COST(3, 5) is outside the range of the array; it does not exist.
COST(2, 6) is outside the range of the array; it does not exist.
COST(-2, -5) is outside the range of the array; it does not exist.

Initializing Arrays   Excluding the zeroth row and column, you may write the following code to initialize to 0, row by row, all the elements in a 4 × 3 array called AREA:

```
200 DIM AREA(4, 3)
210 FOR ROW = 1 TO 4
220    FOR COLUMN = 1 TO 3
230       AREA(ROW, COLUMN) = 0
240    NEXT COLUMN
250 NEXT ROW
```

To initialize to 1 all elements on the main diagonal of a 5 × 5 array called TABLE, you may write the following:

```
300 DIM TABLE(5, 5)
310 FOR ROW = 1 TO 5
320    TABLE(ROW, ROW) = 1
330 NEXT ROW
```

As a result, elements TABLE(1, 1), TABLE(2, 2), TABLE(3, 3), TABLE(4, 4), and TABLE(5, 5) are assigned the value of 1.

Two-dimensional arrays are often used to classify data. For example, if a company makes 5 models of a particular product and the production of each model involves a certain amount of processing time on 6 different machines, the processing time can be summarized in a table of 5 rows and 6 columns, as illustrated in Figure 7.8.

PRODUCT PROCESSING TIME IN MINUTES	MACHINE					
	1	2	3	4	5	6
1	13	30	5	17	12	45
2	23	12	13	16	0	20
MODEL 3	45	12	28	16	10	13
NUMBER 4	21	16	15	22	19	26
5	23	50	17	43	15	18

FIGURE 7.8
A table of the processing time each model spends on a machine.

The following statement reserves storage for the two-dimensional array in Figure 7.8:

```
140 DIM TIME(5, 6)
```

If MODEL represents the model number (the row of the table) and MACHINE represents the machine (the column of the table), then the subscripted variable TIME(MODEL, MACHINE) gives the time it takes for a model to be processed on a particular machine. The value of MODEL can range from 1 to 5, and the value of MACHINE can range from 1 to 6. If MODEL is equal to 4 and MACHINE is equal to 5, the table tells us that the product-processing time is 19 minutes. That is, model number 4 involves 19 minutes of processing on machine 5.

To sum all the elements in row 4 of the table in Figure 7.8 into a running total SUM4 and to sum all the elements in column 2 into a running total SUM2, you can write the following:

```
500 DIM TIME(5, 6)
510 SUM2 = 0
520 SUM4 = 0
530 FOR MODEL = 1 TO 5
540    SUM2 = SUM2 + TIME(MODEL, 2)
550 NEXT MODEL
560 FOR MACHINE = 1 TO 6
570    SUM4 = SUM4 + TIME(4, MACHINE)
580 NEXT MACHINE
```

The last three short partial programs should give you an idea of how to handle elements that appear in various rows and columns of two-dimensional arrays.

Arrays with More Than Two Dimensions

The table in Figure 7.8 is for one product with five different models. Now suppose we want to consider comparable tables for two different products, each of which has five different model numbers and all of which utilize the six machines. To construct such a table, we can modify array TIME so that it is a three-dimensional array:

```
2040 DIM TIME(5, 6, 2)
```

Now the subscripted variable TIME(MODEL, MACHINE, PRODUCT) refers to the time it takes for a given model number (MODEL) on a particular machine (MACHINE) for a specific product (PRODUCT).

Figure 7.9 represents a conceptual view of some of the storage locations for a 5 × 6 × 2 array called TIME. This three-dimensional array contains 5 rows, 6 columns, and 2 planes, for a total of 60 elements.

If we want to take into account the production differences at three different sites, we can make TIME a four-dimensional array:

```
2040 DIM TIME(5, 6, 2, 3)
```

Now the subscripted variable TIME(MODEL, MACHINE, PRODUCT, SITE) refers to the processing time it takes for a given model number on a particular machine for a specific product at a given site. If more factors besides site, product, model, and machine are required, we can add even more dimensions.

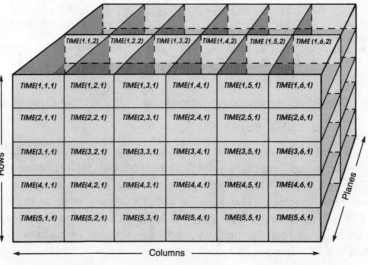

FIGURE 7.9
Conceptual view of some of the storage locations reserved for a 5 × 6 × 2 three-dimensional array called TIME.

7.7

SORTING

Sorting data into alphabetical or numerical order is one of the more frequently executed operations in a business data-processing environment. It is also a time-consuming operation, especially when large amounts of data are involved. Computer scientists have spent a great deal of time developing algorithms to speed up the sorting process. Usually, the faster the process, the more complex the algorithm. In this section, we will discuss two of the more common sort algorithms: the **bubble sort** and the **Shell sort** (named after its author, Donald Shell). Figure 7.10 illustrates the difference between unsorted data and the same data in ascending and descending sequence. Data that is in sequence from lowest to highest in value is in **ascending sequence**. Data that is in sequence from highest to lowest in value is in **descending sequence**.

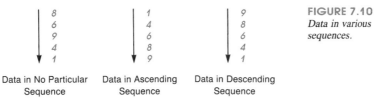

FIGURE 7.10
Data in various sequences.

The Bubble Sort

The bubble sort is a straightforward method of sorting data items that have been placed in an array. To illustrate the logic of a bubble sort, we will sort the data found in Figure 7.10 into ascending sequence. Assume that the data has been assigned to array B, as illustrated below:

B(1)	8
B(2)	6
B(3)	9	Original Order of Unsorted Data in Array B
B(4)	4
B(5)	1

The bubble sort involves comparing adjacent elements and **swapping** (i.e., interchanging) the values of those elements when they are out of order. For example, B(1) is compared to B(2). If B(1) is less than or equal to B(2), no swap occurs. If B(1) is greater than B(2), the values of the 2 elements are swapped. B(2) is then compared to B(3), and so on, until B(4) is compared to B(5). One complete time through the array is called a **pass**. At the end of the first pass, the largest value is in the last element of array B, as illustrated in Figure 7.11. Its box has been shaded to show that it is in its final position and will not move again.

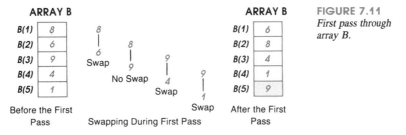

FIGURE 7.11
First pass through array B.

The maximum number of passes necessary to sort the elements in an array is equal to the number of elements in the array less 1. Since array B has 5 elements, at most four passes are made on the array. Figures 7.12, 7.13, and 7.14 on the following page illustrate the second, third, and fourth passes made on array B. On the fifth pass, no elements are swapped. The swapping pushes the larger values down in the illustrations, and as a side effect, the smaller numbers "bubble" up to the top of the array.

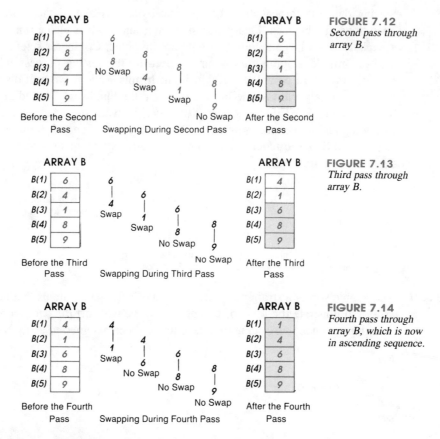

FIGURE 7.12
Second pass through array B.

FIGURE 7.13
Third pass through array B.

FIGURE 7.14
Fourth pass through array B, which is now in ascending sequence.

The SWAP Statement

To exchange the values of two storage locations in a program, we use the SWAP statement. The general form of the SWAP statement is shown in Table 7.8.

_____TABLE 7.8 The SWAP Statement_____

General Form:	SWAP variable₁, variable₂ where **variable₁** and **variable₂** are of the same type.
Purpose:	Exchanges the values of two variables or two elements of an array.
Examples:	1000 SWAP OLDBAL, NEWBAL 2000 SWAP ARR(SUB), ARR(SUB + 1) 3000 SWAP CODE1$(I, I), CODE2$(I, I)

In Table 7.8, line 1000 exchanges the values of the two simple variables OLDBAL and NEWBAL. Prior to the execution of line 1000, if OLDBAL is equal to 500 and NEWBAL is equal to 600, then after its execution, OLDBAL is equal to 600 and NEWBAL is equal to 500.

In line 2000 of Table 7.8, the values of the two subscripted variables ARR(SUB) and ARR(SUB + 1) are exchanged. Exchanging the values of two adjacent elements of an array is a common practice with sort algorithms.

Finally, line 3000 in Table 7.8 exchanges the values of the two corresponding string elements of tables CODE1$ and CODE2$.

Implementing the Bubble Sort

The statement that compares two adjacent elements in an array and exchanges them when necessary is

```
3070 IF B(I) > B(I + 1)
        THEN SWAP B(I), B(I + 1)
```

One pass on the array, which compares all adjacent elements, can be implemented by using the following For loop:

```
3060 FOR I = 1 TO 4
3070    IF B(I) > B(I + 1)
           THEN SWAP B(I), B(I + 1)
3080 NEXT I
```

Finally, as illustrated in Figures 7.11 through 7.14, the elements of the array are sorted by completing four passes on the array. This can be accomplished with a pair of nested For loops:

```
3050 FOR J = 1 TO 4
3060    FOR I = 1 TO 4
3070       IF B(I) > B(I + 1)
              THEN SWAP B(I), B(I + 1)
3080    NEXT I
3090 NEXT J
```
Inefficient Sort Algorithm

Although the nested For loops in the above partial program sort the elements in array B, the algorithm is highly inefficient because it is not always necessary to make the maximum number of passes on the array. For example, the elements in the array may already be in ascending sequence before the sort routine is initiated. This inefficient technique would still make four passes on the sorted array.

To minimize the number of passes it takes to sort an array, a variable called a **switch** is required. The switch is used to halt the sort routine when the array is sorted. The switch is a simple string variable that takes on two values during the duration of the loop. If SWITCH$ is the variable that represents the switch, then when the switch is on (SWITCH$ equals the value ON) another pass is required. When the switch is off (SWITCH$ equals the value OFF), the array is sorted and the loop is terminated. The switch is turned on whenever two adjacent elements are exchanged, and this means that another pass is required. If a pass is made (all adjacent elements are compared) and the switch remains off, then the array is sorted.

In the previous algorithm, the outer For loop controlled the number of passes. If a switch is used to control the number of passes, then the outer For loop should be replaced by a While loop. The following partial program will efficiently sort the elements of array B into ascending sequence.

```
3000 ' *****************************
3010 ' *         Bubble Sort       *
3020 ' *****************************
3030 SWITCH$ = "ON"
3040 WHILE SWITCH$ = "ON"
3050    SWITCH$ = "OFF"
3060    FOR I = 1 TO 4
3070       IF B(I) > B(I + 1)
              THEN SWAP B(I), B(I + 1) :
                 SWITCH$ = "ON"
3080    NEXT I
3090 WEND
3100 RETURN
3110 '
```

The variable SWITCH$ controls whether another pass will be done on the array. Line 3030 assigns SWITCH$ a value of ON. Since SWITCH$ equals ON, line 3040 passes control into the body of the While loop. Line 3050 assigns SWITCH$ a value of OFF just before the For loop makes a pass on the loop. If SWITCH$ is not modified later in the loop (line 3070), the values in the array are in sequence and the next time that line 3040 is executed, control transfers to line 3100.

The FOR statement in line 3060 initializes I to 1. The first element B(1) is then compared to B(2). If B(1) is greater than B(2), the THEN clause swaps the values of the two elements and assigns SWITCH$ a value of ON. Next, B(2) is compared to B(3) and so on. The number of comparisons per pass is equal to the number of elements to compare minus 1. Since the number of data items to sort is 5, the limit parameter in the FOR statement is set to 4.

PROGRAM 7.12

```
1000 ' Program 7.12
1010 ' Sorting Numeric Data Using the
1020 ' Bubble Sort Technique
1030 ' ****************************
1040 ' *        Main Module        *
1050 ' ****************************
1060 GOSUB 2000   ' Call Initialization
1070 GOSUB 3000   ' Call Bubble Sort
1080 GOSUB 4000   ' Call Display Sorted Array
1090 END
1100 '
2000 ' ****************************
2010 ' *       Initialization      *
2020 ' ****************************
2030 OPTION BASE 1
2040 DIM B(5)
2050 PRINT "Unsorted -";
2060 FOR I = 1 TO 5
2070    READ B(I)
2080    PRINT B(I);
2090 NEXT I
2100 PRINT : PRINT
2110 RETURN
2120 '
3000 ' ****************************
3010 ' *        Bubble Sort        *
3020 ' ****************************
3030 SWITCH$ = "ON"
3040 WHILE SWITCH$ = "ON"
3050    SWITCH$ = "OFF"
3060    FOR I = 1 TO 4
3070       IF B(I) > B(I + 1)
              THEN SWAP B(I), B(I + 1) :
                   SWITCH$ = "ON"
3080    NEXT I
3090 WEND
3100 RETURN
3110 '
4000 ' ****************************
4010 ' *    Display Sorted Array   *
4020 ' ****************************
4030 PRINT "Sorted   -";
4040 FOR I = 1 TO 5
4050    PRINT B(I);
4060 NEXT I
4070 RETURN
4080 '
4090 ' ******** Data Follows ********
4100 DATA 8, 6, 9, 4, 1
4110 ' ******* End of Program *******

RUN

Unsorted - 8  6  9  4  1

Sorted   - 1  4  6  8  9
```

Program 7.12, on the previous page, incorporates the logic found in this partial program to sort 8, 6, 9, 4, and 1. Line 2040 reserves storage for array B. The For loop made up of lines 2060 through 2090 loads and displays the unsorted elements of the array. The Bubble Sort Module (lines 3000 through 3110) sorts the numeric array. The Display Sorted Array Module (lines 4000 through 4080) displays the elements after the array has been sorted.

TRY IT YOURSELF

Load Program 7.12 (PRG7-12) from the Student Diskette. Change the relation in line 3070 from "greater than" to "less than." Execute the program. Compare the sequence of the sorted numbers to that originally displayed by Program 7.12. Now do you understand the difference between ascending sequence and descending sequence?

To make the sort algorithm more general, a variable for the size of the array and a variable number of elements can be used. This generalization is illustrated on the following page in Program 7.13, which uses the same techniques as Program 7.12 to sort string data items.

In program 7.13, the string array FIRST.NAME$ is dimensioned to NUM elements in line 2050. Line 2040 assigns the variable NUM the number of data items to be sorted. The limit value in each of the FOR statements in Program 7.12 (lines 2060, 3060 and 4040) is changed from 5, 4, and 5 to NUM, NUM – 1, and NUM. Program 7.13 can sort from 1 to NUM data items, depending on the value assigned to the variable NUM.

The advantage to studying sort algorithms is that they raise the question of algorithm efficiency. In the next section, we will discuss the Shell sort, which offers a vast improvement over the bubble sort algorithm.

The Shell Sort The bubble sort algorithm works well for a small number of data items, but it can take too much processing time for a large number of data items. The problem with this algorithm is that the smaller data items move only one position at a time because only adjacent elements are compared. The Shell sort provides a faster means of sorting a large number of data items. For example, for five hundred items, the Shell sort reduces the processing time by a factor of 5. For a thousand items, it reduces the processing time by a factor of 10. The longer the list to be sorted, the greater the advantage of the Shell sort over the bubble sort.

The Shell sort is similar to the bubble sort, but instead of comparing and swapping adjacent elements B(I) and B(I + 1), it compares and swaps nonadjacent elements B(I) and B(I + GAP), where GAP starts out considerably greater than 1.

Prior to the loop that swaps the elements, GAP is set to one half the length of the array. When a swap is made, a big improvement takes place. When no swap is made on a pass, the Gap is halved again for the next pass. Finally, the Gap becomes 1, as in the bubble sort, and adjacent elements are compared and swapped.

The Shell sort is used in Program 7.14, on page 259, to sort a list of fifteen data items. In the Shell Sort module, line 3030 begins by assigning the Gap to one half the size of the list. Line 3040 initiates a loop that has as its body the bubble sort with some minor modifications. Within the For loop (lines 3080 through 3100) the integer 1 in the bubble sort algorithm is replaced by the variable GAP.

PROGRAM 7.13

```
1000 ' Program 7.13
1010 ' Sorting String Data Using the
1020 ' Bubble Sort Technique
1030 ' *****************************
1040 ' *           Main Module        *
1050 ' *****************************
1060 GOSUB 2000    ' Call Initialization
1070 GOSUB 3000    ' Call Bubble Sort
1080 GOSUB 4000    ' Call Display Sorted Array
1090 END
1100 '
2000 ' *****************************
2010 ' *          Initialization       *
2020 ' *****************************
2030 OPTION BASE 1
2040 READ NUM
2050 DIM FIRST.NAME$(NUM)
2060 PRINT "Unsorted - ";
2070 FOR I = 1 TO NUM
2080    READ FIRST.NAME$(I)
2090    PRINT FIRST.NAME$(I); " ";
2100 NEXT I
2110 PRINT :PRINT
2120 RETURN
2130 '
3000 ' *****************************
3010 ' *          Bubble Sort         *
3020 ' *****************************
3030 SWITCH$ = "ON"
3040 WHILE SWITCH$ = "ON"
3050    SWITCH$ = "OFF"
3060    FOR I = 1 TO NUM - 1
3070       IF FIRST.NAME$(I) > FIRST.NAME$(I + 1)
               THEN SWAP FIRST.NAME$(I), FIRST.NAME$(I + 1) :
                  SWITCH$ = "ON"
3080    NEXT I
3090 WEND
3100 RETURN
3110 '
4000 ' *****************************
4010 ' *    Display Sorted Array     *
4020 ' *****************************
4030 PRINT "Sorted   - ";
4040 FOR I = 1 TO NUM
4050    PRINT FIRST.NAME$(I); " ";
4060 NEXT I
4070 RETURN
4080 '
4090 ' ******** Data Follows ********
4100 DATA 8
4110 DATA Jim, John, Louis, Fran
4120 DATA Tom, Andy, Lou, Mark
4130 ' ******* End of Program *******

RUN

Unsorted - Jim John Louis Fran Tom Andy Lou Mark

Sorted   - Andy Fran Jim John Lou Louis Mark Tom
```

Program 7.14 makes reference to the integer function (INT) in lines 3030 and 3120. The INT function returns the largest integer not greater than the argument. For example, INT(9.78) returns the value 9, and INT(-3.67) returns the value –4. The integer function is described in detail in chapter 8 on page 308.

PROGRAM 7.14

```
1000 ' Program 7.14
1010 ' Sorting Numeric Data Using the
1020 ' Shell Sort Technique
1030 ' ****************************
1040 ' *          Main Module          *
1050 ' ****************************
1060 GOSUB 2000    ' Call Initialization
1070 GOSUB 3000    ' Call Shell Sort
1080 GOSUB 4000    ' Call Display Sorted Array
1090 END
1100 '
2000 ' ****************************
2010 ' *          Initialization          *
2020 ' ****************************
2030 OPTION BASE 1
2040 READ NUM
2050 DIM B(NUM)
2060 PRINT "Unsorted -";
2070 FOR I = 1 TO NUM
2080     READ B(I)
2090     PRINT B(I);
2100 NEXT I
2110 PRINT : PRINT
2120 RETURN
2130 '
3000 ' ****************************
3010 ' *          Shell Sort          *
3020 ' ****************************
3030 GAP = INT(NUM / 2)
3040 WHILE GAP <> 0
3050     SWITCH$ = "ON"
3060     WHILE SWITCH$ = "ON"
3070         SWITCH$ = "OFF"
3080         FOR I = 1 TO NUM - GAP
3090             IF B(I) > B(I + GAP)
                     THEN SWAP B(I), B(I + GAP) :
                          SWITCH$ = "ON"
3100         NEXT I
3110     WEND
3120     GAP = INT(GAP / 2)
3130 WEND
3140 RETURN
3150 '
4000 ' ****************************
4010 ' *     Display Sorted Array     *
4020 ' ****************************
4030 PRINT "Sorted    -";
4040 FOR I = 1 TO NUM
4050     PRINT B(I);
4060 NEXT I
4070 RETURN
4080 '
```

(continued)

```
4090 ' ******** Data Follows ********
4100 DATA 15
4110 DATA 18, 13, 6, 4, 19, 12, 67, 1
4120 DATA 11, 13, 27, 32, 2, 17, 55
4130 ' ******* End of Program *******
RUN

Unsorted - 18  13  6  4  19  12  67  1  11  13  27  32  2  17  55
Sorted   - 1  2  4  6  11  12  13  13  17  18  19  27  32  55  67
```

TRY IT YOURSELF

Load Program 7.14 (PRG7-14) from the Student Diskette. Display and execute the program. Add the following line:

```
3105   GOSUB 4000 : PRINT
```

Execute the program. Note from the intermediate sorted results how the PC interchanges the elements each time through the inner While loop until they are finally in ascending sequence.

⊞ 7.8

TABLE PROCESSING

Many applications call for the use of data that is arranged in tabular form. Rates of pay, tax brackets, parts cost, and insurance rates are examples of tables that contain systematically arranged data. Arrays make it easier to write programs for applications involving tables.

Table Organization

Tables are organized on the basis of how the data items (also called **table functions**) are to be referenced. In **positionally organized tables**, table functions can be accessed by their position in the table. In **argument-organized tables**, table functions are accessed by the value that corresponds to the desired table function.

Positionally Organized Tables

To illustrate a positionally organized table, a program can be written that displays the name of the month in response to a month number, 1 through 12. Figure 7.15 shows the basic concept behind accessing a table function in a positionally organized table.

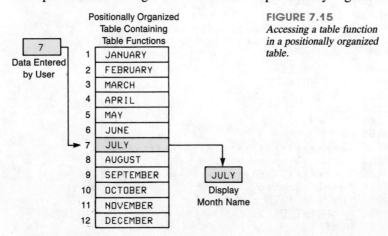

FIGURE 7.15
Accessing a table function in a positionally organized table.

In Figure 7.15, the month name is selected from the table on the basis of its location. A value of 1, entered by the user, equates to January, 2 to February, and so on. To write a program that uses table processing techniques, you must do the following:

1. define the table by declaring an array;
2. load the table functions into the array; and
3. write statements to access the table entries.

Program 7.15 illustrates how to declare, load, and access the table of month names described in Figure 7.15. Line 2040 defines the table by declaring the one-dimensional array MONTH$ to 12. Lines 2050 through 2070 load the table functions — in this case, the month names — into the array. Line 3440 in the Access the Table Function Module accesses the desired table function.

The routine to access the table function in Program 7.15 is rather straightforward. The user enters a value for NUM, and line 3440, on the following page, references the corresponding element of the array that contains the table functions. Figures 7.16 and 7.17 show the results displayed as a result of entering the month numbers 7 and 12 in response to a request by Program 7.15.

PROGRAM 7.15

```
1000 ' Program 7.15
1010 ' Accessing Functions in a Positionally Organized Table
1020 ' ********************************************************
1030 ' *                     Main Module                      *
1040 ' ********************************************************
1050 GOSUB 2000      ' Call Initialization
1060 GOSUB 3000      ' Call Process a Request
1070 GOSUB 4000      ' Call Wrap-up
1080 END
1090 '
2000 ' ********************************************************
2010 ' *                   Initialization                     *
2020 ' ********************************************************
2030 OPTION BASE 1
2040 DIM MONTH$(12)            ' Declare the Table
2050 FOR NUM = 1 TO 12
2060    READ MONTH$(NUM)       ' Load the Table
2070 NEXT NUM
2080 KEY OFF  ' Clear 25th Line
2090 RETURN
2100 '
3000 ' ********************************************************
3010 ' *                 Process a Request                    *
3020 ' ********************************************************
3030 CONTROL$ = "Y"
3040 WHILE CONTROL$ = "Y" OR CONTROL$ = "y"
3050    GOSUB 3200   ' Call Accept Operator Input
3060    GOSUB 3400   ' Call Access the Table Function
3070 WEND
3080 RETURN
3090 '
3200 ' ********************************************************
3210 ' *               Accept Operator Input                  *
3220 ' ********************************************************
3230 CLS  ' Clear Screen
3240 LOCATE 5, 15
3250 INPUT "Month Number (Enter 1 through 12) =====> ", NUM
3260 WHILE NUM < 1 OR NUM > 12
3270    LOCATE 6, 15 : PRINT "Month Number Invalid, Please Reenter"
3280    LOCATE 5, 56 : PRINT SPC(15)
3290    LOCATE 5, 56 : INPUT "", NUM
3300    LOCATE 6, 15 : PRINT SPC(40)
3310 WEND
3320 RETURN
3330 '
```

(continued)

```
3400 ' *****************************************************
3410 ' *               Access the Table Function           *
3420 ' *****************************************************
3430 LOCATE 7, 15
3440 PRINT "Month Name ============================> "; MONTH$(NUM)
3450 LOCATE 9, 15
3460 INPUT "Enter Y to process another month number, else N... ", CONTROL$
3470 RETURN
3480 '
4000 ' *****************************************************
4010 ' *                     Wrap-up                        *
4020 ' *****************************************************
4030 CLS  ' Clear Screen
4040 PRINT : PRINT "Job Complete"
4050 RETURN
4060 '
4070 ' ************* Table Entries Follow ***************
4080 DATA January, February, March, April, May, June, July
4090 DATA August, September, October, November, December
4100 ' **************** End of Program *****************

RUN
```

```
Month Number (Enter 1 through 12) =====> 7

Month Name ============================> July

Enter Y to process another month number, else N... y
```

FIGURE 7.16
*The display by Program
7.15 due to entering the
month number 7.*

```
Month Number (Enter 1 through 12) =====> 12

Month Name ============================> December

Enter Y to process another month number, else N... n
```

FIGURE 7.17
*The display by Program
7.15 due to entering the
month number 12.*

Positionally organized tables such as MONTH$ in Program 7.15 are not difficult to understand. Unfortunately, few tables can be constructed on the basis of the relative position of the table functions. Months, days of the week, and job classes are examples of systematic data that can be organized into positional tables.

Try It Yourself

Load Program 7.15 (PRG7-15) from the Student Diskette. Display and execute the program. Enter the following month numbers: 1, 7, 0, 13, and 9.

Argument-Organized Tables

In most applications, tables are characterized by entries made up of multiple functions. Multiple-function entries are accessed by means of a **search argument**. The search argument is entered by the user much as the month number was in Program 7.15. The search argument is compared to the **table argument**, a table entry, to retrieve the corresponding table function. Figure 7.18 illustrates the composition of a table that is organized by arguments.

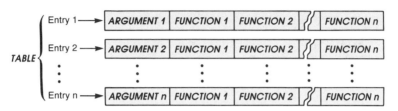

FIGURE 7.18
Conceptual view of an argument-organized table.

The table argument is assigned to a one-dimensional array. Functions are assigned to parallel arrays. Unlike a positionally organized table, in which the value entered is used to obtain the table function, an argument-organized table must be searched until the search argument agrees with one of the table arguments. This search is a **table search** or a **table lookup**.

There are two methods for searching a table: the **serial search** and the **binary search**. A serial search begins by comparing the search argument to the first table argument. If the two agree, the search is over. If they do not agree, then the search argument is compared to the second table argument, and so on. In the serial search, the table arguments may be either in sorted or unsorted order.

In general, a binary search begins the search in the middle of the table and determines whether the table argument that agrees with the search argument is in the upper half or the lower half of the table. The half that contains this table argument is then halved again. This process continues until there is nothing left to divide in half. At that point, the binary search is complete. The binary search, which requires that the table arguments be in ascending or descending sequence, will be discussed in greater detail later.

Serial Search

A serial search is a procedure that all of us use in everyday life. Suppose, for example, that you have a parts list that contains the part numbers and corresponding part descriptions and part costs. If you have a part number, one method for finding the part description and cost is to read through the part number list until you find the part number you are searching for. You can then read off the description and cost that correspond to the part number. Figure 7.19 illustrates the basic concept of a serial search.

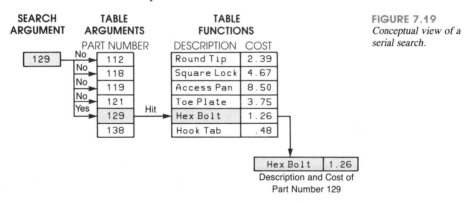

FIGURE 7.19
Conceptual view of a serial search.

The search argument is tested against each of the table arguments, beginning with the first, until a *hit* is made. At that point, the corresponding part description and part cost are selected from the table.

A program that completes the serial search illustrated in Figure 7.19 first needs to have the table defined. Since each entry is made up of a table argument and two functions, we declare three parallel arrays — PART, DESC$, and COST, as shown in line 2050. The variable ENTRIES is assigned the number of parts in the parts list.

```
2030 OPTION BASE 1
2040 READ ENTRIES
2050 DIM PART(ENTRIES), DESC$(ENTRIES), COST(ENTRIES) 'Declare the Table
```

Array PART is assigned the part numbers, array DESC$ the part descriptions, and array COST the part costs. A For loop is used to load the table, as follows:

```
2060 FOR NUM = 1 TO ENTRIES
2070     READ PART(NUM), DESC$(NUM), COST(NUM)              ' Load the Table
2080 NEXT NUM
```

Each time the READ statement is executed, one entry is loaded into the parallel arrays. Each entry in the table consists of an argument and two functions.

The following partial program searches the argument table and causes either the part description and part cost or a diagnostic message to be displayed. Assume that the user has assigned the part number that is to be looked up to the variable PART.NUM, the search argument.

```
3400 ' ******************************************************
3410 ' *                Access the Table Function           *
3420 ' ******************************************************
3430 SWITCH$ = "OFF"
3440 FOR NUM = 1 TO ENTRIES
3450     IF PART.NUM = PART(NUM)
             THEN GOSUB 3600 :
                  SWITCH$ = "ON" : NUM = ENTRIES  ' Process a Table Hit
3460 NEXT NUM
3470 IF SWITCH$ = "OFF"
         THEN PRINT "** Error **"; PART.NUM; "is an Invalid Part Number"
3480 LOCATE 11, 15
3490 INPUT "Enter Y to look up another part number, else N... ", CONTROL$
3500 RETURN
3510 '
3600 ' ******************************************************
3610 ' *                Display Table Function              *
3620 ' ******************************************************
3630 PRINT "Description =====> "; DESC$(NUM)
3640 LOCATE 9, 15
3650 PRINT USING "Cost ============> $$#.##"; COST(NUM)
3660 RETURN
3670 '
```

A For loop (lines 3440 through 3460) is used to implement the serial search algorithm. Prior to the For loop, a switch (SWITCH$) is assigned a value of OFF. The switch is assigned a value of ON within the loop when a hit is made. If the switch is not on when the For loop terminates, then there is no part number in the table which corresponds to the part number entered by the user, and a diagnostic message is displayed.

The IF statement in line 3450 compares the part number entered by the user against the part numbers in the table. If a search is successful, the subscript value is used in lines 3630 and 3650 to display the corresponding part description and part cost found in the parallel arrays. Furthermore, when a search is successful, line 3450 assigns SWITCH$ a value of ON and the loop variable a value equal to the limit value, that is, NUM = ENTRIES. Assigning the loop variable a value that is equal to the limit value causes the For loop to terminate immediately following a successful look-up. The complete program follows.

PROGRAM 7.16

```
1000 ' Program 7.16
1010 ' Serial Search of an Argument Organized Table
1020 ' *********************************************************
1030 ' *                    Main Module                        *
1040 ' *********************************************************
1050 GOSUB 2000    ' Call Initialization
1060 GOSUB 3000    ' Call Process a Request
1070 GOSUB 4000    ' Call Wrap-up
1080 END
1090 '
2000 ' *********************************************************
2010 ' *                  Initialization                       *
2020 ' *********************************************************
2030 OPTION BASE 1
2040 READ ENTRIES
2050 DIM PART(ENTRIES), DESC$(ENTRIES), COST(ENTRIES) ' Declare the Table
2060 FOR NUM = 1 TO ENTRIES
2070    READ PART(NUM), DESC$(NUM), COST(NUM)              ' Load the Table
2080 NEXT NUM
2090 KEY OFF  ' Clear 25th Line
2100 RETURN
2110 '
3000 ' *********************************************************
3010 ' *                Process a Request                      *
3020 ' *********************************************************
3030 CONTROL$ = "Y"
3040 WHILE CONTROL$ = "Y" OR CONTROL$ = "y"
3050    GOSUB 3200   '  Call Accept Operator Input
3060    GOSUB 3400   '  Call Access the Table Function
3070 WEND
3080 RETURN
3090 '
3200 ' *********************************************************
3210 ' *              Accept Operator Input                    *
3220 ' *********************************************************
3230 CLS  ' Clear Screen
3240 LOCATE 5, 15
3250 INPUT "Part Number =====> ", PART.NUM
3260 LOCATE 7, 15
3270 RETURN
3280 '
3400 ' *********************************************************
3410 ' *            Access the Table Function                  *
3420 ' *********************************************************
3430 SWITCH$ = "OFF"
3440 FOR NUM = 1 TO ENTRIES
3450    IF PART.NUM = PART(NUM)
           THEN GOSUB 3600 :
               SWITCH$ = "ON" : NUM = ENTRIES  ' Process a Table Hit
3460 NEXT NUM
3470 IF SWITCH$ = "OFF"
        THEN PRINT "** Error **"; PART.NUM; "is an Invalid Part Number"
3480 LOCATE 11, 15
3490 INPUT "Enter Y to look up another part number, else N... ", CONTROL$
3500 RETURN
3510 '
```

(continued)

```
3600 ' **********************************************************
3610 ' *                   Display Table Function              *
3620 ' **********************************************************
3630 PRINT "Description =====> "; DESC$(NUM)
3640 LOCATE 9, 15
3650 PRINT USING "Cost ============> $$#.##"; COST(NUM)
3660 RETURN
3670 '
4000 ' **********************************************************
4010 ' *                        Wrap-up                        *
4020 ' **********************************************************
4030 CLS   ' Clear Screen
4040 PRINT : PRINT "Job Complete"
4050 RETURN
4060 '
4070 ' **************** Table Entries ********************
4080 DATA 6
4090 DATA 112, Round Tip,  2.39, 118, Square Lock, 4.67
4100 DATA 119, Access Pan, 8.5,  121, Toe Plate,   3.75
4110 DATA 129, Hex Bolt,   1.26, 138, Hook Tab,     .48
4120 ' **************** End of Program ********************

RUN
```

Figure 7.20 illustrates the display that is due to a part number of 129, and Figure 7.21 illustrates the display that is due to the invalid part number 122.

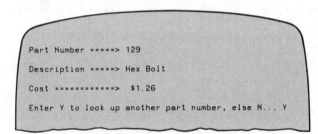

FIGURE 7.20
The display from Program 7.16 due to a part number of 129.

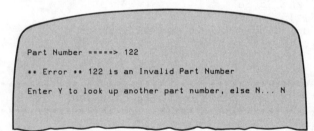

FIGURE 7.21
The display from Program 7.16 due to the invalid part number 122.

Ordering the Table Arguments for a Serial Search

For a serial search, it is not always necessary that the table arguments be in sequence. If it is known that some table entries are requested more often than others, then the table entries requested most often should be placed at the beginning of the table. For example, assume that a frequency analysis uncovered the pattern of requests, shown at the top of the next page, regarding the part-number table entries illustrated earlier in Figure 7.19:

Part Number	% Requested
112	10
118	4
119	15
121	40
129	25
138	6

According to the frequency analysis, the description and cost for part number 121 are requested 40% of the time, and the description and cost for part number 118 are requested only 4% of the time.

If we load the table according to the frequency analysis, then the table entry for part number 121 is at the beginning of the table and the table entry for part number 118 is at the end of the table. This is shown in Figure 7.22. Note that in contrast to the search done earlier in Figure 7.19, the same search takes three fewer comparisons in Figure 7.22. Furthermore, if we load the table according to the frequency analysis, 65% of the requests will require at most two comparisons.

FIGURE 7.22
A serial search of a table loaded according to a frequency analysis.

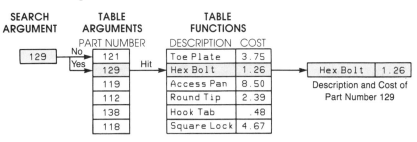

Binary Search   A serial search is useful for short tables but not for long ones. For example, suppose the names in a telephone book were not listed alphabetically. If there were 15,000 names, it would take, on the average, 7,500 comparisons to find a specific telephone number. Some numbers might require only a few comparisons to find, while others might require nearly 15,000 comparisons.

Because telephone books are arranged alphabetically, any name listed therein can be located quickly and easily. When the arguments in a table are in alphabetical or numerical order, an efficient algorithm known as the binary search can be used. A binary search begins the search in the middle of the table. If the search argument is less than the middle table argument, the search continues by halving the lower-valued half of the table. If the search argument is greater than the middle table argument, the search continues by halving the higher-valued half of the table. If the search argument is equal to the middle table argument, the search is over. The binary search algorithm continues to narrow the table until it either finds a match or determines that there is no match.

Figure 7.23 illustrates how the binary search algorithm works with a

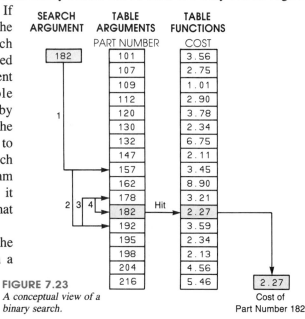

FIGURE 7.23
A conceptual view of a binary search.

table of part numbers and corresponding part costs. Follow carefully the arrows numbered 1 to 4.

Part number 182 is first compared against the 9th element of the 17-element array. Since 182 is greater than 157, the match is located in the higher-valued half of the table. Part number 182 is next compared to the 13th element (halfway between 10 and 17). The part number is less than 192, and the confined area between 10 and 13 is halved again. On the next comparison, 182 is greater than 178 and the area is reduced by half. On the fourth comparison, a match is found. A serial search for part number 182 would have taken 12 comparisons before a match was found. The difference in the number of comparisons between the two algorithms becomes even greater as the size of the table increases.

The following partial program illustrates a binary search.

```
3400 ' *************************************************
3410 ' *              Access the Table Function        *
3420 ' *************************************************
3430 LOW = 1
3440 HIGH = ENTRIES
3450 NUM = 1
3460 WHILE PART.NUM <> PART(NUM) AND LOW <= HIGH
3470     NUM = INT((LOW + HIGH) / 2)
3480     IF PART.NUM < PART(NUM)
             THEN HIGH = NUM - 1
3490     IF PART.NUM > PART(NUM)
             THEN LOW  = NUM + 1
3500 WEND
3510 IF PART.NUM = PART(NUM)
         THEN PRINT USING "Cost =============> $$#.##"; COST(NUM)
         ELSE PRINT "** Error **"; PART.NUM; "is an Invalid Part Number"
3520 LOCATE 11, 15
3530 INPUT "Enter Y to look up another part number, else N... ", CONTROL$
3540 RETURN
3550 '
```

The variables LOW and HIGH point to the beginning and end of that part of the array PART to which the search is confined. Line 3430 initializes LOW to 1. Line 3440 initializes HIGH to ENTRIES, which is equal to the number of entries in the table. Line 3450 initializes NUM to 1 to ensure that PART(NUM), in line 3460, is within the range of the array.

Program 7.17 employs the binary search algorithm to search the table described in Figure 7.23.

____PROGRAM 7.17

```
1000 ' Program 7.17
1010 ' Binary Search of an Argument-Organized Table
1020 ' *************************************************
1030 ' *                 Main Module                   *
1040 ' *************************************************
1050 GOSUB 2000    ' Call Initialization
1060 GOSUB 3000    ' Call Process a Request
1070 GOSUB 4000    ' Call Wrap-up
1080 END
1090 '
2000 ' *************************************************
2010 ' *                Initialization                 *
2020 ' *************************************************
2030 OPTION BASE 1
2040 READ ENTRIES
2050 DIM PART(ENTRIES), COST(ENTRIES)       ' Declare the Table
```

(continued)

```
2060 FOR NUM = 1 TO ENTRIES
2070   READ PART(NUM), COST(NUM)              ' Load the Table
2080 NEXT NUM
2090 KEY OFF  ' Clear 25th Line
2100 RETURN
2110 '
3000 ' *******************************************************
3010 ' *                 Process a Request                   *
3020 ' *******************************************************
3030 CONTROL$ = "Y"
3040 WHILE CONTROL$ = "Y" OR CONTROL$ = "y"
3050   GOSUB 3200  '  Call Accept Operator Input
3060   GOSUB 3400  '  Call Access the Table Function
3070 WEND
3080 RETURN
3090 '
3200 ' *******************************************************
3210 ' *              Accept Operator Input                  *
3220 ' *******************************************************
3230 CLS  ' Clear Screen
3240 LOCATE 5, 15
3250 INPUT "Part Number =====> ", PART.NUM
3260 LOCATE 7, 15
3270 RETURN
3280 '
3400 ' *******************************************************
3410 ' *              Access the Table Function              *
3420 ' *******************************************************
3430 LOW = 1
3440 HIGH = ENTRIES
3450 NUM = 1
3460 WHILE PART.NUM <> PART(NUM) AND LOW <= HIGH
3470   NUM = INT((LOW + HIGH) / 2)
3480   IF PART.NUM < PART(NUM)
         THEN HIGH = NUM - 1
3490   IF PART.NUM > PART(NUM)
         THEN LOW  = NUM + 1
3500 WEND
3510 IF PART.NUM = PART(NUM)
       THEN PRINT USING "Cost =============> $$#.##"; COST(NUM)
       ELSE PRINT "** Error **"; PART.NUM; "is an invalid part number"
3520 LOCATE 9, 15
3530 INPUT "Enter Y to look up another part number, else N... ", CONTROL$
3540 RETURN
3550 '
4000 ' *******************************************************
4010 ' *                   Wrap-up                           *
4020 ' *******************************************************
4030 CLS  ' Clear Screen
4040 PRINT : PRINT "Job Complete"
4050 RETURN
4060 '
4070 ' ************* Table Entries Follow *****************
4080 DATA 17
4090 DATA 101, 3.56, 107, 2.75, 109, 1.01, 112, 2.9,  120, 3.78
4100 DATA 130, 2.34, 132, 6.75, 147, 2.11, 157, 3.45, 162, 8.9
4110 DATA 178, 3.21, 182, 2.27, 192, 3.59, 195, 2.34, 198, 2.13
4120 DATA 204, 4.56, 216, 5.46
4130 ' **************** End of Program ********************

RUN
```

In Program 7.17, lines 3400 through 3550 carry out the search. The compound condition in line 3460 terminates the While loop when PART.NUM is equal to PART(NUM) or when LOW exceeds HIGH. If the search ends because PART.NUM is equal to PART(NUM), the search is successful. If the search ends because LOW exceeds HIGH, the search is unsuccessful. Immediately following the While loop, line 3510 tests to determine which of the two conditions caused the loop to terminate.

Figure 7.24 shows the results that are displayed when a part number of 182 is entered by the user. This corresponds to the example illustrated earlier, in Figure 7.23. Figure 7.25 shows the results that are displayed when an invalid part number is entered.

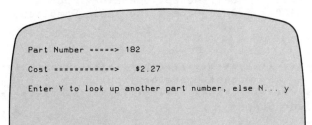

FIGURE 7.24

The display from Program 7.17 due to entering the part number 182.

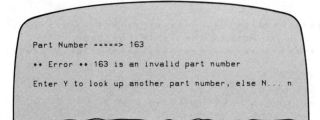

FIGURE 7.25

The display from Program 7.17 due to an invalid part number.

TRY IT YOURSELF

Load Program 7.17 (PRG7-17) from the Student Diskette. Turn on the trace feature of MS BASIC by pressing the function key F7.

Execute the program and enter the same part numbers shown in Figures 7.24 and 7.25. See if you can follow the sequence of statements executed in Program 7.17 from the displayed results.

Press the function key F8 to turn off the trace. See Appendix C, page C.1, for a discussion of the tracing features of MS BASIC.

Combining Table-Access Methods

By itself, a binary search is not always the best method for searching large tables. This is especially true if the most sought-after entries can be isolated. For example, the following frequency analysis of a part-number table with 650 table entries suggests that the table be divided into two tables — one small table in which the 6 most-requested entries are ordered by request, and one large table containing 644 entries, in which the arguments are in ascending sequence.

Part Number	% Requested
112	8
118	4
119	10
121	40
129	25
138	6
Remaining 644 Part Numbers	7

A serial search is employed with the smaller table first. If this search is unsuccessful, then a binary search is used on the larger table. This concept can be expanded further to include several tables and an algorithm that searches one table (i.e., a directory table), in order to determine which table contains the entry and is to be searched next.

⊞ 7.9 WHAT YOU SHOULD KNOW

1. The FOR and NEXT statements are used to set up counter-controlled loops.
2. If the increment value following the keyword STEP is positive or the keyword STEP is not used, then the PC executes the For loop until the loop variable exceeds the limit value. If the increment value is negative, the test is reversed. The value of the loop variable is decremented each time through the loop, and the loop is executed until the loop variable is less than the limit value.
3. The FOR statement may be located anywhere in the program before the corresponding NEXT statement.
4. A valid initial entry into a For loop can be accomplished only by transferring control to the FOR statement.
5. If the range of a For loop includes another For loop, all the statements that are in the range of the inner For loop must also be within the range of the outer For loop.
6. When one For loop is within another, the name of the control variable for each For loop must be different.
7. An array is a variable that allocates a specified number of storage locations, each of which can be assigned a unique value.
8. The elements in the array are distinguished from one another by subscripts. The subscript, written in parentheses, can be a numeric constant, a numeric variable, or a numeric expression.
9. The dimension of an array is the number of subscripts required to reference an element in an array.
10. Before an array can be used in a program, the DIM statement should be used to declare the number of storage locations in main storage that must be reserved for the array.
11. The DIM statement may be located anywhere before the first appearance of a subscripted variable in a program.
12. Several arrays may be dimensioned in the same DIM statement.
13. The OPTION BASE statement is used to assign a lower bound of 0 or 1 to all arrays in a program. If the OPTION BASE statement is not used, the lower bound for all arrays is set to zero.
14. The ERASE statement is used to eliminate previously defined arrays from a program. This statement may be used when a program is short of main storage or when an array must be redimensioned.
15. The subscript that references an array element must be within the range of the array. The range is the number of elements in the array.
16. Noninteger subscripts are rounded to the nearest integer.
17. An array is usually loaded with data using a READ or INPUT statement inside a For loop.
18. Parallel arrays are two or more arrays that have corresponding elements.
19. MS BASIC permits arrays to be dynamically allocated. In the DIM statement, a variable is placed within the parentheses to indicate the size of the array. Before the DIM statement, the variable is assigned a value to which the array is then dimensioned.
20. A two-dimensional array is one that requires two subscripts to reference any element. The first subscript designates the row of that element, and the second subscript designates the column of that element.
21. MS BASIC allows up to 255 dimensions. One- and two-dimensional arrays are the most commonly used arrays in business applications.
22. Sorting is the arranging of data in accordance with some certain order or sequence. Data that is in sequence from lowest to highest is in ascending sequence; data that is in sequence from highest to lowest is in descending sequence.
23. The SWAP statement is used to interchange the values of two variables or elements of an array.
24. Both the bubble sort and Shell sort algorithms work on arrays that contain numeric or string data.
25. Regardless which sort algorithm is used, three steps are required in a program to sort data: dimension the array; load the array with data; and apply an algorithm to manipulate the elements in the array.

26. Tables are organized on the basis of how the data is to be referenced. In positionally organized tables, table functions can be accessed by their position in the table. In argument-organized tables, table functions are accessed by looking up a desired value that corresponds to them. To retrieve these corresponding table functions, a search argument is compared against the table argument. When the search argument matches the table argument, the corresponding table functions are selected and used.

27. To utilize table-processing techniques in a program, you must (1) declare the table by dimensioning arrays for the table entries; (2) use a READ or an INPUT statement inside a For loop to load the table entries; and (3) code appropriate statements to access the table entries.

28. Serial and binary search methods are normally used to access data that is stored in tables.

29. A serial search, which normally begins at the top of the table, does not require that the data be in any sequence.

30. A binary search, which begins in the middle of the table, requires that the data be in ascending or descending sequence.

⊞ 7.10 TEST YOUR BASIC SKILLS (Even-numbered answers are at the back of the book, before the index.)

1. Consider the four valid programs listed below. What is displayed if each program is executed?

a.
```
100 ' Exercise 7.1a
110 LESS50 = 0
120 BETWEEN50.100 = 0
130 GREATER100 = 0
140 READ NUM
150 FOR I = 1 TO NUM
160    READ SCORE
170    IF SCORE >= 0 AND SCORE < 50
          THEN LESS50 = LESS50 + 1
180    IF SCORE >= 50 AND SCORE <= 100
          THEN BETWEEN50.100 = BETWEEN50.100 + 1
190    IF SCORE > 100
          THEN GREATER100 = GREATER100 + 1
200 NEXT I
210 PRINT LESS50, BETWEEN50.100, GREATER100
220 DATA 10, 150, 99, 100, 50, 0, 25, 88
230 DATA 42, 101, 10
240 END
```

b.
```
100 ' Exercise 7.1b
110 F = 0
120 FOR I = 1 TO 3
130    G = 0
140    F = F + 1
150    FOR J = 1 TO 4
160       G = G + F
170       PRINT F, G
180    NEXT J
190 NEXT I
200 END
```

c.
```
100 ' Exercise 7.1c
110 CLS : KEY OFF  ' Clear Screen
120 OPTION BASE 1
130 DIM A(5), B(5), C(5)
140 FOR I = 1 TO 5
150    READ A(I), B(I)
160 NEXT I
170 FOR I = 1 TO 5
180    C(I) = A(I) * B(I)
190    PRINT C(I);
200 NEXT I
210 DATA 1, 4, 2, 3, 4, 4, 2, 4, 3, 5
220 END
```

d.
```
100 ' Exercise 7.1d
110 CLS : KEY OFF   ' Clear Screen
120 OPTION BASE 1
130 READ X, Y
140 DIM A(X, Y)
150 FOR I = 1 TO X
160    FOR J = 1 TO Y
170       READ A(I, J)
180       PRINT A(I, J);
190    NEXT J
200    PRINT
210 NEXT I
220 DATA 4, 3, 2, 1, 6, 9, 5
230 DATA 6, 2, 1, 3, 8, 4, 2
240 END
```

2. Assume that the lower bound is 1 and that array L is declared to have 5 rows and 5 columns. The elements of array L are assigned the following values:

ARRAY L

2	5	14	30	50
7	12	21	70	10
5	15	70	60	0
19	20	30	10	20
22	45	20	40	50

Write the subscripted variable name that references the following values found in array L.

a. 12 b. 70 c. 15 d. 45 e. 60 f. 7 g. 14 h. 22

3. Identify the syntax and logic error(s), if any, in each of the following FOR statements.

   a. `100 FOR AMOUNT = -1 TO -10`   b. `200 FOR VAR = 1 TO 6 STEP -1`
   c. `300 FOR VECTOR = 1 TO 25 ^ (1 / 2)`   d. `400 FOR PINT$ = 0 TO 7`
   e. `450 FOR VALUE = 10 TO 1`   f. `500 FOR QUAD = A TO B STEP -B`

4. Explain what the following partial program does.

```
100 ' EXERCISE 7.4
110 OPTION BASE 1
120 DIM A(3, 4), B(3, 4)
      .
      .
      .
180 FOR I = 1 TO 3
190    FOR J = 1 TO 4
200       B(I, J) = A(I, J)
210    NEXT J
220 NEXT I
230 ERASE A
```

5. Assume that array A has 4 rows and 4 columns and that the elements of array A are assigned the following values:

   ARRAY A

1	2	3	4
5	6	7	8
9	10	11	12
13	14	15	16

   Note: A(1, 1) = 1 and A(3, 2) = 10.

   What will be the final arrangement of array A after the following partial program is executed? Select your answer from the choices below.

```
100 ' Exercise 7.5
110 FOR I = 1 TO 4
120    FOR J = 1 TO 4
130       A(I, J) = A(J, I)
140    NEXT J
150 NEXT I
```

   a.
1	2	3	4
5	6	7	8
9	10	11	12
13	14	15	16

   b.
16	15	14	13
12	11	10	9
8	7	6	5
4	3	2	1

   c.
1	2	2	4
5	6	6	8
9	10	10	12
13	14	14	16

   d.
1	5	9	13
5	6	10	14
9	10	11	15
13	14	15	16

   e. None of these.

6. Refer to the initial array A given in exercise 5. What will be the final arrangement of array A after each of the following partial programs is executed? Select your answers from the choices given in Exercise 5.

   a.
```
100 ' Exercise 7.6a
110 FOR I = 1 TO 4
120    A(I, 3) = A(I, 2)
130 NEXT I
```

   b.
```
100 ' Exercise 7.6b
110 J = 2
120 FOR I = 1 TO 4
130    A(I, J + 1) = A(I, J)
140 NEXT I
```

   c.
```
100 ' Exercise 7.6c
110 FOR I = 1 TO 4
120    A(I, I) = A(I - 2, I + 2)
130 NEXT I
```

   d.
```
100 ' Exercise 7.6d
110 FOR I = 1 TO 4
120    FOR J = 1 TO 4
130       A(I, J) = A(I, J)
140    NEXT J
150 NEXT I
```

7. Refer to the initial array A given in exercise 5. What will be the final arrangement of array A after the following partial program is executed? Select your answer from the choices given in exercise 5. Assume that array B has been declared the same as array A.

```
100 ' Exercise 7.7
110 FOR I = 1 TO 4
120    FOR J = 1 TO 4
130       B(I, J) = A(I, J)
140    NEXT J
150 NEXT I
160 X = 0
170 FOR I = 4 TO 1 STEP -1
180    Y = 0
190    X = X + 1
200    FOR J = 4 TO 1 STEP -1
210       Y = Y + 1
220       A(X, Y) = B(I, J)
230    NEXT J
240 NEXT I
```

8. Given the one-dimensional array NUM, consisting of 50 elements, write a partial program that will count the number of elements in array NUM that have a value between 0 and 18, inclusive, between 26 and 29, inclusive, and between 42 and 47. Use the following counters:

   LOW: count of elements with a value between 0 and 18, inclusive
   MID: count of elements with a value between 26 and 29, inclusive
   HIGH: count of elements with a value between 42 and 47

   Use the subscript I to help reference the elements.

9. Given an array F that has been declared to have 100 elements, assume that each element of array F has been assigned a value. Write a partial program to shift all the values up one location. That is, assign the value of F1 to F2, F2 to F3, and F100 to F1. Do not use any array other than array F. Be careful not to destroy a value before it is shifted.

10. Given the three arrays A, B, and C, each declared to have 50 elements, assume that the elements of arrays A and B have been assigned values. Write a partial program that compares each element of array A to its corresponding element in array B. Assign a 1, 0, or –1 to the corresponding element in array C, as follows:

   1 if A is greater than B
   0 if A is equal to B
   –1 if A is less than B

11. Identify the error(s), if any, in each of the following partial programs:

   a.
   ```
   100 ' Exercise 7.11a
   110 DIM X(300)
   120 FOR I = 1 TO 500
   130    READ X(I)
   140 NEXT I
   150 ERASE X, Y
   ```

   b.
   ```
   100 ' Exercise 7.11b
   110 DIM X(700)
   120 FOR K = 700 TO 1 STEP -1
   130    READ X(K)
   140 NEXT K
   ```

12. Identify the error(s), if any, in each of the following variables and their subscripts.

   a. SUM(8)   b. AMT(6 - 8)   c. BAL(K)   d. F(I(K))
   e. X(3.7)   f. DESC$(5, 6, 7)   g. QUIT(K, A)   h. PAY(3)
   i. LOAN(6.6, 9)   j. Y(I * 3 / J, K + M ^ P)

13. A program utilizes four arrays, B(I), K(J), L(I), and M(Q, J), where the maximum value of I, J, and Q are 15, 36, and 29. Write a correct DIM statement.

14. How many lines will be displayed by the following program?

```
100 ' Exercise 7.14
110 FOR C = 1 TO 20
120    FOR A = 1 TO 10
130       FOR Q = 1 TO 8
140          PRINT C, A, Q
150       NEXT Q
160    NEXT A
170 NEXT C
180 END
```

15. Write a program for each of the following expressions, and display the result.

    a. $1 + 1/2 + 1/4 + 1/8 + \ldots + 1/2^{10}$
    b. $1^1 + 2^2 + 3^3 + 4^4 + 5^5$

16. Given the one-dimensional array A, consisting of 50 elements, write the DIM statement and the For loop to count the number of elements with negative, positive, and zero values in the array.

17. Write a program to find the salesperson who has the greatest total sales for a given period. Assume that the total sales are in array SALES, that the corresponding salesperson's names are in array PERS$, and that each array has been dimensioned to 50 elements.

18. Write a program to find the salesperson who has the least total sales for a given period. Use the same arrays as in exercise 17.

19. Write a program to determine the number of times the letter I is the character value of a string array ALPHA$ that has been previously dimensioned to 50 elements.

20. Write a program to display the item number and gross sales for all items that have a gross sales greater than $3,000. Assume that the item number is stored in array ITEM$ and that the corresponding gross sales are stored in array SALES. Declare a lower bound of 1, and dimension the arrays with an upper-bound value of 200. Do not write the code to load the arrays.

21. Consider the valid program below. What displays when the program is executed?

```
100 ' Exercise 7.21
110 OPTION BASE 1
120 DIM FIB(10)
130 PRINT "N", "NTH FIBONACCI NO."
140 FIB(1) = 1
150 FIB(2) = 1
160 PRINT 1, FIB(1)
170 PRINT 2, FIB(2)
180 FOR NUM = 3 TO 10
190    FIB(NUM) = FIB(NUM - 2) + FIB(NUM - 1)
200    PRINT NUM, FIB(NUM)
210 NEXT NUM
220 END
```

22. Given two two-dimensional arrays, R and S, each of which has 10 rows and 10 columns, write a program to compute the sum of the products of the elements of the arrays with common subscripts. That is, find the following:

$$SUM = \sum_{j=1}^{10} \left(\sum_{k=1}^{10} R_{jk} S_{jk} \right)$$

23. Write a program to generate the first 6 rows of Pascal's triangle. Each entry in a given row of the triangle is generated by adding the two adjacent entries in the immediately preceding row. For example, the third entry in row 4 is the sum of the second and third entries in row 3. The first 6 rows of Pascal's triangle are as follows:

```
            1
          1   1
        1   2   1
      1   3   3   1
    1   4   6   4   1
  1   5  10  10   5   1
```

To eliminate the complexity of spacing, display each row starting in column 1.

24. Use the Student Diskette to complete the Try It Yourself exercises on pages 230, 233, 234, 238, 245, 257, 260, 262, and 270.

⊞ 7.11 BASIC PROGRAMMING PROBLEMS

1. Sum of a Series of Numbers

Purpose: To become familiar with the implementation of counter-controlled loops by means of the FOR and NEXT statements.

Problem: Write five different programs, as described below.

Part A: Construct a program to compute and display the sum of the following series: $1 + 2 + 3 + \ldots + 100$. Use a For loop to create these integers, and sum them.

Part B: Same as Part A except sum all the even numbers from 2 to 100, inclusive.

Part C: Same as Part A except input the lower and upper limits.

Part D: Same as Part C except include a variable step.

Part E: Same as Part A except construct a one-statement BASIC program to compute directly, instead of iteratively, the sum of the numbers from 1 to 100.

Input Data: For Parts A, B, and E, there is no input. For C, input a lower limit of 15 and an upper limit of 42. For Part D, input a lower limit of 20, an upper limit of 75, and a step of 5.

Output Results: Display the result of each program in sentence form. For Parts A and E, the sum is 5050; for Part B, the sum is 2550; for Part C, the sum is 798; for Part D, the sum is 570.

2. Credit Card Verification

Purpose: To become familiar with declaring, loading, and serially searching a table.

Problem: Write a program that will accept a 6-digit credit card number and verify that this number is in a table. If the credit card number is in the table, display a message indicating that the credit card number is valid. If the credit card number is not in the table, display a message indicating that the credit card is invalid; alert the manager; and beep the speaker several times. Declare the credit card-number table to N elements. Use the following 15 credit card numbers.

131416	238967	384512	583214	172319
345610	410001	672354	194567	351098
518912	691265	210201	372198	562982

The 15 credit card numbers are stored in a sequential file under the name EX72CARD.TBL on the Student Diskette.

Input Data: Use the following sample data.

> 372198 518912 102002 672354 210200

Output Results: The following results are shown for credit card numbers 372198 and 210200.

```
              Credit Card Verification

Credit Card Number ••••••> 372198

Credit Card Number is valid

Enter Y to verify another Credit Card Number, else N... Y
```

```
              Credit Card Verification

Credit Card Number ••••••> 210200

•• Error •• Credit Card Number is invalid — Alert Your Manager

Enter Y to verify another Credit Card Number, else N... N
```

3. Windchill Table Lookup

Purpose: To become familiar with accessing data from a positionally-organized table.

Problem: As every resident of Alaska knows, the real enemy in terms of the weather is not the near-zero temperatures, but the windchill factor. Meteorologists in Alaska and in many other states give both the temperature and the windchill factor. So important is the windchill factor that calm air at –40° Fahrenheit is less likely to cause frostbite than air just below freezing that is blowing at gale forces. Basically, two factors determine the windchill factor: the velocity of wind and the temperature. Write a program that accepts from the user a temperature between −20°F and 15°F and a wind velocity between 5 mph and 30 mph, both in multiples of 5. The program should look up the windchill factor in a positionally organized table and display it. Use the following table of windchill factors.

Table of Windchill Factors

Temperature in Fahrenheit	Wind Velocity in Miles per Hour					
	5	**10**	**15**	**20**	**25**	**30**
−20	−26	−46	−58	−67	−74	−79
−15	−21	−40	−51	−60	−66	−71
−10	−15	−34	−45	−53	−59	−64
−5	−10	−27	−38	−46	−51	−56
0	−5	−22	−31	−39	−44	−49
5	0	−15	−25	−31	−36	−41
10	7	−9	−18	−24	−29	−33
15	12	−3	−11	−17	−22	−25

In your program, use the INPUT #n statement and the sequential file EX73TABL.TBL on the Student Diskette to fill the table.

Input Data: Use the following sample data.

Temperature (°F)	Wind Velocity (mph)
−15	10
5	30
−5	40
−40	25
15	10

Output Results: The following results are shown for the first set of data items.

```
Windchill Table Lookup

Temperature (Between -20 and 15) ======>  -15

Velocity (Between 5 and 30) ==========>   10

Windchill Factor ====================>  -40

Enter Y to determine another windchill factor, else N... N
```

4. Week-Ending Department and Store Receipts

Purpose: To become familiar with the use of arrays for determining totals.

Problem: Businesses are usually subdivided into smaller units for the purpose of better organization. The Tri-Quality retail store is subdivided into four departments. Each department submits its receipts at the end of the day to the store manager. Using an array consisting of 5 rows and 6 columns, write a program that is assigned the daily sales. Use the 5th row and 6th column to accumulate the totals. After accumulating the totals, display the entire array.

Input Data: Use the following sample data.

Dept.	Monday	Tuesday	Wednesday	Thursday	Friday
1	$2,146	$6,848	$8,132	$8,912	$5,165
2	8,123	9,125	6,159	5,618	9,176
3	4,156	5,612	4,128	4,812	3,685
4	1,288	1,492	1,926	1,225	2,015

In your program, use the INPUT #n statement and the sequential file EX74SAL.DAT to fill the array. EX74SAL.DAT is stored on the Student Diskette.

Output Results: The following results are displayed.

```
                Week-Ending Store Receipts

   Dept    Mon.     Tues.     Wed.     Thur.     Fri.     Total
   ---------------------------------------------------------------
    1     2,146    6,848    8,132    8,912    5,165    31,203
    2     8,123    9,125    6,159    5,618    9,176    38,201
    3     4,156    5,612    4,128    4,812    3,685    22,393
    4     1,288    1,492    1,926    1,225    2,015     7,946
    T    15,713   23,077   20,345   20,567   20,041    99,743

   Job Complete
```

5. Merging Lists

Purpose: To become familiar with the operation of merging.

Problem: Merging is the process of combining two sorted lists into a single sorted list. Obviously, one list can be appended to the other and the new list can then be sorted. This process, however, is not always the most efficient. Write a program that merges two arrays, X and Y, into array Z. Assume that arrays X and Y have been presorted and are in ascending sequence. Declare array X to have N elements, array Y to have M elements, and array Z to have N + M elements. Display the contents of array Z as part of the end-of-job routine.

(Hint: Be sure to take into consideration that the two arrays are not the same size. That is, when the shorter of the two arrays has been processed, assign the remaining elements of the longer array to array Z.)

Input Data: Use the following sample data.

> Array X: 15 elements — 6, 9, 12, 15, 22, 33, 44, 66, 72, 84, 87, 92, 96, 98, 99
> Array Y: 10 elements — 4, 8, 12, 16, 24, 31, 68, 71, 73, 74

Output Results: The following results are displayed.

```
   The merged array, Z, has 25 elements. Their values are:
    4   6   8   9  12  12  15  16  22  24  31  33  44  66  68  71  72  73  74  84  87
   92  96  98  99

   Job Complete
```

6. Sorting Customer Numbers

Purpose: To become familiar with sorting data into ascending or descending sequence and to gain a better understanding of the bubble and Shell sort algorithms.

Problem: Write a program that requests the selection from a menu of functions for sorting the customer records by customer number. Use the file EX67CUS.DAT described in chapter 6, BASIC Programming Problem 7, page 223, and sort it into either ascending or descending sequence. Use the bubble sort algorithm to sort the customer numbers into ascending sequence. Use the Shell sort algorithm to sort the customer numbers into descending sequence. Declare the customer number array to have 100 elements. Note that there are only 43 records in the customer file. Assume that the number of customer records varies from 1 to 100.

Input Data: Use the data stored in the sequential file EX67CUS.DAT on the Student Diskette.

Output Results: The following is displayed on the screen.

```
   Menu for Sorting Customer Numbers
   ----------------------------------

   Code            Function
   ----            --------
    1              Ascending Sequence
    2              Descending Sequence
    3              End Program

   Enter a Code 1 through 3 =====> 2

   Press the Enter key when the printer is ready...
```

The following partial results for the descending sort of the customer records by customer number are printed on the attached printer.

```
    Sorted Customer List
    --------------------
    Customer       Balance
    --------       -------
       3096         27.95
       3095         56.75
         .            .
         .            .
         .            .
       3012        132.00
       3000         43.25

    Report Complete
```

7. Determining the Mean, the Variance, and the Standard Deviation

Purpose: To apply the concepts of array elements to a statistical problem.

Problem: Construct a program to find the mean (average), the variance, and the standard deviation of a variable number of student grades. Use the following three formulas,

Mean: $$M = \frac{\sum_{j=1}^{n} X_j}{n}$$ Variance: $$V = \sum_{j=1}^{n} \frac{(X_j - M)^2}{n-1}$$ Standard Deviation: $$SD = \sqrt{V}$$

where n is the total number of grades and X_j represents the grade of each student.

Input Data: Enter the number of students via the INPUT statement. Use DATA statements for the student grades.

Number of students: 10

Student grades: 97, 90, 87, 93, 96, 88, 78, 95, 96, 87

Output Results: The following results are displayed.

```
    Statistical Analysis of Student Grades
    --------------------------------------

    Mean ===============> 90.7
    Variance ============> 35.12222
    Standard Deviation ==> 5.9264
    Job Complete
```

8. Payroll Problem VI: Bonus Table Lookup Computations

Purpose: To become familiar with table utilization and program modification.

Problem: Modify Payroll Problem V in chapter 6, BASIC Programming Problem 8, page 224, to compute a bonus for each employee. Add the bonus to the gross pay defined in Payroll Problem V. Adjust the report to include the bonus. Also, print the total bonus paid to all employees.

The bonus is computed by multiplying a factor times the original gross pay. The factor is based on a job class that is found in each employee payroll-transaction record. After computing the gross pay for an employee, use the job class to search the bonus table for the bonus factor to multiply times the gross pay to determine the bonus. If the job class is not in the table, assign the employee a bonus of $25.00. The bonus table follows:

Job Class	Bonus Factor	Job Class	Bonus Factor
01	.025	09	.05
03	.0315	10	.0525
06	.04	12	.055
07	.045		

The data that makes up the bonus table is stored under the name EX78RATE.TBL on the Student Diskette. The very first data item in EX78RATE.TBL is 7, the number of table entries. Use this value to dynamically dimension the parallel arrays used to store the table.

Each record in the transaction file contains an employee number, the number of hours worked, and a job class. The transaction file contains the following eight records.

Employee Number	Hours Worked	Job Class	Employee Number	Hours Worked	Job Class
123	88	06	134	80	12
124	96	03	167	70.5	02
125	72	07	210	80	03
126	80	07	234	32	09

The transaction file is stored under the name EX78TRA.DAT on the Student Diskette.

The employee master file (EX61PAY.DAT) is the same as for Payroll Problem V in chapter 6, on page 224.

You may assume that the records in EX61PAY.DAT and EX78TRA.DAT are in ascending sequence and that there is exactly one record in each file per employee (i.e., each record in EX61PAY.DAT has a match in EX78TRA.DAT).

Input Data: Use the following three sequential files, described under **Problem** and stored on the Student Diskette.

File Name	Description
EX78RATE.TBL	Bonus Table Entries
EX61PAY.DAT	Employee Payroll Master File
EX78TRA.DAT	Employee Payroll-Transaction File

Output Results: A master employee payroll file, as described in Payroll Problem V in chapter 6, is newly created as EX78PAY.DAT. Do not include a year-to-date bonus amount in the employee records written to EX78PAY.DAT. The following report is printed on the printer.

```
                    Biweekly Payroll Report         Page:  1

    Employee
    Number    Bonus   Gross Pay   Fed. Tax   Soc. Sec.    Net Pay
    --------  -----   ---------   --------   ---------    -------
       123    46.00   1,196.00     223.82       85.51     886.67

       124    58.97   1,930.97     378.50       19.66   1,532.81

       125    42.12     978.12     187.93        0.00     790.19

       126    16.20     376.20       6.01       26.90     343.29

       134    38.50     738.50     147.70       52.80     538.00

       167    25.00     758.20     128.56       54.21     575.42
```

```
                    Biweekly Payroll Report         Page:  2

    Employee
    Number    Bonus   Gross Pay   Fed. Tax   Soc. Sec.    Net Pay
    --------  -----   ---------   --------   ---------    -------
       210    22.18     726.18      99.08       51.92     575.17

       234    10.80     226.80      29.98       16.22     180.61


    Total Bonus ============>        259.76
    Total Gross Pay ========>      6,930.96
    Total Withholding Tax ==>      1,201.58
    Total Social Security ==>        307.22
    Total Net Pay ==========>      5,422.16

    End of Payroll Report
```

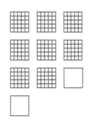

MORE ON STRINGS AND FUNCTIONS

Computers were originally built to perform mathematical calculations. Today, they are still used for that purpose; however, more and more applications require computers to process string data as well. Section 3.5 briefly introduced four string functions — LEFT$, MID$, RIGHT$ and LEN — giving some indication of the ability of MS BASIC to manipulate string data. As you shall see in this chapter, MS BASIC includes several additional string functions, string statements, and special variables that place it among the better programming languages for manipulating letters, numbers, words, and phrases.

MS BASIC also includes numeric functions to handle common mathematical calculations. For example, it is often necessary in programming to obtain the square root or the logarithm of a number. In this chapter, we will discuss the two numeric functions that handle these two calculations, as well as fourteen others.

A second type of function that will be discussed in this chapter is the **user-defined function**. With a function that is defined by the user, numeric or string functions can be created to perform a task that is often needed by the programmer.

Finally, this chapter introduces you to **system-event trapping**. This activity requires that the PC check for the occurrence of an event — for example, the user pressing one of the function keys — as it executes a program. When the event occurs, the PC immediately transfers control to an event-assigned subroutine. Once the subroutine has been completed, the PC continues execution of the program where it left off when the event occurred.

A list of the string functions and a list of the special variables that are available in MS BASIC, along with their areas of use, are shown in Tables 8.1 and 8.2, respectively. To be used, these functions and special variables need only be referred to by name in a LET, PRINT, or IF statement.

The major difference between functions and special variables is that functions require a built-in routine to be executed in order to generate the value returned to your program, whereas special variables don't. Special variables point to addresses in main storage that already contain the desired information.

_____TABLE 8.1 MS BASIC String Functions_____

FUNCTION	FUNCTION VALUE
ASC(X$)	*Returns a two-digit numeric value that is equivalent in ASCII code to the first character of the string argument X$.*
CHR$(N)	*Returns a single string character that is equivalent in ASCII code to the numeric argument N.*
INPUT$(N)	*Suspends execution of the program until N number of characters from the keyboard are entered.*
INSTR(P,X$,S$)	*Returns the beginning position of the substring S$ in string X$. P indicates the position the search begins in X$ and may be omitted from the argument list. If the search for S$ in X$ is unsuccessful, INSTR returns a value of zero.*
LEFT$(X$, N)	*Extracts the leftmost N characters of the string argument X$.*
LEN(X$)	*Returns the length of the string argument X$.*
MID$(X$, P, N)	*Extracts N characters of the string argument X$ beginning at position P.*
RIGHT$(X$, N)	*Extracts the rightmost N characters of the string argument X$.*
SPACE$(N)	*Returns N number of spaces.*
SPC(N)	*Displays N spaces. May be used only in an output statement.*
STR$(N)	*Returns the string equivalent of the numeric argument N.*
STRING$(N, X$)	*Returns N times the first character of X$.*
VAL(X$)	*Returns the numeric equivalent of the string argument X$.*

_____TABLE 8.2 MS BASIC Special Variables_____

SPECIAL VARIABLE	SPECIAL VARIABLE USE
CSRLIN	*Equal to the vertical (row) coordinate of the cursor.*
DATE$	*Equal to the current date as a string in the form mm-dd-yyyy.*
ERL	*Equal to the line number of the last error. Used for error trapping. For a detailed discussion, see Appendix C, section C.2.*
ERR	*Equal to the error code of the last error. Used for error-trapping. For a detailed discussion, see Appendix C, section C.2.*
INKEY$	*Equal to the last character entered through the keyboard.*
TIME$	*Equal to the current time of day in 24-hour notation as a string in the form hh:mm:ss.*

Concatenation, Substrings and Character Counting Revisited — +, LEN, LEFT$, RIGHT$ and MID$

The extraction of substrings from a large string and the combining of two or more strings are important in manipulating nonnumeric data. In section 3.5, on page 74, the concatenation operation + and the LEN, LEFT$, RIGHT$, and MID$ functions were briefly introduced. You'll recall that concatenation is the only string operation allowed in MS BASIC. It joins two strings to form a new string. For example,

```
500 JOIN$ = "ABC" + "DEF"
```

assigns JOIN$ the value ABCDEF. The second string is joined to the right end of the first string to form the result, which is then assigned to JOIN$. More than one concatenation operator may appear in a single assignment statement. For example, if PHRASE1$ = Resistb and PHRASE2$ = the urgeb and PHRASE3$ = to code where b represents a blank character, then

```
600 PHRASE$ = PHRASE1$ + PHRASE2$ + PHRASE3$
```

assigns PHRASE$ the string Resist the urge to code.

The LEN function returns the length of the argument. The argument may be a string constant, a string variable, or a string expression. Table 8.3 and Program 8.1 illustrate the use of the LEN function.

_____TABLE 8.3 Examples of the LEN Function_____

VALUE OF VARIABLE	THE STATEMENT	RESULTS IN
COMP1$ = IBM PC AT	100 LEN1 = LEN(COMP1$)	LEN1 = 9
COMP2$ = Zenith	200 LEN2 = LEN(COMP2$)	LEN2 = 6
	300 LEN3 = LEN("Clone")	LEN3 = 5
	400 LEN4 = LEN("")	LEN4 = 0
NOTH$ = *null char.*	500 LEN5 = LEN(NOTH$)	LEN5 = 0

PROGRAM 8.1

```
100 ' Program 8.1
110 ' Examples of the use of the LEN function
120 ' *****************************************
130 WORD1$ = "Structured"
140 WORD2$ = "Programming"
150 LENGTH = LEN(WORD1$)
160 PRINT WORD1$; " has"; LENGTH; "characters."
170 PRINT WORD2$; " has"; LEN(WORD2$); "characters."
180 PRINT WORD1$ + " " + WORD2$; " has";
        LEN(WORD1$ + " " + WORD2$); "characters."
190 END

RUN

Structured has 10 characters.
Programming has 11 characters.
Structured Programming has 22 characters.
```

In Program 8.1, LEN(WORD1$) in line 150 assigns the variable LENGTH a value of 10. In line 170, LEN(WORD2$) is displayed as 11. In line 180, the LEN function returns the length of the string expression WORD1$ + " " + WORD2$ as 22.

The LEFT$, MID$, and RIGHT$ string functions may be used to extract substrings from a string constant, a string variable, or a string expression. A substring is a part of a string. For example, some substrings of Return of the Jedi are Return, Jedi, of t, and ed. All three functions reference substrings on the basis of the position of characters within the string argument, where the leftmost character of the string argument is position 1, the next is position 2, and so on. For example, in the string Return of the Jedi, the substring Return begins in position 1, and the substring Jedi begins in position 15.

LEFT$(X$, N) extracts a substring starting with the leftmost character (position 1) of the string X$. The length of the substring is determined by the integer value of the length argument N. For example, the following statement assigns SUB1$ the value Return

```
300 SUB1$ = LEFT$("Return of the Jedi", 6)
```

Return begins in position 1 and has a length of 6. The quotation marks are not part of the string.

RIGHT$(X$, N) extracts a substring starting with the rightmost character of the string argument X$. The length of the substring is determined by the value of the length argument N. For example, if MOVIE$ is equal to the string Raiders of the Lost Ark, then the following statement assigns SUB2$ the substring Ark

```
400 SUB2$ = RIGHT$(MOVIE$, 3)
```

MID$(X$, P, N) extracts a substring beginning with the character in position P of X$. The length of the substring is determined by the value of the length argument N. For example, if PHRASE$ is equal to the string Every dog must have his day, then the following statement assigns SUB3$ the substring dog must have

```
500 SUB3$ = MID$(PHRASE$, 7, 13)
```

If the length argument is not included in the list for the MID$ function, then the PC returns a substring that begins with the position argument and ends with the last character in the string argument. For example, if PHRASE$ is equal to the string Today is the tomorrow I worried about yesterday, then the following statement assigns SUB4$ the substring I worried about yesterday:

```
600 SUB4$ = MID$(PHRASE$, 23)
```

Table 8.4 illustrates the use of the LEFT$, RIGHT$, and MID$ functions.

TABLE 8.4 Examples of the LEFT$, RIGHT$, and MID$ Functions

THE STATEMENT	RESULTS IN
Assume S$ is equal to: If something can go wrong, it will	
100 C$ = LEFT$(S$, 12)	C$ = If something
200 F$ = LEFT$(S$, 1.7)	F$ = If
300 H$ = LEFT$(S$, 0)	H$ = null char.
400 J$ = RIGHT$(S$, 7)	J$ = it will
500 P$ = RIGHT$(S$, -1)	Illegal function call
600 R$ = RIGHT$(S$, 50)	R$ = S$
700 T$ = MID$(S$, -1, 6)	Illegal function call
800 U$ = MID$(LEFT$(S$, 4), 2, 1)	U$ = f
900 V$ = MID$(S$, 75, 4)	V$ = null char.
950 X$ = MID$(S$, 18)	X$ = go wrong, it will
980 Y$ = MID$(S$, 256)	Illegal function call

In line 200 of Table 8.4, the argument 1.7 is rounded to 2. In line 300, the numeric argument 0 causes the PC to assign H$ the null string. In line 500, the negative argument causes the PC to display a diagnostic message. Line 500 is invalid. Line 600 shows that if the length argument is greater than the length of the string argument, the function returns a substring that begins at the specified position and includes the remaining portion of the string.

In line 700, the position argument, -1, is invalid. Line 800 shows that you may include a string function as the string argument. Line 900 illustrates that a null string is returned when the specified beginning position in the MID$ function is greater than the length of the argument string. Line 950 shows that when the length argument is not included in the MID$ function, the PC returns a substring beginning with the specified position and ending with the last character of the string argument. Finally, line 980 causes a diagnostic message to display because the position argument is greater than 255. The position argument must be in the range 1 to 255.

The PC interprets the position argument P and the length argument N of the LEFT$, MID$, and RIGHT$ function according to the following rules:

String Function Rule 1: If the position argument P or the length argument N is a decimal fraction, the value of N or P is rounded to an integer.

String Function Rule 2: If the length argument N is less than 0 or greater than 255, then the function call is illegal. If N is equal to zero, the function returns a null string.

String Function Rule 3: If the length argument N is greater than the remaining length of the string argument, the function returns a substring that begins at the specified position and includes the remaining portion of the string.

String Function Rule 4: If the position argument P is greater than the length of the string argument, the function returns a null string. If the position argument P is less than 1 or greater than 255, then the function call is illegal.

Program 8.2 makes use of the LEN and MID$ functions. The basic purpose of the program is to search for words in a sentence. Each time a word is found, the program displays it on a separate line. The program assumes that each word, except for the last, is followed by a space.

PROGRAM 8.2

```
100 ' Program 8.2
110 ' Displaying Each Word in a Sentence
120 ' **********************************
130 PRINT "Enter the sentence without punctuation:"
140 PRINT : INPUT "", SENTENCE$
150 BEG = 1
160 PRINT : PRINT "Words in the sentence:"
170 FOR CHAR = 1 TO LEN(SENTENCE$)
180    IF MID$(SENTENCE$, CHAR, 1) = " "
          THEN PRINT TAB(23); MID$(SENTENCE$, BEG, CHAR - BEG) :
             BEG = CHAR + 1
190 NEXT CHAR
200 ' ****** Display the Last Word *****
210 PRINT TAB(23); MID$(SENTENCE$, BEG)
220 PRINT "Job Complete"
230 END
RUN

Enter the sentence without punctuation:

If an experiment works something has gone wrong


Words in the sentence:
                       If
                       an
                       experiment
                       works
                       something
                       has
                       gone
                       wrong
Job Complete
```

When Program 8.2 is executed, line 130 displays a prompt message. Line 140 accepts the sentence and assigns it to the variable SENTENCE$. In line 150, the variable BEG is assigned a value of 1. This variable is used later, in line 180 to indicate the beginning position of each word and in line 210 to display the last word in the sentence.

Line 180 in the For loop tests each character in the sentence to determine whether it is a space. If a character is a space, then the word beginning at position BEG with length of CHAR – BEG is displayed and BEG is set equal to a value that is equivalent to the beginning position of the next word. Since the last word in the sentence does not end with a space, line 210 instead of line 180 is used to display the last word.

TRY IT YOURSELF

Load Program 8.2 (PRG8-2) from the Student Diskette. Display and execute the program. Enter the following sentence in response to the INPUT statement:

```
When things just can't get any worse they will
```

Delete line 210. Execute the program again and enter the same sentence. Compare the results to those displayed prior to deleting line 210. Do you understand the importance of line 210?

Substring Searching and Replacement — INSTR Function and MID$ Statement

MS BASIC includes the INSTR function to search a string argument for a particular substring. INSTR(P, X$, S$) returns the beginning position of the substring S$ in X$. The search begins at position P of X$. For example, the following partial program causes the variable CNT1 to be assigned the value 4:

```
490 PHRASE$ = "To be or not to be"
500 CNT1 = INSTR(1, PHRASE$, "be")
```

Line 500 assigns CNT1 the position of the first character of the substring be in string PHRASE$. If there are no occurrences of the substring, INSTR returns the value zero.

The INSTR function always returns the leftmost position of the first occurrence of the substring. If the following statement is added to the previous partial program,

```
510 CNT2 = INSTR(5, PHRASE$, "be")
```

then CNT2 is assigned a value of 17. The first occurrence of be is bypassed because the search begins at position 5 in line 510.

The position argument P may be omitted from the list of arguments. For example, the following statement is identical to the previous line 500:

```
500 CNT1 = INSTR(PHRASE$, "be")
```

That is, the search begins at position 1 (by default) and assigns CNT1 a value of 4. Table 8.5 illustrates some additional examples of the INSTR function.

TABLE 8.5 Examples of the INSTR Function

THE STATEMENT	RESULTS IN
Assume that S$ is equal to Rally 'round the flag, boys, rally once again	
100 POS1 = INSTR(1, S$, ",")	POS1 = 22
200 POS2 = INSTR(START, S$, "rally")	POS2 = 30 *(assume START = 22)*
300 POS3 = INSTR(S$, "'")	POS3 = 7

The MID$ statement is used for substring replacement. Do not confuse the MID$ statement with the MID$ function. The MID$ function returns a substring, but the MID$ statement replaces a series of characters within a string with a designated substring. The general form of the MID$ statement is given in Table 8.6 on the opposite page.

As illustrated by the general form in Table 8.6, a substring of X$, specified by the beginning position P and the length N, is replaced by the substring S$. For example, if PHRASE$ is equal to Inprocment and SUBSTR$ is equal to vest, then the following statement,

```
100 MID$(PHRASE$, 3, 4) = SUBSTR$
```

assigns PHRASE$ the value Investment. The substring vest replaces the substring proc.

_____TABLE 8.6_ The MID$ Statement_____

General Form:	`MID$(X$, P, N) = S$`
	*where **X$** is the string in which the replacement takes place;*
	***P** is the position at which the replacement begins;*
	***N** is the number of characters to replace; and*
	***S$** is the replacement substring.*
Purpose:	*Replaces a substring within a string.*
Examples:	`100 MID$(PHRASE$, 3, 4) = SUBSTR$`
	`200 MID$(WORD1$, 1, 5) = "Y"` *(1 character replaced)*
	`300 MID$(WD1$, 30, 2) = "abcde"` *(2 characters replaced)*
	`400 MID$(E$, 4, 5) = A$ + B$`

In Table 8.6, line 200 shows that if the replacement substring is shorter than the substring designated by the length argument in the `MID$` statement, then only those characters which are designated by the replacement substring are actually replaced. For example, if WORD1$ is equal to `Beast`, then the statement

```
200 MID$(WORD1$, 1, 5) = "Y"
```

assigns WORD1$ the value `Yeast`.

If the replacement substring has a length greater than that specified by N in the `MID$` statement, then the PC replaces only N characters. The rightmost excess characters in the replacement substring are not used.

Program 8.3 modifies a line of text through the use of the `INSTR` function and the `MID$` statement. The program searches for all occurrences of the substring `ne`. Each time the substring is found, it is replaced with the substring `in`.

PROGRAM 8.3

```
100 ' Program 8.3
110 ' Searching and Replacing Strings
120 ' *******************************
130 PHRASE$ = "The rane in Spane stays manely in the plane"
140 PRINT "Old text ===> "; PHRASE$
150 POSITION = INSTR(PHRASE$, "ne")
160 WHILE POSITION <> 0
170    MID$(PHRASE$, POSITION, 2) = "in"
180    POSITION = INSTR(POSITION + 2, PHRASE$, "ne")
190 WEND
200 PRINT
210 PRINT "New text ===> "; PHRASE$
220 END

RUN

Old text ===> The rane in Spane stays manely in the plane

New text ===> The rain in Spain stays mainly in the plain
```

Line 150 in Program 8.3 assigns the variable POSITION the value 7, which is the beginning position of the first occurrence of the substring `ne`. Line 170 replaces the substring `ne` that begins in position 7 with the substring `in`. Line 180 searches for the next occurrence of the substring `ne`. The search begins one position to the right of the previous occurrence. The next occurrence of the substring `ne` begins at position 16. Therefore, the `INSTR` function assigns POSITION a value of 16. The loop continues, with line 170 making the next replacement.

This process continues until all the occurrences of ne have been changed to in. At this point, line 180 assigns POSITION a value of zero and the loop terminates. The modified value of PHRASE$ is then displayed by line 210.

If PHRASE$ is assigned a value without the substring ne, the While loop (lines 160 through 190) will not execute. The INSTR function in line 150 returns a value of zero when the substring is not found. With POSITION equal to zero, the WHILE statement in line 160 causes execution to continue at line 200. In this case, the new text and old text are identical.

TRY IT YOURSELF

> Load Program 8.3 (PRG8-3) from the Student Diskette. In line 170, change the string in to en. Execute the program and compare the results to those displayed by Program 8.3.

Converting Character Codes— ASC and CHR$

The ASC and CHR$ functions facilitate the manipulation of individual characters. ASC(X$) returns a two-digit numeric value that corresponds to the ASCII code for the first character of the string argument X$. As explained in chapter 5 and illustrated in Appendix D, Table D.2, each character in MS BASIC has a corresponding ASCII numeric code that the PC uses for storing the character in main storage or on auxiliary storage. For example, the character A has an ASCII code of 65, the character B has an ASCII code of 66, and so on. The following statement displays the result 67:

```
PRINT ASC("C")
 67
```

CHR$(N) can be described as the reverse of the ASC function. It returns a single string character that is equivalent in ASCII code to the numeric argument N. For example, the following statement displays the character B:

```
PRINT CHR$(66)
 B
```

A total of 256 different characters are represented by the ASCII code. The CHR$ function allows you to enter any of the 256 characters by using the corresponding ASCII code as the argument. For example, the following partial program,

```
300 FOR I = 1 TO 10
310    PRINT CHR$(7);
320 NEXT I
330 PRINT CHR$(12)
```

causes the PC to beep ten times and clear the first 24 lines of the screen because the ASCII code 7 corresponds to the character BEL (Bell) and the ASCII code 12 corresponds to the character FF (Form Feed).

The ASC function is used to convert a single character string into a numeric value, which can later be manipulated arithmetically. For example, the partial program on the top of the opposite page changes the single character string assigned to UPPER$ from uppercase to lowercase:

```
490 UPPER$ = "A"
500 UPPER  = ASC(UPPER$)
510 LOWER  = UPPER + 32
520 LOWER$ = CHR$(LOWER)
530 PRINT "Uppercase: "; UPPER$
540 PRINT "Lowercase: "; LOWER$
        .
        .
        .
RUN

Uppercase: A
Lowercase: a
```

In this partial program, the ASCII code for a lowercase character is equal to the corresponding uppercase numeric code plus 32. Line 500 assigns the variable UPPER the numeric value 65, which is equal to the ASCII code for the character A. Line 510 assigns LOWER the value 97. Line 520 assigns LOWER$ the character a, which has an ASCII code of 97. Lines 530 and 540 display the values of UPPER$ and LOWER$.

Table 8.7 illustrates several examples of the ASC and CHR$ functions. Programming Case Study 15, below, makes use of both functions to decipher a coded message.

TABLE 8.7 Examples of the ASC and CHR$ Functions

VALUE OF	THE STATEMENT	RESULTS IN
	100 CODE1= ASC("5")	CODE1 = 53
C$ = *null char.*	200 D1 = ASC(C$)	Illegal function call
D$ = ABC	300 E = ASC(D$)	E = 65
	400 KAY$ = CHR$(75)	KAY$ = K
D = -3	500 Y$ = CHR$(D)	Illegal function call

Programming Case Study 15: Deciphering a Coded Message

Messages are often coded by having one letter represent another. The coded message is called a **cryptogram**, and an algorithm is used to decipher the message into readable form.

The objective here is to take a coded message and have the PC display the corresponding deciphered message. The algorithm calls for subtracting 3 from the numeric code that represents each character in the coded message. Obviously, the algorithm can be, and usually is, more complex.

The coded message is

W K H # V K D G R Z # N Q R Z V

Following is a list of program tasks; a program solution; and a discussion of the program solution.

Program Tasks

1. Clear the screen.
2. Accept a message from the user.
3. Use a For loop to process each character in the message. The For loop includes the following:

    a. an initial parameter of 1
    b. a limit parameter of LEN(message)
    c. the MID$ function to extract each character
    d. the ASC function to determine the numeric value that is equivalent to the ASCII code of the extracted character

e. subtraction of 3 from the numeric value determined in 3.d

f. the CHR$ function to change the numeric value in 3.e to a character

g. display of the character

Program Solution   The following program corresponds to the preceding tasks.

PROGRAM 8.4

```
100 ' Program 8.4
110 ' Deciphering a Coded Message
120 ' *************************
125 CLS : KEY OFF  ' Clear Screen
130 PRINT : INPUT "Coded message ========> ", CODE$
140 PRINT : PRINT "The message is =======> ";
160 FOR CHAR = 1 TO LEN(CODE$)
170    NUM = ASC(MID$(CODE$, CHAR, 1))
180    NUM = NUM - 3
190    LETTER$ = CHR$(NUM)
200    PRINT LETTER$;
210 NEXT CHAR
220 PRINT
230 END

RUN

Coded message ========> WKH#VKDGRZ#NQRZV

The message is =======> THE SHADOW KNOWS
```

Discussion of the   Program 8.4 accepts a coded message, deciphers it one character at a time, and displays the
Program Solution corresponding message one character at a time.

In line 160, LEN(CODE$) is the limit value for the For loop. Line 170 determines the numeric value that corresponds to the ASCII code for the character selected by the MID$ function. It is valid for a string function to be part of the argument for another string function. Line 180 subtracts 3 from the value of NUM, and in line 190 the CHR$ function returns the corresponding character.

TRY IT YOURSELF

Load Program 8.4 (PRG8-4) from the Student Diskette. Delete lines 170 through 200 and insert the following statement:

```
170 PRINT CHR$(ASC(MID$(CODE$, CHAR, 1)) - 3);
```

Execute the program and enter the following coded message:

```
ZKR#LV#WKH#VKDGRZB
```

Do you agree that it is valid to have functions as the arguments of other functions?

Modifying Data   The PC cannot add a string value to a numeric value. The STR$ and VAL functions allow this
*Types — STR$*   restriction to be circumvented. The STR$(N) function returns the string equivalent of the
and VAL   numeric value N. VAL(X$) returns the numeric equivalent of the string X$. Thus,
STR$(52.3) returns the string "52.3" and VAL("310.23") returns the numeric value

310.23. If the argument is negative, the STR$ function returns a leading negative sign. If the argument for the VAL function does not represent a number, the function returns a value of 0. For example, the value displayed by the following statement is zero.

```
PRINT VAL("CHICAGO")
 0
```

Table 8.8 gives examples of both the STR$ and VAL functions. These two functions are used primarily in instances where a substring of numeric digits within an identification number — like a credit card number or an invoice number — need to be extracted for computational purposes and the result has to be transformed back as a string value.

TABLE 8.8 Examples of the STR$ and VAL Functions

VALUE OF	THE STATEMENT	RESULTS IN
	100 A$ = STR$(34)	A$ = 34
B = 64.543	200 S$ = STR$(B)	S$ = 64.543
C = -3.21	300 Z$ = STR$(C)	Z$ = -3.21
	400 F = VAL("766.321")	F = 766.321
K$ = 12E-3	500 Q = VAL(K$)	Q = 12E-3
P$ = ABC	600 W = VAL(P$)	W = 0

Note: *Any numeric value that is assigned to a string variable is actually a string, not a number.*

Duplicating Strings — SPACE$ and STRING$

The SPACE$ and STRING$ functions are used to duplicate string data. SPACE$(N) returns N spaces or blank characters. It is similar to the SPC function which was discussed in chapter 4. For example, the two statements

```
700 PRINT "DEC"; SPC(4); "Micro VAX"
```

and

```
710 PRINT "DEC"; SPACE$(4); "Micro VAX"
```

display identical results. The advantage of the SPACE$ function over the SPC function is that SPACE$ may be used in statements other than the PRINT statement. For example, the following statement,

```
720 SP$ = SPACE$(25)
```

assigns SP$ a string value of 25 spaces. If the argument is equal to or less than zero, the function returns the null string.

The STRING$(N, X$) function returns N times the first character of the string X$. The STRING$ function may be used to duplicate any character. For example, the following statement,

```
730 PRINT STRING$(72, "*")
```

displays a line of 72 asterisks. The second argument may also be represented in ASCII code. That is, the statement

```
740 PRINT STRING$(72, 42)
```

is identical to line 730, since 42 is the ASCII code representation for the asterisk character.

Table 8.9, on the following page, gives examples of both the SPACE$ and STRING$ functions.

TABLE 8.9 Examples of the SPACE$ and STRING$ Functions

VALUE OF	THE STATEMENT	COMMENT
NUM = 50	100 PRINT SPACE$(NUM); "A"	*Displays 50 spaces, followed by the character A in position 51.*
	200 SP$ = SPACE$(12)	*Assigns 12 spaces to SP$.*
	300 NULL$ = SPACE$(0)	*Assigns NULL$ the null string.*
CNT = 45	400 PRINT STRING$(CNT, "-")	*Displays 45 minus signs.*
	500 A$ = STRING$(5, 65)	*Assigns A$ the string value AAAAA.*
	600 IF EMP$ = SPACE$(15) THEN END	*Terminates execution of the program if EMP$ is equal to 15 spaces.*

Accessing the System Time and Date — The Special Variables DATE$ and TIME$

The special variables DATE$ and TIME$ are automatically equal to the system date and system time, respectively. The special variable DATE$ is equal to the current system date as a string value in the form mm-dd-yyyy. The first two characters, mm, represent the month. The fourth and fifth characters, dd, represent the day. The last four characters, yyyy, represent the year. For example, if the system date is initialized to December 25, 1991, then the statement

```
800 TODAYS.DATE$ = DATE$
```

assigns TODAYS.DATE$ the string 12-25-1991.

The special variable TIME$ is equal to the system's time of day, in 24-hour notation, as a string value in the form hh:mm:ss. The first two characters, hh, represent the hours (range 00–23). The fourth and fifth characters, mm, represent the minutes (range 00–59). The last two characters, ss, represent the seconds (range 00–59). If the PC's internal clock is equal to 11:35:42 *at the instant* the statement

```
PRINT "The time is "; TIME$
```

executes, then the following is displayed:

```
The time is 11:35:42
```

The key phrase in the last sentence is "at the instant," since, as part of the start-up procedures, the PC's internal clock automatically maintains the time after it is entered by the operator.

Table 8.10 gives examples of both special variables DATE$ and TIME$.

TABLE 8.10 Examples of the Special Variables DATE$ and TIME$

THE STATEMENT	RESULTS IN
Assume DATE$ = 09-15-1991 and TIME$ = 15:26:32	
100 TD$ = DATE$	TD$ = 09-15-1991
200 TT$ = TIME$	TT$ = 15:26:32
300 MONTH$ = MID$(DATE$, 1, 2)	MONTH$ = 09
400 DAY$ = MID$(DATE$, 4, 2)	DAY$ = 15
500 YEAR$ = MID$(DATE$, 9, 2)	YEAR$ = 91
600 HOUR$ = MID$(TIME$, 1, 2)	HOUR$ = 15
700 MINUTE$$ = MID$(TIME$, 4, 2)	MINUTE$ = 26
800 SECOND$ = MID$(TIME$, 7, 2)	SECOND$ = 32

Note: Any numeric value that is assigned to a string variable is actually a string, not a number.

TRY IT YOURSELF

Enter the following statements and note the values displayed:

```
? DATE$
? TIME$
? MID$(TIME$, 4, 2)
```

The DATE$ and TIME$ functions are often used to display the date and time as part of report headings. The DATE$ function may also be used in business-related applications to verify that a payment date, birth date, or hire date is valid.

Programming Case Study 16: *Validating Payment Dates*

The following program solution illustrates how to verify that a payment date is the present date or an earlier date, not a future date.

Problem: The following customer payment records are stored in the sequential file ACCREC.DAT:

Customer Number	Customer Payment	Payment Date
31245381	$101.55	091592
46371230	95.25	061291
71209824	25.00	062491
96012567	38.00	053091

The payment dates are of the form mmddyy.

The accounts-receivable department has requested that a program be written to verify that the payment date for each record in ACCREC.DAT is not a date in the future. The program should verify each payment date against today's date. If today's date is greater than or equal to the payment date, then the payment date is valid. If today's date is less than the payment date, then the payment date is invalid. For each record, print on the printer the customer number, the payment, the payment date, and a message indicating whether the payment date is valid or invalid. The results are to be in report form, with one line printed for each record read. Assume that today's date is June 22, 1991. (You may reboot the PC to enter this date or use the DATE$ statement, which is discussed on page 296.)

To compare the two dates, the most significant part of the date (years) must be at the far left, followed by the next most significant part (months), followed by the least significant part (days). That is, the program must rearrange the two dates before it can compare them, as follows:

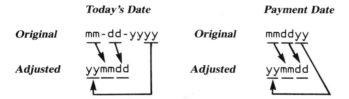

To rearrange the substrings within each date, the MID$ function and the concatenation operator may be used. Once the two fields have been adjusted, today's date can be compared against the customer payment date.

Following are a list of the program tasks; a program solution; and a discussion of the program solution.

Program Tasks 1. Initialization

   a. Set the variable TD$ (today's date) to DATE$.
   b. Use the following statement to rearrange today's date:

   ```
   TODAY$ = MID$(TD$, 9, 2) + MID$(TD$, 1, 2) + MID$(TD$, 4, 2)
   ```

   c. Clear the screen and display a message requesting the user to turn on the printer.
   d. Print a report title and column headings.
   e. Open the sequential file ACCREC.DAT for input.

2. Process File — Establish a While loop that processes the records in ACCREC.DAT until the end-of-file mark is sensed. Within the loop, do the following:

   a. Read an accounts-receivable record. Use the following variable names:

   CUS.NUM$ = customer number
   CUS.PAY   = customer payment
   CUS.DATE$ = customer payment date

   b. Adjust the customer payment date (CUS.DATE$). Use the following statement:

```
ADJ.DATE$ = MID$(CUS.DATE$, 5, 2) + MID$(CUS.DATE$, 1, 2) + MID$(CUS.DATE$, 3, 2)
```

   c. If the adjusted today's date (TODAY$) is greater than or equal to the customer adjusted payment date (ADJ.DATE$), then assign MESSAGE$ the statement Date OK. Otherwise, assign MESSAGE$ the statement Date NOT OK.
   d. Print the customer number, the payment, the payment date, and the message. Format the payment date in the form mm-dd-yy. Use the LEFT$, MID$, and RIGHT$ functions to extract the substrings from the payment date. (Note that the extraction of these substrings may be accomplished solely by means of the MID$ function.)

3. Wrap-up

   a. Close ACCREC.DAT.
   b. Print an end-of-job message.
   c. Clear the screen and display an end-of-job message.

Program Solution The following program solution corresponds to the preceding tasks.

PROGRAM 8.5

```
1000 ' Program 8.5
1010 ' Validating Payment Dates
1020 ' ************************************************************
1030 ' *                     Main Module                          *
1040 ' ************************************************************
1050 GOSUB 2000   ' Call Initialization
1060 GOSUB 3000   ' Call Process File
1070 GOSUB 4000   ' Call Wrap-up
1080 END
1090 '
2000 ' ************************************************************
2010 ' *                   Initialization                         *
2020 ' ************************************************************
2030 TD$    = DATE$
2040 TODAY$ = MID$(TD$, 9, 2) + MID$(TD$, 1, 2) + MID$(TD$, 4, 2)
2050 CLS : KEY OFF  ' Clear Screen
```

(continued)

```
2060 LOCATE 12, 15 : PRINT "Validating Payment Dates"
2070 LOCATE 14, 15
2080 INPUT "Press the Enter key when the printer is ready...", CONTROL$
2090 LPRINT    "   Validating Payment Dates For "; DATE$
2100 LPRINT SPC(3); STRING$(39, "-")
2110 LPRINT
2120 LPRINT    "Customer                   Payment"
2130 LPRINT    "Number     Payment        Date         Comment"
2140 LPRINT    "--------   -------        -------      -------"
2150 FORMAT$ = "\         \   #,###.##      \\-\\-\\     \            \"
2160 OPEN "ACCREC.DAT" FOR INPUT AS #1
2170 RETURN
2180 '
3000 ' *******************************************************
3010 ' *                    Process File                     *
3020 ' *******************************************************
3030 WHILE NOT EOF(1)
3040    INPUT #1, CUS.NUM$, CUS.PAY, CUS.DATE$
3050    ADJ.DATE$ = MID$(CUS.DATE$, 5, 2) + MID$(CUS.DATE$, 1, 2) +
                    MID$(CUS.DATE$, 3, 2)
3060    IF TODAY$ >= ADJ.DATE$
            THEN MESSAGE$ = "Date OK"
            ELSE MESSAGE$ = "Date NOT OK"
3070    LPRINT USING FORMAT$; CUS.NUM$, CUS.PAY, LEFT$(CUS.DATE$, 2),
              MID$(CUS.DATE$, 3, 2), RIGHT$(CUS.DATE$, 2), MESSAGE$
3080 WEND
3090 RETURN
3100 '
4000 ' *******************************************************
4010 ' *                      Wrap-up                        *
4020 ' *******************************************************
4030 CLOSE #1
4040 LPRINT : LPRINT "End of Report"
4050 CLS
4060 LOCATE 12, 34 : PRINT "Job Complete"
4070 RETURN
4080 ' ***************** End of Program ******************

RUN
```

Discussion of the Program Solution

In Program 8.5, line 2030 assigns TD$ today's date. Line 2040 rearranges the substrings of TD$ in the format yymmdd and assigns the result to TODAY$. Line 3050 rearranges the substrings of the customer payment date into the same format. Line 3060 compares today's date to the customer payment date. If TODAY$ is greater than or equal to ADJ.DATE$, then MESSAGE$ is set equal to Date OK. If TODAY$ is less than ADJ.DATE$, then the payment date is a future date and MESSAGE$ is set equal to Date NOT OK. Pay particular attention to lines 2040 and 3050. Rearranging substrings is a common characteristic of programs that validate dates.

The report that Program 8.5 generates is shown in Figure 8.1. Note that the payment

```
Validating Payment Dates For 06-22-1991
----------------------------------------


Customer                 Payment
Number     Payment       Date         Comment
--------   -------       -------      -------
31245381    101.55       09-15-92     Date NOT OK
46371230     95.25       06-12-91     Date OK
71209824     25.00       06-24-91     Date NOT OK
96012567     38.00       05-30-91     Date OK


End of Report
```

FIGURE 8.1
The report generated by Program 8.5.

dates are formatted on the basis of the descriptor field in line 2150 and the use of the string functions in line 3070.

Setting the Time and Date — The DATE$ and TIME$ Statements

Whereas the special variables DATE$ and TIME$ are equal to the system's current date and time, the DATE$ and TIME$ statements allow you to set the system's date and time. These two statements override the date and time entered during start-up procedures. The general forms for the DATE$ and TIME$ statements are given in Tables 8.11 and 8.12.

_____TABLE 8.11 The DATE$ Statement_____

General Form:	DATE$ = *string expression*
	where **string expression** is one of the following forms:
	    mm-dd-yy
	    mm-dd-yyyy
	    mm/dd/yy
	    mm/dd/yyyy

Purpose:	*To set the system date.*
Examples:	300 DATE$ = "07-06-90" 400 DATE$ = "7/6/1990" 500 DATE$ = "06-22-2005" 600 DATE$ = "1/25/91" 700 DATE$ = CUR.DATE$
Note:	*The year must be in the range 1980 to 2099. If you enter a two-digit year, then the PC assumes 19yy. You may enter one digit for the month or day. If only one digit is entered, then the PC assumes a leading zero.*

_____TABLE 8.12 The TIME$ Statement_____

General Form:	TIME$ = *string expression* where **string expression** is one of the following forms:	
	hh	Set the hour (range 0 to 23).
	hh:mm	Set the hour and minutes (minute range 0 to 59).
	hh:mm:ss	Set the hour, minute, and second (second range 0 to 59).
Purpose:	*To set the system time.*	
Examples:	800 TIME$ = "10" 850 TIME$ = "1:23" 900 TIME$ = "20:00:23" 950 TIME$ = "0:25" 975 TIME$ = CUR.TIME$	
Note:	*You may enter one digit for the hour, minute, or second. If one digit is entered, then the PC assumes a leading zero.*	

If you assign values that are out of the designated ranges described in Tables 8.11 and 8.12, the PC will display the following diagnostic message:

```
Illegal function call
```

If the expression assigned to the DATE$ or TIME$ statements is not a valid string, the PC displays the following diagnostic message:

```
Type mismatch
```

Accepting String Data — LINE INPUT Statement, INKEY$ Variable, and INPUT$ Function

The LINE INPUT statement accepts a line entered from the keyboard as a string value and assigns it to a string variable. The LINE INPUT statement ignores the usual delimiters, namely, the quotation mark and the comma. That is, if the string value

```
She said, "Terminate the program!"
```

is entered in response to the statement

```
300 LINE INPUT "What did she say? "; STATE$
```

then STATE$ is assigned the entire string of characters

```
She said, "Terminate the program!"
```

including the comma and the quotation marks.

The general form of the LINE INPUT statement is shown in Table 8.13.

_____**TABLE 8.13** The LINE INPUT Statement_____

General Form:	LINE INPUT *string variable* *or* LINE INPUT *"input prompt message"; string variable* *or* LINE INPUT #n, *string variable*
Purpose:	*Provides for the assignment to a string variable of an entire line (up to 255 characters), including commas and quotation marks, entered from an external source, such as the keyboard or auxiliary storage.*
Examples:	**Data from an**
	LINE INPUT Statement **External Source**
	100 LINE INPUT CUS.REC$ "123","Adams Joe",44,0520
	200 LINE INPUT "What? "; STAT$ "Don't do it", Amanda Said
	300 LINE INPUT "Weight ===> "; WGT$ 126.5 lbs.
	400 LINE INPUT #2, LIN$ "John Smith", 46, "3", 12
Note:	*A question mark is not displayed as part of the prompt unless it is included in the input prompt message.*

The major differences between the LINE INPUT statement and the INPUT statement are as follows:

1. The LINE INPUT statement does not automatically prompt the user with the question mark and trailing space, as the INPUT statement does.
2. The LINE INPUT statement can accept data for only one string variable. The INPUT statement can have more than one variable in the list, and they may be either numeric or string.
3. The LINE INPUT statement cannot accept leading or trailing spaces. The INPUT statement can accept leading or trailing spaces provided quotation marks are used to surround the string.

When executed, an INPUT or LINE INPUT statement instructs the PC to suspend execution of the program until the Enter key is pressed. That is, with these two statements, we must always signal the PC by pressing the Enter key when we have finished entering the requested data. The special variable INKEY$ and the INPUT$ function do not require that the Enter key be pressed for the PC to accept input.

The special variable INKEY$ *does not* suspend execution of the program; instead, it checks the keyboard to determine whether a character is pending — that is, whether a key was recently pressed. The following statement,

```
100 PENDING$ = INKEY$
```

assigns PENDING$ the character that corresponds to the last key pressed. If no character is pending, then INKEY$ assigns the null string to PENDING$.

Consider the following example, in which the INKEY$ function is used to control a looping process. The values of NUM and NUM MOD 7 are displayed until the user presses a key or until an overflow condition occurs.

```
500 NUM = 1
510 WHILE INKEY$ = ""
520    PRINT NUM, NUM MOD 7
530    NUM = NUM + 1
540 WEND
```

In this partial program, the INKEY$ function is used in the WHILE statement to control the loop. As long as there is no character pending from the keyboard, the PC continues to execute the loop.

The special variable INKEY$ is useful for applications that require that a program not be interrupted and yet accept responses from the keyboard. This method of processing is essential for video game programs, like Space Invaders or Missile Command. In these games, objects on the monitor are in constant motion, and at the same time the games must check for user input, like the firing of a phaser or torpedo. Later in this chapter, we will study additional statements that can be used to trap similar events.

The INPUT$(N) function is even more sophisticated than the variable INKEY$, because it accepts N characters from the keyboard. However, unlike INKEY$, INPUT$ suspends execution of the program until the user has pressed N number of keys. For example, the statement

```
300 CHAR$ = INPUT$(1)
```

causes the PC to suspend execution of the program and wait until a key is pressed.

The characters entered in response to the INPUT$ function are not displayed on the screen. To display the response, the statement that contains the function should be followed with a PRINT statement. For example,

```
400 CHAR$ = INPUT$(5)
410 PRINT CHAR$
```

displays the five characters entered by the user.

Table 8.14 illustrates examples of the special variable INKEY$ and the INPUT$ function.

TABLE 8.14 Examples of the Special Variables INKEY$ and the INPUT Function

THE STATEMENT	KEYBOARD RESPONSE	RESULTS IN
100 PENDING$ = INKEY$	J	PENDING$ = J
200 KEYBOARD$ = INKEY$	*No Response*	KEYBOARD$ = *null char.*
300 CHAR$ = INPUT$(4)	A1B2	CHAR$ = A1B2
400 ONE.CHAR$ = INPUT$(1)	3	ONE.CHAR$ = 3

A common use of the INPUT$ function is to suspend the execution of a program at the conclusion of a task so that the information on the screen may be read before it disappears.

For example, if a program is displaying a long list of items, you may want to suspend execution of the program after every 20 or so lines are displayed. The message

```
Press any key to continue...
```

is often used in this context. The INPUT$ simplifies the entry by not requiring that the Enter key be pressed. The following partial program shows how to incorporate this technique into a BASIC program.

```
1000 PRINT "Press any key to continue..."
1010 CHAR$ = INPUT$(1)
```

Line 1000 displays the message, and line 1010 suspends execution of the program. Execution continues when the user presses any key on the keyboard except Ctrl-Break.

8.3

NUMERIC FUNCTIONS

The numeric functions that are part of MS BASIC are listed in Table 8.15. In the discussion that follows, several examples of each numeric function are presented.

TABLE 8.15 MS BASIC Numeric Functions

FUNCTION	FUNCTION VALUE
ABS(N)	*Returns the absolute value of the argument N.*
ATN(N)	*Returns the angle in radians whose tangent is the value of the argument N.*
COS(N)	*Returns the cosine of the argument N where N is in radians.*
EXP(N)	*Returns e(2.718281...) raised to the argument N.*
FIX(N)	*Returns the value of N truncated to an integer.*
FRE(N)	*Returns the number of unused bytes within BASIC's data space.*
INT(N)	*Returns the largest integer that is less than or equal to the argument N.*
LOG(N)	*Returns the natural log of the argument N where N is greater than 0.*
POS(N)	*Returns the current cursor column position.*
RND	*Returns a random number between 0 (inclusive) and 1 (exclusive).*
SCREEN(R, C)	*Returns the ASCII code for the character at the specified row (R) and column (C) on the screen.*
SGN(N)	*Returns the sign of the argument N: –1 if the argument N is less than 0; 0 if the argument N is equal to 0; or + 1 if the argument N is greater than 0.*
SIN(N)	*Returns the sine of the argument N where N is in radians.*
SQR(N)	*Returns the square root of the positive argument N.*
TAN(N)	*Returns the tangent of the argument N where N is in radians.*
TIMER	*Returns a value equal to the number of seconds elapsed since midnight.*

Arithmetic Functions — ABS, FIX, INT, and SGN

The functions classified as **arithmetic** include ABS (absolute value), FIX(fixed integer), INT(integer), and SGN(sign).

The ABS function takes any numeric expression and returns its positive value. For example, if N is equal to –4, then ABS(N) is equal to 4. Additional examples of the ABS function are shown in Table 8.16 on the following page.

The FIX(N) function returns the integer portion of the argument N. When the argument is positive, the FIX function is identical to the INT function. For example, if N is equal to 13.45, then FIX(N) returns 13. However, when the argument is negative, the two functions return a different result. For example, if N is equal to –4.45, then FIX(N) returns –4 and INT(N) returns –5. The INT function returns an integer that is less than or equal to the argument. Additional examples of the FIX and INT functions are shown in Table 8.16.

The SGN(N) function returns a value of + 1 if the argument N is positive, 0 if the argument is 0, and –1 if the argument N is negative. Table 8.16 shows examples of the SGN function.

_____**TABLE 8.16** Examples of the ABS, FIX, INT, and SGN Functions_____

VALUE OF VARIABLE	THE STATEMENT	RESULTS IN
NUM = -3	100 P = ABS(NUM)	P = 3
CNT = 4.5	200 C = ABS(CNT)	C = 4.5
C = 4, D = -6	300 A = C + ABS(D)	A = 10
G = 25.567	400 F = FIX(G)	F = 25
G = -25.567	500 F = FIX(G)	F = -25
G = -25.567	600 I = INT(G)	I = -26
G = -25.567	700 K = INT(ABS(G))	K = 25
D = 4	800 E = SGN(D)	E = 1
P = -5	900 F = 5 + SGN(P)	F = 4

A Generaliz Procedure for Rounding and Truncation

Although MS BASIC allows for automatic rounding through the use of the PRINT USING statement, it is sometimes more convenient for the programmer to control the process of rounding and truncation. The FIX and SGN functions may be used to write generalized expressions for rounding or truncating a number to any decimal place. The generalized expression for rounding numbers is:

FIX(N * 10 ^ E + SGN(N) * .5) / 10 ^ E

and for truncating numbers:

FIX(N * 10 ^ E) / 10 ^ E

where N is the value to be rounded, and
E is the number of decimal places desired

To determine what value should be assigned to E, begin counting from the decimal point as illustrated below.

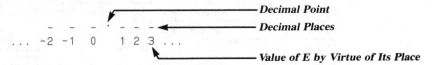

For example, if you wish to round a result N to the nearest hundredths place, you assign E a value of 2. The generalized expression for rounding to the nearest hundredths place becomes:

FIX(N * 10 ^ 2 + SGN(N) * .5) / 10 ^ 2

or:

FIX(N * 100 + SGN(N) * .5) / 100

For truncating a result N to the nearest hundredths place, the generalized expression becomes:

FIX(N * 10 ^ 2) / 10 ^ 2

or:

FIX(N * 100) / 100

See BASIC Programming Problem 3 at the end of this chapter for an example of the use of these generalized expressions for rounding and truncating values.

Exponential Functions — SQR, EXP, and LOG

The functions classified as **exponential** include the SQR (square root), EXP (exponential), and LOG (logarithmic).

The SQR(N) function computes the square root of the positive argument N. Table 8.17 shows several examples of computing the square root of a number.

_____TABLE 8.17_ Examples of the SQR Function_____

VALUE OF VARIABLE	THE STATEMENT	RESULTS IN
	`100 ROOT = SQR(9)`	`ROOT = 3`
`VALUE = 0`	`200 R1 = SQR(VALUE)`	`R1 = 0`
`CUBE = 625`	`300 R2 = SQR(SQR(CUBE))`	`R2 = 5`
`SUB(1) = 1.15129`	`400 R3 = SQR(SUB(1))`	`SUB = 1.072982`
`X = 3, Y = 4`	`500 HYP = SQR(X ^ 2 + Y ^ 2)`	`HYP = 5`
`NEG = -49`	`600 POSI = SQR(ABS(NEG))`	`POSI = 7`
`NUM = -25`	`700 ROOT = SQR(NUM)`	`Illegal Function Call`

The symbol **e** in mathematics represents 2.718281..., where the three dots show that the fractional part of the constant is not a repeating sequence of digits. In MS BASIC, the keyword EXP is used to represent this constant, which is raised to the power given as the argument in parentheses following the function name. The EXP function can be used, for example, to determine the value of $e^{1.14473}$. The following statement,

    210 PI = EXP(1.14473)

results in the variable PI being assigned a value of 3.141593, which is a close approximation of π. If the value of the argument for the EXP function exceeds 88.02968, then an overflow condition occurs.

The natural log ($\log_e$ or ln) of a number can be determined by using the LOG function. For example, the value of X in the equation

$$e^x = 3.141593$$

can be determined by using the following statement:

    310 X = LOG(3.141593)

The resulting value of X is 1.14473 and, therefore,

$$e^{1.14473} = 3.141593$$

This function can also be used to determine the logarithm to the base 10 by multiplying the LOG function by 0.434295. For example, in the statement

    410 LOG10 = 0.434295 * LOG(3)

LOG10 is assigned the value 0.4771219, the base 10 logarithm of 3.

Of the three exponential functions, programmers use the square root function more often than the exponential or logarithmic. However, the latter two functions are essential in some advanced applications. The following Programming Case Study is an example of the use of the LOG function.

Programming Case Study 17: *Determining the Time It Takes to Double an Investment*

The formula for computing the amount of an investment compounded annually for a given number of years is $A = P(1 + J)^N$ where A is the total amount, P is the initial investment, J is the annual rate of interest, and N is the number of years.

This formula can be rewritten to solve for the number of years N:

$$N = \frac{\log \frac{A}{P}}{\log(1 + J)}$$

If the number of years it takes to double an investment is to be determined, then the amount A is equal to twice the investment P, or A = 2P. The formula for determining the number of years to double an investment can further be simplified to the following:

$$N = \frac{\log 2}{\log(1 + J)}$$

The ensuing problem uses the LOG function to compute the number of years it takes to double an investment.

Problem: The WESAVU National Bank requests that a program be written to display a table of annual interest rates and the corresponding years it will take to double an investment compounded annually for integer interests rates from 8 through 18, inclusive. Display the number of years to the nearest tenths place.

Following are an analysis of the problem; a program solution; and a discussion of the program solution.

Program Tasks   1. Initialization

    a. Clear the screen.
    b. Call the Print Report and Column Headings Module.

2. Generate Table

    a. Set NUMERATOR equal to LOG(2).
    b. Use a For loop to generate the annual interest rates (INTEREST) from 8 through 18. Within the loop perform the following tasks:
        (1) Determine the number of years (TIME) it takes to double an investment at INTEREST percent, using the statement:

        TIME = NUMERATOR / LOG(1 + INTEREST / 100).

        (2) Display the interest rate (INTEREST) and the number of years it takes to double an investment (TIME) to the nearest tenths place.

3. Wrap-up — display an end-of-job message.

Program Solution   The following program corresponds to the preceding tasks.

PROGRAM 8.6

```
1000 ' Program 8.6
1010 ' Determining the Time to Double an Investment
1020 ' *********************************************
1030 ' *              Main Module                  *
1040 ' *********************************************
1050 GOSUB 2000   ' Call Initialization
1060 GOSUB 3000   ' Call Generate Table
1070 GOSUB 4000   ' Call Wrap-up
1080 END
2000 ' *********************************************
2010 ' *              Initialization               *
2020 ' *********************************************
2030 CLS : KEY OFF   ' Clear Screen
2040 GOSUB 2200      ' Call Print Report and Column Headings
2050 RETURN
2060 '
```

(continued)

```
2200 ' *********************************************
2210 ' *      Print Report and Column Headings    *
2220 ' *********************************************
2230 PRINT     "Doubling an Investment"
2240 PRINT     "----------------------"
2250 PRINT
2260 PRINT     "Interest    Number"
2270 PRINT     "Rate in %   of Years"
2280 PRINT     "---------   --------"
2290 FORMAT$ = "    ##          ##.#"
2300 RETURN
2310 '
3000 ' *********************************************
3010 ' *                Generate Table            *
3020 ' *********************************************
3030 NUMERATOR = LOG(2)
3040 FOR INTEREST = 8 TO 18
3050    TIME = NUMERATOR / LOG(1 + INTEREST / 100)
3060    PRINT USING FORMAT$; INTEREST, TIME
3070 NEXT INTEREST
3080 RETURN
3090 '
4000 ' *********************************************
4010 ' *                  Wrap-up                 *
4020 ' *********************************************
4030 PRINT : PRINT "End of Report"
4040 RETURN
4050 ' ************* End of Program *************

RUN

Doubling an Investment
----------------------

Interest    Number
Rate in %   of Years
---------   --------
    8         9.0
    9         8.0
   10         7.3
   11         6.6
   12         6.1
   13         5.7
   14         5.3
   15         5.0
   16         4.7
   17         4.4
   18         4.2

End of Report
```

Discussion of the Program Solution

With slight modifications to the values in the FOR statement in Program 8.6, the number of years it takes to double an investment that is compounded annually can be determined for a variety of interest rates. The argument in the first reference to the LOG function in line 3030 may be changed to other numbers, like 3 or 4, to determine how long it takes to triple or quadruple an investment that is compounded annually. See BASIC Programming Problem 3 at the end of this chapter to determine the number of years it takes to double an investment that is compounded quarterly.

> Load Program 8.6 (PRG8-6) from the Student Diskette. Change the argument of the LOG function in line 3030 to 10 so that the PC determines the number of years it takes to increase an investment tenfold at the given interest rates.

Trigonometric Functions — SIN, COS, TAN, and ATN

In MS BASIC, the SIN, COS, and TAN functions can be used to determine the sine, cosine, and tangent of the angle X expressed in radians. For these functions to work correctly, the angle X *must* be expressed in radians. Since angles are usually expressed in degrees, the following statements relating angles and radians should prove helpful:

$$1 \text{ radian} = 180 / \pi \text{ degrees} = 180 / 3.141593 \text{ degrees}$$
$$1 \text{ degree} = \pi / 180 \text{ radians} = 3.141593 / 180 \text{ radians}$$

When using these three functions, remember that if the argument is in units of degrees, it must first be multiplied by 3.141593 / 180 in order to convert it into units of radians before the function can evaluate it. In mathematics, if the equation X = sin 30° is evaluated, then X = 0.5. Evaluating the same equation in MS BASIC requires the following:

```
510 RADS = 30 * 3.141593 / 180
520 X = SIN(RADS)
```

or:

```
510 X = SIN(30 * 3.141593 / 180)
```

MS BASIC does not have corresponding functions for the cosecant, the secant and the cotangent. These three trigonometric functions must be evaluated by combinations of the SIN, COS, and TAN functions. Table 8.18 illustrates the combinations.

TABLE 8.18 Determining the Cosecant, Secant and Cotangent

TO FIND THE	USE
Cosecant	1 / SIN(X)
Secant	1 / COS(X)
Cotangent	1 / TAN(X)

The fourth trigonometric function that is available in MS BASIC is the arctangent. The ATN function returns a value that is the angle (in units of radians) that corresponds to the argument. For example,

```
610 ANGLE = ATN(1)
```

results in ANGLE being assigned the value of 0.7853982 radians. Multiplying this number by 180/3.141593 yields an angle of 45°.

Utility Functions — FRE, POS, SCREEN, and the Special Variable CSRLIN

When the argument is any numeric value, the FRE function returns the number of unused bytes within **BASIC's data space**. BASIC's data space is defined as that part of main storage which is allocated to MS BASIC by the PC, less the reserved portion of the interpreter work area. The following statement

```
700 BYTES = FRE(0)
```

assigns the variable BYTES the amount of available data space.

When the argument is any string, the function causes the PC to collect and compress any fragmented string data that is stored in BASIC's data space before returning the number of free bytes. The end result is more data space available to a program. For example, the statement

```
710 FREE.SPACE = FRE("X")
```

performs housekeeping on BASIC'S data space and then assigns FREE.SPACE the number of free bytes.

This function can be useful with programs that manipulate large amounts of string data and terminate owing to a lack of main storage. Note that the argument within parentheses following the keyword FRE is required even though it is not used.

The POS function returns the current column position of the cursor relative to the left edge of the display screen. The value returned is an integer in the range 1 to 40 or 1 to 80, depending on the current screen-width setting. For example,

```
800 WIDTH 80
810 PRINT TAB(15);
820 PRINT POS(0)
```

causes the PC to display the value 15. The value of the argument plays no role in the value returned by the POS function.

The special variable CSRLIN is equal to the current row (line) the cursor is on relative to the top of the display screen. The value of CSRLIN varies in the range 1 to 25. For example, the following statement entered in the immediate mode,

```
LOCATE 5, 6 : PRINT CSRLIN
 5
```

displays the current line position.

The special variable CSRLIN and the POS function are used in applications where a value must be displayed at a position on the screen other than the current one, followed by the return of the cursor to the former position. Consider the following partial program.

```
820 ROW = CSRLIN
830 COL = POS(0)
840 LOCATE 1, 20 : PRINT "Aim the arrow carefully"
850 LOCATE ROW, COL
```

Line 820 assigns ROW the line the cursor is on. Line 830 assigns COL the column the cursor is in. Line 840 moves the cursor to column 20 of line 1 and displays the message. Line 850 returns the cursor to its former position on the screen.

The SCREEN function allows you to determine what character is currently displayed at the intersection of a row and a column on the screen. The function returns the ASCII code for the character found at the specified location. For example, the following partial program assigns CHAR the value 66, since that is the ASCII code for the character B.

```
900 WIDTH 80
910 LOCATE 15, 16 : PRINT "B"
920 CHAR = SCREEN(15, 16)
```

This function may also be used to return the color attribute at the intersection of the specified row and column. See the MS BASIC manual for more details.

Performance Testing — The TIMER Function

The TIMER function returns a single-precision numeric value that represents the number of seconds that have elapsed since midnight. The For loop on the top of the following page illustrates values returned by the TIMER function.

Line 100 resets the system time to 12:00 noon (43,200 seconds past midnight). In the For loop, line 120 displays both the system time and the number of seconds elapsed since midnight. A close look at the results shows that, on the average, it takes 0.11 seconds to make a pass on the For loop defined by lines 110 through 130.

```
100 TIME$ = "12:00:00"
110 FOR I = 1 TO 10
120     PRINT "Time = "; TIME$, "Timer ="; TIMER
130 NEXT I

RUN
```

```
Time = 12:00:00          Timer = 43200.1
Time = 12:00:00          Timer = 43200.21
Time = 12:00:00          Timer = 43200.32
Time = 12:00:00          Timer = 43200.43
Time = 12:00:00          Timer = 43200.54
Time = 12:00:01          Timer = 43200.6
Time = 12:00:01          Timer = 43200.71
Time = 12:00:01          Timer = 43200.82
Time = 12:00:01          Timer = 43200.93
Time = 12:00:01          Timer = 43201.04
```

The time it takes to make a pass on a given loop will vary slightly between runs. For this reason, when **benchmarking** an algorithm, you should take the average duration of time it takes to accomplish the same task over many runs of the program under the same conditions. Benchmarking is the activity of comparing the performance of algorithms or applications that are running under similar conditions on one or more computer systems.

In chapter 6, we made the claim that a For loop uses less main storage and executes faster than a While loop. This claim is supported through the use of the TIMER and FRE functions in Programs 8.7 and 8.8. Both programs, which were executed on an IBM PC with 644K bytes of main storage, display the sum of the first 250 integers.

PROGRAM 8.7

```
100 ' Program 8.7
110 ' Timing a While Loop
120 ' *****************
130 CLS : KEY OFF  ' Clear Screen
140 SUM   = 0
145 COUNT = 1
150 '
160 START = TIMER
170 WHILE COUNT <= 250
180    SUM   = SUM + COUNT
185    COUNT = COUNT + 1
190 WEND
200 FINISH = TIMER
210 '
220 DURATION = FINISH - START
230 PRINT "While loop time ==>";
240 PRINT DURATION; "seconds"
250 PRINT : PRINT "Sum ==>"; SUM
260 PRINT : PRINT "Bytes free ==>";
270 PRINT FRE(0)
280 END

RUN

While loop time ==> 2.199219 seconds

Sum ==> 31375

Bytes free ==> 60420
```

PROGRAM 8.8

```
100 ' Program 8.8
110 ' Timing a For Loop
120 ' *****************
130 CLS : KEY OFF  ' Clear Screen
140 SUM   = 0
150 '
160 START = TIMER
170 FOR COUNT = 1 TO 250
180    SUM = SUM + COUNT
190 NEXT COUNT
200 FINISH = TIMER
210 '
220 DURATION = FINISH - START
230 PRINT "For loop time ==>";
240 PRINT DURATION; "seconds"
250 PRINT : PRINT "Sum ==>"; SUM
260 PRINT : PRINT "Bytes free ==>";
270 PRINT FRE(0)
280 END

RUN

For loop time ==> 1.160156 seconds

Sum ==> 31375

Bytes free ==> 60461
```

The duration of time it takes for the IBM PC to execute the While loop is 2.199219 seconds. With the For loop in Program 8.8, the duration of time is 1.160156 seconds. In other words, the For loop executes about twice as fast as the While loop.

The amount of main storage that is available to BASIC following the execution of Program 8.7 is 60,420 bytes, versus 60,461 bytes for Program 8.8, a difference of 41 bytes. These two programs are nearly identical; the only significant difference is that Program 8.7 requires two extra lines — line 145 for initialization and line 185 for incrementation.

In Programs 8.7 and 8.8, line 160 sets the variable START to the value returned by the TIMER function. At the conclusion of each loop, the variable FINISH is set equal to TIMER. In both programs, line 220 assigns DURATION the time required to execute the particular loop.

In chapter 3, we also made the claim that integer arithmetic is faster than single-precision arithmetic. Consider Program 8.9, which is nearly identical to Program 8.8 except that the For loop is in integer mode.

PROGRAM 8.9

```
100 ' Program 8.9
110 ' Timing a For Loop
120 ' ****************
130 CLS : KEY OFF  ' Clear Screen
140 SUM%  = 0
150 '
160 START = TIMER
170 FOR COUNT% = 1 TO 250
180    SUM% = SUM% + COUNT%
190 NEXT COUNT%
200 FINISH = TIMER
210 '
220 DURATION = FINISH - START
230 PRINT "For loop time ==>";
240 PRINT DURATION; "seconds"
250 PRINT : PRINT "Sum ==>"; SUM%
260 PRINT : PRINT "Bytes free ==>";
270 PRINT FRE(0)
280 END

RUN

For loop time ==> .9296875 seconds

Sum ==> 31375

Bytes free ==> 60457
```

The duration of time it takes the IBM PC to execute the For loop in Program 8.8 is 1.160156 seconds; in Program 8.9, it is 0.9296875 seconds. Hence, if you desire to speed up the execution of For loops in your program, you may want to declare the loop variable as type integer.

Load Program 8.7 (PRG8-7) from the Student Diskette. Change the value that COUNT is compared to in line 170 from 250 to 1, 10, 100, and 1000. Execute the program for each new value and write down the duration of time it takes the PC to execute the loop.

(continued)

> *TRY IT YOURSELF (continued)*
>
> Load Program 8.8 (PRG8-8) from the Student Diskette. Change the limit value in line 170 to 1, 10, 100, and 1000, then execute the program for each new value and compare the results to those obtained earlier by the modified Program 8.7.
>
> Reload Program 8.7 (PRG8-7). Enter the following line to reset the system time:
>
>   135 TIME$ = "23:59:58"
>
> Execute the program. Can you explain why the program displayed a negative time?

Random Number Function and the RANDOMIZE Statement

The RND function is important to the programmer who is involved in the development of programs that simulate situations described by a random process. The owners of a shopping mall, for example, might want a program written to simulate the number of cars that would enter their parking lots during a particular period of the day. Or, the manager of a grocery store might want a program to model unpredictable values that represented people standing in line waiting to check out. The unpredictable values could be supplied by the RND function. Actually, the random numbers generated by the PC are provided by a repeatable process, and for this reason they are often called **pseudo-random numbers**.

The RND function returns an unpredictable decimal fraction number between 0 (inclusive) and 1 (exclusive). Each time the function is referenced, any number between 0 and <1 has an equal probability of being returned by the function. For example, the statement

    200 NUM = RND

assigns NUM a random number. Program 8.10 illustrates the generation of five random numbers.

PROGRAM 8.10

```
100 ' Program 8.10
110 ' Generating Random Numbers
120 ' ************************
130 FOR I = 1 TO 5
140     PRINT RND,
150 NEXT I
160 END
RUN
 .7151002      .683111      .4821425      .9992938      .6465093
```

Each time the RND function is referenced in line 140 of the loop, a random number between 0 and <1 is displayed.

The INT (or FIX) and RND functions can be combined to create random digits over a specified range. The following expression allows for the generation of random digits over the range $C \leq n \leq D$:

    INT((D - C + 1) * RND + C)

For example, to generate random digits over the range 1 to 10, inclusive, change line 140 in Program 8.10 to:

```
140 PRINT INT((10 - 1 + 1) * RND + 1)
```

or:

```
140 PRINT INT(10 * RND + 1)
```

Program 8.11, Version A, simulates tossing a coin 20 times. The expression INT (2 * RND) returns a zero (heads) or a one (tails). The expression in line 160 returned 13 zeros (heads) and 7 ones (tails).

PROGRAM 8.11   Version A

```
100 ' Program 8.11, Version A
110 ' Simulation of Coin Tossing
120 ' 0 is a Head and 1 is a Tail
130 ' The Coin is Tossed 20 Times
140 ' *************************
150 FOR I = 1 TO 20
160    PRINT INT(2 * RND);
170 NEXT I
180 END

RUN

1 0 1 0 0 0 1 1 0 1 0 0 0 0 0 1 0 0 1 0 0
```

Program 8.11, Version A, can be enhanced to allow a user to enter the number of simulated coin tosses desired and to display the total number of heads and tails. This is illustrated in Program 8.11, Version B.

PROGRAM 8.11   Version B

```
100 ' Program 8.11, Version B
110 ' Simulation of Coin Tossing
120 ' 0 is a Head and 1 is a Tail
130 ' User Enters Number of Times Coin Is Tossed
140 ' *******************************************
145 CLS : KEY OFF   ' Clear Screen
150 HEAD = 0
160 TAIL = 0
170 INPUT "How many tosses ===> ", TOSSES
180 FOR NUM = 1 TO TOSSES
190    RANDOM = INT(2 * RND)
200    IF RANDOM = 0
            THEN HEAD = HEAD + 1
            ELSE TAIL = TAIL + 1
210 NEXT NUM
220 PRINT "Number of Heads ===>"; HEAD
230 PRINT "Number of Tails ===>"; TAIL
240 END

RUN

How many tosses ===> 500
Number of Heads ===> 259
Number of Tails ===> 241
```

TRY IT YOURSELF

Load Program 8.11, Version B (PRG8-11B), from the Student Diskette. Execute the program for the following number of tosses: 50, 100, 1000.

When executed, Program 8.11, Version B, requests that the user enter the number of coin tosses to be simulated. Line 200 increments HEAD (head counter) or TAIL (tail counter) by 1, depending upon the value assigned to RANDOM. At the conclusion of the For loop, lines 220 and 230 display the total number of heads and total number of tails. As illustrated by the results of Program 8.11, Version B, out of 500 simulated coin tosses, 259 were heads and 241 were tails.

Every time Program 8.11, Version B, is executed, it will display the same results, because the PC generates random numbers from a starting value called the **seed**. Unless the seed is changed, the PC continues to generate the same set of random numbers in the same sequence each time the same program is executed. Once a program containing the RND function is ready for production, the RANDOMIZE statement can be used to instruct the PC to generate random numbers from a different seed each time the program is executed. The general form of the RANDOMIZE statement is shown in Table 8.19.

_____TABLE 8.19 The RANDOMIZE Statement_____

General Form:	RANDOMIZE _or_ RANDOMIZE _numeric expression_
Purpose:	_To supply a new seed for the generation of random numbers by the_ RND _function._
Example:	100 RANDOMIZE 200 RANDOMIZE TIMER 300 RANDOMIZE 396.5 400 RANDOMIZE VAL(RIGHT$(TIME$,2))
Note:	_If you do not include a parameter following the keyword_ RANDOMIZE, _then the PC suspends execution of the program and requests a value between –32768 and 32767. You may also reseed the random-number generator by using a negative argument with the_ RND _function, as in_ RND(-1). _This method is not used in this book._

The rule for the execution of the RANDOMIZE statement in a program is as follows:

> **_RANDOMIZE Rule 1:_** The RANDOMIZE statement must be executed prior to any reference to the RND function.

Program 8.12 simulates a popular guessing game, in which the player attempts to guess a number between 1 and 100. The RANDOMIZE statement is included so that the RND function will return a new set of random numbers each time the program is executed.

PROGRAM 8.12

```
1000 ' Program 8.12
1010 ' Guess a Number Between 1 and 100
1020 ' ******************************************
1030 ' *            Main Module                 *
1040 ' ******************************************
1050 GOSUB 2000   ' Call Initialization
1060 GOSUB 3000   ' Call Guess a Number
1070 GOSUB 4000   ' Call Wrap-up
1080 END
1090 '
```

(continued)

```
2000 ' *****************************************
2010 ' *              Initialization          *
2020 ' *****************************************
2030 CLS : KEY OFF  ' Clear Screen
2040 RANDOMIZE TIMER
2050 RANDOM = INT(100 * RND + 1)
2060 CNT = 1
2070 PRINT "***********************************"
2080 PRINT "*                                 *"
2090 PRINT "* Guess a number between 1 and 100. *"
2100 PRINT "* I will tell you if your guess is  *"
2110 PRINT "* too high or too low.             *"
2120 PRINT "*                                 *"
2130 PRINT "***********************************"
2140 PRINT
2150 RETURN
2160 '
3000 ' *****************************************
3010 ' *              Guess a Number          *
3020 ' *****************************************
3030 INPUT "Guess a number ====> ", GUESS
3040 GUESS.COUNT = 1
3050 WHILE GUESS <> RANDOM
3060    IF GUESS > RANDOM
           THEN PRINT "Too High"
           ELSE PRINT "Too Low"
3070    INPUT "Guess a number ====> ", GUESS
3080    GUESS.COUNT = GUESS.COUNT + 1
3090 WEND
3100 RETURN
3110 '
4000 ' *****************************************
4010 ' *              Wrap-up                 *
4020 ' *****************************************
4030 PRINT : PRINT "Your guess is correct."
4040 PRINT "It took you"; GUESS.COUNT; "guesses."
4050 ' *********** End of Program **************

RUN

***********************************
*                                 *
* Guess a number between 1 and 100. *
* I will tell you if your guess is  *
* too high or too low.             *
*                                 *
***********************************

Guess a number ====> 50
Too Low
Guess a number ====> 75
Too Low
Guess a number ====> 87
Too Low
Guess a number ====> 95
Too High
Guess a number ====> 93
Too Low
Guess a number ====> 94

Your guess is correct.
It took you 6 guesses.
```

When the RUN command is issued for Program 8.12, line 2040 in the Initialization Module ensures that the program does not generate the same set of random numbers it generated the last time the program was executed. The seed is based on the value returned by the TIMER function. The chances of generating the same set of random numbers from one run of Program 8.12 to the next is very rare.

Line 2050 assigns RANDOM the number to be guessed (94). Lines 2070 through 2130 display the instructions for the game. Line 3030 in the Guess a Number Module accepts a guess (GUESS) from the user. Line 3040 sets the guess counter (GUESS.COUNT) to 1. If GUESS is equal to RANDOM in line 3050, the program terminates after 1 guess. If GUESS does not equal RANDOM, the PC executes the While loop and displays an appropriate message before requesting the next guess and incrementing GUESS.COUNT. When the user finally guesses the number, control passes to line 4000 and a message and the value of GUESS.COUNT are displayed.

TRY IT YOURSELF

Load Program 8.12 (PRG8-12) from the Student Diskette and try your luck at guessing a number between 1 and 100. If you get bored with the game, modify PRG8-12, lines 2050 and 2090, to guess a number between 1 and 1,000.

⊞ 8.4

USER-DEFINED FUNCTIONS

In addition to numeric and string functions, MS BASIC allows you to define new string or numeric functions that relate to a particular application. This type of function, known as a **user-defined function**, is written directly into the program as a one-line statement. MS BASIC recognizes a user-defined function by the keywords DEF FN (for "define function"), which are incorporated in the function statement just to the right of the line number. For example, the DEF FN statement

```
150 DEF FNY(X) = X * (X + 1) / 2
```

defines a function, $x(x + 1) / 2$, whose name is FNY. The parentheses following the name of the function surround a simple variable known as a **function parameter**. The expression to the right of the equal sign indicates the operations that are to be performed with the value of X when the function is referenced in such statements as LET, PRINT, ON-GOSUB, and IF. For example, either

```
200 RESULT = FNY(VALUE) + 5
```

or

```
210 PRINT FNY(PT / 3)
```

found in the same program with the previous line 150 will reference the FNY function.

Defining your own function reduces programming effort and makes your program "compact" and efficient. Instead of writing a common formula over and over again, you simply define it once as a function, give it a name, and then reference it by that name whenever you need it.

The DEF FN Statement

Table 8.20 (opposite) shows that the DEF FN statement permits the creation of user-defined functions. The name of the function follows DEF, and it must begin with the two letters FN, followed by a variable name that is consistent with the rules used for naming variables.

_____TABLE 8.20_ The DEF FN Statement_____

General Form:	DEF FN*x*(p_1, ..., p_n) = *expression* *where **x** is a simple variable that must agree in type with the expression, and p_1 through p_n are simple variables. A function may be defined with a null list of function parameters.*
Purpose:	*To define a function that is relevant to a particular application that can be referenced as frequently as needed in the program in which it is defined.*

Examples:	`100 DEF FNCUBE(Y, Z) = Y ^ 3 + Z ^ 3`
	`200 DEF FNPI = 3.141593`
	`300 DEF FNSUB$(STNG$, P, N) = MID$(STNG$, P, N)`
	`400 DEF FNRADIAN%(DEG) =  DEG * (FNPI / 180)`
	`500 DEF FNRANDOM(X) = INT(10 * RND)`
	`600 DEF FNVOL#(L#, W#, H#) = L# * W# * H#`

Note:	*A user-defined numeric function is declared integer type, single precison, or double precision on the basis of the following:*

Special Character Appended to Name	**Type**
Percent Sign (%)	*Integer*
Exclamation Point (!)	
or no special character	*Single precision*
Number Sign (#)	*Double precision*

The parameters in a user-defined function are sometimes called **dummy variables**, since they are assigned the values of the corresponding arguments when reference is made to the function. For example, the following partial program contains two user-defined functions. The first one, in line 200, rounds the value assigned to NUM to the nearest cent. The second one, in line 210, truncates the value assigned to NUM to the nearest cent.

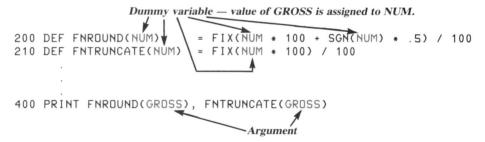

Dummy variable — value of GROSS is assigned to NUM.

```
200 DEF FNROUND(NUM)    = FIX(NUM * 100 + SGN(NUM) * .5) / 100
210 DEF FNTRUNCATE(NUM) = FIX(NUM * 100) / 100
    .
    .
    .
400 PRINT FNROUND(GROSS), FNTRUNCATE(GROSS)
```

Argument

The value of the variable GROSS in line 400 is used in place of the variable NUM in line 200 when the user-defined function FNROUND is called. The same applies when the user-defined function FNTRUNCATE is called by the second item in the list in line 400.

The dummy variable(s) assigned as the parameter in a DEF FN statement are local to the function definition. That is, they are distinct from any variable with the same name outside of the function definition. For example, consider the following partial program.

```
200 DEF FNSENIOR(CUS.SEN) = CUS.SEN * 7 / 0.82
    .
    .
    .
410 READ CUS.NUM$, CUS.SEN, CUS.BIRTH$
```

The dummy variable CUS.SEN in line 200 is not affected when the variables in line 410 are assigned values.

It is possible to define functions through the use of variables other than the parameters. For example, in the following partial program,

```
300 DEF FNC(A) = A * B * C
        .
        .
        .
510 READ A, B, C
```

the variables B and C in line 300 are the same as the variables B and C in line 510. That is, when line 510 is executed, the variables B and C in line 300 are assigned values. The dummy variable A in line 300, however, is not assigned a value when line 510 is executed.

A function with no parameters may be defined. Such functions may be used to define constants or expressions that do not require a variable, as shown below.

```
100 DEF FNPI#    = 3.14159265
200 DEF FNCENTI  = 2.54
300 DEF FNRANDOM = INT(10 * RND + 1)
```

Line 100 defines FNPI# equal to pi (π). Line 200 defines FNCENTI equal to the number of centimeters in an inch. Line 300 defines FNRANDOM so it returns a random number between 1 and 10.

The rules regarding DEF FN statements in a program are:

> **DEF FN Rule 1:** A user-defined function must be executed to define a function before a program can call that function.

> **DEF FN Rule 2:** The same function may be defined as often as required. The last definition executed is used.

> **DEF FN Rule 3:** A function definition cannot reference itself.

Referencing User-Defined Functions

User-defined functions are referenced in the same way that numeric functions are.

The following program determines the effective rates of interest for the nominal rates 5.5%, 6.5%, 7.5%, 8.5%, and 9.5%, using the following formula:

$$R = \left(1 + \frac{J}{C}\right)^{C} - 1$$

where R is the effective rate;
C is the number of conversions per year; and
J is the nominal rate.

The program calculates and displays the effective rates to two decimal places for nominal rates converted semiannually, quarterly, monthly, and daily (assume 365 days per year).

When the RUN command is issued for Program 8.13 (opposite), the display shown in Figure 8.2 is generated. The usefulness of the DEF statement is apparent in this program. Instead of your having to code the formula four times to determine the corresponding effective rates for a nominal rate, the DEF FN statement allows you to code the formula once (line 2030) and then reference it four times (line 3040). The constant used as the argument in each function reference in line 3040 is assigned to COMP in the DEF FN statement in line 2030.

PROGRAM 8.13

```
1000 ' Program 8.13
1010 ' Determining the Effective Rate of Interest
1020 ' Using a User-Defined Function
1030 ' ****************************************
1040 ' *              Main Module             *
1050 ' ****************************************
1060 GOSUB 2000   ' Call Initialization
1070 GOSUB 3000   ' Call Generate Table
1080 GOSUB 4000   ' Call Wrap-up
1090 END
1100 '
2000 ' ****************************************
2010 ' *            Initialization            *
2020 ' ****************************************
2030 DEF FNRATE(COMP) = 100 * ((1 + INTEREST / (COMP * 100)) ^ COMP - 1)
2040 CLS : KEY OFF    ' Clear Screen
2050 GOSUB 2200       ' Call Display Report and Column Headings
2060 RETURN
2070 '
2200 ' ****************************************
2210 ' *  Display Report and Column Headings  *
2220 ' ****************************************
2230 PRINT    "                   Effective Rates Compounded"
2240 PRINT    "              --------------------------------------"
2250 PRINT    "Nominal Rate  Semiannually  Quarterly  Monthly  Daily"
2260 PRINT    "------------  ------------  ---------  -------  -----"
2270 FORMAT$ = "   ##.##          ##.##        ##.##     ##.##   ##.##"
2280 RETURN
2290 '
3000 ' ****************************************
3010 ' *            Generate Table            *
3020 ' ****************************************
3030 FOR INTEREST = 5.5 TO 9.5
3040    PRINT USING FORMAT$; INTEREST; FNRATE(2), FNRATE(4), FNRATE(12),
                            FNRATE(365)
3050 NEXT INTEREST
3060 RETURN
3070 '
4000 ' ****************************************
4010 ' *               Wrap-up                *
4020 ' ****************************************
4030 PRINT : PRINT "End of Report"
4040 RETURN
4050 ' ************ End of Program **************
```

RUN

```
                   Effective Rates Compounded
              --------------------------------------
Nominal Rate  Semiannually  Quarterly  Monthly  Daily
------------  ------------  ---------  -------  -----
    5.50          5.58        5.61      5.64    5.65
    6.50          6.61        6.66      6.70    6.72
    7.50          7.64        7.71      7.76    7.79
    8.50          8.68        8.77      8.84    8.87
    9.50          9.73        9.84      9.92    9.96

End of Report
```

FIGURE 8.2
The display due to the execution of Program 8.13.

TRY IT YOURSELF

Load Program 8.13 (PRG8-13) from the Student Diskette. In the FOR statement in line 3030, change the initial value to 10.5 and the terminal value to 21.5, and add an increment value of 0.5. Execute the program and see what happens.

Programming Case Study 18: *Computer Simulation*

The following Programming Case Study incorporates the use of both the RND function and a user-defined function.

Problem: Beat the House Roller is a simple but popular dice game, in which the house roller throws a pair of dice. The customer then throws the dice, trying to roll a higher score. If the customer rolls a lower score or the same score as the house roller, the house wins. The bet is $5.00 for each game.

An accumulator is included to keep track of the customer's winnings. Also, the customer's winnings are displayed at the end of each roll. A means of temporarily stopping the game is included so the customer can decide if he or she desires to continue playing. Following are an analysis of the problem; a program solution; and a discussion of the program solution.

Program Tasks

1. Initialization

   a. Clear the screen.
   b. Reseed the random number generator by using the following statement:

   ```
   RANDOMIZE TIMER
   ```

   c. Use the RND function to generate random numbers for the purpose of simulating the actual throw of the dice. There are six sides to a die, each with an equal probability of showing up. For each die, provide separate random numbers between 1 and 6. Use the following user-defined function to generate random numbers between 1 and 6:

   ```
   DEF FNRANDOM = INT(6 * RND + 1)
   ```

   d. Set the winnings accumulator (WINNINGS) to zero.

2. Roll the Dice

   a. Set CONTROL$ to the value Y.
   b. Establish a While loop that executes until the user assigns CONTROL$ the value N. Within the loop, do the following:
      (1) Reference the user-defined function twice in succession for the house roller. The sum of the two simulated rolls of a die determines the house roller's score (HOUSE). Display the house roller's score. Determine and display the customer's score (CUSTOMER) in the same manner.
      (2) Determine the winner by comparing the house roller's score and the customer's score. The house wins all ties. Increment or decrement by $5.00 the accumulator WINNINGS. Display the accumulator WINNINGS.
      (3) Use an INPUT statement to determine whether the customer wants to continue playing. A response of Y or y indicates that the customer wants to continue the game.

3. Wrap-up — Display a message on the basis of the customer's winnings. If the customer owes money, display the message Better luck next time! If the customer does not owe any money, display the message You are pretty lucky!

Program Solution The following program solution corresponds to the preceding tasks.

PROGRAM 8.14

```
1000 ' Program 8.14
1010 ' Computer-Simulated Dice Game
1020 ' ****************************************
1030 ' *              Main Module             *
1040 ' ****************************************
1050 GOSUB 2000   ' Call Initialization
1060 GOSUB 3000   ' Call Roll the Dice
1070 GOSUB 4000   ' Call Wrap-up
1080 END
1090 '
2000 ' ****************************************
2010 ' *             Initialization           *
2020 ' ****************************************
2030 CLS : KEY OFF   ' Clear Screen
2040 RANDOMIZE TIMER
2050 DEF FNRANDOM = INT(6 * RND + 1)
2060 WINNINGS = 0
2070 RETURN
2080 '
3000 ' ****************************************
3010 ' *             Roll The Dice            *
3020 ' ****************************************
3030 CONTROL$ = "Y"
3040 WHILE CONTROL$ = "Y" OR CONTROL$ = "y"
3050    ' **** Determine House Roller Score ****
3060    HOUSE    = FNRANDOM + FNRANDOM
3070    PRINT : PRINT "The house rolls ========>"; HOUSE
3080    ' **** Determine the Customer's Score ****
3090    CUSTOMER = FNRANDOM + FNRANDOM
3100    PRINT "Your score =============>"; CUSTOMER
3110    ' **** Determine the Winner ****
3120    IF CUSTOMER > HOUSE
           THEN WINNINGS = WINNINGS + 5
           ELSE WINNINGS = WINNINGS - 5
3130    PRINT USING "Your winnings ==========>$$##.##"; WINNINGS
3140    INPUT "Enter Y to roll the dice again, else N... ", CONTROL$
3150 WEND
3160 RETURN
3170 '
4000 ' ****************************************
4010 ' *                Wrap-up               *
4020 ' ****************************************
4030 PRINT : PRINT
4040 IF WINNINGS > 0
        THEN PRINT "You are pretty lucky!"
        ELSE PRINT "Better luck next time!"
4050 RETURN
4060 ' ************ End of Program ***********

RUN

The house rolls ========> 6
Your score =============> 9
Your winnings ==========>  $5.00
Enter Y to roll the dice again, else N... y
```

(continued)

```
The house rolls ========> 7
Your score ============> 11
Your winnings ==========> $10.00
Enter Y to roll the dice again, else N... Y

The house rolls ========> 7
Your score ============> 4
Your winnings ==========>  $5.00
Enter Y to roll the dice again, else N... y

The house rolls ========> 9
Your score ============> 11
Your winnings ==========> $10.00
Enter Y to roll the dice again, else N... n

You are pretty lucky!
```

Discussion of the Program Solution

The solution to the Computer-Simulated Dice Game is represented by Program 8.14, which includes the following significant points.

1. Line 2050 of the Initialization Module defines a function that is referenced four times (lines 3060 and 3090 of the Roll the Dice Module) for each pass through the loop.
2. Line 3120 of the Roll the Dice Module tests to determine whether the running total WINNINGS should be incremented or decremented by $5.00.
3. Line 4030 of the Wrap-up Module displays an end-of-game message. The message displayed is dependent on the value of WINNINGS.

TRY IT YOURSELF

Load Program 8.14 (PRG8-14) from the Student Diskette. Execute the program and try your luck at Beat the House Roller.

⊞ 8.5

TRAPPING EVENTS

Some applications require that the PC halt execution of a routine and execute a subroutine when a specific event has occurred. The RETURN statement in the subroutine transfers control back to the line number the PC was about to execute when control was transferred to the subroutine. Table 8.21 summarizes the event-trapping statements that are available in MS BASIC.

TABLE 8.21 A Summary of Event-Trapping Statements

STATEMENT	PURPOSE
ON COM(n) GOSUB *line number*	Transfers control to line number when there is data filling the communications buffer (n).
ON ERROR GOTO *line number*	Enables error trapping. See Appendix C, section C.2.
ON KEY(n) GOSUB *line number*	Transfers control to line number when the function key or cursor control key (n) is pressed.
ON PEN GOSUB *line number*	Transfers control to line number when the light pen is activated.
ON PLAY(n) GOSUB *line number*	Plays continuous background music. Transfers control to line number when a note (n) is sensed.
ON STRIG(n) GOSUB *line number*	Transfers control to line number when one of the joystick buttons (n) is pressed.
ON TIMER(n) GOSUB *line number*	Transfers control to line number when the specified period of time (n) in seconds has passed.

Event-trapping statements should be executed prior to the first possible occurrence of the event. For this reason, the statement is usually placed at the beginning of the Initialization Module.

All of the statements in Table 8.21, except the ON ERROR GOTO, require the execution of a second statement to activate the trap. The corresponding statement that activates the trap for the ON KEY(n) GOSUB statement is shown in line 2040.

```
2030 ON KEY(3) GOSUB 6000
2040 KEY(3) ON
```

Line 2030 informs the PC of the subroutine to branch to when the F3 key is pressed. Line 2040 instructs the PC to begin checking for the event that is specified in line 2030.

When the F3 key is pressed following the execution of line 2040, the PC saves the line number of the line it was about to execute. It then branches to line 6000 and executes the subroutine. The RETURN statement transfers control to the line number saved by the PC when the event was encountered.

As another example, consider the use of the ON TIMER (n) GOSUB statement. In some menu-driven applications, it is useful to display an accurate system time on the screen. The following example illustrates how you can instruct the PC to refresh the time displayed on the screen every minute without interfering with the interaction between the operator and the program.

```
2000 ************************************************************
2010 *                    Initialization                       *
2020 ************************************************************
2030 CLS : KEY OFF :  ' Clear Screen
2040 LOCATE 1, 76 : PRINT TIME$
2050 ON TIMER (60) GOSUB 6000
2060 TIMER ON
         .
         .
         .
6000 ************************************************************
6010 *                    Refresh Time                          *
6020 ************************************************************
6030 ROW = CSRLIN
6040 COL = POS(0)
6050 LOCATE 1, 76 : PRINT TIME$
6060 LOCATE ROW, COL
6070 RETURN
```

Line 2030 clears the screen, and line 2040 displays the system time in the format hh:mm:ss. Line 2050 establishes the subroutine to branch to every minute. Note that the time interval, n, is specified in seconds. The value n may range between 1 and 86,400.

Line 2060 activates the interval-timer trap. Thereafter, as long as the program is executing, the PC branches to the subroutine beginning at line 6000 every 60 seconds and refreshes the time displayed on the screen.

If you desire, you may decrease the value of the time interval, n, to 30 seconds or something smaller in order to display the time more frequently and more accurately. However, be aware that if the value of n is too small, the performance of your program may degrade because the PC is being used to frequently update the time on the screen.

Note how the special variable CSRLIN and the POS(0) function are used in lines 6030 and 6040 to determine the current position of the cursor. Then in line 6060, the cursor is moved back to the position it had before control passed to the subroutine.

You may also instruct the PC to turn off an event or to continue keeping track of the event but bypass trapping it. For example,

    3050 TIMER OFF

causes the PC to stop tracking TIMER activity and no trapping takes place. The following statement,

    4050 TIMER STOP

also instructs the PC to disregard trapping the interval timer. However, with the latter statement, TIMER activity is still tracked, so an immediate trap occurs when TIMER ON is later executed.

For additional information on trapping events, including the restrictions placed on the parameter n, see the MS BASIC manual.

⊞ 8.6   WHAT YOU SHOULD KNOW

1. MS BASIC includes several string functions, statements, and special variables that place it among the better programming languages for manipulating letters, numbers, words, and phrases.
2. The LEN(X$) function returns the length of the string argument X$.
3. The LEFT$(X$, N) function extracts a substring beginning with the leftmost character (position 1) of the string argument X$ for a length of N characters.
4. The RIGHT$(X$, N) function extracts a substring beginning with the rightmost character of the string argument X$ for a length of N characters.
5. The MID$(X$, P, N) function extracts a substring beginning with the character in position P of X$ for a length of N characters.
6. The INSTR(P, X$, S$) function returns the beginning position of the substring S$ in string X$. P indicates the position in which the search begins in X$.
7. The MID$ statement replaces a substring within a string.
8. The ASC(X$) function returns a two-digit numeric value that is equivalent in ASCII code to the first character of the string argument X$.
9. The CHR$(N) function returns a single string character that corresponds to the ASCII code for the numeric value N.
10. The STR$(N) function returns the string equivalent of the numeric value N.
11. The VAL(X$) function returns the numeric equivalent of the string X$.
12. The SPC(N) function displays N spaces and may be used only in an output statement.
13. The SPACE$ and STRING$ functions are used to duplicate strings.
14. The special variables DATE$ and TIME$ are automatically equal to the current system date and system time.
15. The DATE$ and TIME$ statements may be used to set the system time and date.
16. The LINE INPUT statement accepts an entire line from the keyboard as a string value and assigns it to a specified variable name.
17. The special variable INKEY$ is used to assign a single character from the keyboard to a string variable without suspending execution of the program.
18. The INPUT$(N) function suspends execution of the program and accepts N characters from the keyboard without requiring that the Enter key be pressed.
19. The numeric functions that are classified as arithmetic include ABS (absolute value), FIX (fixed integer), INT (integer), and SGN (sign).
20. The numeric functions classified as exponential include SQR (square root), EXP (exponential), and LOG (logarithmic).
21. The numeric functions classified as trigonometric include SIN (sine), COS (cosine), TAN (tangent), and ATN (arctangent).
22. The FRE function returns the number of unused bytes within BASIC's data space.
23. The POS function returns the current column position of the cursor relative to the left edge of the display screen. The special variable CRSLIN is equal to the current row (line) the cursor is on relative to the top of the display screen.
24. The SCREEN(R, C) function returns the ASCII code for the character located on the screen at the intersection of column C and row R.
25. The TIMER function returns a single-precision value that represents the number of seconds that have elapsed since midnight.

26. The RND function returns an unpredictable decimal fraction number between zero and less than 1.
27. The RANDOMIZE statement supplies a new seed for the generation of random numbers by the RND function.
28. In addition to the built-in functions, MS BASIC allows you to define other numeric and string functions that relate to a particular application. This second type of function, known as a user-defined function, is written directly into the program as a one-line statement. The one-line statement is the DEF FN statement.
29. All user-defined function names begin with the two letters FN, followed by a variable name that is consistent with the rules used for naming numeric variables.
30. User-defined functions are called upon in a LET, PRINT, ON-GOSUB or IF statement in the same way that numeric and string functions are called upon.
31. MS BASIC includes several event-trapping statements that instruct the PC to interrupt its normal execution of a program and execute a subroutine when a certain event has occurred.

⊞ 8.7 TEST YOUR BASIC SKILLS (Even-numbered answers are at the back of the book, before the index.)

1. Consider the valid programs below. What is displayed if each program is executed?

a.
```
100 ' Exercise 8.1a
110 CLS : KEY OFF  ' Clear Screen
120 STATE$ = "Mississippi"
130 FOR I = 1 TO LEN(STATE$)
140    LOCATE I, I : PRINT LEFT$(STATE$, I)
150 NEXT I
160 END
```

b. The system time is exactly 15:34:56.
```
100 ' Exercise 8.1b
110 CLOCK = VAL(LEFT$(TIME$, 2))
120 IF CLOCK < 12
        THEN ID$ = "am" : IF CLOCK = 0 THEN CLOCK = 12 ELSE
        ELSE ID$ = "pm" : IF CLOCK <> 12 THEN CLOCK = CLOCK - 12
130 TI$ = STR$(CLOCK) + MID$(TIME$, 3, 6) + SPACE$(1) + ID$
140 PRINT "The time is "; TI$
150 END
```

c.
```
100 ' Exercise 8.1c
110 CODE$ = "08<NC74N0AA>FN20A45D;;H"
120 PRINT "Coded message ======> "; CODE$
130 PRINT : PRINT "The message is =====> ";
140 FOR I = 1 TO LEN(CODE$)
150    MESG = ASC(MID$(CODE$, I, 1))
160    MESG = MESG + 17
170    CHAR$ = CHR$(MESG)
180    PRINT CHAR$;
190 NEXT I
200 END
```

d.
```
100 ' Exercise 8.1d
105 CLS : KEY OFF  ' Clear Screen
110 PHRASE1$ = "TODAY IS THE TOMORROW YOU"
120 PHRASE2$ = " WORRIED ABOUT YESTERDAY"
130 PHRASE3$ = PHRASE1$ + PHRASE2$
140 LOCATE 12, 15 : PRINT LEFT$(PHRASE3$, 1);
150 FOR I = 2 TO LEN(PHRASE3$)
160    UPPER = ASC(MID$(PHRASE3$, I, 1))
170    IF UPPER <> 32 THEN
            UPPER = UPPER + 32
180    LOWER$ = CHR$(UPPER)
190    PRINT LOWER$;
200 NEXT I
210 PRINT "."
220 END
```

2. Evaluate each of the following. Assume that PHR$ is equal to the following string:

```
If I have seen further it is by standing upon the shoulders of giants
```

 a. LEN(PHR$)
 b. RIGHT$(PHR$, 100)
 c. LEFT$(PHR$, 5)
 d. MID$(PHR$, 11, 4)
 e. VAL("36.8")
 f. ASC(MID$(PHR$, 4, 1))
 g. CHR$(71)
 h. STRING$(14, "^")
 i. STR$(-13.691)
 j. INSTR(10, PHR$, "i")
 k. MID$(PHR$, 64, 7) = "midgets"
 l. SPACE$(4)

3. Evaluate each of the following. Assume that NUM is equal to 2 and that PHR$ is equal to the following string:

```
GOTO is a four letter word
```

 a. LEN(PHR$)
 b. RIGHT$(PHR$, 4)
 c. RIGHT$(PHR$, 30)
 d. LEFT$(PHR$, 50)
 e. LEFT$(PHR$, 1.5)
 f. LEFT$(PHR$, NUM)
 g. MID$(PHR$, NUM, 3)
 h. MID$(PHR$, NUM ^ 3, 2)
 i. MID$(PHR$, 1, 5 * NUM)
 j. INSTR(PHR$, "is")
 k. INSTR(NUM, PHR$, "t")
 l. INSTR(2 * NUM, PHR$, "r ")

4. Evaluate each of the following.

 a. VAL("99")
 b. ASC("+")
 c. CHR$(63)
 d. STR$(48.9)
 e. CLS : PRINT CSRLIN
 f. CLS : ? "B" : ? SCREEN(1, 1)
 g. CHR$(37)
 h. ASC(":")
 i. PRINT , POS(0)
 j. LOCATE 23, 46 : ? POS(0) + CSRLIN

5. What does the following program display when executed? What value must be assigned to CONTROL$ to terminate the program?

```
100 ' Exercise 8.5
110 CHAR$ = "a"
120 CONTROL$ = ""
130 WHILE CONTROL$ <> "&"
140    FOR I = 1 TO 80
150       PRINT CHAR$;
160    NEXT I
170    CONTROL$ = INKEY$
180    IF CONTROL$ <> ""
          THEN CHAR$ = CONTROL$
190 WEND
200 END
```

6. Write a series of statements that will display the sum of the digits in the customer number NUM$. Assume that NUM$ is equal to the string value 1698.

7. Assuming that the system time is exactly 11:59:59pm and that the system date is December 1, 1992, evaluate each of the following.

 a. CLOCK$ = TIME$
 b. DAY$ = DATE$
 c. SEC = TIMER

8. What does the following program display when executed? Explain the algorithm that is used in this program.

```
100 ' Exercise 8.8
110 CLS : KEY OFF   ' Clear Screen
120 PRINT "Prime numbers between 1 and 100 -";
130 PRINT 2;
140 FOR I = 3 TO 100
150    FOR K = 2 TO INT(SQR(I))
160        IF I = K * INT(I / K)
              THEN K = 12
170    NEXT K
180    IF K < 12
          THEN PRINT I;
190 NEXT I
200 END
```

9. What does the following program display when executed?

```
100 ' Exercise 8.9
110 CLS : KEY OFF   ' Clear Screen
120 FOR K = 1 TO 24
130    FOR J = 1 TO 10
140        LOCATE 12, 36 : PRINT "Wake Up ";
150        FOR I = 1 TO 5
160            PRINT CHR$(7);
170        NEXT I
175        LOCATE 12, 36 : PRINT SPC(7)
180    NEXT J
190    PRINT
200 NEXT K
210 END
```

10. Write a single BASIC statement for each of the following. Use numeric functions wherever possible. Assume that the value of X is a real number.

   a. $p = \sqrt{a^2 + b^2}$ b. $b = \sqrt{|\tan X - 0.51|}$

   c. $q = 8 \cos^2 X + 4 \sin X$ d. $y = e^x + \log_e (1 + X)$

11. What is the numeric value of each of the following?

   a. INT(-18.5) b. ABS(-3)
   c. INT(16.9) d. ABS(6.7)
   e. EXP(1) f. LOG(0)

12. Write separate BASIC statements for each of the following:

   a. determine the sign of $2X^3 + 3X + 5$;
   b. determine the integer part of $4X + 5$; and
   c. round X to two decimal places; to one decimal place.

13. Write a program that displays the values for X and SIN X where X varies between 0° and 180°. Increment X in steps of 5.
14. Explain the purpose of the FRE, POS, and SCREEN functions and the special variable CSRLIN.
15. Characterize the four methods of accepting input through the keyboard—INPUT, LINE INPUT, INKEY$, and INPUT$(N) — in terms of suspension of program execution; type and length of data that may be assigned; and whether the Enter key must be pressed.
16. Write a program that will generate and display 100 random numbers between 1 and 52, inclusive.
17. Explain the purpose of the RANDOMIZE statement. Why is the TIMER function a good choice for determining the seed?

18. Write a user-defined function that will determine a 10% discount on the amount of purchase PUR in excess of $200.00. The discount applies to the excess, not the entire purchase.

19. Explain the function of the following partial program.

```
2030 ON KEY(5) GOSUB 7000
2040 KEY(5) ON
```

20. Is the following program valid or invalid? If it is invalid, indicate why.

```
100 ' Exercise 8.20
110 DEF FNX(B) = FNA(B) + 5
120 DEF FNA(B) = FNW(B) * 7
130 DEF FNW(B) = B ^ 4
140 PRINT FNX(5)
150 END
```

21. Given the following program:

```
100 ' Exercise 8.21
110 FOR I = 1 TO 5
120    READ X
130      PRINT TAB(5); X,   (Complete this portion)
140 NEXT I
150 DATA 1.1, 10000.5, 100.3, 1000.4, 10.2
160 END
```

Complete line 130 so that the results displayed in the second column are right-justified, as shown below:

```
1.1            1.1
10000.5        10000.5
100.3          100.3
1000.4         1000.4
10.2           10.2
```

Do not use the PRINT USING statement. (**Hint:** Use the LOG function.)

22. Use the Student Diskette to complete the Try It Yourself exercises on pages 286, 288, 290, 293, 297, 304, 307, 309, 312, 316, and 318.

8.8 BASIC PROGRAMMING PROBLEMS

1. Palindromes

Purpose: To become familiar with the manipulation of strings through the use of the LEN and MID$ functions.

Problem: A palindrome is a word or phrase that is the same when read either backward or forward. For example, *noon* is a palindrome, but *moon* is not. Write a program that requests the user to enter a string of characters (uppercase) and that determines whether the string is a palindrome.

Input Data: Use the following sample data.

```
9876556789
ABLE WAS I ERE I SAW ELBA
I
BOB DID BOB
WOW LIL DID POP
OTTO
RADAR
!@#$$@#!
( )
A PROGRAM IS A MIRROR IMAGE OF THE MIND
```

Output Results: The following partial results are shown.

```
String? 9876556789
9876556789 is a palindrome.

Enter Y to continue, else N... Y
      .
      .
      .
String? WOW LIL DID POP
WOW LIL DID POP is not a palindrome.

Enter Y to continue, else N... Y
```

2. English to Pig-Latin Conversion

Purpose: To become familiar with string manipulation.

Problem: In pig Latin, a word such as *computer* is converted to *omputercay*. For this BASIC Programming Problem, the translation from English to pig Latin calls for taking the first consonant of the word and moving it to the end of the word, followed by an appended *ay*. If a word begins with a vowel, then the vowel remains in its beginning position and the string *way* is appended to the end of the word. For example, *apple* becomes *appleway*.

Write a program that displays the pig Latin translation for a string of English words (uppercase). Also display the number of words that begin with a vowel, the total number of words in the string, and the percentage of words that begin with a vowel. Do not include punctuation.

Input Data: Use the following sample data.

> EVERY PROGRAM IS A SELF PORTRAIT OF THE PERSON WHO WROTE IT
> AUTOGRAPH YOUR WORK WITH EXCELLENCE

Output Results: The following results are displayed.

```
Enter the English Sentence Without Punctuation
-------------------------------------------------
EVERY PROGRAM IS A SELF PORTRAIT OF THE PERSON WHO WROTE IT AUTOGRAPH
YOUR WORK WITH EXCELLENCE

The Sentence in Pig Latin is:
-----------------------------
EVERYWAY ROGRAMPAY ISWAY AWAY ELFSAY ORTRAITPAY OFWAY HETAY ERSONPAY
HOWAY ROTEWAY ITWAY AUTOGRAPHWAY OURYAY ORKWAY ITHWAY EXCELLENCEWAY

Words beginning with a vowel ========>   7
Total number of words ===============>  17
Percentage beginning with a vowel ===>  41.2

Job Complete
```

3. Time to Double an Investment Compounded Quarterly

Purpose: To become familiar with the use of numeric functions and user-defined functions, and the concepts of rounding and truncation.

Problem: Write a program that will determine the time it takes to double an investment compounded quarterly for the following annual interest rates: 6%, 7%, 8% and 9%. The formula for computing the time is:

$$N = \frac{\log 2}{M(\log(1 + J)/M))}$$

where N = time in years
J = annual interest rate
M = number of conversion periods

Once the time has been determined for a given interest rate, use the generalized expressions for rounding and truncation given in section 8.3 on page 300 to round and truncate the answer to two decimal places. Define both expressions as user-defined functions in your program.

Input Data: None.

Output Results: The following results are displayed.

```
           Time to Double an Investment
               Compounded Quarterly
           ----------------------------

                   Years           Years
     Annual        to Double       to Double
     Interest      (Rounded)       (Truncated)
     --------      ---------       -----------
       6%            11.64           11.63
       7%             9.99            9.98
       8%             8.75            8.75
       9%             7.79            7.78

     Job Complete
```

4. Order Entry Simulation

Purpose: To become familiar with the use of the random number function (RND), the RANDOMIZE statement, the TIMER function, the INPUT$ function, and computer simulation.

Problem: Order entry is the process of receiving customer orders and producing shipping orders. The Oldtown Company has three clerks in its Order Entry Department. On the average, the three clerks can process 197 customer orders a day. Management has requested the Data-processing Department to simulate the activities of the Order Entry Department over a four-week period (20 working days). The following statistics were compiled over the same four-week period during the previous year:

Customer Orders Received	Frequency in Days	Relative Frequency	Cumulative Frequency
185	1	0.05	0.05
190	5	0.25	0.30
195	6	0.30	0.60
200	4	0.20	0.80
205	3	0.15	0.95
210	1	0.05	1.00

Assuming that the four-week period (day 1 through day 20) begins with no backlog order, write a program that will print on the printer the simulation of the following:

1. the number of orders received each day;
2. the number of orders processed (the day's order plus backlog orders);
3. the orders not processed; and
4. the number of days in which orders go unprocessed.

The orders received are to be simulated by employing the RND function. Once the program is working properly, add the statement RANDOMIZE TIMER so that a new seed will be used to generate the random numbers each time the program is executed.

The random number returned by the RND function should be passed through a series of IF statements, which test to determine whether it is less than or equal to the cumulative frequencies for orders compiled from the previous year. The logic for these tests is shown in Figure 8.3.

FIGURE 8.3
The logic for Order-Entry Simulation.

Input Data: None.

Output Results: Display the following message to the user.

```
Press any key when the printer is ready...
```

The following illustrates a sample run. Answers will vary, depending on the random numbers generated on the basis of the value of TIMER.

```
                Order-Entry Simulation
          Maximum Orders Processed per Day 197

              Orders        Orders       Orders Not
       Day    Received      Processed    Processed
       ---    --------      ---------    ----------
        1        190           190           0
        2        200           197           3
        3        190           193           0
        .         .             .            .
        .         .             .            .
        .         .             .            .
       18        190           190           0
       19        195           195           0
       20        205           197           8

     Number of days orders went unprocessed ======> 10
```

5. Cryptograms

Purpose: To become familiar with concatenation, table searching, and string manipulation of cryptograms.

Problem: In section 8.2, on page 289 you were introduced to a method of substituting characters in a coded message and determining the contents of the message. The direct substitution method, based on a table of substitutes, may also be used with cryptograms. Write a program that uses the following table of substitutes to decode a given message.

```
Coded  Characters:   9 G Q 6 V L P N W X A 8 T # H Z J M ( U 3 ) R I S B F K D
Regular Characters:  A B C D E F G H I J K L M N O P Q R S T U V W X Y Z - ƀ .
```

The coded characters and their corresponding regular characters are stored in EX85CODE.TBL on the Student Diskette. Use the TYPE command to display EX85CODE.TBL in order to determine the order in which the data is stored. Assume that all coded messages are in uppercase. The character ƀ represents the blank character.

Input Data: Use the following sample coded messages.

Message 1: G9(WQKW(KV9(S

Message 2: LW#6W#PKUNVK6VVZK(WTZ8WQWUWV(KW#K9K
QHTZ8WQ9UV6KQH88VQUWH#KHLKUNW#P(K
UHKGVK6H#(VKW#(KUNVK(UNVVZ)WUK(UNVV)8WTTW)8WT(
ZMHPM9TTW#PKFKND6DTW88(

Output Results: The following is shown for message 1.

```
Enter the coded message ====> G9(WQKW(KV9(S

The message is =============> BASIC IS EASY

Job Complete
```

6. Soundex Code

Purpose: To become familiar with character transformation, Soundex, and the use of the LINE INPUT statement.

Problem: Frequently, companies that allow their customers to phone or write for information regarding their account status have only the customer's name to aid them in locating a record in the account file. Sometimes the name itself is not clear, owing to illegible handwriting or to poor voice communications in a phone conversation. Also, when customers call to request information about their account, some companies like to ask as few questions as possible in order to give callers the impression that they are special customers. Soundex is the name of a method for transforming the sound of a name into a successful and efficient search for a customer record. Developed by M. Odell and R. Russell, the method involves assigning a code (called the **Soundex code**) to a surname when a record is first added to a file, and placing this code in the record for access purposes. The Soundex code for a name is determined from the following rules:

1. Retain the first letter and drop all occurrences of a, e, h, i, o, u, w, and y in other positions of the name.
2. Assign the following digits to the remaining letters:

Digits	Letters
1	b, f, p, v
2	c, g, j, k, q, s, x, z
3	d, t
4	l
5	m, n
6	r

3. If two or more letters with the same code are adjacent in the *original* name, drop all but the first letter.
4. Convert the name to the form "letter, digit, digit, digit" by adding trailing zeros if there are less than three digits, or by dropping rightmost digits if there are more than three digits. The following examples of names have these corresponding Soundex codes:

Last Name	Code	Last Name	Code
Case	C200	Knuth	K530
Cash	C200	Smith	S530
Caise	C200	Smyth	S530
Gauss	G200	Smythe	S530

This system will work for most Anglo-Saxon names. Similar systems are available for other types of names, such as Asian or Spanish. These systems may not always work, but they speed up the searching of many records.

Write a program that builds an account file in which each record contains the customer number, customer name, Soundex code, and balance due. The program should request from the operator the customer number, name, and balance due. From the last name, the program should determine the Soundex code and display it. Then the program should write the record to a sequential file (EX86DATA.DAT).

Input Data: Use the following sample data. Be sure to include the comma (,) as part of the customer name.

Customer Number	Customer Name	Balance Due	Customer Number	Customer Name	Balance Due
1783	Allen, John	$55.00	3401	Smith, Amanda	$45.00
1934	Smit, Joan	0.00	3607	Cas, Louise	0.00
2109	Case, Jeff	5.00	4560	Smythe, Alice	4.00
2134	Alien, Bill	35.00	5590	Ellen, Boyd	7.80
2367	Allan, Fred	65.00	6498	Caes, Nikole	5.30
2568	Caise, Edie	87.00	7591	Kase, Judy	0.00

Output Results: The following results are displayed for the first customer.

```
Customer Number =====> 1783
Customer Name =======> Allen, John
Balance =============> 55.00
Soundex Code ========> A450

Enter Y to add another account, else N... Y
```

The records are also written to the sequential file EX86DATA.DAT.

7. The Check Digit Problem

Purpose: To illustrate the concepts of generating check digits.

Problem: Construct a program to verify a six-digit part number by validating the units position for a check digit. A check digit is an addition to a number that requires validation; this addition can be used to verify the rest of the digits. A check digit is effective for catching the most common mistakes made in entering a number.

The computation of the check digit for this problem involves multiplying every other digit of the original number by 2 and then adding these values and the remaining digits of the number together. The units digit of the result obtained is then subtracted from 10 to obtain the check digit.

To illustrate the process, let's form the part number by computing the check digit for the number 72546. The alternate digits are first multiplied by 2:

```
    7    5    6
         ×    2
   ------------
   14   10   12
```

Then the remaining digits (2 and 4) are included and all above digits are added:

$$1 + 4 + 1 + 0 + 1 + 2 + 2 + 4 = 15$$

The check digit is the units position of the sum, or 5. The part number 72546 becomes 725465.

This algorithm is quite sophisticated, since it can detect invalid part numbers that have digits reversed, such as 752465 instead of 725465.

Hint: The 6 digits must be separated. You may separate digits through the use of the INT function. For example, the leftmost digit (D6) can be determined from the following, where PART is the 6-digit value:

```
D6 = INT(PART / 100000)
```

and the second leftmost digit (D5) is equal to:

```
D5 = INT((PART - D6 * 100000) / 10000)
```

Continue in this fashion until all 6 digits have been extracted.

Input Data: Prepare and use the following part numbers. Check to see whether the rightmost digit is the correct check digit.

725465, 752465, 033332, 098792, 098798
089798, 000000, 000001, 999999, 999995

Output Results: The following results are displayed for 725465.

```
Validation of Check Digit

Enter Part Number ======> 725465

Part Number is Valid

To Continue Y, else N... Y
```

8. Payroll Problem VII: Spelling Out the Net Pay

Purpose: To become familiar with table utilization, use of the zero element of an array, the INT and STR$ functions, and spelling out numbers.

Problem: Construct a program that spells out the net pay for check-writing purposes. For example, the net pay $5,078.45 is written out on a check as follows:

Five Thousand Seventy-Eight Dollars and 45 Cents

Assume that the net pay does not exceed $9,999.99.

Hint: Use the INT function to separate the integer portion of the net pay into single digits. Use the single digits to access the words from one of two positionally organized tables. If the digit represents the thousands, hundreds, or units position, then access the word from the following table:

Digit	Word	Digit	Word
0	Null	10	Ten
1	One	11	Eleven
2	Two	12	Twelve
3	Three	13	Thirteen
4	Four	14	Fourteen
5	Five	15	Fifteen
6	Six	16	Sixteen
7	Seven	17	Seventeen
8	Eight	18	Eighteen
9	Nine	19	Nineteen

If the digit represents the tens position, then access the word from the following table:

Digit	Word	Digit	Word
0	Null	5	Fifty
1	Ten	6	Sixty
2	Twenty	7	Seventy
3,	Thirty	8	Eighty
4	Forty	9	Ninety

The word entries for both tables are found in the sequential file EX88TAB.TBL on the Student Diskette. The entries for the thousands, hundreds, and units table are first in the sequential file, followed immediately by the entries for the tens table.

Use the INT and STR$ functions to determine the fraction portion of the net pay. Use the concatenation operator to string the words together. If there are no dollars or cents, display the word "No" accordingly.

Input Data: Use the sequential file EX88DATA.DAT found on the Student Diskette. The data file includes the following sample data.

Employee Number	Net Pay	Employee Number	Net Pay
123	$8,462.34	127	$1,003.00
124	987.23	128	4,037.00
125	78.99	129	4.67
126	6,000.23	130	0.02

Output Results: The following results are displayed.

```
Employee
Number    Net Pay    Net Pay Spelled Out
--------  -------    -------------------
   123    8,462.34   Eight Thousand Four Hundred Sixty-Two Dollars and 34 Cents
   124      987.23   Nine Hundred Eighty-Seven Dollars and 23 Cents
   125       78.99   Seventy-Eight Dollars and 99 Cents
   126    6,000.23   Six Thousand  Dollars and 23 Cents
   127    1,003.00   One Thousand Three Dollars and No Cents
   128    4,037.00   Four Thousand Thirty-Seven Dollars and No Cents
   129        4.67   Four Dollars and 67 Cents
   130        0.02   No Dollars and 2 Cents

Job Complete
```

FILE MAINTENANCE, RANDOM FILE PROCESSING, AND SIMULATED-INDEXED FILES

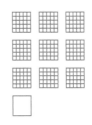

In chapter 6, you were introduced to sequential file processing. Topics included writing reports to auxiliary storage and building and processing sequential data files. In this chapter, we will discuss **file maintenance**. File maintenance means updating files in one or more of the following ways:

1. *adding* new records;
2. *deleting* unwanted records; and
3. *changing* data within records.

This chapter also concentrates on two additional methods of file organization — random and simulated-indexed files.

Random Files

A file that is organized randomly is called a **random file** or a **relative file**. The sequence of processing a random file has no relationship to the sequence in which the records are stored in it. If the tenth record in a file is required by a program, the record can be directly accessed without processing the previous nine records. However, the program must indicate to the PC the location of the record relative to the beginning of the file. For example, to access the tenth record instead of the third or fourth record, the program must explicitly indicate to the PC that the tenth record is requested for processing.

Indexed Files

A third type of file organization, known as **indexed**, is also widely used in data processing. A file organized by an index is an **indexed file**. An indexed file is organized around a specified data item, the **key**, which is common to each record. In an airline reservation file, the key may be the flight number. In an inventory file, the key may be the part number or a part description.

Indexed files have one advantage over random files: the program need only supply the key of the record to be accessed instead of the record's relative location. Although indexed files are not available with MS BASIC, this method of organization may be simulated by using both a sequential file and a random file; this is illustrated in Programming Case Study 23.

Indexed files and random files are used primarily for on-line activities where the applications call for random processing of the data. In airline reservation systems, inventory systems, management information systems, and customer credit checks, indexed or random organization of a file has important advantages over sequential organization.

⊞ 9.2

FILE MAINTENANCE

File maintenance is one of the most important activities in data processing. The programming techniques that are used to update a file are usually based on the type of file organization under which the file was created. To update sequential files, the record additions, deletions, and changes are normally entered into another sequential file called a **transaction file**. A transaction file, therefore, contains data of a temporary or transient nature. Once the updates have been completed, the transaction file can be deleted.

The file that is updated is called the **master file**. A master file contains data that is for the most part permanent. **Current master file** refers to the master file before updating, and **new master file** refers to the updated version of the current master file. A file maintenance program that updates a sequential file must deal with at least three files, as illustrated in the **system flowchart** in Figure 9.1.

FIGURE 9.1
A system flowchart representing file maintenance of a sequential file.

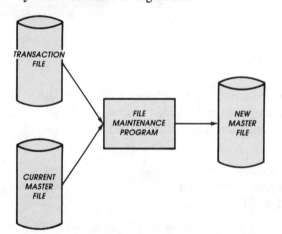

A system flowchart shows, in graphic form, the files, flow of data, equipment, and programs involved in a particular application. The cylinder-like symbols in Figure 9.1 symbolize auxiliary storage devices, like floppy diskette units. The rectangle represents a computer system. The arrows in the system flowchart indicate that data is read from two files and that the results of the program are written to another file.

To employ the file-maintenance technique described in Figure 9.1, both the master and transaction files must be in the same sequence, based upon one of the data items common to both files. For example, an inventory master file and a corresponding inventory transaction file may be in sorted ascending sequence by stock number.

For the sake of simplicity, the presentation of file maintenance has been divided into two problems and two corresponding program solutions. In the first set, Programming Case Study 19, a method of adding records to the current master file to form a new master file will be illustrated. In Programming Case Study 20, record deletion and changing data within records will be illustrated. BASIC Programming Problem 9.1 at the end of this chapter requires the completion of all the file maintenance in one program.

Programming Case Study 19: File Maintenance I — Adding Records by Merging Files

Problem: Programming Case Study 11, on page 195 in chapter 6, created a sequential data file called INVNTORY.DAT from the inventory data shown in Table 9.1 on the opposite page.

New stock items are to be added to the inventory master file INVNTORY.DAT created by Program 6.2 on page 196. The new stock items are shown in Table 9.2 on the opposite page and are in the file TRAINV.DAT. The program should **merge** the records of the two files to create the new inventory master file. Merging is the process of combining two or more files that are *in the same sequence* into a single file that maintains that same sequence for a given data item found in each record. The two files are each in ascending sequence according to the stock number.

_____TABLE 9.1 Inventory Data Used to Create the Master File INVNTORY.DAT_____

STOCK NUMBER	WAREHOUSE LOCATION	DESCRIPTION	UNIT COST	SELLING PRICE	QUANTITY ON HAND
C101	1	Roadhandler	97.56	125.11	25
C204	3	Whitewalls	37.14	99.95	140
C502	2	Tripod	32.50	38.99	10
S209	1	Maxidrill	88.76	109.99	6
S416	2	Normalsaw	152.55	179.40	1
S812	2	Router	48.47	61.15	8
S942	4	Radialsaw	376.04	419.89	3
T615	4	Oxford-Style	26.43	31.50	28
T713	2	Moc-Boot	24.99	29.99	30
T814	2	Work-Boot	22.99	27.99	56

_____TABLE 9.2 Inventory Data in the Transaction File TRAINV.DAT_____

STOCK NUMBER	WAREHOUSE LOCATION	DESCRIPTION	UNIT COST	SELLING PRICE	QUANTITY ON HAND
C103	2	Saw-Blades	5.06	6.04	15
C206	1	Square	4.56	5.42	34
S210	3	Microscope	31.50	41.99	8
S941	2	Hip-Boot	26.95	32.50	12
T615	4	Oxford-Style	26.43	31.50	28
T731	1	Sandals	6.75	9.45	52

The transaction file can be created by modifying line 2050 in Program 6.2 as follows,

```
2050 OPEN "TRAINV.DAT" FOR OUTPUT AS #1
```

and entering the records in Table 9.2 in response to the modified Program 6.2.

Also assume that the name of the current master file, INVNTORY.DAT, has been changed to CURINV.DAT, using the system command NAME from Table 2.10 on page 39 to change file names. For example,

```
NAME "INVNTORY.DAT" AS "CURINV.DAT"
```

By changing the name of the current master file, its former name, INVNTORY.DAT, can then be assigned to a new master file.

It is an error for a record in the transaction file to have the same stock number as a record in the current master file. If this happens, an appropriate diagnostic message, including the stock number and description, should be displayed. Also, a count of the number of records in the new master file should be displayed before the program is terminated.

A top-down chart showing what must be done to solve the problem is illustrated in Figure 9.2 on the following page. You'll recall that recurring subtasks are identified by darkening the upper right-hand corner of the process symbol. At implementation time, recurring subtasks are coded once and called upon as often as needed. Following are the program tasks that correspond to the top-down chart in Figure 9.2; a program solution; and a discussion of the program solution.

Program Tasks 1. Initialization

    a. Set RECORD.COUNT to zero. Increment this counter each time a record is written to the new master file.

    b. Set two end-of-file switches, MAS.EOF$ for the current master file and TRA.EOF$ for the transaction file, to the value OFF. Set either switch to the value ON when the end-of-file mark is sensed in the corresponding file.

    c. Open CURINV.DAT, TRAINV.DAT, and INVNTORY.DAT.

    d. Clear the screen and display an appropriate screen title.

2. Process Files

    a. Read the first record in the current master file and the first record in the transaction file. Use the following variable names.

Current Master File			Transaction File		
STOCK$	=	stock number	TRA.STOCK$	=	stock number
LOCATION$	=	location	TRA.LOCATION$	=	location
DESC$	=	description	TRA.DESC$	=	description
COST	=	cost	TRA.COST	=	cost
PRICE	=	price	TRA.PRICE	=	price
QUANTITY	=	quantity	TRA.QUANTITY	=	quantity

    b. Establish a While loop that executes until either MAS.EOF$ or TRA.EOF$ is equal to the value ON (i.e., the end-of-file mark has been sensed on one of the input files). Within the While loop, compare STOCK$ to TRA.STOCK$.

      (1) If STOCK$ is equal to TRA.STOCK$, then display a diagnostic message and read the next transaction record.

      (2) If STOCK$ is less than TRA.STOCK$, then write the current master record to the new master file, increment counter RECORD.COUNT by 1, and read the next current master record.

      (3) If STOCK$ is greater than TRA.STOCK$, then write the transaction record to the new master file, increment counter RECORD.COUNT by 1, and read the next transaction record.

3. Wrap-up

    a. One of the two input files may still contain records that need to be written to the new master file. This procedure is often referred to as **flushing the files**.

    b. Close all files.

    c. Display the value of RECORD.COUNT as well as the following message:

```
INVNTORY.DAT Update Complete
```

Program Solution   Program 9.1, on the opposite page, corresponds to the top-down chart in Figure 9.2 and to the preceding program tasks.

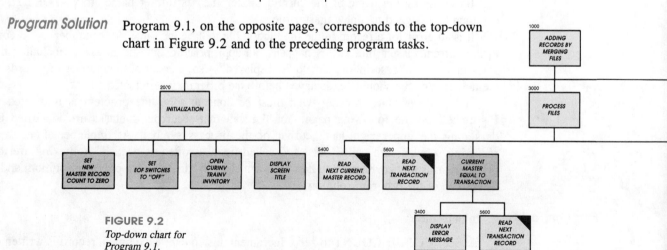

FIGURE 9.2
Top-down chart for Program 9.1.

PROGRAM 9.1

```
1000 ' Program 9.1
1010 ' File Maintenance I  - Adding Records by Merging Files
1020 ' Current Master File = CURINV.DAT
1030 ' Transaction File    = TRANSACT.DAT
1040 ' New Master File      = INVNTORY.DAT
1050 ' ************************************************************
1060 ' *                        Main Module                        *
1070 ' ************************************************************
1080 GOSUB 2000   ' Call Initialization
1090 GOSUB 3000   ' Call Process Files
1100 GOSUB 4000   ' Call Wrap-up
1110 END
1120 '
2000 ' ************************************************************
2010 ' *                      Initialization                       *
2020 ' ************************************************************
2030 RECORD.COUNT = 0
2040 MAS.EOF$ = "OFF"
2050 TRA.EOF$ = "OFF"
2060 OPEN "CURINV.DAT"   FOR INPUT  AS #1
2070 OPEN "TRAINV.DAT"   FOR INPUT  AS #2
2080 OPEN "INVNTORY.DAT" FOR OUTPUT AS #3
2090 CLS : KEY OFF  ' Clear Screen
2100 LOCATE 5, 15 : PRINT "Adding Records to Inventory File"
2110 LOCATE 6, 15 : PRINT "------------------------------"
2120 RETURN
2130 '
3000 ' ************************************************************
3010 ' *                      Process Files                        *
3020 ' ************************************************************
3030 GOSUB 5400   ' Call Read Next Current Master Record
3040 GOSUB 5600   ' Call Read Next Transaction Record
3050 WHILE MAS.EOF$ = "OFF" AND TRA.EOF$ = "OFF"
3060    IF STOCK$ <> TRA.STOCK$
            THEN GOSUB 3200
            ELSE GOSUB 3400 : GOSUB 5600
3070 WEND
3080 RETURN
3090 '
3200 ' ************************************************************
3210 ' *           Determine Record to Write to Master File        *
3220 ' ************************************************************
```

(continued)

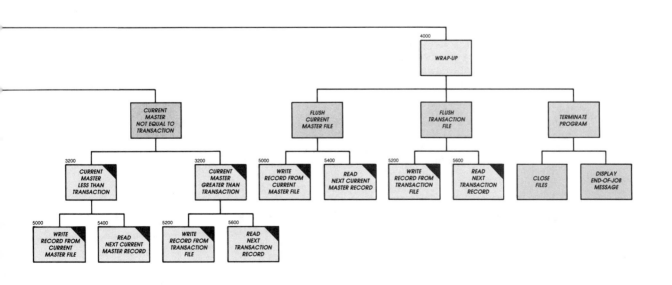

```
3230 IF STOCK$ < TRA.STOCK$
        THEN GOSUB 5000 : GOSUB 5400
        ELSE GOSUB 5200 : GOSUB 5600
3240 RETURN
3250 '
3400 ' ****************************************************************
3410 ' *                   Display Error Message                     *
3420 ' ****************************************************************
3430 PRINT
3440 PRINT "********** Transaction Record Already in Current Master File"
3450 PRINT "*  ERROR  * Stock Number = "; TRA.STOCK$
3460 PRINT "********** Description  = "; TRA.DESC$
3470 RETURN
3480 '
4000 ' ****************************************************************
4010 ' *                        Wrap-up                              *
4020 ' ****************************************************************
4030 WHILE MAS.EOF$ = "OFF"
4040    GOSUB 5000  ' Call Write Record from Current Master File
4050    GOSUB 5400  ' Call Read Next Current Master Record
4060 WEND
4070 WHILE TRA.EOF$ = "OFF"
4080    GOSUB 5200  ' Call Write Record from Transaction File
4090    GOSUB 5600  ' Call Read Next Transaction Record
4100 WEND
4110 CLOSE
4120 PRINT
4130 PRINT "The number of records in the new master file is"; RECORD.COUNT
4140 PRINT
4150 PRINT "INVNTORY.DAT Update Complete"
4160 RETURN
4170 '
5000 ' ****************************************************************
5010 ' *           Write Record from Current Master File             *
5020 ' ****************************************************************
5030 WRITE #3, STOCK$, LOCATION$, DESC$, COST, PRICE, QUANTITY
5040 RECORD.COUNT = RECORD.COUNT + 1
5050 RETURN
5060 '
5200 ' ****************************************************************
5210 ' *           Write Record from Transaction File                *
5220 ' ****************************************************************
5230 WRITE #3, TRA.STOCK$, TRA.LOCATION$, TRA.DESC$, TRA.COST,
             TRA.PRICE, TRA.QUANTITY
5240 RECORD.COUNT = RECORD.COUNT + 1
5250 RETURN
5260 '
5400 ' ****************************************************************
5410 ' *           Read Next Current Master Record                   *
5420 ' ****************************************************************
5430 IF EOF(1)
        THEN MAS.EOF$ = "ON"
        ELSE INPUT #1, STOCK$, LOCATION$, DESC$, COST, PRICE, QUANTITY
5440 RETURN
5450 '
5600 ' ****************************************************************
5610 ' *           Read Next Transaction Record                      *
5620 ' ****************************************************************
5630 IF EOF(2) THEN TRA.EOF$ = "ON"
             ELSE INPUT #2, TRA.STOCK$, TRA.LOCATION$, TRA.DESC$,
                         TRA.COST, TRA.PRICE, TRA.QUANTITY
5640 RETURN
5650 ' ***************** End of Program *********************

RUN
```

*Discussion of the
Program Solution*

Because merging two files into one is a complex process, we recommend that particular attention be paid to the top-down chart in Figure 9.2 on pages 334 and 335. Stepping through both the program tasks and the top-down chart will give a better understanding of the algorithm used to merge the two files.

Figures 9.3 and 9.4 show the contents of the current master file, CURINV.DAT, and the transaction file, TRAINV.DAT.

```
"C101","1","Roadhandler",97.56,125.11,25
"C204","3","Whitewalls",37.14,99.95,140
"C502","2","Tripod",32.5,38.99,10
"S209","1","Maxidrill",88.76,109.99,6
"S416","2","Normalsaw",152.55,179.4,1
"S812","2","Router",48.47,61.15,8
"S942","4","Radialsaw",376.04,419.89,3
"T615","4","Oxford-Style",26.43,31.5,28
"T713","2","Moc-Boot",24.99,29.99,30
"T814","2","Work-Boot",22.99,27.99,56
```

FIGURE 9.3
A list of the records in the current master file, CURINV.DAT.

```
"C103","2","Saw-Blades",5.06,6.04,15
"C206","1","Square",4.56,5.42,34
"S210","3","Microscope",31.50,41.99,8
"S941","2","Hip-Boot",26.95,32.50,12
"T615","4","Oxford-Style",26.43,31.50,28
"T731","1","Sandals",6.75,9.45,52
```

FIGURE 9.4
A list of the records in the transaction file, TRAINV.DAT.

When the RUN command is issued for Program 9.1, line 1080 in the Main Module calls the Initialization Module that begins at line 2000. Line 2030 initializes RECORD.COUNT to 0. RECORD.COUNT is equal to the number of records written to the new master file, INVNTORY.DAT. Lines 2040 and 2050 assign the end-of-file switches, MAS.EOF$ and TRA.EOF$, the value of OFF. These two switches are used to control the While loops in the program.

Lines 2060 and 2070 open for input the two files CURINV.DAT and TRAINV.DAT. Line 2080 opens for output the new master file, INVNTORY.DAT. Line 2090 clears the screen and lines 2100 and 2110 display a screen title.

Following the return of control to the Main Module, line 1090 calls the Process Files Module. Lines 3030 and 3040 cause the PC to read the first record in each file. Within the While loop, line 3060 compares the stock number (STOCK$) in the record read from the master file to the stock number (TRA.STOCK$) in the record read from the transaction file. The comparison determines which record will be written to the new master file, INVNTORY.DAT. The logic proceeds as follows:

1. If STOCK$ is equal to TRA.STOCK$, then control transfers to the Error Module (lines 3400 through 3480) and a diagnostic message is displayed indicating that the record from TRAINV.DAT already exists in CURINV.DAT. The next record in TRAINV.DAT is read before the WEND statement in line 3070 returns control to the WHILE statement in line 3050.
2. If STOCK$ does not equal TRA.STOCK$, then control passes to the Determine Record to Write to Master File Module beginning at line 3200, and another comparison is made between the two variables to determine which record should be written to the new master file. The following procedure is used:
   a. If STOCK$ is less than TRA.STOCK$, then control transfers to the Write Record from Current Master File Module (lines 5000 through 5060), which writes the record from CURINV.DAT. The counter RECORD.COUNT is incremented by 1 before control returns to line 3230 and the next record in CURINV.DAT is read. Control then returns to the Process Files Module.

b. If STOCK$ is greater than TRA.STOCK$, then control transfers to the Write Record from Transaction File Module (lines 5200 through 5260), which writes the record from TRAINV.DAT. The counter RECORD.COUNT is incremented by 1 before control returns to line 3230 and the next record in TRAINV.DAT is read. Control then returns to the Process Files Module.

When the PC senses the end-of-file mark on either file, the end-of-file switch representing the exhausted file is assigned a value of ON and control returns to the Main Module. Line 1100 in the Main Module transfers control to the Wrap-up Module.

If the end of file is sensed on TRAINV.DAT, then lines 4030 through 4060 flush any records remaining in CURINV.DAT. If the end of file is sensed on CURINV.DAT, then the While loop (lines 4070 through 4100) flushes any records that remain in TRAINV.DAT.

It is important to note that the main While loop in the Process Files Module and both While loops that flush the files in the Wrap-up Module are controlled by switches, not by the EOF function. If we use the EOF function rather than the two switches to directly control the loops, the last record in each file may not be written to the new master file.

A close look at Figures 9.3 and 9.4 on the previous page reveals that the fifth record in TRAINV.DAT has the same stock number as the eighth record in CURINV.DAT. This causes the display of a diagnostic message, as shown in Figure 9.5.

FIGURE 9.5
The results displayed owing to the execution of Program 9.1.

```
Adding Records to Inventory File
--------------------------------

**********  Transaction Record Already in Current Master File
*  ERROR  *  Stock Number = T615
**********  Description = Oxford-Style

The number of records in the new master file is 15

INVNTORY.DAT Update Complete
```

Figure 9.6 shows the contents of the new master file, INVNTORY.DAT, created by Program 9.1.

```
"C101","1","Roadhandler",97.56,125.11,25
"C103","2","Saw-Blades",5.06,6.04,15
"C204","3","Whitewalls",37.14,99.95,140
"C206","1","Square",4.56,5.42,34
"C502","2","Tripod",32.5,38.99,10
"S209","1","Maxidrill",88.76,109.99,6
"S210","3","Microscope",31.5,41.99,8
"S416","2","Normalsaw",152.55,179.4,1
"S812","2","Router",48.47,61.15,8
"S941","2","Hip-Boot",26.95,32.5,12
"S942","4","Radialsaw",376.04,419.89,3
"T615","4","Oxford-Style",26.43,31.5,28
"T713","2","Moc-Boot",24.99,29.99,30
"T731","1","Sandals",6.75,9.45,52
"T814","2","Work-Boot",22.99,27.99,56
```

FIGURE 9.6
A list of the records in the merged new master file, INVNTORY.DAT.

TRY IT YOURSELF

Load Program 9.1 (PRG9-1) from the Student Diskette. Rename CURINV.DAT as CURINVSA.DAT. Rename INVNTORY.DAT as CURINV.DAT. Execute the program and note the diagnostic messages. Don't forget to rename the files with their original names when you're finished.

Programming Case Study 20: *File Maintenance II — Deleting and Changing Records by Matching Records*

In Programming Case Study 19, you were introduced to one category of file maintenance — adding new records to the master file. In the following Programming Case Study, you will be introduced to the two remaining categories of file maintenance — deletion of unwanted records and changing data within records in the master file. Here again, records will be read from two files, the current master file and a transaction file, and a new master file will be created. A process known as **matching records** will be used. Matching records involves processing two or more related files that are in the same sequence according to a common data item.

As records are read from the two related files, the PC acts upon them in the following manner:

1. If the stock numbers in both records are equal, then the action indicated on the transaction record is carried out. Either the current master record is deleted by not writing it to the new master file, or the data is changed in the current master record, as indicated on the transaction record, and the modified current master record is written to the new master file.
2. If the stock number in the current master record is less than the stock number in the transaction record (i.e., if the transaction file contains no modifications to the current master record), then the current master record is written to the new master file.
3. If the stock number in the current master file is greater than the stock number in the transaction record (i.e., if the transaction record has no match), then the transaction record is in error and a diagnostic message is displayed.

This process of matching records is illustrated in the following problem.

Problem: Given the current master file shown in Figure 9.6, on the opposite page, and the transaction file shown in Table 9.3, a program that updates the current master file and creates a new master file will be illustrated. Both the current master file and the transaction file are in ascending sequence by stock number.

_____**TABLE 9.3** Inventory Data in the Transaction File TRAINV–2.DAT_____

STOCK NUMBER	TRANSACTION CODE	WAREHOUSE LOCATION	DESCRIPTION	UNIT COST	SELLING PRICE	QUANTITY ON HAND
C204	D	Null Char.	Null Char.	–1	–1	–1
C402	C	3	Null Char.	33.50	40.50	–1
S812	C	Null Char.	ROUTER-II	–1	–1	12
T615	D	Null Char.	Null Char.	–1	–1	–1
T731	C	Null Char.	Null Char.	6.50	–1	–1

Change the name of the current master file in Figure 9.6 to CURINV-2.DAT. Use the name TRAINV-2.DAT to identify the transaction file in Table 9.3. Call the new master file INV-2.DAT.

With respect to the contents of the transaction file TRAINV-2.DAT:

1. The transaction code D indicates that the corresponding record in the current master file is to be deleted, and the code C indicates changes.
2. Data items that are *not* to be changed in the current master file are designated in the transaction file with a value of –1 if the item is numeric and by a null character if the item is a string.
3. In order for the INPUT statement to read the transaction file properly, all data items are assigned a value, including those within records representing a delete.
4. With minor modifications, Program 6.2, on page 196, can be used to build the transaction file TRAINV-2.DAT.

If a record in the transaction file has no matching record in the current master file, then the diagnostic message

```
** ERROR ** Transaction record with stock number XXXX has no match
```

is displayed. As part of the end-of-job routine, the total number of records deleted and the number of records changed are displayed.

Since the algorithm for matching records is similar to the algorithm for merging files that was presented in Programming Case Study 19, a top-down chart and a list of the program tasks are not included in this Programming Case Study. The program solution follows.

Program Solution   The following program matches records between the current master file, CURINV-2.DAT, and the transaction file, TRAINV-2.DAT, and builds the new master file, INV-2.DAT.

PROGRAM 9.2

```
1000 ' Program 9.2
1010 ' File Maintenance II -  Deleting Records and Changing Fields
1020 ' Current Master File =  CURINV-2.DAT
1030 ' Transaction File    =  TRAINV-2.DAT
1040 ' New Master File      =  INV-2.DAT
1050 ' **********************************************************************
1060 ' *                        Main Module                                 *
1070 ' **********************************************************************
1080 GOSUB 2000   ' Call Initialization
1090 GOSUB 3000   ' Call Process Files
1100 GOSUB 4000   ' Call Wrap-up
1110 END
1120 '
2000 ' **********************************************************************
2010 ' *                       Initialization                               *
2020 ' **********************************************************************
2030 DELETE.COUNT = 0
2040 CHANGE.COUNT = 0
2050 RECORD.COUNT = 0
2060 MAS.EOF$ = "OFF"
2070 TRA.EOF$ = "OFF"
2080 OPEN "CURINV-2.DAT" FOR INPUT  AS #1
2090 OPEN "TRAINV-2.DAT" FOR INPUT  AS #2
2100 OPEN "INV-2.DAT"    FOR OUTPUT AS #3
2110 CLS : KEY OFF  ' Clear Screen
2120 PRINT "Deleting Records and Changing Fields in Inventory File"
2130 PRINT "------------------------------------------------------"
2140 RETURN
2150 '
3000 ' **********************************************************************
3010 ' *                       Process Files                                *
3020 ' **********************************************************************
3030 GOSUB 5400   ' Call Read Next Current Master Record
3040 GOSUB 5600   ' Call Read Next Transaction Record
3050 WHILE MAS.EOF$ = "OFF" AND TRA.EOF$ = "OFF"
3060    IF STOCK$ = TRA.STOCK$
           THEN GOSUB 3200
           ELSE GOSUB 3800
3070 WEND
3080 RETURN
3090 '
```

(continued)

```
3200 ' ***************************************************************
3210 ' *                  Determine Maintenance Type               *
3220 ' ***************************************************************
3230 IF TRA.TYPE$ = "D"
         THEN GOSUB 3400
         ELSE GOSUB 3600
3240 RETURN
3250 '
3400 ' ***************************************************************
3410 ' *                     Delete Record                         *
3420 ' ***************************************************************
3430 DELETE.COUNT = DELETE.COUNT + 1
3440 GOSUB 5400   ' Call Read Next Current Master Record
3450 GOSUB 5600   ' Call Read Next Transaction Record
3460 RETURN
3470 '
3600 ' ***************************************************************
3610 ' *                     Change Record                         *
3620 ' ***************************************************************
3630 IF TRA.LOCATION$ <> ""
         THEN LOCATION$ = TRA.LOCATION$
3640 IF TRA.DESC$ <> ""
         THEN DESC$ = TRA.DESC$
3650 IF TRA.COST   <> -1
         THEN COST   = TRA.COST
3660 IF TRA.PRICE <> -1
         THEN PRICE = TRA.PRICE
3670 IF TRA.QUANTITY   <> -1
         THEN QUANTITY = TRA.QUANTITY
3680 CHANGE.COUNT = CHANGE.COUNT + 1
3690 GOSUB 5000   ' Call Write Record to New Master File
3700 GOSUB 5400   ' Call Read Next Current Master Record
3710 GOSUB 5600   ' Call Read Next Transaction Record
3720 RETURN
3730 '
3800 ' ***************************************************************
3810 ' *         Write Current Master or Error Routine            *
3820 ' ***************************************************************
3830 IF STOCK$ < TRA.STOCK$
         THEN GOSUB 5000 : GOSUB 5400
         ELSE GOSUB 5200 : GOSUB 5600
3840 RETURN
3850 '
4000 ' ***************************************************************
4010 ' *                         Wrap-up                           *
4020 ' ***************************************************************
4030 WHILE MAS.EOF$ = "OFF"
4040     GOSUB 5000 ' Call Write Record to New Master File
4050     GOSUB 5400 ' Call Read Next Current Master Record
4060 WEND
4070 WHILE TRA.EOF$ = "OFF"
4080     GOSUB 5200   ' Call Display Error Message
4090     GOSUB 5600   ' Call Read Next Transaction Record
4100 WEND
4110 CLOSE
4120 PRINT
4130 PRINT "Total Number of Records Deleted ==========>";
         DELETE.COUNT
4140 PRINT "Total Number of Records Changed ==========>";
         CHANGE.COUNT
4150 PRINT "Total Number of Records in New Master ====>";
         RECORD.COUNT
4160 PRINT
```

(continued)

```
4170 PRINT "INV-2.DAT Update Complete"
4180 RETURN
4190 '
5000 ' ************************************************************
5010 ' *              Write Record to New Master File            *
5020 ' ************************************************************
5030 WRITE #3, STOCK$, LOCATION$, DESC$, COST, PRICE, QUANTITY
5040 RECORD.COUNT = RECORD.COUNT + 1
5050 RETURN
5060 '
5200 ' ************************************************************
5210 ' *                  Display Error Message                  *
5220 ' ************************************************************
5230 PRINT
5240 PRINT "** ERROR ** Transaction record with stock number ";
5250 PRINT TRA.STOCK$; " has no match."
5260 RETURN
5270 '
5400 ' ************************************************************
5410 ' *              Read Next Current Master Record            *
5420 ' ************************************************************
5430 IF EOF(1)
        THEN MAS.EOF$ = "ON"
        ELSE INPUT #1, STOCK$, LOCATION$, DESC$, COST, PRICE, QUANTITY
5440 RETURN
5450 '
5600 ' ************************************************************
5610 ' *               Read Next Transaction Record              *
5620 ' ************************************************************
5630 IF EOF(2) THEN TRA.EOF$ = "ON"
                ELSE INPUT #2, TRA.STOCK$, TRA.TYPE$, TRA.LOCATION$,
                             TRA.DESC$, TRA.COST, TRA.PRICE, TRA.QUANTITY
5640 RETURN
5650 ' ******************** End of Program ********************

RUN
```

Discussion of the Program Solution   When the RUN command is issued for Program 9.2, line 1080 in the Main Module transfers control to the Initialization Module. Lines 2030 through 2070 initialize counters to zero and end-of-file switches to OFF. Line 2080 opens for input the current master file, CURINV-2. DAT, shown in Figure 9.6 on page 338. Line 2090 opens for input the transaction file, TRAINV-2.DAT. TRAINV-2.DAT contains the records shown in Figure 9.7. Line 2100 opens the new master file, INV-2.DAT. After the screen has been cleared and a title has been displayed, control returns to the Main Module.

```
"C204","D","","",-1,-1,-1
"C402","C", 3,"",33.50,40.50,-1
"S812","C","","ROUTER-II",-1,-1,12
"T615","D","","",-1,-1,-1
"T731","C","","",6.50,-1,-1
```

FIGURE 9.7
A list of the records in the sequential file TRAINV-2.DAT.

Line 1090 transfers control to the Process Files Module. Lines 3030 and 3040 call upon the modules to read the first current master record and the first transaction record. Within the While loop, line 3060 compares the two stock numbers, STOCK$ and TRA.STOCK$. If STOCK$ is equal to TRA.STOCK$, then the transaction represents a change or delete and control passes to line 3200. In line 3230, the transaction type is compared to the value D. If the record represents a delete, then control transfers to the subroutine beginning at line 3400. Otherwise, the record represents a change, and control transfers to the subroutine beginning at line 3600.

If in line 3060, STOCK\$ does not equal TRA.STOCK\$, then control passes to line 3800 and the PC determines whether the current master record should be written to the new master or the transaction record is in error.

In the Change Record Module, lines 3630 through 3670 test each value assigned to the variables that correspond to the transaction record. If any of the numeric variables TRA.COST, TRA.PRICE, or TRA.QUANTITY equal –1, then the corresponding variables in the current master file are *not* changed. If they equal any other value, then the IF statements result in the assignment of new values to the variables making up the current master record. Line 3630 compares TRA.LOCATION\$ to the null character. The null character signifies that the description field in the current master record is not to be changed. If TRA.LOCATION\$ does not equal a null character, then TRA.LOCATION\$ is assigned to LOCATION\$.

After each variable is tested (except for the stock number, which cannot be changed), line 3680 increments the change field counter (CHANGE.COUNT) by 1 and line 3690 causes the PC to write the modified current master record to the new master file. In the Write Record to New Master File Module, line 5040 increments the new master file record count (RECORD.COUNT) by 1. Finally, lines 3700 and 3710 read the next current master record and the next transaction record. Control then returns to the Process Files Module.

Let us now go back to line 3060 and discuss what happens if the current master record and transaction record do not match. If STOCK\$ does not equal TRA.STOCK\$, then control passes to line 3800. Line 3830 determines whether the stock number in the current master record STOCK\$ is less than the stock number TRA.STOCK\$ in the transaction record. If STOCK\$ is less than TRA.STOCK\$, then control transfers to the Write Record to New Master File Module, and the current master record is written to the new master file before RECORD.COUNT is incremented by 1. The last statement in the THEN clause in line 3830 reads the next current master record.

In line 3830, if STOCK\$ is not less than TRA.STOCK\$, then it is greater than TRA.STOCK\$. In this case, control transfers to the Display Error Message Module (lines 5200 through 5270), which displays an appropriate diagnostic message. The diagnostic message states that the transaction record has no corresponding match in the current master file. Following a return from the Display Error Message Module, the PC reads the next transaction record due to the last statement in the ELSE clause in line 3830.

The Process Files Module maintains control of the PC until end of file is sensed on either the current master file or the transaction file. Note here again that switches (MAS.EOF and TRA.EOF), not the EOF function, are used to control the While loops. If the EOF function is used to control the looping, it is possible that the last record in either input file will not be processed.

Once the end-of-file mark is sensed on either input file, the appropriate switch is set equal to the value ON and control passes back to the Main Module. The Wrap-up Module then flushes either file that may have records remaining. If records remain in the current master file, then they are written to the new master file. If records remain in the transaction file, then they have no match and are considered to be in error.

Figure 9.8 shows the display due to the execution of Program 9.2.

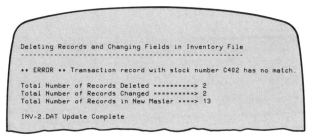

FIGURE 9.8
The display due to the execution of Program 9.2.

In the results displayed following the command RUN, one of the 5 records in the transaction file, stock number C402, does not have a corresponding match in the current master file. Of the other 4 transaction records, 2 call for deleting records and 2 for modifying the current master records. The new master file, INV-2.DAT, contains 13 records, as shown in Figure 9.9.

```
"C101","1","Roadhandler",97.56,125.11,25
"C103","2","Saw-Blades",5.06,6.04,15
"C206","1","Square",4.56,5.42,34
"C502","2","Tripod",32.5,38.99,10
"S209","1","Maxidrill",88.76,109.99,6
"S210","3","Microscope",31.5,41.99,8
"S416","2","Normalsaw",152.55,179.4,1
"S812","2","ROUTER-II",48.47,61.15,12
"S941","2","Hip-Boot",26.95,32.5,12
"S942","4","Radialsaw",376.04,419.89,3
"T713","2","Moc-Boot",24.99,29.99,30
"T731","1","Sandals",6.5,9.45,52
"T814","2","Work-Boot",22.99,27.99,56
```

FIGURE 9.9

A list of the records in the sequential file INV-2.DAT following execution of Program 9.2.

TRY IT YOURSELF

Load Program 9.2 (PRG9-2) from the Student Diskette. In line 2100, change INV-2.DAT to INV-3.DAT. In line 2060, assign the value ON to the variable MAS.EOF$. Execute the program and see what happens.

9.3

RANDOM FILE PROCESSING

As you learned in section 9.1, the sequence of processing a randomly organized file has no relationship to the sequence in which the records are stored in the file. Random files have several advantages over sequential files, even though fewer program steps are required to create and access records within sequential files than for the same procedure within random files. For example, random files require less space in auxiliary storage, because numbers are stored in a compressed format and no commas are required between data items.

The main advantage of random files over sequential files is that their records may be processed randomly. In other words, processing a record in the middle of the file does not require that all the records prior to that one be read. This is true because each record within a random file has a key associated with it. The key indicates the position of the record from the beginning of the random file.

This section presents the file-handling statements and functions that are necessary to create and process files that can be accessed randomly.

Opening and Closing Random Files

As with sequential files, random files must be opened before they are read from or written to. When a program is finished with a random file, it must close the file. The general form of the OPEN statement for random files is shown in Table 9.4. The general form of the CLOSE statement is the same as for sequential files and is shown in Table 6.2 on page 189.

TABLE 9.4 The OPEN Statement for Random Files

General Form:	OPEN *filespec* AS #*filenumber* LEN = *recl*
	where ***filespec*** *is the name of the random file;*
	filenumber *is a numeric expression whose value is between 1 and the maximum number of files allowed (3 by default); and*
	recl *is a value equal to the maximum number of characters in each record.*
Keyword Entry:	*Simultaneously press the Alt and O keys on your keyboard.*

(continued)

_____TABLE 9.4 The OPEN Statement for Random Files *(continued)*_____

Purpose:	*Allows a program to read from or write records to a random file.*
| *Examples:* | ```
100 OPEN "B:WAREHSE.DAT" AS #1 LEN = 59
200 OPEN "ACCOUNT.DAT" AS #2 LEN = 200
300 OPEN FILE$ AS #3 LEN = RECL
400 OPEN "B:EX91PAY.DAT" AS #1
``` |
| *Note:* | *MS BASIC provides a second general form for the* OPEN *statement:*
OPEN "R", #filenumber, filespec, recl
(This second general form is less contemporary than the general form specified in this table, and will therefore not be used in this book.) |

The two primary differences between opening a random file and a sequential file are as follows:

1. For sequential files, it is necessary that the mode of processing (INPUT, OUTPUT, or APPEND) be specified. When a mode is not specified, the PC opens the file as a random file. Once a random file has been opened, a program can read or write records to the file. This leads to the following rule:

OPEN Rule 6: When the mode is not specified in an OPEN statement, the file is opened as a random file.

2. For random files, the record length (i.e., the exact number of characters in each record) should be specified in the OPEN statement. Failure to do so may result in wasted space in auxiliary storage. The default record length for random files is 128 bytes.

   The record length may vary between 1 and 32,767 characters and should correspond to the total number of characters defined in the corresponding FIELD statement.

The following OPEN statement,

```
200 OPEN "ACCOUNT.DAT" AS #2 LEN = 60
```

opens ACCOUNT.DAT on the default drive for random processing as filenumber 2. The record length is 60 characters. If ACCOUNT.DAT does not exist in auxiliary storage, then it is created. If ACCOUNT.DAT already exists as a random file, records may be added, read, and rewritten.

The FIELD Statement   When an OPEN statement such as

```
2040 OPEN "WHSEDATA.DAT" AS #1 LEN = 59
```

is executed, the PC establishes in main storage a buffer, 59 positions (bytes) in length, for sending data to and receiving data from the random file WHSEDATA.DAT. When a program requests a record from WHSEDATA.DAT, the PC reads the record into the buffer. When a record is written to WHSEDATA.DAT, the program must first place the data items into the buffer. When a write statement is executed, the PC transfers the contents of the buffer to auxiliary storage.

MS BASIC includes the FIELD statement so that the program can either move the data out of the buffer following a read or store the data into the buffer before a write. The FIELD statement allows data items to be identified with respect to their size and location within the buffer.
```

Let us assume that the random file WHSEDATA.DAT contains a record for each warehouse that our company owns. Each record includes four data items (i.e., fields):

Data Item	Number of Characters
Warehouse Name	18
Street Address	17
City, State, Zip Code	20
Total Square Feet	4

The following FIELD statement may be used to describe each data item within the buffer:

```
2050 FIELD #1, 18 AS WHSE.NAME$,   17 AS WHSE.ADDRS1$,
               20 AS WHSE.ADDRS2$,  4 AS WHSE.AREA$
```

Line 2050 allocates the first 18 positions in the buffer to the string variable WHSE.NAME$ (warehouse name); the next 17 positions to WHSE.ADDRS1$ (street address); the next 20 positions to WHSE.ADDRS2$ (city, state, zip code); and the last 4 positions to WHSE.AREA$ (total square feet). Each position or byte can hold one character. Therefore, the warehouse name should not exceed 18 characters in length.

After a record is read into the buffer, the data items may be referenced through the use of WHSE.NAME$, WHSE.ADDRS1$, WHSE.ADDRS2$, and WHSE.AREA$. Also, these same variable names may be used to assign data items to the buffer before writing a record.

The general form of the FIELD statement is shown in Table 9.5. As indicated in Table 9.5, the list that defines a buffer in a FIELD statement can include only simple string variables. The following FIELD statement is invalid:

```
400 FIELD #3, 4 AS COUNT$, 10 AS NUM  ' Invalid due to numeric variable NUM
```

This leads to the following rule:

FIELD Rule 1: A FIELD statement can include only simple string variables.

TABLE 9.5 The FIELD Statement

General Form:	FIELD #filenumber, list where each entry in the **list** is of the following form: width AS stringvar where **width** is the number of positions (bytes) in the buffer allocated to the data item; and **stringvar** is the string variable name.
Purpose:	Allocates space for variables in a buffer by defining the location and length (number of characters) of data items and assigns a unique string variable to each data item location. The string variable is used to access or assign a data item in the buffer.
Examples:	100 FIELD #1, 12 AS DESC$, 4 AS PRICE$, 3 AS CODE$ 200 FIELD #2, 45 AS ADDRS$ 300 FIELD #3, 1 AS STA$, 23 AS COMMENT$, 99 AS JOB.DESC$

Shortly, we will discuss how to handle numeric data items when dealing with random files.

It is also important that the sum of the widths in the list of a FIELD statement not exceed the record length specified in the OPEN statement. Otherwise, the following diagnostic message is displayed, followed by termination of the program:

```
Field overflow
```

This leads to the following rule:

> **FIELD Rule 2:** The sum of the widths in the list of a FIELD statement must not exceed the record length in the OPEN statement.

With regard to the placement of the FIELD statement, most programmers place it immediately after the corresponding OPEN statement.

Several FIELD statements that refer to the same random file are allowed in the same program. A number of applications, like accounts receivable, inventory control, and payroll, are often designed around a single file. The file may contain a number of different types of records, such as a **header record** that includes permanent information, followed by related transaction records. Each type of record utilizes a different FIELD statement. A single character in each record identifies it as a header record or transaction record and this character is then used to determine which FIELD statement to use.

The LSET and RSET Statements

The LSET and RSET statements are used to store string data in the buffer before writing a record to a random file. LSET stands for left-justify and RSET for right-justify.

Given this FIELD statement:

```
500 FIELD #1,  9 AS EMP.NUMBER$,  25 AS EMP.NAME$,
              35 AS EMP.ADDRS$,   10 AS EMP.PHONE$
```

the following series of statements assign string data to the buffer:

```
600 LSET EMP.NUMBER$ = TRA.NUMBER$
610 LSET EMP.NAME$   = TRA.NAME$
620 RSET EMP.ADDRS$  = TRA.ADDRS$
630 LSET EMP.PHONE$  = TRA.PHONE$
```

Line 600 left-justifies the value of TRA.NUMBER$ in the 9 positions assigned to EMP.NUMBER$ in the buffer. Likewise, line 610 left-justifies the value of TRA.NAME$ in the 25 positions assigned to EMP.NAME$. Line 630 left-justifies the value of TRA.PHONE$ in the 10 positions assigned to EMP.PHONE$. Line 620 right-justifies the value of TRA.ADDRS$ in the 35 positions assigned in the buffer to EMP.ADDRS$.

The LSET and RSET statements not only justify a value in the buffer, they also append spaces to ensure that the length of the value is equal to the width of the string variable receiving it. If TRA.ADDRS$ is equal to 1458 Tod Ave, then it has a length of 12 characters. On the other hand, in the FIELD statement defined earlier by line 500, EMP.ADDRS$ was defined as having a length of 35 positions. The statement

```
710 LSET EMP.ADDRS$ = TRA.ADDRS$
```

assigns EMP.ADDRS$ the value 1458 Tod Ave *followed by* 23 spaces. The statement

```
720 RSET EMP.ADDRS$ = TRA.ADDRS$
```

assigns EMP.ADDRS$ the value 1458 Tod Ave *preceded by* 23 spaces.

If the string expression is longer than the width, both the LSET and RSET statements truncate the excess characters located on the right.

The LSET statement is used more often than the RSET statement. The following rule summarizes the use of the LSET and RSET statements.

> **LSET and RSET Rule 1:** Before a record is written to a random file, all values must be stored in the buffer through the use of the LSET or RSET statement. It is invalid to assign values to variables in a FIELD statement through the use of the INPUT, LET, or READ statement.

The general forms of the LSET and RSET statements are shown in Table 9.6.

_____TABLE 9.6 The LSET and RSET Statements_____

General Form:	LSET *stringvar* = *string expression* RSET *stringvar* = *string expression* where **stringvar** *is a string variable defined in the FIELD statement, and* **string expression** *is a value that is assigned to stringvar.*
Purpose:	*Moves data into a buffer in preparation for writing a random record.* LSET *left-justifies the string expression in stringvar.* RSET *right-justifies the string expression in stringvar.*
Examples:	500 LSET ACC.NUM$ = TRA.NUM$ 600 RSET INV.DESC$ = "Double-Sided Diskette" 700 LSET PART.COST$ = MKS$(PART.COST)

The MKI$,
MKS$, and MKD$
Functions —
Make a Numeric
Value a String
Value

It is invalid to define a numeric variable in the list of a FIELD statement. So that numeric values may be placed in the buffer, MS BASIC includes the MKI$, MKS$, and MKD$ string functions. These three functions are used to convert numeric values to string values so that they can be assigned to string variables in the buffer prior to writing the record to the random file. The converted string form of the numeric value is also called **compressed format** or **binary format**.

In the FIELD statement, the string variables that receive converted numeric values must be given proper lengths, as described in Table 9.7.

_____TABLE 9.7 Required Length Assignments for String Variables Receiving Numeric Values, Along with the Appropriate Function to Use_____

TYPE OF NUMERIC VALUE	LENGTH IN BYTES OF RECEIVING STRING VARIABLE	APPROPRIATE FUNCTION
Integer	*2*	MKI$
Single precision	*4*	MKS$
Double precision	*8*	MKD$

The MKI$ function is used to convert the value of an integer variable to a 2-byte string value. Likewise, MKS$ is used to change a value that has been assigned to a single-precision variable into a 4-byte string value, and MKD$ is used to change a double-precision value into an 8-byte string value. Table 9.8 illustrates several examples of the use of the MKI$, MKS$, and MKD$ functions in placing numeric values in the buffer of a random file.

_____TABLE 9.8 Examples of the MKI$, MKS$ and MKD$ String Functions_____

THE STATEMENT	RESULTS IN
Assume that the following FIELD statement is employed:	
1070 FIELD #1, 2 AS EMP.DEP$, 4 AS EMP.GROSS$, 8 AS EMP.YTD.GROSS$	
3300 LSET EMP.DEP$ = MKI$(TRA.DEP%)	*The numeric value of the integer variable TRA.DEP% is converted to a string value and assigned to EMP.DEP$.*
3310 LSET EMP.GROSS$ = MKS$(TRA.GROSS)	*The numeric value of the single-precision variable TRA.GROSS is converted to a string value and assigned to EMP.GROSS$.*
3320 LSET EMP.YTD.GROSS$ = MKD$(TRA.YTD.GROSS#)	*The numeric value of the double-precision variable TRA.YTD.GROSS# is converted to a string value and assigned to EMP.YTD.GROSS$.*

The CVI, CVS, and
CVD Functions –
Convert a String
Value to a Numeric
Value

The CVI, CVS, and
CVD Functions –
Convert a String
Value to a Numeric
Value

Before a string value representing a number can be used, it must be converted back to a numeric value. The three numeric functions CVI, CVS, and CVD are used to convert a string value to a numeric value following the read of a record from a random file. The appropriate function to use is shown in Table 9.9.

TABLE 9.9 Appropriate Function to Use Based on the Size Assigned to the String Variable in the FIELD Statement

LENGTH IN BYTES ASSIGNED STRING VARIABLE IN BUFFER	APPROPRIATE FUNCTION
2	CVI
4	CVS
8	CVD

As illustrated in Table 9.9, the CVI function is used to convert the string value assigned to a 2-byte string variable in the buffer to an integer value. The CVS function is used to convert the string value assigned to a 4-byte string variable to a single-precision value. And finally, the CVD function is used to convert the string value assigned to an 8-byte string variable to a double-precision value. Table 9.10 illustrates several examples of the use of the CVI, CVS, and CVD functions.

TABLE 9.10 Examples of the Numeric Functions CVI, CVS, and CVD

THE STATEMENT	RESULTS IN
Assume that the following FIELD *statement is employed:*	
1070 FIELD #1, 2 AS EMP.DEP$, 4 AS EMP.GROSS$, 8 AS EMP.YTD.GROSS$	
4300 PRINT "Dependents ==>"; CVI(EMP.DEP$)	*The string value of EMP.DEP$ is converted to an integer value and is displayed.*
4310 TAX = CVS(EMP.GROSS$) * 0.02	*The string value of EMP.GROSS$ is converted to a single-precision value and is multiplied by 0.02. The product is assigned to TAX.*
4320 YTD.GROSS# = CVD(EMP.YTD.GROSS$)	*The string value of EMP.YTD. GROSS$ is converted to a double-precision value and this value is assigned to YTD.GROSS#.*

The GET and PUT
Statements

The GET statement reads and transfers a record from a random file to the buffer defined by the corresponding FIELD statement. The PUT statement writes a record from the buffer defined by the corresponding FIELD statement to a random file.

The general forms of the GET and PUT statements are shown in Tables 9.11 and 9.12.

TABLE 9.11 The GET Statement

General Form:	*GET #filenumber, record number*
	or
	GET #filenumber
Purpose:	*Reads and transfers a record from the random file (assigned to filenumber) to a buffer defined by a corresponding* FIELD *statement. If the record number is not included in the* GET *statement, then the next record in the random file is read and transferred to the buffer.*
Examples:	400 GET #1, RECORD.NUMBER
	500 GET #2, 47
	600 GET #FILE, REC
	700 GET #3

The following partial program illustrates the relationship between the OPEN, FIELD, and GET statements.

```
490 OPEN "EMPDATA.DAT" AS #1 LEN = 78
500 FIELD #1, 9 AS EMP.NUMBER$,  25 AS EMP.NAME$,
             35 AS EMP.ADDRESS$,  9 AS EMP.PHONE$
        .
        .
        .
900 GET #1, RECORD.NUMBER
```

If RECORD.NUMBER has a value of 29 when line 900 is executed, then the 29th record in the random file EMPDATA.DAT is read into the buffer defined by the FIELD statement in line 500.

Records from a random file may be read sequentially, beginning at any record in the file. For example, if RECORD.NUMBER is assigned the value 26 before the execution of line 500 in the following partial program,

```
500 GET #2, RECORD.NUMBER
        .
        .
        .
600 GET #2
        .
        .
        .
700 GET #2
```

then line 500 reads the 26th record, line 600 the 27th record, and line 700 the 28th record. If the first GET following an OPEN statement has no record number, then the first record in the random file is read and transferred to the buffer. The following partial program reads sequentially a random file with 50 records and sums the numeric value assigned to ACC.AMT$ for each record read.

```
100 SUM = 0
110 OPEN "ACCOUNT.DAT" AS #3 LEN = 41
120 FIELD #3, 14 AS ACC.NUM$, 23 AS ACC.NAME$, 4 AS ACC.AMT$
130 FOR RECORD.NUMBER = 1 TO 50
140    GET #3
150    SUM = SUM + CVS(ACC.AMT$)
160 NEXT RECORD.NUMBER
170 PRINT "The sum is"; SUM
```

Line 140 of the For loop reads the next record in the random file. Line 150 increments the variable SUM by the numeric value of ACC.AMT$ for each record read. Note that CVS(ACC.AMT$) is equal to the numeric value of ACC.AMT$.

_____TABLE 9.12 The PUT Statement_____

General Form:	PUT #filenumber, record number *or* PUT #filenumber
Purpose:	Writes a record to the random file (assigned to filenumber) from the buffer defined by a corresponding FIELD statement. If the record number is not included in the PUT statement, then the next record in the random file is replaced by the contents of the buffer.
Examples:	300 PUT #1, RECORD.NUMBER 400 PUT #2, 567 500 PUT #FILENUM, COUNT 600 PUT #3

As indicated in Table 9.12, the PUT statement writes the contents of the buffer to a random file. Thus the statement

```
800 PUT #2, 62
```

writes the contents of the buffer assigned to filenumber 2 as record 62.

Remember to use the LSET and RSET statements to assign the data to the variables in the FIELD statement before the PUT statement is executed.

The LOC and LOF Functions

The LOC(n) function returns the record number of the last record read or written to the random file assigned to filenumber n. For example, in the following partial program,

```
500 GET #3, RECORD.NUMBER
510 LAST.RECORD = LOC(3)
```

the variable LAST.RECORD is assigned the value of RECORD.NUMBER, since RECORD.NUMBER is the record number of the last record read from the random file assigned to filenumber 3. The LOC function may also be used with a sequential file to determine the total number of records read and written since the file was last opened.

The LOF(n) function returns information regarding the character size of the random file assigned to filenumber n. This value may then be used to determine the number of records in a random file by dividing whatever the LOF function returns by the record length defined in the OPEN statement. This expression can be important when processing a random file sequentially.

Programming Case Study 21: *Creating a Random File*

In earlier Programming Case Studies, each record in INVNTORY.DAT included a number to indicate the warehouse in which the stock item was located. The warehouse location numbers varied between 1 and 4. The following problem creates a random file in which each record includes a warehouse name, an address, and a total number of square feet for each of the four warehouses.

Problem: The PUC Company requests a program that creates a random file in which each record represents one of its warehouses. Each record includes the following data items:

Data Item	Type	No. of Characters
Warehouse Name	String	18
Street Address	String	17
City State Zip Code	String	20
Total Square Feet	Numeric, single precision	4
Total Record Character Count		59

The actual data for each record is shown below:

Warehouse Location	Warehouse Name	Street Address	City, State, Zip Code	Total Square Feet
1	PUC Gyte Whse	1498 Baring Ave.	Whitley IN 46325	80,000
2	PUC Anderson Whse	612 45th St.	Calcity IL 60618	220,000
3	PUC Potter Whse	1329 Olcot St.	Pointe IN 46367	85,900
4	PUC Porter Whse	15 E 63rd St.	Polk IN 45323	92,500

The user enters the warehouse location number to indicate the record that is to be created. The warehouse location number *is not* to be part of the record.

Following are the program tasks in outline form; a program solution; and a discussion of the program solution.

Program Tasks   1. Initialization

   a. Turn off the 25th line.
   b. Open the file WHSEDATA.DAT for random access as filenumber 1 with a record length of 59 characters.
   c. Use the following FIELD statement:

   ```
   FIELD #1, 18 AS WHSE.NAME$,  17 AS WHSE.ADDRS1$,
             20 AS WHSE.ADDRS2$, 4 AS WHSE.AREA$
   ```

   where WHSE.NAME$ = warehouse name
         WHSE.ADDRS1$ = street address
         WHSE.ADDRS2$ = city, state, zip code
         WHSE.AREA$ = total square feet

2. Create Random File

   a. Set CONTROL$ equal to the value Y.
   b. Establish a While loop that executes until CONTROL$ does not equal the value Y or y. Within the While loop, do the following:
      (1) Call the Accept a Warehouse Record Module. In this module, do the following:
         (a) Clear the screen.
         (b) Display a program title.
         (c) Use INPUT statements to accept the warehouse number (TRA.LOCATION); warehouse name (TRA.NAME$); warehouse street address (TRA.ADDRS1$); warehouse city, state, zip code (TRA.ADDRS2$); and warehouse square feet (TRA.AREA).
      (2) Call the Write a Warehouse Record Module. In this module, do the following:
         (a) Use the LSET statement to assign the four data items to the buffer. Use the MKS$ function to convert the numeric value of TRA.AREA to a string value.
         (b) Write the record to the random file WHSEDATA.DAT, using the PUT statement with the key TRA.LOCATION.
      (3) Use an INPUT statement to assign CONTROL$ the value Y or y if the user wants to enter another record.

3. Wrap-up

   a. Close the random file WHSEDATA.DAT.
   b. Display an end-of-job message.

Program Solution   The following program corresponds to the preceding tasks.

PROGRAM 9.3

```
1000 ' Program 9.3
1010 ' Creating a Random File
1020 ' Random File Created = WHSEDATA.DAT
1030 ' *********************************
1040 ' *          Main Module          *
1050 ' *********************************
1060 GOSUB 2000   ' Call Initialization
1070 GOSUB 3000   ' Call Create Random File
1080 GOSUB 4000   ' Call Wrap-up
1090 END
1100 '
```

```
2000 ' *********************************
2010 ' *          Initialization        *
2020 ' *********************************
2030 KEY OFF   ' Clear the 25th Line
2040 OPEN "WHSEDATA.DAT" AS #1 LEN = 59
2050 FIELD #1, 18 AS WHSE.NAME$,  17 AS WHSE.ADDRS1$,
                20 AS WHSE.ADDRS2$, 4 AS WHSE.AREA$
2060 RETURN
2070 '
3000 ' *********************************
3010 ' *          Create Random File      *
3020 ' *********************************
3030 CONTROL$ = "Y"
3040 WHILE CONTROL$ = "Y" OR CONTROL$ = "y"
3050    GOSUB 3200  ' Call Accept a Warehouse Record
3060    GOSUB 3400   ' Call Write a Warehouse Record
3070    LOCATE 14, 10
3080    INPUT "Enter Y to add another record, else N... ",
             CONTROL$
3090 WEND
3100 RETURN
3110 '
3200 ' *********************************
3210 ' *    Accept a Warehouse Record    *
3220 ' *********************************
3230 CLS  ' Clear Screen
3240 LOCATE  2, 10
3250 PRINT "Warehouse Location Random File Create"
3260 LOCATE  4, 10
3270 INPUT "Warehouse Number =============> ", TRA.LOCATION
3280 LOCATE  6, 10
3290 INPUT "Warehouse Name ===============> ", TRA.NAME$
3300 LOCATE  8, 10
3310 INPUT "Warehouse Street =============> ", TRA.ADDRS1$
3320 LOCATE 10, 10
3330 INPUT "Warehouse City, State, Zip ===> ", TRA.ADDRS2$
3340 LOCATE 12, 10
3350 INPUT "Warehouse Total Square Feet ==> ", TRA.AREA
3360 RETURN
3370 '
3400 ' *********************************
3410 ' *     Write a Warehouse Record    *
3420 ' *********************************
3430 LSET WHSE.NAME$   = TRA.NAME$
3440 LSET WHSE.ADDRS1$ = TRA.ADDRS1$
3450 LSET WHSE.ADDRS2$ = TRA.ADDRS2$
3460 LSET WHSE.AREA$   = MKS$(TRA.AREA)
3470 PUT #1, TRA.LOCATION
3480 RETURN
3490 '
4000 ' *********************************
4010 ' *             Wrap-up             *
4020 ' *********************************
4030 CLOSE #1
4040 LOCATE 16, 10 : PRINT "Random file WHSEDATA.DAT created"
4050 LOCATE 18, 10 : PRINT "Job Complete"
4060 RETURN
4070 ' ********* End of Program *********

RUN
```

Discussion of the
Program Solution

When the RUN command is issued for Program 9.3, line 2040 opens the random file WAREHSE.DAT as filenumber 1. Line 2050 defines the buffer for filenumber 1. As shown in Figure 9.10, the Accept a Warehouse Record Module (lines 3200 through 3370) accepts the operator's responses. Lines 3430 through 3460 of the Write a Warehouse Record Module assigns the data items to the buffer. The PUT statement in line 3470 writes the record that corresponds to the warehouse location (TRA.LOCATION). Finally, line 3080 in the Create Random File Module accepts a user response that determines whether the program should continue.

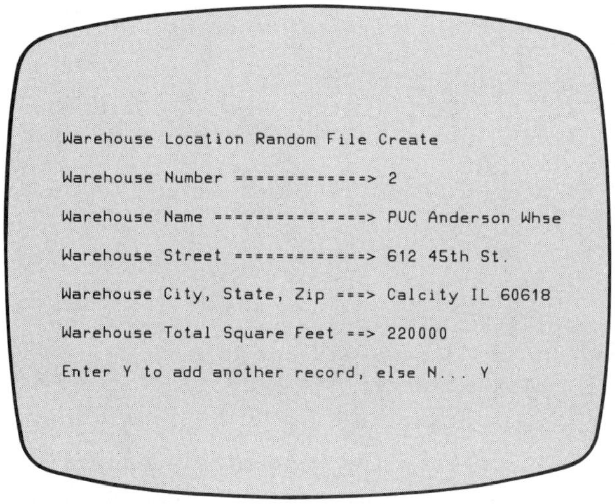

FIGURE 9.10
*Display from the
execution of Program
9.3 for warehouse
location 2.*

```
Warehouse Location Random File Create

Warehouse Number ==============> 2

Warehouse Name ===============> PUC Anderson Whse

Warehouse Street =============> 612 45th St.

Warehouse City, State, Zip ===> Calcity IL 60618

Warehouse Total Square Feet ==> 220000

Enter Y to add another record, else N... Y
```

Program 9.3 can be rewritten without the operator being required to enter the warehouse location number TRA.LOCATION. In the rewritten version, line 3470 is modified to 3470 PUT #1. A PUT statement without a record number writes the buffer as the next record. However, the operator would then be required to enter the records in sequence. As it stands now, Program 9.3 will properly create the random file regardless of the order in which the records are entered. For example, warehouse location number 4 can be entered before warehouse location number 1.

Because it requests a warehouse location number, Program 9.3 can later be used to add new warehouse records or to modify existing warehouse records. For example, if a fifth warehouse is added by the PUC Company, Program 9.3 can be used to add this new record. Unlike sequential files, whose contents are automatically deleted when opened for output, random files exist until they are deleted by a system command.

In the creation of random files, it is not necessary that a record be entered for every record number. It is valid to number warehouses 1, 3, 6, and 10. When a random file like that is created without contiguous record numbers, the PC reserves areas for records 2, 4, 5, 7, 8, and 9. These areas are called **empty cells**.

Try It Yourself

Load Program 9.3 (PRG9-3) from the Student Diskette. Execute the program and add record number 6. Use your first name as the name of the warehouse; your address; and a square-foot area of 100,000.

Programming Case Study 22: *Accessing Records in a Random File*

The following problem requires a program that accesses records in the random file WHSEDATA.DAT, which was created in Programming Case Study 21.

Problem: The PUC Company has requested that a program be written to access and display records from the random file WHSEDATA.DAT.

Following are the program tasks in outline form; a program solution; and a discussion of the program solution.

Program Tasks   1. Initialization

    a. Turn off the 25th line.

    b. Open the file WHSEDATA.DAT for random access as filenumber 1 with a record length of 59 characters.

    c. Use the following FIELD statement:

```
FIELD #1, 18 AS WHSE.NAME$,  17 AS WHSE.ADDRS1$,
          20 AS WHSE.ADDRS2$, 4 AS WHSE.AREA$
```

    where WHSE.NAME$ = warehouse name
           WHSE.ADDRS1$ = street address
           WHSE.ADDRS2$ = city, state, zip code
           WHSE.AREA$ = total square feet

2. Process a Request

    a. Set CONTROL$ equal to the value Y.

    b. Establish a While loop that executes until CONTROL$ does not equal the value Y or y. Within the While loop, do the following:

        (1) Call the Accept a Request Module. Within the module, clear the screen, display a program title, and use the INPUT statement to accept the warehouse location number (TRA.LOCATION).

        (2) Call the Get and Display Record Module. Within this module, use the GET statement to access the requested record (TRA.LOCATION). Next display the variables described in the FIELD statement in step 1c. Use the CVS function to display the numeric value of WHSE.AREA.

        (3) Use an INPUT statement to assign CONTROL$ the value Y or y if the user wants to display another record.

3. Wrap-up

    a. Close the random file WHSEDATA.DAT.

    b. Clear the screen.

    c. Display an end-of-job message.

Program Solution   The following program corresponds to the preceding tasks.

PROGRAM 9.4

```
1000 ' Program 9.4
1010 ' Accessing Records in a Random File
1020 ' Random File = WHSEDATA.DAT
1030 ' *********************************
1040 ' *          Main Module          *
1050 ' *********************************
1060 GOSUB 2000  ' Call Initialization
1070 GOSUB 3000  ' Call Process a Request
1080 GOSUB 4000  ' Call Wrap-up
1090 END
1100 '
```

(continued)

```
2000 ' ********************************
2010 ' *          Initialization          *
2020 ' ********************************
2030 KEY OFF  ' Clear the 25th Line
2040 OPEN "WHSEDATA.DAT" AS #1 LEN = 59
2050 FIELD #1, 18 AS WHSE.NAME$,  17 AS WHSE.ADDRS1$,
               20 AS WHSE.ADDRS2$, 4 AS WHSE.AREA$
2060 RETURN
2070 '
3000 ' ********************************
3010 ' *          Process a Request        *
3020 ' ********************************
3030 CONTROL$ = "Y"
3040 WHILE CONTROL$ = "Y" OR CONTROL$ = "y"
3050    GOSUB 3200  ' Call Accept a Request
3060    GOSUB 3400  ' Call Get and Display Record
3070    LOCATE 14, 10
3080    INPUT "Enter Y to access another record, else N... ",
              CONTROL$
3090 WEND
3100 RETURN
3110 '
3200 ' ********************************
3210 ' *          Accept a Request         *
3220 ' ********************************
3230 CLS  ' Clear Screen
3240 LOCATE 2, 10
3250 PRINT "Warehouse Location Random File Access"
3260 LOCATE 4, 10
3270 INPUT "Warehouse Number ==============> ", TRA.LOCATION
3280 RETURN
3290 '
3400 ' ********************************
3410 ' *       Get and Display Record       *
3420 ' ********************************
3430 GET #1, TRA.LOCATION
3440 LOCATE  6, 10
3450 PRINT "Warehouse Name ===============> "; WHSE.NAME$
3460 LOCATE  8, 10
3470 PRINT "Warehouse Street =============> "; WHSE.ADDRS1$
3480 LOCATE 10, 10
3490 PRINT "Warehouse City, State, Zip ===> "; WHSE.ADDRS2$
3500 LOCATE 12, 10
3510 PRINT USING "Warehouse Total Square Feet ==> ###,###";
               CVS(WHSE.AREA$)
3520 RETURN
3530 '
4000 ' ********************************
4010 ' *             Wrap-up              *
4020 ' ********************************
4030 CLOSE #1
4040 LOCATE 16, 10 : PRINT "Job Complete"
4050 RETURN
4060 ' ********* End of Program *********

RUN
```

*Discussion of the
Program Solution*   Figure 9.11 shows the results displayed when warehouse location number 2 is entered for
Program 9.4. Line 3430 in the Get and Display Record Module reads the record that
corresponds to the number entered by the user and that was assigned to TRA.LOCATION in
line 3270. Lines 3450 through 3490 show that the values found in a record can be displayed

by using the variable names in the FIELD statement. It is not necessary to use any special assignment statement when displaying the values of string variables that do not represent numeric values in a FIELD statement. In line 3510, the CVS function is used to convert the total square feet (WHSE.AREA$) to a numeric value.

It is important to note that records in WHSEDATA.DAT may be accessed in any order desired. After displaying warehouse location number 2, you may request 1, 3, 4, or 2 again and the PC can respond immediately without rewinding the file or reading records between the previously accessed record and the next record.

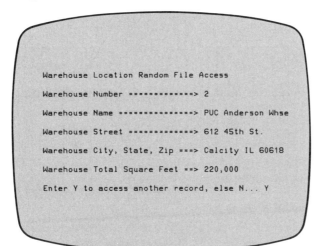

FIGURE 9.11
Results displayed due to entering warehouse location number 2 for Program 9.4.

<u>*TRY IT YOURSELF*</u>

Load Program 9.4 (PRG9-4) from the Student Diskette. Execute the program and request record number 6 — the one you added in the previous Try It Yourself. After record number 6 displays, request record number 5 and see what happens. Can you explain the display?

⊞ 9.4
SIMULATED-INDEXED FILES

Provided the record number is known, any record can be accessed in a random file. Unfortunately, few applications use integers like 1, 2, and 3 to represent the employee numbers, customer numbers, or stock numbers that commonly identify the record to be accessed in a file. More often, these keys are made up of several digits and letters that have no relationship to the location of the record in a random file. However, many applications require random access on the basis of these types of keys.

In many programming languages, like COBOL and PL/I, a third type of file organization, indexed files, allows a relationship between a key and the record location to be automatically established. With MS BASIC, indexed files are not available, and therefore the relationship between the key and the record location must be handled by the programmer.

Programming Case Study 23: *Using a Simulated-Indexed File for Inventory Retrieval and Update*

Problem: The Stores department of the PUC Company has requested computerized access to inventory records by stock number. Their request involves the creation of a simulated-indexed file as illustrated in the system flowchart in Figure 9.12 on the following page.

Two programs are required. The first program should create an index (for up to 100 keys) and a corresponding random file from the sequential file INV-2.DAT created earlier by Program 9.2 and shown in Figure 9.9 on page 344. The second program should permit the user to display, add, change, and delete records in the file, provided the stock number is known.

Following are the program tasks for part 1 of the problem; the program 1 solution; and a discussion of the program 1 solution.

FIGURE 9.12
A system flowchart representing Programs 9.5 and 9.6.

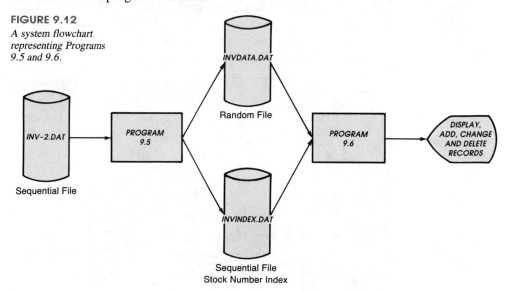

Program 1 Tasks: Build Index File

1. Initialization

   a. Clear screen.
   b. Declare array INDEX$ to 100 elements.
   c. Use a For loop to set each element in array INDEX$ equal to the string value Empty.
   d. Set RECORD.NUMBER to zero.
   e. Open INV-2.DAT and INVDATA.DAT. Records will be read from the sequential file INV-2.DAT and written to the random file INVDATA.DAT. Assign a length of 32 characters to each random record. This character count is based on the following:

Data Item	Maximum No. of Characters	Master File Names	Random File Names
Stock Number	4	MAS.STOCK$	STOCK$
Warehouse Location	1	MAS.LOCATION$	LOCATION$
Description	15	MAS.DESC$	DESC$
Unit Cost	4	MAS.COST	COST$
Selling Price	4	MAS.PRICE	PRICE$
Quantity on Hand	4	MAS.QUANTITY	QUANTITY$
Total Character Count	32		

   f. Use the following FIELD statement:

```
2120 FIELD #2, 4 AS STOCK$, 1 AS LOCATION$, 15 AS DESC$,
              4 AS COST$, 4 AS PRICE$, 4 AS QUANTITY$
```

2. Build Data Portion of Index File

   a. Establish a While loop that executes until end of file on INV-2.DAT. Within the While loop, do the following:
      (1) Read a record from INV-2.DAT.
      (2) Call the Assign Key to INDEX$(RECORD.NUMBER) Module. In this module, increment RECORD.NUMBER by 1 and set INDEX$(RECORD.NUMBER) equal to MAS.STOCK$.

(3) Call the Write Record to INVINDEX.DAT Module. In this module, use the LSET statement and MKS$ function to assign the data items in the record read from INV-2. DAT to the random file buffer. Use the PUT statement to write the record (RECORD.NUMBER) to the random file INVDATA.DAT.

3. Wrap-up

    a. Close the random file INVDATA.DAT.

    b. Display the number of records (RECORD.NUMBER) written to INVDATA.DAT.

    c. Call the Create File of Keys Module. In this module, open the sequential file INVINDEX.DAT. Use a For loop to write the elements of array INDEX$ to INVINDEX.DAT. Finally, close INVINDEX.DAT.

    d. Display the message Job Complete.

PROGRAM 9.5

```
1000 ' Program 9.5
1010 ' Create Initial Sequential Index File and Random File
1030 '
1040 ' This program reads the sequential file INV-II.DAT and creates
1050 ' the random file INVDATA.DAT.  The stock number (STOCK$) is
1060 ' assigned to the element in array INDEX$ that corresponds to
1070 ' the record number.  As part of the end-of-file routine, array
1080 ' INDEX$ is written to the sequential file INVINDEX.DAT.  The
1090 ' maximum no. of records that INVINDEX.DAT can contain is 100.
1100 '
1110 ' ****************************************************************
1120 ' *                        Main Module                          *
1130 ' ****************************************************************
1140 GOSUB 2000   ' Call Initialization
1150 GOSUB 3000   ' Call Build Data Portion of Index File
1160 GOSUB 4000   ' Call Wrap-up
1170 END
1180 '
2000 ' ****************************************************************
2010 ' *                      Initialization                         *
2020 ' ****************************************************************
2030 CLS : KEY OFF   ' Clear Screen
2040 OPTION BASE 1
2050 DIM INDEX$(100)
2060 FOR RECORD.NUMBER = 1 TO 100
2070    INDEX$(RECORD.NUMBER) = "Empty"
2080 NEXT RECORD.NUMBER
2090 RECORD.NUMBER = 0
2100 OPEN "INV-2.DAT" FOR INPUT AS #1
2110 OPEN "INVDATA.DAT" AS #2 LEN = 32
2120 FIELD #2, 4 AS STOCK$, 1 AS LOCATION$, 15 AS DESC$, 4 AS COST$,
                4 AS PRICE$, 4 AS QUANTITY$
2130 RETURN
2140 '
3000 ' ****************************************************************
3010 ' *              Build Data Portion of Index File               *
3020 ' ****************************************************************
3030 WHILE NOT EOF(1)
3040    INPUT #1, MAS.STOCK$, MAS.LOCATION$, MAS.DESC$, MAS.COST,
                  MAS.PRICE,  MAS.QUANTITY
3050    GOSUB 3200   ' Call Assign MAS.STOCK$ to INDEX$(RECCNT)
3060    GOSUB 3400   ' Call Write Record to INVINDEX.DAT
3070 WEND
3080 RETURN
3090 '
```

(continued)

```
3200 ' ***********************************************************************
3210 ' *                 Assign Key to INDEX$(RECORD.NUMBER)                 *
3220 ' ***********************************************************************
3230 RECORD.NUMBER = RECORD.NUMBER + 1
3240 INDEX$(RECORD.NUMBER) = MAS.STOCK$
3250 RETURN
3260 '
3400 ' ***********************************************************************
3410 ' *                    Write Record to INVINDEX.DAT                     *
3420 ' ***********************************************************************
3430 LSET STOCK$ = MAS.STOCK$
3440 LSET LOCATION$ = MAS.LOCATION$
3450 LSET DESC$ = MAS.DESC$
3460 LSET COST$ = MKS$(MAS.COST)
3470 LSET PRICE$ = MKS$(MAS.PRICE)
3480 LSET QUANTITY$ = MKS$(MAS.QUANTITY)
3490 PUT #2, RECORD.NUMBER
3500 RETURN
3510 '
4000 ' ***********************************************************************
4010 ' *                              Wrap-up                                *
4020 ' ***********************************************************************
4030 CLOSE
4040 PRINT "The number of records in the file is"; RECORD.NUMBER
4050 GOSUB 4200   ' Call Create File of Keys
4060 PRINT : PRINT "Job Complete"
4070 RETURN
4080 '
4200 ' ***********************************************************************
4210 ' *                        Create File of Keys                          *
4220 ' ***********************************************************************
4230 OPEN "INVINDEX.DAT" FOR OUTPUT AS #1
4240 FOR RECORD.NUMBER = 1 TO 100
4250    WRITE #1, INDEX$(RECORD.NUMBER)
4260 NEXT RECORD.NUMBER
4270 CLOSE
4280 RETURN
4290 ' ********************* End of Program *********************

RUN

The number of records in the file is 13

Job Complete
```

Discussion of the Program 1 Solution

When the RUN command is issued for Program 9.5, line 1140 calls the Initialization Module. After the screen is cleared and the array INDEX$ is declared, lines 2060 through 2080 initialize all elements of array INDEX$ to the string value Empty. Following the For loop, the record counter (RECORD.NUMBER) is set equal to zero and the files are opened.

The Build Data Portion of the Index File Module maintains control of the program until the end-of-file mark is sensed on the master file INV-2.DAT. Within the loop, a record from INV-2.DAT is read; the stock number (MAS.STOCK$) is assigned to the next element in INDEX$; and the data portion of the master record is written to INVDATA.DAT. Note the relationship established between the RECORD.NUMBER element of array INDEX$ and the RECORD.NUMBER record in the random file INVDATA.DAT.

As part of the Wrap-up Module, array INDEX$ is written to the sequential file INVINDEX.DAT. This file contains 100 data items, some of which are equal to stock numbers and others of which are equal to the string value Empty. In part 2 of this Programming Case Study, array INDEX$ is used to determine the locations of records with corresponding stock numbers. The fact that unused elements of array INDEX$ are equal to the string value Empty will be helpful both for adding and for deleting records.

Program 2 This second program displays and updates records in the simulated indexed file created by Program 9.5. This is as shown in Figure 9.12 on page 358. A top-down chart (Figure 9.13); a list of the corresponding program 2 tasks; the program 2 solution; and a discussion of the program 2 solution follow.

Since Program 9.6 is one of the more complex programs in this textbook, you are encouraged to load it (PRG9-6) from the Student Diskette and execute it with the suggested data in this section.

FIGURE 9.13
A top-down chart for Program 9.6.

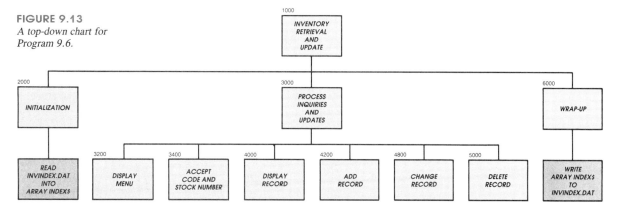

Program 2 Tasks: Display and Update Records in a Simulated Indexed File

The following tasks correspond to the top-down chart in Figure 9.13.

1. Initialization

   a. Clear the screen.
   b. Declare array INDEX$ to 100 elements.
   c. Open the sequential file INVINDEX.DAT and random file INVDATA.DAT. INVINDEX.DAT contains the stock numbers; INVDATA.DAT contains the data that corresponds to the stock numbers.
   d. Use a For loop to read the 100 stock numbers in INVINDEX.DAT into array INDEX$.
   e. Close INVINDEX.DAT.

2. Process Inquiries and Updates

   a. Call the Display Menu Module. In this module, display a menu with the following valid codes:

Code	Function
1	Display Record
2	Add Record
3	Change Record
4	Delete Record
5	End Program

   b. Call the Accept Code and Stock Number Module. In this module, accept a function code (CODE) and stock number (TRA.STOCK$). Both CODE and TRA.STOCK$ must be validated. CODE must equal one of the valid function codes displayed by the menu.

   The stock number TRA.STOCK$ is validated by comparing it to the elements of array INDEX$. If the function code CODE equals 1, 3, or 4, then TRA.STOCK$ must equal the value of one of the elements of INDEX$. The subscript of the element of array INDEX$ that is equal to the stock number is used in the Display Record, Change Record, and Delete Record Modules to access the corresponding record in the random file INVDATA.DAT.

     If the function code equals 2 (add record), then the stock number must *not* equal the value of an element in array INDEX$.

     Control remains in this module until a valid function code and a valid stock number are entered by the user.

c. On the basis of the value of the function code, use an ON-GOSUB statement to call the Display Record, Add Record, Change Record, or Delete Record Module. Following return of control from one of these modules, the Display Menu Module is called to initiate the next user request.

  (1) The function of the Display Record Module is to display the record that corresponds to the stock number entered by the user. In this module, do the following:

    (a) Read the RECORD.NUMBER record in the random file INVDATA.DAT. RECORD.NUMBER is set equal to the record number by line 3650 in the validation process.

    (b) Display the record read from INVDATA.DAT.

    (c) Use the INPUT$ function to suspend execution so that the user may view the record before the menu is displayed again.

  (2) The function of the Add Record Module is to add a record to INVDATA.DAT and a corresponding stock number to array INDEX$. In this module, do the following:

    (a) Redisplay the stock number entered by the user.

    (b) Determine the first element of INDEX$ that is equal to the string value Empty.

    (c) If no element of INDEX$ is equal to the string value Empty, then the array is full, an appropriate diagnostic message is displayed, and control is returned to the menu.

    (d) If an element of INDEX$ equals the value Empty, then request the remaining items that belong to this new record and assign the stock number (TRA.STOCK$) to the RECORD.NUMBER element of INDEX$.

    (e) Use the PUT statement to write the record to INVDATA.DAT which corresponds to RECORD.NUMBER. The record is written to INVDATA. DAT only after the user is given the opportunity to terminate the addition.

  (3) The function of the Change Record Module is to allow the user to change any item in the record except the stock number. In this module, do the following:

    (a) Use the GET statement to read the record in the random file INVDATA.DAT which corresponds to RECORD.NUMBER.

    (b) Request the user to enter changes. If an item is to remain the same in the record, then the user responds by entering a –1 for the item in question.

    (c) Check each response. If a response is not equal to –1, use the LSET and MKS$ functions to assign the corresponding variable in the buffer the new value.

    (d) Write the modified record to INVDATA.DAT only after the user has been given the opportunity to terminate the record change.

  (4) The function of the Delete Record Module is to delete an unwanted record. To delete a record, assign INDEX$(RECORD.NUMBER) the string value Empty only after giving the user the opportunity to terminate the record deletion. Note that nothing is done to the corresponding record in INVDATA.DAT. However, since INDEX$(RECORD.NUMBER) is assigned the string value Empty, this element may be used for a record addition at a later date; at this time, the record in the random file is changed.

3. Wrap-up

    a. Close the random file INVDATA.DAT.

    b. Open the sequential file INVINDEX.DAT for output.

    c. Use a For loop to write the 100 elements of array INDEX$ to INVINDEX.DAT.

    d. Close the sequential file INVINDEX.DAT.

    e. Display an end-of-job message.

PROGRAM 9.6

```
1000 ' Program 9.6
1010 ' Inventory Retrieval and Update
1020 '
1030 ' This program displays or updates records in a simulated-indexed file.
1040 ' The data for the simulated-indexed file is located in the random file
1050 ' INVDATA.DAT.  The records in the random file are accessed by a key
1060 ' (stock number) that is entered by the user.  Records may be displayed,
1070 ' added to the file, deleted from the file, or changed.
1080 '
1090 ' *********************************************************************
1100 ' *                        Main Module                              *
1110 ' *********************************************************************
1120 GOSUB 2000   ' Call Initialization
1130 GOSUB 3000   ' Call Process Inquiries and Updates
1140 GOSUB 6000   ' Wrap-up
1150 END
1160 '
2000 ' *********************************************************************
2010 ' *                        Initialization                           *
2020 ' *********************************************************************
2030 CLS : KEY OFF   ' Clear Screen
2040 OPTION BASE 1
2050 DIM INDEX$(100)
2060 OPEN "INVINDEX.DAT" FOR INPUT AS #1
2070 OPEN "INVDATA.DAT" AS #2 LEN = 32
2080 FIELD #2, 4 AS STOCK$, 1 AS LOCATION$, 15 AS DESC$, 4 AS COST$,
              4 AS PRICE$, 4 AS QUANTITY$
2090 FOR RECORD.NUMBER = 1 TO 100
2100    INPUT #1, INDEX$(RECORD.NUMBER)   ' Read Stock Numbers into Array
2110 NEXT RECORD.NUMBER
2120 CLOSE #1
2130 RETURN
2140 '
3000 ' *********************************************************************
3010 ' *              Process Inquiries and Updates                      *
3020 ' *********************************************************************
3030 GOSUB 3200      ' Call Display Menu
3040 GOSUB 3400      ' Call Accept Code and Stock Number
3050 WHILE CODE <> 5
3060    ON CODE GOSUB 4000, 4200, 4800, 5000   ' Call Process Inquiry
3070    GOSUB 3200   ' Call Display Menu
3080    GOSUB 3400   ' Call Accept Code and Stock Number
3090 WEND
3100 RETURN
3110 '
```

(continued)

```
3200 ' ********************************************************************
3210 ' *                        Display Menu                            *
3220 ' ********************************************************************
3230 CLS
3240 LOCATE  2, 19 : PRINT "Menu for Inventory Retrieval and Update"
3250 LOCATE  3, 19 : PRINT "---------------------------------------"
3260 LOCATE  5, 19 : PRINT "   Code              Function"
3270 LOCATE  6, 19 : PRINT "   ----              --------"
3280 LOCATE  7, 19 : PRINT "    1                Display Record"
3290 LOCATE  9, 19 : PRINT "    2                Add Record"
3300 LOCATE 11, 19 : PRINT "    3                Change Record"
3310 LOCATE 13, 19 : PRINT "    4                Delete Record"
3320 LOCATE 15, 19 : PRINT "    5                End Program"
3330 RETURN
3340 '
3400 ' ********************************************************************
3410 ' *                 Accept Code and Stock Number                  *
3420 ' ********************************************************************
3430 SWITCH$ = "ON"
3440 WHILE SWITCH$ = "ON"
3450    SWITCH$ = "OFF"
3460    LOCATE 17, 52 : PRINT SPC(10)
3470    LOCATE 17, 19 : INPUT "Enter a Code 1 through 5 ======> ", CODE
3480    WHILE CODE < 1 OR CODE > 5
3490       BEEP : BEEP : BEEP : BEEP
3500       LOCATE 18, 19 : PRINT "Code out of range, please reenter"
3510       LOCATE 17, 52 : PRINT SPC(10)
3520       LOCATE 17, 52 : INPUT "", CODE
3530       LOCATE 18, 19 : PRINT SPC(40)
3540    WEND
3550    IF CODE <> 5
          THEN LOCATE 19, 19 : INPUT "Stock Number ==================> ",
          TRA.STOCK$ : GOSUB 3600 'Call Determine If Stock Number Is Valid
3560 WEND
3570 CLS
3580 RETURN
3590 '
3600 ' ********************************************************************
3610 ' *            Determine If Stock Number Is Valid                  *
3620 ' ********************************************************************
3630 RECORD.NUMBER = 0
3640 FOR I = 1 TO 100
3650    IF TRA.STOCK$ = INDEX$(I)
          THEN IF CODE = 2 THEN GOSUB 3800
                           ELSE RECORD.NUMBER = I : I = 100
3660 NEXT I
3670 IF RECORD.NUMBER = 0 AND CODE <> 2
        THEN GOSUB 3800   ' Call Stock Number Error Routine
3680 RETURN
3690 '
3800 ' ********************************************************************
3810 ' *                 Stock Number Error Routine                    *
3820 ' ********************************************************************
3830 BEEP : BEEP : BEEP : BEEP
3840 IF CODE = 2
        THEN LOCATE 20, 19 : PRINT "Stock Number Already Exists"
        ELSE LOCATE 20, 19 : PRINT "Stock Number Is Invalid"
3850 LOCATE 22, 19
3860 PRINT "Press any key to reenter Code and Stock Number..."
3870 A$ = INPUT$(1)
3880 LOCATE 17, 52 : PRINT SPC(10)
3890 LOCATE 19, 52 : PRINT SPC(10)
3900 LOCATE 20, 19 : PRINT SPC(50)
```

(continued)

```
3910 LOCATE 22, 19 : PRINT SPC(50)
3920 SWITCH$ = "ON"
3930 RETURN
3940 '
4000 ' *********************************************************************
4010 ' *                        Display Record                             *
4020 ' *********************************************************************
4030 GET #2, RECORD.NUMBER
4040 PRINT : PRINT "Stock Number =============> "; TRA.STOCK$
4050 PRINT : PRINT "Warehouse Location =======> "; LOCATION$
4060 PRINT : PRINT "Description ==============> "; DESC$
4070 PRINT : PRINT USING "Unit Cost ================>#,###.##"; CVS(COST$)
4080 PRINT : PRINT USING "Selling Price ============>#,###.##";CVS(PRICE$)
4090 PRINT : PRINT USING "Quantity on Hand =========>#,###";CVS(QUANTITY$)
4100 PRINT : PRINT "Press any key to continue..."
4110 A$ = INPUT$(1)
4120 RETURN
4130 '
4200 ' *********************************************************************
4210 ' *                         Add Record                                *
4220 ' *********************************************************************
4230 PRINT : PRINT "Stock Number =============> "; TRA.STOCK$
4240 RECORD.NUMBER = 0
4250 FOR I = 1 TO 100   ' Search for "Empty" element in array INDEX$
4260    IF INDEX$(I) = "Empty"
           THEN RECORD.NUMBER = I : I = 100 : GOSUB 4400
4270 NEXT I
4280 IF RECORD.NUMBER = 0
        THEN PRINT : PRINT "** ERROR ** Index is full" :
           PRINT : PRINT "Press any key to continue..." : A$ = INPUT$(1)
4290 RETURN
4300 '
4400 ' *********************************************************************
4410 ' *                  Request Remaining Data Items                     *
4420 ' *********************************************************************
4430 PRINT : INPUT "Warehouse Location =======> ", TRA.LOCATION
4440 PRINT : INPUT "Description ==============> ", TRA.DESC$
4450 PRINT : INPUT "Unit Cost ================> ", TRA.COST
4460 PRINT : INPUT "Selling Price ============> ", TRA.PRICE
4470 PRINT : INPUT "Quantity on Hand =========> ", TRA.QUANTITY
4480 PRINT : INPUT "Enter Y to add record, else N... ", CONTROL$
4490 IF CONTROL$ = "Y" OR CONTROL$ = "y"
        THEN GOSUB 4600   ' Call Write Record
4500 RETURN
4510 '
4600 ' *********************************************************************
4610 ' *                      Call Write Record                            *
4620 ' *********************************************************************
4630 LSET STOCK$    = TRA.STOCK$
4640 LSET LOCATION$ = TRA.LOCATION$
4650 LSET DESC$     = TRA.DESC$
4660 LSET COST$     = MKS$(TRA.COST)
4670 LSET PRICE$    = MKS$(TRA.PRICE)
4680 LSET QUANTITY$ = MKS$(TRA.QUANTITY)
4690 INDEX$(RECORD.NUMBER) = TRA.STOCK$
4700 PUT #2, RECORD.NUMBER
4710 RETURN
4720 '
```

(continued)

```
4800 ' ************************************************************************
4810 ' *                           Change Record                            *
4820 ' ************************************************************************
4830 GET #2, RECORD.NUMBER
4840 PRINT : PRINT "Stock Number =============> "; TRA.STOCK$
4850 PRINT
4860 PRINT "**** Enter a -1 if you do not want to change a data item ****"
4870 PRINT : INPUT "Warehouse Location =======> ", TRA.LOCATION$
4880 IF TRA.LOCATION$ <> "-1"
        THEN LSET LOCATION$ = TRA.LOCATION$
4890 PRINT : INPUT "Description ==============> ", TRA.DESC$
4900 IF TRA.DESC$     <> "-1"
        THEN LSET DESC$ = TRA.DESC$
4910 PRINT : INPUT "Unit Cost ================> ", TRA.COST
4920 IF TRA.COST      <> -1
        THEN LSET COST$ = MKS$(TRA.COST)
4930 PRINT : INPUT "Selling Price ============> ", TRA.PRICE
4940 IF TRA.PRICE     <> -1
        THEN LSET PRICE$ = MKS$(TRA.PRICE)
4950 PRINT : INPUT "Quantity on Hand =========> ", TRA.QUANTITY
4960 IF TRA.QUANTITY  <> -1
        THEN LSET QUANTITY$ = MKS$(TRA.QUANTITY)
4970 PRINT : INPUT "Enter Y to update record, else N... ", CONTROL$
4980 IF CONTROL$ = "Y" OR CONTROL$ = "y"
        THEN PUT #2, RECORD.NUMBER
4990 RETURN
4995 '
5000 ' ************************************************************************
5010 ' *                           Delete Record                            *
5020 ' ************************************************************************
5030 PRINT
5040 PRINT "Are you sure you want to delete stock number "; TRA.STOCK$
5050 PRINT : INPUT "Enter Y to delete record, else N... ", CONTROL$
5060 IF CONTROL$ = "Y" OR CONTROL$ = "y"
        THEN INDEX$(RECORD.NUMBER) = "Empty"
5070 RETURN
5080 '
6000 ' ************************************************************************
6010 ' *                              Wrap-up                                *
6020 ' ************************************************************************
6030 CLOSE
6040 OPEN "INVINDEX.DAT" FOR OUTPUT AS #1
6050 FOR RECORD.NUMBER = 1 TO 100  ' Write New Index to INVINDEX.DAT
6060     WRITE #1, INDEX$(RECORD.NUMBER)
6070 NEXT RECORD.NUMBER
6080 CLOSE
6090 PRINT "Inventory Retrieval and Update Program Terminated"
6100 PRINT : PRINT "Job Complete"
6110 RETURN
6120 ' ********************** End of Program *************************

RUN
```

Discussion of the
Program 2 Solution

When the RUN command is issued for Program 9.6, the menu in Figure 9.14 on the opposite page is displayed.

If a function code of 1 through 4 is entered, then line 3550 requests the user to enter a stock number by displaying the following message:

```
Stock Number ==================>
```

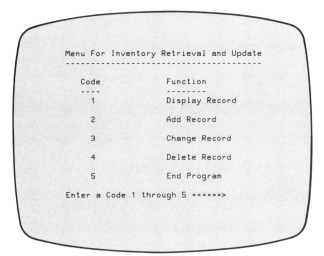

FIGURE 9.14
Menu displayed for Program 9.6.

The Determine If Stock Number Is Valid Module (lines 3600 through 3690) verifies the stock number. If a function code of 2 is entered, then the stock number TRA.STOCK$ must not equal the value of any of the elements of array INDEX$. If a function code of 1, 3, or 4 is entered, then the stock number TRA.STOCK$ must be equal to one of the elements of array INDEX$. An additional function of this validation process, when the function code is 1, 3, or 4, is to establish the record number (RECORD.NUMBER) of the corresponding record to be displayed, changed, or deleted.

If a function code of 1 and the stock number S941 are entered by the user, then the Display Record Module (lines 4000 through 4130) displays the information shown in Figure 9.15.

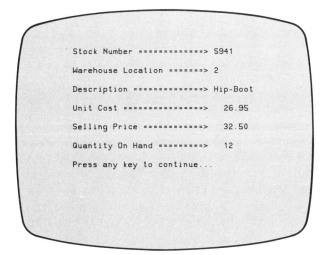

FIGURE 9.15
The display from entering a function code of 1 (Display Record) and the stock number S941.

If a function code of 2 and the stock number S429 are entered by the user, then the Add Record Module and its subordinates (lines 4200 through 4720) request the remaining items that make up this new record. This is shown in Figure 9.16 on the following page.

FIGURE 9.16
The display from entering a function code of 2 (Add Record) and the data items for stock number S429.

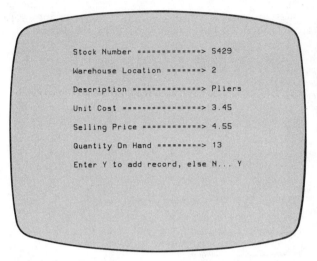

```
Stock Number ==============> S429

Warehouse Location =======> 2

Description ===============> Pliers

Unit Cost ================> 3.45

Selling Price ===========> 4.55

Quantity On Hand =========> 13

Enter Y to add record, else N... Y
```

Lines 4250 through 4270 determine the first element of INDEX$ that is equal to the string Empty. The subscript of this element is then used to indicate the record number in the PUT statement in line 4700. Just before line 4700, line 4690 assigns the stock number TRA. STOCK$ to INDEX$ (RECORD. NUMBER).

If a function code of 3 and the stock number T814 are entered, then the Change Record Module (lines 4800 through 4995) reads the record that corresponds to RECORD. NUMBER; requests changes; and rewrites the record. Figure 9.17 shows the display for changing the selling price to 29.95 and the quantity on hand to 32 for record T814.

FIGURE 9.17
The display from entering a function code of 3 (Change Record) and the stock number T814.

```
Stock Number ==============> T814

**** Enter a -1 if you do not want to change a data item ****

Warehouse Location =======> -1

Description ==============> -1

Unit Cost ================> -1

Selling Price ===========> 29.95

Quantity on Hand =========> 32

Enter Y to update record, else N... Y
```

If a function code of 4 and the stock number of C206 are entered, then the Delete Record Module (lines 5000 through 5080) assigns the string Empty to the element of INDEX$ that corresponds to RECORD.NUMBER. Note that the data record in INVDATA.DAT is not changed in any way. Later, when a new record is added, the record deleted in INVDATA.DAT is changed to the new record. The following is displayed by the Delete Record Module:

```
Are you sure you want to delete stock number C206

Enter Y to delete record, else N... Y
```

If a function code of 5 is entered, then the Wrap-up Module writes the array INDEX$ to the sequential file INVINDEX.DAT; closes the files; and displays the following:

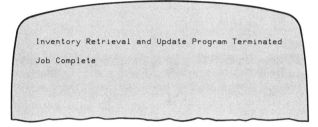

```
Inventory Retrieval and Update Program Terminated

Job Complete
```

TRY IT YOURSELF

Load Program 9.6 (PRG9-6) from the Student Diskette. Add the following as line 2025:

```
1025 COLOR 15, 1, 4
```

(The COLOR statement will be discussed in detail in chapter 10.) Execute the program and see what happens. Display, change, delete, and add several records to the file. Refer to Figure 9.9 on page 344 for a list of the records in the original file.

⊞ 9.5 WHAT YOU SHOULD KNOW

1. MS BASIC allows for two types of file organization — sequential and random. A file that is organized sequentially is limited to sequential processing. A file that is organized randomly can be processed either sequentially or in a random fashion. The sequence in which a random file is processed bears no relationship to the sequence in which the records are stored in it.
2. A third type of organization, indexed, is also widely used in data processing. It is not available in MS BASIC. Indexed files may be simulated by using both a sequential file and a random file.
3. File maintenance is the process of updating files in one or more of the following ways:

   a. adding new records
   b. deleting unwanted records
   c. changing data within records

4. A transaction file contains data of a temporary nature.
5. A master file contains data that is, for the most part, permanent.
6. A file maintenance program that updates a sequential file must deal with at least three files: a transaction file, the current master file, and a new master file.
7. A system flowchart shows, in graphic form, the files, the flow of data, the equipment, and the programs involved in a particular application.
8. Merging is the process of combining two or more files that are in the same sequence into a single file that maintains that same sequence for a given data item in each record.
9. Matching records involves two or more related files that are in the same sequence according to a common data item. If a record in the transaction file matches a record in the current master file, then the current master record may be updated. If there is no match, appropriate action must be taken, depending on the application.
10. Like sequential files, random files must be opened before they are read from or written to. When a program finishes with a random file, it must close the file. The OPEN statement for a random file must include a record length. Never write a record that is longer than the assigned record length. You can, however, write records that are shorter than the length that is specified in the OPEN statement.
11. Whenever a file is opened for random access, the record length must be specified.
12. The FIELD statement is used to define data items with respect to their size and location within the buffer.
13. Only string variables can be used in a FIELD statement to define the buffer.
14. A random file must be opened before a corresponding FIELD statement is executed.

15. The sum of the widths in the list of a FIELD statement must not exceed the record length specified in the OPEN statement.
16. The LSET and RSET statements are used to store string data in the buffer.
17. So that numeric values may be placed in and removed from a buffer, MS BASIC includes the MKS$ and CVS functions. The MKS$(N) function converts the numeric value N to a 4-character string value for the purpose of placing the numeric value into the buffer. The CVS(X$) function converts the string variable X$, defined in the FIELD statement, to a numeric value.
18. The GET #n, r statement reads the rth record from the random file assigned to filenumber n.
19. The PUT #n, r statement writes the rth record to the random file assigned to filenumber n.
20. If the second parameter in a GET or PUT statement is not included, then the PC reads or writes the next record in sequence in the random file.
21. The LOC(n) function returns the record number of the last record read or written to the random file assigned to filenumber n.
22. The LOF(n) function returns information regarding the size of the random file assigned to filenumber n.

9.6 TEST YOUR BASIC SKILLS (Even-numbered answers are at the back of the book, before the index.)

1. If the last record accessed in a program was record 10 of a random file assigned previously to filenumber 1, which record is accessed next by the following GET statements? (Assume that each GET statement is affected by the previous one.)

   a. GET #1   b. GET #1, 22   c. GET #1   d. GET #1, 96   e. GET #1

2. Fill in the following:
   a. The GET statement reads a record into the _____ defined by the _____ statement.
   b. Only _____ variables may be used in a FIELD statement.
   c. The sum of the characters in a FIELD statement must be _____ than or equal to the sum of the length of the record defined in the OPEN statement.
   d. The _____ function returns the record number of the last record read or written to the random file assigned as the argument.

3. Construct a FIELD statement with the following variables and corresponding types and sizes.

Variable	Type	Size
SOC$	String	9
CODE$	String	1
VALUE1$	Numeric	Double Precision
VALUE2$	Numeric	Single Precision
VALUE3$	Numeric	Integer

4. Explain the difference between the LSET statement and the RSET statement.
5. The number of active records in a random file varies between 0 and 100 each day. Active records begin with 1 and continue by 1 until the last active record is reached. The number of the last active record in the random file TABLE.DAT is always located in record 101. This record contains only one data item, RECNO$. The active records each contain three data items, defined in the FIELD statement by the names ITEM1$, ITEM2$, and ITEM3$.

   Write a partial program that first reads record 101 in TABLE.DAT, then dynamically dimensions the parallel arrays ITEM1, ITEM2, and ITEM3 to the numeric value of RECNO$. Finally, read the active records in the random file TABLE.DAT and assign the three values in each record to the elements of arrays ITEM1, ITEM2, and ITEM3 in the order in which the values are located in the record. Use filenumber 1.
6. Which of the following are invalid file-handling statements? Why?

   a. 100 OPEN "SALE.DAT" AS 1 LEN = -23   b. 200 GET #2   c. 300 GET #1, RECNO
   d. 400 GET #2, RECNO$ e. 500 PUT #3   f. 600 LSET COST$ = COST
   g. 700 RSET MKS$(N) = N$ h. 800 GET #1, LOC(1)   i. 900 LSET PRICE$ = CVS(PRICE)

7. Explain the difference between the CVI, CVS, and CVD functions.
8. Describe how a sequential file, a random file, and an array are used to simulate an indexed file.
9. Write a statement that assigns the random file PURCHASE.DAT to file number 1. The maximum number of characters in a record in the random file is 239.
10. Use the Student Diskette to complete the Try It Yourself exercises on pages 338, 344, 354, 357, and 369.

⊞ 9.7 BASIC PROGRAMMING PROBLEMS

1. Adding, Changing, and Deleting Records in the Master File

Purpose: To become familiar with the maintenance of a sequential file.

Problem: Write a program to match and merge the current payroll master file EX61PAY.DAT (see BASIC Programming Problem 1 in chapter 6 on page 220) with the transaction file EX91TRA.DAT (see Input Data below) and create a new payroll master file EX91PAY.DAT. Include the following diagnostic messages:

```
**ERROR** Addition Invalid    - Employee XXX already in master file.
**ERROR** Transaction Invalid - Employee XXX not in master file.
```

Display as part of the end-of-job routine the total number of additions, changes, deletions, errors, and transactions and the number of records in the new master file.

Input Data: The master file EX61PAY.DAT and the transaction file EX91TRA.DAT are on the Student Diskette. The contents of the transaction file, EX91TRA.DAT, are shown in Figure 9.18. The transaction code A represents an addition, C a record change, and D a record delete. "Null" represents the null character.

Transaction Code	Employee No.	Employee Name	Dependents	Marital Status	Rate of Pay	Year-to-Date Gross Pay	Year-to-Date Federal With. Tax	Year-to-Date Social Security Tax	
C	124	Null	4	Null	-1	$6,345.20	-1	-1	
A	126	Fish, Joe	1	M	$6.00	0	0	0	
D	134	Null	-1	Null	-1	-1	-1	-1	
A	143	Byrd, Ed	3	S	9.00	0	0	0	**FIGURE 9.18**
C	167	Null	0	Null	-1	-1	-1	-1	*Contents of the*
C	225	Null	-1	S	-1	-1	-1	-1	*transaction file*
D	250	Null	-1	Null	-1	-1	-1	-1	*EX91PAY.DAT.*

Output Results: The new master file EX91PAY.DAT is created. The following results are displayed.

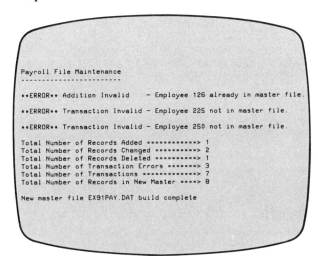

```
Payroll File Maintenance
------------------------

**ERROR** Addition Invalid    - Employee 126 already in master file.

**ERROR** Transaction Invalid - Employee 225 not in master file.

**ERROR** Transaction Invalid - Employee 250 not in master file.

Total Number of Records Added ·············> 1
Total Number of Records Changed ···········> 2
Total Number of Records Deleted ···········> 1
Total Number of Transaction Errors ········> 3
Total Number of Transactions ··············> 7
Total Number of Records in New Master ·····> 8

New master file EX91PAY.DAT build complete
```

2. Creating a Random File for Quarterly Payroll Totals

Purpose: To become familiar with creating a random file.

Problem: Write a program that creates a random file with four records. Each record contains payroll information with respect to the following time periods:

Record Number	Time Period
1	January – March
2	April – June
3	July – September
4	October – December

Each record is made up of the following quarterly employee totals: gross pay, withholding tax, and social security tax. To ensure accuracy, use double-precision variables. Define the variables in the FIELD statement as having a width of 8 bytes, and assign values to the buffer by means of the MKD$ function. Call the random file EX92DATA.DAT.

Input Data: Use the following sample data.

Quarter	Gross Pay	Withholding Tax	Social Security
1	$11,231.12	$3,998.34	$1,121.45
2	8,345.23	2,456.23	913.75
3	13,891.75	2,554.64	1,585.11
4	0.00	0.00	0.00

Output Results: The random file EX92DATA.DAT is created in auxiliary storage. The following is displayed for the first record entered.

```
Quarterly Payroll Random File Create

Quarter =================> 1

Gross Pay ==============> 11231.12

Withholding Tax =========> 3998.34

Social Security Tax =====> 1121.45
```

3. Random Access of Quarterly Payroll Totals

Purpose: To become familiar with accessing records in a random file.

Problem: Write a program that will randomly access any record in the random file EX92DATA.DAT created in the previous exercise. If the user enters 2, then the program should display the payroll totals for the second quarter. If the user enters 1, then the program should display the payroll totals for the first quarter.

Input Data: Use the random file EX92DATA.DAT created in BASIC Programming Problem 2.

Output Results: The following results are displayed for quarter 2.

```
Quarterly Payroll Random File Access

Quarter =================> 2

Gross Pay ==============>    8,345.23

Withholding Tax =========>    2,456.23

Social Security Tax =====>      913.75
```

4. Employee Record Retrieval and Update — A Simulated-Indexed File

Purpose: To become familiar with the use of indexed files.

Problem: Construct two programs. The first program is to take the file EX61DATA.DAT created in BASIC Programming Problem 1 of chapter 6 and build an index in a sequential file made up of the employee numbers. The program should also build a corresponding random file made up of the data in EX61PAY.DAT. Declare 200 elements for the array written to the sequential file. (**Hint:** See Program 9.5 on page 359.)

Call the sequential file EX94INDX.DAT and the random file EX94DATA.DAT. Use the following FIELD statement for the random file:

```
FIELD #2, 3 AS EMP.NUMBER$, 20 AS EMP.NAME$, 4 AS EMP.DEP$,
          1 AS EMP.STATUS$,  4 AS EMP.RATE$, 4 AS EMP.YTD.GR$,
          4 AS EMP.YTD.TAX$, 4 AS EMP.YTD.SOC$
```

Note: Ask your instructor whether the first program is required. Copies of EX94INDX.DAT and EX94DATA.DAT are on the Student Diskette.

The second program is to be a menu-driven program that allows the user to display, add, change, and delete records on a random basis. The user informs the PC of the record to access by entering the employee number.

(**Hint:** See Program 9.6 on page 363.)

The menu-driven program should accept the following function codes:

Code	Function	Code	Function
1	Display record	4	Delete record
2	Add record	5	End program
3	Change record		

Input Data: Update the payroll file with the sample data given in BASIC Programming Problem 1 of this chapter.

Output Results: The program should generate results similar to those generated by Program 9.6 on page 363.

5. Payroll Problem VIII: Matching Records

Purpose: To become familiar with matching records.

Problem: Modify Payroll Problem V in chapter 6 on page 224 (BASIC Programming Problem 8) to display diagnostic messages when there is no match between the record in the master file and the record in the transaction file. If a record in the master file has no corresponding match in the transaction file, write the current master record to the new master file and display the message

    ** NOTE ** Employee XXX has no time card

If a record in the transaction file has no corresponding match in the master file, display the message

    ** ERROR ** Employee XXX has no master record

(**Hint:** The logic regarding matching records is similar to the logic in Program 9.2 on page 340.)

Input Data: Use EX61PAY.DAT as the current master file. This is the same file that was used in Payroll Problem V. The transaction file EX95TRA.DAT is on the Student Diskette. The transaction file contains the following records:

Employee Number	Hours Worked
123	88
125	72
126	80
134	80
167	70.5
168	68
210	80
234	32

Output Results: A new master payroll file is created as EX95PAY.DAT. The following results are printed on the printer.

```
                         Preliminary
                   Biweekly Payroll Report

Employee
Number      Gross Pay       Fed. Tax     Soc. Sec.    Net Pay
--------    ---------       --------     ---------    -------
  123        1,150.00        214.62         82.23      853.15
** NOTE ** Employee 124 has no time card
  125          936.00        179.51          0.00      756.49
  126          360.00          2.77         25.74      331.49
  134          700.00        140.00         50.05      509.95
  167          733.20        123.56         52.42      557.22
** ERROR ** Employee 168 has no master record
  210          704.00         94.65         50.34      559.01
  234          216.00         27.82         15.44      172.74

Total Gross Pay ========>    4,799.20
Total Withholding Tax ==>      782.93
Total Social Security ==>      276.22
Total Net Pay ==========>    3,740.05

End of Payroll Report
```

COMPUTER GRAPHICS AND SOUND

10

The value of the computer for displaying information in the form of charts, figures, and graphs as opposed to printed characters, has long been recognized. For many years, however, the cost of equipment kept most users from incorporating **computer graphics** into their programs. With the advent of the PC, more and more users are displaying the results from their programs pictorially.

As you will see in this chapter, MS BASIC has statements that provide a considerable graphics capability. Figures 10.1 through 10.4 show a variety of different business-type charts, figures, and graphs that can be displayed on your PC. Business-type graphics are commonly used to summarize data. They are an effective way to show amounts and/or trends. Figure 10.5, on page 377, shows non-business-type graphics that may also be displayed on your PC. Although no attempt is made here to present sophisticated graphics, at the conclusion of this chapter you will have enough knowledge of the graphics features of MS BASIC to start using them in the programs you write.

This chapter also explores the MS BASIC statements that allow you to play music and create sound effects.

FIGURE 10.1
Line graphs (used to show business trends).

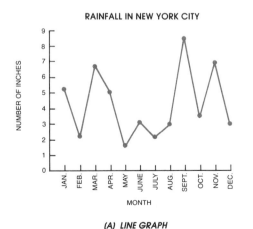

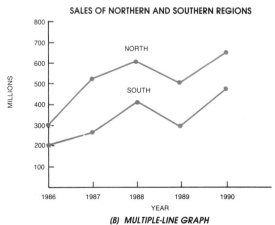

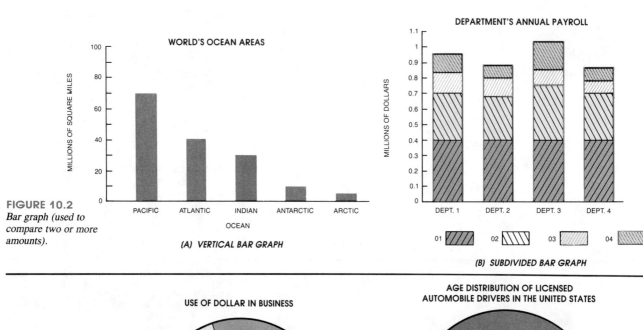

FIGURE 10.2
Bar graph (used to compare two or more amounts).

(A) VERTICAL BAR GRAPH

(B) SUBDIVIDED BAR GRAPH

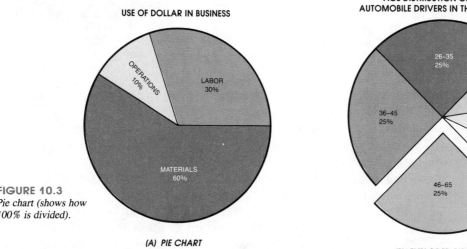

FIGURE 10.3
Pie chart (shows how 100% is divided).

(A) PIE CHART

(B) EXPLODED PIE CHART

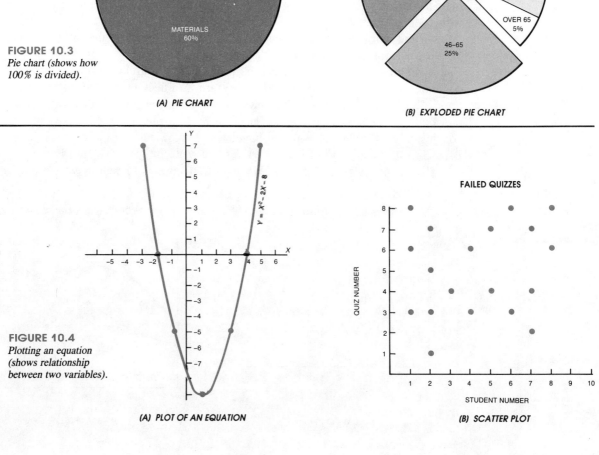

FIGURE 10.4
Plotting an equation (shows relationship between two variables).

(A) PLOT OF AN EQUATION

(B) SCATTER PLOT

FIGURE 10.5
Logo and animation.

(A) LOGO   *(B) ANIMATION*

PC Graphics Modes   The PC provides three graphics modes. They are **text**, **medium resolution**, and **high resolution**. As described in Table 10.1, the text mode is available on all PCs. Medium-resolution and high-resolution graphics are available only if you have a **color/graphics interface board** in your PC.

TABLE 10.1 Graphics Capabilities with Different Hardware Configurations

DISPLAY DEVICE	DISPLAY INTERFACE BOARD	GRAPHICS CAPABILITIES
1. IBM Compatible Monochrome (Black and White) Display	IBM Compatible Monochrome Display Interface	Only text mode with a width of 40 or 80 characters. Black and white character graphics.
2. IBM Compatible Monochrome (Black and White) Display	Color/Graphics Interface	Shades of black and white graphics in text, medium resolution, and high resolution.
3. IBM Compatible Color Monitor	Color/Graphics Interface	Color graphics in text and medium resolution. Black and white graphics in high resolution.

The text mode is the one used throughout this book. In this mode, the screen is divided into either 25 rows and 80 columns or 25 rows and 40 columns, as illustrated in Figures 10.6(A) and 10.6(B) on page 379. At the intersection of each row and column, the PC can display any one of the 256 characters shown in Table D.2 in Appendix D. Each intersection of a row and column is called a **character position**. In this mode, the PRINT statement and the ASCII character set are used to display figures and graphs as well as nongraphic information such as words and sentences. If you have the proper hardware, you can also display the characters in 16 different colors. The text mode is often used to create logos and simple animated designs.

With medium-resolution graphics, the screen is divided into 200 rows and 320 columns (see Figure 10.6(C) on page 379). Each intersection of a row and column represents a small dot, also called a **pixel** (picture element). The total number of pixels is 64,000 (200 x 320). Forty characters per line are displayed in this mode. If you have a color monitor, each pixel can be assigned any one of 16 colors. In medium resolution you can plot points, draw figures, and create high-quality animated designs.

The high-resolution graphics mode divides the screen into 200 rows and 640 columns, as shown in Figure 10.6(D) on page 379. The total number of pixels is 128,000 (200 x 640). The larger number of pixels across the screen allows you to draw figures that require finer detail than is available with medium resolution. Eighty characters per line are displayed in this mode. Only monochrome colors are available in high resolution — black and white or amber or green.

All the programs presented thus far can be executed in any one of the three modes as long as you recognize the different default width settings (80 for text and high resolution, 40 for medium resolution).

The SCREEN Statement

When MS BASIC is started, the PC is in the text mode. The SCREEN statement may then be used to select among the three modes as follows:

SCREEN 0 (text mode)
SCREEN 1 (medium-resolution graphics mode)
SCREEN 2 (high-resolution graphics mode)

The statement may be entered without a line number or as part of a program. Each time the SCREEN statement is executed, the screen is erased and the color is set to white on black. However, nothing is changed on the screen if the mode in the SCREEN statement is the same as the current one. If there is a BASIC program in main storage, it is not erased when you switch from one mode to another.

The general form of the SCREEN statement is shown in Table 10.2.

_____TABLE 10.2 The SCREEN Statement_____

General Form:	SCREEN *mode, color switch, active page, visual page*
	where **mode** *is 0 (text), 1 (medium resolution) or 2 (high resolution);*
	color switch *is 0 (disables color) or any other number (enables color) in the text mode. With medium resolution, 0 enables color and any other number disables color;*
	active page *is an integer expression (in the range 0 to 7 for width 40 characters, and 0 to 3 for width 80) which specifies the page to be written to by output statements; and*
	visual page *is an integer expression in the same range as active page that selects the page to be displayed.*
Purpose:	*Selects the screen attributes to be used by subsequent output statements.*
Keyword Entry:	*Press the F10 key or press simultaneously the Alt and S keys on your keyboard.*
Examples:	2030 SCREEN 1
	3030 SCREEN ,,2, 3
	4030 SCREEN 0, 1, 1, 0
	5030 SCREEN 0,, 0, 1
	6030 SCREEN 1, 1
	7030 SCREEN 2
Note:	*The parameters active page and visual page are valid only in the text mode, i.e., mode = 0.*

Line 2030 in Table 10.2 clears the screen and switches to the medium-resolution mode. If any parameter is omitted in the SCREEN statement, the PC maintains the current status for the omitted parameter.

In line 3030, the mode remains the same, and all future output statements are directed to page 2. Page 3 is immediately displayed. Here, the term *page* refers to a 2K (width = 40) or 4K (width = 80) byte area of the 16K display buffer. Note that in this example we are preparing to have the PC build one page (page 2) while displaying another (page 3). This form of flip-flopping the screens may be used in the text mode to create animations.

In line 4030 of Table 10.2, the mode is switched to text; color is enabled; all future output statements are directed to page 1; and page 0 is displayed. In line 5030, the mode is switched to text; color maintains its status; future output statements are directed to page 0; and page 1 is displayed. Line 6030 switches the PC to medium resolution and the color is disabled. Finally, line 7030 switches the PC to high resolution.

Figure 10.6, on the opposite page, illustrates how the screen is subdivided for the various modes.

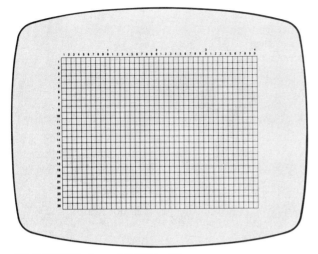

(A) SCREEN 0 : WIDTH 40
  Mode: Text
  Rows: 25
  Columns: 40
  Colors: 16 Foreground
          8 Background
          16 Border

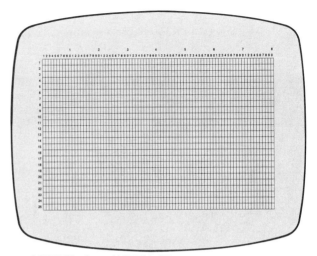

(B) SCREEN 0 : WIDTH 80
  Mode: Text
  Rows: 25
  Columns: 80
  Colors: 16 Foreground
          8 Background
          16 Border

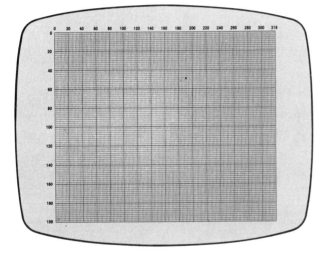

(C) SCREEN 1
  Mode: Medium Resolution
  Rows: 200
  Columns: 320
  Characters per line: 40
  Colors: 8 Foreground
          16 Background

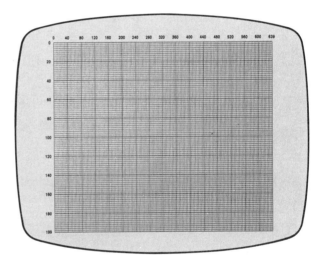

(D) SCREEN 2
  Mode: High Resolution
  Rows: 200
  Columns: 640
  Characters per line: 80
  Colors: Black and White

FIGURE 10.6
Layout of the screen and color availability for the text mode, medium-resolution graphics mode, and high-resolution graphics mode.

▦ **10.2**

TEXT-MODE
GRAPHICS

You can produce interesting and useful graphics on any PC with the PRINT and PRINT USING statements, the CHR$ function, and the ASCII character set. Some elementary text-mode graphics using the typewriter keys (letters, numbers, and punctuation marks) were presented in chapter 4, exercises 12 and 13, on page 127.

Program 10.1, on the following page, shows how you can access additional graphics characters (ASCII codes 128 through 255, also called the **USA character set**) through the use of the CHR$ function. You'll recall from chapter 8 that the CHR$ function returns a character that is equivalent in ASCII code to the numeric argument.

PROGRAM 10.1

```
100 ' Program 10.1
110 ' Displaying the Last Half of the ASCII Character Set
120 ' ***********************************************
130 CLS : KEY OFF  ' Clear Screen
140 FOR CODE = 128 TO 255
150    PRINT USING "###  !"; CODE, CHR$(CODE)
160 NEXT CODE
170 END
```

When the RUN command is issued for Program 10.1, the For loop (lines 140 through 160) causes the PC to display the last half of the ASCII character set, as shown in Table D.2 in Appendix D. Through the use of the CHR$ function, these characters may be used in the text mode to draw various figures. Besides characters made up of curved lines, you can choose characters that range from a solid dark color (codes 219 thru 223) to a lighter shade (code 176, 177, and 178) for drawing bar graphs.

TRY IT YOURSELF

Load Program 10.1 (PRG10-1) from the Student Diskette. Display and execute the program. Change the PRINT USING statement in line 150 to an LPRINT USING statement. See the printer user's manual regarding the proper switch settings for displaying the USA character set. When the printer is ready, execute the modified version of Program 10.1 and compare the output to Table D.2 in Appendix D on page D.4.

Programming Case Study 24: *Logo for the Bow-Wow Dog Food Company*

The following Programming Case Study pertains to the display of a logo that employs some of the graphics characters that make up the last half of the ASCII character set.

Problem: On a recent tour through the main office, Mr. Beagle, president of the Bow-Wow Dog Food Company, noticed the large number of PCs in use. To brighten the office area, he has requested that the Data Processing Department display the company logo, shown in Figure 10.7, on all idle PCs.

The program that displays the logo must **chain to** (call) a menu-driven program called MAINMENU when the operator presses any key. For a discussion of how a program chains to another program, see section C.4 in Appendix C.

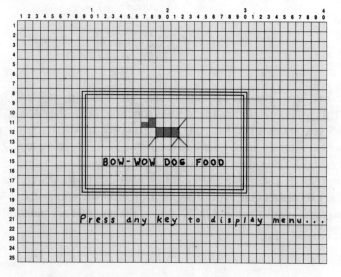

FIGURE 10.7
The Bow-Wow Dog Food Company logo designed on a screen layout form with a width of 40 characters.

Following are a top-down chart (Figure 10.8); a list of the program tasks in outline form; a program solution; and a discussion of the program solution.

FIGURE 10.8
A top down chart for Program 10.2.

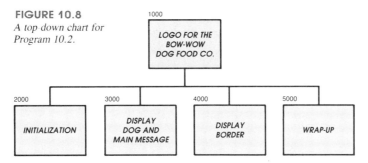

Program Tasks   The following program tasks correspond to the top-down chart in Figure 10.8.

1. Initialization

   a. Clear the screen.
   b. Use the WIDTH statement to set the display mode of the screen to 40 characters per line.

2. Display Dog and Message

   Use the LOCATE and PRINT statements to position the dog and main message on the screen. Use the CHR$ function and the following ASCII character codes for the dog's body parts:

Body Part	ASCII Code	Body Part	ASCII Code
Nose	220	Tail	47
Head	219	Legs pointing left	47
Body	219 (three)	Leg pointing right	92

3. Display Border

   Use the LOCATE and PRINT statements to display the border surrounding the dog and the main message. Use the CHR$ function and the following ASCII character codes for the border:

Border Part	ASCII Code	Border Part	ASCII Code
Upper-left corner	201	Lower-right corner	188
Lower-left corner	200	Vertical border	186
Upper-right corner	187	Horizontal border	205

4. Wrap-up

   a. Display the message Press any key to display menu...
   b. Use the INPUT$ function to suspend execution until a key is pressed by the operator.
   c. Set the display mode of the screen to 80 characters per line.

   Use the following statement in place of the END statement in the Main Module to chain to MAINMENU:

```
CHAIN "MAINMENU"
```

Program Solution   The following program corresponds to the top-down chart in Figure 10.8 and to the preceding program tasks.

PROGRAM 10.2

```
1000 ' Program 10.2
1010 ' Logo for Bow-Wow Dog Food Company
1020 ' *******************************
1030 ' *            Main Module           *
1040 ' *******************************
1050 GOSUB 2000   ' Call Initialization
1060 GOSUB 3000   ' Call Display Dog and Main Message
1070 GOSUB 4000   ' Call Display Border
1080 GOSUB 5000   ' Call Wrap-up
1090 CHAIN "MAINMENU"    ' Call Program MAINMENU
1100 '
2000 ' *******************************
2010 ' *           Initialization           *
2020 ' *******************************
2030 CLS : KEY OFF   ' Clear Screen
2040 WIDTH 40        ' Switch to 40-Column Display
2050 RETURN
2060 '
3000 ' *******************************
3010 ' *  Display Dog and Main Message  *
3020 ' *******************************
3030 LOCATE 11, 17 : PRINT CHR$(220); CHR$(219); SPC(3); CHR$(47)
3040 LOCATE 12, 19 : PRINT STRING$(3, 219)
3050 LOCATE 13, 18 : PRINT CHR$(47); SPC(2); CHR$(47); CHR$(92)
3060 LOCATE 15, 12 : PRINT "BOW-WOW DOG FOOD"
3070 RETURN
3080 '
4000 ' *******************************
4010 ' *           Display Border           *
4020 ' *******************************
4030 LOCATE 8, 9 : PRINT CHR$(201); STRING$(20, 205); CHR$(187)
4040 FOR I = 9 TO 17
4050    LOCATE I,  9 : PRINT CHR$(186)
4060    LOCATE I, 30 : PRINT CHR$(186)
4070 NEXT I
4080 LOCATE 18, 9 : PRINT CHR$(200); STRING$(20, 205); CHR$(188)
4090 RETURN
4100 '
5000 ' *******************************
5010 ' *              Wrap-up              *
5020 ' *******************************
5030 LOCATE 21, 9 : PRINT "Press any key to display menu...";
5040 HALT$ = INPUT$(1)
5050 WIDTH 80   ' Switch to 80-Column Display
5060 RETURN
5070 ' ******** End of Program ********

RUN
```

Discussion of the   When Program 10.2 is executed, the Initialization Module clears the screen and switches the
Program Solution   screen to the 40-column display mode. The Display Dog and Main Message Module uses the CHR$ function to display the various graphics characters. Note that in line 3040, the STRING$ function causes three solid dark characters to display.

   The Display Border Module, lines 4000 through 4100, uses a For loop to display the vertical lines. In the Wrap-up Module, the INPUT$ function is used to suspend execution until the operator wants to display the main menu. Line 1090 of the Main Module chains to MAINMENU before Program 10.2 terminates execution. The logo displayed by Program 10.2 is shown in Figure 10.9.

FIGURE 10.9
The logo displayed through the execution of Program 10.2.

Programming Case Study 25: Horizontal Bar Graph of Monthly Sales

The program solution to the following problem illustrates the capability of MS BASIC to display information in the form of a horizontal bar graph.

Problem: The Sales Analysis Department of the ISCP Company wishes to display a horizontal bar graph to illustrate the monthly sales trends of the previous year. Each month name and its corresponding sales are stored in the sequential file MONSALES.DAT. The contents of MONSALES.DAT are as follows:

Month	Sales	Month	Sales
January	$41,000	July	$30,000
February	33,000	August	25,000
March	21,000	September	33,000
April	11,000	October	38,000
May	17,000	November	46,000
June	23,000	December	53,000

The desired bar graph is shown in Figure 10.10.

FIGURE 10.10
Output for Program 10.3 designed on a screen layout form.

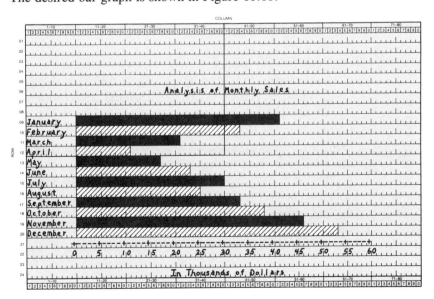

Following are a top-down chart; a list of the program tasks in outline form; a program solution; and a discussion of the program solution.

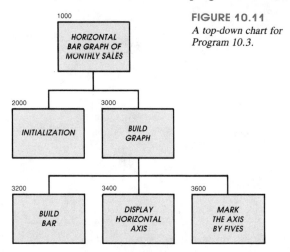

FIGURE 10.11
A top-down chart for Program 10.3.

Program Tasks The following program tasks correspond to the top-down chart in Figure 10.11.

1. Initialization

   a. Dimension the parallel arrays MONTH$ and SALES to 12.
   b. Open MONSALES.DAT for input.
   c. Use a For loop to read the month names and corresponding sales into the parallel arrays MONTH$ and SALES.
   d. Close MONSALES.DAT.
   e. Clear the screen and display the bar graph title.

2. Build Graph

   a. Call the Build Horizontal Bars Module: Within this module, use a For loop with a loop variable of MON to display the 12 monthly names and corresponding bars. Use alternate shadings for each bar. Use the ASCII code 219 to shade the first bar (January). Use ASCII code 177 to shade the next bar (February). Set the variable CHAR$ to CHR$(219) prior to the loop. Within the For loop, do the following:
      (1) Display the month name and tab to column 11. Hold the cursor at column 11.
      (2) Use another For loop to display the bar for the month being processed. In the For loop, use the loop variable NUM, an initial value of 1, and a limit value of SALES(MON)/1000. Within the loop, print CHAR$ and keep the cursor on the same line.
      (3) Following the inner For loop, use an IF statement to switch the value of CHAR$. This causes the next bar to be a different shade. If CHAR$ is equal to CHR$(219), then assign CHAR$ the value CHR$(177); otherwise, assign CHAR$ the value CHR$(219).
   b. Call the Display Horizontal Axis Module: Tab to column 10. Use a For loop with a loop variable of PO, an initial value of 0, and a limit value of 60. Within the For loop, use an IF statement to display a minus sign if PO is not a multiple of 5. If PO is a multiple of 5, then display a plus sign. In either case, the PRINT statement should end with a semicolon so that the cursor remains on the same line. The plus sign marks off the horizontal line in multiples of 5. These marks are called **ticks**.
   c. Call the Mark the Axis by Fives Module: Use a For loop with a loop variable of MARK, an initial value of 0, and a limit value of 60. Within the loop, use a PRINT

statement and TAB function to display multiples of 5, beginning with 0 for each tick. At the conclusion of the For loop, label the horizontal axis as described in Figure 10.10.

Program Solution   The following program corresponds to the top-down chart in Figure 10.11 and to the preceding program tasks.

PROGRAM 10.3

```
1000 ' Program 10.3
1010 ' Horizontal Bar Graph of Monthly Sales
1020 ' *****************************************************
1030 ' *                  Main Module                      *
1040 ' *****************************************************
1050 GOSUB 2000   ' Call Initialization
1060 GOSUB 3000   ' Call Build Graph
1070 END
1080 '
2000 ' *****************************************************
2010 ' *                  Initialization                   *
2020 ' *****************************************************
2030 OPTION BASE 1
2040 DIM MONTH$(12), SALES(12) ' Dim month names and month sales arrays
2050 OPEN "MONSALES.DAT" FOR INPUT AS #1
2060 ' ** Read Names and Sales into Arrays MONTH$ and SALES **
2070 FOR MON = 1 TO 12
2080    INPUT #1, MONTH$(MON), SALES(MON)
2090 NEXT MON
2100 CLOSE #1
2110 CLS : KEY OFF   ' Clear Screen
2120 LOCATE 6, 29 : PRINT "Analysis of Monthly Sales"
2130 LOCATE 9
2140 RETURN
2150 '
3000 ' *****************************************************
3010 ' *                  Build Graph                      *
3020 ' *****************************************************
3030 GOSUB 3200   ' Call Build Horizontal Bars
3040 GOSUB 3400   ' Call Display Horizontal Axis
3050 GOSUB 3600   ' Call Mark the Axis by Fives
3060 RETURN
3070 '
3200 ' *****************************************************
3210 ' *                  Build Horizontal Bars            *
3220 ' *****************************************************
3230 CHAR$ = CHR$(219)
3240 FOR MON = 1 TO 12
3250    PRINT MONTH$(MON); TAB(11);
3260    FOR NUM = 1 TO SALES(MON)/1000
3270       PRINT CHAR$;
3280    NEXT NUM
3290    PRINT
3300    IF CHAR$ = CHR$(219)
            THEN CHAR$ = CHR$(177)
            ELSE CHAR$ = CHR$(219)
3310 NEXT MON
3320 RETURN
3330 '                                          (continued)
```

```
3400 ' ***********************************************************
3410 ' *                Display Horizontal Axis                 *
3420 ' ***********************************************************
3430 PRINT TAB(10);
3440 FOR TICKS = 0 TO 60
3450    IF TICKS / 5 = INT(TICKS / 5)
             THEN PRINT "+";
             ELSE PRINT "-";
3460 NEXT TICKS
3470 PRINT
3480 RETURN
3490 '
3600 ' ***********************************************************
3610 ' *                Mark the Axis by Fives                  *
3620 ' ***********************************************************
3630 FOR MARK = 0 TO 60 STEP 5
3640    PRINT TAB(MARK + 9); MARK;
3650 NEXT MARK
3660 PRINT
3670 PRINT : PRINT TAB(30); "In Thousands of Dollars"
3680 RETURN
3690 ' **************** End of Program ********************

RUN
```

Discussion of the Program Solution

When the RUN command is issued for Program 10.3, the Initialization Module fills the parallel arrays MONTH$ and SALES with the 12 month names and corresponding monthly sales.

In the Build Horizontal Bars Module, line 3230 assigns CHAR$ the dark-shaded graphics character with an ASCII code 219. The outer FOR loop (lines 3240 through 3310) builds a bar on each pass. The inner For loop (lines 3260 through 3280) builds each individual bar. After each bar is displayed, line 3300 switches the shade of the character assigned to CHAR$. The new shade is used to build the next bar.

The Display Horizontal Axis Module (lines 3400 through 3490) displays the horizontal axis. Finally, the Mark the Axis by Fives Module (lines 3600 through 3680) assigns a multiple of 5, beginning with 0, to each tick.

The horizontal bar graph displayed by Program 10.3 is shown in Figure 10.12 on the opposite page.

TRY IT YOURSELF

1. Load Program 10.3 (PRG10-3) from the Student Diskette. Delete line 3300. Execute the program and see what happens.

2. Reload PRG10-3. Replace the three occurrences of CHR$(219) in lines 3230 and 3300 with CHR$(14). Execute the program and see what happens.

The COLOR Statement for the Text Mode

If your PC has a color monitor and color/graphics interface board, then you can enhance your screen displays with color. There are two COLOR statements, one for the text mode and another for the medium-resolution graphics mode. In this section, we will discuss the COLOR statement for the text mode.

The COLOR statement allows you to select colors for the foreground, background, and border of the screen. As illustrated in Figure 10.13 on the opposite page, the **background** is that part of the screen against which the characters are displayed. Displayed characters are the **foreground**. The **border** is the edge of the screen.

FIGURE 10.12
The horizontal bar graph displayed through the execution of Program 10.3.

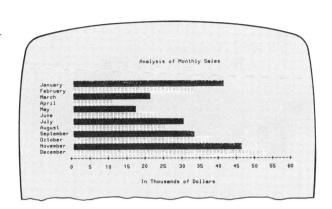

FIGURE 10.13
The background, foreground, and border of the screen.

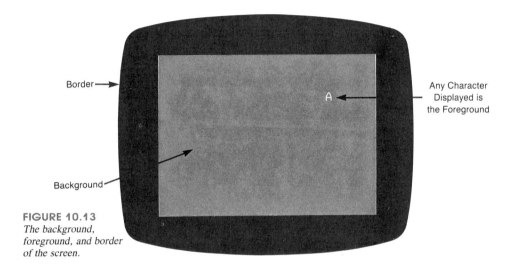

When the system command BASICA is first keyed in, the color is set to white on black; that is, the foreground is set to white and the background and border are set to black. The COLOR statement may then be used in the immediate mode or as a statement in a program to change colors as often as desired. The general form of the COLOR statement for the text mode is shown in Table 10.3.

_____**TABLE 10.3** The COLOR Statement for the Text Mode_____

General Form:	COLOR *foreground, background, border*
	where **foreground** *is a numeric expression in the range 0 to 31;*
	background *is a numeric expression in the range 0 to 7; and*
	border *is a numeric expression in the range 0 to 15.*
Purpose:	*Sets the color for the foreground, background, and border of the screen. The foreground and border may be set equal to any of the 16 colors described in Table 10.4 on the following page. Adding the number 16 to the foreground value causes the characters to blink in that color. Only the colors with numbers 0 through 7 may be selected for the background.*
Keyword Entry:	*Press simultaneously the Alt and C keys on your keyboard.*
Examples:	300 COLOR 14, 2, 6 ' Yellow on Green with a Brown Border
	350 COLOR 12 ' Light Red Foreground
	400 COLOR ,, 14 ' Yellow Border
	450 COLOR 7, 0, 0 ' White on Black
	500 COLOR 0, 7 ' Black on White
	550 COLOR 0, 0, 0 ' Black on Black

_____TABLE 10.4 The 16 Colors Available with a Color Monitor and Color/Graphics
Interface Board_____

COLOR	NUMBER	COLOR	NUMBER	COLOR	NUMBER
Black	0	Brown	6	Light Red	12
Blue	1	White	7	Light Magenta	13
Green	2	Grey	8	Yellow	14
Cyan	3	Light Blue	9	Bright White	15
Red	4	Light Green	10		
Magenta	5	Light Cyan	11		

Line 300 in Table 10.3 sets a yellow foreground, a green background, and a brown border screen. Line 350 changes the foreground to light red; the background and border colors remain as they were. Line 400 changes only the border color to yellow. Line 450 resets the colors to the normal white on black. In this case, the background and border are the same. Line 500 reverses the colors; that is, it changes them to black on white. With line 550, the foreground, background, and border are the same color, and, therefore, character images sent to the screen will not display.

When the COLOR statement is executed, all previously displayed characters remain in the original color. The new colors are used for future displays. For this reason, the COLOR statement is often followed by the CLS statement. The CLS statement causes the entire background and border to immediately display in the newly assigned colors. For example,

```
COLOR 14, 7, 2 : CLS
```

instructs the PC to change the screen immediately to a white background and green border. All characters displayed as a result of listing or executing a program will display in the color yellow.

You may instruct the PC to blink characters by adding the number 16 to the foreground color. For example,

```
COLOR 31, 4 : CLS
```

causes the PC to blink bright white characters on a red background.

If you have a monochrome display (black and white or green or amber color) and a color/graphics interface board, the color settings in Table 10.4 are still useful, but the different colors will appear in various patterns of shading on your screen.

The COLOR statement improves substantially the quality of the results displayed by a program. For example, if the following statement,

```
2035 COLOR 15, 1, 4
```

is added to any of the previous menu-driven programs, then the main menu displays in bright white on a blue background with a red border. Other color combinations can be considered for submenus and the results displayed by a program.

Programming Case Study 26: Animating an Inchworm Creeping Across the Screen

We can use the SCREEN statement in the text mode to build different pages and display them one after another. As illustrated in the following Programming Case Study, this page switching allows us to instruct the PC to animate objects formed with characters.

Problem: Use the SCREEN statement to animate an inchworm creeping across the screen in a left-to-right direction. The five positions of the inchworm are shown by the filled-in squares in Figure 10.14 on the opposite page.

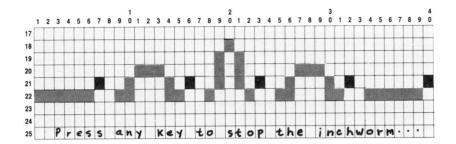

FIGURE 10.14
The five positions of the creeping inchworm.

Use the 40-column display and build each position of the inchworm on a different page. Once all the pages have been built, display the pages in sequence until the operator intervenes.

Following are a top-down chart; a list of the program tasks in outline form; a program solution; and a discussion of the program solution.

FIGURE 10.15
A top-down chart for Program 10.4.

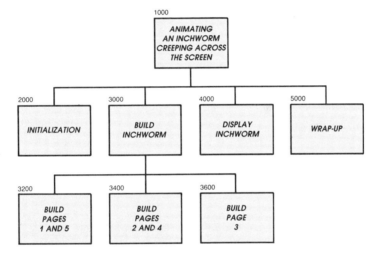

Program Tasks The following program tasks correspond to the top-down chart in Figure 10.15.

1. Initialization

   a. Use the SCREEN statement to select the text mode.
   b. Set the width of a line to 40 characters.
   c. Turn off the cursor.
   d. Clear the screen.

2. Build Inchworm

   Build each position of the inchworm on a separate page. Note the identicalness of positions 1 and 5 and positions 2 and 4. By adjusting the columns and the page number, the same code may be used to build the identical positions of the inchworm.

   a. Call the Build Pages 1 and 5 Module: Use the SCREEN statement to write to page 1 or 5 while displaying page 0 (page 0 is blank). For page 1, set the column to 1. For page 5, set the column to 34. Use the LOCATE and PRINT statements and the shaded rectangle (ASCII code = 219) to build the inchworm. Color the body green (COLOR 2) and the head red (COLOR 4). The message that is located on line 25 of Figure 10.14 is then written to page 5.
   b. Call the Build Pages 2 and 4 Module: Use the SCREEN statement to write to pages 2 and 4 while displaying page 0. For page 2, set the column to 9. For page 4, set the column to 25. Use the same statements and colors described in 2a to build the inchworm.

c. Call the Build Page 3 Module: Use the SCREEN statement to write to page 3 while displaying page 0. Use the same statements and colors described in 2a to build the inchworm.

3. Display Inchworm

Establish a While loop that executes until the operator presses a key. Use the statement WHILE INKEY$ = "" to control the loop. Within the While loop, use a nested For loop like the one below to display pages 1 through 5.

```
4050 FOR PAGE = 1 TO 5
4060    SCREEN ,,,PAGE
4070      FOR TIME.DELAY = 1 TO 250 : NEXT TIME.DELAY
4080 NEXT PAGE
```

The SCREEN statement displays pages 1 through 5. The inner For loop delays the display of the next page for half a second. The display of the pages in sequence at a set time interval animates the inchworm creeping across the screen in a left-to-right direction.

4. Wrap-up

a. Use the SCREEN statement to write to page 0 and display page 0.
b. Set the width of a line to 80 characters.
c. Set the color to white on black.
d. Clear the screen.

Program Solution The following program corresponds to the top-down chart in Figure 10.15 and to the preceding program tasks.

PROGRAM 10.4

```
1000 ' Program 10.4
1010 ' Animating an Inchworm Creeping Across the Screen
1020 ' ***********************************************
1030 ' *                Main Module                  *
1040 ' ***********************************************
1050 GOSUB 2000  ' Call Initialization
1060 GOSUB 3000  ' Call Build Inchworm
1070 GOSUB 4000  ' Call Display Inchworm
1080 GOSUB 5000  ' Call Wrap-up
1090 END
1100 '
2000 ' ***********************************************
2010 ' *                Initialization               *
2020 ' ***********************************************
2030 SCREEN 0 : WIDTH 40  ' Set to Text Mode and 40 Character Width
2040 LOCATE ,, 0 : CLS : KEY OFF  ' Make Cursor Invisible and Clear Screen
2050 RETURN
2060 '
3000 ' ***********************************************
3010 ' *                Build Inchworm               *
3020 ' ***********************************************
3030 PAGE = 1 : GOSUB 3200    ' Call Build Page 1
3040 PAGE = 2 : GOSUB 3400    ' Call Build Page 2
3050 PAGE = 3 : GOSUB 3600    ' Call Build Page 3
3060 PAGE = 4 : GOSUB 3400    ' Call Build Page 4
3070 PAGE = 5 : GOSUB 3200    ' Call Build Page 5
3080 RETURN
3090 '
```

(continued)

```
3200 ' ************************************************
3210 ' *              Build Pages 1 and 5            *
3220 ' ************************************************
3230 SCREEN ,, PAGE, 0
3240 IF PAGE = 1 THEN COL = 1 ELSE COL = 34
3250 LOCATE 22, COL : COLOR 2 : PRINT STRING$(6, 219);
3260 LOCATE 21, COL + 6 : COLOR 4 : PRINT CHR$(219)
3270 IF PAGE = 5
         THEN LOCATE 25, 3 : COLOR 15 :
             PRINT "Press any key to stop the inchworm..."
3280 RETURN
3290 '
3400 ' ************************************************
3410 ' *              Build Pages 2 and 4            *
3420 ' ************************************************
3430 SCREEN ,, PAGE, 0
3440 IF PAGE = 2 THEN COL = 9 ELSE COL = 25
3450 LOCATE 22, COL : COLOR 2 : PRINT STRING$(2,219);SPC(3);STRING$(2,219)
3460 LOCATE 21, COL + 1 : PRINT CHR$(219); SPC(3); CHR$(219)
3470 LOCATE 20, COL + 2 : PRINT STRING$(3, 219)
3480 LOCATE 21, COL + 7 : COLOR 4 : PRINT CHR$(219)
3490 RETURN
3500 '
3600 ' ************************************************
3610 ' *                Build Page 3                 *
3620 ' ************************************************
3630 SCREEN ,, PAGE, 0
3650 LOCATE 22, 18 : COLOR 2 : PRINT CHR$(219); SPC(3); CHR$(219)
3660 LOCATE 21, 19 : PRINT CHR$(219); SPC(1); CHR$(219)
3670 LOCATE 20, 19 : PRINT CHR$(219); SPC(1); CHR$(219)
3680 LOCATE 19, 19 : PRINT CHR$(219); SPC(1); CHR$(219)
3690 LOCATE 18, 20 : PRINT CHR$(219)
3700 LOCATE 21, 23 : COLOR 4 : PRINT CHR$(219)
3710 RETURN
3720 '
4000 ' *************************************************
4010 ' *               Display Inchworm               *
4020 ' *************************************************
4030 WHILE INKEY$ = ""
4050   FOR PAGE = 1 TO 5
4060     SCREEN ,,,PAGE
4070     FOR TIME.DELAY = 1 TO 250 : NEXT TIME.DELAY
4080   NEXT PAGE
4090 WEND
4100 RETURN
4110 '
5000 ' *************************************************
5010 ' *                    Wrap-up                   *
5020 ' *************************************************
5030 SCREEN ,, 0, 0 : WIDTH 80 : COLOR 7 ' Reset Screen
5040 CLS : KEY ON  ' Clear Screen and Turn on 25th Line
5050 RETURN
5060 ' ************** End of Program ***************

RUN
```

When Program 10.4 is executed, the five positions of the inchworm shown in Figure 10.16 are displayed from left to right, one after the other.

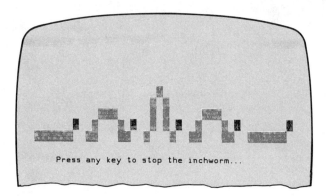

FIGURE 10.16
The five positions of the inchworm creeping across the screen, superimposed on one screen.

Discussion of the Program Solution

Here are some important points to note about Program 10.4:

1. In line 2040 of the Initialization Module, the LOCATE statement is used to make the cursor invisible for all pages displayed.
2. The five positions of the inchworm are each built on a separate page, owing to the calls made in the Build Inchworm Module. Each subroutine called from this module begins with a SCREEN statement that establishes the page to write to and the page to display. It is important that we include the parameter 0 for the visual page, since the visual page defaults to the active page if no value is specified.
3. In the Display Inchworm Module, the While loop causes the inchworm to creep across the screen from left to right, over and over again, until the operator presses a key on the keyboard. Within the loop, the five pages are displayed one after the other. The For loop in line 4070 delays the display of the next page for about half a second.

TRY IT YOURSELF

Load Program 10.4 (PRG10-4) from the Student Diskette. Change the limit value in the FOR statement in line 4070 to 50. Execute the program and see what happens. Try other values for the limit. Can you explain the function of this statement?

In Programming Case Study 26, we were able to build all the required positions on separate pages before displaying the animation. This is not always possible, because most animations require more pages than are available (eight pages for 40-column display and four pages for 80-column display). When the number of required positions exceeds the number of available pages, the program must build one page while displaying another page.

⊞ 10.3

MEDIUM-RESOLUTION AND HIGH-RESOLUTION GRAPHICS

To change to the medium-resolution graphics mode, enter the statement SCREEN 1. In this mode, the screen is divided into 200 rows and 320 columns (see Figure 10.6c on page 379). To change to the high-resolution graphics mode, the statement SCREEN 2 is entered. In the high-resolution graphics mode, the screen is divided into 200 rows and 640 columns (see Figure 10.6d on page 379).

Here are some important points regarding the medium-resolution and high-resolution graphics modes:

1. These two graphics modes are available only if your PC has a color/graphics interface board.

2. To send graphical designs to the printer, you must have one that emulates the IBM graphics printer. Also, you must enter the PC command GRAPHICS before you enter the PC command BASICA. For example, if you have changed the default drive to B, then after the B> prompt enter

```
B> A:GRAPHICS
B> A:BASICA
```

3. With a color monitor, medium-resolution graphics allow us to color objects on the screen. High-resolution graphics allow displays only in black and white, but with much greater detail.

4. In either of the two graphics modes, the intersection of a row and column is a point, or pixel. We plot points and draw lines and curves by instructing the PC to turn on selected pixels.

5. We give the PC information about the points, lines, and curves to draw in the form of coordinates like (x, y), where x is the column (horizontal axis) and y is the row (vertical axis).

6. Coordinates are specified with the column first, then the row. This is different from the LOCATE statement in the text mode, which requires the row first, then the column.

7. Rows and columns are numbered beginning with 0, rather than 1.

8. There are two ways to indicate the coordinates of a point on the screen: absolute form and relative form. Coordinates of the form (x, y) are absolute in relation to the origin (0, 0). Coordinates of the form STEP(x, y) are relative to the last point referenced by the last graphics statement executed.

9. If you enter WIDTH 80 in the medium-resolution graphics mode, the PC will switch to the high-resolution graphics mode. If you enter WIDTH 40 in the high-resolution graphics mode, the PC will switch to the medium-resolution graphics mode.

In the sections that follow, several graphics statements and examples are presented.

The COLOR Statement for the Medium-Resolution Graphics Mode

The general form of the COLOR statement for the medium-resolution graphics mode is given in Table 10.5.

TABLE 10.5 The COLOR Statement for the Medium-Resolution Graphics Mode

General Form:	COLOR *background, palette* where **background** *is a numeric expression in the range 0 to 15, and* **palette** *is a numeric expression. If the expression is an even number, then palette 0 is selected for the foreground; otherwise, palette 1 is selected.*
Purpose:	*Sets the background color of the screen and selects one of two palettes of color for the foreground. The background may be set equal to any of the 16 colors described in Table 10.4 on page 388. The choice of palettes for the foreground is as follows:*

Palette 0	*Palette 1*	*Number*
Background Color	*Background Color*	*0*
Green	*Cyan*	*1*
Red	*Magenta*	*2*
Brown	*White*	*3*

Keyword Entry:	*Press simultaneously the Alt and C keys on your keyboard.*
Examples:	500 COLOR 9, 1 600 COLOR , 0 700 COLOR BACK, PAL
Note:	*The COLOR statement selects the palette (0 or 1) for the foreground. Graphics statements that follow the COLOR statement select the color number from the palette. If no color number is selected, then the default color number 3 is used for medium resolution and the color number 1 is used for high resolution. In medium resolution the border is always the same color as the background.*

In Table 10.5, line 500 sets the background color to light blue and selects palette 1 for the foreground. Graphics statements that follow line 500 may select cyan (color number 1 in Table 10.5), magenta (2), white (3), or the background color (0) for the foreground. Selecting the background color turns off the referenced pixel(s).

Line 600 leaves the background color the same and palette 0 is selected for the foreground. Graphics statements that follow line 600 may select the foreground color from green (1), red (2), brown (3), or the background color (0). Finally, line 700 in Table 10.5 selects the background color on the basis of the value of BACK and a palette on the basis of whether PAL is odd (palette 1) or even (palette 0).

The PSET and PRESET Statements

The PSET (point set) and PRESET (point reset) statements can be used to set a point (pixel) on the screen to one of the four colors on the active palette. The general forms of the PSET and PRESET statements are given in Table 10.6.

TABLE 10.6 The PSET and PRESET Statements

General Form:	PSET (x, y), color
	and
	PRESET (x, y), color
	where **(x, y)** are the coordinates of the point to be plotted (turned on), and **color** is an integer expression in the range 0 to 3. The color number selects the color from the active palette (see Table 10.5 on the previous page).
Purpose:	Draws a point on the screen.
Examples:	700 PSET (34, 72), 2
	750 PSET (COL, ROW)
	800 PSET STEP (X, 5), 0
	850 PRESET STEP (40, 90), KOLOR
	900 PRESET (34, 72)
Note:	1. The coordinates (x, y) may be absolute or relative.
	2. The PC ignores points referenced outside the range of the screen.
	3. PSET and PRESET are identical statements except for the default color number when the color parameter is not included. With the PSET statement, the color number defaults to 3. With the PRESET statement, the color number defaults to 0, the background color. Thus, PSET (X, Y), 0 is identical to PRESET (X, Y).

Line 700 in Table 10.6 plots the point at the intersection of column 34 and row 72. Depending on which palette is active, the point is colored red or magenta. Line 750 plots the point (COL, ROW), using the default color number 3 on the active palette. Lines 800 and 900 in Table 10.6 erase the point defined by the specified coordinates. You'll recall that a color number of 0 or a lack of the color parameter in the PRESET statement instructs the PC to use the background color (i.e., the pixel is turned off). Line 850 plots the point that is 40 columns and 90 rows from the last point referenced. The color of the point is based upon the value of KOLOR and the active palette.

Consider Program 10.5 and the results due to its execution in Figure 10.17. Line 140 switches the PC to the medium-resolution graphics mode and clears the screen. Line 150 sets the background color to yellow and selects palette 0. The For loop (lines 160 through 180) draws a green vertical line. The color number in line 170 selects the color green from palette 0. Lines 190 and 200 plot two points, using the color red on the left and right sides of the green vertical line. Finally, the second For loop (lines 210 through 230) erases part of the line drawn by the first For loop.

As we shall see in the next section, MS BASIC has a LINE statement that simplifies drawing lines like the one drawn by Program 10.5 in Figure 10.17.

FIGURE 10.17
Plotting a line and points.

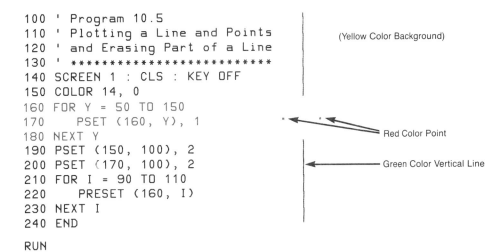

```
100 ' Program 10.5
110 ' Plotting a Line and Points
120 ' and Erasing Part of a Line
130 ' *************************
140 SCREEN 1 : CLS : KEY OFF
150 COLOR 14, 0
160 FOR Y = 50 TO 150
170    PSET (160, Y), 1
180 NEXT Y
190 PSET (150, 100), 2
200 PSET (170, 100), 2
210 FOR I = 90 TO 110
220    PRESET (160, I)
230 NEXT I
240 END

RUN
```

(Yellow Color Background)

Red Color Point

Green Color Vertical Line

TRY IT YOURSELF

Load Program 10.5 (PRG10-5) from the Student Diskette. Delete lines 190 through 230. In line 160, change the initial value to 1 and the limit value to 1000. Replace line 170 with the following:

```
170 PSET(INT(319 * RND + 1), INT(199 * RND + 1))
```

Execute the program and see what happens.

The LINE Statement   The LINE statement can be used to draw a line or a box on the screen. The general form of the LINE statement is given in Table 10.7.

__TABLE 10.7 The LINE Statement__

General Form:	LINE (x_1, y_1) – (x_2, y_2), *color, box, style*
	where (x_1, y_1) is the starting point;
	(x_2, y_2) is the ending point;
	color selects the color for the line from the active palette;
	***box** is B or BF,*
	*where **B** instructs the PC to draw a box, rather than a line, with (x_1, y_1)*
	and (x_2, y_2) as opposite coordinates; and
	***BF** is similar to B, except that the box is filled with color; and*
	***style** determines the type of line (dashed or solid) to be drawn. (The style*
	parameter is optional and will not be used in this book.)
Purpose:	*Connects two points with a line or draws a box (filled or unfilled) on the screen.*
Examples:	100 LINE (50, 70) - (90, 100), 2
	200 LINE - (65, 90)
	300 LINE (0, 0) - (319, 199), 3
	400 LINE (0, 199) - (319, 0), 1, B
	500 LINE (COL1, ROW1) - (COL2, ROW2),, BF
Note:	*Lines that extend beyond the range of the screen are **clipped**; that is, the PC determines the intersection of the line with the edge of the screen and draws the line up to the edge.*

In Table 10.7, line 100 draws a line from the point defined by the intersection of column 50 and row 70 to the point defined by the intersection of column 90 and row 100. The color of the line is either red (palette 0) or magenta (palette 1). Line 200 draws a line from the last point referenced to the point (65, 90) in the default color on the active palette.

Line 300 in Table 10.7 draws a diagonal line from the upper left-hand corner to the lower left-hand corner of the screen. If palette 0 is active, then the color of the line is brown. Line 400 draws a box around the outer edge of the screen. If palette 0 is active, then the lines making up the box are colored green. Otherwise, the lines of the box are colored cyan. Line 500 also draws a box. The location of the box on the screen is dependent on the values assigned to COL1, ROW1, COL2, and ROW2. The parameter BF instructs the PC to fill the box with the default color for the active palette.

Consider Program 10.6 in Figure 10.18 and the right triangle displayed as a result of its execution. In Program 10.6, line 130 switches the PC to the medium-resolution graphics mode and clears the screen. Line 140 changes the background of the screen to blue and selects palette 1. Line 150 draws the base of the triangle. Line 160 draws the altitude, and line 170 draws the hypotenuse. Since none of the LINE statements includes a color number, the default color number 3 (white for palette 1) is used. Note also that lines 160 and 170 both draw lines from the last point referenced.

FIGURE 10.18
Drawing a right triangle.

```
100 ' Program 10.6
110 ' Drawing a Right Triangle
120 ' ************************
130 SCREEN 1 : CLS : KEY OFF
140 COLOR 1, 1
150 LINE (20, 75) - (100, 75)
160 LINE - (100, 25)
170 LINE - (20, 75)
180 END

RUN
```

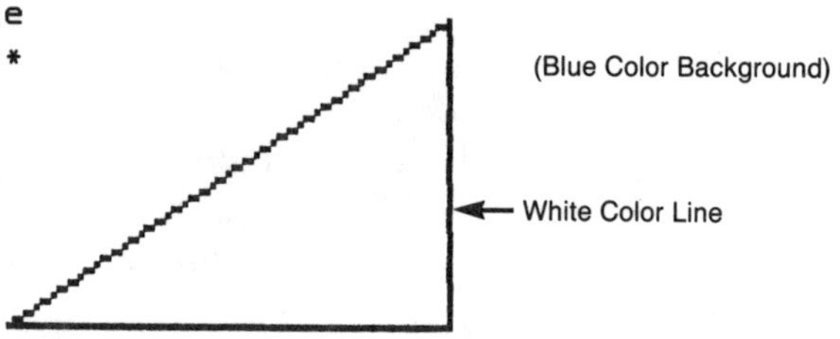

(Blue Color Background)

← White Color Line

TRY IT YOURSELF

Load Program 10.6 (PRG10-6) from the Student Diskette. Change the background color to 0 and the palette to 0. Add the following line:

```
171 LINE - (100, 125) : LINE - (100, 75)
```

Execute the program and see what happens.

As another example of the use of the LINE statement, consider Program 10.7 in Figure 10.19 on the opposite page. This program instructs the PC to draw 5 boxes (one of which is inside another). Line 130 switches the PC to the medium-resolution graphics mode and clears the screen. Line 140 selects a black background and palette 0.

The first LINE statement in Program 10.7 draws the small, unfilled, square box with opposite coordinates of (20, 10) and (40, 30), using the color green. Line 160 draws the large square box, using the color red. Next, line 170 draws a filled square within the square drawn by line 160. Because the background color is used in line 170, the red pixels are turned off to leave an unfilled square within the large red square.

Line 180 in Program 10.7 draws the filled vertical box, using the color green. Finally, line 190 draws the filled horizontal box, using the default color brown on palette 0.

TRY IT YOURSELF

Load Program 10.7 (PRG10-7) from the Student Diskette. Change the background color to blue and the active palette to 1. Delete the color parameters in lines 150 through 180. Execute the program and see what happens.

FIGURE 10.19
Drawing boxes.

```
100 ' Program 10.7
110 ' Drawing Boxes
120 ' ******************
130 SCREEN 1 : CLS : KEY OFF
140 COLOR 0, 0
150 LINE (20, 10) - (40, 30), 1, B
160 LINE (20, 40) - (60, 80), 2, BF
170 LINE (30, 50) - (50, 70), 0, BF
180 LINE (70, 0) - (90, 80), 1, BF
190 LINE (110, 20) - (170, 40),, BF
200 END

RUN
```

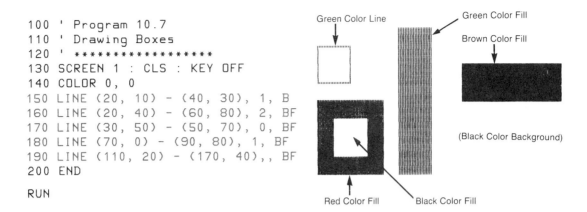

The CIRCLE Statement

The CIRCLE statement draws circles, ellipses, arcs, and wedges. The general form of the CIRCLE statement is given in Table 10.8.

_____TABLE 10.8 The CIRCLE Statement_____

General Form:	CIRCLE *(x, y), radius, color, start, end, shape*
	*where **(x, y)** is the center of the curved figure;*
	radius *is the distance from the center to the outer edge of the curved figure, as measured in points (pixels);*
	color *selects the color for the curved figure from the active palette;*
	start *and **end** are the two ends of the arc to be drawn (The measures are angles in radians and can range between –2*PI and 2*PI where PI = 3.141593. Negative values [–0 is not allowed] cause a wedge or pie slice to be drawn. If these two parameters are omitted, the PC draws the entire curved figure.); and*
	shape *is the ratio of the radius in the y direction to the radius in the x direction (height/width). This parameter is used to draw ellipses. If this parameter is omitted, the PC draws a partial or complete circle, depending on the start and end parameters.*
Purpose:	*Draws circles, ellipses, arcs, and wedges.*
Examples:	200 CIRCLE (160, 100), 20
	300 CIRCLE (60, 40), 30, 1
	400 CIRCLE (20, 20), 50
	500 CIRCLE (X, Y), RAD, KOLOR
	600 CIRCLE (120, 120), 35,, 0, 1.5708
	700 CIRCLE (160, 100), 50, 1, -3.141593, -4.7124
	800 CIRCLE (100, 100), 40,,,,5/18
Note:	*The last point referenced after the CIRCLE statement is executed is the center point (x, y).*

In Table 10.8, line 200 instructs the PC to draw a circle with a center at column 160 and row 100 and with a radius of 20 points. The default color number 3 on the active palette is used to draw the circle. In line 300, a circle with a center at (60, 40) with a radius of 30 points is drawn in green or cyan.

Line 400 in Table 10.8 draws a circle that is clipped, because part of the circle goes beyond the screen. Line 500 causes a circle to be drawn, using the color number KOLOR, with center at (X, Y) and a radius of RAD points.

Line 600 in Table 10.8 draws an arc from 0^0 to 90^0, with a center at (120, 120) and a radius of 35 points. The default color on the active palette is used to color the curved figure. Line 700 draws a wedge. The negative start and end parameters instruct the PC to connect the center to the ends of the arc to form a wedge. The wedge extends from 180^0 to 270^0. Figure 10.20, on the following page, shows the relationship between radians and slices of a circle.

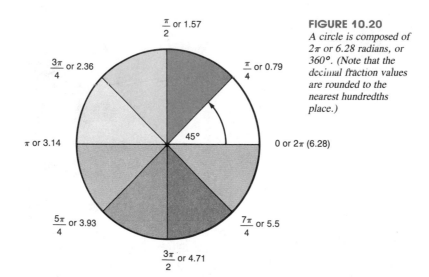

FIGURE 10.20

A circle is composed of 2π or 6.28 radians, or 360°. (Note that the decimal fraction values are rounded to the nearest hundredths place.)

Line 800 in Table 10.8 draws a horizontal (flatter) ellipse. The center of the ellipse is at (100, 100). Because the shape is less than 1, the radius parameter is the x radius. The product of the shape (5/18) and the radius parameter is the y radius.

In mathematics, when the shape is equal to 1, a circle is defined. A shape that is less than 1 causes the ellipse to be horizontal (flatter). A shape greater than 1 causes the ellipse to be vertical (taller).

Because the pixel length for the PC screen is not the same in both the x and y direction (320 x 200 for medium resolution), the default value of the shape that draws a circle is 5/6 (5 rows for every 6 columns) in medium resolution and 5/12 (5 rows for every 12 columns) in high resolution. With this in mind, you must adjust slightly the mathematical definition of the term *shape*. For example, the following statement,

```
900 CIRCLE (160, 100), 50,,,, 1
```

does not result in a circle, even though the shape is 1. Line 900 draws an ellipse that is slightly taller than it is wide. The following statement draws a circle because the PC uses a *default value* of 5/6 for the shape.

```
950 CIRCLE (160, 100), 50
```

See Program 10.8 in Figure 10.21 on the opposite page for additional examples of CIRCLE statements that draw ellipses.

The PAINT Statement

Another color statement that is available with MS BASIC is the PAINT statement. This statement paints (fills) an area on the screen with the selected color. The general form of the PAINT statement is given in Table 10.9 on the opposite page.

Assuming that in medium resolution palette 0 is active, line 600 in Table 10.9 paints the area with the color red that is bounded by the color green in which the point with coordinates (50, 25) is located. If there is no green boundary surrounding (50, 25), then the entire screen is painted red. Line 600 is invalid in high resolution because the paint parameter is not 0 or 1.

In either medium resolution or high resolution, line 700 paints the area encompassing the point with coordinates (COL, ROW) and bounded by the color number EDGE with the color associated with KOLOR. Line 800 colors the area that includes the point with coordinates (200, 100) with the default color (3 in medium resolution and 1 in high resolution). If the edge of the area is not equal to the default color, then the entire screen is painted.

_____TABLE 10.9_ The PAINT Statement_____

General Form:	PAINT *(x, y)*, *paint*, *boundary*
	where *(x, y)* are the coordinates of a point within the area to be filled with color; ***paint*** is a numeric expression or a string expression (If paint is a numeric expression, then it must be within the range 0 to 3 for medium resolution and 0 or 1 for high resolution. The numeric expression determines the color the PC uses to paint the area on the screen. The default for medium resolution is 3 and for high resolution 1. If paint is a string expression, then it describes a tiling pattern for the area.); and ***boundary*** is a numeric expression that defines the color of the edges of the area to be filled.
Purpose:	Paints an area defined by the boundary color on the screen with the selected color.
Examples:	600 PAINT (50, 25), 2, 1 700 PAINT (COL, ROW), KOLOR, EDGE 800 PAINT (200, 100) 900 PAINT (100, 150), TILE$
Note:	1. The area defined by the boundary color must be completely enclosed or the entire screen is painted. 2. In high resolution, the paint parameter should not be different from the boundary parameter.

Consider Program 10.8 and the results due to its execution, which are shown in Figure 10.21.

```
100 ' Program 10.8
110 ' Drawing Circles, Arcs,
120 ' Wedges, and Ellipses
130 ' ********************
140 PI = 3.141593
150 SCREEN 1 : CLS : KEY OFF
160 COLOR 1, 0
170 ' **** Draw Circle ****
180 CIRCLE (40, 40), 20, 1
190 PAINT (40, 40), 3, 1
200 ' ****** Draw Arc *****
210 CIRCLE (80, 40), 20, 1, 0, PI/2
220 ' **** Draw Wedge *****
230 CIRCLE (120,40),20,3,-2*PI,-PI/2
240 PAINT (125, 35), 1, 3
250 ' ** Draw Horizontal Ellipse **
260 CIRCLE (40, 100), 30, 3,,,7/18
270 PAINT (40, 100), 2, 3
280 ' ** Draw Vertical Ellipse **
290 CIRCLE (90, 100), 30, 3,,,18/7
300 PAINT (95, 95), 1, 3
310 ' ** Draw Circle Within Box **
320 LINE (120, 70)-(180, 130), 3, B
330 CIRCLE (150,100), 20, 3
340 PAINT (125, 75), 2, 3
350 END

RUN
```

FIGURE 10.21
Examples of the COLOR and PAINT statements.

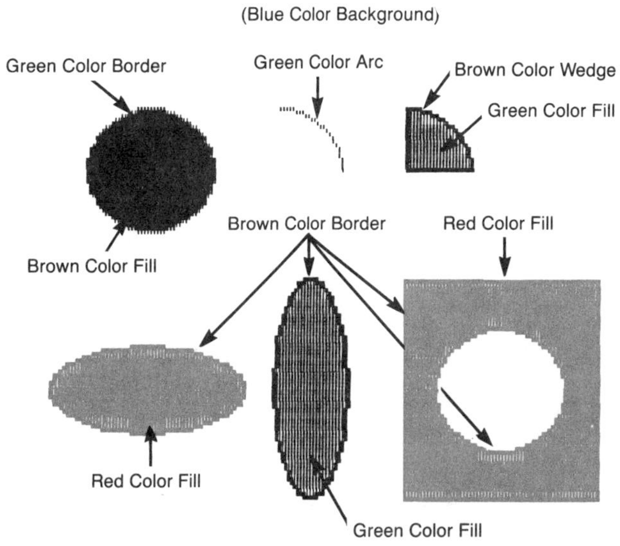

In Figure 10.21, line 150 switches the PC to the medium-resolution graphics mode. The color statement in line 160 selects a blue background and activates palette 0. Line 180 draws the circle in the upper-left corner of the output results. Line 190 paints the circle brown.

Note that the boundary parameter in line 190 is equal to the color number used to draw the circle in line 180.

Line 210 in Program 10.8 draws an arc from $0°$ to $90°$ with a center at (80, 40). Line 230 draws the wedge illustrated in Figure 10.21. Line 240 paints the wedge green. You'll recall that the negative start and end parameters instruct the PC to draw lines from the center point to the end points of the arc to form a wedge. A start parameter of –2 * PI, which is the same as $0°$, is used (–0 is invalid).

Line 260 draws a horizontal ellipse. Line 290 draws a vertical ellipse. Both ellipses are shown in the output results in Figure 10.21. Each of the two CIRCLE statements is followed by a PAINT statement that paints the ellipses. Line 270 paints the horizontal ellipse the color red, and line 300 paints the vertical ellipse the color green.

The lower-right figure in Figure 10.21 is displayed because of lines 320 through 340. Line 320 draws the box. Line 330 draws the circle within the box. Both figures are drawn using the color brown (palette 0, color 3). Line 340 uses the color red to paint the area within the box and outside the circle. Painting continues in all directions until the brown border is reached.

Tiling   Line 900 in Table 10.9, on the previous page, causes the area to be tiled rather than painted. **Tiling** involves covering a specified area on the screen with a pattern. The pattern is uniformly repeated over the entire area.

The pattern of the tile is based on a series of binary digits assigned to the paint parameter in the form of a string expression. The string expression may contain from 1 to 64 bytes. Each byte, called a **tile mask**, contains 8 binary digits. A single tile mask is formed in a BASIC program by means of the CHR$ function, as follows:

CHR$(Decimal Number Representing the Tile Mask)

A series of tile masks is assigned to a string variable that is used as the paint parameter. An example of a tile pattern is shown in Figure 10.22. Each tile represents a single row of pixels.

	Bit Pattern		
	7 6 5 4 3 2 1 0	CHR$ Argument	
Tile 0	1 0 1 0 1 0 1 0	170	
Tile 1	1 1 1 1 1 1 1 1	255	
Tile 3	0 1 0 0 0 1 0 0	68	

130 TILE$ = CHR$(170) + CHR$(255) + CHR$(68)

FIGURE 10.22
An example of a tile pattern and the corresponding string expression assigned to the paint parameter TILE$.

With high resolution, every bit represents a pixel. If the bit is on (1), then the corresponding pixel is turned on; otherwise, the bit is assigned the background color (turned off). By scanning the bit pattern in Figure 10.22, you can get a feel for what each row in the pattern looks like in high resolution.

With medium resolution, every 2 bits represent a pixel, for a total of 4 pixels across per tile byte. Table 10.10 (opposite) shows the binary color numbers for the foreground colors found on the two palettes and the equivalent CHR$ decimal representation for drawing solid lines. A solid line is defined as a single row of pixels.

Consider Programs 10.9 and 10.10 and their corresponding output results in Figure 10.23 on the opposite page.

In Program 10.9 of Figure 10.23, line 170 tiles the box defined by line 160. The pattern of the tile is assigned to the string variable TILE$ in line 130 and corresponds to the one described earlier in Figure 10.22. TILE$ describes a pattern of three lines. The first two are solid lines, and the third is of alternating colors. The first line is in the color magenta. The second line is in the color white. The third line is alternating between cyan and the background color blue.

_____TABLE 10.10 The Binary Color Numbers
for Tiling and Equivalent CHR$ Decimal Values for Solid Lines_____

PALETTE 0	PALETTE 1	BINARY COLOR NUMBER	SOLID LINE PATTERN	CHR$ DECIMAL REPRESENTATION FOR SOLID LINE
Background	*Background*	*00*	*00000000*	*0*
Green	*Cyan*	*01*	*01010101*	*85*
Red	*Magenta*	*10*	*10101010*	*170*
Brown	*White*	*11*	*11111111*	*255*

FIGURE 10.23
Programs 10.9 and 10.10 and their corresponding output results.

```
100 ' Program 10.9
110 ' Tiling a Box in Medium Resolution
120 ' *********************************
130 TILE$ = CHR$(170) + CHR$(255) + CHR$(68)
140 SCREEN 1 : CLS : KEY OFF
150 COLOR 1, 1
160 LINE (40, 70) - (120, 120), 3, B
170 PAINT (117, 80), TILE$, 3
180 END

RUN
```

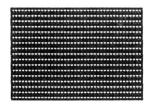

```
100 ' Program 10.10
110 ' Tiling a Wedge in High Resolution
120 ' *********************************
130 PI = 3.141593
140 TILE$ = CHR$(170) + CHR$ (170)
            + CHR$(255) + CHR$(68) + CHR$(68)
150 SCREEN 2 : CLS : KEY OFF
160 CIRCLE (320, 100), 150,, -3 * PI / 4, -PI
170 PAINT (300, 95), TILE$
180 END

RUN
```

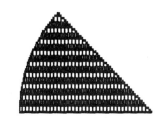

In Program 10.10 of Figure 10.23, line 140 defines the pattern of the tile. Line 150 switches the PC to high resolution. Line 160 instructs the PC to draw a wedge. Finally, line 170 tiles the wedge by turning on the pixels described by the series of binary digits described in line 130.

Developing reasonable tile patterns becomes easier with practice. We suggest that you load Programs 10.9 and 10.10 from the Student Diskette and experiment with changing the patterns in the two programs.

The DRAW Statement

The DRAW statement instructs the PC to draw an object defined by a string expression. The string expression is made up of a series of easy-to-code commands (see Table 10.12 on the following page). The commands can be used to draw lines, plot points, set colors, and perform other special operations — all within one statement. For example, the following statement executed in medium or high resolution,

```
DRAW "L75 U100"
```

draws a horizontal line 75 columns (pixels) long in a left direction from the last point referenced. It then draws a line 100 points long upward toward the top of the screen, beginning at the leftmost point of the first line. The last point referenced is based on the most recently executed graphics statement or it is at the center of the screen following the execution of a CLS statement or the system command RUN. You'll recall that the center of the screen is at (160, 100) for medium resolution and (320, 100) for high resolution (see Figure 10.6 on page 379).

The general form for the DRAW statement is shown in Table 10.11. The list of commands that can be assigned to the string expression in the DRAW statement is given in Table 10.12.

_____TABLE 10.11 The DRAW Statement_____

General Form:	DRAW *string expression*
	where **string expression** *is a command or series of commands as described in Table 10.12.*
Purpose:	*Draws an object as specified in the string expression.*
Examples:	300 DRAW "BM75,120 M200,50 M100,150 M75,120" 400 DRAW "U100 R100 D100 L100" 500 DRAW "E=S1; F=S2; L=S3" 600 DRAW DESIGN$
Note:	*The commands within the string expression may be separated from each other by a blank character or a semicolon.*

_____TABLE 10.12 DRAW Commands_____

COMMAND	FUNCTION	EXAMPLES
M x,y	*Move and draw to (x,y).*	M20,50
M ±x, ±y	*Move and draw to (X + x, Y + y), where (X,Y) is the last referenced point.*	M+30,+50
Un	*Move and draw up n rows.*	U70
Dn	*Move and draw down n rows.*	D35
Rn	*Move and draw right n columns.*	R45
Ln	*Move and draw left n columns.*	L27
En	*Move and draw diagonally up and right, where n = diagonal distance.*	E40
Fn	*Move and draw diagonally down and right, where n = diagonal distance.*	F90
Gn	*Move and draw diagonally down and left, where n = diagonal distance.*	G10
Hn	*Move and draw diagonally up and left, where n = diagonal distance.*	H36
B	*Causes the next move command to move without drawing.*	BM20,50
N	*Instructs the PC to return to the current point after the next move command.*	NR75
An	*Set angle n, where n ranges from 0 to 3. 0 = 0 degrees, 1 = 90 degrees, 2 = 180 degrees, and 3 = 270 degrees. Rotates next object drawn through the specified angle.*	A2
Tn	*Turn angle n for subsequent drawings, where n is in the range –360 to 360; n > 0 turns angle counterclockwise, n < 0 turns angle clockwise.*	T30
Sn	*Scale subsequent drawings, where n varies between 1 and 255 (all line lengths are multiplied by n/4).*	S24
Cn	*Selects color from active palette.*	C2
Pp,b	*Fills area, using color number p to boundary b.*	P1,2
Xv	*Execute a subcommand, where v is a string variable containing additional commands. Allows a series of commands to exceed the string expression limit of 255 characters.*	XDESIGN2$

Programs 10.11 and 10.12 in Figure 10.24 illustrate the use of the DRAW statement to instruct the PC to draw two simple figures — a bicycle wheel and a sailboat.

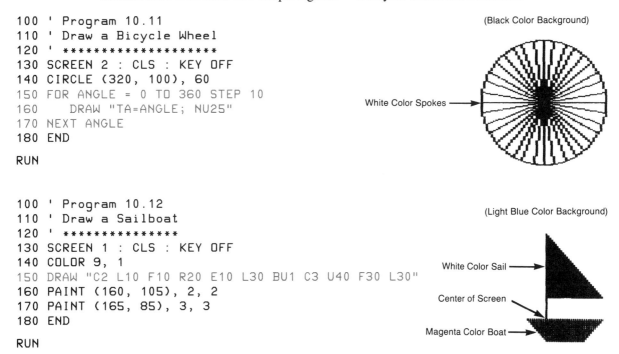

```
100 ' Program 10.11
110 ' Draw a Bicycle Wheel
120 ' ********************
130 SCREEN 2 : CLS : KEY OFF
140 CIRCLE (320, 100), 60
150 FOR ANGLE = 0 TO 360 STEP 10
160    DRAW "TA=ANGLE; NU25"
170 NEXT ANGLE
180 END

RUN
```

(Black Color Background)

White Color Spokes

```
100 ' Program 10.12
110 ' Draw a Sailboat
120 ' **************
130 SCREEN 1 : CLS : KEY OFF
140 COLOR 9, 1
150 DRAW "C2 L10 F10 R20 E10 L30 BU1 C3 U40 F30 L30"
160 PAINT (160, 105), 2, 2
170 PAINT (165, 85), 3, 3
180 END

RUN
```

(Light Blue Color Background)

White Color Sail

Center of Screen

Magenta Color Boat

FIGURE 10.24
Examples of the DRAW statement.

Program 10.11 in Figure 10.24 employs the DRAW statement in the high-resolution graphics mode to draw the bicycle wheel shown to the right of the program. Line 140 draws the rim with a center at (320, 100) and a radius of 60 points. The For loop (lines 150 through 170) draws the spokes. The loop variable ANGLE starts at 0 and steps by 10 until it reaches 360. Each time through the loop, the TA command in line 160 causes the PC to rotate counterclockwise the direction of the next line drawn. Note that the ratio of the length of a spoke (25 points) to the radius of the circle (60 points) is equal to 5/12. This ratio is required because the screen does not have the same number of rows (200) as columns (640).

Program 10.12 in Figure 10.24 uses the DRAW statement in medium resolution to draw a sailboat on a light blue background. The boat is drawn first, then the sail. The color of the boat is magenta, and the sail is white. The 11 commands in the string expression of the DRAW statement in line 150 do this: (1) C2 — select the color magenta for the boat; (2) L10 — move from the center of the screen (160, 100) and draw to the left 10; (3) F10 — move and draw down and to the right 10; (4) R20 — move and draw right 20; (5) E10 — move and draw up and to the right 10; (6) L30 — move and draw left 30; (7) BU1 — move up one row; (8) C3 — select the color white for the sail; (9) U40 — draw and move up 40; (10) F30 — draw and move down and to the right 30; (11) L30 — move and draw to the left 30.

Two important points to remember about Program 10.12: First, prior to the DRAW statement, the last point referenced is the center of the screen. Hence, the second command moves and draws a line 10 columns to the left of the center. Second, command 7 (BU1) is required so that the sail does not intersect the boat. If the sail intersects the boat, then the color magenta used in line 170 to paint the boat would leak out and would cover the entire screen except for the sail.

TRY IT YOURSELF

1. Load Program 10.12 (PRG10-12) from the Student Diskette. Add the command S12 (scale by 12) prior to the first command in the string expression in line 150. The command S12 causes the size of the boat to increase by a factor of 3. Also try S2 and see what happens. See Table 10.11 on page 402 for a description of the S command.

2. Reload PRG10-12 and remove the command BU1 in line 150. Execute the modified version of Program 10.12 and observe the color on the screen.

The WINDOW Statement

The WINDOW statement redefines the coordinates of the screen. In both medium resolution and high resolution, the physical coordinates are such that the upper-left corner is the origin (0, 0) and the coordinate system extends down and to the right. This is called the **physical coordinate system**.

The WINDOW statement allows us to draw graphs and other objects in a different coordinate space called the **world coordinate system**. Once the WINDOW statement modifies the coordinate system, subsequent figures are scaled to the new system. MS BASIC automatically converts the world coordinates into the normal physical coordinates so that the figure can be displayed on the screen.

The general form of the WINDOW statement is given in Table 10.13.

——TABLE 10.13 The WINDOW Statement——

General Form:	WINDOW $(x_1, y_1) - (x_2, y_2)$
	or
	WINDOW SCREEN $(x_1, y_1) - (x_2, y_2)$
	where (x_1, y_1) are the upper-left coordinates and (x_2, y_2) are the lower-right coordinates of the screen, as described below.

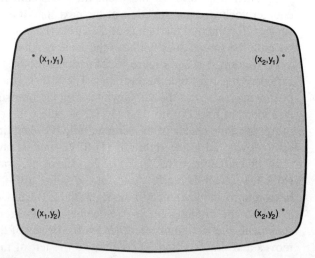

Active window coordinates are mapped onto any viewports subsequently opened by the VIEW *statement.*

If the SCREEN *parameter is not included, then the screen is the normal Cartesian coordinate system, with x increasing to the right and y increasing upward. Furthermore, if the x and y values have the same magnitude, then the origin (0, 0) of the newly defined coordinate system is at the center of the screen. If the* SCREEN *parameter is included, then the coordinates are not inverted and y values increase downward from the origin.*

(continued)

_____TABLE 10.13 The WINDOW Statement *(continued)*_____

Purpose:	*Redefines the coordinates of the viewport. Allows one to "zoom" and "pan" a figure. Subsequent* PSET, PRESET, LINE, *and* CIRCLE *statements reference the new coordinate system.*
Examples:	200 WINDOW (-1, 1) - (1, - 1) 300 WINDOW (-4, 4) - (4, 4) 400 WINDOW (0, 9) - (10, 0) 500 WINDOW SCREEN (0, 0) - (10, 9)
Note:	1. *All possible pairs of x and y are valid. The only restriction is that x_1 cannot equal x_2 and y_1 cannot equal y_2. The* RUN, SCREEN, *or* WINDOW *statement, with no parameters, returns the screen to its normal physical coordinates with the origin (0, 0) at the upper-left corner.* 2. *The* DRAW *statement always references the physical coordinates of the screen.*

FIGURE 10.25
Viewing the graph of the function $y = x^2$ through different window coordinates.

Figure 10.25 illustrates the view of the graph of the function $y = x^2$ through the various WINDOW statements in Table 10.12. Study Figure 10.25 closely. Larger-value coordinates tend to miniaturize the figure, as in (b), while smaller-value coordinates force clipping and only a portion of the figure to be displayed and magnified, as in (c) and (d).

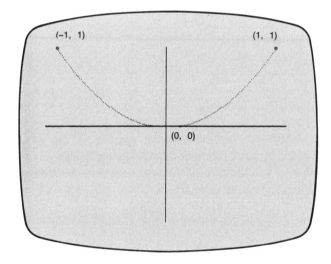

(A) 200 WINDOW (-1, 1) - (1, -1)

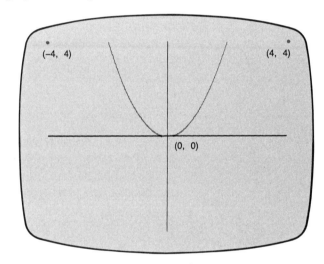

(B) 300 WINDOW (-4, 4) - (4, -4)

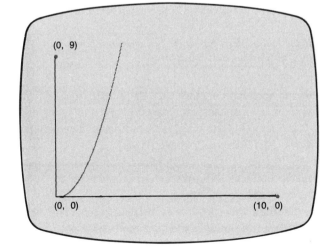

(C) 400 WINDOW (0, 9) - (10, 0)

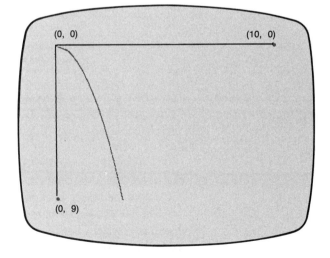

(D) 500 WINDOW SCREEN (0, 0) - (10, 9)

The PMAP and POINT Functions

The PMAP and POINT functions are useful for determining screen characteristics when the WINDOW statement is used to change the coordinate system of the screen.

The PMAP function maps the specified physical coordinate to a world coordinate or a specified world coordinate to a physical coordinate. That is, you can determine the physical coordinate that corresponds to a world coordinate, and vice versa. The general form of the PMAP function is

numeric variable = PMAP(c, n)

where c is the x or y coordinate of the point that is to be mapped from one coordinate system to the other and n is in the range 0 to 3. The descriptions of the permissible values of n are given in Table 10.14.

TABLE 10.14 Descriptions of the Permissible Values for n for the PMAP Function

VALUE OF N	DESCRIPTION
0	*Returns the physical coordinate that corresponds to the world coordinate x.*
1	*Returns the physical coordinate that corresponds to the world coordinate y.*
2	*Returns the world coordinate that corresponds to the physical coordinate x.*
3	*Returns the world coordinate that corresponds to the physical coordinate y.*

The POINT function has two general forms, as follows:

numeric variable = POINT(x, y)

or

numeric variable = POINT(n)

For the first general form, the PC returns the foreground color attribute of the point (x, y). If a WINDOW statement is active, then the point refers to the world coordinates.

The second general form returns the x or y coordinate of the last point referenced. The descriptions of the permissible values of n are given in Table 10.15.

TABLE 10.15 Descriptions of the Permissible Values for n for the POINT Function

VALUE OF N	DESCRIPTION
0	*Returns the physical x coordinate of the last point referenced.*
1	*Returns the physical y coordinate of the last point referenced.*
2	*Returns the world x coordinate that corresponds to the last point referenced (physical x coordinate if no WINDOW statement is active).*
3	*Returns the world y coordinate that corresponds to the last point referenced (physical y coordinate if no WINDOW statement is active).*

VIEW Statement

The VIEW statement defines a **viewport** or rectangular subset of the screen onto which figures can be displayed. The active window coordinates are mapped onto the viewport. Subsequent figures drawn in the viewport are scaled to the window coordinates. The general form of the VIEW statement is given in Table 10.16 on the opposite page.

Consider Program 10.13 in Figure 10.26 (opposite) and the results displayed from its execution. Line 140 clears the screen and selects the medium-resolution graphics mode. Line 150 colors the screen background light blue and selects palette 0.

The WINDOW statement in line 160 redefines the coordinates of the screen. The new coordinate system has its origin (0, 0) exactly in the middle of the screen, with both the x axis and y axis extending from –1 to 1. The screen represents the Cartesian coordinate system magnified near the origin.

_____TABLE 10.16 The VIEW Statement_____

General Form:	VIEW $(x_1, y_1) - (x_2, y_2)$, *color, boundary* *or* VIEW SCREEN $(x_1, y_1) - (x_2, y_2)$, *color, boundary* *where (x_1, y_1) is the upper left and (x_2, y_2) is the lower right coordinates of the viewport (the coordinates must be defined in terms of the actual physical coordinates of the screen);* **color** *is a number (0 to 3 for medium resolution and 0 or 1 for high resolution) which corresponds to a color that is used to paint the viewport; and* **boundary** *is a number (0 to 3 for medium resolution and 0 or 1 for high resolution) which corresponds to a color that is used to draw a boundary around the viewport. If the* SCREEN *parameter is omitted, all points are relative to the viewport; otherwise, they are absolute.*
Purpose:	*Defines a viewport or rectangular subset of the screen onto which figures can be displayed. The* VIEW *statement causes subsequent figures to be scaled to fit the viewport.*
Examples:	600 VIEW (75, 75) - (200, 100), 2, 3 700 VIEW (100, 100) - (150, 150) 800 VIEW SCREEN (25, 50) - (100, 150)
Note:	*1. Only one viewport is active at a time. The* CLS *statement only clears the active viewport.* RUN *and* SCREEN *disable the viewports.* VIEW *with no parameters defines the entire screen as the viewport.* *2. A viewport is scaled according to the most recently executed* WINDOW *statement.*

Line 170 of Program 10.13 defines and activates a second viewport with upper-left coordinates of (100, 50) and lower-right coordinates of (250, 150). These coordinates are not based on the coordinate system established by the WINDOW statement in line 160. They relate to the original coordinate system, where the origin is at the upper-left corner. However, except for its being scaled down, the coordinate system in the viewport is identical to the one ‚defined by the WINDOW statement in line 160. The viewport has a green background and a brown border.

Since only one viewport is active at a time, lines 180 and 190 draw red lines representing the x and y axes within the second viewport defined by line 170. The For loop (lines 200 through 220) graphs the equation $y = x^2$ between $x = -1$ and $x = 1$, with a point plotted every one-hundredth of a unit. The points making up the graph are colored brown.

```
100 ' Program 10.13
110 ' The Graph of y = x ^ 2 Between x = -1
120 ' and x = 1 Drawn in a Secondary Viewport
130 ' ****************************************
140 SCREEN 1 : CLS : KEY OFF
150 COLOR 9, 0
160 WINDOW (-1, 1) - (1, -1)
170 VIEW (100, 50) - (250, 150), 1, 3
180 LINE (-1, 0) - (1, 0), 2
190 LINE (0, 1) - (0, -1), 2
200 FOR X = -1 TO 1 STEP .01
210    PSET (X, X ^ 2)
220 NEXT X
230 END
RUN
```

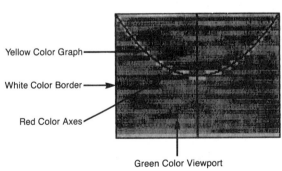

(Blue Color Background)

Yellow Color Graph

White Color Border

Red Color Axes

Green Color Viewport

FIGURE 10.26
Multiple viewports.

> Load Program 10.13 (PRG10-13) from the Student Diskette. Change the viewport coordinates in line 170 to (0, 0) – (160, 100). Execute the program and see what happens. Add an apostrophe (') prior to the keyword VIEW in line 170 and execute the program again.

The GET and PUT Statements for Graphics

The GET and PUT statements are used for high-speed object motion. With these two statements, you can save and recall the contents of any rectangle on the screen. The activity of saving and recalling images in medium or high resolution can be very useful for producing high-quality computer animation.

The GET statement reads the colors of the points in the specified area of the screen into an array. The PUT statement writes the colors of the points in the array onto an area of the screen. The idea behind these two statements is that we can instruct the PC to draw a figure on the screen, use the GET statement to store the figure in a numeric array, then move the figure from one location to another with the PUT statement. The general forms of the GET and PUT statements are given in Tables 10.17 and 10.18 on the opposite page.

With the PUT statement, the action parameter XOR is the most interesting, because if you use it twice in succession, the original scene within the specified area will reappear. This is critical to computer animation when you are required to move an object across the screen. Before we can move an image to a new location on the screen, we must return the current location to its old scene. Two successive PUTs with the XOR action parameter and a slight time delay in between gives us the desired action.

Here is a step-by-step algorithm for moving an object across the screen:

1. Draw the desired image on the screen.
2. Use the GET statement to store the image into an array.
3. Clear the screen.
4. Draw background figures that will remain constant during the animation.
5. Establish a For loop that determines the coordinates at which the image is to appear. Within the loop, do the following:
   a. Use the PUT statement with the action parameter XOR to put the image at the desired location.
   b. Use a For loop to delay execution of the next statement so that the figure may be seen.
   c. Use the PUT statement with the action parameter XOR to erase the image at the current location.

Consider the animation of a bus traveling on a highway, right to left, produced in the medium-resolution graphics mode by Program 10.14 in Figure 10.27 on page 410. Lines 180 through 240 plot the bus in the upper-left corner of the screen. Line 260 stores the points within the rectangle defined by the coordinates (26, 40) and (71, 53) into the integer array BUS%.

The formula given in Table 10.17 is used to determine the size of BUS%. For example, from lines 180 through 220 it can be determined that the minimum-size rectangle that includes the bus (plus the wheels) is $76 - 26 + 1 = 46$ points wide and $53 - 40 + 1 = 14$ points high. Furthermore, we are working in medium resolution, which requires 2 bits per point. Hence, the formula after substitution looks like this:

$$4 + 14 * INT((46 * 2 + 7) / 8) = 172$$

_____TABLE 10.17 The GET Statement for Graphics_____

General Form:	GET (x_1, y_1) – (x_2, y_2), *array name*
	where (x_1, y_1) and (x_2, y_2) are the opposite coordinates of a rectangle on the screen (the coordinates may be absolute or relative); and
	array name *is the name of a numeric array into which the* GET *statement reads the information about the points in the specified area.*
Purpose:	*Reads the colors of the points in the specified area on the screen into an array.*
Examples:	300 GET (250, 50) - (300, 100), ANIMAT1
	400 GET (0, 0) - (319, 199), SCREEN1%
	500 GET (0, 100) - (160, 199), ANIMAT2
Note:	*The required size of the array in bytes is:*
	$4 + H * INT((W * bits + 7) / 8)$
	*where **H** is the height (number of rows) of the rectangle;*
	***W** is the width (number of columns) of the rectangle; and*
	***bits** is 2 in medium resolution and 1 in high resolution. You'll recall that there are 2 bytes per element in an integer array; 4 bytes per element in a single-precision array; and 8 bytes per element in a double-precision array.*

_____TABLE 10.18 The PUT Statement for Graphics_____

General Form:	PUT *(x, y), array name, action*
	*where **(x, y)** are the coordinates of the top-left corner of the rectangular area on the screen, where the pixel pattern in **array name** is displayed; and*
	***action** specifies the manner in which the pixel pattern is displayed on the existing screen background. The action parameter may be one of the following:*
	PSET – *Put the pixel pattern on the screen exactly as defined in array name.*
	PRESET – *Put the inverse pixel pattern in array name (negative image) on the screen.*
	AND – *Turn "on" those pixels that are both "on" in array name and "on" on the screen.*
	OR – *Superimpose the pixel pattern in array name onto the existing pattern on the screen.*
	XOR – *Turn "on" those pixels that are "on" in array name and "off" on the screen or "off" in array name and "on" on the screen. (If the action parameter is not used, then* XOR *is the default value.)*
Purpose:	*Writes the colors of the points in the array onto an area of the screen.*
Examples:	300 PUT (25, 50), ANIMAT1
	400 PUT (0, 0), SCREEN1%, XOR
	500 PUT (0, 50), ANIMAT2, OR
	600 PUT (160, 100), ARR1, PSET

With an integer array, divide the byte requirement by 2. The result is that 86 elements are required in BUS%.

Lines 280 through 340 of Program 10.14 clears the screen, displays a message, and then draws the highway and telephone poles. Finally, lines 360 through 420 animate the bus driving on the highway over and over again until the operator presses any key on the keyboard.

The first PUT statement (line 380) in the For loop plots the bus to the far right and just above the highway. Line 390 delays the next PUT statement (line 400) for a fraction of a second. This second PUT statement erases the bus plotted by line 380. The next time line 380 is executed, it plots the bus 50 points to the left. This plotting and erasing continues until the bus is near the left side of the screen. At this point, the While loop starts the bus back at the right side of the screen. This animation continues until the operator intervenes.

TRY IT YOURSELF

Load Program 10.14 (PRG10-14) from the Student Diskette. Modify line 390 by replacing the limit value of 50. Try a limit value of 200. Notice how the bus has slowed down. Now try a limit value of 1 and see what happens.

FIGURE 10.27
Computer animation in the medium-resolution graphics mode of a bus traveling down a highway, right to left.

```
100 ' Program 10.14
110 ' Animating a Moving Bus
120 '**********************
130 OPTION BASE 1
140 DIM BUS%(86)
150 CLS : SCREEN 1 : KEY OFF
160 COLOR 0, 0
170 '******** Draw Bus Body ********
180 LINE (31, 40) - (71, 50), 2, BF
190 LINE (26, 45) - (31, 50), 2, BF
200 '****** Draw Bus Wheels ******
210 CIRCLE (29, 50), 3, 3
220 CIRCLE (66, 50), 3, 3
230 PAINT (29, 50),3, 3
240 PAINT (66, 50),3, 3
250 '****** Store Bus Image ******
260 GET (26, 40) - (71, 53), BUS%
270 '*** Draw Highway with Telephone Poles ***
280 CLS
290 LOCATE 15, 7 : PRINT "Press any key to stop bus..."
300 LINE (0, 100) - (319, 100), 2
310 FOR COL = 5 TO 319 STEP 40
320     LINE (COL, 100) - (COL, 85)
330     LINE (COL - 3, 88) - (COL + 2, 88)
340 NEXT COL
350 ' ******** Animate Bus ********
360 WHILE INKEY$ = ""
370     FOR ANIM = 250 TO 0 STEP -50
380         PUT (ANIM, 87), BUS%, XOR
390             FOR TIME.DELAY = 1 TO 50 : NEXT TIME.DELAY
400         PUT (ANIM, 87), BUS%, XOR
410     NEXT ANIM
420 WEND
430 END

RUN
```

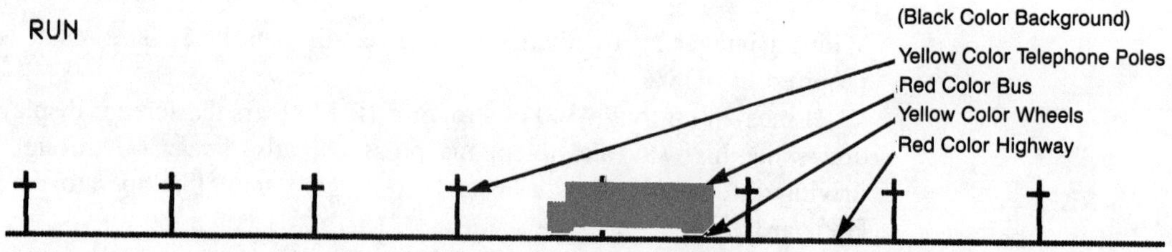

(Black Color Background)
Yellow Color Telephone Poles
Red Color Bus
Yellow Color Wheels
Red Color Highway

```
Press any key to stop bus...
```

⊞ 10.4

SOUND AND MUSIC

A speaker is located in the left corner of the system unit of the PC (see Figure 1.6 on page 5 in chapter 1). Though this speaker is small, it is capable of producing a variety of sounds. For example, in chapter 5 we used the BEEP statement to produce a high-pitched sound to draw the operator's attention to data-entry errors. In this section, we will explore two additional statements that can activate the speaker under program control. They are the SOUND and PLAY statements.

The SOUND Statement

The SOUND statement is used to create a sound of variable frequency and duration. The general form of the SOUND statement is given in Table 10.19. Program 10.15, following the table, illustrates the use of the SOUND statement to generate a siren sound. Line 130 clears the screen. Line 140 selects a blinking red foreground on a black background with a blue border. The second statement in line 140 turns off the cursor. Lines 150 and 160 display messages. The While loop (lines 170 through 210) executes until the user presses a key on the keyboard.

The For loop (lines 180 through 200) in Program 10.15 generates a siren-like sound, using the PC's speaker. Each time through the For loop, the frequency increases until it reaches 1100 Hertz (cycles per second).

_____TABLE 10.19 The SOUND Statement_____

General Form:	SOUND *frequency, duration*
	where **frequency** *is a numeric expression between 37 and 32767; and* **duration** *is a numeric expression in the range 0 to 65535. The expression represents the duration in clock ticks, and there are 18.2 clock ticks per second. A duration of zero turns off the current sound.*
Purpose:	*Generates sound through the PC's speaker.*
Examples:	500 SOUND 1000, 85 600 SOUND 32767, 0 700 SOUND FREQ, DUR
Note:	*The frequency is measured in Hertz (cycles per second).*

PROGRAM 10.15

```
100 ' Program 10.15
110 ' Using the Speaker as a Siren
120 ' ***************************
130 WIDTH 40 : KEY OFF
140 COLOR 20, 0, 1 : LOCATE ,, 0
150 LOCATE 13, 8 : PRINT "EMERGENCY!!  EMERGENCY!!"
160 LOCATE 24, 4 : PRINT "Press any key to stop the siren...";
170 WHILE INKEY$ = ""
180    FOR FREQ = 500 TO 1100 STEP 20
190       SOUND FREQ, .05
200    NEXT FREQ
210 WEND
220 WIDTH 80 : COLOR 7, 0, 0 : KEY ON
230 END

RUN
```

TRY IT YOURSELF

Load Program 10.15 (PRG10-15) from the Student Diskette. Execute the program. Now modify the initial, terminal, and step values in line 180 and the duration parameter in line 190. See if you can get the program to cause the speaker to sound more like a police-car siren.

The PLAY Statement

The PLAY statement converts your PC into a piano. Like the DRAW statement, the PLAY statement instructs the PC to play music that is defined by a string expression. The string is made up of a series of easy-to-code commands (see Table 10.21 on the opposite page). The music you compose may be as simple as a single note or as complex as the counterpoint in Bach or a symphony by Beethoven. The general form of the PLAY statement is shown in Table 10.20.

————TABLE 10.20 The PLAY Statement————

General Form:	PLAY *string expression* where **string expression** *is a command or series of commands, as described in Table 10.21.*
Purpose:	*Plays music as specified in the string expression.*
Examples:	100 PLAY "C D E F G A B >C C< B A G F E D C" 200 PLAY "L4 C D E2 L4 E D L2 C D E C" 300 PLAY MUSIC$ 400 PLAY "L=LENGTH; XCHORUS$; XBRIDGE$; XCHORUS$;"
Note:	*The commands within the string expression may be separated from each other by blank characters or a semicolon, except that a semicolon is not allowed after* MF, MB, MN, ML, *or* MS.

Line 100 in Table 10.20 plays the C scale. The greater than sign (>) causes the PC to climb to the next octave. The less than sign (<) has the opposite effect.

Line 200 plays the song "Stepping Up Stepping Down." The L command establishes the length of all subsequent notes played. The command E2 changes the length only for that note.

Line 300 in Table 10.20 plays the tune definition assigned to the string variable MUSIC$. The first command in line 400 sets the length of the notes that follow to the value assigned to LENGTH. Line 400 also illustrates how you can instruct the PC to execute a series of subcommands. This can be useful when you want to play a chorus after each bridge.

As a sample program that uses the PLAY statement, consider Program 10.16. This program plays the tune "Twinkle Twinkle Little Star" over and over again until the user presses a key on the keyboard. Both the chorus and the bridge are defined prior to the PLAY statement in lines 160 and 180. In line 210, the PLAY statement employs the X command to reference the subcommands assigned to CHORUS$ and BRIDGE$.

PROGRAM 10.16

```
100 ' Program 10.16
110 ' Twinkle Twinkle Little Star
120 ' ***************************
130 'CLS : KEY OFF
140 'LOCATE 13, 25 : PRINT "Press any key to stop the song..."
150 ' ****** Define Chorus ******
160 CHORUS$ = "L4 C C G G A A L2 G L4 F F E E D D L2 C"
170 ' ****** Define Bridge ******
180 BRIDGE$ = "L4 G G F F E E L2 D L4 G G F F E E L2 D"
190 ' ******** Play Song ********
200 WHILE INKEY$ = ""
210    PLAY "XCHORUS$; XBRIDGE$; XCHORUS$;"
220 WEND
230 END

RUN
```

TRY IT YOURSELF

Load Program 10.16 (PRG10-16) from the Student Diskette. Execute the program and listen to it play "Twinkle Twinkle Little Star." Double the parameter following each L command. Execute the program and listen to the sound. Now triple the original values and execute the program again.

TABLE 10.21 PLAY Commands

COMMAND	FUNCTION	EXAMPLES
A to G with optional #, +, or –	Plays the specified note in the current octave. A number sign (#) or plus sign (+) appended to the letter indicates a sharp; a minus sign (–) indicates a flat.	C A+ D–
On	Sets the octave for the notes that follow. There are 7 octaves, numbered 0 to 6. Octave 4 is the default. Each octave goes from C to B, and octave 3 starts with middle C.	O2
>n or <n	The greater than sign (>) instructs the PC to climb to the next octave and play note n. The less than sign (<) lowers the octave by 1. Either sign affects all notes that follow.	>C <D–
Nn	Play note n, where n ranges from 0 to 84. This serves as an alternative to using the O command followed by the note name. N0 is a "rest."	N27 N0
Ln	Sets the length of the notes that follow. The parameter n can range from 1 to 64. The PC interprets n as 1/n. The length of a note may also follow the note. For example, C4 is the same as L4C.	L4 L=S;
Pn	Pause. The parameter n can range from 1 to 64. As with the L command, the PC interprets n as 1/n.	P16 P=R;
.	Dot. Placed after a note, the dot causes the note to be played as a dotted note. Multiple dots are valid.	A. C+..
Tn	Tempo. Defines the number of quarter notes per minute. The parameter n can range from 32 to 255. The default is 120.	T110 T=NU;
MF	Music foreground. The music created by the SOUND or PLAY statement runs in the foreground. The program is put into a wait state until the music statement is finished. A note does not start until the previous note is finished. MF is the default.	MF
MB	Music background. The music created by the SOUND or PLAY statement runs in the background. That is, the BASIC program continues to execute while the music plays in the background.	MB
ML	Music legato. Each note that follows plays the full period set by L.	ML
MN	Music normal. Each note that follows plays 7/8 of the time specified by L. Default between MN, ML, and MS.	MN
MS	Music staccato. Each note that follows plays 3/4 of the time specified by L.	MS
Xv;	Execute a subcommand, where v is a string variable containing additional commands. Allows a series of commands to exceed the string expression limit of 255 characters.	XMUSIC$;

⊞ 10.5   WHAT YOU SHOULD KNOW

1. The PC provides three graphics modes — text, medium resolution, and high resolution. The latter two are available only if your PC has a color/graphics interface board.
2. When the system command BASICA is entered, the PC is in the text mode. In this mode, the screen has 25 lines (rows) of 80 columns each. You can switch to the 40-column display by using the WIDTH statement.
3. The SCREEN statement can be used to switch between the text, medium-resolution, and high-resolution graphics modes. The SCREEN statement can also be used in the text mode to do simple animation through the use of the active and visual pages.
4. In the medium-resolution graphics mode, the screen is divided into 200 rows and 320 columns. In the high-resolution graphics mode, the screen is divided into 200 rows and 640 columns. Each intersection of a column and row defines a point (pixel), which can be turned on or off.
5. The text mode is often used to create logos and simple animations. The medium-resolution graphics mode is used to plot points, draw figures, and create sophisticated animated designs. The high-resolution graphics mode allows you to draw very detailed designs.
6. In the text mode, you can produce interesting and useful graphics with the PRINT and PRINT USING statements, the CHR$ function, and the ASCII character set.
7. If you have a color monitor and a color/graphics interface board, then you may enhance your displays in the text and medium-resolution graphics modes with a variety of colors. With high resolution, figures can be displayed only in black and white or green or amber.
8. In the text mode, the COLOR statement sets the color for the foreground, background, and border. The foreground and border can be set to 16 different colors and the background to 8 colors. By adding the number 16 to the foreground color number, all characters displayed will blink.
9. In the text mode, a CLS statement should follow the COLOR statement to ensure that the color takes effect immediately over the entire screen.
10. To send graphics designs to the printer, you must have one that emulates the IBM graphics printer. You must also enter the system command GRAPHICS before you enter the system command BASICA.
11. In both medium resolution and high resolution, we plot points and draw lines by instructing the PC to turn on pixels. We define lines and curves in the form of coordinates, like (x, y) where x is the column and y is the row. Each pixel has a unique set of coordinates.
12. There are two ways to indicate the coordinates of a point: absolute form and relative form.
13. The COLOR statement for medium resolution allows one to select from 16 different background colors and 1 of 2 palettes of colors for the foreground. Each palette carries 4 colors, numbered 0 through 3.
14. The PSET and PRESET statements are used to turn individual points (pixels) on or off. The PC turns off a point by assigning it the background color.
15. The LINE statement is used to draw lines and boxes in a color selected from the active palette. When the LINE statement is used to draw a box, you can also instruct the PC to fill the box with the color selected from the active palette. In high resolution, the active palette has no meaning.
16. The CIRCLE statement is used to draw circles, ellipses, arcs, and wedges.
17. The PAINT statement can be used to paint an enclosed area. In medium resolution, the colors on the active palette are available. In high resolution, only black and white are available.
18. The PAINT statement can also be used to tile an enclosed area on the screen. The tile pattern is based on the binary value of the tile mask. The CHR$ function is used to establish the tile mask in a program.
19. The DRAW statement is used to draw complicated objects on the basis of commands assigned to a string expression.
20. The normal coordinates of the screen are called physical coordinates. The WINDOW statement can be used to redefine the coordinates into what are called world coordinates. Any viewport subsequently opened by the VIEW statement is defined in terms of the world coordinates.
21. Depending on the argument, the PMAP and POINT functions return either physical or world coordinates.
22. The GET and PUT statements are used for high-speed object motion. These statements can be very useful in producing high-quality computer animation.
23. The SOUND statement generates sound through the PC's speaker.
24. The PLAY statement converts your PC into a piano. The music you compose in the form of a string expression may be as simple as a single note or as complex as the counterpoint in Bach or a symphony by Beethoven.

⊞ 10.6 TEST YOUR BASIC SKILLS (Even-numbered answers are at the back of the book, before the index.)

1. Consider the two valid programs below. What is displayed if each is executed?

  a.
```
100 ' Exercise 10.1a
110 SCREEN 2 : CLS : KEY OFF
120 WINDOW (-100, 100) - (100, -100)
130 LINE (-100, 0) - (100, 0)
140 LINE (0, 100) - (0, -100)
150 FOR X = -50 TO 50 STEP 1
160    Y = X + 8
170      PSET (X, Y)
180 NEXT X
190 END
```

  b.
```
100 ' Exercise 10.1b
110 SCREEN 1 : CLS : KEY OFF
120 COLOR 1, 0
130 WINDOW (-10, 10) - (10, -10)
140 LINE (-10, 0) - (10, 0)
150 LINE (0, 10) - (0, -10)
160 FOR X = 1 TO 7
170    CIRCLE (0, 0), X, 2
180 NEXT X
190 END
```

2. Use PSET, LINE, and CIRCLE statements to draw the following figures. Assume that the PC is in the medium-resolution graphics mode.

  a.
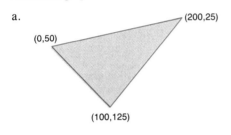

  b.
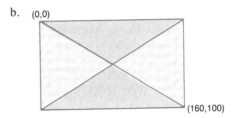

  c.
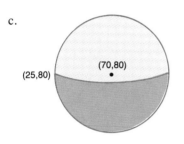

  d.
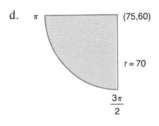

3. Use the DRAW statement to draw the figures in 2a and 2b. Use the scale factor to double the size of each figure.

4. Assume you are working with a PC that has a color/graphics interface board and color monitor. Describe the appearance of the screen after each of the following is executed.

  a.
```
200 SCREEN 0 : KEY OFF
300 COLOR 4, 1, 0 : CLS
```

  b.
```
400 SCREEN 1 : CLS : KEY OFF
500 COLOR 0, 0
```

5. Describe the display of characters following the execution of a COLOR statement with a foreground color number of 20 in the text mode.

6. Fill in the following:

  a. In the medium- and high-resolution graphics modes, the intersection of a row and column is called a _____ or _____ .

  b. If you plan to print a graphics display, then you must enter the system command _____ before entering BASICA.

  c. If you enter WIDTH _____ in the medium-resolution graphics mode, the PC will switch to the high-resolution graphics mode.

  d. Use the _____ function to describe a tile pattern for the PAINT statement.

  e. To draw a wedge with the CIRCLE statement, add a _____ before the start and end parameters.

  f. The _____ and _____ statements are used in the medium- and high-resolution graphics modes to produce high-quality computer animation.

  g. There are _____ bytes per element in an integer array; _____ bytes per element in a single-precision array; and _____ bytes per element in a double-precision array.

7. Consider the valid program below and then answer the three questions that follow.

```
100 ' Exercise 10.7
110 INPUT "Density (0 to 1) ===> ", DENSITY
120 COLOR 4, 0, 0 : CLS
130 KEY OFF : WIDTH 40
140 RANDOMIZE TIMER
150 FOR ROW = 1 TO 24
160    FOR COL = 1 TO 40
170       IF RND <= DENSITY
              THEN LOCATE ROW, COL :
                 PRINT CHR$(219);
180    NEXT COL
190 NEXT ROW
200 LOCATE 25, 1
210 INPUT "Press the Enter key to quit...", A$
220 COLOR 7, 0, 0 : WIDTH 80 : KEY ON
230 END
```

   a. What is displayed if this program is executed?
   b. What are the foreground, background, and border colors that are due to line 120?
   c. What is the purpose of line 220?

8. Write a program that draws the following three-dimensional box in the medium-resolution graphics mode, using the color brown. Color the background blue and activate palette 0. Paint the face of the figure red, the side brown, and the top green.

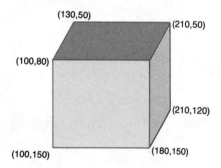

9. Evaluate each of the following. Assume that the statements are executed in the high-resolution graphics mode.

   a. 100 PSET (320, 100)
   b. 200 GET (23, 46) - (75, 80), A%
   c. 300 PUT (72, 96) - (125, 130), A%
   d. 400 CIRCLE (50, 50), 15,, -3, -4
   e. 500 CIRCLE (320, 160), 30,,,, 5/8
   f. 600 LINE - (40, 30)
   g. 700 LINE (0, 0)-(160, 100)
   h. 800 DRAW "BM320,160 NR45 D45"
   i. 900 SOUND 200, .03
   j. 950 PLAY "XMUS$;"

10. Use the PRINT statement, the CHR$ function, and ASCII code 219 to draw a box with the following characteristics in the text mode. Assume that the screen is set to the 40-column display mode.

   a. Horizontal lines at rows 4 and 22.
   b. Vertical lines at columns 9 and 32.

11. Write a program that uses the WINDOW statement with coordinates (−25, 25) – (25, −25) in the high-resolution graphics mode to establish the Cartesian coordinate system. Draw the x and y axes and the graph of the equation $y = 3x + 2$ between x = 20 and x = −20. Plot points, using the PSET statement every 0.01 units.

12. Identify each of the following PLAY commands.

   a. A−   b. L8   c. >C   d. XM$;   e. N0
   f. T100   g. P8   h. MS   i. ML   j. O3

13. Identify each of the following DRAW commands.

   a. BM 10, 20   b. M+3, +5   c. C1   d. F5   e. E20
   f. A3   g. U75   h. H5   i. L20   j. NL20

14. With respect to the PUT statement, define the action parameters PSET, AND, and XOR.
15. Determine the required size for the integer array ANIM% in the following GET statement. Assume that the statement is executed in the high-resolution graphics mode.

```
300 GET (20, 30) - (80, 100), ANIM%
```

16. Use the Student Diskette to complete the Try It Yourself exercises on pages 380, 386, 392, 395, 396, 404, 408, 410, 411, and 413.

⊞ 10.7 Basic Programming Problems

1. Horizontal Bar Graph of Annual Sales for the Past Ten Years

Purpose: To become familiar with graphing in the text mode.

Problem: A graph gives the user of a report a pictorial view of the information. Consider the following problem, which has as its defined output a horizontal bar graph. The Sales Analysis Department of the PUC Company requests from the Data Processing Department a report in the form of a horizontal bar graph representing the company's annual sales trend for the ten-year period 1981 through 1990. The annual sales are as follows:

Year	Sales (in millions)	Year	Sales (in millions)
1981	$22	1986	$43
1982	26	1987	40
1983	28	1988	45
1984	35	1989	50
1985	40	1990	48

Include the following characteristics in the graph:

1. Display the bar graph horizontally in the 80-column display mode.
2. Display vertically the column that represents the years.
3. Use a series of asterisks to represent the sales for each year.
4. Mark off the horizontal axis in increments of 5, beginning with 0 and ending with 55. Each unit represents a million dollars.

(Hint: See Program 10.3 on page 385.)

Input Data: Use the ten-year PUC Company data shown above. The data (year and sales) for each year is in the sequential file EX101SAL.DAT on the Student Diskette.

Output Results: The following results are displayed.

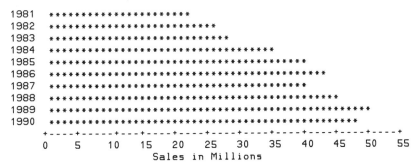

2. Graphing a Function

Purpose: To become familiar with using the PSET statement to graph a function on a world coordinate system in the high-resolution graphics mode.

Problem: Graph the function $y = 2x^3 + 6x^2 - 18x + 6$. Use a WINDOW statement with coordinates (–6, 70) – (6, –70) to define the Cartesian coordinate system with its origin at the center of the screen. Graph the function between $x = -5$ and $x = 3$. Plot points every 1/100th of a unit. Label the axes as shown in the Output Results.

(Hint: See Program 10.13 in Figure 10.26 on page 407.)

Input Data: None.

Output Results: The following results are displayed.

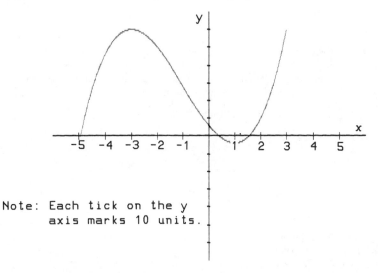

```
Note: Each tick on the y
      axis marks 10 units.
```

3. Animating Push-Ups

Purpose: To become familiar with simple animation through the use of the GET and PUT statements in the medium-resolution graphics mode.

Problem: Draw an animation of the Mechanical Man doing push-ups. Phase 1 and phase 2 of the animation are illustrated in Figure 10.28. Draw phase 1 and use the GET statement to store it in an array. Do the same with phase 2. Have the Mechanical Man do 50 push-ups by switching from one figure to another. Color the Mechanical Man's torso red and his head brown.

(Hint: See Program 10.14 in Figure 10.27 on page 410.)

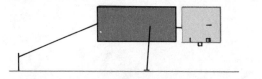

FIGURE 10.28
Positions of the Mechanical Man doing push-ups.

Phase 1: The Mechanical Man in position 1.

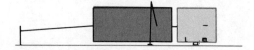

Phase 2: The Mechanical Man in position 2.

Input Data: None.

Output Results: The display of the Mechanical Man will switch between phase 1 and phase 2 fifty times.

4. Drawing a Design

Purpose: To become familiar with the LINE, CIRCLE, and PAINT statements.

Problem: Construct a program that draws the design shown in the Output Results. Draw the design in the medium-resolution graphics mode. Use the PAINT statement to color and tile the various sections of the design.

Input Data: None.

Output Results: The following results are displayed.

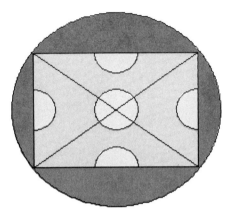

5. Playing the Musical Score "Yankee Doodle" on the PC

Purpose: To become familiar with the PLAY statement.

Problem: Obtain a song sheet of "Yankee Doodle." Use a For loop to play the song seven times, starting at octave 0 and ending at octave 6.

Input Data: None.

Output Results: The PC plays the song "Yankee Doodle" seven times, each time at a higher octave.

PROGRAM FLOWCHARTING AND TOP-DOWN DESIGN

APPENDIX A

The purpose of this appendix is to concentrate on preparing, using, and reading program flowcharts and top-down charts. Upon successful completion of this appendix, you will be able to develop program flowcharts that describe the logic and operations of computer programs and top-down charts that illustrate the decomposition of large, complex problems.

A **program flowchart** shows in graphic form the algorithm (method of solution) used in a program. By depicting a procedure for arriving at a solution, a program flowchart also shows how the application or job is to be accomplished. The term *flowchart* will be used throughout this appendix to mean program flowchart.

Purpose of Flowcharting

A flowchart is used by programmers and analysts as

1. an aid in developing the logic of a program;
2. an aid in breaking the program into smaller units, sometimes called modules, if a top-down or modular approach is used;
3. a verification that all possible conditions have been considered in a program;
4. a means of communicating with others about the program;
5. a guide in coding the program; and
6. documentation for the program.

Flowchart Notation

Eight basic symbols are commonly used in flowcharting a program. They are given in chapter 1, Table 1.4 on page 12, with their names and meanings and with some of the MS BASIC statements that are represented by them. In a flowchart, the process, input/output, decision, terminal, connector, and predefined process symbols are connected by solid lines. These solid lines, called flowline symbols, show the direction of flow. The annotation symbol, on the other hand, is connected by a broken line to any one of the other flowchart symbols (including any of the flowline symbols).

One rule that is fundamental to all flowcharts concerns direction. In constructing a flowchart, start at the top (or left-hand corner) of a page. The flow should be top to bottom or left to right. If the flow takes any other course, arrowheads must be used. No curved or diagonal flowline symbols are ever drawn. Although arrowheads are shown in Figure A.1 and in other flowcharts throughout this book, they need not be used in these cases, since their usage is optional when flow is both left to right and top to bottom.

Inside each of the symbols, except the flowline symbols, write either English-sentence-type notation, mathematical notation or program language statements. These notations are arbitrary, and their use depends on the kind of program being flowcharted, on the experience of the person constructing the flowchart and on the standards that are used in the computer installation. One symbol or abbreviated description may represent more than one MS BASIC statement. The annotation symbol, with comments written inside it, is optional and is used whenever additional information is desired for the sake of clarity.

The first symbol in a flowchart is usually a terminal symbol with Start written inside it. This corresponds to no MS BASIC *statement* but is used solely to provide aid in finding the beginning point to a person who is unfamiliar with the flowchart.

Figure A.1 illustrates the logic of Program A.1, which calculates the state income tax. Two versions of the flowchart are given to show that the choice of the written contents inside each symbol is an arbitrary matter. Both versions have the same logic, since the number, type, and arrangement of flowchart symbols are identical. The flowchart in Figure A.1(A) is more like English, and it would be used to communicate with a nonprogrammer, while the flowchart in Figure A.1(B) is more like BASIC and would be used to communicate with a programmer who is familiar with BASIC. A slight disadvantage in using English-sentence-type notation is that ordinary English can become wordy and, at times, even unclear.

PROGRAM A.1

```
100 ' Program A.1
110 ' Computation of State Tax
120 ' ***********************
130 CLS : KEY OFF   ' Clear Screen
140 INPUT "Please enter the salary =================> ", SALARY
150 INPUT "Please enter the number of dependents ==> ", DEP
160 TAX = 0.02 * (SALARY - 500 * DEP)
170 PRINT
180 PRINT "The state tax is =======================> $"; TAX
190 END

RUN

Please enter the salary =================> 19500
Please enter the number of dependents ==> 5

The state tax is =======================> $ 340
```

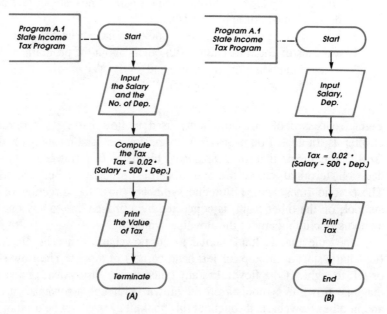

FIGURE A.1
Flowcharts for Program A.1 (A), English-like, and A.1 (B), BASIC-like.

The advantage of using BASIC-like notation rather than English-like notation is that it permits the description of the operation to be presented in a compact and precise form. Table A.1 lists common notations, including mathematical ones, used in flowcharts.

_____TABLE A.1_ Some Common Notations Used in Flowcharts_____

SYMBOL OR NOTATION	EXPLANATION	SYMBOL OR NOTATION	EXPLANATION
+	_Addition or Positive Value_	$\leq$	_Is Less Than or Equal To_
−	_Subtraction or Negative Value_	| |	_Absolute Value_
* or ×	_Multiplication_	¬	_Negation_
/	_Division_	_EOF_	_End of File_
\	_Integer Division_	_HI_	_High_
^	_Exponentiation_	_LO_	_Low_
←	_Is Replaced By or Is Assigned To_	_EQ_	_Equal_
=	_Is Equal To_	_MOD_	_Modulo_
≠ or ¬=	_Is Not Equal To_	_Yes or Y_	
:	_Comparison_	_No or N_	
>	_Is Greater Than_	_On_	
$\geq$	_Is Greater Than or Equal To_	_Off_	_Self-Explanatory_
<	_Is Less Than_	_True or T_	
		False or F	

The advantage of using program-language statements in a flowchart is that this type of flowchart can improve communication among programmers who are familiar with the given language. This book, which favors a combination of English-sentence-type, mathematical, and BASIC–type notation, will use whichever notation renders a given operation clear and unambiguous.

⊞ A.3

GUIDELINES FOR PREPARATION OF FLOWCHARTS

Before the flowchart can be drawn, a thorough analysis of the problem, the data, and the desired output results must be performed. Also, the logic required to solve the problem must be determined. On the basis of this analysis, a **general flowchart** of the main path of the logic can be sketched. This can then be refined until the overall logic is fully determined. Then this general flowchart is used to make one or more **detailed flowcharts** of the various parts and levels in and exceptions to the main path of logic. After each detailed flowchart has been freed of logical errors and other undesirable features, like unnecessary steps, the actual coding of the program in a computer language can be undertaken.

Straight-Line Flowcharts

Figure A.2 illustrates a general flowchart that is **straight-line**. A straight-line flowchart is one in which the symbols are arranged sequentially (one after the other), without any deviations or looping, until the terminal symbol that represents the end of the flowchart is reached. Once the operation indicated in any one symbol has been performed, that operation is never repeated.

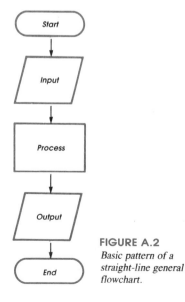

FIGURE A.2
Basic pattern of a straight-line general flowchart.

Flowcharts with Looping   A general flowchart that illustrates an iterative or repeating process known as looping is shown in Figure A.3. The logic illustrated by this flowchart is in three major parts: initialization, process, and wrap-up. A flowline exits from the bottom symbol in Figure A.3 and enters above the diamond-shaped decision symbol that determines whether the loop is to be executed again. This flowline forms part of a loop inside which some operations are repeatedly executed until specified conditions are satisfied. This flowchart shows the input, process, and output pattern; it also uses a decision symbol that shows where the decision is made to continue or stop the looping process.

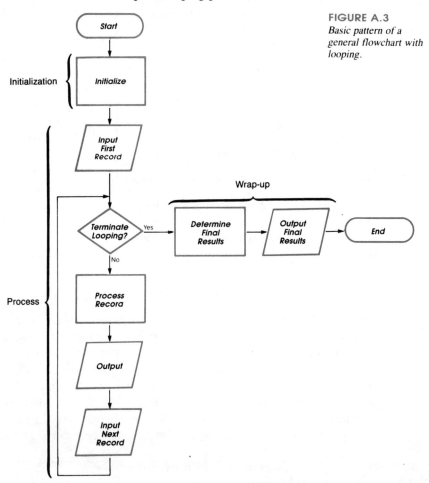

FIGURE A.3
Basic pattern of a general flowchart with looping.

The flowchart in Figure A.3 also contains two braces that show initialization and wrap-up operations. For example, setting the program counters to 0 may represent an initialization operation, and displaying the values of counters may represent a wrap-up operation.

Like the straight-line flowchart, a flowchart with looping need not have all the symbols shown in Figure A.3, or a flowchart can have many more symbols. For example, the process symbol within the loop in Figure A.3, when applied to a particular problem, may expand to include branching forward to bypass a process or backward to redo a process. It is also possible that through the use of decision symbols, the process symbol in Figure A.3 could be shown expanded to several loops, some of which might be independent from each other and some of which might be within other loops.

The main point to remember is that the flowchart shows a process that is carried out. Flowcharts are flexible; they can show any process no matter how complex it may be, and they can show it in whatever detail is needed.

The two flowcharts illustrated in Figure A.4 represent the same program; that is, the program simply reads and then prints a record. Then the program loops back to the reading operation and repeats the sequence, reading and printing for any number of records.

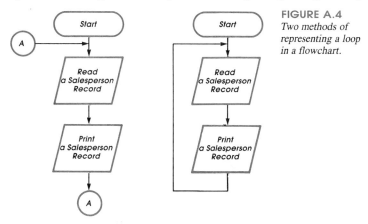

FIGURE A.4
Two methods of representing a loop in a flowchart.

Although the flowcharts in Figure A.4 illustrate two ways a loop can be represented, the particular loop that is shown is an **endless** or **infinite loop**. This type of loop should be avoided in constructing programs. In order to make a program like the one shown in Figure A.4 finite, you must define it so that it will terminate when specified conditions are satisfied. For example, if 15 aging accounts are to be processed, the program can be instructed to process no more than 15 and then stop. Figure A.5 illustrates the use of a counter in terminating the looping process. Note that the counter is first set to 0 in the initialization step. After an account is read and a message of action is printed, the counter is incremented by 1 and tested to find whether it is now equal to 15. If the value of the counter is not 15, the looping process continues. If the value of the counter is 15, the looping process terminates.

For the flowchart used in Figure A.5, the exact number of accounts to be processed must be known beforehand. In practice, this will not always be the case, since the number of accounts may vary from one run to the next.

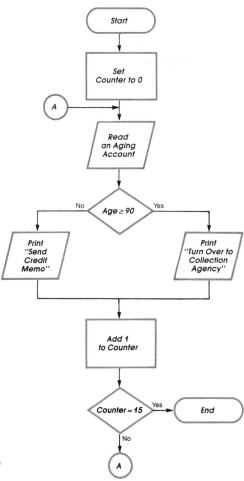

FIGURE A.5
Termination of a loop by use of a counter.

A way to solve this type of problem is shown in Figure A.6, which illustrates the use of an end-of-file test to terminate the looping process. The value –999999 has been chosen to be the last account number. This kind of value is sometimes known as the **sentinel value**, because it "guards" against reading past the end of file. Also, the numeric item chosen for the last value cannot possibly be confused with a valid item — it is outside the range of the account numbers. Programs using an end-of-file test like the one shown in Figure A.6 are far more flexible and far less limited than programs that do not, such as those illustrated in Figures A.4 and A.5.

Two more flowcharts with loops are shown in Figures A.7 and 1.15 on page 13. Figure A.7 illustrates the concept of counting, and Figure 1.15 illustrates the computations required to compute the average commission paid a company's sales personnel. Both flowcharts incorporate the end-of-file test.

FIGURE A.6
Termination of a loop by testing for the end of file.

FIGURE A.7
Flowchart with looping, illustrating the concept of counting the number of records in an inventory file.

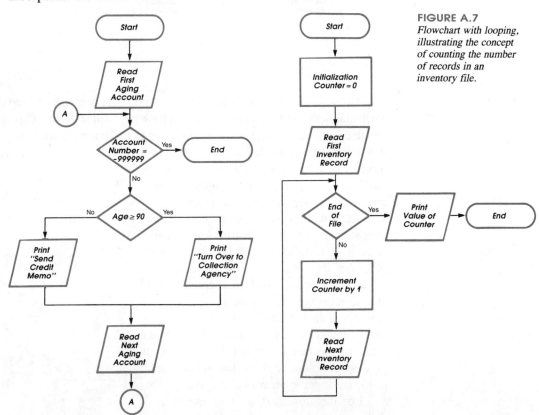

The technique of flowcharting may not be very useful in simple computer programs like Program A.1 on page A.2. However, as programs become more complex, with many different paths of execution, a flowchart is not only useful but sometimes is a prerequisite for successful analysis and coding of the program. Indeed, developing the problem solution by arranging and rearranging the flowchart symbols can lead to a more efficient computer program.

⊞ A.4

CONTROL STRUCTURES

Computer scientists agree that high-quality programs can be constructed from the following three basic logic structures:

1. Sequence
2. If-Then-Else or Selection
3. Do-While or Repetition

The following are two common extensions to these logic structures:

4. Do-Until or Repeat-Until
5. Case (an extension of the If-Then-Else logic structure)

The **Sequence structure** is used to show one action or one action followed by another and is illustrated in Figure A.8. Every flowchart in this text includes this control structure.

The **If-Then-Else** structure represents a two-way decision, with action specified for each of the two alternatives. This logic structure is shown in Figure A.9. The flowcharts presented earlier in Figures A.5 and A.6 include this logic structure. The action can be null for one alternative, as shown in Figure A.9(B).

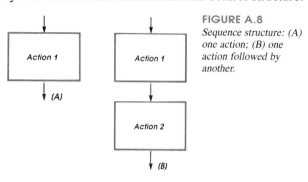

FIGURE A.8
Sequence structure: (A) one action; (B) one action followed by another.

The **Do-While structure** is the logic structure most commonly used to create a process that will repeat as long as the condition is true. The Do-While structure is illustrated in Figure A.10 and has been used earlier, in Figures A.3, A.6, and A.7. Because the decision to perform the action within the structure is at the top of the loop, it is possible that the action may not be done.

FIGURE A.9
If-Then-Else structure: (A) action specified for each of the two alternatives (true or false); (B) additional action taken for one alternative.

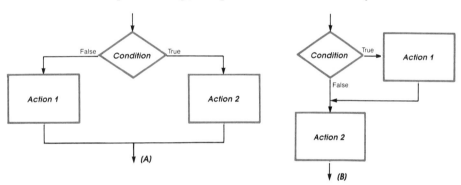

The **Do-Until structure** is also used for creating a process that will be repeated. The major differences between the Do-Until and the Do-While structures are that (1) the action within the structure of a Do-Until will always be executed at least once, and (2) the decision to perform the action within the structure is at the bottom of the loop. Figure A.11 illustrates the Do-Until structure, and the flowchart presented in Figure A.5 included a Do-Until structure.

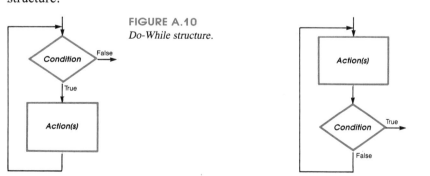

FIGURE A.10
Do-While structure.

FIGURE A.11
Do-Until structure.

The **Case structure** is similar to the If-Then-Else structure except that it provides more than two alternatives. Figure A.12 illustrates the Case structure.

A high-quality program can be developed through the use of just these five logic structures. The program will be easy to read, easy to modify, and reliable; most important of all, the program will do what it is intended to do!

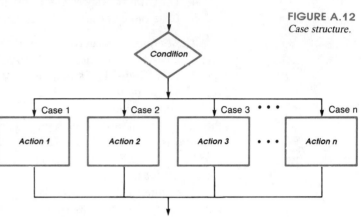

FIGURE A.12
Case structure.

⊞ A.5

PROPER PROGRAMS

A **proper program** is one that has the following characteristics:

1. It has one entry point.
2. It has one exit point.
3. It has no unreachable code.
4. It has no infinite loops.

A program constructed with just the five logic structures will form the basis for a proper program. Figure A.13 illustrates the breaking up — the decomposition — of a

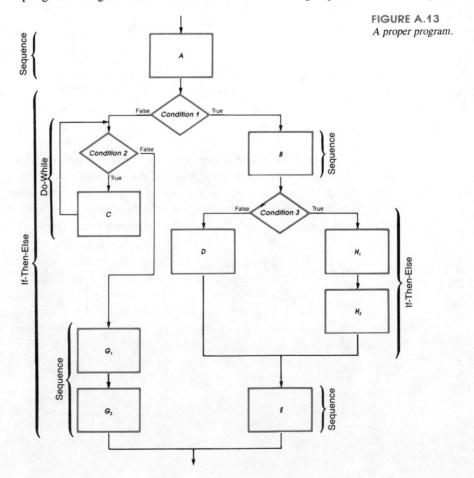

FIGURE A.13
A proper program.

program into some of the control structures presented in the previous section. On the other hand, Figure A.14 illustrates a program that will result in an improper program.

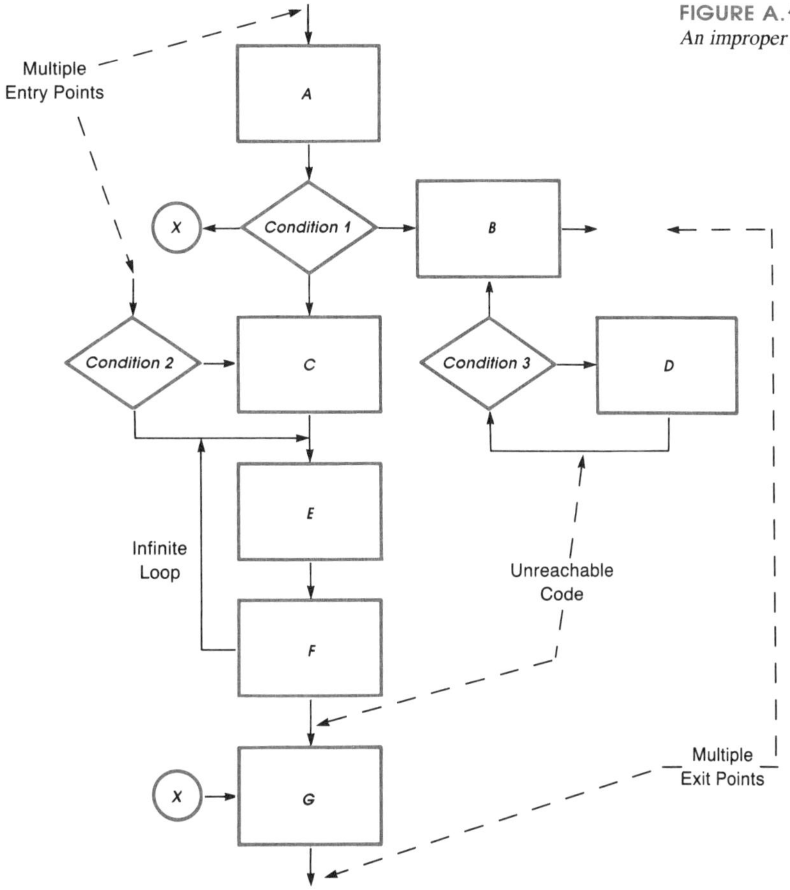

FIGURE A.14
An improper program.

This book stresses the construction of proper programs. However, you should be aware that in the real world the characteristics of a proper program may be relaxed or even intentionally violated.

⊞ **A.6**

FLOWCHARTING
TIPS

Shown below are a few flowchart suggestions. These suggestions assume that the input, processing, and output of the problem are defined properly.

1. Sketch a general flowchart and the necessary detail flowcharts before coding the problem. Repeat this step until you are satisfied with your flowcharts.
2. Use the control structures described in section A.4.
3. Put yourself in the position of the reader, keeping in mind that the purpose of the flowchart is to improve communications between one person and another concerning the method of solution for the problem.
4. Show the flow of processing from top to bottom and from left to right. When in doubt, use arrowheads, as required, to indicate the direction of flow.
5. Draw the flowchart so that it is neat and clear. Use the connector symbols to avoid excessively long flowlines.
6. Choose notation and wording that explain the function of each symbol in a clear and precise manner.
7. Do your best to avoid endless loops; construct loops so that they will be terminated when specific conditions are satisfied.

The reason that flowcharts are so important is simple: the difficulties in programming lie mostly in the realm of logic, not in the syntax and semantics of the computer language. In other words, most computer-use errors are mistakes in logic, and a flowchart aids in detecting logic mistakes!

▦ A.7

THE TOP-DOWN CHART AND TOP-DOWN DESIGN

A graphic representation of the top-down approach is a **top-down chart** (a **hierarchy** or **VTOC chart — Visual Table of Contents chart**). Figure A.15 represents a top-down chart of a task that is broken down into subtasks. If necessary, the subtasks are further refined into smaller subtasks. The overall task and each of the subtasks are represented by a process symbol with a short description written inside it. The top-down chart is read from top to bottom, and in general from left to right.

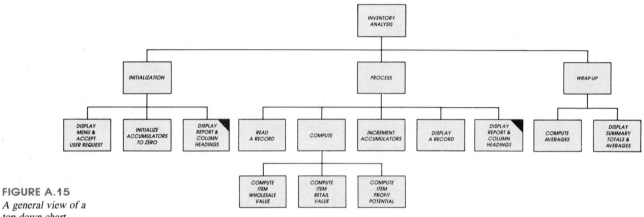

FIGURE A.15
A general view of a top-down chart.

A top-down chart differs from a program flowchart in that it does not show decision-making logic or flow of control. A program flowchart shows procedure, but a top-down chart shows organization. A top-down chart allows you to concentrate on defining *what* needs to be done in the program before deciding *how* and *when* it is to be done, which is represented in a program flowchart.

A top-down chart is very similar to a company's organization chart: each subtask carries out a function for its superior. Think of the higher-level subtasks as vice presidents of the organization, who perform the controlling functions for that organization. Also think of the lower-level sub-subtasks as workers of the organization, who perform the **repetitive** kinds of work for that organization.

In the top-down approach, the execution of both the design and the programming begins with the general and moves to the specific. Consider a problem in which a file must be processed. Each time a record is read, accumulators are incremented and a record is displayed. At the end of job, averages and summary totals are also displayed. To design a solution to this problem, use a top-down chart like the one in Figure A.15.

As you design from top to bottom (general to specific), the subtasks are connected to their superior tasks by vertical lines. Each subtask is subordinate to the one above it and superior to any that are below it.

Top-down programming is based on the idea that the subtasks, especially the higher-level ones, are implemented into the program as internal subroutines, or modules. For example, the Main Module at the top in Figure A.15 may be implemented in a BASIC program as three GOSUB statements. The function of the first GOSUB is to call upon the Initialization Module. At the completion of its prescribed task, the Initialization Module returns control to the Main Module. The second GOSUB references the Process Module, which maintains control until the file is processed. The final GOSUB in the Main Module references the Wrap-up Module, which computes the averages and displays the summary totals and averages. Upon completion of its task, the Wrap-up Module returns control to the Main Module and the program terminates.

Not all lower-level subtasks in a top-down chart become subroutines in a program. A top-down chart attempts to illustrate *what must be done and not necessarily how to implement it*. A subtask that ends up being one or two lines of code is usually placed in its superior module. If the subtask Display a Record in Figure A.15 is one line of code, then the subtask may be implemented directly into the Process Module.

The same subtask may be subordinate to more than one superior task. This is illustrated in Figure A.15. Recurring subtasks are identified by darkening the upper-right-hand corner of the process symbol. At implementation, recurring subtasks are coded once and called as often as needed.

A top-down chart is not a program flowchart, nor does it replace the program flowchart in designing algorithms. A top-down chart is a tool that is used early in the design stage to decompose, in an orderly fashion, a large task into subtasks, and to some extent to show the flow of control between these subtasks. The result is a graphic view of what must be done to solve the overall problem.

The emphasis in the top-down approach is on careful analysis. The first top-down chart a programmer thinks of is seldom the one that is implemented. Typically, a top-down chart is reviewed and refined several times before it is considered acceptable. In many companies, top-down charts are submitted to a **peer review group**, composed of programmers and analysts, for further review and refinement before a programmer is allowed to proceed with the next step of program development. This process of review and refinement is sometimes referred to as a **structured walk-through**.

⊞ A.8   TEST YOUR BASIC SKILLS   (Even-numbered answers are at the back of the book, before the index.)

1. What is the first step in solving a problem that uses a computer?
2. Which of the flowchart symbols given in chapter 1, Table 1.4 on page 12, are not required, in that any program may be flowcharted without using them?
3. Can one flowchart symbol be used to represent, simultaneously, two or more MS BASIC statements?
4. In the flowchart in Figure A.16, what is the value of I and the value of J at the instant just after the statement J = J + 1 is executed for the fifth time? The value of I and J after the statement I = I + 2 is executed the tenth time? (A statement such as J = J + 1 is valid and is read as "the new value of J equals the old value of J plus one" or, equivalently, "the value of J is to be replaced by the value of J plus one.")
5. Consider the flowchart portion in Figure A.17. It assumes that a relatively intelligent person is going to work. This individual usually has the car keys but occasionally forgets them. Does the flowchart portion in Figure A.17 incorporate the most efficient method of representing the actions to be taken? If not, redraw the flowchart portion given in Figure A.17.

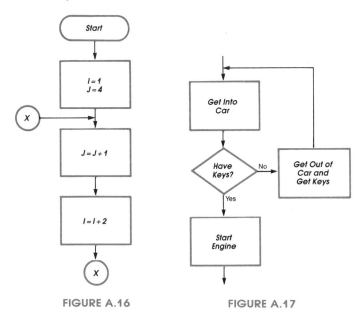

FIGURE A.16   FIGURE A.17

6. In the flowchart in Figure A.18, of a valid though trivial program, what values of I and of J are printed when the output symbol is executed for the fiftieth time?
7. What are the values of I and J just as the output symbol is executed for the thousandth time in the flowchart of Figure A.18?
8. What is wrong with the flowchart in Figure A.19?

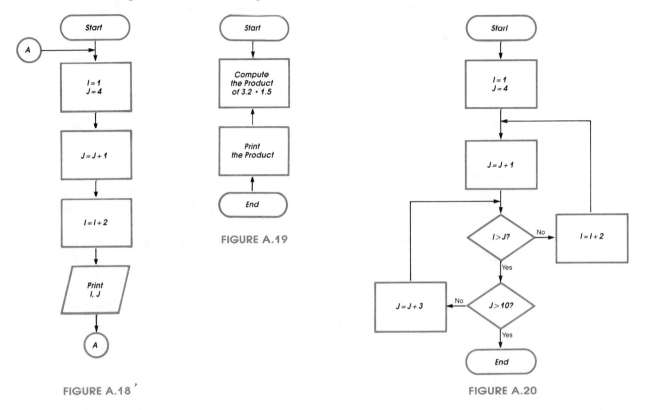

FIGURE A.19

FIGURE A.18

FIGURE A.20

9. Two numbers, R and S, located in the main storage of a computer, are to be replaced by their squares. Construct the flowchart to represent this action.
10. Construct an efficient flowchart to solve for the roots of the following equation:

$$ax^2 + bx + c = 0 \text{ using the following formula: } x = \frac{-b \pm \sqrt{b^2 - 4ac}}{2a}$$

Input three values containing the coefficients a, b, and c, respectively. Print the values of the two real roots. If complex roots exist ($b^2 - 4ac < 0$), print a message to that effect. If the roots are equal, print one root. (Assume that the coefficient a does not have a value of zero so that an attempted division by zero will not occur.)
11. Two numbers, U and V, located in the main storage, are to be interchanged. Construct the flowchart to represent this interchange.
12. Construct a flowchart for the following problem: Input two values for a and b. If the quotient a/b exists, display its value. If the quotient does not exist, display an appropriate message.
13. An opaque urn contains three diamonds, four rubies, and two pearls. Construct a flowchart that describes the following events: Draw a gem from the urn. If it is a diamond, lay it aside. If it is not a diamond, return it to the urn. Continue in this fashion until all the diamonds have been removed. After all the diamonds have been removed, repeat the same procedure until all the rubies have been removed. After all the rubies have been removed, continue in the same fashion until all the pearls have been removed.
14. In the flowchart represented by Figure A.20, what is the value of I and the value of J at the instant the terminal symbol with the word End is reached?
15. Part I
Draw one flowchart, and only one, that will cause the "mechanical mouse" to go through any of the four mazes shown in Figure A.21 on the opposite page. At the beginning, an operator will place the mouse on the entry side of the maze, in front of the entry point, facing "up" toward the maze. The instruction "Move to next cell" will

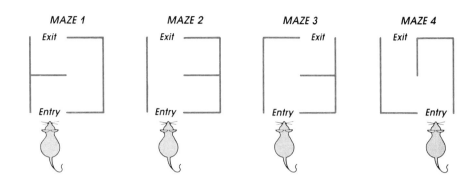

FIGURE A.21

put the mouse inside the maze. Each maze has four cells. After that, the job is to move from cell to cell until the mouse emerges on the exit side. If the mouse is instructed to "Move to next cell" when there is a wall in front of it, it will hit the wall and blow up. Obviously, the mouse must be instructed to test whether it is "Facing a wall" before any "Move." The mechanical mouse's instructions set consists of the following:

A. Physical movement:
   1. Move to next cell (the mouse will move in the direction it is facing).
   2. Turn right.
   3. Turn left.
   4. Turn around (all turns are made in place, without moving to another cell).
   5. Halt.

B. Logic:
   1. Facing a wall? (Through this test, the mouse determines whether there is a wall immediately in front of it, that is, on the border of the cell it is occupying and in the direction it is facing.)
   2. Outside the maze?
   3. On the entry side?
   4. On the exit side?

Part II (Extra Credit)
If your flowchart can cause the mechanical mouse to go through all of the mazes in part I without blowing up, then try your flowchart for mazes 5, 6, and 7 in Figure A.22. See whether you can produce one flowchart that will work for mazes 1 through 7.

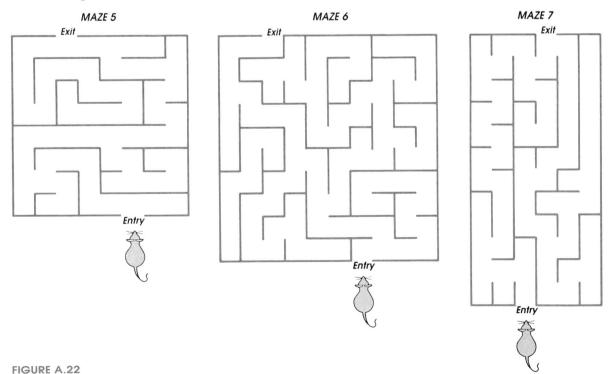

FIGURE A.22

PSEUDOCODE AND OTHER LOGIC DESIGN TOOLS

APPENDIX B

In recent years, many useful techniques have been developed to aid the problem-solver in the design and documentation of computer programs. Two of these were presented earlier: top-down charts in chapter 3 and Appendix A and the more traditional program flowcharts in chapter 1 and Appendix A. In this appendix, three additional logic tools will be surveyed: pseudocode, Nassi-Schneiderman charts, and Warnier-Orr diagrams.

Pseudocode is a program-design technique that uses natural English and resembles BASIC code. It is an intermediate notation that allows for the logic of a program to be formulated without diagrams or charts. Pseudocode resembles BASIC in that specific operations can be expressed, as the following three examples demonstrate:

Read employee record
Add 1 to male counter
Display employee record

What makes pseudocode appealing to many is that it has no formal syntactical rules, which allows the programmer to concentrate on the design of the program rather than on the peculiarities of the logic tool itself.

Although pseudocode has no formal rules, the following are commonly accepted:

1. Begin pseudocode with a program title statement.

   Program: Monthly Sales Analysis Report

2. End pseudocode with a terminal program statement.

   End: Monthly Sales Analysis Report

3. Begin each statement on a new line. Use simple and short imperative sentences that contain a single transitive verb and a single object.

   Open employee file

   Subtract 10 from quantity

4. Express assignment as a formula or as an English-like statement.

   Withholding tax = 0.20 × (gross pay − 38.46 × dependents)

   or

   Compute withholding tax

5. To implement the design, try to avoid using logic structures not available in the programming language to be used.

6. For the If-Then-Else structure, use the following conventions:

   a. Indent the true and false tasks.
   b. Use "End-If" as the structure terminator.

These conventions for the If-Then-Else structure are illustrated in Figures B.1 and B.2.

```
If balance < 500
   Then Display credit ok
   Else Display credit not ok
End-If
```

FIGURE B.1

```
If  sex code = male
   Then Add 1 to male count
      If age > 21
         Then Add 1 to male adult count
         Else Add 1 to male minor count
      End-If
   Else Add 1 to female count
      If age > 21
         Then Add 1 to female adult count
         Else Add 1 to female minor count
      End-If
End-If
```

FIGURE B.2

7. For the Do-While structure, use the following conventions:
   a. If the structure represents a counter-controlled loop, begin the structure with "Do."
   b. If the structure does not represent a counter-controlled loop, begin the structure with "Do-While."
   c. Specify the condition on the Do-While or Do line.
   d. Use "End-Do" as the last statement of the structure.
   e. Align the Do-While or Do and the End-Do vertically.
   f. Indent the statements within the loop.

The conventions for the Do-While structure are illustrated in Figures B.3 and B.4.

```
Program: Employee File List
Display report and column headings
Set employee count to 0
Read first employee record
Do-While not end-of-file
   Add 1 to employee count
   Display employee record
   Read next employee record
End-Do
Display employee count
Display end-of-job message
End: Employee File List
```

FIGURE B.3

```
Program:  Sum first 100 Integers
Set sum to 0
Do integer = 1 to 100
   Add integer to sum
End-Do
Display sum
Display end-of-job message
End: Sum first 100 Integers
```

FIGURE B.4

8. For the Do-Until structure, use the following conventions:
   a. Begin the structure with "Do-Until."
   b. Specify the condition on the Do-Until line.
   c. Use "End-Do" as the last statement of the structure.
   d. Align the Do-Until and the End-Do vertically.
   e. Indent the statements within the loop.

The conventions for the Do-Until structure are illustrated in Figure B.5.

Program: Sum first 100 Integers	*Start-Case customer code*
Set sum to 0	*Case 100*
Set integer to 1	*Add 1 to high-risk customer count*
Do-Until integer > 100	*Case 200*
Add integer to sum	*Add 1 to risk customer count*
Add 1 to integer	*Case 300*
End-Do	*Add 1 to regular customer count*
Display sum	*Case 400*
Display end-of-job message	*Add 1 to special customer count*
End: Sum first 100 Integers	*End-Case*

FIGURE B.5   FIGURE B.6

9. For the Case structure, use the following conventions:
   a. Begin the structure with "Start-Case," followed by the variable to be tested.
   b. Use "End-Case" as the structure terminator.
   c. Align "Start-Case" and "End-Case" vertically.
   d. Indent each alternative.
   e. Begin each alternative with "Case," followed by the value of the variable that equates to the alternative.
   f. Indent the action of each alternative.

These conventions are illustrated in Figure B.6.

For an additional example on using pseudocode, see Figure 1.20 in chapter 1 on page 12.

⊞ B.3

NASSI-SCHNEIDERMAN CHARTS

Nassi-Schneiderman charts (also called N-S charts) are often referred to as structured flowcharts. Unlike program flowcharts, they contain no flowlines or flowchart symbols and thus have no provision to include a GOTO statement.

N-S charts are made up of a series of rectangles. The flow of control always runs top to bottom. The sequence structure in an N-S chart is illustrated in Figure B.7.

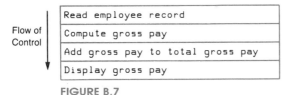

FIGURE B.7   FIGURE B.8

The If-Then-Else structure is shown by three triangles within a rectangle and a vertical line separating the true and false tasks, as shown in Figure B.8. The N-S chart indicates a decision (age ≥ 21) and the actions to be taken for an adult and minor. If a person's age is greater than or equal to 21, then the actions specified for the true case are processed. If a person's age is less than 21, then the actions specified for the false case are processed. It is not possible for both the true and false tasks to be processed for the same person.

The Do-While structure (test at the top of the loop) is referred to by a rectangle within a rectangle, as shown in Figure B.9.

The diagram indicates that the statements within the inner rectangle are to be processed in sequence as long as it is not end of file. When the end of file is sensed, control passes to the statement below the Do-While structure.

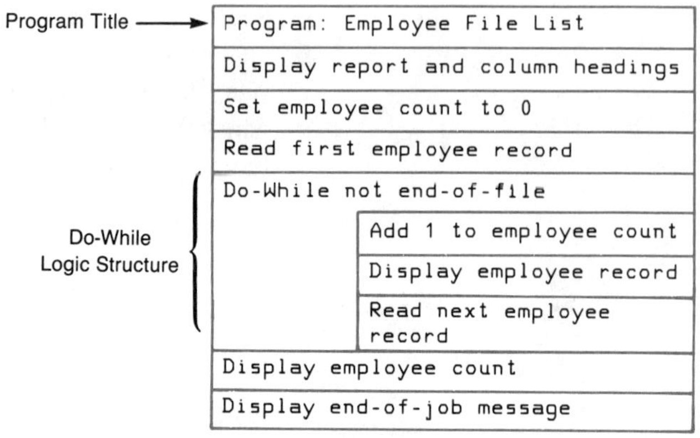

The Do-Until structure (test at the bottom of the loop) is

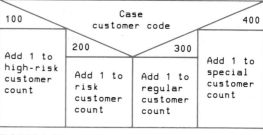

FIGURE B.9

similarly referred to by a rectangle within a rectangle, as shown in Figure B.10.

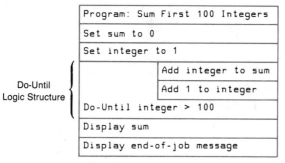

FIGURE B.10

FIGURE B.11

The Case structure is represented as shown in Figure B.11. As with the If-Then-Else structure, only one of the actions specified will be processed for each customer.

Those who advocate N-S charts claim they are quite useful in all phases of the program development cycle, especially for system and program documentation. Nassi and Schneiderman go even further. They write:

> Programmers who first learn to design programs with these symbols never develop the bad habits which other flowchart notation systems permit. . . . Since no more than fifteen or twenty symbols can be drawn on a single sheet of paper, the programmer must modularize his program into meaningful sections. The temptation to use off-page connectors, which lead only to confusion, is eliminated. Finally, the ease with which a structured flowchart can be translated into a structured program is pleasantly surprising.*

Others argue that N-S charts are nothing more than pseudocode with lines and rectangles around it.

⊞ B.4

WARNIER-ORR DIAGRAMS

In some respects, a Warnier-Orr diagram is similar to a top-down chart laid on its side. Both place a heavy emphasis on the idea of hierarchies. Warnier-Orr diagrams, however, go one step further and place an equal emphasis on flow of control.

You'll recall from chapter 3 and Appendix A that a top-down chart is used primarily to show functionality or *what* must be done to solve a problem. Once a top-down chart is complete, an intermediate tool, like a program flowchart, an N-S chart, or pseudocode, must be used to show the flow of control or *how* and *when* things are to be done in the framework of a solution. With Warnier-Orr diagrams, no such intermediate step is required.

---

*I. Nassi and B. Schneiderman, "Flowchart Techniques for Structured Programming," SIGPLAN, Notices of the ACM, v.8, n. 8, August 1973: 12-16.

As with N-S charts, solutions are constructed by means of the three basic logic structures: sequence, selection (If-Then-Else or Case), and repetition (Do-While or Do-Until).

A Warnier-Orr diagram is made up of a series of left braces, pseudocode-like statements, and a few special symbols, as shown in Table B.1.

_____**TABLE B.1** Warnier-Orr Symbols and Their Meanings_____

SYMBOL	MEANING
{	*The brace is used to enclose logically related events.*
(0, 1)	*An event is done zero or one time. Notation for selection structure.*
(0, n) or (n)	*An event is done n times. Notation for Do-While structure.*
(1, n)	*An event is done one to n times. Notation for Do-Until structure.*
blank or (1)	*An event is done one time.*
⊕	*Exclusive OR. Used in conjunction with the notation (0, 1) to show a Selection structure.*

The Sequence structure is illustrated in a Warnier-Orr diagram by listing the sequence of events from top to bottom within a brace, as shown in Figure B.12.

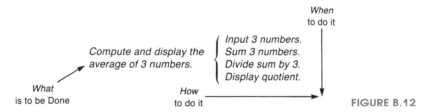

FIGURE B.12

The left brace points to what is to be done. Within the brace is the list of events that show how to do it and, from top to bottom, when each event is to take place.

The If-Then-Else structure is shown by the use of the notation (0, 1) and the exclusive OR symbol (see Figure B.13). The Case structure is shown in a similar fashion (see Figure B.14).

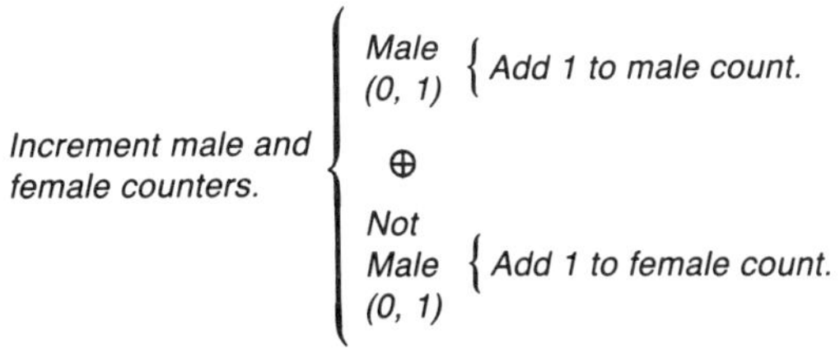

FIGURE B.13 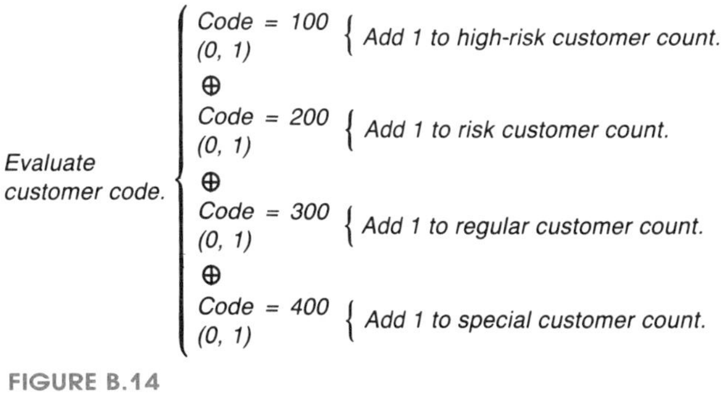   FIGURE B.14

The Warnier-Orr diagram in Figure B.15 on the following page shows a solution for reading an employee file and computing the gross pay for each employee. The solution includes a Do-While structure.

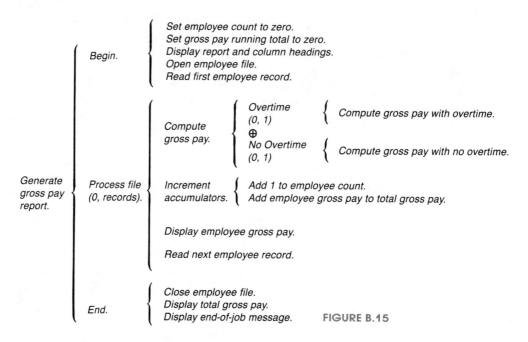

FIGURE B.15

The event "Process file (0, records)" illustrates a Do-While structure. The "0" within parentheses means that the loop can be executed zero times if, for example, the employee file is empty. The term *records* within parentheses indicates the number of times the loop is to be executed. It is also valid to write the notation for the Do-While structure as (*records*), rather than (*0, records*).

The notation used to represent a Do-Until structure is similar to that of the Do-While structure, except that the notation below the event is written as (1, n) rather than (0, n), because the Do-Until structure is executed at least one time.

DEBUGGING TECHNIQUES, PROGRAMMING TIPS, AND CHAINING

APPENDIX C

⊞ C.1

DEBUGGING TECHNIQUES

Although the top-down approach and structured programming techniques help minimize errors, they by no means guarantee error-free programs. Owing to carelessness or insufficient thought, program portions can be constructed which do not work as anticipated and which give erroneous results. When such problems occur, techniques are needed to isolate the errors and correct the erroneous program statements.

MS BASIC can detect many different grammatical errors and can display appropriate diagnostic messages. However, no BASIC system can detect all errors, since literally hundreds of possible coding errors can be made. Some of these errors can go undetected by MS BASIC until either an abnormal end occurs during execution or the program terminates with the results in error.

There are several techniques for attempting to discover the portion of the program that is in error. These methods are called **debugging techniques**. The errors themselves are **bugs**, and the activity involved in their detection is **debugging**.

Tracing (TRON and TROFF)

The TRON (TRace ON) instruction in MS BASIC provides a means of tracing the path of execution through a program in order to determine which statements are executed. The instruction TROFF (TRace OFF) turns off the tracing. These instructions may be inserted into a program as BASIC statements, or they may be used as system commands before the RUN command is issued. Pressing the F7 key enters the instruction TRON, and pressing the F8 key enters the instruction TROFF.

The TRON instruction activates tracing, and the PC displays the line number of each statement executed. The line numbers appear enclosed in square brackets to prevent them from being confused with other results the program may produce.

For example, if a PC with tracing activated executes a program portion consisting of lines 250, 260, 270, and 280, the output displayed will be as follows:

```
[250] [260] [270] [280]
```

The TROFF instruction deactivates tracing. Both the TRON and TROFF instructions may be used any number of times in a BASIC program.

Program C.1 has the TRON and TROFF statements in lines 125 and 195. When the RUN command is issued, all statements between lines 125 and 195 are traced, and their line numbers and corresponding output are displayed accordingly.

PROGRAM C.1

```
100 ' Program C.1
110 ' Illustrating Use of the
115 ' TRON and TROFF Instructions
120 ' **************************
125 TRON
130 SUM = 0
140 I = 1
150 WHILE I < 4
160     SUM = SUM + I
170     I = I + 1
180 PRINT I; SUM
190 WEND
195 TROFF
200 END

RUN

[130] [140] [150] [160] [170] [180] 2   1
[190] [160] [170] [180]   3   3
[190] [160] [170] [180]   4   6
[190] [195]
```

Program C.2 is similar to Program C.1. When this program is executed, the PC displays the value of 1 for I over and over. The program has a bug, which results in an infinite loop when the program is run.

PROGRAM C.2

```
100 ' Program C.2
110 ' This Program Contains a Bug
120 ' **************************
130 SUM = 0
140 I = 1
150 WHILE I < 4
160     SUM = SUM + I
170     T = I + 1          ' This line contains an error
180 PRINT I; SUM
190 WEND
200 END
```

If the TRON instruction is used as a system command, the following output occurs during tracing:

```
TRON
RUN

[100] [110] [120] [130] [140] [150] [160] [170] [180] 1   1
[190] [160] [170] [180]   1   2
[190] [160] [170] [180]   1   3
[190] [160] [170] [180]   1   4
[190]...
```

From the output, we can see the repetition of the following sequence of line numbers:

```
[190][160][170][180]
```

This output reveals that the program executes lines 160, 170, 180, and 190 repeatedly in the While loop.

The condition in the WHILE statement in line 150 cannot be satisfied, since the value of I will always be less than 4. Line 170 has been incorrectly written. In order to satisfy the condition in the WHILE statement, use:

```
170    I = I + 1      instead of:    170    T = I + 1
```

Examining Values (STOP, PRINT, and CONT)

Another useful debugging technique is to stop a program, examine the values of various variables within the program, and then continue the execution of the program. All this can be accomplished through the use of the STOP, PRINT, and CONT (continue) statements. Consider partial Program C.3.

PROGRAM C.3

```
100 ' Program C.3
110 ' Illustrating the Use of STOP, PRINT, and CONT
120 ' *********************************************
130 .
     .
     .
300 V1 = 10 * 12.15
310 A1 = 2 * 24.3
320 S1 = 36.9 / 3
325 STOP
     .
     .
     .
RUN

Break in 325          (displayed when STOP statement is executed)

PRINT V1              (entered by user)
 121.5                (displayed result from PRINT statement)

PRINT A1; S1          (entered by user)
 48.6   12.3          (displayed result from PRINT statement)

CONT                  (entered by user)
```

When the STOP statement is executed in line 325, the program will stop and the message Break in 325 will be displayed. Now the values of various variables can be examined by using a PRINT statement without a line number.

After the values of V1, A1, and S1 are displayed, the CONT is issued and the remaining program is executed. CONT should not be placed directly into a BASIC program; instead, it should be entered as a command from the keyboard by the user.

Intermediate Output

In some instances, including intermediate PRINT statements as a part of the program may be preferable to using STOP statements and displaying the values of variables in the immediate mode.

Appropriate PRINT statements may be inserted after each statement or series of statements involving computations. This technique is called **source language debugging** or the **intermediate output method**. Intermediate results are displayed until the specific portion of the program that is in error can be deduced.

If a program produces little output to begin with, the intermediate-output method should be used, since the outputs from the intermediate PRINT statements will be easy to distinguish from the regular output. If a program produces a great deal of output, then the technique involving the STOP, PRINT, and CONT statements should be utilized to minimize the amount of output to the display unit.

⊞ C.2
TRAPPING USER ERRORS (ON ERROR GOTO AND RESUME)

Most abnormal terminations in a production environment are due to user errors, not programmer errors. This is especially true for programs that interact with the user. User errors fall into two basic categories:

1. erroneous data that is entered in response to INPUT statements
2. failure to follow the instructions given in the user's manual

Good programmers will attempt to trap as many user errors as possible. Errors that fall into the first category can be trapped by validating incoming data to ensure that it is reasonable or within limits.

The second category of user errors includes both **soft errors** and **hard errors**. A soft error is any error that causes the system to display a diagnostic message followed by continued execution of the program. Entering string data in response to an INPUT statement with a numeric variable is an example of a soft error. MS BASIC will display an error message and request that the data be reentered.

A hard error is any error that causes the PC to display a diagnostic message followed by termination of the program's execution. Examples of hard errors include the following:

1. not placing a diskette in the disk drive
2. not closing the door on the disk drive
3. using a defective diskette
4. using a diskette that has not been formatted

In some situations, it is preferable to handle hard or soft errors within the program through the use of the ON ERROR GOTO and RESUME statements. The ON ERROR GOTO provides a common branch point for any error that occurs following its execution in a program. The branch point and the statements that follow it are an **error-handling routine**. In an error-handling routine, it is often desirable to resume execution of the program at a specified point. The RESUME statement is used for this purpose. The general forms of the ON ERROR GOTO and RESUME statements are shown in Tables C.1 and C.2.

Once the ON ERROR GOTO statement is inserted in a program, any error that normally terminates execution now causes the PC to transfer control to the error-handling routine. MS BASIC provides two special variables, ERL and ERR, that are automatically assigned values before control transfers to the error-handling routine. ERL is assigned the line number of the statement that caused the error; ERR is assigned an error code.

TABLE C.1 The ON ERROR GOTO Statement

General Form:	ON ERROR GOTO *line number*
Purpose:	*Activates error trapping and specifies the line number of an error-handling routine to transfer control to when an error occurs.*
	When line number = 0, as in ON ERROR GOTO 0, error trapping is deactivated and a diagnostic message is displayed, followed by termination of the program.
Examples:	1100 ON ERROR GOTO 5000 1200 ON ERROR GOTO 6000 1300 ON ERROR GOTO 0
Note:	*In the error-trapping routine, the special variables ERR and ERL may be tested, where ERR represents the error code of the last error, and ERL represents the line number of the statement that caused the error.*

_____TABLE C.2 The RESUME Statement_____

General Form:	RESUME *n* *where n may be null, zero, line number, or the keyword* NEXT.
Purpose:	*Continues execution of the program after an error-handling routine has been performed.* RESUME *or* RESUME 0 *resumes execution at the statement that caused the error.* RESUME NEXT *resumes execution at the statement immediately following the one that caused the error.* RESUME *line number resumes execution at the specified line number.*
Examples:	1150 RESUME 3350 RESUME 0 4000 RESUME NEXT 6250 RESUME 5550
Note:	*This statement should not be executed unless the* ON ERROR GOTO *statement has been previously executed.*

Table C.3 lists the error description and corresponding error code that the ON ERROR GOTO statement will trap. The table entries are alphabetized by error description. For an in-depth discussion of the error descriptions, see Appendix A in the MS BASIC user's manual.

_____TABLE C.3 Error Descriptions and Their Corresponding Error Codes_____

ERROR DESCRIPTION	ERROR CODE	ERROR DESCRIPTION	ERROR CODE	ERROR DESCRIPTION	ERROR CODE
Advanced feature	*73*	*Duplicate definition*	*10*	*Overflow*	*6*
Bad file mode	*54*	*Field overflow*	*50*	*Path/file access error*	*75*
Bad file name	*64*	*File already exists*	*58*	*Path not found*	*76*
Bad file number	*52*	*File already open*	*55*	*Rename across disks*	*74*
Bad record number	*63*	*File not found*	*53*	RESUME *without error*	*20*
Can't continue	*17*	FOR *without* NEXT	*26*	RETURN *without* GOSUB	*3*
Communication buffer overflow	*69*	*Illegal direct*	*12*	*String formula too complex*	*16*
Device fault	*25*	*Illegal function call*	*5*	*String too long*	*15*
Device I/O error	*57*	*Input past end*	*62*	*Subscript out of range*	*9*
Device timeout	*24*	*Internal error*	*51*	*Syntax error*	*2*
Device unavailable	*68*	*Line buffer overflow*	*23*	*Too many files*	*67*
Direct statement in file	*66*	*Missing operand*	*22*	*Type mismatch*	*13*
Disk full	*61*	NEXT *without* FOR	*1*	*Undefined line number*	*8*
Disk media error	*72⁻*	*No* RESUME	*19*	*Undefined user function*	*18*
Disk not ready	*71*	*Out of data*	*4*	*Undocumented error*	*—*
Disk write protect	*70*	*Out of memory*	*7*	WEND *without* WHILE	*30*
Division by zero	*11*	*Out of paper*	*27*	WHILE *without* WEND	*29*
		Out of string space	*14*		

Through the use of IF statements, a decision can be made in the error-handling routine to terminate execution or resume execution at some point in the program. The ON ERROR GOTO 0 statement directs the PC to disable error trapping, display the error message, and terminate execution. On the other hand, the RESUME statement may be used to transfer control to any point in the program to continue execution. If execution is to resume following an error, an error-recovery procedure such as displaying a message or assigning a value to a variable is performed before execution is resumed outside the error-handling routine. The ON ERROR GOTO statement must be placed in a program in such a way that it is executed before the lines in which errors are to be trapped.

Program C.4 uses the ON ERROR GOTO statement to trap user errors. In the error-handling routine, the special variable ERR is tested. If ERR is equal to 25 (Device fault, such as printer not ready) or 27 (Out of paper), a recovery procedure is executed. If ERR equals any other code, then a message is displayed requesting the user to copy down the program name, the line number in which the error occurred, and the error code, and to transmit this information to the person who is in charge of resolving the error.

PROGRAM C.4

```
1000 ' Program C.4
1010 ' Illustrating the Use of
1020 ' the ON ERROR GOTO Statement
1030 ' **************************
1040 ON ERROR GOTO 2000
1050 LPRINT "Number", "Amount"
1060 LPRINT
1070 READ NUM$, AMT
1080 WHILE NUM$ <> "EOF"
1090    LPRINT NUM$, AMT
1100    READ NUM$, AMT
1110 WEND
1120 LPRINT "Job Complete"
1130 STOP
2000 ' *************************
2010 ' *  Error-Handling Routine *
2020 ' *************************
2030 CLS : KEY OFF  ' Clear Screen
2040 IF ERR = 25 OR ERR = 27
        THEN GOSUB 2200 : RESUME
        ELSE GOSUB 2400 : ON ERROR GOTO 0
2050 RETURN
2060 '
2200 ' ***** Printer Error *******
2210 PRINT "Please check the printer."
2220 PRINT "It may be turned off, out of"
2230 PRINT "paper, or improperly"
2240 PRINT "connected."
2250 PRINT
2260 INPUT "Press the Enter key when the printer is ready...", CONTROL$
2270 RETURN
2280 '
2400 ' *** Irrecoverable Error ***
2410 BEEP : BEEP : BEEP : BEEP
2420 PRINT "An Irrecoverable error has occurred"
2430 PRINT "Please copy down the following:"
2440 PRINT "line number and error code. Transmit"
2450 PRINT "these and the program name to someone"
2460 PRINT "in charge of resolving the error."
2470 PRINT
2480 PRINT "Error in line =====> "; ERL
2490 PRINT "Error code ========> "; ERR
2500 PRINT : PRINT "Thank You"
2510 RETURN
2520 '
2530 ' ****** Data Follows *******
2540 DATA 123, 124.89, 126, 145.91, 134, 234.78
2550 DATA 210, 567.34, 235, 435.12, 345, 192.45
2560 DATA EOF, 0
2570 END
```

C.3

PROGRAMMING
TIPS

With MS BASIC, you can code a program in many different ways and still obtain the same results. This section presents several tips for coding a program; their use will improve a program's performance, efficiency, structure, and clarity.

Each tip is explained and then applied accordingly. You are encouraged to add other tips to the ones that are provided in this section.

Tip 1: *Use Simple Arithmetic*

Addition is performed faster than multiplication, which in turn is faster than division or exponentiation. For example, use the code on the left side rather than on the right side below:

```
150 AREA = BASE * HEIGHT * .5       150 AREA = BASE * HEIGHT / 2
160 LENGTH = SIDE1 + SIDE1          160 LENGTH = 2 * SIDE1
170 VOL = LEN1 * LEN1 * LEN1        170 VOL = LEN1 ^ 3
```

Tip 2: *Avoid Repetitive Evaluations of Expressions*

If identical computations are performed in several statements, evaluate the common expression once and save the result in a variable for use in later statements. For example, use the code on the left side rather than on the right side below:

```
200 DISC = SQR(B * B - 4 * A * C)       200 ROOT1 = -B + SQR(B * B - 4 * A * C)
210 ROOT1 = -B + DISC                   210 ROOT2 = -B - SQR(B * B - 4 * A * C)
220 ROOT2 = -B - DISC
```

Tip 3: *Avoid Recomputation of Constants Within a Loop*

Do not make unnecessary computations. Remove the unnecessary code from a loop, including expressions and statements that do not affect the loop. Place such code before the loop. For example, use the code on the left side rather than on the right side below:

```
300 PI = 3.141598                  300 PI = 3.141598
310 K = 4 * PI                     310 FOR RAD = 1 TO 500
320 X = Y + 2                      320    PRINT 4 * PI * RAD * RAD
330 FOR RAD =  1 TO 500            330    X = Y + 2
340    PRINT K * RAD * RAD         340 NEXT RAD
350 NEXT RAD
```

Regardless of the value of RAD, 4π is always constant. Instead of calculating 4π five hundred times, remove this expression from the loop and compute it once. It is also not necessary to compute the value of X each time through the loop, since the loop never changes the value of X.

Tip 4: *Use Functions and Subroutines*

Use functions and subroutines wherever possible, since in many cases they conserve main storage and always execute faster than the same capability written in MS BASIC. For example, do the following:

```
400 DISC = SQR(B * B - 4 * A * C)
```

instead of:

```
400 DISC = (B * B - 4 * A * C) ^ (0.5)
```

Tip 5: *Write Clearly and Avoid Clever or Tricky Code*

Resist the temptation to write clever or tricky code that is difficult to understand. Later modification by someone else may take additional time and may be costly in the long run.

For example, do the following:

```
600 FOR ROW = 1 TO 10
610    FOR COLUMN = 1 TO 10
620       IF ROW = COLUMN
                THEN ARRAY(ROW, COLUMN) = 1
                ELSE ARRAY(ROW, COLUMN) = 0
630    NEXT COLUMN
640 NEXT ROW
```

instead of:

```
600 FOR ROW = 1 TO 10
610    FOR COLUMN = 1 TO 10
620       ARRAY(ROW, COLUMN) = INT(ROW / COLUMN) * INT(COLUMN / ROW)
630    NEXT COLUMN
640 NEXT ROW
```

This section of code generates an array called ARRAY, where 1s are placed on the main diagonal and zeros everywhere else.

Tip 6: *Avoid Needless IF Statements Whenever Possible*

You can avoid the need for more IF statements and additional code if you use compound conditions in IF statements. For example, use the code on the left side rather than on the right side below:

```
700 IF I = J AND K = L          700 IF I = J
        THEN A = 99                     THEN IF K = L THEN A = 99
```

Tip 7: *Avoid Using IF and GOTO Statements for Looping*

Use WHILE and WEND statements whenever possible for looping. For example, use the code on the left side rather than on the right side below:

```
800 SUM = 0                     800 SUM = 0
810 K = 1                       810 K = 1
820 WHILE K <= 100              820 IF K > 100 THEN 860
830    SUM = SUM + K            830    SUM = SUM + K
840    K = K + 1                840    K = K + 1
850 WEND                        850 GOTO 820
860 PRINT SUM                   860 PRINT SUM
```

⊞ C.4

WRITING LARGE PROGRAMS: THE CHAIN AND COMMON STATEMENTS

Another technique that may be used to implement the top-down approach, especially when the programs are very large, involves writing external subroutines that are linked together by the CHAIN statement. The CHAIN statement may be used within a BASIC program to instruct your PC to stop executing the current program, then to load another program from auxiliary storage and start executing it.

The COMMON statement is used in conjunction with the CHAIN statement to pass selected variables from the current program (also called the **chaining program**) to the new program (also called the **chained-to** program).

The general form of the CHAIN statement is shown in Table C.4 on the opposite page.

In the first example in Table C.4, the statement

```
3000 CHAIN "B:PROG2"
```

terminates execution of the current program (the chaining program), loads and executes PROG2.BAS from the B drive, and begins execution at the first executable statement of PROG2. PROG2 is the chained-to program. Note that you are not required to include the extension in the program name. The CHAIN statement assumes that the extension is BAS. Unless otherwise specified in a COMMON statement, none of the variables defined in the chaining program are available to PROG2, the chained-to program.

_____TABLE C.4 The CHAIN Statement_____

General Form:	CHAIN *"program name"*, *line number*, ALL
	where **program name** *is the name of the program loaded from auxiliary storage and executed;*
	line number *is an optional parameter indicating the line number in the chained-to program where execution begins; and*
	ALL *is an optional parameter that instructs the PC to pass* all *the variables to the chained-to program as defined in the chaining program.*
Purpose:	*Instructs the PC to stop executing the current program, then load another program from auxiliary storage and start executing it.*
Examples:	3000 CHAIN "B:PROG2" 4000 CHAIN "PROG3.BAS", 2000 5000 CHAIN "MODULE2",, ALL 6000 CHAIN "MODULE3", 2040, ALL

In the second example in Table C.4, the statement

```
4000 CHAIN "PROG3.BAS", 2000
```

initiates execution at line 2000 in program PROG3. Since a device name is not specified in line 4000 in Table C.4, the PC loads PROG3 off the default drive.

Specifying a line number is a common technique for chaining back to another program that has already been partially executed. For example, a program may chain to a subordinate program that carries out a sub-task. When the subordinate program is finished, it chains back to a specified line number in its superior program (the original chaining program).

Care must be taken when using the READ and DATA statements in a chained-to program that may be called a number of times. Each time a chained-to program is executed, the pointer is moved back to the beginning of the data-sequence holding area. However, files that are opened in a chaining program remain opened, with the pointer at the same position in the file.

Line 5000 in Table C.4 shows how a chaining program may pass *all* the variables to the chained-to program. As illustrated in this example, when the line number is not used in the CHAIN statement, two commas are required between the program name and the parameter ALL.

Finally, in the last example in Table C.4, all variables are passed to the chained-to program and execution begins at line 2040.

The COMMON Statement

Whereas the ALL parameter in the CHAIN statement allows you to pass all the variables in the chaining program to the chained-to program, the COMMON statement allows you to be selective in your choice of variables that are passed to the chained-to program.

The general form of the COMMON statement is shown in Table C.5.

_____TABLE C.5 The COMMON Statement_____

General Form:	COMMON *variable, ..., variable*
	where the list of variables is defined in the chaining program.
Purpose:	*Passes selected variables from the chaining program to a chained-to program.*
Examples:	1020 COMMON SUM, COUNT, AMOUNT 1030 COMMON EMP.NAME$, ADDRESS$, CREDIT 1040 COMMON RATE()
Note:	*A* COMMON *statement may be used to pass arrays to a chained-to program. Arrays are specified by appending adjacent open and close parentheses ( ) to the right side of the array name. It is not required that arrays be dimensioned in the chained-to program.*

Any number of COMMON statements may appear in a program. For example, the following statement,

```
2040 COMMON GROSS, TAX, DEPENDENTS
```

is the same as the following list of statements:

```
3040 COMMON GROSS
3050 COMMON TAX
3060 COMMON DEPENDENTS
```

However, it is invalid to list the same variable name in more than one COMMON statement in the same program.

Although COMMON statements may be located anywhere in a program, it is recommended that they appear at the beginning, as illustrated in Programs C.5 and C.6.

Assume that Program C.5 is in main storage. Furthermore, assume that Program C.5, as well as Program C.6, resides in auxiliary storage.

PROGRAM C.5

```
100 ' Program C.5
110 ' The Chaining Program
120 ' ********************
130 COMMON A, B, SUM
140 A = 3
150 B = 5
160 C = 7
170 SUM = 0
180 FOR I = 1 TO 99 STEP 2
190     SUM = SUM + I
200 NEXT I
210 PRINT "PRGC-5 Value of SUM ===================>"; SUM
220 CHAIN "PRGC-6"
230 PRINT : PRINT "PRGC-5 Value of GRAND from PRGC-6 =====>"; GRAND
240 END
```

PROGRAM C.6

```
100 ' Program C.6
110 ' The Chained-To Program
120 ' *********************
130 COMMON GRAND
140 TOTAL = 0
150 FOR J = 2 TO 100 STEP 2
160     TOTAL = TOTAL + J
170 NEXT J
180 D = A + B
190 PRINT : PRINT "PRGC-6 Sum of A and B from PRGC-5 =====>"; D
200 PRINT : PRINT "PRGC-6 Value of TOTAL ==================>"; TOTAL
210 GRAND = SUM + TOTAL
220 CHAIN "PRGC-5", 230
230 END
```

When the RUN command is issued for Program C.5, the following displays.

```
PRGC-5 Value of SUM ===================> 2500

PRGC-6 Sum of A and B from PRGC-5 =====> 8

PRGC-6 Value of TOTAL ==================> 2550

PRGC-5 Value of GRAND from PRGC-6 =====> 5050
```

Examine closely the results displayed by Programs C.5 and C.6. The first output displayed is due to line 210 in Program C.5. Line 220 instructs the PC to stop executing Program C.5 and to load and execute Program C.6.

Line 130 in Program C.5 passes the variables A, B, and SUM to Program C.6. Some programming languages allow you to rename the variables that are passed from one program to another. With MS BASIC, the variable names in the chained-to program must be the same as those which are listed in the COMMON statement of the chaining program.

Line 190 of Program C.6 displays the sum of the variables A and B passed from Program C.5. Line 200 causes the third line of the output to display. Line 220 chains back to Program C.5 and begins execution at the line just below the original CHAIN statement. Note that line 130 of Program C.6 passes the variable GRAND, which is displayed by line 230 in Program C.5 as the fourth line of output.

Keep in mind that when Program C.5 originally chained to Program C.6, it was removed from main storage. Therefore, when Program C.6 chains back to Program C.5, the chained-to program must be reloaded from auxiliary storage.

In most beginning BASIC programming classes, programs seldom reach the size that would require the use of the CHAIN and COMMON statements and the chaining concept. However, in the real world of programming, programs that use the techniques described in Programs C.5 and C.6 are the rule rather than the exception.

TRY IT YOURSELF

Load Program C.5 (PRGC-5) from the Student Diskette. Delete line 130. Execute the program and compare the results to those displayed by Programs C.5 and C.6. Explain the significance of line 130 in Program C.5.

FORMATTING A DISKETTE, DOS COMMANDS, ASCII CHARACTER SET, AND PC LITERATURE

APPENDIX D

⊞ D.1

INTRODUCTION

This appendix presents a series of topics that relate specifically to the PC. Included are the operating instructions to format a diskette; MS DOS commands; and a list of popular magazines, newspapers, and manuals for the PC.

⊞ D.2

FORMATTING A DISKETTE

You must format a diskette before the PC can use it for the first time. Initializing is the process of marking off a diskette into sections in which programs or data can be stored. Later, these numbered sections are used by the PC to recall information. For example, when you save a program, the name of the program and its location are recorded by the PC in the diskette's directory. Then when you instruct the PC to load the program back into main storage, it searches the directory for the name and corresponding location.

A diskette has to be formatted only once. If you format a diskette that contains programs or data, they will be lost; the formatting process erases any information that is on the diskette.

To format a diskette, ask your instructor for a system diskette. The system diskette contains the operating system (MS DOS or PC DOS) and a number of utilities (programs supplied by the computer manufacturer). One of the utilities is called FORMAT, and it is used to format a diskette. With the system diskette and the diskette to be formatted in hand, do the following:

1. Boot the PC, using steps 1 through 8 as outlined in Table 2.6 on page 33.
2. Enter the following command to the right of the A>:

      FORMAT B: (Press the Enter key.)

   Be sure to include the colon (:).

3. Insert the diskette to be formatted in the B drive.
4. Press any key.
5. After a short time, the PC will display the number of bytes that are available on the newly formatted diskette and will respond with the following question:

      Format another (Y/N)?

   Enter N to quit the FORMAT utility or Y to format another diskette.

⊞ D.3

MS DOS COMMANDS

The commands listed in Tables 2.8 and 2.10, on pages 37 and 39–40, respectively, allow you to operate your PC under MS BASIC. However, you can enter MS DOS commands to list, rename, delete, and copy files. Also, there are several commands, that are not available under MS BASIC, but are available with the MS DOS operating system.

There are two categories of MS DOS commands — **internal** and **external**. Internal commands, like `COPY` and `DIR`, are part of the operating system program `COMMAND.COM`. External commands, like `FORMAT` and `DISKCOPY`, are separate from `COMMAND.COM`; they are utilities that normally reside on the system diskette. For example, when you list the files on the system diskette, `FORMAT.COM` and `DISKCOPY.COM` will list along with `COMMAND.COM`. If these utilities do not show up in a listing of the files on the system diskette, then the commands are not available to you.

Two of the most important DOS commands are `COPY` and `DIR`. A discussion of these two MS DOS commands follows, and a summary of some additional ones are given in Table D.1.

COPY   The `COPY` command is used to copy files from one diskette to another. It may also be used to copy files to the same diskette, provided a different file name is used for the duplicate. The general form for the `COPY` command is

> `COPY`   source-file   target-file

Here are some examples.

1. `COPY B:LAB2-1.BAS   A:`

   `LAB2-1.BAS` on the diskette in the B drive is copied to the diskette in the A drive as `LAB2-1.BAS`.

2. `COPY B:*.BAS   A:`

   All the files on the diskette in the B drive which have an extension of BAS are copied to the diskette in the A drive. The asterisk (`*`) and question mark (`?`) are global characters. The asterisk indicates that any character can occupy that position and all the remaining positions in the file name or extension. The question mark indicates that any character can occupy that position only.

3. `COPY A:*.*   B:`

   Copies all files on the diskette in the A drive to the diskette in the B drive.

4. `COPY LAB2-?.* A:`

   Copies all files with 6-character file names beginning with `LAB2-` from the diskette in the default drive to the diskette in the A drive. If the A drive is the default drive, an error message will display, since you cannot copy files to the same diskette unless you specify new names for the duplicate files.

5. `COPY B:LAB2-3.BAS   B:LAB2-4.BAS`

   Copies `LAB2-3.BAS` on the same diskette in the B drive under the file name `LAB2-4.BAS`.

DIR   The `DIR` (DIRectory) command is used to list information about a diskette in the specified drive. Depending on how the command is entered, the information displayed may include a list of the file names; the size of each file (in bytes); the date and time each file was created; the number of files listed; and the amount of free area left on the diskette (in bytes).

Here are some examples.

1. `DIR`

   Lists, one to a line, the names of the files on the diskette in the default drive and all relevant information concerning the files and the diskette.

2. `DIR B:.BAS`

   Lists, one to a line, the names of the files that have an extension of `BAS` on the diskette in the B drive and all relevant information concerning the listed files and the diskette.

3. `DIR /P`

   Lists one screenful at a time, one to a line, the names of the files on the diskette in the default drive and all relevant information concerning the files and the diskette. Press any key to continue with the directory listing.

4. `DIR B:/W`

   The `/W` parameter lists the file names five to a line (wide display). Additional information about each file (size, time, and date) is not included in the display.

Summary of Important DOS Commands

Table D.1 summarizes the important DOS commands. For examples of how to use these commands, see the Disk Operating System User's manual.

TABLE D.1 Summary of Important DOS Commands

DOS COMMAND	FUNCTION
CD	Changes the current directory of the specified or default drive. CD\CHAP78 changes the current directory to CHAP78. CD\ changes the current directory to the root (main) directory on the default drive.
CLS	Clears the screen and places the cursor in the upper-left corner.
COPY	Copies one or more files from the diskette in the source disk drive to the diskette in the target disk drive.
DATE	Displays the current system date and allows you to enter a new date.
DEL	Deletes one or more files from the diskette in the specified disk drive. Same as the ERASE command.
DIR	Lists all files which meet a criterion in a directory on the specified disk drive.
DISKCOPY	Duplicates the diskette in the source disk drive to the diskette in the target disk drive. DISKCOPY is a utility; it is not part of COMMAND.COM. Therefore, this command will work only if the system diskette contains DISKCOPY.COM.
ERASE	Deletes one or more files from the diskette in the specified disk drive. Same as the DEL command.
FORMAT	Prepares a diskette so that the PC can read and write data and information to the diskette. FORMAT is a utility; it is not part of COMMAND.COM. Therefore, this command will only work if the system diskette contains FORMAT.COM.
MODE	MODE 40 sets the display mode of the screen to 40 characters per line. MODE 80 sets the display mode to 80 characters per line.
PRINT	Prints the specified ASCII file on the attached printer. PRINT is a utility; it is not part of COMMAND.COM. Therefore, this command will work only if the system diskette contains PRINT.COM.
RENAME	Changes the name of the specified file.
TIME	Displays the current system time and allows you to enter a new time.
TYPE	Displays the specified ASCII file on the screen.

▦ D.4

ASCII CHARACTER CODES

Table D.2 lists all 256 ASCII decimal codes and their corresponding characters. Each time you press a key, the *character* is displayed on the screen and the associated *decimal code* is transmitted to main storage. Special characters may be displayed on the screen by using PRINT CHR$(n), where n is the corresponding decimal code. See Program 10.1 on page 380.

ASCII decimal codes 126 to 255 represent the USA character set. However, foreign character sets may also be represented by these decimal codes.

TABLE D.2 ASCII Character Set

DECIMAL CODE	CHARACTER	DECIMAL CODE	CHARACTER	DECIMAL CODE	CHARACTER	DECIMAL CODE	CHARACTER	DECIMAL CODE	CHARACTER
000	(null)	052	4	104	h	156	£	208	╨
001	☺	053	5	105	i	157	¥	209	╤
002	☻	054	6	106	j	158	Pt	210	╥
003	♥	055	7	107	k	159	ƒ	211	╙
004	♦	056	8	108	l	160	á	212	╘
005	♣	057	9	109	m	161	í	213	╒
006	♠	058	:	110	n	162	ó	214	╓
007	(beep)	059	;	111	o	163	ú	215	╫
008	▫	060	<	112	p	164	ñ	216	╪
009	(tab)	061	=	113	q	165	Ñ	217	┘
010	(line feed)	062	>	114	r	166	ª	218	┌
011	(home)	063	?	115	s	167	º	219	█
012	(form feed)	064	@	116	t	168	¿	220	▄
013	(carriage return)	065	A	117	u	169	⌐	221	▌
014	♫	066	B	118	v	170	¬	222	▐
015	☼	067	C	119	w	171	½	223	▀
016	►	068	D	120	x	172	¼	224	α
017	◄	069	E	121	y	173	¡	225	β
018	↕	070	F	122	z	174	«	226	Γ
019	‼	071	G	123	{	175	»	227	π
020	¶	072	H	124	|	176	░	228	Σ
021	§	073	I	125	}	177	▒	229	σ
022	▬	074	J	126	~	178	▓	230	µ
023	↨	075	K	127	⌂	179	│	231	τ
024	↑	076	L	128	Ç	180	┤	232	Φ
025	↓	077	M	129	ü	181	╡	233	Θ
026	←	078	N	130	é	182	╢	234	Ω
027	→	079	O	131	â	183	╖	235	δ
028	(cursor right)	080	P	132	ä	184	╕	236	∞
029	(cursor left)	081	Q	133	à	185	╣	237	Ø
030	(cursor up)	082	R	134	å	186	║	238	∈
031	(cursor down)	083	S	135	ç	187	╗	239	∩
032	(space)	084	T	136	ê	188	╝	240	≡
033	!	085	U	137	ë	189	╜	241	±
034	"	086	V	138	è	190	╛	242	≥
035	#	087	W	139	ï	191	┐	243	≤
036	$	088	X	140	î	192	└	244	⌠
037	%	089	Y	141	ì	193	┴	245	⌡
038	&	090	Z	142	Ä	194	┬	246	÷
039	'	091	[	143	Å	195	├	247	≈
040	(	092	\	144	É	196	─	248	°
041	)	093	]	145	æ	197	┼	249	●
042	*	094	^	146	Æ	198	╞	250	•
043	+	095	_	147	ô	199	╟	251	√
044	,	096	`	148	ö	200	╚	252	ⁿ
045	-	097	a	149	ò	201	╔	253	²
046	.	098	b	150	û	202	╩	254	■
047	/	099	c	151	ù	203	╦	255	(blank)
048	0	100	d	152	ÿ	204	╠		
042	1	101	e	153	Ö	205	═		
050	2	102	f	154	Ü	206	╬		
051	3	103	g	155	¢	207	╧		

⊞ D.5

PC MAGAZINES, NEWSPAPERS, AND MANUALS

This section contains a selected list of some of the popular magazines, newspapers, and manuals for the PC. Many libraries have copies of these, and you are encouraged to look them over.

You can subscribe to the following magazines by contacting the publisher at the addresses listed below.

PC Magazines

1. *LOTUS*, P.O. Box 5289, Boulder, Colorado 80321
2. *LAN*, 12 West 21st St., New York, New York 10010
3. *PC Magazine*, P.O. Box 2443, Boulder, Colorado 80321
4. *PC Tech Journal*, P.O. Box 2966, Boulder, Colorado 80321
5. *PC World*, P.O. Box 51833, Boulder, Colorado 80321
6. *Personal Computing*, P.O. Box 386, Dalton, Massachusetts 01227
7. *SIGSMALL/PC Notes*, 11 West 42nd St., New York, New York 10036
8. *Today's Office*, 645 Stewart Ave., Garden City, New York 11530

PC Newspapers

There are a number of newspapers that cover a variety of topics concerning the PC. As with PC magazines, you can subscribe to these newspapers by contacting the publisher.

1. *Computerworld*, P.O. Box 1016, Southeastern, Pennsylvania 19398
2. *Info World*, P.O. Box 1018, Southeastern, Pennsylvania 19398
3. *MIS Week*, P.O. Box 2036, Mahopac, New York 10541
4. *PC Week*, One Park Avenue, 4th Floor, New York, New York 10016
5. *Network*, One Park Avenue, 4th Floor, New York, New York 10016

PC Manuals

The IBM Corporation publishes dozens of manuals that cover BASIC, DOS, and the various IBM PC models and peripherals. These manuals may be purchased from your authorized IBM Personal Computer dealer or by writing to IBM Corp., P. O. Box 1328-C, Boca Raton, Florida 33432.

The manuals listed below are part of the IBM PC Computer Language Series. They all relate specifically to topics covered in this book.

1. The IBM Personal Computer *BASIC: Quick Reference*
2. The IBM Personal Computer *BASIC Reference*
3. The IBM Personal Computer *BASIC Handbook: General Programming Information*
4. The IBM Personal Computer *Guide to Operations*
5. The IBM Personal Computer *Disk Operating System*
6. The IBM Personal Computer *Disk Operating System: Technical Reference*
7. The IBM Personal Computer *Technical Reference*
8. The IBM Personal Computer *Disk Operating System: User's Guide*

If you have an IBM PC compatible, contact your dealer or write to the manufacturer for a list of available manuals.

⊞ CHAPTER 1

2. The basic subsystems of a computer are input, main storage, central processing unit, auxiliary storage, and output.

Input — a device that allows programs and data to enter into the computer system.

Main Storage — a subsystem that allows for the storage of programs and data for the CPU to process at a given time.

Central Processing Unit (CPU) — the unit that controls and supervises the entire computer system and performs the arithmetic and logical operations on data that is specified by the stored program.

Auxiliary Storage — a subsystem that is used to store programs and data for immediate recall.

Output — a device that allows the computer system to communicate the results of a program to the user.

4. A floppy diskette unit and a hard disk unit both serve as input and output devices.

6. Hardware is the physical equipment of a computer system. The subsystems as described in 2 above are hardware. Software refers to the programs, languages, written procedures, and documentation concerned with the operation of a computer system.

8. 1024

10. network

12. a. 700   b. 300   c. An error message will be displayed because the value of C is zero and division by zero is not permitted.

14.

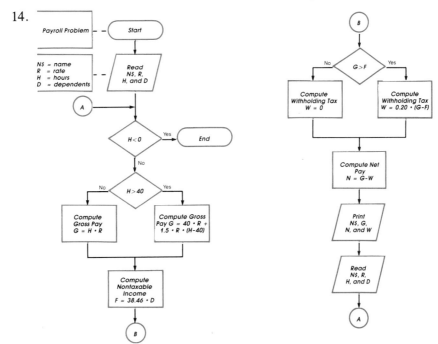

⊞ CHAPTER 2   2.

Line	W	X	Y	Displayed
100	4	0	0	
110	4	2	0	
120	4	2	6	
130	4	2	6	6
140	5	2	6	
150	5	30	6	
160	5	30	6	30
170	5	9	6	
180	5	9	4	
190	5	9	4	4
200	5	0	4	
210	5	0	4	0
220	5	0	4	

4. a. `100 T = 3`   b. `200 X = T - 2`   c. `300 P = T * X`
   d. `400 T = 3 * T`   e. `500 A = P / X`   f. `600 X = X + 1`
   g. `700 R = R ^ 3`
          or
      `700 R = R * R * R`

6. a. `100 Y = 21`   b. `110 PRINT S`
      `110 PRINT Y`
      `120 END`
   c. `120 END` (optional for   d. `105 PRINT S`
      MS BASIC)
   e. `110 PRINT A1`   f. `100 Z1 = 1` or `110 PRINT Z`
      `120 END`

8. (1) Insert the data as constants in the `LET` statement that is used to calculate a result.
   (2) Assign each data item to a variable. Use these variables in the `LET` statement to calculate a result.
   (3) Use the `INPUT` statement to assign the data items to variables. Use these variables in the `LET` statement to calculate a result.

10. `AUTO`   — automatically starts a BASIC program with a line number.
    `FILES`   — instructs the PC to list the names of the programs and data files on the default drive.
    `LIST`   — instructs the PC to list the source statements of the current program.
    `NEW`   — instructs the PC to delete the current program from main storage.
    `RUN`   — instructs the PC to execute the current program in main storage.
    `RENUM`   — renumbers the entire program uniformly.

12. Yes. See Program 2.4 on page 24.
14. No. Although line 140 displays the correct result (270), it does not display the value of PAY. If the rate of pay (RATE) or the hours (HOURS) are assigned different values, the program will still display the following: `The gross pay is 270`.
16. Enter 150 and press the Enter key.
18. Yes. MS BASIC will accept lines that are out of order and will place them in their proper sequence.

⊞ CHAPTER 3

2. 568962500000
   The error is 17,824.

4. a. –6.333334   b. 23   c. 8

6. c: INT is a reserved word (keyword). A list of the MS BASIC reserved words is on page R.5 of the reference card at the back of this book.
   e: First character is not a letter.
   f: PRINT is a reserved word.
   g: First character is not a letter.
   h: FOR is a reserved word.

8. The formation of a numeric expression concerns the proper placement of constants, variables, function references, parentheses, and arithmetic operators in a numeric expression. The evaluation of a numeric expression is concerned with the manner in which a validly formed numeric expression is to be evaluated by the PC.

10. a. 11   b. 1   c. –.6666667   d. 262144   e. 17   f. 2320

12. a. `110 Q = (D + E) ^ (1 / 3)`
    b. `120 D = (A ^ 2) ^ 3.2`
    c. `130 B = 20 / (6 - S)`
    d. `140 Y = A1 * X + A2 * X ^ 2 + A3 * X ^ 3 + A4 * X ^ 4`
    e. `150 H = X + X / (X - Y)`
    f. `160 S = 19.2 * X ^ 3`
    g. `170 V = 100 - (2 / 3) ^ (100 - B)`
    h. `180 T = (76234 / (2.37 + D)) ^ (1 / 2)`
    i. `190 V = 1234E-4 * M - (.123458 ^ 3 / (M - N))`
    j. `200 Q = ((F - M * 1000) ^ (2 * B)) / (4 * M) - 1 / E`

14. a, b, c, d, e, f, g, i

16. a. D = –1, A and B do not change in value.
    b. A = –2.2, B = 2, E1 = 1, E2 = 3.2, E3 = 5

18. a. Owing to lines 110 and 130, the variable A is assigned a value of zero. In line 140, division by zero causes a fatal error. Modify line 110 or line 130 so that A does not equal zero when line 140 is executed.
    b. Because of lines 110 and 120, the numeric expression in line 130 cannot be evaluated by the PC. It is invalid to raise a negative integer to a decimal fraction power. Modify line 110 or line 120 so that the PC is not requested to raise a negative integer to a decimal fraction power.

20. ```
    Principal ===> 100
    Rate in % ===> 15
    Amount ======> 115
    ```

⊞ CHAPTER 4

2. d, f, h

4. ```
   2050 LOCATE 1,  7 : PRINT A
   2060 LOCATE 4, 45 : PRINT B
   ```

6. ```
   2050 PRINT USING "The amount is **$####.##+"; AMOUNT
   ```

8. ```
   2050 CLS : KEY OFF
   2060 LOCATE 6, 6 : PRINT 6
   ```

10. The cursor is located in column 1 of line 14.

12.
```
   VVVVV
  X     X
 X  O O  X
 X       X
 X   U   X
 X (   ) X
 X   -   X
  X     X
   XXXXX
```

14. a. 3050 PRINT USING "!"; LAST.NAME$
     b. 4050 PRINT USING "&"; LAST.NAME$
     c. 5050 PRINT USING "\   \"; LAST.NAME$
     d. 6050 PRINT USING "\\"; LAST.NAME$

16. Assume that Ƀ represents a blank character.

    a. Ƀ25   b. ƀƀƀ38.40
    c. ƀƀƀ$22.60-   d. $ƀƀ425.89
    e. ****88.76   f. %637,214.0
    g. Ƀ3.98Ƀ   h. %-123.80
    i. ƀƀƀƀ12.614   j. Ƀ2.66E+02
    k. A   l. ABCD
    m. AB   n. ABCD

⊞ CHAPTER 5

2. 100 X = 0   a. 130 X = X + 1   b. 150 X = X + 7
    110 T = 10   140 T = T + 1   160 T = T + 7

    c. 170 X = X + 2   d. 190 X = 2 * X   e. 210 X = X - 1
       180 T = T + 2   200 T = 2 * T   220 T = T - 1

4. a. Q value greater than 8 or Q value equal to 3.
    b. Q value greater than or equal to 0.
    c. Q value less than 27.
    d. Q may be equal to any value that is within the limits of the PC.

6. a. 200 IF AGE >= 21   b. 300 IF SEX.CODE$ = "M"
            THEN C = C + 1   THEN M = M + 1
      210 S = S + 1   ELSE F = F + 1

8. a.

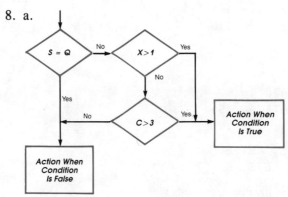

b.

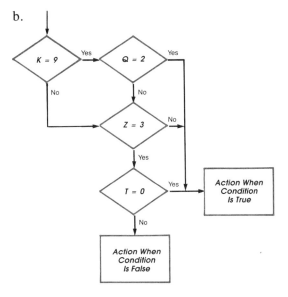

10. a.
```
200 INPUT "Percent (0 < Percent <= 25) =====> "; PERCENT
210 WHILE PERCENT < 0 OR PERCENT > 25
220    BEEP : BEEP : BEEP : BEEP
230    PRINT "Percent"; PERCENT; "is in error, please reenter"
240    INPUT "Percent (0 < Percent <= 25) =====> "; PERCENT
250 WEND
```

b.
```
200 INPUT "Balance ($550.99 < Balance < $765.50) =====> "; BALANCE
210 WHILE BALANCE <= 550.99 OR BALANCE >= 765.50
220    BEEP : BEEP : BEEP : BEEP
230    PRINT "Balance"; BALANCE; "is in error, please reenter"
240    INPUT "Balance ($550.99 < Balance < $765.50) =====> "; BALANCE
250 WEND
```

Also line 210 may be written as follows:

```
210 WHILE NOT(BALANCE >= 550.99 AND BALANCE <= 765.50)
```

c.
```
200 INPUT "Code (A, D, E or F) =====> "; CODE$
210 WHILE NOT(CODE$ = "A" OR CODE$ = "D" OR CODE$ = "E" OR CODE$ = "F")
220    BEEP : BEEP : BEEP : BEEP
230    PRINT "Code "; CODE$; " is in error, please reenter"
240    INPUT "Code (A, D, E or F) =====> "; CODE$
250 WEND
```

d.
```
200 INPUT "Customer =====> "; CUSTOMER$
210 WHILE MID$(CUSTOMER$, 3, 1) <> "4"
220    BEEP : BEEP : BEEP.: BEEP
230    PRINT "Customer"; CUSTOMER$; "is in error, please reenter"
240    INPUT "Customer =====> "; CUSTOMER$
250 WEND
```

```
12. 100 ' Exercise 5.12 Solution
    110 NEGA = 0
    120 ZERO = 0
    130 POSI = 0
    140 READ NUM
    150 WHILE NUM <> -1E37
    160    IF NUM < 0 THEN NEGA = NEGA + 1
                      ELSE IF NUM = 0
                            THEN ZERO = ZERO + 1 ELSE POSI = POSI + 1
    170    READ NUM
    180 WEND
    190 PRINT NEGA, ZERO, POSI
    200 ' ********** Data Follows **********
    210 DATA 4, 2, 3, -9, 0, 0, -4, -6, -8, 3
    220 DATA 2, 0, 0, 8, -3, 4, -1E37
    230 END
```

Line 160 may also be written as follows:

```
160 IF NUM < 0 THEN NEGA = NEGA + 1
163 IF NUM = 0
        THEN ZERO = ZERO + 1
        ELSE POSI = POSI + 1
```

```
14. 100 ' Exercise 5.14 Solution
    110 CLS : KEY OFF   ' Clear Screen
    120 INPUT "Number of Fibonacci Numbers ===> ", X
    130 FIB1 = 1
    140 FIB2 = 1
    150 PRINT
    160 PRINT FIB1;
    170 PRINT FIB2;
    180 NUM = 3
    190 WHILE NUM <= X
    200    FIB3 = FIB2 + FIB1
    210    PRINT FIB3;
    220    FIB1 = FIB2
    230    FIB2 = FIB3
    240    NUM = NUM + 1
    250 WEND
    260 PRINT : PRINT : PRINT "Job Complete"
    270 END
```

```
16. 190 ' Exercise 5.16 Solution
    200 IF U < V
        THEN IF U < W THEN S = U ELSE S = W
        ELSE IF V < W THEN S = V ELSE S = W
```

18. a. X   b. COUNT = 0; SUM = 68   c. 4
    d. 68   e. −2

20. 3040 ' Exercise 5.20 Solution
    3050 IF C = 0 AND D = 0
              THEN A = -1
              ELSE IF C <> 0 AND D <> 0 THEN A = -2 ELSE A = -3

22. a. S > 0 OR A > 0 OR T > 0

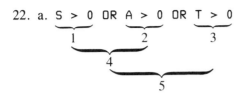

   b. S > 0 AND A > 0 AND NOT T > 0

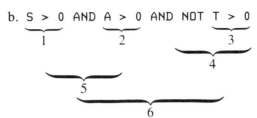

   c. S > 0 IMP A > 0 EQV T > 0 AND P > 0

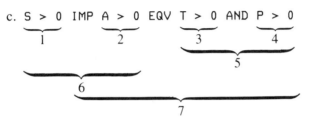

   d. NOT S > 0 AND T > 0 XOR P > 0

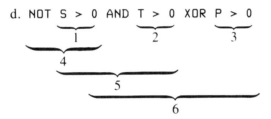

⊞ CHAPTER 6

2. a. OPEN, OUTPUT, APPEND   b. OPEN, INPUT
   c. closed   d. EOF(n)
   e. APPEND

4. 2050 OPEN "B:SALES1.DAT" FOR INPUT AS #1
   2060 OPEN "B:SALES2.DAT" FOR INPUT AS #2
   2070 OPEN "B:SALES3.DAT" FOR INPUT AS #3

6. a: Filespec must precede the mode.
   e: Comma must immediately follow filenumber.
   g: Filenumber must not be preceded by a number sign (#).
   h: Comma at the end of the list is invalid.

8. a. 3450 LINE.COUNT = LINE.COUNT + 1
   b. 3450 LINE.COUNT = LINE.COUNT + 2
   c. 3450 LINE.COUNT = LINE.COUNT + 3

⊞ CHAPTER 7

2. a. L(2, 2)   b. L(3, 3) or L(2, 4)   c. L(3, 2)
    d. L(5, 2)   e. L(3, 4)   f. L(2, 1)
    g. L(1, 3)   h. L(5, 1)

4. The partial program assigns the value of each element of array A to the corresponding element in array B and then eliminates array A from the program.

6. a. c   b. c   c. e   d. a

8.
```
2000 ' Exercise 7.8 Solution
2010 OPTION BASE 1
2020 DIM NUM(50)
        .
        .
        .
3030 LOW  = 0
3040 MID  = 0
3050 HIGH = 0
3060 FOR I = 1 TO 50
3070    IF NUM(I) >=   0 AND NUM(I) <= 18
           THEN LOW  = LOW + 1
3080    IF NUM(I) >= 26 AND NUM(I) <= 29
           THEN MID  = MID + 1
3090    IF NUM(I) >  42 AND NUM(I) <   47
           THEN HIGH = HIGH + 1
3100 NEXT I
```

10.
```
2000 ' Exercise 7.10 Solution
2010 OPTION BASE 1
2020 DIM A(50), B(50), C(50)
        .
        .
        .
3030 FOR I = 1 TO 50
3040    IF A(I) < B(I) THEN C(I) = -1
                ELSE IF A(I) = B(I) THEN C(I) = 0
                            ELSE C(I) = 1
3050 NEXT I
```

Line 3040 may also be written as follows:

```
3040    IF A(I) < B(I) THEN C(I) = -1
3042    IF A(I) = B(I) THEN C(I) =  0
3045    IF A(I) > B(I) THEN C(I) =  1
```

12. Assuming that the variable names that represent subscripts are positive values, all are valid except for b, which has a negative subscript.

14. 1600

16.
```
2000 ' Exercise 7.16 Solution
2010 OPTION BASE 1
2020 DIM A(50)
        .
        .
        .
```

(continued)

```
3000 POSI = 0
3010 ZERO = 0
3020 NEG  = 0
3030 FOR I = 1 TO 50
3040    IF A(I) > 0 THEN POSI = POSI + 1
3050              ELSE IF A(I) = 0 THEN ZERO = ZERO + 1
3060                         ELSE NEG  = NEG + 1
3070 NEXT I
```

You may also write line 3040 as follows:

```
3040 IF A(I) > 0 THEN POSI = POSI + 1
3042 IF A(I) = 0 THEN ZERO = ZERO + 1
3045 IF A(I) < 0 THEN NEG  = NEG  + 1
```

18.
```
2000 ' Exercise 7.18 Solution
2010 OPTION BASE 1
2020 DIM SALES(50), PERS$(50)
        .
        .
        .

3000 GRSALES = SALES(1)
3010 NAME$ = PERS$(1)
3020 FOR I = 2 TO 50
3030    IF SALES(I) < GRSALES
           THEN NAME$ = PERS$(I) : GRSALES = SALES(I)
3040 NEXT I
3050 PRINT NAME$, GRSALES
```

20.
```
2200 ' Exercise 7.20 Solution
2210 OPTION BASE 1
2220 DIM ITEM$(200), SALES(200)
        .
        .
        .
3000 FOR I = 1 TO 200
3010 IF SALES(I) > 3000
        THEN PRINT ITEM$(I), SALES(I)
3020 NEXT I
```

22.
```
2000 ' Exercise 7.22 Solution
2010 OPTION BASE 1
2020 DIM R(10, 10), S(10, 10)
        .
        .
        .
3000 SUM = 0
3010 FOR J = 1 TO 10
3020    FOR K = 1 TO 10
3030       SUM = SUM + R(J, K) * S(J, K)
3040    NEXT K
3050 NEXT J
```

## CHAPTER 8

2. a. 69

b. The entire string.

c. Ifкiк (where к indicates a blank character)

d. seen

e. 36.8

f. 73

g. G

h. AAAAAAAAAAAAAA

i. "-13.691"

j. 24

k. The word giants is replaced by the word midgets in the string assigned to PHR$.

l. кккк (where к indicates a blank character)

4. a. 99   b. 43   c. ?   d. "48.9"   e. 1

   f. 66   g. %   h. 58   i. 15   j. 69

6.
```
100 ' Exercise 8.6 Solution
110 NUM$ = "1698"
120 NUM  = VAL(NUM$)
130 D4   = INT(NUM / 1000)
140 D3   = INT((NUM - D4 * 1000) / 100)
150 D2   = INT((NUM - D4 * 1000 - D3 * 100) / 10)
160 D1   = INT(NUM  - D4 * 1000 - D3 * 100 - D2 * 10)
170 SUM  = D4 + D3 + D2 + D1
180 PRINT "The sum of the digits is"; SUM
190 END
```

Also, lines 120 to 160 may be written as follows:

```
120 D1 = VAL(MID$(NUM$, 1, 1))
130 D2 = VAL(MID$(NUM$, 2, 1))
140 D3 = VAL(MID$(NUM$, 3, 1))
150 D4 = VAL(MID$(NUM$, 4, 1))
```

8. The program displays the prime numbers between 1 and 100. Any whole number greater than 1 that has no factors other than 1 and itself is called a prime number. In number theory, it can be proven that if a number has no factors between 2 and the square root of the number, then the number is prime. The program uses this method for finding the prime numbers between 1 and 100.

10. a. 100 P = SQR(A ^ 2 + B ^ 2)

b. 200 B = SQR(ABS(TAN(X) - .51))

c. 300 Q = 8 * (COS(X)) ^ 2 + 4 * SIN(X)

d. 400 Y = EXP(X) + LOG(1 + X)

12. a. 500 SIGN = SGN(2 * X ^ 3 + 3 * X + 5)

b. 600 INTEGER = INT(4 * X + 5)

c. 700 ROUNDED.2 = INT((X + .005) * 100) / 100

   710 ROUNDED.1 = INT((X + .05) * 10) / 10

14. FRE   — returns the number of unused bytes within BASIC's data space.

    POS   — returns the current column position of the cursor relative to the left edge of the display screen.

    SCREEN   — returns the ASCII code for the character found at the specified location.

    CSRLIN   — equal to the current row position of the cursor relative to the top of the display screen.

16.
```
100 ' Exercise 8.16 Solution
110 RANDOMIZE TIMER
120 FOR R = 1 TO 100
130    PRINT INT(52 * RND + 1)
140 NEXT R
150 END
```

18.
```
100 DEF FNDISCOUNT(PURCHASE.AMT) = .10 * (PURCHASE.AMT - 200)
```
20. The program is valid and displays the value 4380.

CHAPTER 9

2. a. buffer, FIELD   b. string   c. less   d. LOC(n)

4. The LSET and RSET statements are used to store data in the buffer before a record is written to a random file. LSET left-justifies the value in the specified area of the buffer. RSET right-justifies the value in the specified area of the buffer.

6. a: A negative record length is invalid.

    d: A string variable as the second parameter in a GET statement is invalid.

    f: It is invalid to assign the value of a numeric variable to a string variable. The statement should read 600 LSET COST$ = MKS$(COST).

    g: It is invalid to have the MKS$ function on the left of the equal sign in an RSET statement. The statement should read 700 RSET N$ = MKS(N).

    i: The function CVS should be replaced by MKS$.

8. The sequential file contains the keys that are read into an array by the Initialization Module. The random file contains the data records that are accessed by using the subscript of the element in the array that has the key as its value.

CHAPTER 10

2. a.
```
100 ' Exercise 10.2a Solution
110 SCREEN 1 : CLS : KEY OFF
120 PSET (0, 50)
130 LINE -(200, 25)
140 LINE -(100, 125)
150 LINE -(0, 50)
160 END
```

   b.
```
100 ' Exercise 10.2b Solution
110 SCREEN 1 : CLS : KEY OFF
120 LINE (0, 0) - (160, 100),, B
130 LINE -(0, 0)
140 LINE (160, 0) - (0, 100)
150 END
```

```
c. 100 ' Exercise 10.2c Solution
   110 SCREEN 1 : CLS : KEY OFF
   120 PI = 3.141593
   130 CIRCLE (70, 80), 45
   140 PSET (70, 80)
   150 CIRCLE (70, 80), 45,, PI, 2 * PI, 1/6
   160 END

d. 100 ' Exercise 10.2d Solution
   110 SCREEN 1 : CLS : KEY OFF
   120 PI = 3.141593
   130 CIRCLE (75, 60), 70,, -PI, -3 * PI / 2
   140 END
```

4. a. Following the execution of lines 200 and 300, the screen has a blue background, a black border, and a red foreground.

   b. Following the execution of lines 400 and 500, the screen has a black background and border and a brown foreground, the default color on palette 0.

6. a. point, pixel   b. GRAPHICS   c. 80
   d. CHR$ e. minus sign   f. GET, PUT
   g. 2, 4, 8

```
8. 100 ' Exercise 10.8 Solution
   110 SCREEN 1 : CLS : KEY OFF
   120 COLOR 1, 0
   130 LINE (100, 80) - (180, 150), 3, B
   140 PAINT(140, 135), 2, 3
   150 LINE (100, 80) - (130, 50), 3
   160 LINE -(210, 50), 3
   170 LINE -(180, 80), 3
   180 PAINT (140, 65), 1, 3
   190 LINE (210, 50) - (210, 120), 3
   200 LINE -(180, 150), 3
   210 PAINT (185, 135), 3, 3
   220 END
```

```
10. 100 ' Exercise 10.10 Solution
    110 CLS : KEY OFF : WIDTH 40
    120 LOCATE 4, 9
    130 FOR I = 9 TO 32
    140     PRINT CHR$(219);
    150 NEXT I
    160 LOCATE 22, 9
    170 FOR I = 9 TO 32
    180     PRINT CHR$(219);
    190 NEXT I
    210 FOR I = 4 TO 22
    220     LOCATE I, 9 : PRINT CHR$(219)
    230 NEXT I
    240 FOR I = 4 TO 22
    250     LOCATE I, 32 : PRINT CHR$(219)
    260 NEXT I
    270 END
```

12. a. Causes the note A flat to be played.
    b. Sets all notes that follow to lengths of 1/8.
    c. Sets all notes that follow to the next octave and causes the C note to be played.
    d. Executes the subcommand M$, which contains additional commands.
    e. Rest.
    f. Sets the tempo to 100 quarter notes per minute.
    g. Pause a length of 1/8.
    h. Music staccato—each note that follows plays 3/4 of the time specified by L.
    i. Music legato—each note that follows plays the full period set by L.
    j. Sets the octave to 3.

14. PSET   —   Put the pixel array on the screen exactly as defined in the array named in the PUT statement.

    AND   —   Within the specified area on the screen, turn "on" those pixels that are "on" in the array named in the PUT statement and "on" on the screen.

    XOR   —   Within the specified area, turn "on" those pixels that are "on" in the array name in the PUT statement and "off" on the screen or "off" in the array name and "on" on the screen.

⊞ APPENDIX A

2. The annotation, terminal, and connector symbols.
4. Part I: I = 9, J = 9
   Part II: I = 21, J = 14

6. I = 3, J = 5
8. The arrowheads point the wrong way between the process symbol and output symbol and between the output symbol and terminal symbol representing End.
10.   12.

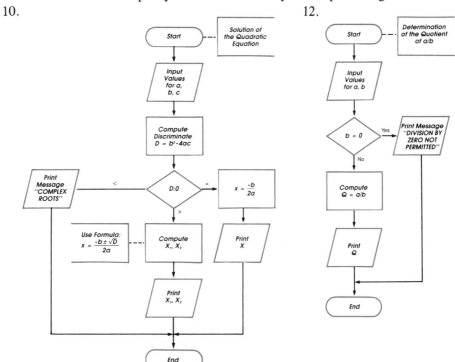

14. I = 17 and J = 16

INDEX

MICROSOFT BASIC REFERENCE CARD

Legend: *Uppercase letters are required keywords. You must supply items within < >s. You must select one of the entries within { }'s. Items within [ ]'s are optional. Three ellipsis points (...) indicate that an item may be repeated as many times as you wish. The symbol ᵬ represents a blank character.*

Summary of BASIC Statements

STATEMENT	PAGE	
BEEP	162	Causes the speaker on the PC to beep for a quarter of a second.
CHAIN <"filespec"> [,line number] [,ALL]	C.9	Instructs the PC to stop executing the current program, then load another program from auxiliary storage and start executing it.
CIRCLE <(x, y), radius> [,color [,start,end [,shape]]]	397	Causes the PC to draw an ellipse, circle, arc, or wedge with center at (x, y).
CLOSE [#] [filenumber] [,[#] [filenumber]]...	189	Closes specified files.
CLS	28	Erases the information on the first 24 lines of the screen and places the cursor in the upper-left corner of the screen.
COLOR [background] [,palette]	398	In medium-resolution graphics mode, sets the color for the background and palette of colors.
COLOR [foreground] [,background] [,border]	387	In the text mode, defines the color of the foreground characters, background, and border around the screen.
COM(n) {ON/OFF/STOP}	319	Enables or disables trapping of communications activity on adaptor n.
COMMON <variable> [,variable]...	C.9	Passes specified variables to a chained program.
DATA <data item> [,data item]...	95	Provides for the creation of a sequence of data items for use by the READ statement.
DATE$ = mm{/ -}dd{/ -}yy[yy]	296	Sets the system date, where mm = month, dd = day, yy = year, yyyy = 4-digit year.
DEF FN <name> [(variable [,variable...])] = <expression>	313	Defines and names a function that can be referenced in a program as often as needed.
DIM <array name(size)> [,array name(size)]...	241	Reserves storage locations for arrays.
DRAW <string expression>	401	Causes the PC to draw the object that is defined by the value of the string expression.
END	21	Terminates program execution and closes all opened files.
ERASE <array name> [,array name]...	243	Eliminates previously defined arrays.
FIELD <#filenumber, width AS string variable> [,width AS string variable]...	346	Allocates space for variables in a random file buffer.
FOR numeric variable = initial TO limit [STEP increment]	229	Causes the statements between the FOR and NEXT statements to be executed repeatedly until the value of the numeric variable exceeds the value of the limit.
GET <(x₁, y₁) - (x₂, y₂)>, array name>	408	Reads the colors of the points in the specified area on the screen into an array.
GET [#][filenumber] [,record number]	349	Reads the specified record from a random file and transfers it to the buffer that is defined by the corresponding FIELD statement.
GOSUB <line number>	76	Causes control to transfer to the subroutine represented by the specified line number. Also retains the location of the next statement following the GOSUB statement.
GOTO <line number>	150	Causes an unconditional branch to the line number.
IF <condition> THEN [clause]	136	Causes execution of the THEN clause if the condition is true.
IF <condition> THEN [clause] ELSE [clause]	136	Causes execution of the THEN clause if the condition is true. Causes execution of the ELSE clause if the condition is false.
INPUT [;][,]["prompt message"{;/,}] <variable> [,variable]...	26	Provides for the assignment of values to variables from a source external to the program, like the keyboard.
INPUT [#filenumber, variable> [,variable]...	199	Provides for the assignment of values to variables from a sequential file in auxiliary storage.
KEY {ON/OFF}	38	Turns the display of the ten function keys on line 25 of the screen to on or off.
KEY(n) {ON/OFF/STOP}	319	Activates or deactivates trapping of specified key n.
[LET] <variable> = <expression>	65	Causes the evaluation of the expression, followed by the assignment of the resulting value to the variable to the left of the equal sign.
LINE [(x₁, y₁)] -(x₂, y₂)> [,color] [,B[F]][,Style]	401	Draws a line or a box on the screen.
LINE INPUT [;][;"prompt message";] <string variable> or **LINE INPUT** [#filenumber, > <string variable>	297	Provides for the assignment of a line of up to 255 characters from a source external to the program, like the keyboard or a sequential file.
LOCATE [row] [,column] [,cursor] [,start] [,stop]	110	Positions the cursor on the screen. Can also be used to make the cursor visible or invisible and to control the size of the cursor.
LPRINT [item] [{;/,} item]...	105	Provides for the generation of output to the printer.
LPRINT USING <string expression; > <item> [{;/,} item]...	114	Provides for the generation of formatted output to the printer.
LSET <string variable> = <string expression>	347	Moves string data left-justified into an area of a random file buffer that is defined by the string variable.
MID$ <(string var, start position [,number]) > = <substring>	286	Replaces a substring within a string.
NEXT [numeric variable] [,numeric variable]...	229	Identifies the end of the For loop(s).
ON COM(n) GOSUB <line number>	318	Causes control to transfer to the line number when data is filling the communications buffer (n).
ON ERROR GOTO <line number>	C.4	Enables error trapping and specifies the first line number of an error-handling routine that the PC is to branch to in the event of an error. If the line number is zero, error trapping is disabled.
ON <numeric expression> GOSUB <line number> [,line number]...	164	Causes control to transfer to the subroutine represented by the selected line number. Also retains the location of the next statement following the ON-GOSUB statement.
ON <numeric expression> GOTO <line number> [,line number]...	173	Causes control to transfer to one of several line numbers according to the value of the numeric expression.
ON KEY(n) GOSUB <line number>	318	Causes control to transfer to the line number when the function key or cursor control key (n) is pressed.
ON PEN GOSUB <line number>	318	Causes control to transfer to the line number when the light pen is activated.
ON PLAY(n) GOSUB <line number>	318	Plays continuous background music. Transfers control to the line number when a note (n) is sensed.

(BASIC Statements continued on page R.2 in left column)

MICROSOFT BASIC REFERENCE CARD

Summary of BASIC Statements (continued)

STATEMENT	PAGE	
ON STRIG(n) GOSUB <line number>	318	Causes control to transfer to the line number when one of the joystick buttons (n) is pressed.
ON TIMER(n) GOSUB <line number>	318	Causes control to transfer to the line number when the specified period of time (n) in seconds has elapsed.
OPEN <filespec> FOR <mode> AS <[#]filenumber> [LEN = record length] or OPEN <mode>, [#]filenumber, filespec> [,record length]	187 and 344	Allows a program to read or write records to a file. If record length is specified, then the file is opened as a random file. If the record length is not specified, then the file is opened as a sequential file.
OPTION BASE {0 / 1}	242	Assigns a lower bound of 0 or 1 to all arrays.
PAINT <(x, y)> [[,paint] [,boundary]]	398	Paints an area on the screen with the selected color.
PEN(n) {ON / OFF / STOP}	319	Enables or disables the PEN read function used to analyze light pen activity.
PLAY <string expression>	412	Causes the PC to play music according to the value of the string expression.
PRESET <(x, y)> [,color]	394	Draws a point in the color specified at (x, y). If no color is specified, it erases the point.
{PRINT / ?} [item] [{, / ; / b}item]...	101	Provides for the generation of output to the screen.
{PRINT / ?} <#filenumber,> [item] [{, / ; / b}item]...	190	Provides for the generation of output to a sequential file.
PRINT USING <string expression;> <item>[{, / ; / b}item]...	106	Provides for the generation of formatted output to the screen.
PRINT #filenumber,> USING <string expression;> <item>[{, / ; / b}item]...	191	Provides for the generation of formatted output to a sequential file.
PSET <(x, y)> [,color]	394	Draws a point in the color specified at (x, y).
PUT <(x$_1$, y$_1$), array name> [,action]	349	Writes the colors of the points in the array onto an area of the screen.

STATEMENT	PAGE	
PUT <[#]filenumber> [,record number]	408	Writes a record to a random file from a buffer defined by the corresponding FIELD statement.
RANDOMIZE [numeric expression]	310	Reseeds the random number generator.
READ <variable> [,variable]...	97	Provides for the assignment of values to variables from a sequence of data items created from DATA statements.
{REM / '} [comment]	31	Provides for the insertion of comments in a program.
RESTORE [line number]	99	Allows the data items in DATA statements to be reread.
RESUME {line number / NEXT / 0 / b}	C.4	Continues program execution at the line number, or the line following that which caused the error, after an error-recovery procedure.
RETURN [line number]	77	Causes control to transfer from a subroutine back to the statement that follows the corresponding GOSUB or ON-GOSUB statement.
RSET <string variable> = <string expression>	347	Moves string data right-justified into an area of a random file buffer that is defined by string variable.
SCREEN [mode] [,color switch] [,active page] [,visual page]	378	Sets the screen attributes for text mode, medium-resolution graphics, or high-resolution graphics.
SOUND <frequency, duration>	411	Causes the generation of sound through the PC speaker.
STOP	C.3	Stops execution of a program. Unlike the END statement, files are left open.
STRIG(n) {ON / OFF / STOP}	319	Enables or disables trapping of the joystick buttons.
SWAP <variable, variable$_2$>	254	Exchanges the values of two variables or two elements of an array.
TIME$ = hh[:mm[:ss]]	296	Sets the system time where hh = hours, mm = minutes, and ss = seconds.
TIMER {ON / OFF / STOP}	319	Enables or disables trapping of timed events.
VIEW [[SCREEN] (x$_1$, y$_1$) – (x$_2$, y$_2$)] [,color] [,boundary]	407	Defines a viewport.

STATEMENT	PAGE	
WEND	93	Identifies the end of a While loop.
WHILE <condition>	93	Identifies the beginning of a While loop. Causes the statements between WHILE and WEND to be executed repeatedly while the condition is true.
WIDTH {40 / 80}	29	Erases the information on the first 24 lines of the screen, sets the width of the line on the screen to 40 or 80 characters, and places the cursor in the upper-left corner of the screen.
WINDOW <[SCREEN] (x$_1$, y$_1$) – (x$_2$, y$_2$) >	404	Redefines the coordinates of the viewport. Allows you to draw objects in space and not be bounded by the limits of the screen.
WRITE [expression list]	194	Writes data to the screen. Identical to the PRINT statement except that it causes commas to be inserted between items displayed; causes strings to be delimited with quotation marks; and positive numbers are not preceded by blanks.
WRITE <#filenumber, > [item] [{, / ; / b} item]...	195	Writes data to a sequential file. Causes the PC to insert commas between the items written to the sequential file.

Summary of BASIC Commands

COMMAND	PAGE	
AUTO [line number] [,increment]	40	Automatically starts a BASIC line with a line number. Each new line is assigned a systematically incremented line number.
CLEAR	39	Assigns all numeric variables the value zero and all string variables the null value.
CONT	39	Resumes a system activity, like the execution of a program, following interruption due to pressing the Control and Break keys simultaneously or execution of the STOP or END statement.
DELETE [lineno$_1$] [-lineno$_2$]	39	Deletes line numbers lineno$_1$ through lineno$_2$ in the current program.
EDIT <line number>	39	Displays a line for editing purposes.
FILES ["device name:]	40	Lists the names of all programs and data files in auxiliary storage as specified by the device name.

(BASIC Commands continued on page R.3 in left column)